1001
REALLY COOL
WEB SITES

Edward J. Renehan, Jr.

D1601744

JP

JAMSA
P·R·E·S·S™
...a computer user's best friend™

a division of Kris Jamsa Software, Inc.

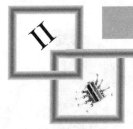

1001 Really Cool Web Sites

Published by
Jamsa Press
2975 S. Rainbow, Suite I
Las Vegas, NV 89102
U.S.A.

For information about the translation or distribution of any Jamsa Press book, please write to Jamsa Press at the address listed above.

1001 Really Cool Web Sites

Printed in the United States of America.
98765432

ISBN 1-884133-22-3

Publisher Debbie Jamsa	**Technical Advisor** Phil Schmauder	**Cover Design** Design Studio
Composition Caroline Kinsey	**Cover Photograph** O'Gara/Bissell	**Proofers** Tammy Funk Heather Grigg
Indexer Linda Linssen	**Copy Editors** Tammy Funk Heather Grigg	Tami Kahrs Rosemary Pasco
Site Collection Stephanie Jamsa Kris Cope	Larry Letournean Rosemary Pasco	

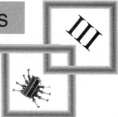

III

WELCOME TO "WEB COOL"

For all its mystique, the World Wide Web may at first seem intimidating to the lay person, the non-programmer. I admit that I am just such an animal. I am an historian and biographer by trade. Thus, I am among the many who consider the computer a useful tool, though not an inherent pleasure. What is it about "the Web" that stops me and other non-techies, making us pause for a moment before we finally give in and embrace it and its myriad resources?

Is the problem that those few of us who are still sensitive to the weight and meaning of words, feel threatened by the analogy that lies at the heart of that term: the Web? After all, most webs are of use only to the spiders who spin and maintain them. Other beasts simply get stuck in the threads of the web and wait there to be devoured. Or, is the problem simply an irrational fear of the unknown, in this case, the technical unknown? Is that why we initially hesitate to mix our metaphors and "surf" the "links" of the "Web"?

In due course, however, the alluring World Wide Web becomes harder and harder to resist. We are intrigued by its descriptions in *Time* magazine and the *Wall Street Journal*. We are constantly invited to enter the Web, and thus the future, via increasingly user-friendly "on ramps" to the "Information Super Highway," of which, the Web (to continue mixing metaphors) is a part.

SO WHAT IS THE WEB REALLY?

But what is the Web, exactly? Here, my friend, is the sound-bite that you can trot out at the next cocktail party in your future: The World Wide Web is an open system of millions of linked hypertext documents that form a "web" of information spanning the globe.

As shown in Figure 1, the Web consists of hyperlinked (or interconnected) "documents" (which often include graphics, animation, video, and sound) that reside on hundreds of thousands of host computer systems in more than 150 countries around the world. These "documents" are bibliographies, magazines, multimedia exhibits, databases, digital travel agencies, on-line stores, and a hundred other things. They are all connected in one way or another. And they are all available to you on the Web.

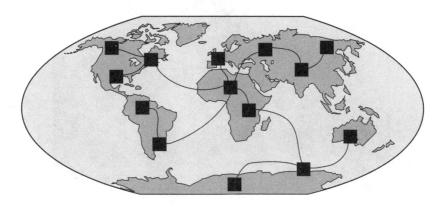

Figure 1 The Web consists of millions of interconnected documents.

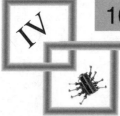
What makes the Web unique is the ease with which you can move from one hyperlinked document to another. As you use (the experts call it "surf") the Web, you view a Web document's contents on your computer screen. Although your computer displays the document's contents, the document actually resides at another computer (a Web site) which can be located anywhere in the world. Assume, for example, you are reading a Web document that discusses President Lincoln. You and your computer may be in New York City. The document, however, might reside on a Web site at a university in Illinois, or possibly within a government computer in Washington D.C. The magic and power of the Web is that you don't need to know, unless you care, where the document actually resides.

As you read through a Web document, you will very likely encounter highlighted (underlined or bold) text, called a hyperlink. Should you click your mouse on the highlighted text, your Web browsing software (which is currently displaying the document) will display a second, related document. This related information, called a link, may reside at the same Web site as your previous document, or at an unrelated Web site somewhere across the world.

When you surf the Web, you don't care where the documents actually reside. Instead, you simply move from one document to another, by clicking your mouse on the corresponding links. During one of my last Web tours, I started with a document that discussed Microsoft. Within that document, I found a link to the Comdex computer convention held each fall in Las Vegas. As I viewed information about this year's Comdex, I encountered a list of shows playing on the Las Vegas strip, one of which featured Elvis impersonators. As I read a description of the show, I noticed a link to Graceland, on which I clicked my mouse and soon found myself on a tour of Presley's Memphis home.

In short, the links you encounter within Web documents may lead you to many sites that are strangely related to your original topic. Figure 2 illustrates a typical Web document, which contains text and graphics. As you traverse the Web, moving from one site to another, you will display new documents, or *homepages*. In short, think of a homepage as the first document you display, when you begin your search for information on a specific topic.

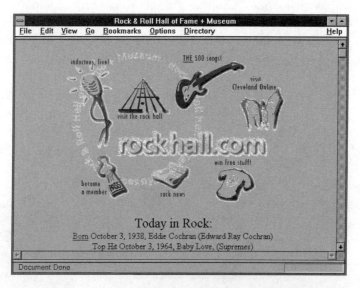

Figure 2 *Web documents (homepages) consist of text, graphics, and links to other documents which reside throughout the Web.*

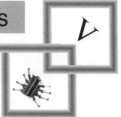

IS THE INTERNET THE WEB, OR IS THE WEB THE INTERNET?

Each day, users are overwhelmed by newspaper, magazine, and TV references to the Internet and the World Wide Web. If you are like most new users, you may be wondering, "What's the difference between the Internet and the Web?" To start, the Internet is a huge collection of computers, connected across 150 countries worldwide. Think of the Internet as nothing more than a huge computer network. Each day, millions of users, worldwide, use the Internet to exchange electronic mail, to transfer files, and, as you will learn, to access the World Wide Web.

Across the Internet, there are millions of documents whose contents discuss a wide variety of topics. You can, for example, find documents that discuss the latest scientific and medical research, electronic versions of classic novels, such as *Moby Dick,* or reviews of movies, hotels, books, and much more. The problem with the Internet is that because of the huge number of documents (almost 100,000 new documents are added each day), finding the information you need can be difficult at best.

To simplify the process of finding information on the Internet, software programmers created a visual interface (one that presents documents using text and pictures) that lets you display documents on your screen and move easily from one related document to another by clicking your mouse on highlighted text (called links) that appear within the document. In short, this new means of information retrieval is the World Wide Web.

As such, you can think of the World Wide Web as sitting on top of the Internet. In general, the links between the millions of documents form a Web that interconnects documents worldwide. When you access the World Wide Web, you are using the Internet (remember, the Internet is the collection of networked computers across which you access Web documents).

Because of the Web's explosive popularity, many people now think of the Internet as simply the Web. However, keep in mind that the Web is only one activity you can perform on the Internet. Other activities include e-mail and on-line chat sessions, as well as other information retrieval systems such as Gopher, Archie, and Veronica.

THINGS YOU CAN DO ON THE WEB

There seems to be no limit to what you can see and do on the Web. If you would care to read hypertext editions of *The New York Times,* or any of hundreds of other newspapers and magazines in various languages originating in dozens of different countries and cities, you can do so. Your other options include shopping for almost anything your heart (or head) desires, accessing financial information and executing financial transactions including stock purchases and sales, tracking your favorite sports teams, or entertaining your kids with wonderful on-line games and learning resources. The secret to successfully using the Web to find the information you need, lies in knowing the address of related site's. That's where this book comes in.

Across the Web, there are tens of thousands of Web sites. I devised *1001 Really Cool Web Sites* as your guide to the best of the best (and therefore the "coolest") of these many options. In short, I designed this book to save you time (I've done the thousands of hours of surfing for you) and effort as you look for the information you need.

1001 Really Cool Web Sites

Each document on the Web has a unique address (the old timers call Web addresses URLs, or *unique resource locators*). To view a Web document's contents using your browser, you simply tell your browser the address of the site you desire. Throughout this book, I describe over 1,000 sites across the Web. If you examine each site description closely, you will find a site title, followed by a line beginning with a series of strange characters (http://). The line that contains these characters is the site's Web address. The letters *http* are an abbreviation for *hypertext transport protocol*, which defines the set of rules Web site designers follow to create documents through which you can browse. Each Web document has a unique address that begins with the letters *http*. This book doesn't just give you the address of random documents on the Web, it gives you the addresses of sites I personally regard as cool!

Just What is Cool?

Finding quality on the Web remains something of a dicey business. While there are a great many informationally rich, graphically beautiful, and navigationally excellent places on the Web, there is also a great deal that is trivial or, even worse, vulgar. One can spend hours (sometimes even days) selecting diamonds from among the many pieces of costume jewelry on the Web. The fact, is that there are tens of thousands of homepage addresses on the Web, the vast majority of which have not qualified for inclusion in this book.

You are asking, I am sure, what my criteria for "cool" is, and how I selected the Web sites that appear in this book. Here is your answer. There are, to my mind, four aspects of Web "cool." The first of these is navigational coolness. This flavor of coolness is inherent in a Web site where the document's organization of data (whether that data is text, graphics, audio, video, or a mix of all these things) is such that a user unfamiliar with the site, can quickly, easily, and intuitively find his or her way to desired locations and files within the document.

The second aspect of Web "cool" is graphical. As you examine the sites presented in this book, you will find that the Web's hypertext technology allows for rich graphics and visually attractive page design. Graphical coolness is inherent in a site that uses this Web capability in such a way as to create pages that are attractive to the eye, in the same way that the pages of a well-designed magazine cause you to stop and take notice.

And the third aspect of Web coolness? This is the informational aspect. The Web enables the presentation of vast amounts of data, and thus makes sites that offer minimal amounts of information on topics they purport to "cover" seem all the more trivial and absurd. Thus, I define informational coolness by depth of data, which should go as deep as the technology allows. And, that is pretty deep if done right: fathoms below the *Titanic*, so far as I am concerned.

The fourth and final aspect of Web coolness, and the most important, is attitude. This label speaks for itself. Open, positive sharing of information is cool. Hate mongering is not cool. Inclusion is cool. Exclusion is not cool. Positive, constructive criticism is cool. Biting sarcasm is not cool. Freedom of speech is cool. Censorship is uncool. Like the sign says: "It is a question of attitude."

To make my list of *1001 Really Cool Web Sites,* a homepage has had to qualify for at least one of the above four categories of coolness, with the paramount coolness of attitude being an absolute requirement. (For example, the "Friends of the Earth" page on the Web does not strike me as being particularly well designed, either graphically or navigationally, but the site has attitudinal cool and the depth of information provided is impressive. Thus, it makes the list.)

Ideally, the perfect Web site should (as do many of the sites included in this book) embrace all four forms of coolness: navigational, graphical, informational, and attitudinal.

Another aspect of this book that I hope you will find cool is the CD-ROM which accompanies it. This CD-ROM provides:

- both PC and Mac browsing software that lets you access the Web;

- offers from on-line services and providers for free connect time;

- a full-color electronic version of this book that you can view on your PC or Mac and search for sites that contain the information you need;

- a demo version of a pretty cool, Windows-based program by PF.Magic called Dogz, which brings to your PC, your own live-in pet. If you are using a Mac, you will have to check out PF.Magic's homepage, discussed later in this section.

How to Access the World Wide Web

To access hypertext documents on the World Wide Web, you use a piece of software called a "browser." The CD-ROM that accompanies this book includes browser programs for both the PC or Mac platforms. Via your browser, you specify the Web address of the document you wish to access. After taking a few moments to find the document on the Web, your browser will then display the "homepage" (or initial page) of the document.

From the homepage, you may encounter links to other pages within the site you are accessing, or to related pages at other sites on the Web. For example, the homepage for an art museum will probably not only include direct links to that institution's own "virtual" galleries and electronic gift shop, but also links to the homepages of similar institutions on the Web. It is your navigation (movement from one to another) of these cascading pages and documents that is termed "surfing" the Web.

A Bit More about Hypertext

I hear you saying, "Okay Ed, what button do I push? Where do I click? How do I make my surfboard move to the next wave and carry me further down the coast? How do I use these 'links' you are talking about?" Homepages represent links as either icons or underlined text, and sometimes as both. Simply click your mouse on the link you desire and your browser will do the rest, bringing up the linked page for you to peruse with all its information and, probably, even more links from which to choose. Just keep pointing and clicking and you will be officially surfing the Web! Doesn't that sound easy?

First You Have to Make a Connection

Before you surf, you must buy a board and get yourself to the beach. In other (and more direct) words, you have to connect your PC or Mac to the Internet via a modem. You do this by using your modem, connected to a standard phone-line, to dial into an Internet provider (such as those described on the CD-ROM that accompanies this book) or an on-line service (such as CompuServe, America Online, or Prodigy).

Internet providers are companies that will let you access the Internet (thus, also the Web) through their host computer, which is connected to the Internet. There are many providers out there; the monthly fees are usually reasonable--although it does pay to do some comparison shopping before you sign up. In addition to base pricing, look into whether or not the provider offers a dial-up number that is a local call from where you will work. Otherwise, those phone bills mount up, once you start surfing. To help you perform such "provider comparisons," the CD-ROM, that accompanies this book, discusses the simple steps you need to perform in order to try out several providers for free.

Another attractive option for connecting to the Web is to use an on-line service, such as CompuServe or Prodigy. An on-line service is by far your cheapest way to go. Additionally, for the casual (and perhaps technophobic?) lay-computer user, on-line services offer user-friendly interfaces that make the Internet, in general (and the Web in particular), easier to negotiate and navigate than might otherwise be the case. (Generally, most Internet providers now let you connect to the Web with a few mouse clicks.)

The real price you pay for the economically and technically "safe" connection to the Internet offered by an on-line service is speed. Most Web documents, being graphically intense, represent large amounts of information (many bytes of data). If your Internet connection is not fast enough (for example, if you are logged into on-line service at a rate of 2,400 baud, as opposed to the minimum 14,400 baud that is recommended for all Web usage), you are going to be in for some extremely slow surfing. Depending on the speed of your connection, it may take your browser several minutes to display a homepage that a user with a faster provider-direct connection (say, at 28,800 baud) may be able to download in less than 30 seconds. As you start to surf the Web, you will realize quickly, that waiting for your browser to display graphic images can become quite frustrating.

TRY OUT THE WORLD WIDE WEB FREE!

The good people at Jamsa Press have arranged with several major Internet providers and on-line services to offer readers of *1001 Really Cool Web Sites* some really cool deals. They have made it easy for you to get, in some cases, free access time on the Internet, and in other cases, significantly reduced start-up costs.

The process is simple. Use the software provided on the accompanying CD-ROM to connect to the Web and to great deals for Web access. The CD-ROM includes software for various providers and services, each of which offers different levels of Web support and access. None of them are the right option for everyone. But, at least one is bound to be the right option for you! "Test drive" the various providers and services courtesy of the special offers you'll find described on the *1001 Really Cool Web Sites* disc, then choose the Information Super Highway "on ramp" that you think best suits your needs.

Within the CD-ROM, you will find instructions which will help you get connected to the Internet using the provider or on-line service you choose. To begin, insert the CD-ROM in your drive. Next, examine the CD-ROM for a file named README. Open and print the README file using your word processor.

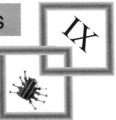

USING THE CD-ROM VERSION OF THIS BOOK

As briefly discussed, the CD-ROM that accompanies this book contains software you can use to connect to the Internet using Windows or a Mac. In addition, the CD-ROM contains an electronic version of this book! Every site you'll encounter on the pages of this book appears on the CD-ROM, with one major difference--the CD-ROM displays each site's screen image in full color! It's really cool. Using the CD-ROM, you can read the electronic book much like you would this one; you can read sequentially, moving from one site to the next, or you can search for sites that discuss a specific topic. If you are using a Mac, simply insert the CD-ROM disc and click on the document named **1001Cool**. If you are using Windows, you must first install the CD-ROM software discussed next.

INSTALLING THE CD-ROM SOFTWARE FOR WINDOWS 3.1

Before you can use the *1001 Really Cool Web Sites* CD-ROM, you must first install software that lets you view the CD-ROM files from within Windows. To install this software within Windows 3.1, perform these steps:

1. Place the *1001 Really Cool Web Sites* CD-ROM in your drive.

2. Select the Program Manager File menu and choose Run. Windows will display the Run dialog box.

3. Within the Run dialog box, type the command D:\SETUP, replacing the drive letter D with the drive letter that corresponds to your CD-ROM drive. For example, if your CD-ROM is drive E, you would type E:\SETUP.

4. Choose OK. The SETUP program will install the files on to your hard drive.

To run the *1001 Really Cool Web Sites* CD-ROM double click your mouse on the *1001 Really Cool Web Sites* icon. Windows will start the program displaying the opening screen shown in Figure 2.

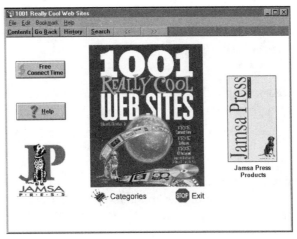

Figure 2 1001 Really Cool Web Sites opening screen.

BROWSING WEB SITES USING THE CD-ROM

When you view Web sites using the CD-ROM, you are not connected to the Web. Instead, you use the CD-ROM to look up sites that contain the information you desire. Think of the *1001 Really Cool Web Sites* CD-ROM as a phone book. Before you place a phone call, you use the phone book to look up phone numbers. Likewise, before you connect to the Web, you can use the CD-ROM to locate the sites you need. Just as you can use a phone book to look up numbers while you place other calls, you can use the *1001 Really Cool Web Sites* CD-ROM to lookup sites while you are connected to the Web. For example, assume that you are surfing the Web looking for movie reviews. Using the CD-ROM, you can search for sites that discuss movies or films. After you find a site on the CD-ROM, you can type in the site's address into your browser to view the site's document.

VIEWING SITES BY CATEGORY

The CD-ROM lists over 1,001 Web sites that I've grouped into categories. To view sites by category, click your mouse on the Categories button. The CD-ROM, in turn, will display its list of site categories as shown in Figure 3.

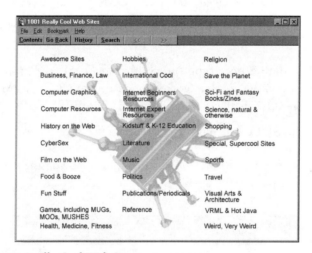

Figure 3 Categories within 1001 Really Cool Web Sites.

To display the sites within a category, simply click your mouse on the category you desire. For example, if you are simply browsing the CD-ROM, you might start with the Awesome Sites category. The *1001 Really Cool Web Sites* CD-ROM, in turn, will display the first site in the category, which in this case, is the Andy Warhol Museum shown in Figure 4.

The toolbar near the top of the window contains two buttons you can use to move forward and backward through a category's sites. If you click your mouse on the button containing the right-facing arrows (>>), the CD-ROM will display the next site in the category list. If you click your mouse on the left-facing arrows (<<), the CD-ROM will display the previous site. If either of these buttons becomes dim, you have reached either the first or last site in the category list and you cannot move further in that direction.

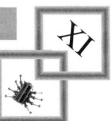

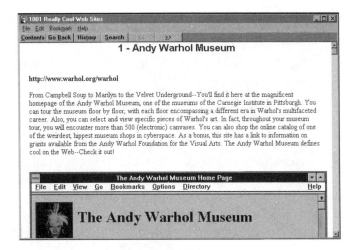

Figure 4 *The first site in the Awesome Site category--Andy Warhol Museum.*

INSTALLING THE CD-ROM UNDER WINDOWS 95

You can use the *1001 Really Cool Web Sites* CD-ROM under Windows 95 just as you would Windows 3.1. The steps you must perform to install the *1001 Really Cool Web Sites* files under Windows 95 are very similar to those just discussed:

1. Place the *1001 Really Cool Web Sites* CD-ROM in your drive.

2. Click your mouse on the Start menu and choose Run. Windows 95 will display the Run dialog box.

3. Within the Run dialog box, type the command D:\SETUP, replacing the drive letter D with the drive letter that corresponds to your CD-ROM drive. For example, if your CD-ROM is drive E, you would type E:\SETUP.

4. Choose OK. The SETUP program will install the files on to your hard drive.

To run the *1001 Really Cool Web Sites* CD-ROM from within Windows 95, select the Start menu and choose Programs. Within the menu of program options, select the *1001 Really Cool Web Sites* entry. Windows 95 will start the program, displaying the opening screen previously shown in Figure 2.

RETURNING TO THE CATEGORY LIST

You can return to the category list from a site at any time by clicking your mouse on the toolbar Contents button. To return to the *1001 Really Cool Web Sites* CD-ROM main window, click your mouse on the Contents button from within the category list window.

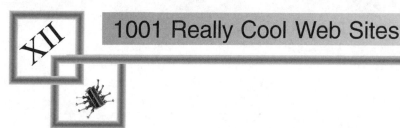

PRINTING A SITE

When you find a site within the *1001 Really Cool Web Sites* CD-ROM that you later want to visit using your browser, you can write down the site's address, or you can print a copy of the site and its address. To print the current site, select the Web Directory File menu and choose Print Topic.

SEARCHING FOR A WEB SITE

The fastest way to list Web sites that discuss your topic of interest is to click your mouse on the Search button. The *1001 Really Cool Web Sites* CD-ROM, in turn, will display the Search dialog box. Within the Search by Word field, type in your topic of interest. If you are interested in movies, for example, you would type in Movies and press Enter. The CD-ROM, in turn, will display a Search Results dialog box that lists the titles of sites that discuss Movies. By sizing the Search Results dialog box, you can view each site's complete title. To size the window, simply drag the window frame using your mouse.

Within the Search Results sites list, double click your mouse on the title of the site you desire. The CD-ROM will display the site's text and graphics. If the site contains the information you desire, click your mouse on the Cancel button to close the Search Results dialog box. Otherwise, double click your mouse on a second site.

ANNOTATING A SITE ADDRESS

Over time, Web sites may change or cease to exist. If you are using the book version of the *1001 Really Cool Web Sites*, you can make an appropriate note on the page of the book that contains the site. Likewise, if you are using the CD-ROM, you can make annotations to a site. To annotate the current CD-ROM site, select the Edit menu Annotate option. The CD-ROM, in turn, will display the Annotate dialog box. Type in your annotation, such as a new site address, and select Save. The *1001 Really Cool Web Sites* CD-ROM, in turn, will display a small paper clip above the left-hand corner of the site's screen image. To display the annotation, click your mouse on the paper clip.

VIEWING A PREVIOUSLY VIEWED SIGHT

As you click through the sites in the *1001 Really Cool Web Sites* CD-ROM, there may be times when you want to view a site that you saw earlier, but whose category you no longer remember. In such cases, click your mouse on the toolbar History button. The CD-ROM, in turn, will display the History dialog box that contains a list of sites you have previously viewed. Double click your mouse on the site you desire.

MARKING YOUR FAVORITE SITES

If you use the book version of *1001 Really Cool Web Sites*, you may find yourself marking the pages of the sites you use on a regular basis. In a similar way, you can place bookmarks on your favorite sites within the *1001 Really Cool Web Sites* CD-ROM. After you assign a bookmark to a site, you can select the site quickly from the Bookmark menu. To assign a bookmark to the current site, select the Bookmark menu and choose Define. The CD-ROM will display the Define dialog box. Choose OK.

EXITING THE *1001 REALLY COOL WEB SITES* CD

To exit the *1001 Really Cool Web Sites* CD-ROM, select the File menu Exit option or click your mouse on the Exit menu button that appears on the opening window.

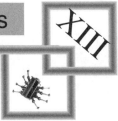

A DOG ON MY DESKTOP? COOL!

Throughout this book, I've given you a list of what I consider the coolest sites on the World Wide Web. As I was surfing the Web in search of this book's sites, I came across software that I was pretty sure Happy, the Dalmatian who appears in the Jamsa Press logo, would think is pretty cool! I was sure, however, that most of you would find the Dogz program quite a bit of fun.

Dogz is a program from P.F.Magic that unleashes a pet dog on your Windows or Mac screen. As shown in Figure 5, your pet dog comes complete with a ball, bone, food, and water, as well as other essentials.

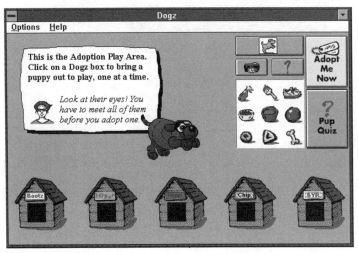

Figure 5 Dogz on the desktop!

If you want, you can stop what you are doing and play fetch or hide and seek. If you are really busy, your dog will simply take a nap in the corner of your desktop. Over time, your dog will get to know you and the things you like to do (such as how often you want to play ball).

If you are a Windows user, you will be happy to find out that we have included a demo copy of Dogz on the CD-ROM that accompanies this book (sorry Mac users, the demo wasn't ready when we went to press). To install the demo software on your system, perform these steps:

1. Select the File menu Run option. Windows will display the Run dialog box.

2. Within the Run dialog box, type in the command D:\DOGZ\SETUP, replacing the drive letter D with the drive letter that corresponds to your CD-ROM drive. For example, if your CD-ROM is drive E, you would type E:\DOGZ\SETUP.

3. Choose OK. The setup program will install the Dogz software on your system.

After you pick the dog you like, you will want to adopt him by contacting PF.Magic. That's where the Web comes back into play. You can adopt your dog using the PF.Magic Web site at http://www.pfmagic.com/dogz/adopt (as shown in Figure 6, or you can contact PF.Magic the old-fashioned way at 1-800-48-ADOPT.

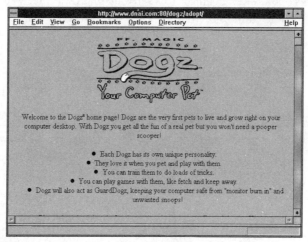

Figure 6 Adopting a Dog from PF.Magic.

Take the demo program for a test drive. I think you will agree that Dogz, which has been featured worldwide in magazine reviews, is pretty cool!

UNDERSTANDING THE WEB'S DYNAMICS

Each day, thousands of new sites (homepages) appear on the Web. As new sites come, other sites move (possibly to a new location) or simply go away (when the person who maintains the site learns just how much work a Web site really is). A danger in writing a book that gives readers Web addresses is that, over time, the addresses may change. When I chose sites for this book, I made my best effort to select sites that looked stable. In other words, I tried to choose sites I thought would not move, or worse yet, go away. I then worked with the folks at Jamsa Press to establish a way (using the Jamsa Press Web site) for you to get updated addresses, should a site move.

If, while you are surfing the cool sites I've listed in this book, you find that a site has gone away, connect to the Jamsa Press Web site (http://www.jamsa.com) and find the icon for *1001 Really Cool Web Sites*. When you click your mouse on the icon, you will encounter a list of updated addresses for sites that have moved. As you examine the sites in this book, you will find that I have grouped them by category. At the end of each site category, I have included a list of additional sites, to which you might want to surf, as you look for information on a specific topic. By combining these additional site lists with the on-line addresses at Jamsa Press, I'm happy to announce that you should have no problem getting to the cool sites!

I'll be seeing you in cyberspace.

Edward J. Renehan, Jr.
Wickford, North Kingstown, RI
10 October 1995

Andy Warhol Museum

http://www.warhol.org/warhol

From Campbell Soup to Marilyn to the Velvet Underground—You'll find it here at the magnificent homepage of the Andy Warhol Museum, one of the museums of the Carnegie Institute in Pittsburgh. You can tour the museum floor by floor, with each floor encompassing a different era in Warhol's multifaceted career. Also, you can select and view specific pieces of Warhol's art. In fact, throughout your museum tour, you will encounter more than 500 (electronic) canvases. You can also shop the online catalog of one of the weirdest, hippest museum shops in cyberspace. As a bonus, this site has a link to information on grants available from the Andy Warhol Foundation for the Visual Arts. The Andy Warhol Museum defines cool on the Web—Check it out!

Figure 1.1 Encounter Andy Warhol himself.   *Figure 1.2 Three Marilyns in Cyberspace.*

Babbage's Best of the Internet

http://www.bbcnc.org.uk/babbage/

Who is Babbage? He's the BBC's (British Broadcasting Company's) duly-appointed Internet guide (Webmaster to the Queen, I suppose that means: Royal Order of the Cybergarter). He is named after Charles Babbage, the eminent Victorian inventor of the Difference Engine (the first mechanical computer). What Babbage provides is an indispensable hypertext guide to the Internet. Babbage's links (more than 300 of them) are broken down by categories that include business, broadcasters, computer resources, culture, fine arts, the Internet, and more. The site also has its own forms-based interface for many Web search engines. Check out Babbage and his choice picks of the best in cyberspace. Splendid!

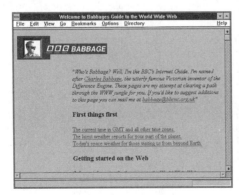 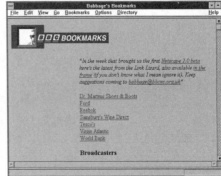

Figure 2.1 Babbage's many options.   *Figure 2.2 Babbage's bookmarks.*

John Perry Barlow (from the Grateful Dead to the Electronic Frontier)

http://www.eff.org/~barlow

A character whose life appears out of the writings of both Ken Kesey and William Gibson, John Perry Barlow left ranching in Wyoming to become a lyricist for the Grateful Dead. Now, in his third incarnation as co-founder of the Electronic Frontier Foundation, Barlow wanders online to philosophize about computer freedom and ethics in the digital age. Access Barlow's wisdom and humanity by visiting the Electronic Frontier Foundation homepage (address above) and then choosing the link entitled "Boardmembers, Staff & Volunteer Home Pages." A long menu of names will appear, including not just Barlow, but also Esther Dyson, who is certainly worth a point and a click herself.

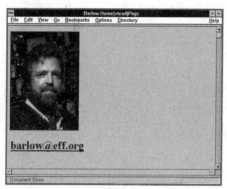

Figure 3.1 Mr. Barlow himself.

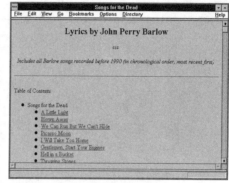

Figure 3.2 All of Barlow's songs.

Berlin and Prague: A Journey in Photographs

http://www-swiss.ai.mit.edu/philg/berlin-prague/book-cover.html

Access Philip Greenspun's beautiful documentary of a journey down the Elbe in search of lost Jewish culture. For me, the most engaging part of the voyage was its start at the perennial wreck that is East Berlin. Greenspun's penetrating photographs of this city reveal a shattered monument to the last great battle of the European War. These photos also make a statement about the forty-year socialist administration which failed, decade after decade, to raise the streets and buildings out of the rubble and disrepair that accompanied defeat. However, Greenspun's journey does have a lighter side. He also takes us with him when he meets and courts a beautiful blonde Czech woman, who alone is worth the price of admission.

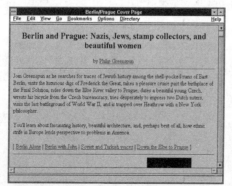

Figure 4.1 Greenspun's memorials and memories.

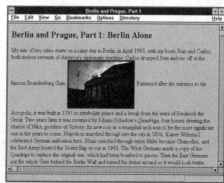

Figure 4.2 The start of the journey.

Computer Animation Edge

http://www.rezn8.com

ReZn8 Productions is an animation/video graphics group working on some of the best film projects of the decade. At this site, they give you sample graphics to demonstrate the "hows and whats" of their work. "Technological advances are rapidly blurring the distinction between all traditional forms of media," the homepage announces. "With each passing minute, the world beneath our feet is compressing. As the world compresses, a fusion occurs." There are few finer examples of the fusion of digital art, motion, and sound than what you will find here, where unreality is reality. At this site, audio and visual inertia stop, and turns on its head. So, if you feel the need to have your assumptions challenged, surf to this spot on the Web.

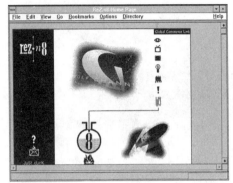

Figure 5.1 State-of-the-art graphics.   *Figure 5.2* View golf video clips.

6

Best of the Web Award Recipients

http://wings.buffalo.edu/contest/awards/

The "Best of the Web Awards" (established by Brandon Plewe—plewe@acsu.buffalo.edu) highlight sites which best show the versatility and power of the Web, demonstrating the outer limits of Web programming. The 1994 awardees, who await you here, were announced at the International W3 Conference in Geneva on May 26, 1994. Nominations were open and were received from users across the Web. Voting was managed in the same way. Come check out the Best Overall Site, Best Educational Site, and Best Institutional Site, as well as winners of a host of other awards, including Best Navigational Aid. You'll also find information on the upcoming Best of the Web '95.

 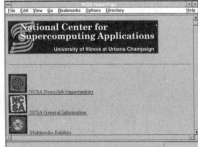 

Figure 6.1 Best of Web '94.   *Figure 6.2* Best Overall Site.   *Figure 6.3* MTV gets honorable mention.

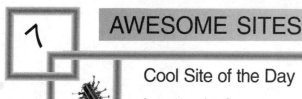

AWESOME SITES

Cool Site of the Day

http://cool.infi.net

Every day it is something new. The link changes punctually at midnight (I've checked). Here you will find zines (electronic magazines), cool commercial sites, and the nooks and crannies of the Web where classic rock-n-roll lingers. You'll experience special-interest sites ranging from Harley-Davidson motorcycles to weather forecasting. Some sites seem more cool than others, but it is hard to complain because cool is a subjective thing. As my late father once said when looking in the window of a gallery in Soho, "One person's garbage is another person's art."

Figure 7.1 Stay up to date with Cool sites.

Figure 7.2 The year's coolest site!

Crash-Site: A Journey to the Edge

http://www.crashsite.com/Crash

The homepage explains itself: "At the Crash-Site, fiction overwhelms reality. Screams replace whispers. Activism replaces passivity. Littered with consumer products and spectator sports, the inner and outer landscapes helplessly hurtle toward one another. The Crash-Site, where music, art, and machine meet, is the point of impact." Using the latest VRML and Hot Java programming, the "Crash-Site" makes cool site number 5 seem as tame and conservative as the *Saturday Evening Post*. (By the way, the world thus created is not one that you should journey in without Netscape. For information on downloading Netscape, see http://www.netscape.com). Awesome.

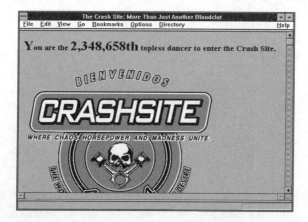

Figure 8 The shock of the new at Crash-Site.

CyberKind: Prosaics & Poetics for a Wired World

http://sunsite.unc.edu/shannon/ckind/title.html

CyberKind is a Web magazine (a zine) that includes fiction, nonfiction, poetry, and digital art—all related in some way to the Internet. If I may, I will encourage you in particular to read one ongoing series of stories written by Redmon Barbry and entitled "One Night on the Internet." The story chronicles a number of online dialogues between an unnamed cyberhero and none other than God, who has been found lurking on the Net. "Are you out there?" asks the hero. "Yes, yes, I am here," replies God as a prelude to a remarkable chat session.

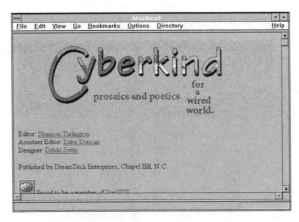

Figure 9 Cyberkind's "neterature."

Phrack Magazine

http://freeside.com/phrack.html

Since 1985, the electronic magazine (zine) *Phrack* has provided hackers with info on networking technologies and telephony, as well as "relaying other topics of interest to the international computer underground." It has also been the target of several federal investigations, as described by Bruce Sterling in *The Hacker Crackdown*. (To subscribe to *Phrack* and at the same time enroll yourself on a watch-list that the FBI probably thinks is secret, send e-mail to Phrack@well.com.) As the editors say, "Submissions to the above e-mail address may be encrypted with the following key, not that we use PGP or encourage its use or anything. Heavens no. That would be politically-incorrect. Maybe someone else is decrypting our mail for us on another machine that isn't used for *Phrack* publication. Yeah, that's it."

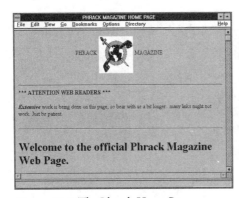 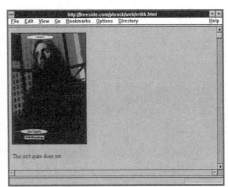

Figure 10.1 The Phrack Home Page.   *Figure 10.2* Phrack's editor strikes a pose.

AWESOME SITES

11

The Eden Matrix Cartoon Cornucopia

http://www.eden.com

When I was little, my parents would not let me read comic books. Good thing Mom hasn't seen this site! From this page, the alternative comic-strip junkie will fall delightedly through dozens of Web sites containing the golden harvest of today's digital renaissance of comic strips. Check out Adhesive comics that include *Too Much Coffee Man*, *Eyebeam*, *JAB*, and, of course, *The Eden Matrix*. You will also encounter Mojo Press which offers such horror comics as *Creature Features* and *Weird Business*. And don't forget the complete *Deep Girl Digital Ashcan* flipbook, featuring, well, the story of *Deep Girl #3* by Ariel Bordeaux. Only the most ravenously comic-hungry geek will leave this site unsatisfied. If you are concerned about society, check out this site to confirm your fears.

Figure 11.1 The Eden Matrix cornucopia.

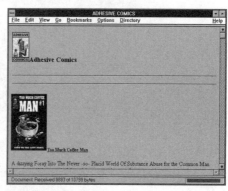

Figure 11.2 Adhesive bestsellers.

12

Escher: Images that Defy the Laws of Time and Space

http://orangutan.cv.nrao.edu/images/fantasy

See GIF and JPEG images of a great collection of Escher's most popular prints including *Belvedere*, *Moebius*, *Montage*, *Planetoid*, *Relativity*, and, of course, *Waterfall*, which is the classic illustration for a six-step endlessly falling loop. The site also includes a number of other great fantasy images. Who is Escher? I'm glad you asked! For the best description of Escher, turn to the book *Godel, Escher, Bach: An Eternal Golden Braid—A metaphorical fugue on minds and machines in the spirit of Lewis Carroll*, which won the 1980 Pulitzer Prize for general non-fiction. For now, however, check the images below and surf over to the Escher homepage.

Figure 12.1 Escher: Moebius

Figure 12.2 Escher: Waterfall

Figure 12.3 Escher: Belvedere

5-D Stereogram Graphic Weirdness

http://www.ais.net:80/netmall/bma

5-D stereograms take advantage of the manner in which your brain interprets similar, but slightly offset, images to produce a 3-D image. In a 5-D stereogram, the information for two different views of the same scene is hidden within the piece of art. This homepage includes links to three stereogram images (Vanishing Wolf, Vanishing Manatee, and Basketball) you can view. To see each image on your screen, you must relax your eyes and allow your point of focus to move behind the screen surface. When your focus reaches the correct point, the hidden multi-dimensional image will come into focus automatically. Voila! Oh my God, it is a Manatee with a basketball! I think I've done something wrong.

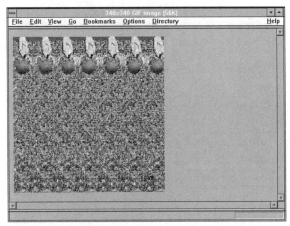

Figure 13 The Manatee with a basketball.

Harpsichord Sonatas from Scarlatti

http://www.win.tue.nl/scarlatti

Though an Italian, Domenico Scarlatti (1685-1757) spent much of his life at the Spanish court as a keyboard teacher. Scarlatti is best known for his more than 500 sonatas written to exercise musical skills, while at the same time please the ear. Some are easy, some tough. Some are boring; and others will stay with the listener for a lifetime. Including 10 pictures and 174 sound fragments totaling 39 minutes of listening, this archive allows you to look up sonatas by number or by musical characteristics, and then play/view the first few bars of each piece. Marvelous. Now, if I only had a harpsichord.

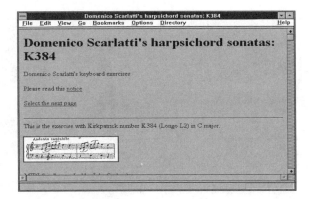

Figure 14 Search sonatas by number or key.

AWESOME SITES

Jurassic Heaven: Dinosaur Museum

http://www2.ios.com/~dinosaur

Perspective Visuals is a commercial multimedia software firm. At this site, you'll find demos of several of Perspective Visuals' products, including *Dinosaur Museum* (which is why my son Billy, a dinosaur nut and *Jurassic Park* fan, insisted that I cover this site). Developed in conjunction with the Smithsonian Institution, *Dinosaur Museum* includes 3-D photographs that make dinosaur dioramas, skeletons, and skulls jump out from your computer screen, as well as fabulous interactive graphic "curiosity learning screens" that help illustrate dinosaur myths, facts, and trivia. The software includes some of the best animation movies ever created (for Macintosh and for Windows).

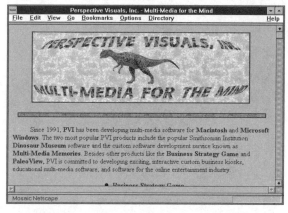

Figure 15 Dinosaurs on the Web.

Kaleidospace Multimedia Gallery

http://Kspace.com

Enter a great digital performance space for multimedia artists. You'll find it all here: interactive media, digital movies, hypertext books with multimedia, downloadable multimedia tools, and digital music videos. On the day I visited, the spotlight artist was Bruce Nunnaly, and the current artists-in-residence included none other than Clive Barker! In a "studio," you can look at multimedia works in progress. Any multimedia artists lurking out there? Find the sign-up sheet to display your wares. The represented artists are searchable by name, genre, and medium. And you can download copies of the "works" in this exhibit for a fee. I think I'll submit a piece myself, but first, I'll apply for a grant.

Figure 16.1 A multimedia cornucorpia.

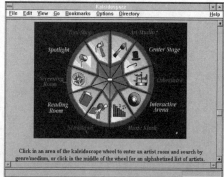

Figure 16.2 Picking topics from the kaleidoscope.

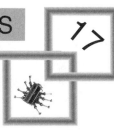

MovieLink: The Ultimate Cyber-Entertainment Luxury

http://www.movielink.com

Movies? What's playing? Check out this site. To start, choose your city from the clickable U.S. map, or simply enter your five-digit zip code and survey listings of movie showing schedules with a search by movie title, neighborhood, or showtime. In some cities, you can even reserve tickets using your American Express card. One minor criticism: the listings seem biased toward large commercial cinemas and films, and do not include many small art-houses. But if you are like the rest of the world, and your heart's desire is to see the big, action-packed suspense thrillers, then this site is for you.

Figure 17 This guy does not look comfortable.

Library of Congress Cultural Exhibits

http://lcweb.loc.gov/homepage/exhibits.html

As a historian by trade, I thoroughly enjoyed this site, which includes electronic editions of nine great Library of Congress exhibits. Included here are such exhibits as "Declaring Independence: Drafting the Documents," "Temple of Liberty: Building the Capitol for a New Nation," and an exhibit on the Gettysburg Address. Take the Gettysburg Address exhibit as an example. It has facsimiles of each of Lincoln's several drafts of the speech, a facsimile of his invitation to come to Gettysburg in the first place, and last, but not least, the only known photograph of Lincoln at Gettysburg on the day he made the speech. Extraordinary.

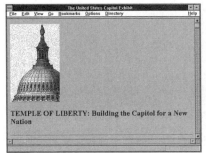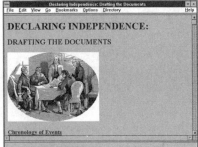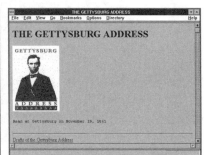

Figure 18.1 Temple of Liberty.   *Figure 18.2 Ben Franklin and company.*   *Figure 18.3 Abe's day out.*

AWESOME SITES

19

Planet Earth Home Page Virtual Library

http://www.nosc.mil/planet_earth/info.html

This is literally *the* homepage for the planet earth. From here you can branch to thousands of resources through a neatly arranged, intuitive tree structure. In short, this one URL address gets you to more data than the Library of Congress. You will begin with a selection of 13 rooms from which to begin your intuitive quest. Need statistics, maps? Try one of the World Region rooms. For other needs, start at the Multimedia Room, the Government Room, the Science Room, the Education Room, or . . . well, you get the picture. That's it, the homepage for my favorite planet. Love it or leave it.

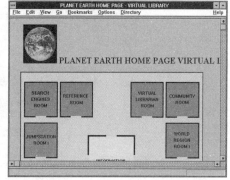

Figure 19.1 My favorite planet.   *Figure 19.2 The library map.*

20

Music Kitchen: Musical Munchies

http://www.nando.net/music/gm

Mom's cooking up something good. Choose from Bonnie Raitt, Redd Cross, Meat Puppets, Rock-It Comix, the Wild Colonials, World Domination Records, or any of several other cool links. We've got it all, boys and girls. We've got discographies. We've got press releases, photos, and tour schedules. We've also got Sonic Youth, Tracy Chapman, and even Stephen Stills (yes, unlike Jerry Garcia, he is still alive). What's missing? Lawrence Welk and the King Family Singers. But then, if they weren't missing, this site would not rate as cool. (Actually, my grandmother loved Lawrence Welk. Sorry, Grandma.)

Figure 20.1 Mom as you remember her.   *Figure 20.2 Bonnie as you remember her.*   *Figure 20.3 Meat Puppets, such nice young people.*

The San Francisco Exploratorium

http://www.exploratorium.edu

What? You've never been to the Exploratorium in the Palace of Fine Arts in San Francisco? Well, stop here for your chance to get a taste. The exhibits are fascinating, and constantly changing. When I visited, the featured presentation was something entitled "Diving Into the Gene Pool," a multimedia exploration of genetics and the Human Genome Project. By the time you stop by, something else will probably be on display. One thing you should be sure to check out is the interesting illustrated history of the Palace of Fine Arts, one of the most beautiful buildings in the world. Explore.

Figure 21.1 Exploratorium Home Page.

Figure 21.2 A sobering exhibit.

NASA

http://hypatia.gsfc.nasa.gov/NASA_homepage.html

Use your Web browser to roam through the Kennedy, Goddard, Ames, Dryden, and Langley space centers. You can also access the NASA Strategic Plan and a great file on NASA history, as well as information on NASA educational programs, NASA online educational resources, and NASA procurement (business opportunities, awards, forecasts, etc.). But wait! That's not all! You also get a set of Ginsu knives (just kidding). You get access to the NASA Technical Report Server, and a complete searchable index to NASA information resources by subject. Right now I'm searching for the shuttle ride sign-up screen.

Figure 22.1 What a lousy logo.

Figure 22.2 Who is that masked man?

Figure 22.3 Shuttle sign-up sheet!

AWESOME SITES

Sounds Out of Chaos

http://www.ccsr.uiuc.edu/People/gmk/Papers/ChuaSndRef.html

Chua's Oscillator Circuit is a chaotic system that generates sounds stranger than those that vibrate and rattle cars filled with high-school students. Tune in and hear the audio equivalent of a fractal graphic. Chua's Circuit is one of the few physical systems for which the presence of chaos has been observed experimentally, verified by computer simulations, and proven mathematically. Learn how to use the circuit to generate musical signals. Also check out the bifurcation diagrams related to the circuit, as well as the recurrence diagrams that reveal the dynamic structure in the chaos of Chua's oscillator. I wonder if random sounds will become a category at the Grammy Awards.

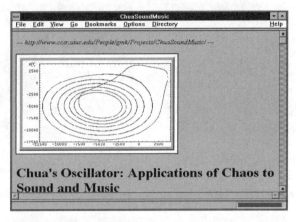

Figure 23 Chun's big idea.

The Nine Planets: A Multimedia Tour of the Solar System

http://seds.lpl.arizona.edu/billa/tnp

Treat yourself to a 60-page hypermedia excursion through a stunning collection of solar-system images, movies, and facts. The site describes and illustrates each of the planets and major moons with movies and stills taken by NASA spacecraft. This regularly updated site includes an "Express Tour" of the ten best worlds, a general overview of the solar system, and also the "Grand Tour Deluxe," embracing details on some 64 heavenly bodies, including such small bodies as comets, the Kuiper Belt, and that weird little bugger, the Oort Cloud.

Figure 24.1 Mao's favorite: The Red Planet.

Figure 24.2 A comet, and I don't mean the reindeer.

Figure 24.3 The Voyager Probe.

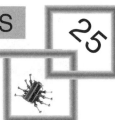

Stalking the Wily Hacker

http://town.hall.org/university/security/stoll/cliff.html

Check out this great multimedia presentation given by Cliff Stoll at the Cisco Networkers '94 Conference, wherein he tells the same tale recounted in his book *The Cuckoo's Egg.* The book is a true account of how Stoll, tracking down a 75-cent computer error, followed a lead all the way back to a ring of KGB spies. In addition to being technically adept and a gifted writer, Stoll is just downright funny as he explains how he stumbled onto one of the most inept covert operations ever launched, comparing the KGB spy-mavens to Keystone cops. You'll find this both a fun and educational stop on the Web. Stoll is about as hip as they come.

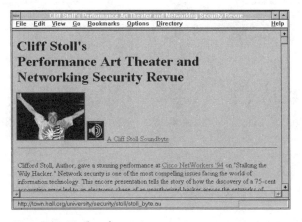

Figure 25 Hackers beware!

Stock Market Data from MIT

http://www.ai.mit.edu/stocks

This site is a great resource for recent stock market information, including previous day's closing prices and one-year graphs of historical prices. The site includes stock charts of price and volume movement updated daily, mutual fund charts of price movement, top stocks (i.e., the most frequently graphed stocks of late), ticker symbols sorted by company and by symbol, a directory of historical data files extracted and used to draw the graphs at the site, information about how the stock graphs have been drawn, and more. Wow! Thurston Howell, III meets cyberspace. Buy! Sell!

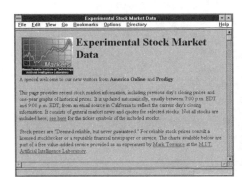

Figure 26.1 Gotta love the NASDAQ.

Figure 26.2 Mutual Fund performance.

AWESOME SITES

Mandarin Films Virtual Theatre

http://www.mandarin.films.hk/

Mandarin Films keeps on cranking out these movies and part of the reason why they can do it is they are all the same movie: not just the same plot and actors, but also the same costumes and fake interiors. But that's part of the allure: the fun. You not only get to make fun about how absurd the hand-painted scene of a park outside a fake windows looks, but you also get to joke about how it looked just as bad in the film you say last week. Come to think of it, the scene was very similar as well, but this week's bad fat guy was a good fat guy last week, and this week's good thin guy was a bad thin guy.

Figure 27.1 Welcome to Mandarin Films.

Figure 27.2 You'll find options in the lobby.

SunSITE: Eclectic Resource Links

http://sunsite.unc.edu/

SunSITE at the University of North Carolina, Chapel Hill, is one of the most extraordinary places on the Web and links to an outstanding number of eclectic resources. Just a few samples: Use Sun's "Iconbrowser" to do fast searches of more than 7,000 public domain icons that you are invited to download. Join "radio vets" Dave Rabbit and Pete Sadler and access audio files that let you experience a bit of the unofficial history of the Vietnam War: sound clips from a pirate radio station that operated in South Vietnam (ca. 1971). Or experience a multimedia exhibit entitled "Free Burma" that is a tool designed to hasten the downfall of the current military government there, which is guilty of many atrocities.

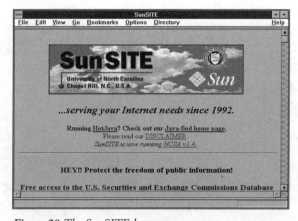

Figure 28 The SunSITE home page.

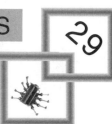

Top Ten Signs Your WWW Page is Not Cool

http://www.galcit.caltech.edu/~joe/coolpage.html

Want to know what others will think of your homepage? Check out this site to learn the signs that your site may not be cool. Just a few of the signs? How about number 8: "Disney wants to buy the rights to use it in *Mighty Ducks III*." Or number 3: "Nancy Kerrigan says it's the corniest page she's ever seen." The witty author of this site also gives you links to other examples of his creativity, including two small Doom WADs (computer game environments) called "The Missions of Rocket Jones," a terrific *Lost In Space* episode guide with digital clips, and an interesting something entitled "Madman Loose in Disneyland."

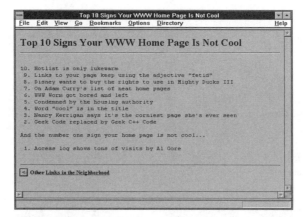

Figure 29 The ten signs.

Urban Desires: An Interactive Magazine of Metropolitan Passions

http://desires.com/issues.html

This zine (electronic magazine) offers fascinating interactive stories, incredible art, fantastic graphics, and brilliant social commentary. You will find fiction, as well as art criticism, technotoy reviews of cutting edge software (everything from virtual gardens to new arcade games), and reports from the outer fringe of both amateur and professional sex in major metropolitan areas. Hmmm. Don't ask . . . don't tell. Here you will also find reviews of music along with the work of performance-artists (including digital movie clips), considerations of style in all its forms (architecture, fashion, interior design), and some of the best travel writing being published today.

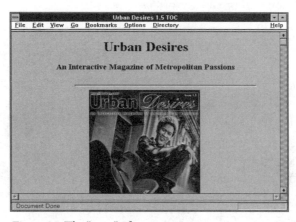

Figure 30 The "cover" of a recent issue.

AWESOME SITES

Voyager-cum-Laurie Anderson and *The Paris Review*

http://www.voyagerco.com

Courtesy of the Voyager Company, take an amazing trip through graphics, prose, and sound. Our electronic diva of the digital age, Laurie Anderson, has her own room here, as does George Plimpton's *Paris Review*. The option of having portions of *The Paris Review* here, on my PC, to read at my leisure, is for me the very definition of luxury. Eloquence, grace, and wit all wrapped up together in one elegant bundle of fine writing. It almost seems too good to be true. You will also find information on the range of great electronic publications from Voyager, which, of course, you can order online.

Figure 31 The Paris Review *goes digital.*

VRML Arc Gallery: The Next Generation of Graphics

http://www.arc.org/vrml/index.html

What? You missed the last Interactive Media Festival in LA? Well, my lucky friend, you can still enjoy the exhibits in this wild VRML Arc Gallery. "What is VRML?" you ask. Virtual Reality Modeling Language, of course. Briefly, VRML is a new standard on the Net that lets you model and navigate within a 3-D environment that mimics the real world. Very cool. For more info, see the discussion of VRML that serves as a prologue to the comprehensive VRML section later in this book. By the way, you need a special browser to view VRML files—but it is a free download. Once again, check out the VRML section of this book for details.

Figure 32.1 Denne: CyberSurfer in VRML.   *Figure 32.2* Collier: Burn Cycle.

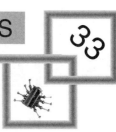

Marius Watz's World Wide Web Pages

http://www.uio.no/~mwatz/

This splendid set of links focuses on philosophy, the avant-garde, cyberculture, cyberpunk, and other aspects of the technical and cultural fringe. Marius Watz's eclectic list of offerings includes a link to sites related to Hakim Bey, Bolo, computer-generated writing, computer art, the "fiction of philosophy," the future culture list, memetics, the Nexus Project, and the Persistence of Vision (POV) ray-tracer. Aiming at where the transcendental and the technical meet, Watz has assembled a great set of links and pointers. When you visit, bring your karma and an open mind.

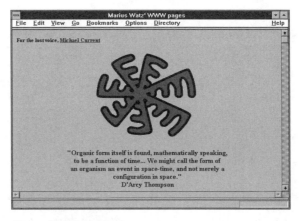

Figure 33 Watz's opening page.

34

Weather, Weather Everywhere

http://www.atmos.uiuc.edu/wxworld/html/general.html

If you just can't get enough information on the weather, if you watch the Weather Channel for hours and still want more, this site is for you. Maintained by the University of Illinois, it provides far more weather information than any normal person would ever reasonably need to have. Still, lots of this stuff is cool and fun, such as the constant flow of current satellite images, the interactive weather maps, and the many animations offering real-time graphical descriptions of weather situations around the globe. Anyone who watches television knows how much these weather-geeks enjoy their computer graphics. At this site, you'll find more state-of-the-art evidence to support that statement.

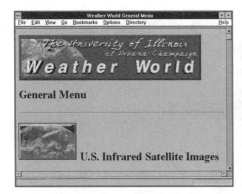

Figure 34.1 Weather smorgasbord.

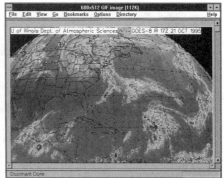

Figure 34.2 Weather patterns over the U.S.

35

Web Wide World of Music

http://american.recordings.com/wwwofmusic/

OK, so I'm almost 40, but I still like Hootie and the Blowfish. What's the big deal? Neil Young is 50, and he is playing with Pearl Jam. So get off my back. One of the 150 or so great band-related sites that you can link to from this page connect directly with Hootie and the boys. What other bands have links here? Well, Neil's buddies in Pearl Jam for one, as well as lots of other relatively new musical arrivals. It seems the only classic rock bands that have their own pages are the Dead, the Stones, and the Beatles. Who's with me that we need a site for The Band, a site for Clapton, and a site for The Who?

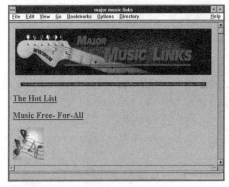

Figure 35.1 Major music links.

Figure 35.2 Hot music, hot stuff.

36

Webster's Weekly

http://www.awa.com/w2/

This great hypertext zine (electronic magazine) features Nick Bruel cartoons, the "Horrorscope," film reviews, and interesting articles on politics, art, and culture (not to mention the politics *of* art and culture). Be sure to check out Jason Ford's great column, "Dialing in from Arlington County," and Ian Finseth's "The Pen Political." Finseth is fabulous. "Let us imagine for a nonce," he writes, "a scenario in which the people of the United States grow increasingly distressed with the government." Yes, let us imagine. This zine also offers music reviews, photography, and poetry. Do yourself a favor and read "Letters from an American Observer" by John Blackburn in Volume 3, Issue 11. The article contains some pretty cool insights.

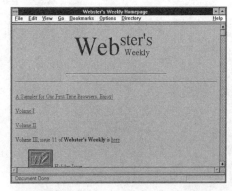

Figure 36.1 Webster's Masthead.

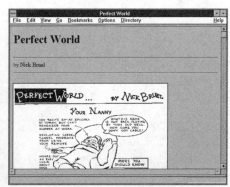

Figure 36.2 Bruel's Perfect World.

Xanadu of the Arts: Edinburgh Festival Fringe

http://www.presence.co.uk/fringe

Every year in late August, the ancient place called Edinburgh, Scotland explodes into fantastic and frenzied life. One of the most beautiful cities in the world is transformed into the largest theater in the world. The old, cobbled streets are alive from dawn until dusk, seven days a week. And Edinburgh reverberates with the music and laughter of over 1,200 shows performed by 700 companies from 32 nations. Get all the information on the upcoming 1996 event (including the draft program, tips on booking tickets, and details on how to arrange to perform or show your art).

Figure 37 Edinburgh Festival home page.

World Art Treasures

http://sgwww.epfl.ch/BERGER/index.html

Available in either French or English versions, this site promulgates the love of classical art with the help of 100,000 slides belonging to the J.E. Berger Foundation. Exhibitions include "Sandro Botticelli: The Enigmas of Painting," "Roman Portraits from Egypt," and "Art from Egypt, China, Japan, India, Myanmar/Burma, Laos, Cambodia, and Thailand." A fourth exhibition recreates the pilgrimage undertaken by Seti I for himself and his people some 3,300 years ago, which was a great journey of exploration and discovery that led to the building of the temple of Adybos. This site of treasures is truly a treasure.

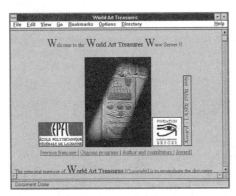

Figure 38.1 Begin your tour here.

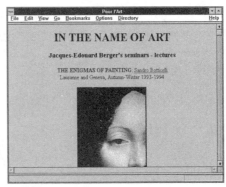

Figure 38.2 A da Vinci portrait.

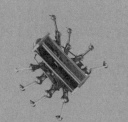

More Awesome Sites

As you surf the Web, you may find that one or more of the site addresses listed in this book have changed. In such cases, connect to Jamsa Press at http://www.jamsa.com and click on the icon that corresponds to the *1001 Really Cool Web Sites* book. Jamsa Press will list replacement addresses (when possible) for sites that have moved. In addition, you can also use the following site list as you search for more awesome sites:

Photos	http://www.cs.ucl.ac.uk/bbrace/bbrace.html
Training	http://s2.com.etj.
Weather Information	http://thunder.met.fsu.edu/~nws/wxhwy.html
Beer on the Web	http://karikukko.pc.helsinki.fi/beerinfo.html
Chocolatier recipe collection	http://www.godiva.com/recipes/chocolatier/index.html
Game Corner	http://susis.usl.hk/#lok/vidgame.html
Internet Magazine	http://www.futurenet.co.uk/games/gamesmaster.html
Total Football	http://www.futurenet.co.uk/Forums/TotalFootball/
Science Museum	http://sln.fi.edu/
Internet Mac Users Group	http://coyote.accessnv.com/dhanley/m3/m3.html
Wolfenstein 3D	http://www.astro.washington.edu/ingram/wolf.html
Wake Shield Project	http://www.svec.uh.edu

39

Advertising Age Magazine

http://www.adage.com/

This zine is the electronic edition of the classic weekly advertising and marketing magazine. Access reference databases on agency portfolios and awards. Read portraits of advertising's rising creative giants. Track personnel comings and goings as the nation's leading advertising talents form new alliances. And check in every morning for the day's top story. Is True North looking to buy Bozell again? Is Ogilvy & Mather about to lose the Campbell Soup account? Who are the superstars of marketing? For an answer to that last question, check *Advertising Age's* "Marketing 100."

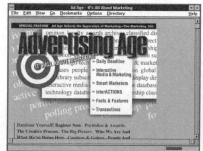

Figure 39.1 Ad Age home page.

Figure 39.2 Interactive media info.

Figure 39.3 Marketing superstars.

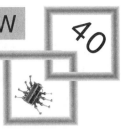

AT&T Toll-Free 800 Directory

http://att.net/dir800

Offering toll-free 800 telephone numbers for literally thousands of corporations and retailers across the US, this elegantly designed Web site lets you find the desired telephone number easily and intuitively with just a few points and clicks. You can conduct a search in several different ways. You can browse by category of service or by type of merchandise offered, or you can do a direct search by individual company name. Additionally, you can browse new numbers to see what might be of interest. You can get an estimate of costs and start the process for getting your own firm's toll-free number listed in the online directory.

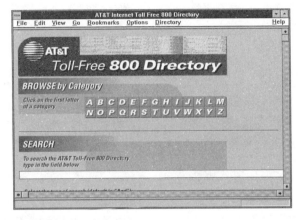

Figure 40 Easy browsing.

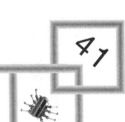

Advertising Law Home Page

http://www.webcom.com/~lewrose/home.html

Maintained by Lewis Rose, who is an advertising and marketing law partner with the Washington firm of Arent Fox Kintner Plotkin & Kahn, this extensive archive includes Federal Trade Commission (FTC) policy statements on advertising substantiation, deception, food advertising, environmental claims, testimonials, use of the word "free," sweepstakes and other contests, 900 numbers, investment marketing, and more. Here you will also find full-text FTC compliance manuals, as well as a link to the FTC's own Web site containing copies of daily press releases, information about the mission and structure of the agency, and the rule-making record for the FTC's proposed telemarketing regulations.

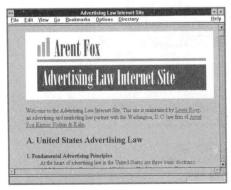

Figure 41.1 Ad Law home page.

Figure 41.2 Your hosts.

Ad Market

http://www.admarket.com

"Ad Market" offers you one-stop shopping for information on costs, reach, and schedules for virtually all domestic and foreign advertising media from television to mailing lists. Here you will also find extensive information on various public relations and advertising firms available for hire. And, you will discover advertising resources you perhaps never before realized existed, such as credit-card billing insert programs and food package container "billboards." Presented by *Hot Wired*, *Advertising Age*, and *Organic Online*, "Ad Market" is a valuable resource you will definitely want to check out.

Figure 42.1 Ad Market home page.   *Figure 42.2 Organic Online.*

Better Business Bureau

http://www.cbbb.org/cbbb

Have a question about the veracity of a firm you are doing business with, or might do business with? Run a check on them using the Better Business Bureau's information resources at this site. In addition to the database, see the BBB's policy statements on advertising self-regulation, alternative dispute resolution, charity monitoring, and donor education. Here you will also find the latest "hot flash" scam alerts and advisories, a directory of all BBB offices in the United States, a directory of corporate members, and a valuable collection of links to other resources of use and value to educated consumers. Rumor has it that Ralph Nader is this site's Webmaster.

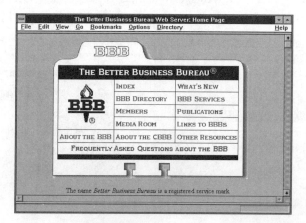

Figure 43 A site on your side.

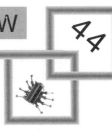

Dreyfus On-line Information Center

http://networth.galt.com/dreyfus/4134

Need strategies for creating your investment portfolio? Want to see what consistent automatic investment at various levels will do to change your retirement outlook? Want to know "The Ten Key Principles" that every investor should always keep in mind? Explore the "Dreyfus On-line Information Center" and get a clear sense of precisely how to achieve your investment objectives. In addition to general information on investing, the "Dreyfus On-line Information Center," of course, provides descriptions of some of the mutual funds offered by Dreyfus, along with related Dreyfus services.

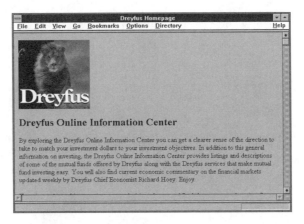

Figure 44 Dreyfus home page.

CommerceNet

http://www.commerce.net

CommerceNet is the quickest and easiest place from which you can link to the homepage of virtually any major national or multi-national corporation. You will see them all here: Apple, Lockheed, Dun & Bradstreet, Bank of America, IBM, Chase Manhattan, and even a little something called Microsoft. You will also find links to stock information, online brokerage companies, economic and statistical data related to the U.S. and world economies, and a link to the very useful Open Market Commercial Sites Index. Want more? How about a cluster of investment bank homepages, along with links to Wharton and other prestigious business schools? An indispensable resource.

  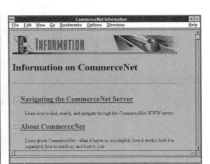

Figure 45.1 CommerceNet home page.   *Figure 45.2* What's new.   *Figure 45.3* CommerceNet info.

Employment Edge

http://sensemedia.net/employment.edge

Employment Edge, which specializes in professional career placement throughout the U.S., assures confidentiality and never charges candidates a fee. Take a look at jobs that companies post at this site, or find out how to place your own "help-wanted" ad. The site categorizes all listings by region and occupation, embracing management, accounting, auditing, engineering, and programming (including MIS and software engineering). Also, you'll find an eclectic assortment of gigs lumped together under the heading "Everything Else." This last category is where you go if you are a snake-charmer or a juggler. No, wait. If you are a snake-charmer or a juggler look under "Management."

Figure 46 *The ultimate "Help Wanted."*

47

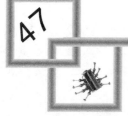

Federal Express

http://www.fedex.com

We've all seen the TV commercial for FedEx in which a woman is getting chewed out over the phone by a client because a FedEx package hasn't arrived at its destination on time. She puts the unhappy client on hold, checks the FedEx package-tracking database using special software, and finds that the package has indeed been delivered and was signed for by some unlucky schmuck in the unhappy client's office who you just know is about to die. Avoid that mess. Just download and use the package-tracking software with which you, too, can emerge victorious from just such an altercation. Arm yourself appropriately. Both PC and Mac software is available.

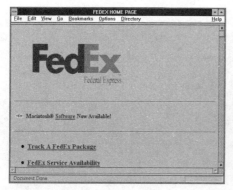

Figure 47.1 *FedEx home page.*

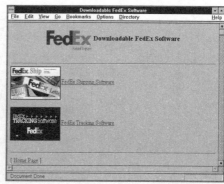

Figure 47.2 *Free software!*

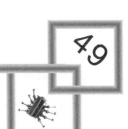

Fidelity Investments Information Center

http://www.fid-inv.com/

Have you ever noticed how all these investment companies have reliable names like "Fidelity" and "Prudential"? Makes sense. It is kind of hard to think of handing over your hard-earned cash for investment with Crapshoot Financial Services, a subsidiary of Tenuous Enterprises, Inc. But Fidelity? That's the ticket! That sounds safe! Despite all that, if you follow investing, you know of Fidelity's tremendous success. Heck, any time I might get information from Peter Lynch, you can count me in. Here you'll find detailed prospectuses on Fidelity's many financial services, toll-free numbers, lists of Fidelity offices, and more. This graphics-intensive site has a convenient "text-only" option for those dial-up users who don't want to sit around waiting for screens to resolve.

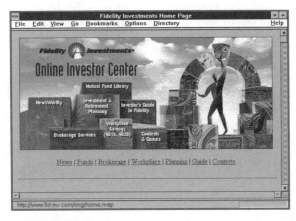

Figure 48 *Fidelity home page.*

First Virtual Holdings Corporation

http://fv.com/

First Virtual Holdings is the world's first electronic-merchant banker. This is a financial services company created specifically to enable anyone with Internet access to buy and sell information worldwide using the Internet. The First Virtual Payment System enables safe transactions for Internet users without the need to purchase or install additional software or equipment. First Virtual's system is secure, accessible, low-cost, convenient, and can handle both large and small transactions. By the way, First Virtual also operates a public-access information server called the InfoHaus, which allows anyone to become an information merchant on the Internet quickly and for almost no cost. See details here.

Figure 49.1 *First Virtual home page.*   ***Figure 49.2*** *First Virtual options.*   ***Figure 49.3*** *All the facts.*

GNN Personal Finance Center

http://gnn.com/meta/finance/

This site has so much great stuff! For starters, check out the link to "NCSA What's New: Investment and Personal Finance," which is your guide to the most recently added server addressing financial concerns. Then also check Frank Armstrong's Q&A chat area which is an adjunct to his "Investment Strategies for the 21st Century." You will also encounter Bob Beaty's "Money Matters," a weekly "News & Notes" column, and Eric Foster's weekly installment from "The Mortgage Applicant's Bible." Convenient links take you to such places as The Company Corporation (providing corporate services to over 110,000 American businesses) and Nolo Press (the leading publisher of self-help law books and software).

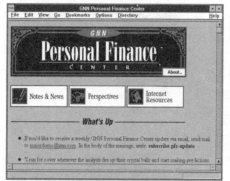

Figure 50.1 GNN home page.

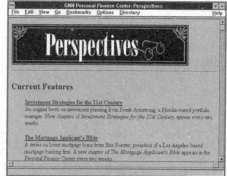

Figure 50.2 GNN perspectives.

Internet Business Center

http://tig.com/IBC/index.html

The Internet Business Center from The Internet Group continually provides the latest, most reliable information about conducting business on the Internet. They have resources to help you understand marketing on the Net, as well as building an in-house Internet publishing system. They also feature a regularly updated list of links to what they consider the "best" commercial sites (with their reasons why!). Plus, you'll find links to important Internet statistics, maps, and charts as well as links to "cool posts" with interesting points of information about conducting business on the Internet. Last, but not least, is a link to "Net Nuggets," which is a list of Internet resources.

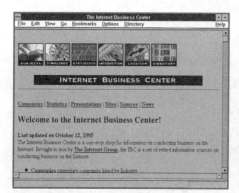

Figure 51.1 IBC home page.

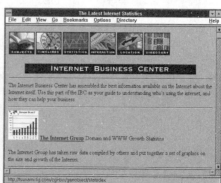

Figure 51.2 IBC statistics pointers.

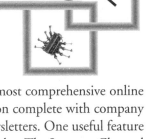
The Investor Channel

http://www.wimsey.com/Magnet/mc/index.html

These folks tout themselves, with some reason, as being the maintainers of "the world's most comprehensive online investor publication." The Investor Channel features free, up-to-date industry information complete with company profiles, news releases, current closing stock quotes, and related investment news and newsletters. One useful feature is a "hotlist" of featured public companies trading on stock exchanges around the world that The Investor Channel finds "interesting" (i.e., poised for a move either south or north). Additionally, you'll find a good list of links to other investment-oriented sites.

Figure 52 Investor Channel home page.

Internal Revenue Service

http://www.ustreas.gov/treasury/bureaus/irs/irs.html

Not everything on the Web is fun. But having access to necessary information is always cool. Here you'll find four main links: Tax Forms and Instructions, Frequently Asked Questions, Where to File, and Where to Get Help. You will also get a kick out of the opening screen, where the "Mission" of the IRS is stated: "The purpose of the Internal Revenue Service is to collect the proper amount of tax revenue at the least cost to the public in a manner warranting the highest degree of public confidence in our integrity, efficiency, and fairness." Yeah, right.

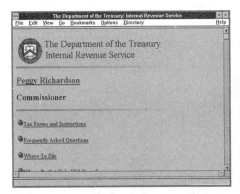

Figure 53.1 IRS home page.

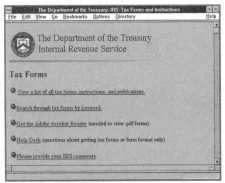

Figure 53.2 Download tax forms.

54

Jerry's Guide to Law

http://www.yahoo.com/Law

I don't know who Jerry is, but this list of links is fabulous. He's got 32 categories including criminal law (65 sites), intellectual property (63 sites), judiciary and supreme court (27 sites), law firms and legal agencies (319 sites), law schools (80 sites), legal research (58 sites), software law (13 sites), and much, much more. You will even find sites on tax law for when you get an unwelcome communication from the gang noted in listing number 53. I doubt if all this information combined can substitute for having your own capable attorney on hand for advice. But at the least, it can make you an informed consumer of legal services. Think of Jerry as your "cyber dream team" . . . with less dressy suits.

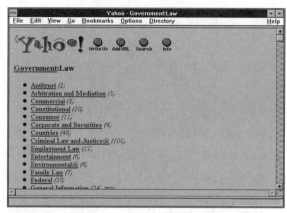

Figure 54 *Yahoo law links.*

55

J.P. Morgan & Company

http://www.jpmorgan.com

Just goes to show you. If you are rich enough, you can be dead for decades and still get your own homepage. But seriously, some very useful information is here, including daily posting of RiskMetric data sets to help you evaluate the risks of potential investments. In addition, regularly updated numbers vis-à-vis the government bond index, the mortgage finance index, the mortgage purchase index, and all major currency indices are at your disposal. If you are an investment professional, you may also want to check the online bulletin board of career opportunities at Morgan.

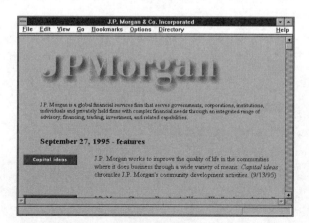

Figure 55 *Morgan home page.*

Legal Information Institute (Cornell)

http://www.law.cornell.edu/

This Web server integrates both the Gopher-based and the Web-based offerings of the Legal Information Institute (LII) of the Cornell Law School. The server offers the LII's hypertext front-end to recent Supreme Court decisions (which are distributed on the day of decision under Project Hermes), the LII's collection of recent decisions of the New York Court of Appeals, the LII's hypertext version of the full U.S. Code (the 50 principle statues of governance that cover everything from congressional functions to the wartime division of the Federal government powers), and many other important legal documents. You also get the electronic edition of the Cornell Law Review, a handy link to the catalog of the Cornell Law Library, and information on applying to the school.

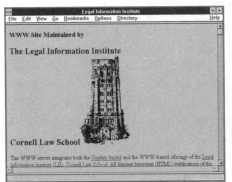

Figure 56.1 Legal Information Institute home page.

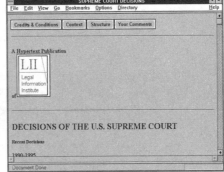

Figure 56.2 Supreme Court decisions.

Monster Jobs on the Web

http://www.monster.com

Go to this site and then sit, poised and ready at your keyboard, with thousands of rewarding career opportunities literally at your fingertips. Here you will find over 450 employers (including Hewlett-Packard, Bay Networks, Compaq, Edgewater Technology, Millipore, and Motorola) offering more than 2,700 (mostly technical) jobs. Visit Monster's "Employer Profiles" to gain a better understanding of what progressive corporations have to offer, and enhance your employment outlook by posting your resume to "Resume On-Line." Want to find the perfect job in the perfect locale? Then search listings by location, industry, company, discipline, or keyword.

Figure 57.1 Monster home page.

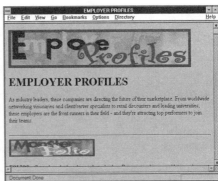

Figure 57.2 Employer profiles.

Mortgage Calculator

http://ibc.wustl.edu/mort.html

One screen does it, but does it so well. Plug in the principal loan balance. Plug in the annual interest rate. Plug in the amortization length (30 years, 15 years, etc.). Register the starting month and year. Also plug in any monthly (or annual) principal prepayments you plan on making. Then just press the calculate button and you get a full amortization table showing exactly how much you will be spending over the life of the loan to pay off the debt with interest. It is intriguing to see how even small principal prepayments can result in large interest savings over the life of a loan. This is an elegant and useful tool. You techies out there will be interested to know that the whole thing was accomplished with just a simple Perl script.

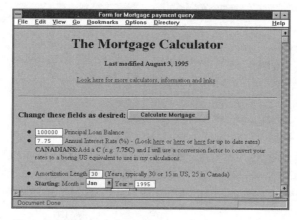

Figure 58 *Plug and play mortgage calculation.*

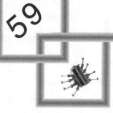

Nest Egg Magazine

http://nestegg.iddis.com/nestegg/nestegg/backnest.html

See the fantastic, interactive edition of the personal finance magazine that boasts some two million subscribers to its paper edition. This site includes indexed links to all articles published in *Nest Egg* to date (searchable by topic, keyword, or author) plus up-to-date mutual fund and securities performance data, and a financial bookstore. *Nest Egg* is produced by Investment Dealers' Digest (IDD), a diversified financial publishing, database, software, and consulting company that specializes in providing up-to-the-minute financial information and analysis.

Figure 59.1 *Nest Egg home page.*

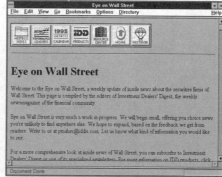

Figure 59.2 *Eye on Wall Street.*

NetWORTH: Mutual Funds a 'Poppin'

http://networth.galt.com/

Interested in mutual funds? This site provides in-depth information on 5,000 of them, including prospectuses and performance figures. You also get pricing quoted direct from the markets via dedicated S&P real-time data feed, and access to the Morningstar Ratings database. You also get listings and samples of the best financial newsletters. Plus, a weekly investor's market outlook report and several interactive question and answer forms, where you can get your concerns addressed by industry professionals, are useful tools as well. Concerned about protecting your confidential financial information? This site uses Netscape's HTTP Secure protocol, with access authentication and encryption.

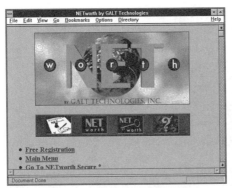

Figure 60.1 NetWorth home page.

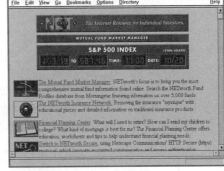

Figure 60.2 NetWorth resources.

Personal Investment and Finance Links

http://www.yahoo.com/Economy/Markets_and_Investments/Personal_Finance/

Do you hide from the mailperson on bill day? Do you get more calls from collection agencies than you do from your family? If "yes," you'll want to check out this site's links, which include Debt Counselors of America (a non-profit organization which assists individuals and businesses that are experiencing financial crisis), a site called "Investing for the Perplexed," the Moneyweb UK Personal Finance site, a site called "Personal Finance Center" that offers links to the vast personal finance and investment resources worldwide, and more. Making bad investments is easier than you think. Before you start investing, use these links as your financial guide.

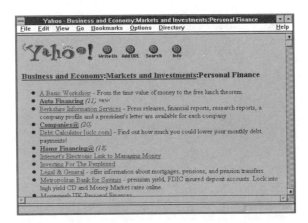

Figure 61 Yahoo investment links.

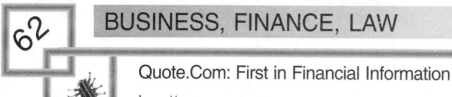

Quote.Com: First in Financial Information

http://www.quote.com

QuoteCom is a service dedicated to providing quality financial market data on the Internet. This includes current quotes on stocks, commodity futures, mutual funds, and bonds. It also includes business news, market analysis and commentary, fundamental (balance sheet) data, and company profiles. QuoteCom includes real-time index data, quotes on NASDAQ Bulletin Board stocks and ADR's, and quotes on stock options for U.S. stocks, indices, and futures. At the moment of writing, QuoteCom can only provide one quote at a time, but by the time you read this they will be able to provide rapid quote chains. Come experience the future of investing.

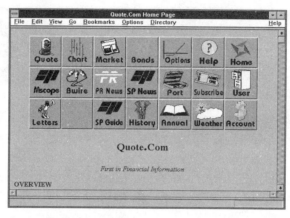

Figure 62 QuoteCom home page.

Standard & Poor's 500 Index

http://www.secapl.com/secapl/quoteserver/sp500.html

The Standard & Poor's Corporation provides investors with a wide range of statistical materials, advisory reports, and other financial information. At this site, you'll find a quick and easy graph system that gives you the most recent day's activity (with just a 15 minute delay after market close, Eastern Standard Time). You can also see a graph for the last 12 months or the last five years. Rumor has it that this site is Louis Rukeyser's favorite quick-stop, and that he has it loaded at the top of his hotlist.

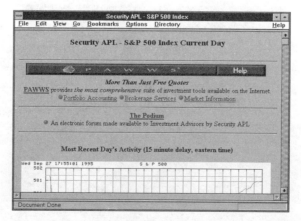

Figure 63 Daily graph of SP 500.

StrategyWeb

http://www.onramp.net/~atw_dhw/home.htm

Access a growing collection of strategy analysts and senior consultants from around the world available for inter-action, discussion, and coaching. These professionals offer the latest concepts and innovative techniques in strategic management. Mix-and-match with one, two, or several consultant contractors. Then, negotiate engagements pri-vately and securely. Specialties include Latin American monetary policy, entry strategies for the Western European market, how to use Australia-New Zealand as a launchpad into Asia, the legal/tax challenges of doing business in Eastern Europe, and more. In short, think of this site as your cyberCFO (chief financial officer).

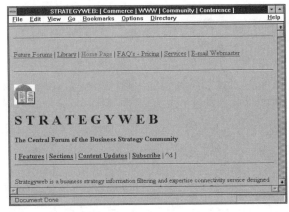

Figure 64 StrategyWeb home page.

Trade Law and International Finance Library

http://ananse.irv.uit.no/law/nav/law_ref.html

Do you need to sort out the vast laws and regulations that accompany international trade and finance? This site has links to the Norwegian International Trade Law Project, the Pace University Institute of International Commercial Law, and the U.S. House of Representatives Internet Law Library (including treaties, references on laws of all juris-dictions arranged by subject, and more). You also get the International Maritime & Commercial Law List at EINet Galaxy, the collections on international law from the Multilaterals Project at the Fletcher School of Law and Diplo-macy (and their trade and commercial relations list), and a set of international-trade-and-finance bookmarks.

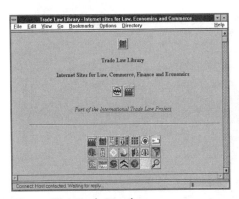

Figure 65.1 Trade Law home page.

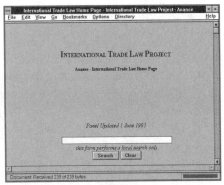

Figure 65.2 International Trade Law Project.

U.S. Department of Commerce

http://www.doc.gov

The Department of Commerce's principle objective is to promote economic growth and foster business research and development. To achieve this objective, the Department of Commerce offers you a number of valuable resources at this site. The "What's New" section provides a comprehensive online calendar of significant Department of Commerce happenings, including reports, press releases, conference announcements, and also announcements of new online databases. "Information from the Secretary's Office" includes press releases and speeches. You can also connect to the Department of Commerce's FTP and Gopher servers to access such resources as STAT-USA, which provides the Budget of the United States Government for Fiscal 1996 (interesting reading, to say the least).

Figure 66.1 Dept. of Commerce home page.

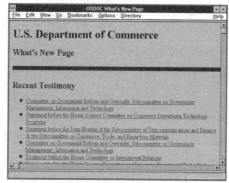

Figure 66.2 What's new.

The WWW Virtual Law Library

http://www.law.indiana.edu/law/lawindex.html

The Virtual Library provides you with links to all sorts of esoteric sites including the ACLU Free Reading Room, the Advertising Law Internet Site, the American Bar Association, the Consumer Law Page, and the E-Law Home Page. You can also link to the Electronic Democracy Information Network, the Franklin Pierce Law Center, Information Law Alert, the Public Policy Network Archives, WWW Multimedia Law, the United Nations Justice Network, West's Legal Directory (including 675,000 profiles of law firms), the Princeton Review Guide to Law Schools, Taxpayers Against Fraud, the Bodleian Law Library, and more. I'm still searching for a link to the "Dancing Itos."

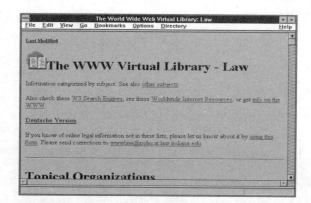

Figure 67 Virtual Law Library home page.

Wall Street Direct

http://www.cts.com/~wallst

If you invest or plan to start, Wall Street Direct is a must-see site. Wall Street Direct provides a staggering array of useful links arranged by topic, some of which are advisory services, brokerage services, charting services, conferences and trade shows, data services, downloadable software, and educational services. In addition, you'll find market predictions, product reviews, publications, seminars and workshops, and statistics. From this starting point, you can make stock or mutual fund investments, access key market indices, track stocks individually or as groups, and even get tutorials on how the market works and why. All these varied resources are indexed by category.

Figure 68.1 Wall Street Direct home page.

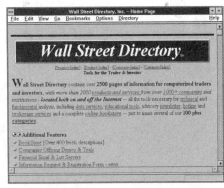

Figure 68.2 Discount financial super store.

The World Bank

http://www.worldbank.org

Here you will find electronic editions of the World Bank's many valuable publications, including the latest Commodity Policy and Analysis Unit "pink-sheet." You can also browse African development studies, publications of the Economic Development Institute, facts and figures from the Economic Growth Project, OED reports on Sri Lanka, reports from the Latin America and Caribbean Region Technical Group, and publications of the Consultative Group on Agricultural Research. Additionally, you have your choice of current events listings, press releases, and specific country/project information. Need to better understand the world market? Start here, at the World Bank.

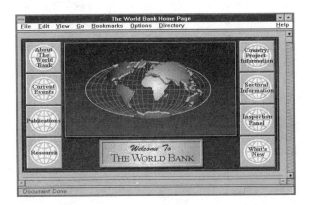

Figure 69 The World Bank home page.

More Business, Finance, Law

As you surf the Web, you may find that one or more of the site addresses listed in this book have changed. In such cases, connect to Jamsa Press at http://www.jamsa.com and click on the icon that corresponds to the *1001 Really Cool Web Sites* book. Jamsa Press will list replacement addresses (when possible) for sites that have moved. In addition, you can also use the following site list as you search for information on business, finance, and law:

GSU RMI Home Page	http://131.96.94.5/gsuweb.htm
Business	http://akebono.stanford.edu/yahoo/Business/
Markets and Investments	http://akebono.stanford.edu/yahoo/Economy/Markets_and_Investments
Business Use of the Internet	http://arganet.tenagra.com/Tenagra/books.html
Branch Business Center	http://branch.com/business.htm#business
Marcus Associates	http://branch.com/marcus
Making Money on Internet	http://cism.bus.utexas.edu/ravi/making_money.html
Internet Transactions	http://com.primenet.com/research/

70

Scientific Visualization Cornucopia

http://www.nas.nasa.gov/RNR/Visualization/annotatedURLs.html

Connect to no less than 55 great labs and commercial concerns doing cutting-edge, super-cool computer graphics development and research. Look at great virtual reality (VR), fractal graphics, and other items by accessing the ParVis Visualization Project at the Australian National University or the TEINAS Project at the University of California (Santa Cruz). Other links take you to the Center for Applied Parallel Processing at the University of Colorado (Boulder), the Visualization Lab at the Cornell Theory Center, the Scientific Visualization Lab at the University of Manchester (UK), and the Coves Project at Northwestern. Let these graphics change your expectation of "Cool!"

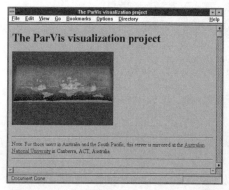

Figure 70.1 One option from among many.   *Figure 70.2 And another.*

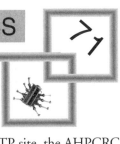

71

Computer Graphics Information

http://mambo.ucsc.edu/psl/cg.html

This site gives you more than fifty great computer graphics sites including the SIGGRAPH FTP site, the AHPCRC Graphics Software, and the Geometry Center of the University of Minnesota. You can also go to the University of Pennsylvania Center for Human Modeling and Simulation, the Bremen Center for Complex Systems and Visualization, the Brown University Computer Graphics Group, the Milan Laboratory of Eidomatics, the University of Waterloo Computer Graphics Laboratory, the University of Toronto Dynamic Graphics Project, the Caltech Computer Graphics Group, or the Microsoft Research Graphics Group. Come see cutting-edge technology in practice.

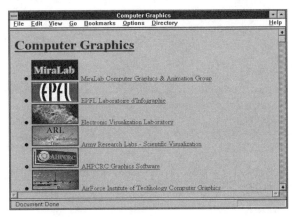

Figure 71 A few of your choices.

72

Cool Demos

http://www-graphics.stanford.edu/demos/

The good folks at the Stanford University Computer Graphics Laboratory provide this cool site. For starters, the neat banner image at the masthead is itself a demo, and Stanford folks describe how they created it. Then you will be treated to several 3-D volume morphs, pictures, and movies of objects painted with a 3-D painting system developed at Stanford, and movies of a zippered polygon mesh model of a plastic toy lion. You also get volume-rendered movies of a human head and an engine block, and images from various college-rendering competitions dating from 1992 to 1995. Excellent.

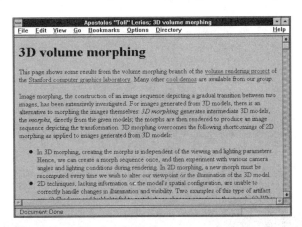

Figure 72 3-D volume morphs.

Figlet Fonts

http://www.inf.utfsm.cl/cgi-bin/figlet

Access this site and download some of the wildest, most exotic fonts you'll ever see. But first, customize them and make them uniquely your own. More than 103 separate fonts are available. The Figlet service is a Perl CGI script that interfaces Figlet through the Web. It was developed by Victor Parada at Universidad Tecnica Federico Santa Maria in Valpraiso, Chile. This service is fun; it is cool; and it is free. And how many things are truly free these days? Not nearly enough, if you ask me. Take China, for example. China really ought to be free. And Cuba. And . . .

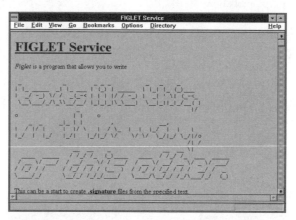

Figure 73 Figlet home page.

74

Fractal Movie Archive

http://www.cnam.fr/fractals/anim.html

You'll see more than 147 fractal animations available in Anim5, FLI, FLC, MPEG, and QuickTime formats. These animations are absolutely beautiful. They include snow flakes in a red Mandelbrot set, galactic clusters in the Mandelbrot set, a cruise through an alien landscape, mitosis within egg cells in the Mandelbrot set, a fast fly through a fractal-generated canyon, and flying over a desert. You also get to see chaotic smoke, a fractal wrapped around a sphere, a Mandelbrot set morphing into a Julia set, webs in a Mandelbrot set, two Mandelbrot sets sliding one on the other, and a back zoom on a triangle Mandelbrot set. Oh . . . just come see them!

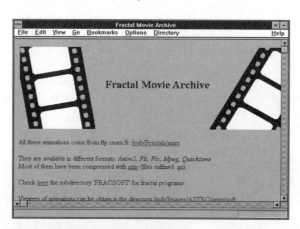

Figure 74 Fractal movie home page.

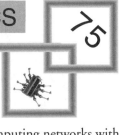

Fractal Microscope

http://www.ncsa.uiuc.edu/Edu/Fractal/Fractal_Home.html

"Fractal Microscope" is an interactive tool for exploring fractal patterns. Combining supercomputing networks with the simple interface of a Macintosh or X-Windows workstation, students and teachers from all grade levels can engage in discover-based exploration. The program is designed to run in conjunction with the NCSA imaging tools DataScope and Collage. With this program, students can enjoy the art of mathematics as they master the science of mathematics. This focus can help one address a wide variety of topics in the K-12 curriculum including scientific notation, coordinate systems and graphing, number systems, convergence, divergence, and self-similarity.

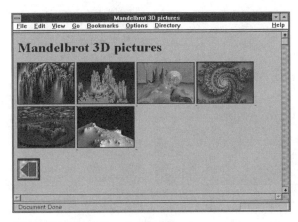

Figure 75 Mandelbrot 3-D gallery.

Fractals and Scale: A Tutorial

http://life.anu.edu.au:80/complex_systems/tutorial3.html

This fascinating, yet brief, tutorial explains how and why Mandelbrot proposed the idea of a fractal as a way to cope with problems of scale in the real world, and defined a fractal to be any curve or surface that is independent of scale. This property, referred to as *self-similarity*, means that any portion of the curve, if blown up in scale, would appear identical to the whole curve. That, in a nutshell, is the story on fractals that is put much more eloquently in the superb hypertext tutorial entitled "Fractals and Scale," by David G. Green of the Australian National University.

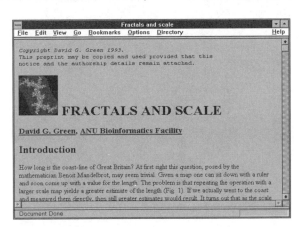

Figure 76 Home page for Green's tutorial.

COMPUTER GRAPHICS

The Geometry Sender

http://synap.neuro.sfc.keio.ac.jp/~aly/polygon/polygon.html

The Geometry Sender of Japan's Keio University is a network file system dedicated to the distribution of geometric structures. Using 3-D viewers, you can download from this site and view a number of interactive software demos, including a VRML/WebOOGL demo and a WebPaint demo that you view using Geomview with Mosaic. This site also contains a W3-D demo for viewing with RenderWare and Mosaic, and a VRML demo using WebSpace and Netscape. Here you will also find instructions for configuring 3-D viewers, an object-formats manual, and a 3-D libraries/languages manual.

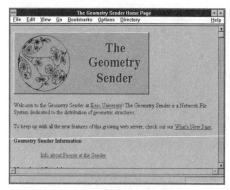

Figure 77.1 Geometry Sender home page.

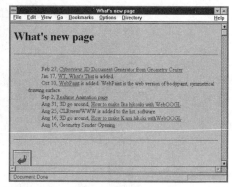

Figure 77.2 What's New.

Hyperbolic & Fractal Movies

http://andro.sfc.keio.ac.jp/~aly/mpeg/mpeg.html

Check out the MPEG animation of the fractal octopus—just watch those tentacles churn. Lots of other wild, weird, and cool stuff here, including manic penguins in crazed hyperbolic motion. When you are done with them, check out the fluid movement of the eerie "Fractal Brain." Then, keep your eye on the flighty hyperbolic dancer (Nureyev on speed and in baggier tights than normal). Then witness "Noh Men" for HyperCard Interactive. It is hard to grasp the scientific point to some of this stuff, but it is all fun to watch.

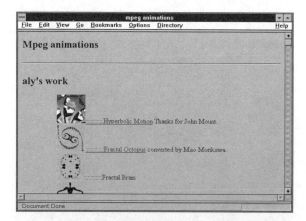

Figure 78 MPEG animation options.

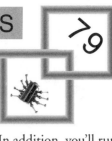

Hyperbolic Tiles

http://www.cs.cmu.edu/Web/People/jmount/moretilings.html

See JPEG images of hyperbolic spheres, tiles of money, and weird patterns in your own home. In addition, you'll run into a hyperbolic portrait of a weird-looking dude who just gets weirder around the edges. You also get an explanation of how (if not why) the images were generated. And you get a C-UNIX source code for the hyperbolic tiler. "What are hyperbolic tiles?" you ask. Did you ever have a kaleidoscope when you were a kid? They are kind of like that, but digital. You don't have to hold anything up to the light. And you certainly do not have to shake up the computer to make the pictures change. Come experience the critical edge of computer graphic strangeness.

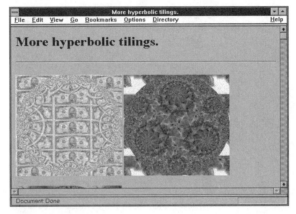

Figure 79 Hyperbolic cash.

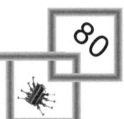

Mandelbrot Explorer

http://www.softlab.ntua.gr/mandel/mandel.html

Think of this site as fractal geometry meets the everyday guy (or girl). Enter a few coordinates, create your own Mandelbrot sets, and then zoom in and out to study the picture. You define the drawing areas and the X and Y minimum/maximum coordinates. This is lots of fun. Or print out your creation, hang it on the wall, and explain it nonchalantly to your friends as, "a fractal graphic I created, a Mandelbrot set devolving into a curved loop." Lots of accomplishment and pleasure await you in the Mandelbrot Explorer.

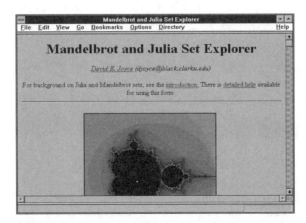

Figure 80 Mandelbrot Explorer.

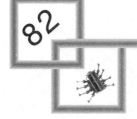

COMPUTER GRAPHICS

Persistence-of-Vision (POV) Ray-Tracing

http://www.uio.no/~mwatz/pov/index.html

POV is ray-tracing freeware with which you can create 3-D photorealistic images. This page gives you links to distribution sites, POV utilities, documentation, the POV source code, a gallery of POV objects, and more. Also valuable are the links to POV galleries, including Marius Watz's organitecture gallery, Adam Wells' picture archive, the POV Hall of Fame, and the Qjulia Page, where you'll find quarternion julia sets rendered with a patch version of POV. Very cool. Also check out Sharky's Art Gallery & House of Graphic Illusions. Then turn to the easy tools with which you can render your own graphic illusions.

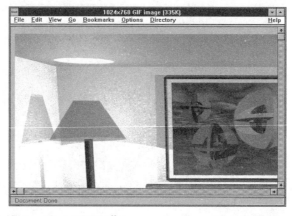

Figure 81 A POV gallery.

Pixel Planes Home Page

http://www.cs.unc.edu/~pxpl/home.html

Access the University of North Carolina's Pixel-Planes Project, and have a ball. This group is dedicated to building graphics engines with an emphasis on scalability and real-time rendering. The project's name reflects one of the principle techniques these folks use for fast rendering . The basic building block of all their systems is a plane of processors, each with a few bytes of its own memory, operating in unison. Each pixel (picture element) on the screen is associated with one unique processor. Get a sneak-peek of the next generation in computer-graphics wizardry.

Figure 82 Pixel-Planes information.

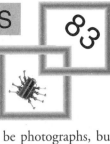

Ray-Tracing Hub

http://www.cm.cf.ac.uk/Ray.Tracing/

Ray-tracing is the computer-graphic technique for creating images that look like they could be photographs, but aren't. From the "Ray-Tracing Hub," you can link to more than 100 great ray-tracing sites, including galleries, software companies, and downloadable ray-tracing packages such as Rayshade, Radiance, Rtrace, and others. Included are the UK Grafix homepage (lots of images), a ray-traced walk-through of a castle, fast parallel volume rendering, and architectural rendering using Radiance. Explore all the dimensions of the UK's digital dream factories via the "Ray-Tracing Hub."

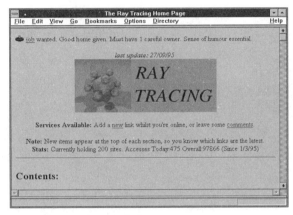

Figure 83 Ray-Tracing hub.

Rob's Multimedia Lab

http://www.acm.uiuc.edu:80/rml/

This site is *packed* with outstanding examples of multimedia graphics and sound. Access the sounds and graphics from *Star Wars, Jurassic Park,* and even *Seinfeld*. In addition, you can link to a slow but rich digital picture gallery, or download computer graphics weather images created with data from the GEOS satellite. Rob's lab also has morphing stuff (morphing uses software to blend one image into another), including morphing freeware that you can download and use on your home PC. Be sure to check out Rob's cornucopia of goodies.

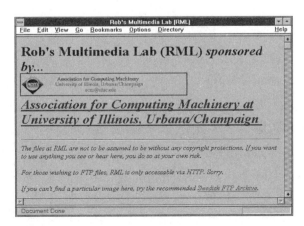

Figure 84 Rob's Multimedia Lab.

COMPUTER GRAPHICS

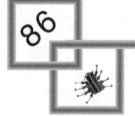

Silicon Graphics Image Gallery

http://www.sgi.com/Fun/free/gallery.html

For years, Silicon Graphics, Inc. (SGI) has been the leader in computer-graphics hardware and software. Most of these images come from SGI customers and partners. Each thumbnail (small version of the image) is hyperlinked to information about exactly how the image was created. You can access a larger version of each thumbnail by clicking on the image. This site has lots of cool graphics including neon flowers, a motorcycle race, paper planes, a globe, robots, and a girl with a painted face. You should also look at the scientific images which include protein on DNA, a bronchial tube, an oceano-graphic image, and the ever-favorite crash dummy. Come take a marvelous tour through the visual delights of this gallery.

Figure 85 Image Gallery home page.

Sonic Art: Contours of the Mind

http://online.anu.edu.au/ITA/ACAT/contours

"Contours of the Mind" is an exhibition of sonic and visual art at the Australian National University Drill Hall Gallery. This gallery offers photographs, computer-generated "still" works, computer animation, video, slides, sculpture, music, and interactive installations. Needless to say, the event brings together a unique blend of visual art, science, and music. Areas explored by the pieces in the show include cellular automata, strange attractors, chaotic dynamics, and iterated function systems. Science and high art have never before met on a higher plane. Come see the intersection of great ideas.

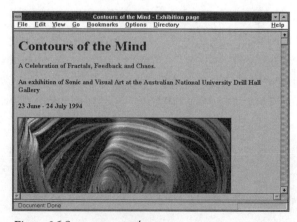

Figure 86 Start your tour here.

Thant's Animations Index

http://mambo.ucsc.edu/psl/thant/thant.html

This rich document contains numerous short descriptions and links to servers on the Web which offer computer generated animations, visualizations, movies, and interactive images. The site is maintained by Thant Nyo, a senior at Towson State University, with the help of a researcher at the Perceptual Science Lab at UCSC, where Thant's documents are hosted. Literally hundreds of options are open to you here, from fractals to cartoons, from ray-traced images to digitized films. Jump from here to sites around the world where the latest technology creates some of the most dynamic images ever to volt through a telephone cable.

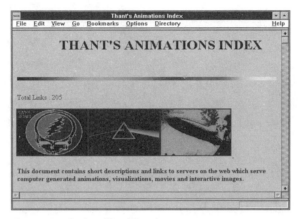

Figure 87 Cool stuff at Thant's.

More Computer Graphics

As you surf the Web, you may find that one or more of the site addresses listed in this book have changed. In such cases, connect to Jamsa Press at http://www.jamsa.com and click on the icon that corresponds to the *1001 Really Cool Web Sites* book. Jamsa Press will list replacement addresses (when possible) for sites that have moved. In addition, you can also use the following site list as you search for information on computer graphics:

Aviation Image Archives	http://adswww.harvard.edu/GA/image_archives.html
PDS Imaging Node - Homepage	http://cdwings.jpl.nasa.gov/PDS/
On Line Catalog Information	http://cdwings.jpl.nasa.gov/PDS/public/catalog_info.html
mandel	http://enigma.phys.utk.edu/mandel/
CURIOUS HOME PAGE	http://found.cs.nyu.edu/CAT/affiliates/curious/curioushp.html
GIF/JPEG Graphics	http://fourier.dur.ac.uk:8000/graphics.html
More pictures	http://fourier.dur.ac.uk:8000/taste.graphic.html
Pictures from Brazil	http://guarani.cos.ufrj.br:8000/Rio/Todas.html
gd 1.1.1	http://siva.cshl.org/gd/gd.html
Last files from alt.binaries.pictures.misc	http://web.cnam.fr/Images/Usenet/abpm/summaries/

COMPUTER RESOURCES

Audio System for Technical Readings (AsTeR)

http://www.cs.cornell.edu/Info/People/raman/aster/aster-toplevel.html

AsTeR is a system for rendering technical documents in audio. This page includes examples generated by AsTeR, as well as specifications and documentation for the project (including a Ph.D. thesis of the project). An AsTeR audio of this thesis is, by the way, being made available by Recordings for the Blind (as the first computer-generated talking book). Each example is made up of three components: the original LaTeX input, the audio formatted output by AsTeR, and the visually formatted version produced by LaTeX and DVIPS (Digital Video Interactive Performance System). Come learn all about this fascinating new technology.

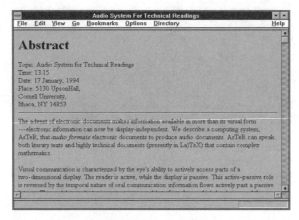

Figure 88 *Summary of Raman's project.*

BTG Incorporated

http://www.btg.com/

This site houses one of the premier companies specializing in open systems development, systems engineering, reusable software, document management, value-added reselling, and the manufacture of customized high-performance computers. Come here to learn how BTG puts you in touch with more than 90,000 hardware and software products from over 350 vendors and how they qualified for GSA purchases. You will also find information on "the world's fastest computer," the BTG AXP275 RISC machine. In short, this site lets you learn to design, implement, and distribute products by following examples from a company that has mastered the process.

Figure 89.1 *BTG home page.*

Figure 89.2 *BTG government marketplace.*

Figure 89.3 *BTG financials.*

Cisco Systems Educational Archives

http://sunsite.unc.edu/cisco/cisco-home.html

The Cisco Education Archives (chosen as one of PC Magazine's Top 100 Web Sites!) provides information designed to help educators and schools connect to the wealth of educational resources available on the World Wide Web. These resources include "The Virtual Schoolhouse," a meta-library of K-12 links categorized by subject. You will also find the "Star CEARCH School of the Month," and the customized Cisco CEARCH engine for ferreting out hidden gold from the depths of the Cisco Educational Archives. A must-see site for parents and educators.

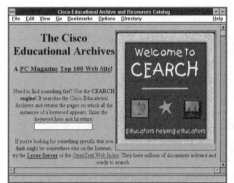

Figure 90.1 Cisco's Educational Archive.

Figure 90.2 Cisco's Virtual Schoolhouse.

Complex Systems Information on the Internet

http://www.seas.upenn.edu/~ale/cplxsys.html

The header for this great list of links related to artificial life (alife) opens with a definition: "Life is, if it dies when you stomp on it." This site has links to more than 50 great alife-related web and gopher sites, as well as newsgroups and journals. You'll find links to the Santa Fe Institute (pretty much the place where all the alife and complex systems research started), the online edition of *Artificial Life* journal, the University of Texas genetic programming lab, the Avida Alife Group at Caltech, and Mark Smucker's evolutionary computation and artificial life page. In other words, this is a site where you can get "alife." Get a life. Get it? Got it. On to the next site.

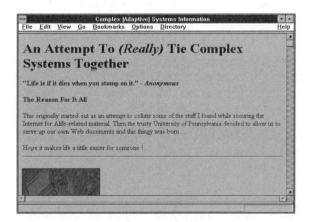

Figure 91 Complex Systems home page.

Computer Professionals for Social Responsibility

http://www.cpsr.org/dox/home.html

Computer Professionals for Social Responsibility (CPSR) is a public-interest alliance of computer scientists and others interested in the impact of computer technology on society. As technical experts, CPSR members provide the public and policymakers with realistic assessments of the power, promise, and limitations of computer technology. As concerned citizens, they direct public attention to critical choices concerning the applications of computing and how those choices affect society. Come here to learn about various CPSR programs or simply to interact with some intelligent, concerned citizens who care enough about their world to want to make a difference. Cool.

Figure 92 CPSR home page.

Computer Security Reference Index

http://www.telstra.com.au/info/security.html

The Telstra Computer Security Reference Index includes links to myriad Web and Gopher resources for creating and maintaining computer security. You'll find information on firewalls, Anon FTP, Pretty Good Privacy (PGP), Riordan's Internet Privacy Enhanced Mail (RIPEM), and more. You will also find information on commercial security products, and security-related mailing lists and newsgroups. You can even download one of several excellent firewall utilities. Come on, gang. You know it is important to practice safe computing. Stop here for the tools you need.

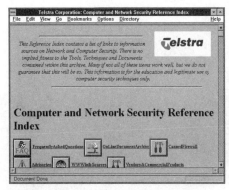 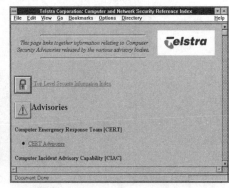

Figure 93.1 Opening page.   *Figure 93.2* Computer security advisories.

Data Communications & Networking Links

http://www.racal.com/networking.html

You have found the launch pad for hundreds of data communications and networking links, including companies, conferences/expositions, FAQs, FTP sites, magazines, mailing lists, tutorials, and newsgroups. Among the items on your menu: links focusing on high-speed networking, the SNMP info site, a great PC-Mac TCP/IP FAQ list, and more. You also get several complete digital books, including Steve Woas's *Modem Workshop* and a very useful tutorial on TCP/IP network administration. As if that were not enough, you will also find tutorials on ISDN, SNA, and ATMEthernet. In sum, this site comprises a marvelous cheat-sheet that covers technology you really need to know.

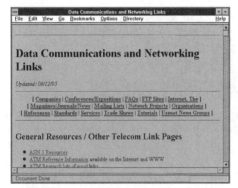

Figure 94.1 DCNL home page.

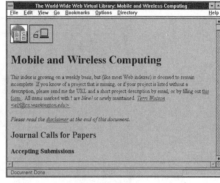

Figure 94.2 Wireless computing information.

Digital Equipment Corporation

http://www.digital.com

For years, Digital Equipment Corporation (DEC) was one of the fastest and most innovative computer companies. Unfortunately, sleeping through the PC revolution almost closed DEC. Today, DEC is rebounding with several high-end PC computer products. Several people, including Microsoft, have begun to take notice. Consider this site the Rosetta Stone (a stone—with parallel inscriptions in Greek, ancient Egyptian demotic, and hieroglyphic characters—that archaeologists used to decipher ancient Egyptian writing) for understanding the products and services of Digital Equipment Corporation (DEC). The site provides complete information on DEC products, company financials, customer periodicals, new technology and research, and also DEC service, training, and support. DEC has risen to the top before and may again. Check out this site and see what's happening at DEC.

Figure 95.1 Digital home page.

Figure 95.2 Digital financials.

FutureCulture

http://www.uio.no/~mwatz/futurec/index.html

FutureCulture is, without a doubt, the ultimate alternative cyberculture links list. Topics addressed here include virtual reality, the computer underground, cyberpunk, media, virtual communities, and social and public policy issues. "FutureCulture is not just another generic cool cyberpunk discussion list, but rather a community," reads the homepage. "Sometimes we discuss artificial life and nanotech, sometimes we discuss the future of monogamy and the misery of breaking up. We're cyborgs, but we're also humans." Touch the humanity at FutureCulture and come away with sometimes useful and new perspectives.

Figure 96 FutureCulture home page.

Fuzzy Systems Tutorial

http://life.anu.edu.au:80/complex_systems/fuzzy.html

James F. Brule's elegant, succinct hypertext tutorial clearly explains *fuzzy systems* as an alternative to traditional notions of set membership and logic. In one artful presentation, Brule explains both fuzzy logic's origins in ancient Greek philosophy *and* its practical application in artificial intelligence programming. Brule also shows that fuzzy sets are not only a viable tool for artificial intelligence, but also for formal mathematics generally. When is vagueness anything but an obstacle to clarity? When it is the vagueness of fuzzy logic, of course.

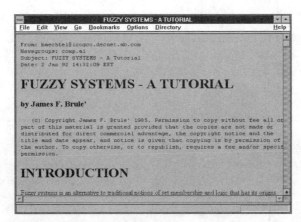

Figure 97 The start of the tutorial.

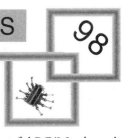

Global Monitor

http://www.monitor.ca/monitor/

From Canada comes a great weekly magazine for PC/Mac users and programmers. You'll find useful PC/Mac buyer's checklists, hardware reviews, software reviews, and more. You'll even find regular coverage of such esoteric topics as OS/2 (including lots of software goodies for the Warp fan). And this page has regular features on DOS and Windows news, MIDI, PC games, FIDO, freenets, and the Internet. This is a new address for the folks at Global Monitor, who celebrated their recent anniversary (their second) with a wonderful present: their own (fast) Web server! But as I've already described, they also have some presents for you, when you visit.

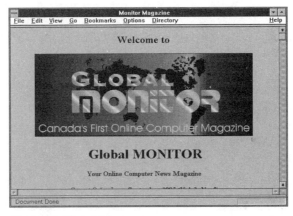

Figure 98 Global Monitor home page.

Illustrated Audio

http://debra.dgbt.doc.ca/ia.html

Illustrated Audio links graphics and text with sound and makes possible the distribution of computer-based slide shows over low-bandwidth networks with pipes (wires) too small (slow) for full-motion video. Here you will find a complete source code, as well as details on the development of the project. You can also download related software, including the iaunpack program (a Bourne shell script that unpacks the data file and launches the player), and the iaplay program (the player that synchronizes the images and the sound-track). Go for it!

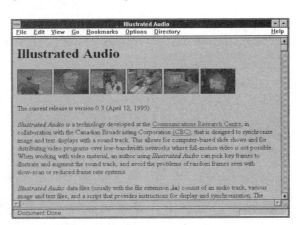

Figure 99 Illustrated Audio details.

Instruction Set Smorgasbord

http://www.comlab.ox.ac.uk/archive/cards.html

Wouldn't it be nice to have a comprehensive collection of microprocessor instruction set cards in a common, easily-accessible format, including chips from RCA, Signetics, National Semiconductor, Rockwell, Motorola, Intel, Texas Instruments, DEC, and Zilog? Well, you've got it. In addition to cards for microprocessors and microcomputers, you get instruction sets for the HP64000 assembler, an HP64000 Pascal compiler summary, a DEC Marco-11 assembler summary, and a Pascal programming language summary. You also get a list of links to resources concerning the Pentium floating point divide bug. Turn to this easy, online reference before you turn to the schematics.

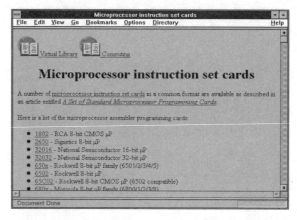

Figure 100 Take your pick.

Internet Computer Index

http://ici.proper.com

Internet Computer Index (ICI) is a great, one-stop, resource-locating service. Using ICI, you can tap the Net's tremendous wealth more easily and efficiently than from most other jumping-off points. (One minor shortfall is that ICI does not have anonymous FTP service, although they do offer a wide variety of files through Gopher and the Web.) Through ICI's simple-to-use menu- and directory-interface, you can access hundreds of worldwide databases, special interest groups, files, and more. Spend a few moments with ICI and wind up with just the resource you need at just the time you need it.

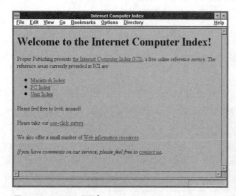

Figure 101.1 Welcome page.

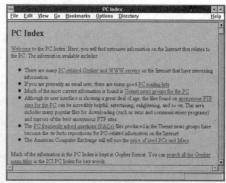

Figure 101.2 PC index.

Macintosh Resources: Welcome to Macintosh

http://www.astro.nwu.edu/lentz/mac/home-mac.html

If you among that enlightened minority that understands the simple equation, *Windows 95 = Macintosh 1984*, this is the place for you. This page entitled "Welcome to Macintosh" is a splendid oasis at the edge of the technical desert that is DOS, and far removed from the mirage of Windows. Among the great items here are the free Aretha release of Frontier, a Mac port of GhostScript, programs from Mac guru John Norstad (including Disinfectant and NewsWatcher), and Mac FAQs. Lentz also provides "Mind Candy" such as great QuickTime movies and a supercool startup-screen. Emerge from the digital desert and join your fellow Mac-heads at this splendid watering hole.

 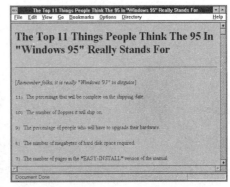

Figure 102.1 Mac Resources home page.   *Figure 102.2 Some Windows 95 jokes.*

Microsoft Research

http://www.research.microsoft.com

Microsoft Research (MSR) was established as a center of research excellence for pursuing innovations in key areas of computer science. MSR includes independent research groups in computer graphics, decision theory, natural languages, operating systems, program analysis, speech technology, user interfaces, and vision technology. All MSR technical reports are available at this site, and they comprise a large and invaluable cache of resources. Here you will also find information on research facilities available at the Microsoft Campus in Redmond, as well as information on MSR staffing and career opportunities . . . and I don't means jobs in the cafeteria.

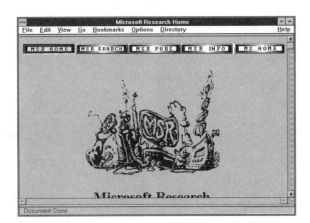

Figure 103 Yet another Microsoft logo.

NEC

http://www.nec.co.jp/

For years, NEC has been a leader in electronic products and a model for efficient corporate organization. Available in both English and Japanese, the NEC homepage gives you information on new product development at NEC, information on the PC-9800 series, and an overview of NEC corporate operations. You also get a valuable newsletter entitled "NEC Today," information on the range of NEC products and services (including online technical support), and information on NEC research and development. While you are here, be sure to access the NEC USA WWW Server. It features information on NEC suppliers/distributors nationwide, detailed English-language tech support for all NEC products, U.S.-based career opportunities with NEC, and more.

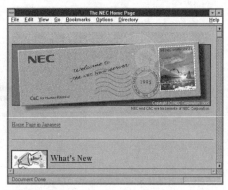

Figure 104.1 NEC home page.

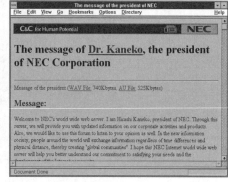

Figure 104.2 NEC overview.

NeuroNet

http://www.neuronet.ph.kcl.ac.uk/

Maintained by the good folks at beautiful King's College, London, NeuroNet represents a mighty gathering of the forces of neural network research and development worldwide. NeuroNet includes a clickable map of NeuroNet managing nodes, a hyperlinked list of homepages for leading neural network researchers across the planet, and more. You will also have access to great neural network software, an open neural network discussion forum, and links to a wealth of papers and technical reports relating to all areas of neural network research and development. This is an essential stop on the Information Superhighway for all who are interested in advanced artificial intelligence.

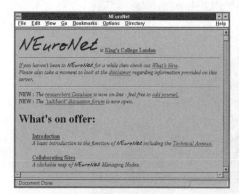

Figure 105.1 NeuroNet home page.

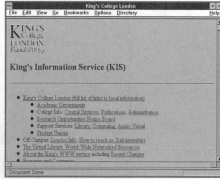

Figure 105.2 Your hosts.

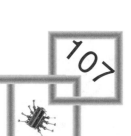

Object Oriented Programming with C++

http://info.desy.de/gna/html/cc/index.html

Winner of the *Best of the Web* '94 Award for Best Educational Service, this self-paced introductory course provides a superb introduction to both the C++ programming language and fundamental concepts of object orientation. The tutorial includes a walk-through that allows you to sample the course without running the entire tutorial, a bootstrap document providing the minimum essential instruction required to access the class, a syllabus with administration information about the class, and, of course, the complete hypertext tutorial. If you want to learn C++, start here.

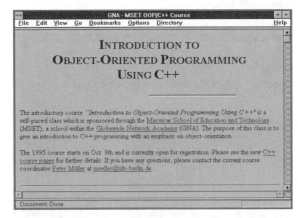

Figure 106 *The place to begin.*

The Parallel Computing Archive

http://www.hensa.ac.uk/parallel/

Although most of us have been conditioned to think of computers as only PCs, high-end computing actually employs a wide variety of multiprocessor-based machines that perform operations in parallel. This site is funded by the London and South East Centre for High Performance Computing and COMETT for *occam* and Transputer training. (A *Transputer* is a fast, UNIX-based processor that enables several massively parallel systems.) Here you will find material on parallel and high-performance computing with special focus on the SGS-Thomson Transputer processor, the *occam* language, and the Transputer User Group. Come here to find the answer to virtually any question about parallel computing.

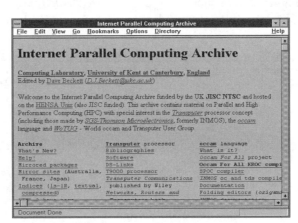

Figure 107 *A plethora of options.*

PC Hardware Tutorial

http://pclt.cis.yale.edu/pclt/pchw/platypus.htm

The PC may be the single most important tool for researchers, educators, and executives. However, because it is purchased in a camera store or a discount warehouse, it is often treated as a commodity item. Purchases are made without reference to important differences in design and architecture among systems. This hypercourse clears the fog and gives you the information you need to understand different prices and configurations and such terms as "Mhz," "upgradable," and "SVGA." Browse a few minutes, and take a valuable step in your education as a consumer of technology. In short, stop here before you buy.

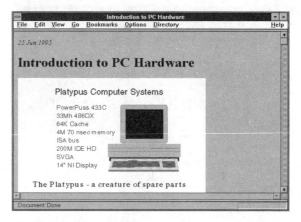

Figure 108 Tutorial home page.

PDS: The Performance Database Server

http://netlib2.cs.utk.edu/performance/html/PDStop.html

Speed. Everyone's concerned with their PC's speed and performance. If you really want to know how your system stacks up against the competition, you can check out the latest statistics (benchmarks) from the Performance Database Server. You can get performance benchmark information on hardware and software *before* you invest in the technology. You can browse these benchmark reports by data tree (selecting the benchmark listed and the machines desired), specify search strings for literal text matching, or display sorted data from various available published benchmark reports. Give yourself the benefit of these comprehensive PC, Mac, SNMP, and LAN benchmarks.

Figure 109.1 PDS home page.

Figure 109.2 Sorted reports.

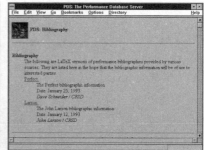

Figure 109.3 PDS bibliography opener.

Rockwell Telecommunications Network Systems

http://www.rns.com/

If you want to preview the technology of tomorrow, check out the Rockwell Telecommunications Network Systems page. This site provides access to Rockwell technical support, product information, sales departments, career opportunities, and new product development. Of current interest is Rockwell's support for the new Power Macintosh 9500, the first of a line of Power Macintosh computers based on the popular 132 megabyte PCI bus. You'll find much information on Rockwell's new 2200 FDDI/PCI driver for that machine, as well as the new Rockwell 2300 Fast Ethernet/PCI adapter. Cool stuff.

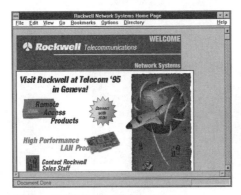

Figure 110.1 Rockwell home page.

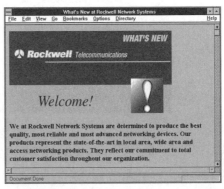

Figure 110.2 What's new.

Santa Cruz Operation

http://www.sco.com/

If you want Windows software, you first think of Microsoft. If you use UNIX software, Santa Cruz Operation is where you want to be. Come here for information on the Santa Cruz Operation's products and services. Your options include a corporate overview, office locations, third-party support information, career opportunities with Santa Cruz, developer support, client integration, and server products. This is also your source for late-breaking information on Wintif 95, Mainsoft Tools, ARCserve, and the SCO ASC program for delivering multivendor support. You'll also get the details on OpenServer Release 5.0, BCS data management for Intel/UNIX platforms, and more. As a bonus, you can review Santa Cruz's quarterly results and annual report. All in all, Santa Cruz's Web site is a tremendous resource for all current and would-be clients.

Figure 111.1 Santa Cruz home page.

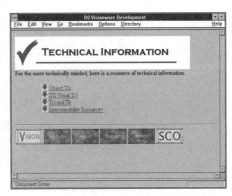

Figure 111.2 Client integration at SCO.

Sound Index

http://www.it.kth.se/sounds

As its name implies, this site is a great collection of .AU sound files divided by topic. Here you have animal noises, sound effects, hal9000 sounds, miscellaneous noises, percussion, and even songs. "Which songs?" I hear you asking. Well, it is a weird, eclectic collection that includes the *Dr. Who* theme song, some hip-hop, and also "Do the Bartman" from *The Simpsons*. You also get the *Hammer* and the *James Bond* themes. The sound effects tend to be sci-fi oriented and completely cool. Slip on your earphones and (literally) have a blast.

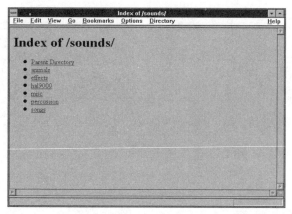

Figure 112 *Your sound menu.*

Sun Microsystems

http://www.sun.com/

When people around the world want to see innovation, they look to Silicon Valley. When folks in Silicon Valley want to see the future of computing, they look to Sun Microsystems. Connect to this site and download a free trial copy of Solaris CDE, Sun's Common Desktop Environment. Get tools and information for migrating from Solaris 1 (SunOS 4.x) to Solaris 2. Visit IDG's *Sunworld Online* magazine. Or simply stick with the great columns and commentary offered by Sun. These include "The Webmaster's Corner" and the "Internet Evangelist," and occasional contributions by Jakob Nielsen. No ride on the Information Superhighway is complete without a stop at Sun, so make the stop.

Figure 113 *Sun home page.*

Techne: Interface, Immersion, and Interactivity Research

http://wimsey.com/anima/TECHNEhome.html

Billing itself as a "forum for experimental research projects, tools, and issues in interface and information design," "Techne" is loaded with cool stuff. Check out Oliver Hockenhull and Jeff Berryman's opus on "Database Technology and Media Art," the engaging "Hypertext Fiction and the Literary Artist," or Derek Dowden's explanation of the CyberCube Project. (This latter is a videographic language system for networked interactive communications space.) You also get a great atlas of interface documents culled from the Net, a FAQ on Ted Nelson's Xanadu, and interesting papers on interface theory and HCI. This is a great example of technological cool converging with cultural cool.

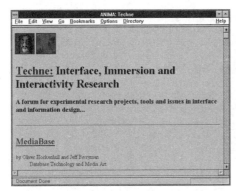
Figure 114.1 Techne home page.

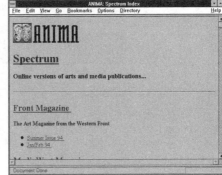
Figure 114.2 Just one Techne option.

Supercomputing Info from the Birthplace of *Mosaic*

http://www.ncsa.uiuc.edu/

Get supercomputing news from the National Center for Supercomputing Applications, the birthplace of Mosaic. Here you will find NCSA news, multimedia exhibits, software tools (including Mosaic), and more. Of special interest are specialized databases for automation of data intensive tasks, as well as information on collaborations in massively parallel code and Grand Challenge research. Additionally, you will get information on training programs for HPCC systems. And you will get details on NCSA's Virtual Environment Group (VEG) for using virtual reality to visualize scientific data. In sum, what awaits you here at the NCSA site is an astonishing array of resources.

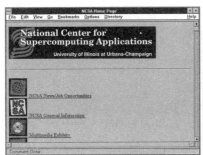
Figure 115.1 NCSA home page.

Figure 115.2 NCSA multimedia exhibits.

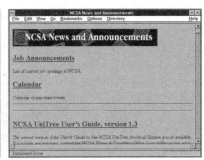
Figure 115.3 NCSA news.

Transputer Archive

http://www.comlab.ox.ac.uk/archive/transputer.html

A *Transputer* is a fast, UNIX-based processor that enables several massively parallel systems. Courtesy of the Oxford University Computing Laboratory, the Transputer Archive contains a wealth of information on the Transputer designed by Inmos (now SGS-Thomson Microelectronics). Included here are Geoff Barrett's account of formal methods used to develop a floating-point unit for the T800 Transputer, the proceedings of the 4th Nordic Transputer Conference on Parallel Computing and Transputers, and a list of Transputer books available from Blackwell's Bookshops. Transport yourself to the Transputer Archive for a taste of some of the most powerful computing on the planet.

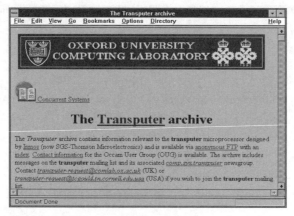

Figure 116 Transputer home page.

Women and Computer Science

http://www.ai.mit.edu/people/ellens/gender.html

This outstanding site is maintained by Ellen Spertus (ellens@ai.mit.edu) and features a wonderful collection of links and resources. Here you will find Nancy Leveson's great essay "Educational Pipeline Issues for Women," Karen Frenkel's study of women and computing, Dale Strok's consideration of women in AI research, and an electronic "reprint" of the article "Sex and the Cybergirl" from *Mother Jones*. I'd also recommend that you look at Ellen Spertus' writings, which include a useful essay entitled "Why Are There So Few Female Computer Scientists?"

Figure 117 Just look at those harmonicas.

Z39.50 Resources: A Pointer Page

http://ds.internic.net/z3950/z3950.html

Stop here and you will find the most exhaustive archive available on the Information Retrieval Service and Protocol Standard, ANSI/NISO Z39.50. What is Z39.50? Oh, nothing much. Just the basis for WAIS (the Internet's Wide Area Information Server). A particularly useful link here is that of Index Data, a software development group in Copenhagen which has developed a toolkit to aid in the implementation of the ISO SR and the Z39.50-1995 protocols. They say, "software is available free of charge, on a liberal license: Commercial re-use is explicitly permitted." Cool! Other goodies? OCLC has made its Z39.50 Client API available, and the National Library of Canada has posted its server code. Plenty more interesting stuff will catch your eye here as well. To find out what, make a visit.

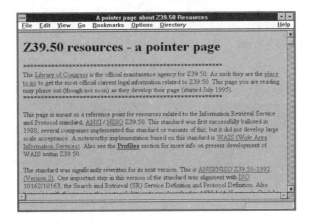

Figure 118 Z39.50 pointer page.

More Computer Resources

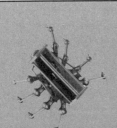
As you surf the Web, you may find that one or more of the site addresses listed in this book have changed. In such cases, connect to Jamsa Press at http://www.jamsa.com and click on the icon that corresponds to the *1001 Really Cool Web Sites* book. Jamsa Press will list replacement addresses (when possible) for sites that have moved. In addition, you can also use the following site list as you search for information on or about computers:

Computer Science Department	http://a.cs.okstate.edu/welcome.html
UNIX Security Topics	http://ausg.dartmouth.edu/security.html
Branch Business Center	http://branch.com/business.htm#computer
ACM SIGMOD	http://bunny.cs.uiuc.edu/README.html
Langley Computer Users	http://cabsparc.larc.nasa.gov/LCUC/lcuc.html
SAT/SAGEM Index	http://catalog.com/satusa/
LANL Information Servers	http://cnls-www.lanl.gov/is.html
CPSR	http://cpsr.org/cpsr/cpsr_membership_info/cpsr.html
Center for Research in Computing	http://crca-www.ucsd.edu/
Univ. of Bonn CS Department	http://cs.uni-bonn.de/
UTEP Welcome (CS Dept)	http://cs.utep.edu/

American Special Collections

http://lcweb.loc.gov/spcoll/spclhome.html

Use the Library of Congress as your jumping-off place for myriad special collections on the history, demography, and geography of the United States. You can view these collections through photographs, maps, drawings, recordings, and books that depict America's towns and great cities, farms and wilderness, home and public buildings. Search this marvelous resource by geographical region, subject terms, or historical/chronological sequence. Here you will find manuscript collections, motion pictures, posters, sound recordings, pamphlets, prints, photographs, pop culture archives, and more. Be sure to treat yourself to something called "America Through the Looking Glass."

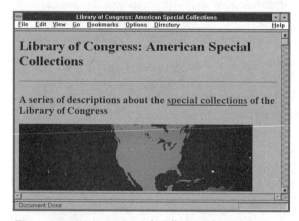

Figure 119 American Special Collections home page.

120

American Memory Collection

http://lcweb2.loc.gov/amhome.html

Access the unparalleled special collections of the Library of Congress including the Carl Van Vechten photographs (1932-64), recently recovered manuscripts from the Thomas Biggs Harned-Walt Whitman Collection, and early motion pictures (1897-1916) that feature President William McKinley, the Pan American Exposition, and San Francisco before the great earthquake. There's also recordings of political speeches made during World War I, an enormous collection of Civil War photographs by Mathew Brady and others, and the Life History Manuscripts from the Folklore Division of the WPA Federal Writers' Project, 1936-40. One more neat item: color photos from the Farm Security Administration and the Office of War Information, 1938-44. Watch these American memories come to life.

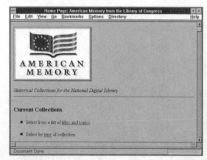

Figure 120.1 American Memory home page.

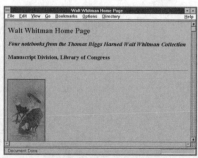

Figure 120.2 Walt Whitman exhibit.

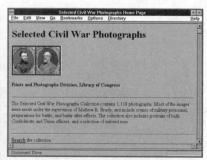

Figure 120.3 Civil War photo archive.

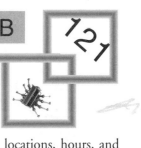

British Museums

http://boom.cs.ucl.ac.uk/local/museums/

Focused on museums in and around the city of London, this useful site provides details on locations, hours, and holdings of many major institutions. You'll encounter information about the British Museum, the Museum of London, the Museum of Mankind, the Museum of the Moving Image (MOMI), the British National Gallery, the Natural History Museum, the Royal Academy of Arts, the Science Museum, and the beautiful Victoria & Albert Museum. You'll also find information on the National Maritime Museum, the Queen's House, the Cutty Sark, and the Royal Observatory of Greenwich. All in all, this site has a lot of history. Dive in.

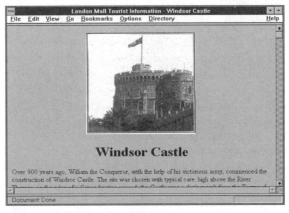

Figure 121 Windsor Castle home page.

Fighters on the Farm Front

http://arcweb.sos.state.or.us/osuhomepage.html

This online exhibit from Oregon State University documents Oregon's Emergency Farm Labor Service, a program sponsored by the Oregon State College Extension Service to ensure an adequate farm labor supply during World War II and the years immediately thereafter. This electronic exhibit is a slightly expanded version of an exhibit currently touring Oregon. Aspects of the exhibit focus on women in the Emergency Farm Labor Service, the role of prisoners-of-war, the Youth Victory Farm Volunteers, the roles of international migrant workers, and Japanese internees.

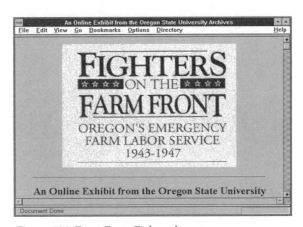

Figure 122 Farm Front Fighters home page.

1492: An Ongoing Voyage

http://sunsite.unc.edu/expo/1492.exhibit/Intro.html

1492. Columbus. What was life like in those areas before 1492? What spurred European expansion? How did European, African, and American people react to each other? What were some of the immediate results of these contacts? "1492: An Ongoing Voyage" addresses such questions, closely examining what happened when the polyglot Mediterranean world collided with the multicultural Western Hemisphere. Your voyage with Columbus will examine controversial aspects of history you may not have learned in school—learn it now.

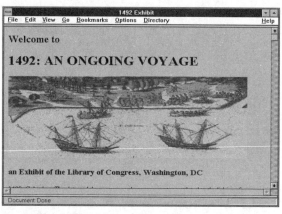

Figure 123 Goodbye, Columbus.

History of Medicine

http://www.nlm.nih.gov/hmd.dir/hmd.html

The History of Medicine Division of the National Library of Medicine (founded 1836) gives you a rich cornucopia of material, starting with nearly 60,000 medical images. One of their many electronic exhibits is "Origins of the National Institutes of Health," which covers topics such as a brief history of Caesarian section, images from the history of the Public Health Service, the Ellis Island Health Service, and more. You'll also find some 70,000 medical pamphlets printed before 1801, ninety early western manuscripts of classic medical texts, more than 200 oral history memoirs from eminent physicians and health officials, and numerous films documenting medical history as of 1917.

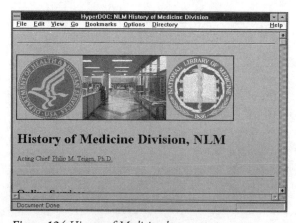

Figure 124 History of Medicine home page.

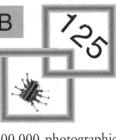

The Mariners' Museum

http://www.seva.net/sevanet/branch/region/mari_museum/mari_museum.html

Welcome to the Mariners' Museum which features more than 35,000 artifacts and over 500,000 photographic images and negatives, as well as the largest maritime library (75,000 volumes) in the Western Hemisphere. One of the world's most prestigious international Maritime museums, the Mariners' Museum is dedicated to preserving the culture of the sea and its tributaries, the history of its conquest by man, and the maritime influence on civilization. Check out the antique boats gallery, the carvings gallery, the Crabtree collection of miniature ships, and more.

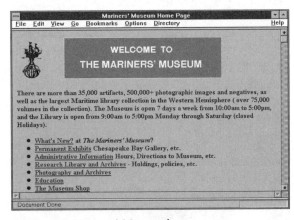

Figure 125 Mariners' Museum home page.

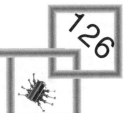

A Roman Palace in the Former Yugoslavia

http://sunsite.unc.edu/expo/palace.exhibit/intro.html

Learn all about a unique structure from the Roman Empire (the "palace" of Diocletian at Split) in this multimedia tour created by Michael Greenhalgh. Incorporating graphical reconstructions as well as contemporary photographs of the ruins, this is an engaging multimedia walk-through. The name "Spalato" (Split) means "little palace," and the emperor Diocletian made his home here during the waning days of the Roman Empire. What remains? The arching vaults below the church of St. Domnus, in which Diocletian himself is said to lie. See structures now and as they were a thousand years ago.

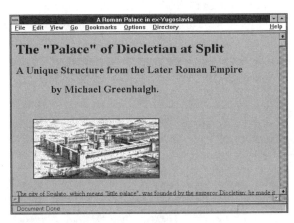

Figure 126 Roman Palace home page.

COOL HISTORY ON THE WEB

Rome Reborn

http://www.ncsa.uiuc.edu/SDG/Experimental/vatican.exhibit/Vatican.exhibit.html

By the fourteenth century, the once-great city of Rome had dwindled to a miserable village. Perhaps 20,000 people clung to the ruins despite the ravages of diseases and invaders. Popes and cardinals had fled to Avignon in southern France. In the Renaissance, however, the popes returned to the See of Saint Peter. They straightened streets, raised bridges across the Tiber, provided hospitals, and built churches and gardens for themselves and for the people. This fabulous electronic exhibit documents that revival, as well as the way in which the papal curia became one of the most efficient governments in Europe and fostered much of the best in Renaissance art, architecture, sculpture, and science.

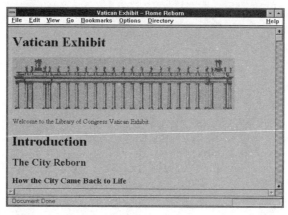

Figure 127 Vatican exhibit home page.

Smithsonian Institution

http://www.si.edu/message/

Something far more important than a mere advance in technology is at the heart of the information revolution. It is the fulfillment of one of the central promises of democracy: to make knowledge available to as many as citizens as want it. In this spirit, the Smithsonian makes its many museums, research centers, and offices accessible from the Information Super Highway. This veritable "Smithsonian without walls" includes homepages for each of the Smithsonian's museums and research centers. Demonstrating excellence in design as well as content, this site seems a more than appropriate way for the Smithsonian to celebrate an upcoming milestone: its 150th anniversary in 1996. Use Cyberspace to enjoy the institute too few of us get to experience in sufficient detail.

Figure 128.1 Smithsonian home page.

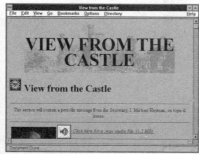

Figure 128.2 The view from the castle.

Figure 128.3 Smithsonian museums on the Mall.

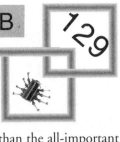

United States Holocaust Memorial Museum

http://www.ushmm.org/

It is hard to believe, but the United States Holocaust Memorial Museum actually does *more* than the all-important job of remembering and honoring the innocent victims of Nazi genocide. Taking the lesson of the Holocaust a step further, the Museum bears witness not just to the old and well-rehearsed crimes of Hitler, but also to contemporary holocausts such as the current tragedy of "ethnic cleansing" in the former Yugoslavia. This is a must-see site.

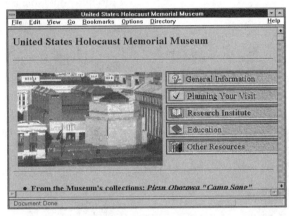

Figure 129 U.S. Holocaust Museum home page.

The Viking Home Page

http://control.chalmers.se/vikings/viking.html

No, we are not talking about the football team. At this site, you can learn all about your favorite barbarians with their weird looking boats and hats. This site includes an overview of the brief "Viking Age" (which began in 793 and ended prematurely in 1066, due to too much partying), a Swedish-Viking-English dictionary, information on Viking food and *drink*, and more. You get links to more than thirty Viking-related sites, including the Norse Film and Pageant Society, the Norse Mythology Web Page, a page dedicated to "the lost art of Viking sailing," information on a Viking theme park (!) in Oslo, and a great link to the Swedish Museum of National Antiquities.

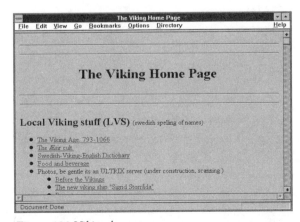

Figure 130 Viking home page.

131

The Simon Wiesenthal Center

http://www.wiesenthal.com

The Simon Wiesenthal Center is an international center for Holocaust remembrance and the defense of human rights. The Center's mandate is a unique combination of social action, public outreach, scholarship, education, and media projects. It imparts the lessons of the Holocaust and develops educational strategies for teaching that most noble of things: *tolerance*. You'll also find the Wiesenthal Center's *CyberWatch* program meant to combat hatred and bigotry, as it manifests itself (and believe me, it does) on the Internet. This is a necessary stop for all thoughtful people on the Information Super Highway.

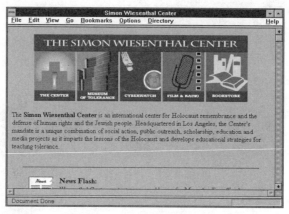

Figure 131 Wiesenthal Center home page.

132

WPA Life Histories Home Page

http://lcweb2.loc.gov/wpaintro/wpahome.html

Experience history through the eyes (writings) of those who lived it. These life histories were written by the staff of the Folklore Project of the Federal Writers' Project for the U.S. WPA from 1936 to 1940. The collection includes 2,900 documents, representing the work of over 300 writers from 24 states. The histories describe the informant's family, education, income, occupation, political views, religion, and personal history. What is particularly cool is that many elderly former slaves and aged Civil War veterans are included here. They seem to speak to you directly out of history itself. Search by region or state, or simply browse and make marvelous discoveries.

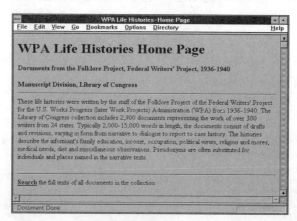

Figure 132 Life Histories home page.

More Cool History On The Web

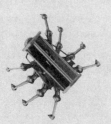

As you surf the Web, you may find that one or more of the site addresses listed in this book have changed. In such cases, connect to Jamsa Press at http://www.jamsa.com and click on the icon that corresponds to the *1001 Really Cool Web Sites* book. Jamsa Press will list replacement addresses (when possible) for sites that have moved. In addition, you can also use the following site list as you search for information on history:

History of Science	http://nearnet.gnn.com:80/wic/histsci.toc.html
American Memory	http://rs6.loc.gov/amhome.html
The Nation's Forum	http://rs6.loc.gov/nfhome.html
Berlin/Prague	http://www-swiss.ai.mit.edu/philg/berlin-prague/book-cover.html
The Palo Alto Historical Assoc.	http://www.commerce.digital.com/palo-alto/historical-assoc/home.html
Anne Frank WWW site	http://www.cs.washington.edu/homes/tdnguyen/Anne_Frank.html
All About Turkey	http://www.ege.edu.tr/Turkiye
AMS/HIS Home Page	http://www.gar.utexas.edu/
Labyrinth WWW Home Page	http://www.georgetown.edu/labyrinth/labyrinth-home.html

Surf-Watch

http://www.surfwatch.com

Surf-Watch is a new type of software which helps parents, educators, and employers reduce the risk of children and others uncovering sexually explicit material on the World Wide Web and other areas of the Internet. This site provides information on the latest revisions of the software for both Windows and Macintosh machines, an automated *Surf-Watch* demonstration, and an invitation to order *Surf-Watch* online. Note that the *Surf-Watch* software is not to be confused with the *Bay Watch* television program, which my son Billy never misses and insists on calling "babe-watch." Agh, to be young again. By the way, you can also contact *Surf-Watch* at: 1-800-458-6600.

Figure 133 Surf-Watch home page.

Ms. Metaverse Pageant

http://virtualvegas.com

Behold the skyline of Virtual Vegas, where getting a room or catching a taxi is never a problem. In addition to being home to a virtual convention center, a virtual casino, and a virtual "lizard" lounge, Virtual Vegas is also home to a virtual beauty pageant: the Ms. Metaverse Pageant. Here you can view the sexy photographs of would-be Ms. Metaverse honorees and then vote for your favorite. You also get various details on their hobbies, occupations, fantasies, etc. The ladies of Virtual Vegas are not the type you will find in a swimsuit on television with Dick Clark, Bert Parks, Ed McMahon, or this year's host of the Miss America Pageant. These ladies are a bit different. Enough said.

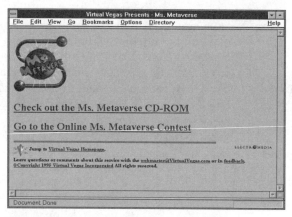

Figure 134 Ms. Metaverse options.

Penthouse Online

http://www.penthousemag.com/home.html

Access the *Penthouse* "Private Collection" of erotic images, order a poster-size centerfold photo, or shop in the erotic toy store. This page also has abbreviated, current, and past editions of *Penthouse* in electronic format; these incorporate not just sexy photographs, but also short stories, music and cinema reviews, and, of course, the legendary Letters to the *Penthouse* Editor. Hmmm. I think I'll write one right now. "Dear Penthouse: You know, I never believed these letters were true until I had a cyber-experience I have to tell you about . . . "

Figure 135 Penthouse home page.

Playboy Magazine

http://www.playboy.com

I was a disadvantaged youth. My father did not have any old or new editions of *Playboy* squirreled away in the bottom of his bedroom closet, like so many of my friends' fathers did. Or perhaps he was just better at hiding them. In any event, my son will be similarly disadvantaged unless, of course, he stumbles on this address while surfing the Net. "Oh, gee, hi Dad. I didn't realize you were home. What's that you ask? What am I looking at on the screen? Hey, did I type *Playboy*? What a goof! I meant to type *Smithsonian*. Yeah, that's it. Gosh, I wonder if something is wrong with the mapping on your keyboard, Dad." The contents? Predictable: playmates, cartoons, "classic interviews" (if you consider G. Gordon Liddy a classic), and an invitation to subscribe.

Figure 136.1 Playboy home page.

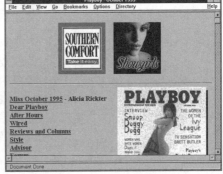
Figure 136.2 Monthly magazine contents.

The SaferSex Page

http://www.cmpharm.ucsf.edu/~troyer/safesex.html

Well, few topics are more important than safe sex. Ranked in the top 5% of Web sites by Point Software, The SaferSex Page has information about condoms, HIV, ways to have unsafe sex even *with* a condom, and more. Want to become involved? A forum for chatting and exchanging information on a host of topics related to safe sex is waiting for you. One interesting topic is "What's in your safe sex kit?" This forum, by the way, is real-time WebChat, courtesy of the Internet Roundtable Society. In sum, this is a marvelous and highly useful gathering of vital information.

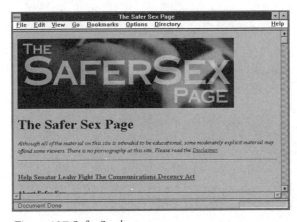
Figure 137 Safer Sex home page.

CYBERSEX

Hustler Online

http://hustler.onprod.com

Preview this month's pictorials, or scan the contents of the current issue before going to the newsstand to pick it up. The "cartoon of the day" emphasizes *Hustler's* own unique, wicked brand of humor. And the tempted will find an online form for subscribing to the magazine. If you want something more than those items mentioned above, become a "member" for a small fee. This lets you gain electronic access to back-issues of the magazine, plus a wide, constantly-growing selection of photographs, which resolve quickly out from *Hustler's* dedicated "members only" T1 server. I saw no end to the supply of "Hustler Honeys." All told, this well-designed site provides a voyeuristic pleasure palace.

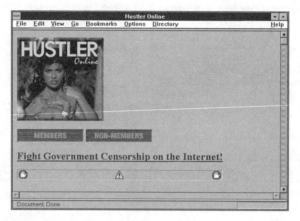

Figure 138 *Hustler home page.*

More Cybersex

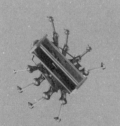

As you surf the Web, you may find that one or more of the site addresses listed in this book have changed. In such cases, connect to Jamsa Press at http://www.jamsa.com and click on the icon that corresponds to the *1001 Really Cool Web Sites* book. Jamsa Press will list replacement addresses (when possible) for sites that have moved. In addition, you can also use the following site list as you search for information on cybersex:

Midnight Graffiti	http://www.xmision.com/~nlifer/mg.html
Cyberbabies	http://www.webcom.com/~cbabes/cyberbabes.html
Aphrodite's Love Palace	http://www.dircon.co.uk/purplet/love.html
Sound Bites	http://www.sirius.com/~fearless/greato.aiff
Recontres	http://www.easynet.co.uk/findlove/index.htm
Poly Home Page	http://www.mit.edu:8001/people/ert/triples/home.html
Dating Game	http://www.cid.com/cid/date/
Fantasies	http://www.fantasies.com/
The Purity Test	http://phenom.physics.wisc.edu/~fosdal/Purity/

Academy of Motion Picture Arts & Sciences

http://www.ampas.org/ampas/

Why don't you take a break from hacking and check out last summer's bust of a movie, *The Net*? Why mention *The Net*? Beats me. Anyway, as it turns out, the annual Academy Awards is not the only thing the Academy of Motion Picture Arts and Sciences does—they've actually put together a cool Web site. At this site, you can find out about the various programs, fellowships, and educational and historical activities with which the Academy is involved. You can also access information on the latest press releases from the organization and catch up on industry gossip. Rumor has it that Martin Scorsese is about to option film rights to *1001 Really Cool Web Sites*. OK, maybe not. But if you check out this site, you'll be in the "Hollywood know."

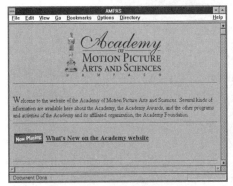

Figure 139.1 The Academy's home page.

Figure 139.2 Index of Academy info.

Blade Runner Archive

http://kzsu.stanford.edu/uwi/br/off-world.html

This great sites includes, as its masthead tells us, "all kinds of stuff" about the film *Blade Runner*. Be sure to check out the hilarious section entitled "Sequels? You bet . . . sadly." "The *Blade Runner* File" is a wonderful compilation of discussion about *Blade Runner* issues and personalities. And there is a list of *Blade Runner* references including magazines, books, posters, and photos. Additionally, you get links to Murray *Chapman's Blade Runner* FAQ, an online version of the *Blade Runner Souvenir Book*, an early draft of the script for the first *Blade Runner* film, a great essay entitled "At Home with Replicants," and Gorm Eriksen's *Blade Runner* pages. A Sci-Fi must see.

Figure 140 Blade Runner heaven.

FILM ON THE WEB

141

The Blues Brothers Page

http://dec36.cs.monash.edu.au:1786/bluesbros/faq.html

Get links not only to *Blues Brothers* sites, but also to detailed information on Dan Aykroyd, John Belushi, and more. You'll find movie stills, posters, sound files, and information on the Disney Channel's *Blues Brothers Special*. This cool site also gives you fan club information, a complete transcript of key scenes (143 of them, to be precise) in the film *The Blues Brothers*, and more. Additionally, you get great Jake and Elwood trivia quizzes, and the lyrics to such songs as "Rawhide," "Stand By Your Man," "She Caught the Katy," "Everybody Needs Somebody," and, of course, "Sweet Home Chicago." By the way: Watch out for the Penguin!

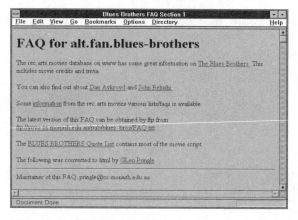

Figure 141 All about the two boys from Detroit.

142

Internet Movie Database

http://www.cm.cf.ac.uk/Movies/

Formerly known as the Cardiff Movie Database, this resource lets you search an exhaustive set of information files by movie title, cast/crew names, character names, MPAA ratings, genres, countries of origin, production companies, filming locations, quotes, soundtracks (who sang what), plot summaries, or years of release. I gave the database a vigorous test by typing in the name of my old high school friend, Steve Buscemi. He is an up-and-coming character actor who has done a fair amount of television and film work (including opposite Sean Connery in *Rising Sun*), and has just finished writing and directing his own film, *Tree's Lounge*. Sure enough, the database had him covered.

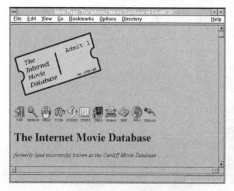

Figure 142.1 Internet movie database.

Figure 142.2 My famous friend!.

CinemaSpace

http://remarque.berkeley.edu:8001/~xcohen/

Published by the Film Studies Program of the University of California at Berkeley, *CinemaSpace* is an electronic journal devoted to all aspects of cinema and new media. Turn to *CinemaSpace* for academic papers on film and new media, essays on film theory and critique, multimedia "lectures" on film art and history, and more. Two current articles and links are "Narrating National Sadness: Cinematic Mapping and Hypertextual Dispersion," and "The Political Aesthetic: Nation and Narrativity on the *Starship Enterprise*." More than an intellectual guide to new media—this site's discussion will keep you at the forefront of this critical technology.

Figure 143 CinemaSpace home page.

The Envelope Please: An Interactive Guide to the Academy Awards

http://guide.oscars.org/TheEvelopePlease.html

Actually a preview of a much more elaborate program, which will be released for the 68th Annual Academy Awards in 1996, this interactive database lets you search through the history of the Oscars by actor, director, screenwriter, cinematographer, film name, or film genre category. The site includes a wonderful collection of film clips—although they are huge, 2.5Mb to 4.5Mb in size. Thus, if you are not connected by ISDN or T1 lines, you might be happier sticking with the handy "mostly-text" option that yields the same rich mixture of information, sans clips. As a perk, you get a fun interactive online Oscar Trivia Game. If it is going on at the Oscars, you will find specifics about here! Come check it out.

Figure 144.1 The Envelope Please.

Figure 144.2 Best-Actor Nominees.

Figure 144.3 Best Actor.

Film & Video Resources

http://http2.sils.umich.edu/Public/fvl/film.html

Maintained by Lisa Wood and Kristen Garlock at the University of Michigan, this great page provides a large collection of links to scholarly discussions, general/popular discussions, and production/technical discussions of film and film art. You'll also find reviews, filmographies/bibliographies, searchable databases, and more. From the first silent films to the latest action thriller, you will find information on all your favorite directors, actors, screenwriters, and producers right here. Let's look up D.W. Griffith (the great silent-screen director) and see if he is related to Andy.

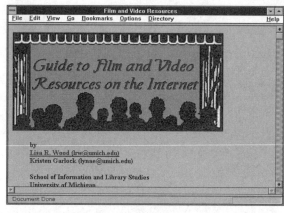

Figure 145 Film & Video home page.

Alfred Hitchcock's WWW with Sex and Suspense

http://nextdch.mty.itesm.mx/~plopezg/Kaplan/Hitchcock.html

The perfect site for the Hitchcock junkie. If you loved *Psycho* and *Rear Window*, you won't think this site is for "*The Birds*." The site includes a wonderful essay entitled "Alfred Hitchcock, The Director: A Rear Window of the Director's Life." It also provides a complete filmography. The site details each and every cameo, fully documenting the when, where, and how of each occurrence of the classic Hitchcockian trademark. Just as intriguing are interviews with people who helped Hitchcock achieve his greatest triumphs, a collection of witty quotes from the director, and great stills that include a suspicious-looking motel with a lonely house on the hill above. "Norman, is that you?"

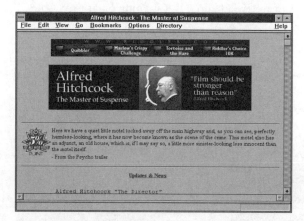

Figure 146 Mr. Alfred Hitchcock.

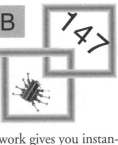

Hollywood Network

http://hollywoodnetwork.com

As seen on *Good Morning America, Inside Edition*, and other television shows, Hollywood Network gives you instantaneous online access to experts in acting, directing, music, producing, screenwriting, and writing. The Hollywood Network's live bulletin boards, insider's tips, and "opportunity desks" let you ask questions of top industry professionals and post your professional profile for potential deals or job placement in the film industry. Got a screenplay to hype? Hype it here. Got a book or film option to hawk? Hawk it here. Tell them Ed sent you.

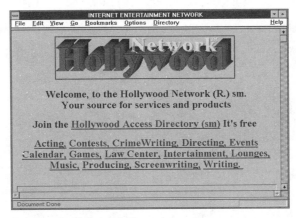

Figure 147 Hollywood Network home page.

Indiana Jones WWW Page

http://dialin.ind.net/~msjohnso/

"Indy! Watch out! There's a huge boulder hurling down the tunnel right at you!" I don't know why I even bother to warn him. He always survives no matter what villains, or nature, or fate throw at him. With links to the official LucasArts Home Page, and a neat new page dedicated to Karen Allen, this is the ultimate *Indiana Jones* trivia site. In addition to scripts, stills, details, and gossip from past films, you also get updates on the (evidently troubled) process of creating the fourth in the series of Indiana Jones films. You also get an entire collection of links which focus on "The Shameless Commercialization of Indy." Commercialization? I'm shocked.

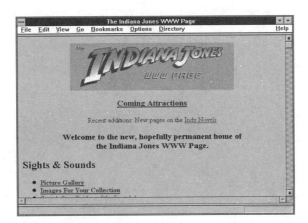

Figure 148 The Indiana Jones page.

MCA/Universal CyberWalk

http://univstudios.com

Enter the ultimate Hollywood screening room: a universe of stellar home entertainment awaits you in your state-of-the-art screening room stocked with current home video hits, classics, and collectibles from MCA/Universal Home Video. Create your very own online home video hit list. Also, have your kids check out the online activities in the Universal Kid's Playroom. Useful, too, is also Universal V/IP. These exclusive Visual/Interactive Previews give you the scoop of all the new and forthcoming Universal releases before they hit the theaters, including clips! Great stuff. The kind of thing that makes me proud to be an entertainment consumer. You must take the MCA/Universal Cyberwalk.

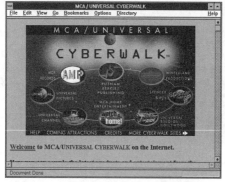

Figure 149.1 MCA/Universal CyberWalk.

Figure 149.2 Universal Pictures information.

Marilyn Monroe (aka Norma Jean, as in *"Goodbye"*)

http://www.infonet.net/showcase/agency/marilyn.html

Yes, we're talking about the little-known actress made famous by Elton John. (The truly hip remember her as the wife of Joe DiMaggio.) Yes, here you'll find a great collection of photographs of *one of* John F. Kennedy's *favorite actresses.* Whatever you want, we've got it. How about leaning back, hands on hips? Yawning? In a nightgown? What about a gold dress with a plunging neckline? How about a swimsuit photo? A bedroom shot? What about kneeling in a strapless red dress? All right. I know what you're looking for. Yes, it is here: naked with just a string of beads. The original *Playboy* centerfold . . . You are *so* predictable.

Figure 150 Jack's favorite actress.

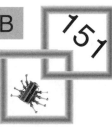

Movie and Film Festivals

http://www.yahoo.com/Entertainment/Movies_and_Films/Festivals

Don't you just hate the way Cannes has gotten in the last few years? All those tourist types crashing the parties that should be reserved for us *real* film people. I don't know about you, but that's why I'm looking for other venues, baby. See details on more than 25 great alternatives to Cannes right here, including the Sundance Festival, the London Film Festival, and festivals in Stockholm, Atlanta, Portland, Aspen, Berlin, Rotterdam, and Philadelphia. Me, I personally prefer watching the clips at Planet Hollywood with an ale or lager.

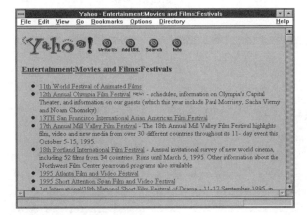

Figure 151 A long list of options.

Movie Information

http://www.cs.cmu.edu/afs/cs.cmu.edu/user/clamen/misc/movies/README.html

What a great collection of links for the film buff! Access hundreds of movie reviews by title. Get film facts from the U.S. National Film Registry. See what films will release this month. Check out the James Bond Movie Page, the Movie Poster Archive, or see what happened on this date in movie history. You will also find the *Financial Times'* "Screen Finance" homepage, the electronic edition of *Film Comment*, and the Independent Film and Video Makers Internet Resource Guide, and the *Depth Probe* archive. This is a must-visit site for movie-goers in the "know."

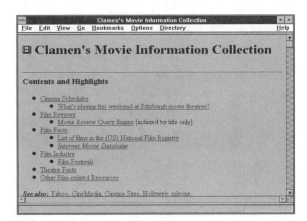

Figure 152 Clamen's Movie Information.

Paramount Pictures

http://www.paramount.com

For over 83 years, legendary directors from Hitchcock to Coppola, famed actors from Gary Cooper to Harrison Ford, and renowned beauties from Grace Kelly to Alicia Silverstone have walked through Paramount's famous Bronson Gate to create some of the most popular films of all time. Now you can point and click your way through that same gate. Go to the Paramount Theatre to see clips from Paramount's latest releases, as well as their newest television shows, including the most recent *Star Trek* series. At the time that I visited, the theatre was showing clips from *Virtuosity, Clueless, The Indian in the Cupboard, Congo*, and *Braveheart*. But there will be new film features when you stop by. My experience? Two thumbs up!

Figure 153.1 The fabled gates.

Figure 153.2 Cher's "Clueless" page.

154

The Meg Ryan Page

http://web.cs.ualberta.ca/~davidw/MegRyan/meg.cgi

Okay, you Meg Ryan nuts out there—your spot on the Web has arrived. This site contains your fan-club survival kit: Meg Ryan bio, Meg Ryan image archive, Meg Ryan audio archive, Meg Ryan's most notable quotes (notable quotes? she's an epigramist all of a sudden?), the Meg Ryan Filmography, etc., etc. When you get bored with Meg, use links to the homepages honoring Gillian Anderson, Alicia Silverstone, Uma Thurman, Helen Hunt, and (give me a break!) Heather Locklear. Now, just who are all these elitist snobs who say the Internet is being trivialized by the onrush of digitized pop culture? I beg to differ. This sort of electronic kitsch is highly entertaining, though for all the wrong reasons.

Figure 154 The Meg tribute.

Screenwriters' and Playwrights' Home Page

http://www.teleport.com/~cdeemer/scrwriter.html

This page, which is frequently updated, is designed to meet the special needs of screenwriters. Here you have good nuts and bolts information on dramatic structure, script format, and script marketing. For inspiration and example, you have access to scripts from everything from *Godzilla* to Hitchcock classics. You also get Jack Stanley's Screenwriters' FAQ, film databases, movie reviews, and agent reference lists. The spirit of this site is embraced by the quote from Anton Chekhov (remember him? the Russian playwright), which decorates the masthead: " . . . only he is an emancipated thinker who is not afraid to write foolish things." No wiser nor more foolish words were ever penned.

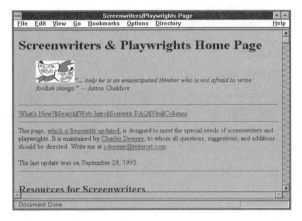

Figure 155 Resources for dramatic writers.

More Film on the Web

As you surf the Web, you may find that one or more of the site addresses listed in this book have changed. In such cases, connect to Jamsa Press at http://www.jamsa.com and click on the icon that corresponds to the *1001 Really Cool Web Sites* book. Jamsa Press will list replacement addresses (when possible) for sites that have moved. In addition, you can also use the following site list as you search for information on film:

MGM/StarGate	http://www.earthlink.net/STARGATE/
MPEG Movie Archive	http://www.eeb.ele.tue.nl/mpeg/
RESERVOIR DOGS : HOME PAGE	http://www.foresight.co.uk/ents/dogs/dogin.html
Pilot Online Movie Guide	http://www.infi.net/pilot/movieguide.html
Festival	http://www.interport.net/festival
The Internet Movie Database at Cardiff UK	http://www.leo.org/Movies/
Links to movie resources	http://www.maths.tcd.ie/pub/films/movie_hypdocs.html
The Internet Movie Database at Mississippi US	http://www.msstate.edu/M/on-this-day
Internet Movie Database	http://www.msstate.edu/Movies/moviequery.html
William Gibson's Alien III Script	http://www.umd.umich.edu/~nhughes/cyber/gibson/alien3.html

Austrian Beer Guide

http://www.lib.uchicago.edu/keith/austrian-beer.html

Graphically beautiful and informationally comprehensive, this great page describes, ranks, and provides the labels for approximately 360 distinct Austrian beers produced by 66 breweries. You can access a list of breweries with their addresses, phone, and fax numbers. A sample of the information you will find here: When in Vienna, remember that the best beers come from the Brauhaus micro-brewery in Nussdorf, and are served only at one tavern, the Bier Heurige. All the beers are top-fermented. (*Top-fermentation* is the method whereby yeast is spread over the top of the brew rather than simply mixed in with it. The result is a brew with a full, rich flavor.) Vienna here I come!

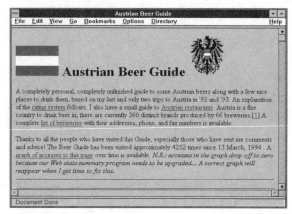

Figure 156 A splendid beer list.

Beer Page

http://www-personal.umich.edu/~spencer/beer/

Geared mostly for home-brewers, this great page includes John Palmer's excellent tutorial on "How to Brew Your First Beer," as well as access to extensive beer "Recipe Files." You also get a library of beer labels, electronic home-brew digests, and links to other beer-related Web pages. This page also provides information on competitions and festivals, not to mention brewery homepages. As a bonus, you also get an electronic edition of the Ann Arbor Brewers Guild newsletter, Michigan being the genesis point of this great site. Hmmm. Do you need a "designated driver" in Cyberspace?

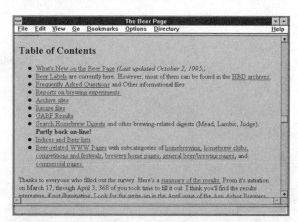

Figure 157 Spencer's Beer Page, a labor of love.

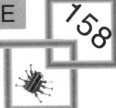

Beer Ratings

http://www.mit.edu:8001/afs/athena.mit.edu/user/m/j/mjbauer/WWW/beer-ratings.html

So what beers are at the bottom of this ratings chart? You guessed it: Budweiser, Coors, and Miller although as the author of this page concedes, "those three do make good cheap slug-killer . . ." Top of the chart for great beers: Theakston Old Peculier, Anchor Porter, Guinness Extra Stout (yes!), Pete's Wicked Ale, Pilsner Urquell, and Samuel Smith Nut Brown Ale. And for "decent" beers we have Dixie Blackened Voodoo Lager, Pete's Wicked Lager, Castlemaine XXXX Export Lager, Celis White, Fuller's ESB English Ale, and Pete's Wicked Summer Brew, just to name a few. Who says that research is not alive and well at MIT?

Figure 158 Try some Theakston "Old Peculier."

Coffee Resources

http://www.cappuccino.com

Downing a pot of coffee won't help you drive home after drinking all the beers itemized at site 158. Coffee does not sober you up. It just makes you a wide-awake drunk. Unfortunately, I find it much easier to order a beer than a "double-lite latte with foam." However you can learn a lot at this coffee-lovers site, formally entitled "Over the Coffee," including coffee recipes. Created by Tim Nemec and inspired by the Usenet coffee newsgroups, "Over the Coffee" seeks to provide a variety of information for both coffee enthusiasts and coffee professionals, and thereby expand upon the concept of the "coffee community." In doing so, it has been rated among the top 5% of all sites on the Web by Netscape Navigator.

Figure 159.1 This site will keep you awake.

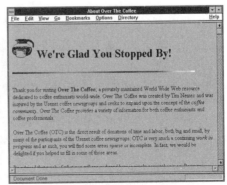

Figure 159.2 A reason for being.

Dining Out on the Web

http://www.ird.net/diningout.html

This is a list of restaurant guides. No recipes, no wine, no beer, no brew pubs, no cafes. The focus is on restaurants, reviews of restaurants, and collections of restaurant menus. Links include the North American Restaurant Guide, the Internet Restaurant Guide, restaurant reviews from across the United States in the Iowa State Spires gopher, and restaurant guides in *CitiLink* and *City Net*. For even more gustatory delights, check out the Kosher restaurant database, the worldwide Sushi restaurant reference, the Chile-Heads "hot" restaurants guide, a comprehensive review index for vegetarian restaurants across the U.S., and Paul & Kay Henderson's list of favorite restaurants. Hungry?

Figure 160 *Restaurant reviews at your fingertips.*

The eGG (Electronic Gourmet Guide)

http://www.2way.com/food/egg/index.html

Welcome to *The eGG*, the Internet e-zine (electronic magazine) devoted to food and cooking. Regular columns include *eGGsalad* by Steve Holzinger, *Aunt Salli's CyberKitchen* by Salli Schwartz, *Global Gourmet* recipes, the *Gourmet Guess* food trivia game, and more. In addition, you'll find a link to a sister publication of *The eGG* entitled *American Wine on the Web*. When I visited, featured articles included profiles of four gourmet companies and how they got their start, and the Aspen Cooking School. The writing is lucid and witty. The graphics are scrumptious.

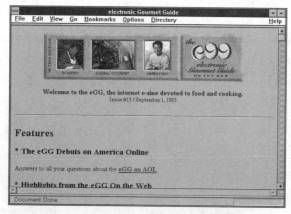

Figure 161 *The eGG home page.*

FoodWare

http://www.novator.com/FOODWARE/FOODWARE.html

FoodWare is a recipe-management software package that lets you access recipes, plan menus, and organize your shopping lists quickly and effortlessly. With FoodWare, you can access your own online recipes, as well as an entire library of cookbooks on disk. What you also get here is a great catalog of generic cookbooks on CD-ROM and a FoodWare demo walk-through. Now, I don't mean to carp, but the kitchen is the second to last place in my house where I'd put a computer. Call me crazy, but all that steam and splattered water and extreme heat just doesn't strike me as optimal. However, I agree with Maslow that food is important. "Honey, where did you place the burger CD?"

Figure 162 Put my computer where?

Godiva Chocolates

http://www.godiva.com

Here Godiva Chocolatier and *Chocolatier Magazine* join forces to satisfy your craving for knowledge, fun, and self-indulgence. Cook up batches of delectable treats using decadent recipes from the Godiva archive. Lick up sprinklings of trivia, tips, facts, and folklore about that timeless treat that is chocolate. First, tease and tempt yourself with Godiva's latest offerings, and then indulge via the online ordering facility. One very handy thing here is the *Forget-Me-Not* Gift Reminder Service. Register for free and ask Godiva to e-mail you with reminders of important dates for birthdays, anniversaries, celebrations, or other occasions when a gift of fine chocolates might be appropriate. Hmmm. "Remind me of my birthday. . ."

Figure 163.1 Godiva heaven.

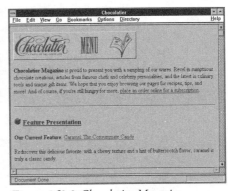

Figure 163.2 Chocolatier Magazine.

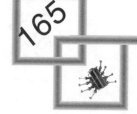

GrapeVine: The Wine Zine

http://bighorn.terra.net/grapevine

GrapeVine is the ultimate e-zine for the wine (not whine) crowd. Use this excellent publication to find everything the layman needs to know to look and sound cool when ordering in a restaurant or browsing in a wine shop. *GrapeVine* is packed with reviews, tutorials, references, interviews, and price-charts that leave few questions unanswered. For those who seek to dive deep into the mystical secrets of wine's genesis, this zine even has articles on wine-making processes, grape science, weather patterns which influence the taste of various grapes and wines, and more. Splendid.

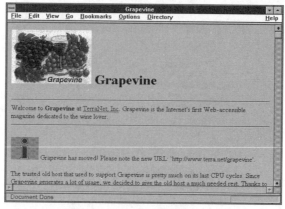

Figure 164 Dedicated to the wine lover.

Hot Hot Hot: The Net's Coolest Hot Sauce Shop!

http://www.hot.presence.com/g/p/H3/index.html

Among culinary adventures, there's an ultimate in thrill seeking: hot sauces. Like bungie jumping over a volcano, hot sauces are unique experiences which skirt the edge of danger. Addressing the special needs of those who court such adventure, "Hot Hot Hot" bills itself as the Internet's first "culinary headshop." Come here for fiery foodstuffs you never thought existed: over 100 "products of fire" with names like Bat's Brew, Nuclear Hell, and Ring of Fire. There's more to hot sauces than just their heat. In fact, a myriad of subtle flavors exist ranging as wide as the imaginations of the alchemists who brew these incendiary potions. It's hot! Check it out.

Figure 165 Hot stuff home page.

International Food Information Council

http://ificinfo.health.org/

Call this the "healthy food site" for short. Here you will find information on healthy eating during pregnancy, children's nutrition, food biotechnology, food-related classroom curricula, pesticides, and more. Recent additions to the site include "Food Biotechnology: Health & Harvest of Our Times," "Ten Tips to Healthy Eating and Physical Activity for You," and an updated version of "Sorting Out the Facts About Fat." An intuitive database format allows you to search files geared to meet the information needs of journalists, health professionals, educators, parents, or consumers. If the steamed veggies don't fill you up, you might check out the Godiva Chocolates at site 163.

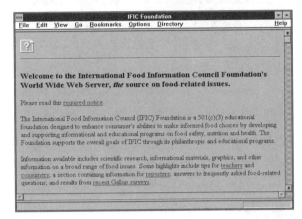

Figure 166 IFIC home page.

Internet Wine Rack

http://www.clark.net/pub/wine/home.html

This is actually far more than just an online wine store. It is, in fact, a comprehensive online catalog for all fine wines and liquors including lager, ale, and stout. The wines of Spain seem to be something of a specialty here, and their presentation is spiced up with much in the way of information about the tradition and history of the regions out of which they emerge. For the novice, "Wine Advocate Best Buy" recommendations are designed to turn you on to the best in moderately-priced, yet rich-tasting and full-bodied, clarets. I'm starting to get thirsty just writing about it.

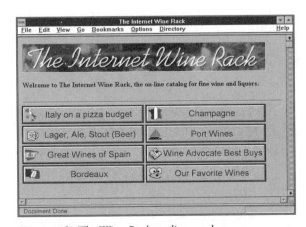

Figure 167 The Wine Rack on-line catalog.

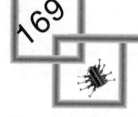

Kool-Aid Enthusiasts Page

http://ugweb.cs.ualberta.ca/~gerald/koolaid/

This site is not for people who are merely interested in Kool-Aid. No, this site is for people who are insanely attached to Kool-Aid, or so the extent of information archived here would suggest. I am reminded of a painting I once saw: a painting of two books side-by-side on a shelf. One great book was entitled *History of the Safety Pin*. Another very small book was entitled *History of Human Civilization*. How much is there to actually *say* about Kool-Aid? Plenty, I guess, if you are into it. How did this site make our cool list? Well, back in college, we used to mix Kool-Aid and vodka . .

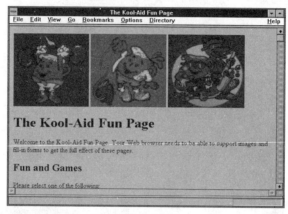

Figure 168 Remember this little guy?

Restaurant Le Cordon Bleu

http://sunsite.unc.edu/expo/restaurant/restaurant.html

Like to cook? Then challenge yourself to master recipes from the world-famous Paris cooking school, Le Cordon Bleu. The recipes available at this site are a selection from the popular cookbook *Le Cordon Bleu at Home*. This site provides recipes and menus for seven complete dinners embracing poultry, fish, and meat dishes, as well as recipes for delectable pastries, soups, and desserts. Sorry, no microwave recipes here, no easy solutions. What you find is a challenge to achieve culinary excellence, and the promise of a delectable reward for your efforts. Call me when you are ready to serve.

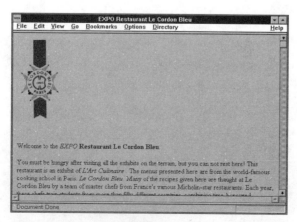

Figure 169 As "uptown" as you can get.

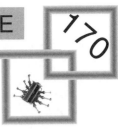

The Official Snapple Home Page

http://www.snapple.com/

Stop by the mailroom and find out what's going on with Snapple, or read the weekly Snapple letter of appreciation. Visit the tree of flavors to find out about, well, flavors. There's also a neat contest. (You'll never guess what the grand prize is.) Once you've put in your contest entry, visit the chat room to converse with fellow Snapple lovers, swap Snapple stories, and arrange to rendezvous at upcoming Snapple conventions (that's right, Snapple conventions). For the history of Snapple or to find out who that strange lady in the TV ads is, go to the Snapple Electronic Archives.

Figure 170 *Have a virtual sip.*

Unusual Foods

http://town.hall.org/food/unusual.html

What we are talking about is monkey brains, turtle eyes, that sort of stuff. One food establishment portrayed at this site is "The Golden Pear," an unusual restaurant in Prague nestled at the end of a winding cobblestone road at the foot of a castle. The specialty of the house? Snail livers, of course. Well, that is what they are called, at least. They look like livers and taste like livers. But of course snails don't have livers. They have *gonads*. Yum, yum. Now me, I am extremely provincial. I not only prefer hamburgers, I prefer them well done with ketchup and a side-order of onion rings. That is about as exotic as I care to be. If you ask me, this site deserves the "Weight Watcher's Seal of Approval."

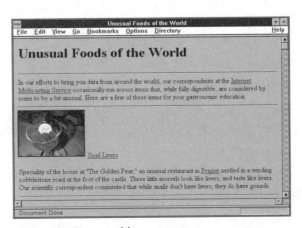

Figure 171 *Try a snail liver.*

The Wine Page

http://augustus.csscr.washington.edu/personal/bigstar-mosaic/wine.html

Over 70,000 users have accessed this extremely popular site since its inception in August of 1994. After my first visit, it is easy to understand why. There is some great stuff here. Check out the digital wine tour of Washington state. Visit the "Tasting Archive" for reviews of hundreds of different vintages. Read the splendid essay on the use of oak in wine fermentation barrels. Join the "Virtual Tasting Group." Or enjoy a profile of wine-guru Robert Parker. You can also link to pages focusing on the wines of Oregon, Hungary, and Slovenia, as well as to The Wine Net News. Salud!

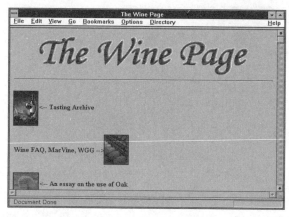

Figure 172 Resources for wine lovers.

More Food & Booze

As you surf the Web, you may find that one or more of the site addresses listed in this book have changed. In such cases, connect to Jamsa Press at http://www.jamsa.com and click on the icon that corresponds to the *1001 Really Cool Web Sites* book. Jamsa Press will list replacement addresses (when possible) for sites that have moved. In addition, you can also use the following site list as you search for information on food and booze:

Miniature Wine Grapevines of California	http://branch.com/dutch/dutch.htm
Forest Hill Vineyard Napa Valley	http://branch.com/wine/wine.html
Lake Tahoe Dining	http://dol.meer.net/locns/tahoe/dining/index.html
Chile Today Hot Tamale	http://eMall.Com/Chile/Chile1.html
The Recipes Folder!	http://english-server.hss.cmu.edu/Recipes.html
Health-Conscious Restaurants	http://gopher.metronet.com:70/1/North-Texas-Free-Net/Directs/Rests
The Beer Page	http://guraldi.itn.med.umich.edu:80/Beer
WWW Vegetarian Sites	http://jalapeno.ucs.indiana.edu/~nazhuret/Fact/recipes-other.html
Chicago Area Restaurant Guide	http://netmedia.com/IMS/chicago/ca_rest_guide.html
Bay Area Restaurants	http://sfgate.com/~sfchron/dining/dining.html

ArtRock Auction: Save the Earth

http://www.commerce.com/save_earth

The Save the Earth Foundation's Internet fund-raising auction (April 22 through May 21, 1995) was such a big success that they've decided to keep it going permanently. Here's your chance to pick up on signed posters from the likes of Santana, Eric Clapton, Roger McGuinn, Guns 'n Roses, Lou Reed, Ozzy Osborne, David Crosby, and others. At any time, you can find several auctions taking place. And all the proceeds go to the Save the Earth Foundation. In other words, the cash goes to plant trees, save rain forests, clean-up waterways, and do other cool stuff like that.

Figure 173 Buy a picture, save a tree.

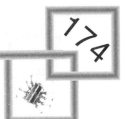

All Magic Guide

http://uelectric.com/allmagicguide.html

Want to learn how to pull a rabbit out of your hat? Saw your partner in half? Pull an endless stream of handkerchiefs (clean, I hope) from out of your mouth? Then turn to the "All Magic Guide." Here, in addition to tricks of the magic trade, you will also get interesting insights on magic history with profiles of such greats as Houdini. Also check out the film and tape library of "The Society of American Magicians." Download the library's promotional video to find out more about its services and to get brief glimpses of such legends as Blackstone, Thurston, Tenkai, Okinu, and Allerton. Additional link options include "Hank Lee's Magic Factory," "The Magic of Christian V. Andersen, " "The Greatest Magic Page on Earth," "The Magic of David Copperfield," and "Merlin's Web."

Figure 174 The All Magic home page.

CBS (as in "television")

http://www.cbs.com

Lots of fun stuff here starting with an archive of David Letterman's "Top Ten" lists, as well as other information on Letterman and his program including lists of upcoming guests. You also get line-ups for Tom Snyder's *Late, Late Show* (What? Ross Perot again?), up-to-the-minute information on broadcasts from CBS Sports (What? Nancy Kerrigan again?), and all sorts of cool inside gossip from Black Rock, the CBS corporate headquarters in New York City. What I was really looking for was an Andy Rooney homepage. That way, I'd have to click on him for an opinion.

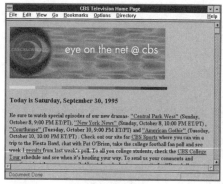

Figure 175.1 CBS home page.

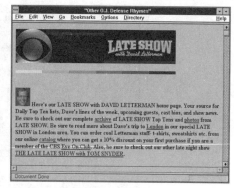

Figure 175.2 Letterman.

Comic Book and Comic Strip Page

http://www.cyberzine.com/webcomics/

The Comic Book and Comic Strip Page comprises the perfect starting point for any comic junkie who wants to explore resources on the Web. This gateway to what are literally hundreds of links includes Teemu Makinen's great European cartoons page, the *Lena Comix Review* homepage, Brad Chamberlain's *Poison Elves*, David Wald's *Comics Information* page, and pages dedicated to the *Superguy*, *Sandman*, *Watchmen*, *Tank Girl* and *Transformers* cartoon series. Additionally, you get links to Steve Thoemke's mutant page, *Aero & Space* (a great 22-page digital comic by Larry Merrill), and the *Myth of America* hypertext comic book by Joe Dubach of Harvard. Al Gore, relax. The information infrastructure must be working.

Figure 176 Comics, comics everywhere.

Discovery Channel On-line

http://www.discovery.com

This fun spot on the Web gives you complete Discovery Channel program listings, as well as neat, engaging background information on how a number of those programs were developed. When I visited, I accessed details on the research and production of the great documentary *Navajo Talkers: WWII's Unbreakable Code*, as well as the Discovery Channel film *Holy Woman of the Himalayas*. This graphically intensive site has been optimized for Netscape and I seriously recommend that you use Netscape when visiting here. Come discover this great site.

Figure 177 Discovery Channel home page.

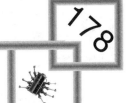

The Doctor Fun Page

http://www.unitedmedia.com/comics/drfun/

Here's the deal. You'll see a new cartoon every day, most often in 24-bit JPEG format. Download it, view it, whatever. Miss a day? Look in the archive of past day's cartoons. The arbiter of this site (a.k.a., Dr. Fun) appears to be David Farley (d-farley@tezcat.com). We don't know the criteria he uses for selecting or creating the cartoons. Perhaps we don't want to know. But we do know this. As his opening page announces: "I am not soliciting ideas for Doctor Fun, thanks." So, please, whatever you do, don't give Dave any *ideas*. Just keep them to yourself. If you must give someone *ideas*, send e-mail to president@whitehouse.gov.

Figure 178 Dr. Fun home page.

F.B.I. (as in *The* F.B.I.)

http://www.fbi.gov/

Call me crazy, but I think this site is riotously funny. Start with the archive of Director Louis J. Freeh's speeches. Then check out the "Ten Most Wanted" profiles (with photographs, *ugly* photographs) and the overview of the mission and history of the bureau, including a profile of that great American hero, J. Edgar Hoover. Hackers will enjoy the F.B.I.'s amazingly revealing (and, I suppose, quite useful) updates on the computer crime investigations of their National Computer Crime Squad. Somewhat less entertaining, of course, are the reports and updates concerning the Unabomber case and the tragic Oklahoma City bombing. Come check out this site, but remember, big brother may be watching.

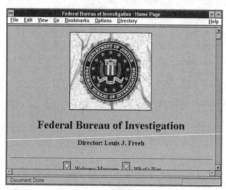

Figure 179.1 FBI home page.

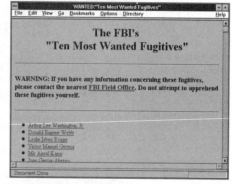

Figure 179.2 One of the ten most wanted. Go get 'im!

Jesse Helms Speaks

http://www.nando.net/sproject/jesse/helms.html

In case you haven't noticed, the senior Senator from the Tar Heel state has a habit of putting his foot into his mouth. Here you'll find such great quotes as, "Mr. Clinton better watch out if he comes down here. He'd better have a body guard." And the classic, "It is a lot easier to throw grenades than it is to catch them." Try his sensitive view of the AIDS crisis: "We've got to have some common sense about a disease transmitted by people deliberately engaging in unnatural acts." You will also find an amusing pictorial tour of Jesse Helms's long career.

Figure 180 Louder, Jesse, louder.

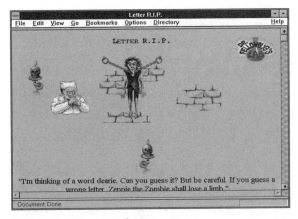

Letter R.I.P. Game

http://www.dtd.com/rip/

Mix *Wheel of Fortune* with *The Texas Chainsaw Massacre* and you get Letter R.I.P., a perverted game of "Hangman" with a sick twist. "I am thinking of a word, Dearie," says the weird nurse who sits beside a zombie chained to a brick wall. "Can you guess the word? But be careful. If you guess a wrong letter, Zeppie the Zombie shall lose a limb." Good luck. Or, more to the point, good luck Zeppie. Click on the button for each letter. Guess correctly, no problem. The mystery word begins to build. Get one wrong, and Zeppie loses an essential body part which is tossed onto a bloody pile. Guess wrong often enough, and things get pretty gross.

Figure 181 Letter RIP home page.

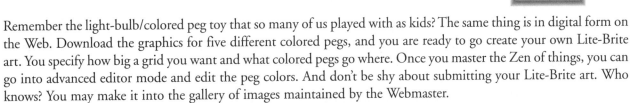

Lite-Brite Do-It-Yourself Artwork

http://www.galcit.caltech.edu/~ta/lb/lb.html

Remember the light-bulb/colored peg toy that so many of us played with as kids? The same thing is in digital form on the Web. Download the graphics for five different colored pegs, and you are ready to go create your own Lite-Brite art. You specify how big a grid you want and what colored pegs go where. Once you master the Zen of things, you can go into advanced editor mode and edit the peg colors. And don't be shy about submitting your Lite-Brite art. Who knows? You may make it into the gallery of images maintained by the Webmaster.

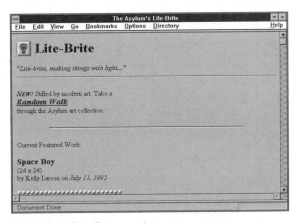

Figure 182 Lite-Brite opening page.

FUN STUFF

183

Number Synthesizer

http://www.cs.yale.edu/cgi-bin/saynumber.au

This simple but elegant site can be entertaining for a few minutes, at least for your kids. The screen is nothing to look at, but the implementation is fun. Briefly, all you do is type in a number and the speech synthesizer at the other end of the Web "articulates" (i.e., *speaks*) the number. The application seems trivial on its face. But I imagine it would be of use for a young child, just learning his or her numbers and needing reinforcement on the fundamentals. Type in a seven, hear the phrase. Type in a nine, hear the phrase. You get the drift. My four-year-old daughter rather liked this one, at least to the extent that it was hard to get her to surrender the keyboard.

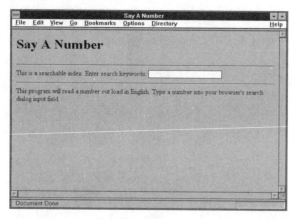

Figure 183 *"Say a number" home page.*

184

NBC (again, as in "television")

http://www.nbc.com

Here you have it. All that is necessary to life as we know it: news, sports, weather, and Leno. Be sure to check out "Peacock Park" where you can download and play NBC's "Peacock Pachinko," sneak a peek at new programs about to premier, sign-up for NBC's e-mail "Xtra" edition, and download your free copy of the NBC screensaver. (Of course, the screensaver is a variation on the classic peacock logo, but then you guessed that already.) You can also enter either the Colgate-Palmolive "Virtual Star" Contest or the Blockbuster/Nintendo "Must See 3D" Contest, each of which features lots of cool prizes for you and me, the dismal products of an era defined by materialism. Oh, well . . .

Figure 184.1 *NBC home page.*

Figure 184.2 *Peacock Park.*

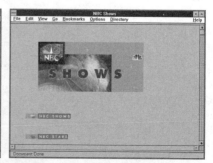
Figure 184.3 *NBC program guide.*

Poems for Disposable Cameras

http://www.wam.umd.edu:80/~sek/wedding/camerapoems.html

Poems for disposable cameras? What the heck does that mean? That's what I wondered. Here's the story. This is a collection of poems composed for the purpose of being placed with the disposable cameras you sometimes discover on guest-tables at wedding receptions. Here you will find such classics as: "I'm your camera; so have some fun./You'll make this album a special one!/Snap away as best you're able./Then leave me off at the gift table!" Lately, I've been inspired and my version of the same poem goes like this: "I'm your camera; so have some fun./Shoot with me instead of your gun./Please enjoy the open bar./But remember, later, you're driving a car."

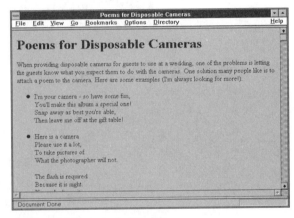

Figure 185 *Not exactly T.S. Eliot.*

Project Galactica Guide

http://www.willamette.edu/pgg/

This is a riotously funny guide to the universe in all its reality and unreality, in the spirit of Douglass Adams (author of *The Hitchhiker's Guide to the Galaxy*). Of course, you should not believe a word of it. But you should enjoy it. Look in on the AAAA (the Anonymous Acronym Abuse Association), ambient video (elevator music for your eyes), and more. You may want to look into what it is like to camp on Antartoth II (i.e., what it is like to see your life flash before your eyes), or learn how to play the game of Beer Hunter, or discover exactly why there are no kangaroos in Austria.

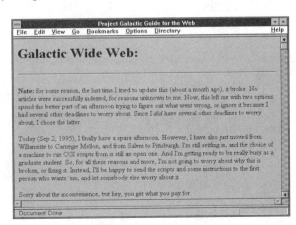

Figure 186 *Project Galactica home page.*

187

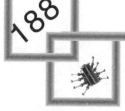

Star Wars Trilogy Trivia

http://www.tcfhe.com/starwars

What a fantastic place to visit! This site has searchable databases on storylines and characters, as well as subplots for *Star Wars, The Empire Strikes Back*, and *Return of the Jedi*. Go to the backlot area and download 3D props from each of the films. Interested in finding out what would happen if you crossed *Star Wars* with *Saturday Night Live's* version of a 60's beach party? Then look into the screening room. When you are done with this site, use the convenient link to visit the homepage for LucasArts Entertainment. Like so many super-cool sites, both the *Star Wars* and the LucasArts sites are viewed best with Netscape.

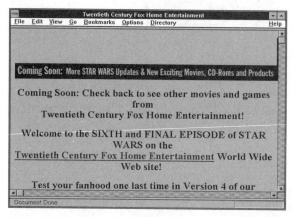

Figure 187 Return of the Jedi home page.

188

Random House Home Page

http://www.RandomHouse.com

Here is a fun page from one of the leading U.S. publishers. In addition to information about books and authors published by Random House and its imprints (including Knopf and Del Rey Books), you also get an electronic edition of Random House's great in-house publicity magazine, *At Random*. This site is packed with author interviews and interesting chapters from newly-published Random House books. At the time I visited, there was an in-depth interview with Norman Mailer concerning *Oswald's Tale*, as well as a chapter on Lenny Bruce ("The Man Who Went Down on America's Conscience") from a collection of articles by the late Kenneth Tynan recently published by Random House as *Profiles*. As a bonus, you'll find great crossword puzzles by Stanley Newman.

Figure 188.1 Random House home page.

Figure 188.2 A star (actually, four-star) author.

Figure 188.3 At Random.

Squashed Bug Zoo

http://albert.ccae.virginia.edu/~dcm3c/zoo.html

Did you like to torture insects, ripping off their wings and burning them under magnifying glasses, when you were young? If so, the Squashed Bug Zoo is for you (just as it was for the 25,000 other people who visited the site in the past six months). Yes, enter the dead bug gallery and view such tantalizing morsels as "roach thing," "large black beetle," and, of course, the ever-popular "blood-engorged tick." But don't just *view* the collection. Do something more than that. Participate. Contribute. Upload your own dead-bug images, you sicko. Grab your Nikon, run out into the backyard, stomp some innocent creature, and then get its mug-shot for posterity. Don't worry. No one will think you're weird, Renfield.

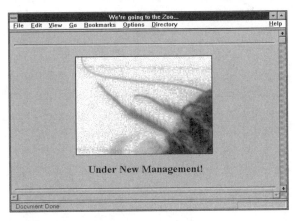

Figure 189 Yum, yum, yum.

More Fun Stuff

As you surf the Web, you may find that one or more of the site addresses listed in this book have changed. In such cases, connect to Jamsa Press at http://www.jamsa.com and click on the icon that corresponds to the *1001 Really Cool Web Sites* book. Jamsa Press will list replacement addresses (when possible) for sites that have moved. In addition, you can also use the following site list as you search for fun stuff:

Upcoming Guests List	http://bingen.cs.csbsju.edu/letterman/guest-list.html
Late Show with David Letterman	http://bingen.cs.csbsju.edu/letterman/show-summary/LSsummary.html
WebWisdom	http://keck.tamu.edu/cgi/staff/webwisdom.html
Humorous Quotations	http://meta.stanford.edu/quotes.html
Jay's Comedy Club	http://paul.spu.edu/~zylstra/comedy/index.html
Taglines Galore!	http://www.brandonu.ca/~ennsnr/Tags/
Johann's Comics Page	http://www.cen.uiuc.edu/~jb2561/comic.html
Some stuff about COMICS	http://www.css.itd.umich.edu/users/kens/comics.html

190

The Atomic Diner

http://atomic.neosoft.com/Atomic.html

The Atomic Diner is the homepage of the *World At War* computer game series from Avalon Hills and Atomic Games. In addition to information on such products as *World At War: Stalingrad*, *World at War: Operation Crusader*, and *Beyond Squad Leader*, this site also provides links to several mailing lists where hundreds of Internet gamers come together to discuss strategy and find play-by-electronic-mail opponents. The Diner also has links to the Atomic Games FTP server, which you can access using a Web browser, and includes patches for *Operation Crusader* (v 2.35) and *Stalingrad* (v 1.85), as well as patches for both *V for Victory* and *World at War* (Mac and PC versions).

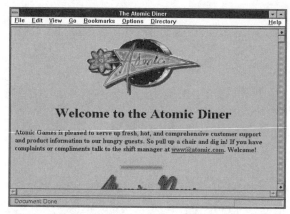

Figure 190 The Atomic home page.

191

Backgammon on the Web

http://www.statslab.cam.ac.uk/~sret1/backgammon/main.html

The Web Backgammon Page provides dozens of pointers to everything from simple backgammon rules sheets to FIBs, the First Internet Backgammon Server, which was developed by Andreas Schneider to let remote partners play real-time Backgammon over the Internet. This site also has links to Long Distance Backgammon (Backgammon by e-mail), the newsgroup rec.games.backgammon (which features a great FAQ), reviews of 17 backgammon books, and a comprehensive archive of annotated matches. Oh, I've got new e-mail—looks like it's my move.

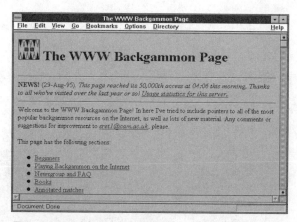

Figure 191 Backgammon Page.

Chess Archives

http://www.traveller.com/chess/

An essential stop for every Chess fiend on the Web, the Chess Archives lets you download graphical representations of the chess board designed to illustrate classic moves: openings, endgames, checkmate scenarios, and chess problems. Along with tactics, this site provides trivia, history, and even special information explaining chess to children. Convenient links connect you to related sites, including the Internet Chess Library, Rudolf Steinkellner's games database, the Nordic Zonal Tournament, Retrograde Analysis and Mathematics Chess, Herbert Groot Jebbink's Chess Page, and even the Alabama Chess Federation. Checkmate!

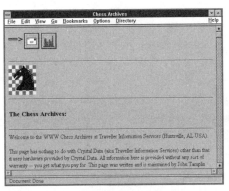

Figure 192.1 Chess Archives home page.

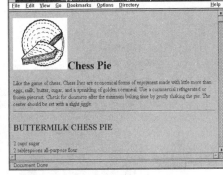

Figure 192.2 Another reason to play chess.

The Connect-4 Game

http://csclub.uwaterloo.ca/u/kppomaki/c4_www/connect.cgi

Few games are simpler than Connect-4. Each of two players has a stack of twenty chips. A 7x6 board propped up vertically between the two players has seven "slots" at the top of it, one slot for each column. When a game chip is dropped into one of the slots, it slides down until either rests at the bottom of the board or on top of another chip. The two players take turns dropping chips into slots. The first player to connect four of his/her color in a row is the winner. The connection can be vertical, horizontal, or diagonal, but it must lie in a straight, continuous line. Sound easy? Guess again. It seems the younger you are, the better luck you have. Hence I always seem to lose. :-(

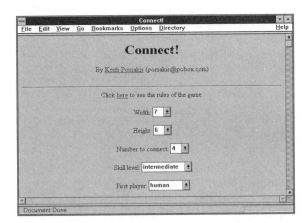

Figure 193 Connect-4 start page.

DoomWeb

http://www.cs.hmc.edu/~tkelly/docs/doom/

Doom is one of those games that my son loves and I hate: Go into a 3D room, shoot a bunch of guys, grab some ammunition. Go into another 3D room, kill more guys, grab more ammunition. You get the picture. On the plus side, *Doom* provides a cunningly-devised virtual world, excellent sound support, powerful support for networked play, and almost unlimited amounts of replay with third-party tools that let you reprogram the game. Agh! He's coming at you! Shoot him! Shoot him! Now grab his ammo. Now head for the door.

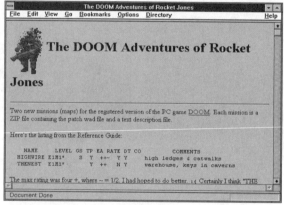

Figure 194 Rocket Jones WAD info.

Fantasy Role-Playing Games

http://www.acm.uiuc.edu/adnd

Primarily meant to serve advanced *Dungeons and Dragons* types, this site includes a fantastic collection of assumable characters, variants of which are available for building into one's own alter-ego. A link gives you easy access to a Web dice server from Irony Games, not to mention a fantastic random village generator. You also get a hyperlist of the most popular game sites. So don your costume and log-in! Note that the above site-address is due to change very shortly, although there will be a forwarding link in place for at least six months once the move is made.

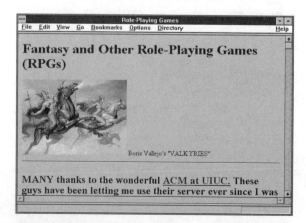

Figure 195 Fantasy home page.

GAMES, INCLUDING MUGs, MOOs, MUSHES

Game Bytes Magazine

Game Bytes is an electronic magazine dedicated to providing reviews, views, and images from all the best new computer games. The reviews are reader-provided, rigorous, and remarkably well-done. The First Look!/Previews, which the e-zine features, lets you see screens from games about to be released or games still in development. Ross Erickson's excellent column, "A View from the Edge," contains cogent observation and a refreshingly astute perspective on various issues in the gaming industry. In short, this is a must-see site for the avid PC gamer.

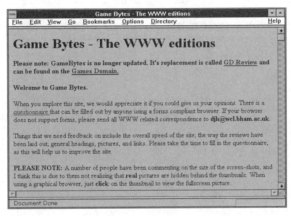

Figure 196 GameBytes home page.

The Game Cabinet

http://web.kaleida.com/u/tidwell/GameCabinet.html

The Game Cabinet gives you rules, rule variants, reviews, and random information about board games from around the world. You remember these games, played variously with cards, dice, dominoes, or sometimes toothpicks. You played them with your grandmother when you were seven. The two of you would sit for hours on the back porch of the summer house in the Adirondacks, the crickets chirping, and the waters of Lake Champlain lapping gently up on the rocks a few hundred yards away. As the years passed, your games evolved to collegiate levels where they included quarters and shot glasses. In any case, you'll find game rules here.

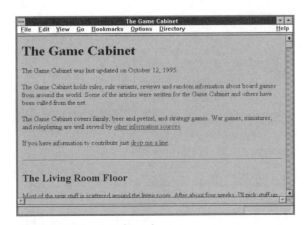

Figure 197 Game Cabinet home page.

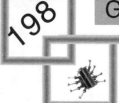

GNU WebChess

http://www.delorie.com/game-room/chess

This fun but graphically intensive site lets you play chess against a computer. You get the edge because it is you who sets the parameters, such as who goes first and how long each player gets to consider a move. You can even ask the computer to give you hints, although it will cost you some dignity. The odds are incredibly good that you are a better player than I, in which case you will have better luck against this king-killing automation. I kept thinking of the computer in *War Games*. Remember that splendid machine? "Let's play a game," it suggested. "What game?" asked Matthew Broderick. "How about thermonuclear war?" answered the computer. At least chess is safer.

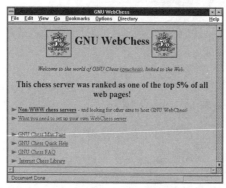

Figure 198 WebChess home page.

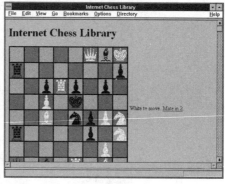

Figure 198.2 Play a game.

Hunt the Wumpus

http://www.bu.edu/htbin/wcl

This interactive game pits you against cyber-players and, of course, the monster Wumpus who (you see this coming, don't you?) lives in a deep, dark, uninviting cave. While hunting the Wumpus, you will also be busy shooting magic arrows and trying to stay out of the many hidden pits. Oh, by the way, you should also try to avoid (1) being eaten by the Wumpus, (2) being riddled with arrows shot by other cyberplayers, or (3) being carried away by the numerous, annoying bats. Survived the first round? Don't worry, an entirely different competition will follow.

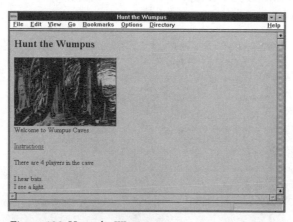

Figure 199 Hunt the Wumpus.

GAMES, INCLUDING MUGs, MOOs, MUSHES

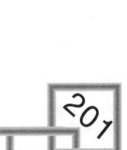

Illuminati Online Games

http://io.com/help/online.games.html

This Web page provides links to a vast array of war games, multiplayer games, brain teasers, card games, dungeon crawlers, adventure games, roll playing games (RPGs), and more. Yes, you can link to "weird" games for adults and simple, "unweird" games for children. Choose from lots of simulation games, puzzles and quizzes, computer card games, virtual pool played in a virtual bar called "Saucy Jack's," digital darts, digital pinball, and more. I'll tell you what. Let's you and I play a round of virtual pool, and loser has to buy the next round of virtual Dewars. Deal?

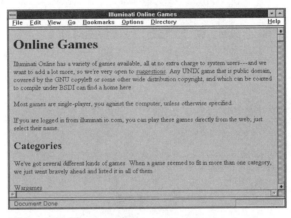

Figure 200 Illuminati home page.

Jackpot: Electronic Slot Machine

http://www.cs.umu.se/cgi-bin/scripts/jackpot

A click is the equivalent of pulling the lever. (Note: Do *not* insert quarters into your floppy disk drive. This *will* damage your computer.) I've been playing for hours. I'm sure I'll start winning pretty soon. If I don't win with this pull, then I will on the next. I can just tell this is a lucky computer; and I just *know* this is my lucky day. Of course, I can stop whenever I want to. It is not as if this is some sort of compulsion or sickness. I could turn and walk away right now if I didn't feel in my heart that my luck is going to start kicking in at any moment now, any moment. Here we go. I *know* I'm gonna win this time. Whoa! *Almost.* I can tell this baby's just about ready to come up with three in a row.

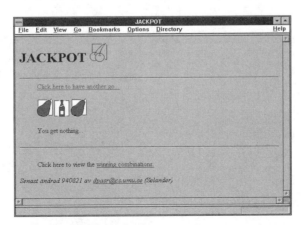

Figure 201 Break the bank.

MUD Resource Collection

http://www.cis.upenn.edu/~lwl/mudinfo.html

This is the perfect spot to find many useful links to sources of MUD (Multi-User Dimension, Dialogue, or Dungeon) information, with a particular emphasis on MUSHes (Multi-User Shared Hallucination), though plenty of general information is available as well. Be sure to check out the Automated MUSH List. You will also find FAQs, documentation, and papers on various MUDs worldwide, some MUDlists and MudWHO links to MUD-related information. Gopher sites and Web pages are available, as well as Web servers with interfaces to games. While you are there, be sure to look at Javelin's Guide for PennMUSH Gods, the great essay on "Wizard Ethics."

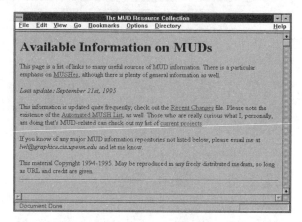

Figure 202 MUD information page.

Nowwhere

http://imagiware.com/imagiware.cgi

Move around a ray-traced (Netscape-friendly) virtual landscape solving puzzles with the help of sound and animation clues. At the beginning, you stand just inside a long, narrow building. Faint light comes through the wooden door to the East. Other than the hall, you see nothing, except for a huge distant wall viewed through the door at the horizon. The open door beckons. You step through it and immerse into a world quite unlike any you've ever known before (unless, of course, you are in the habit of taking mescaline, in which case *Nowwhere* will not seem very strange at all). Rumor has it many "Dead Heads" found the game dull.

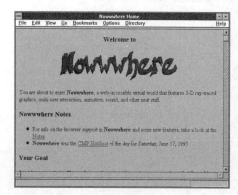

Figure 203.1 Nowwhere "start" page.

Figure 203.2 A few Nowwhere views.

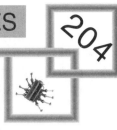

Role-Playing Game Internet Resource Guide

http://www.common.net/~shadow/rpg_index/

I want to be a prince. No, a wizard. No, a dwarf. No, an evil sorcerer. On second thought, I think, I'll just be a historian writing a book about the Internet. But if you'd like to be a prince, or a wizard, or a dwarf, or an evil sorcerer, pick up your identity here. You can also pick up information on White Wolf/Storyteller games, hero games from Iron Crown, FASA games, horror games, and even live action role playing and gaming societies. Also, be sure to look into Paul Tobia's eclectic and wonderful list of his favorite cool gaming resources on the Web. Catch you later, Merlin.

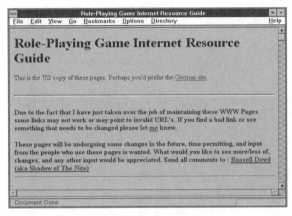

Figure 204 RPG home page.

TrekMUSE

http://grimmy.cnidr.org/trek.html

Learn all about how to play the text-based virtual reality game TrekMUSE which, as the Webmaster responsible for this site points out, owes its existence "to the far-reaching vision of Gene Roddenberry." Roddenberry, of course, is the late great creator of *Star Trek*. Going beyond the now-familiar world of Kirk and Spock, however, TrekMUSE transports you to stand in the presence of empires and wizards, the likes of which the long-voyaging crew of the *Enterprise* could never have even imagined. In other words, simply click your mouse to go where no man has ever gone, to seek out brave new worlds, and to fulfill the cosmic destiny of mankind. Then go have dinner.

Figure 205 TrekMuse home page.

206

Universal Access Blackjack Server

http://www.ua.com/blackjack/bj.html

This graphical blackjack engine lets you bet cyberdollars (safer than real dollars) in amounts ranging from $100 to $5,000. The game rules are the same you would find at Caesar's Palace: dealer stands on soft 17, split on any pair, double on first two cards, no doubling when you get blackjack. Also, if the dealer and the player both have blackjack, it's a push (no winner or loser). A nice option is that you can preload 52 playing-card bitmaps, so that subsequent play will proceed faster. Boy, I'm feeling lucky tonight. Pour me another martini and let's play.

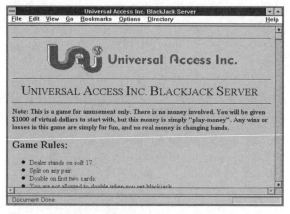

Figure 206 Blackjack server.

207

Vampire: The Masquerade

http://acacia.ens.fr:8080/home/granboul/Vampire/index.html

I have lived for centuries. I have known the long, lonely isolation that is eternity while watching generations rise and fall through the darkness that is my day. I know the pain of loss but also the fantastic climax at the end of the hunt. You may seek me here among my kind; you may reach for me from what may seem the safe digital anonymity of your keyboard. But seek me at your own risk, for I may find you in the night. To some I tell tales of the cities and stories I have known, the characters I've seen pass. To others I tell not a thing. This is my fate. There is no escape for me. I am caught in the undertow of time, and each new thrust of the waves is a millennium. Wow! Now that's an interview.

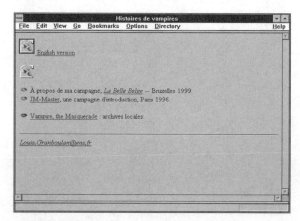

Figure 207 The Masquerade.

AIDS Information Newsletter

http://cornelius.ucsf.edu/~troyer/safesex/vanews/

Targeted to primary health-care professionals, librarians, and trainers/educators, the AIDS Information Newsletter is published biweekly by the U.S. Department of Veterans Affairs. The coverage at this site is comprehensive and rigorous. You'll find tips for counselors who dispense safe-sex information, an in-depth report on women and the spread of HIV, a consideration of the relationship between Tuberculosis and HIV infection, and more. For serious news about a serious subject, turn to the AIDS Information Newsletter. An indispensable reference.

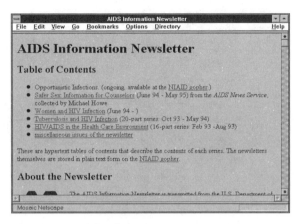

Figure 208 AIDS information page.

Acupuncture

http://www.acupuncture.com/acupuncture

Pins and needles, needles and pins. This site provides one-stop shopping for all information related to acupuncture for the cure of ailments ranging from chronic pain to intestinal fever. In addition to scholarly papers on acupuncture as an alternative form of healing, you also get information on related topics, such as herbology, Chinese nutrition, Chinese medicines, Tui Na and Chinese massage, and more. Additionally, you'll find practitioner referrals, lists of accredited schools where you can study the art of acupuncture, and links to other alternative health care sites. Ouch!

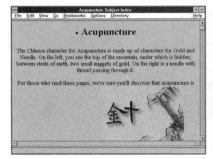 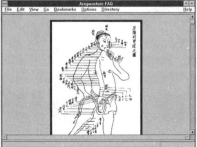 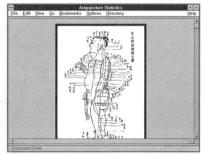

Figure 209.1 Acupuncture page.   *Figure 209.2* And the needle goes where? *Figure 209.3* But does it cure hangovers?

Alcoholics Anonymous

http://www.moscow.com/Resources/SelfHelp/AA/

Maintained by Phil W., a member of Alcoholics Anonymous (AA), this upbeat page provides complete information on that fellowship of men and women who share their experience, strength, and hope in order to conquer their addiction to alcohol. This site includes an electronic edition of the classic book *Alcoholics Anonymous*, as well as other AA-related items such as pamphlets, conference announcements, and links to other recovery resources on the Internet. This is a very positive place on the Web. If you feel you might need to visit this site, I urge you to do so.

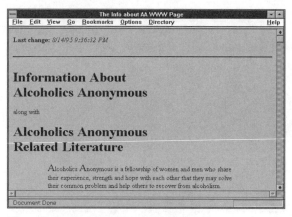

Figure 210 Alcoholics Anonymous info.

211

Alternative Medicine

http://www.yahoo.com/Health/Alternative_Medicine/

Alternative medicine is any diagnosis or treatment technique that falls outside the disciplines taught at mainstream medical schools. Yahoo's list of more than 30 alternative medicine resources includes information on chiropracture, holistic healing, herbal remedies, and lauric acid derivatives. You'll also find links to resources dealing with massage, meditation, Feldenkrais/Somatic Options (including T'ai Chi), and Kombucha tea. The National Alternative Health Referral Network, which is your directory to health practitioners, schools, and product vendors associated with the arts, sciences, and crafts of alternative therapies for a range of ailments, is particularly valuable.

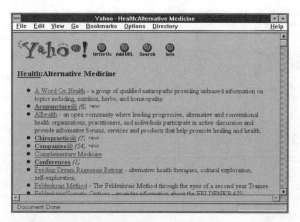

Figure 211 Yahoo's alternative medicine options.

Anatomy Teaching Modules

http://www.rad.washington.edu/AnatomyModuleList.html

From the University of Washington comes five detailed, profusely-illustrated tutorials on fundamental aspects of the human anatomy. The various tutorials include discussion of normal knee anatomy, normal distal-thigh anatomy, temporomandivular joint anatomy (good ol' TMJ), and pre- and post-operative radiographic findings with regard to the hallux valgus. Due to the graphically intensive nature of these tutorials, they take a fairly long time to load, but the wait is worth it. All medical students, as well as instructors, will find the University of Washington's Anatomy Teaching Modules an extremely valuable resource.

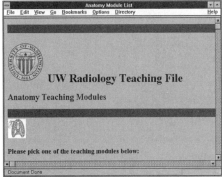
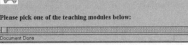

Figure 212.1 Your choices.

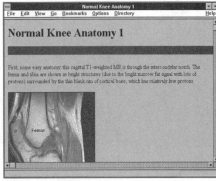

Figure 212.2 Normal knee anatomy.

Attention Deficit Disorder Archive

http://www.seas.upenn.edu/~mengwong/add/

Attention Deficit Disorder is a learning/behavioral disorder characterized by difficulty sustaining attention, excessive activity, and impulsive behavior. This site has the famous "20 questions" that comprise the Hallowell/Ratey informal criteria for Attention Deficit Disorder (ADD) diagnosis; a great speech by Ned Hallowell, M.D., on "The Hidden Gifts of ADD;" the Jasper/Goldberg Adult ADD Screening Examination (Version 5.0); and excerpts from Hallowell and Ratey's splendid book about ADD entitled *Driven to Distraction*. You will also find files on drug therapies for ADD, classroom strategies for coping with ADD, and the latest on the debate over the FDA's opinion on Adderall (Obetrol). A fantastic collection of research about an often overlooked and misunderstood affliction.

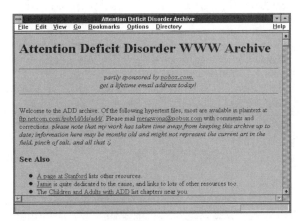

Figure 213 Attention Deficit Disorder information.

HEALTH, MEDICINE, FITNESS

Breast Cancer Information Clearinghouse

http://nysernet.org/bcic

Maintained by the New York State Education and Research Network, the Breast Cancer Information Clearinghouse provides essential data on all aspects of breast cancer. At this site, you will find methods for early detection of the disease, 800-numbers and information hotlines, links to regional breast cancer support groups, and more. You also get information on medical support associations and agencies, reports on possible dietary and environmental contributors to the disease's development, and suggestions for lifestyle changes you can make that will increase your odds of avoiding breast cancer. This site is indispensable for all women, as well as for the men who love them.

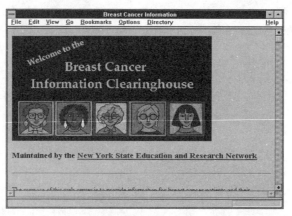

Figure 214 Breast Cancer information.

Deaf World Wide Web

http://deafworldweb.org/deafworld/

The goal of "Deaf World Wide Web" is to maintain all information available on the deaf around the world and to provide free services to the individuals, researchers, and non-profit organizations worldwide working to improve the lives and options of deaf people. At this site, you'll find links related to deaf K-12 education, deaf colleges and universities, signing tutorials, articles, research papers, electronic journals, and more. You'll also find engaging information about how computers, the Internet, and technology in general are changing the lives of the deaf for the better. The Web offers all of us a tremendous opportunity to assist disabled persons and better understand the obstacles they face. This site is a marvelous start.

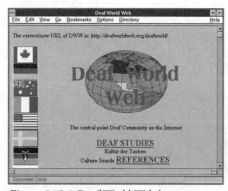

Figure 215.1 Deaf World Web home page.

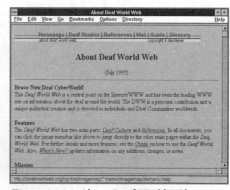

Figure 215.2 About Deaf World Web.

DERWeb: Dental Education on the Web

http://www.shef.ac.uk/uni/projects/der/derweb.html

I hate going to the dentist. I wonder why someone decides he or she wants to be a dentist? Yup, the noise the drill makes, talking after novocain, and spitting in a sink that is always just out of reach . . . these are a few of *my* favorite things. The purpose of DERWeb is to set up a library of dental images for use in teaching and research, along with a variety of teaching materials and other information on educational technology in dentistry. You will also find links to electronic journals, online articles of interest to dentists and dental technicians, and valuable HTML-based teaching materials related to various dental procedures. Additionally, useful links connect you to the British Dental Association, as well as other associated Web resources. What? No Dustin Hoffman and *Marathon Man* links?

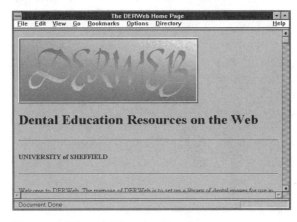

Figure 216 Dental Education Resources page.

Death and Dying

http://www.yahoo.com/Society_and_Culture/Death/

At this site, Yahoo assembles an impressive array of resources related to death, dying, bereavement, and coping with major emotional and physical losses. One particularly interesting item is the weekly morbidity and mortality report from the Centers for Disease Control and Prevention, which is available in .PDF format readable with Adobe Acrobat Reader. (You can obtain an Acrobat Reader from Adobe—see http://www.adobe.com) This site also has pages that cover many end-of-life issues, including the rights of the terminally ill and the ongoing debates over the roles of suicide and euthanasia. Additionally, you will find links to organizations positioned to help you sort out all these things.

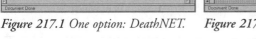

Figure 217.1 One option: DeathNET.

Figure 217.2 DeathNET details.

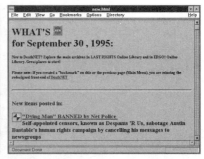

Figure 217.3 What's new at DeathNET.

218

Epilepsy Web Page

http://www.swcp.com/~djf/epilepsy/index.html

Epilepsy, Caesar's falling-down disease, is actually caused by disturbed electrical rhythms in the central nervous system and is often manifested by seizure. If you are the one person in 200 who has epilepsy (or if you care for someone who does), this site is filled with information. The "Epilepsy Web Page" gives you with links to the Massachusetts General Hospital Epilepsy Surgery Unit, the Albert Einstein College of Medicine's Comprehensive Epilepsy Management Center, and the Epilepsy Foundation of America. You can access the Comprehensive Epilepsy Program at Washington University, information on the Ketogenic Diet, and a digital brain scan of an epileptic seizure.

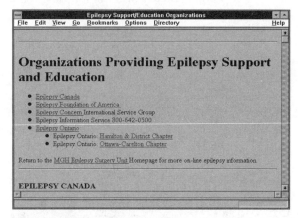

Figure 218 Epilepsy resources.

219

Good Medicine Magazine

http://none.coolware.com/health/good_med/

Good Medicine Magazine is an excellent bimonthly publication on preventive medicine with an emphasis on traditional and holistic approaches. Read in-depth articles on such topics as guided imagery, holistic skin and body care, Reiki (energy healing), and more. You also get detailed herbal recipes for a range of traditional and holistic cures to many ailments. Another plus is the information this site provides about recognized holistic-medicine practitioners who are available to treat what ails you and to train you in the subtle art of "good" medicine.

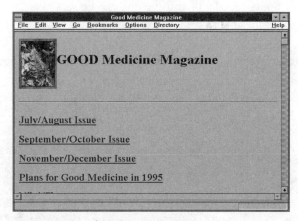

Figure 219 Good Medicine Magazine.

Hemophilia Home Page

http://www.web-depot.com/hemophilia

Michael Davon, a person with hemophilia (a hereditary blood defect, almost exclusive to males, that inhibits blood clotting), created the "Hemophilia Home Page" as a means of serving the hemophiliac community. His helpful page includes information on hemophilia and AIDS, an archive of hemophilia-related articles, and links to related newsgroups and mailing lists. In addition, you'll find information on organizations that provide support for the hemophilia community, links to pertinent Web sites, and a link to the National Hemophilia Foundation.

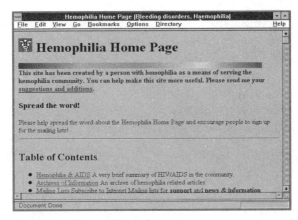

Figure 220 Hemophilia information page.

Homeopathic Education Center

http://homeopathy.com/~educate/

To treat an illness, homeopathic-medicine practitioners administer small doses of a remedy that would in healthy persons produce symptoms similar to those of the illness. Here at the online campus for the study of homeopathic medicine, the British Institute of Homeopathy offers a unique, 300-hour diploma course. This personally tutored study program combines written lessons, audio and video lectures, and interactive e-mail homework assignments. Graduates are entitled to use the initials *DlHom* (Doctor licensed for Homeopathy) and to practice the art of homeopathy in England, although international recognition guidelines vary from country to country.

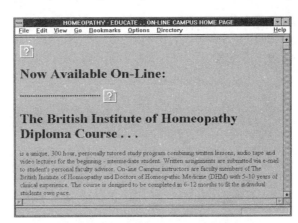

Figure 221 Homeopathic Education Center page.

Home Test Kits

http://kerouac.pharm.uky.edu/KitsHP.html

Is it pink? Is it blue? Is that good? Is your Dad really going to kill me? From the University of Kentucky Pharmacy School comes this wonderful resource: a consumer's guide to home-testing kits for a variety of ailments. Read about blood pressure monitors, colorectal-cancer home testing kits, glucose-monitoring kits, ovulation-prediction kits, and home-pregnancy tests. The Pharmacy School staff provides comparisons of kits from different manufacturers and, for each product, offers technical assistance that goes beyond the terse instructions that come with home-testing kits.

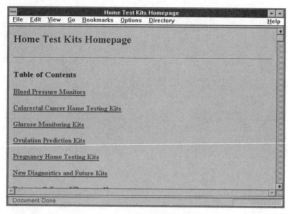

Figure 222 Home test kits homepage.

223

Hyperlexia Page

http://www.iac.net/~whaley/gordy.html

Hyperlexia is a recently diagnosed malady that combines precocious reading ability with a serious lack of power to comprehend what is being read. As the maintainers of this page are quick to inform us, "We are the parents of a hyperlexic child, *not clinical professionals*. We are primarily interested in providing an online resource for other parents, however, speech and other professionals may find this page interesting as well." Thus, for all in need, check out this wonderful collection of resources: journal articles, bibliographies, links to research centers, and even a catalog of toys for special needs kids. Thank you, Ted and Julie Whaley, for an absolutely splendid, caring place on the Web.

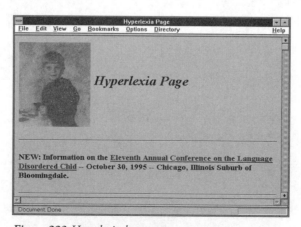

Figure 223 Hyperlexia home page.

Medical Education Information Center

http://hyrax.med.uth.tmc.edu/

Maintained by the good folks at the Department of Pathology and Laboratory Medicine, University of Texas, Houston Medical School, this site provides especially strong coverage of medical informatics issues and how they impact the practice of medicine. Also, be sure to check out the great clinical forum on the art and science of pathology and laboratory medicine. Another useful feature is "Health Explorer," which is billed as "a forum of discovery for our patients and community designed to enlighten and educate." And, of course, you will find links to major medical sites around the Web and around the world. No, I didn't find a link to *Quincy*, and yes, I looked.

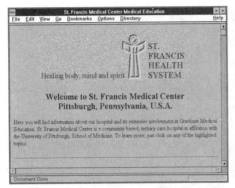
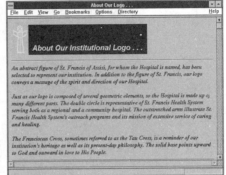

Figure 224.1 One option: St. Francis Health System.

Figure 224.2 About the logo.

MAPS: Multidisciplinary Association for Psychedelic Studies

http://www. maps.org

MAPS focuses on the development of beneficial, socially-sanctioned uses of psychedelic drugs and marijuana. Such uses include psychotherapeutic research and treatment, treatment of addiction, pain relief, spiritual exploration, shamanic healing, psychic research, brain physiology research, and related scientific inquiries. MAPS pursues its mission by helping scientific researchers design, obtain government approval for, fund, conduct, and report on psychedelic research in human volunteers (who, I gather, are not hard to find). At this site, you may even learn how to volunteer for an experiment or two. I believe there is a waiting list.

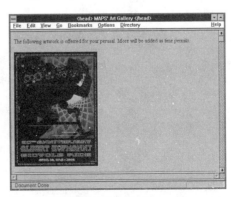

Figure 225.1 MAPS home page.

Figure 225.2 MAPS art gallery.

National Cancer Institute: CancerNet Web

http://www.ncc.go.jp/

The homepage of the National Cancer Center of Tokyo, Japan, CancerNet Web is a quick and easy way to obtain cancer information. At this site, you'll find highly useful treatment summaries in various forms for both health professionals and patients, as well as supportive care summaries, cancer screening/prevention summaries, and drug information summaries. The site discusses all types and varieties of cancer, from blood disorders to lung cancer and skin cancer. Additionally, you have links to electronic editions of journals and abstracts. View these screens in either Japanese or English, as you wish. A tremendous resource.

Figure 226 Japanese National Cancer Center page.

National Clearinghouse for Alcohol & Drug Information

http://www.health.org

The National Clearinghouse for Alcohol and Drug Information is the information service for the Center for Substance Abuse Prevention of the U.S. Department of Health and Human Services. Thus, it is the world's largest resource for current information and materials about alcohol and other drugs. Come here to be empowered with custom searches of annotated bibliographies consisting of over 28,000 records, 8,000 prevention-related publications, and more. These materials, by the way, are culturally-diverse and tailored for use by parents, teachers, youth, communities, and prevention professionals.

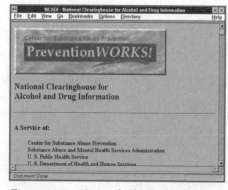

Figure 227.1 National Clearinghouse home page.

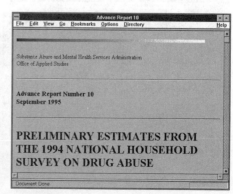

Figure 227.2 1994 Drug Abuse Survey.

National Library of Medicine

http://www.nlm.nih.gov/welcome.html

The National Library of Medicine provides you with the most extensive array of medical information resources on the Web. Be sure to look into the link to the National Information Center on Health Services Research, the Visible Human Project, and the extensive set of links to related sites. Conveniently, you also have National Library of Medicine/National Institutes of Health visitor information, as well as information on seminars, conferences, and complete agency telephone and e-mail directories. From the history of medicine to tomorrow's next-generation innovation, find it here.

Figure 228.1 National Library of Medince home page.

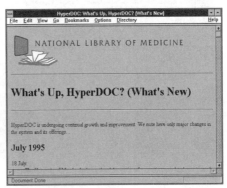

Figure 228.2 What's new.

Nutrition Strategies from Dr. Art Ulene

http://www.vitamin.com

"Nutrition Strategies" offers regularly updated nutrition and weight loss tips from America's favorite family doctor, Dr. Art Ulene. What are the positive effects of antioxidants in combating cancer, and through what kind of diet can you expect to get the best mix of antioxidants? Are beta carotene and vitamin E of value when isolated in vitamin complex products, or only when absorbed directly from foods? These are just the types of questions you will see addressed by Dr. Art Ulene, whose weekly tips will help you lead a long, happy, and active life. Put down that pizza and check this out—it will be good for you.

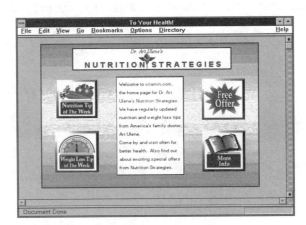

Figure 229 Dr. Art Ulene's Nutrition Strategies.

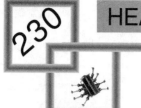

HEALTH, MEDICINE, FITNESS

OncoLink: Oncology Information

http://cancer.med.upenn.edu/

Is there any aspect of cancer prevention or therapy that this comprehensive resource does not address? I doubt it. This site addresses cancer screening in elderly men, a matching directory for bone marrow donors/recipients worldwide, non-surgical approaches to low-grade prostate cancer, clinical trials in antineoplastons, and more. Whether you are a patient, a physician, a primary-care nurse, or a concerned friend or family member, come here for the knowledge to manage, if not master, this potentially devastating disease. A must-see site.

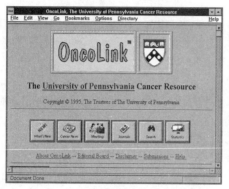

Figure 230.1 OncoLink home page.

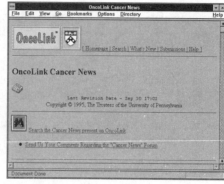

Figure 230.2 Cancer News.

The Parkinson's Web

http://neuro-chief-e.mgh.harvard.edu/parkinsonsweb/Main/PDmain.html

Persons with Parkinson's disease, a progressive nervous condition, often experience muscular tremors, slowing of movement, partial facial paralysis, and impaired muscular control. However, as the maintainers of this useful site make clear, each person with Parkinson's disease has his or her own unique experience, which deserves an individualized treatment plan. What is universal is the need for everyone to know as much as possible about the condition and to understand how certain insights, anticipations, and adjustments lead to more effective living with Parkinson's. This site is dedicated to providing that information. All aspects of the disease are covered, although the site contains an especially useful cache of information on Young Onset Parkinson's disease.

Figure 231.1 Parkinson's home page.

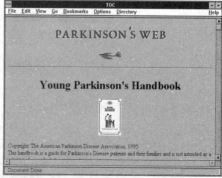

Figure 231.2 Young Parkinson's Handbook.

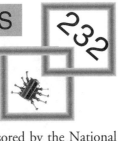

Pediatric Oncology Group

http://pog.ufl.edu/serv/htdocs/pog.html

The Pediatric Oncology Group (POG) is a cooperative of individuals and institutions sponsored by the National Cancer Institute and dedicated to controlling cancer among children and adolescents. The idea is to pool knowledge, experience, case material, and resources in order to better understand the pathobiology of childhood cancer and to improve treatments, survival rates, and quality of life. "Solving the problem of cancer is our goal," they write, "and children with cancer and their families are our inspiration. We are the stewards of their trust."

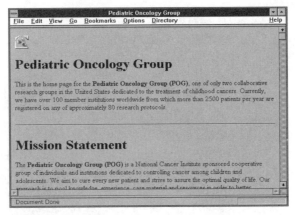

Figure 232 Pediatric Oncology Group home page.

233

Personal Nutrition Profile

http://health.mirical.com/site/Mirical/form3.html

Simply fill out a form (age, sex, height, weight, and profile of your average daily physical activity), and get your recommended daily allowances for 29 key nutrients that include iron, magnesium, phosphorous, potassium, zinc, and vitamins A, B1, B2, B3, B6, B12, C, and E. I am to limit my daily cholesterol to 300 mg, get 220 mg of folacin, and 350 mg of magnesium. Let's see, I suppose that's about what goes into two twinkies and a German beer. Yup, I'm all set. Now, what'll I have for dinner? Maybe some red meat with heavy gravy, if my wife will let me. Nope. Don't worry. She won't.

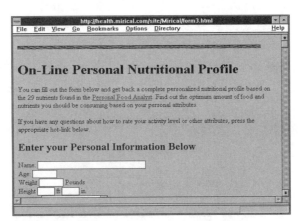

Figure 233 Fill in the info; retrieve the bad news.

234

Primary Care Topics

http://uhs.bsd.uchicago.edu/uhs/topics/uhs-teaching.html

This great list of primary-care teaching topics includes discussion of health promotion and prevention, cardiovascular issues, pulmonary care, gastrointestinal ailments, and renal and urology topics. This site also contains extensive files dealing with hematology, oncology, endocrine medicine, infectious diseases, rheumatology, neurology, gynecology, dermatology, ophthalmology, psychiatry, nutrition, surgery, and geriatrics. Note: these very advanced resources are primarily for students and teachers of medical science, rather than for the lay person or the patient.

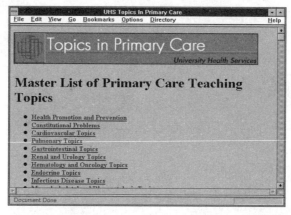

Figure 234 Primary care topics.

235

Public Health Information Guide

http://128.196.106.42/ph-hp.html

Courtesy of the Arizona Health Sciences Center, the "Public Health Information Guide" provides quick and easy access to Internet resources (including Web, Gopher, and FTP sites) related to public health. You get links to text and hypertext materials on public health, epidemiology, and related topics. You will also find links to public health organizations, patient education sites, health consumer fact sheets, and academic sites with strong public health programs. As a bonus, this site provides detailed information on the University of Arizona Graduate Program in Public Health, which is one of the best in the U.S.

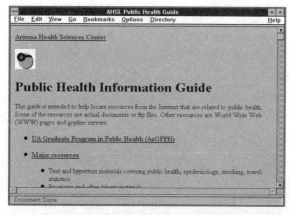

Figure 235 Public health info from Arizona.

TB/HIV Research Laboratory at Brown University

http://www.brown.edu/Research/TB-HIV_Lab/

Brown University's TB/HIV Research Lab is dedicated to research on the prevention and treatment of two infectious diseases of global importance: tuberculosis (TB) and human immunodeficiency virus (HIV), otherwise known as AIDS. Their approach is immunological, through the identification of factors contributing to host susceptibility and immune response to both HIV and TB. It is also epidemiological (through the evaluation of HIV risk behaviors and risk-groups), clinical, and computational (through the design and implementation of novel algorithms contributing to state-of-the-art vaccine design). Learn more about the programs of the Brown TB/HIV Research Lab here.

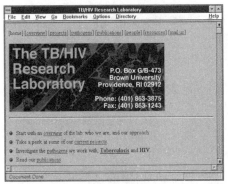 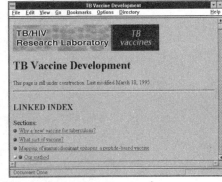

Figure 236.1 Brown TB/HIV Lab home page.   *Figure 236.2 Current research.*

U.S. Department of Health & Human Services

http://www.os.dhhs.gov/

The U.S. Department of Health and Human Services (HHS) protects the health of United States citizens and provides services (federal welfare programs and so on) to those unable to help themselves. Access this page to get all the information you need about the staff, policies, and programs of the U.S. Department of Health and Human Services. You'll find press releases, media advisories and statements for the news media, and past press releases sorted by year. Also, check out the background on current departmental initiatives, major addresses by the HHS Secretary and other Department officials, transcripts of Congressional testimony by HHS representatives, and electronic copies of journal and opinion articles by HHS officials concerning current topics.

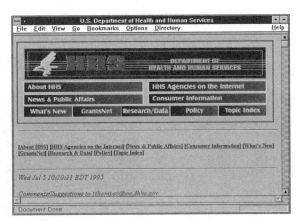

Figure 237 HHS home page.

Victorian Institute of Forensic Pathology

http://www.vifp.monash.edu.au/

The Department of Forensic Medicine at Monash University, Australia, provides this forensic site named for one of the most famous of all dead people: Queen Victoria. (Actually, the site is named after the district in which it resides. The district is named after the old dead queen.) The electronic documents available here include the full text of the book *Law and Ethics in Medicine for Doctors in Victoria*. The Institute also offers the National SIDS (Sudden Infant Death Syndrome) Autopsy Protocol and Database, the Australian National Coroner's Database, and other forensic resources. Quite cheerful, as you can guess.

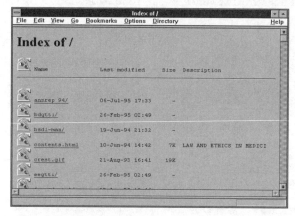

Figure 238 VIFP home page.

VIDIMED Project Gallery

http://www.artcom.de/projects/vidimed/

VIDIMED provides a large gallery of medical images including volume renderings of human CT (Computer Tomography—a non-invasive, computer-graphics-based imaging method for the diagnosis of many medical conditions) data sets done by the *Art-Com* Particle Volume renderer. You also get access to the Interactive Volume Renderer (a Web interface to a subset of the parameters of the Particle Volume Rendering application) and an interactive archive of the Interactive Volume Renderer, showing the most recent images rendered by users. Additionally, the site contains complete documentation for the project, as well as a keyword engine for searching images.

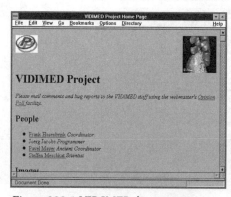

Figure 239.1 VIDIMED home page.

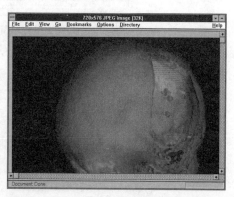

Figure 239.2 Volume renderings of human CT data sets.

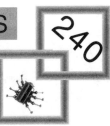

The Virtual Hospital

http://vh.radiology.uiowa.edu/

The "Virtual Hospital" is a project of the Electric Differential Multimedia Laboratory, Department of Radiology, University of Iowa College of Medicine. This continuously updated, medical, multimedia database provides invaluable patient care support and distance-learning to practicing physicians and other healthcare professionals. Additionally, the site's user-friendly *Iowa Health Book* provides information to the general public on a range of important health issues. Stop by and sample the stunning graphics and vital information contained at the "Virtual Hospital."

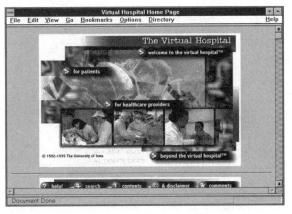

Figure 240 *Virtual Hospital home page.*

The World Health Organization

http://www.who.ch/

This homepage of the World Health Organization, a division of the United Nations located in Geneva, provides vital information on HIV, tuberculosis, malnutrition, the recent E-bola virus outbreak in Africa, and many other world health issues. An archive list of vaccination requirements for various travel destinations around the world is particularly useful. And an absolutely fabulous statistical database system dishes up virtually any disease or mortality statistics one could possibly ask for, broken down by country, region, continent, decade, and so on. In addition to this useful information, you invariably have the requisite hype: press releases, speeches, and other puffs of air.

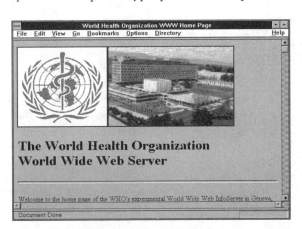

Figure 241 *World Health Organization home page.*

Yoga Paths

http://zeta.cs.adfa.oz.au/Spirit/Yoga/Overview.html

"Yoga Paths" comprises a splendid array of resources related to not only Hindu (Karma, Bhakti, Hatha, Kriya and Astanga) Yoga, but also non-Hindu (Veda) Yoga approaches. The YP site also has a fine synthesis of Taoist philosophy by Barry Pierce, a link to the Chinmaya Mission (which propagates vedantic truths according to Swami Chinmayananda), an edition of the *Bhagavad Gita* in both Sanskrit and English, and an electronic edition of the *Yoga Journal*. Also, check out Dinu Roman's "The Mystery of Meditation." Oh, Ouch! I think my leg is stuck!

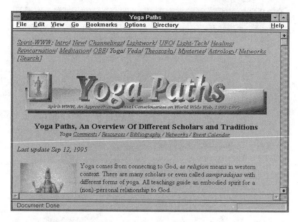

Figure 242 *Yoga Paths home page.*

More Health, Medicine, Fitness

As you surf the Web, you may find that one or more of the site addresses listed in this book have changed. In such cases, connect to Jamsa Press at http://www.jamsa.com and click on the icon that corresponds to the *1001 Really Cool Web Sites* book. Jamsa Press will list replacement addresses (when possible) for sites that have moved. In addition, you can also use the following site list as you search for information on health and medicine:

Health Resources	http://alpha.acast.nova.edu/medicine.html
HSPH Biostatistics Home Page	http://biosun1.harvard.edu/
BWH main entrance	http://bustoff.bwh.harvard.edu/
Department of Food Science & Nutrition	http://fscn1.fsci.umn.edu/fscn.htm
Online Mendelian Inheritance in Man	http://gdbwww.gdb.org/omimdoc/omimtop.html
MycDB	http://kiev.physchem.kth.se/MycDB.html
Alcoholism Research Data Base	http://nearnet.gnn.com/wic/med.02.html
Health & Medicine	http://nearnet.gnn.com/wic/med.toc.html
Cholesterol	http://nearnet.gnn.com/wic/nutrit.02.html
Good Medicine Magazine	http://none.coolware.com:80/health/good_med/

Beekeeping Home Page

http://weber.u.washington.edu/~jlks/bee.html

Come here for some stinging editorials on a honey of a hobby to which folks are just swarming. You will find loads of information here: the different breeds of bees, how to hive them, how to take the honey without having the bees get all that mad, how to get stung, how *not* to get stung, why it is not a good idea to try to raise those deadly African bees, and why having the right kind of bee in your bonnet is not necessarily a problem. You also get links to the Carl Hayden Bee Research Center, the Africanized Honey Bee (yikes!) homepage, and the Eastern Apiculture Society.

Figure 243 Moe, Larry, and Curly.

Birding on the Web

http://www.zender.com/birder/

I know something about birding, as my first book was a biography of that great naturalist, essayist, and birder John Burroughs (1837-1921). This absolutely splendid site includes dozens of links to birding resources and societies around the globe, from the Netherlands to Japan, and from Yosemite to Maine. Share information with birders from North Ireland, Quebec, Paris, and Scotland. Access sitings and statistics for hundreds of different varieties of birds on every continent of the planet. I suspect that old John Burroughs, who was generally (and rightly) skeptical of technology, wouldn't know quite what to make of this fantastic resource. But times change.

Figure 244 Birding home page.

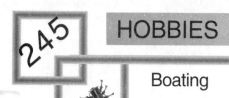

Boating

http://wmi.cais.com/www/boating/index.html

Whether your gig is sailing (hooray!) or motorboating (boo!), you'll find something at this site to interest, amuse, and perhaps even help you. With regard to sailing resources, you have chartering companies, sail makers, rig and hardware vendors, and navigational electronics catalogs. Sail through great links related to saltwater fishing, ocean kayaking, boating instruction and safety, and the Billfish Foundation (an organization which encourages conservation of our waterways). If you are thinking about a new boat, look through catalogs here as well. While you're at it, buy me one.

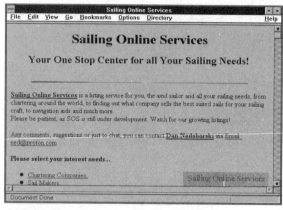

Figure 245 Sailing on-line services.

Camping Trips: Susan and Bob

http://www.amug.org/~kwagunt

Bob Marley (no, not *that* Bob Marley) and Susan Groth help organize non-commercial camping trips around the U.S. and around the world. On Susan and Bob's outings, groups of interested individuals share resources and communally supply all required equipment, planning, labor, and organization in the absence of a professional guide or outfitter. "The elimination of overhead and staff usually enables a private trip to cost approximately one-third of the equivalent commercial trip." Of those who have participated in such expeditions once, 50% have demonstrated their enthusiasm by doing it again. Access this site for more details.

Figure 246 Camp with Susan and Bob.

Canoeing: The Eddyline Echo

http://www.channel1.com/users/scott/

As some of you paddlers know already, excellent canoeing resources are already out on the Net, but they are not all easy to navigate to (or through). Here, you can find race information and results for every canoe sport, enjoy river descriptions, view a slalom/downriver training site, obtain water-release information, and read articles on training and competing. Use the paddler's directory to meet like-minded paddlers in your region and, thus, not get stuck upriver without a paddle(r). See, I did not mention the movie *Deliverance* once!

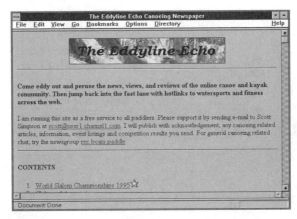

***Figure 247** Canoeing home page.*

Cameron's Climbing Page

http://www.dap.csiro.au/~cameron/climbing/

Maintained by Cameron Simpson (cameron@dap.csiro.au), this page provides everything and anything about rock climbing: techniques, events, maps, hardware, and even climbing glossaries and dictionaries. In addition to details on Australian climbing (Australia being the home of this page), you also get great data on climbing in the U.K. and the U.S. You can use Cameron's links to get information on climbing in Rocky Mountain National Park and contact climbing clubs in Colorado, Michigan, Arkansas, and Arizona. And you get electronic editions of climbing magazines that include *Rock & Ice* and *Expedition News*. Tether yourself to "Cameron's Climbing Page" for world-class climbing information.

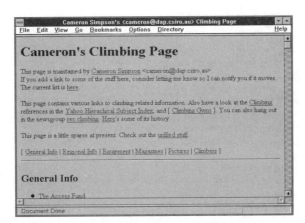

***Figure 248** Cameron's Climbing Page.*

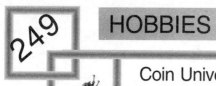

Coin Universe

http://www.coin-universe.com/

"Coin Universe" is your launch pad to the many coin collecting resources on the Web, including coin clubs and associations, coin-collector pages, commercial coin pages, software for coin collecting, and more. Be sure to check out Scott Travers' informative report on "Rare Coin Consumer Protection." You can also access an electronic edition of *Coin Dealer* newsletter. Or, if you really know your stuff, you can participate in a Teletrade certified coin auction. Odds are you can easily outbid me.

Figure 249 Coin Universe.

Fish in Aquariums: The Krib

http://www.cco.caltech.edu/~aquaria/Krib/index.html

Turn off all the lights, save for the one on top of the tank, and watch the Angelfish and guppies gawk out into the dark. Hook the little plastic diver to his airhose, and watch the bubbles foam up from his back. Throw a couple of miniature catfish in there to keep the bottom clean. And like your mother always told you, "Please rinse out that filter and change the charcoal. How can you make those animals live in that filth?" Agh, the joys of an aquarium. At this site, you'll get gobs of information—everything from the fundamentals of setting up a little five-gallon tank to the subtle art of creating artificial reefs. Turn to this site for expert information.

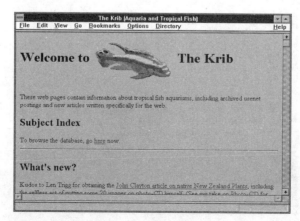

Figure 250 Aquarium heaven.

The Fishing Page

http://www.geo.mtu.edu/~jsuchosk/fish/fishpage

Billed as the world's first Web fishing page, this site has a special emphasis on fly fishing. If you are into creative fly-tying, you will love this site because it has a large gallery of images of various flies, as well as fly-fishing FAQs (frequently asked questions). This page also has a gopher archive connection, as well as links to a range of intriguing options that include the "Women's Fishing Partnership," the "physics of flycasting," the "Aussie Lure Shop," something called the "Virtual Flybox," and, of course, the "Fish Index of the Web Virtual Library." In other words, were Hemingway around, this site would be one of his favorite stops on the Web.

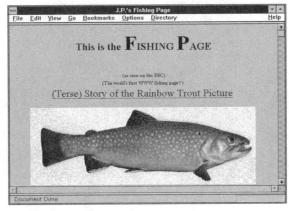

Figure 251 *Fishing home page.*

Garden Encyclopedia

http://www.btw.com/garden_archive/toc.html

The Garden Encyclopedia is an enormous, exhaustive, online reference that provides in-depth information on flowers, plants, fertilizers, soil acids, and more . . . literally leaving no question unanswered. Whether you are planting vegetable gardens or decorative flower plots, evergreens or pansies, this detailed and authoritative reference will prove a vital resource. Authored by leading experts, *The Garden Encyclopedia* is the online equivalent to thousands of pages of text. Dig up all the garden facts you need with *The Garden Encyclopedia*.

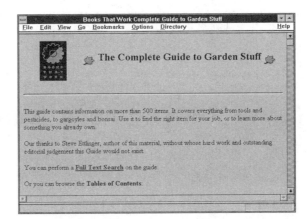

Figure 252 *Your on-line garden encyclopedia.*

Hang-Gliding Server

http://cougar.stanford.edu:7878/HGMPSHomePage.html

Start off with the tremendous gallery of images taken of hang gliders from the ground and by hang gliders from the air. Whoa! Watch out for the rocks. Then, download the free hang-gliding flight simulator and goof around with that until you crash a few times. Next, check out all the other great hang-gliding and paragliding resources from the U.S. and Europe, including coverage of supine flying, sailplaning, and more. In addition, use this server's links to check out hang-gliding clubs in Finland, France, Norway, New Zealand, Italy, Canada, the U.S., and the U.K. Keep in mind that, while you are cordially invited to crash at this site, you should always do your best to fly safe.

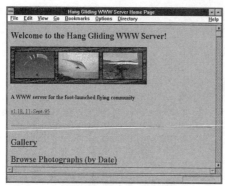

Figure 253.1 Hang-gliding page.

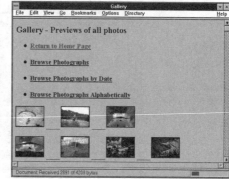

Figure 253.2 Click on the thumbnails enlarge images.

Genealogy: Everton Publishers

http://www.everton.com

Look up your roots. With any luck, you are not descended from John Wilkes Booth. If you want pointers on how to get started tracing your genealogy, this site is the place to visit. Great tools you will find here include Everton's multimedia online genealogical helper and a splendid array of U.S. and non-U.S. resources for genealogists. This site also has connections to genealogical archives and libraries worldwide, global research systems, genealogical software archives, and, of course, Everton's great catalogue of products and services for all current and would-be genealogists and family historians. Now if I could only remember my mother's maiden name, I'd be off to a great start . . .

Figure 254.1 Genealogy page.

Figure 254.2 A useful handbook.

Figure 254.3 And a handy magazine.

Hiking & Camping: The Backcountry

http://io.datasys.swri.edu

Just you alone (or you with a significant other, or you with a party of 16), a backpack, and a lonesome trail cutting narrowly through the wilderness to the cosmic depths of the ultimate in forest solitude. The only sounds are the rush of waterfalls, the chirping of birds, and your radio when you tune in to the Yankees game by the fire at night. The beers are cooling in the rushing water of the otherwise pristine creek. The cans of pre-fab tortellini are on the cookstove. You are a 20th century cyberjock trying, in your own way, to immerse and become one with nature.

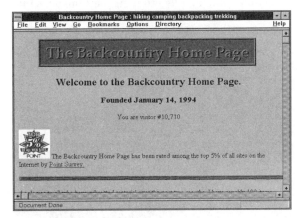

Figure 255 The Backcountry page.

Kites: Jason's Web Kite Site

http://www.latrobe.edu.au/Glenn/KiteSite/Kites.html

This site contains a great collection of JPEG images of single, dual, and quadline kites. "At present, most of the photographs were taken by myself and I retain copyright on them" writes the site's maintainer, Jason Hellwege, "but feel free to download them for whatever non-profit use you have (I think some make damned nice background and startup screens)." Damned right they do, Jason. You will find links to the "NewsGroup Rec.Kites" and the "Hawaii Kite FTP" site. Should you care to send Jason Hellwege some images to include in his gallery, his address is J.Hellwege@latrobe.edu.au. Or simply e-mail him to wish him "fair winds."

Figure 256 Go fly a kite.

The On-line Knitting Magazine

http://www.io.org/~spamily/knit/

Lord, that bathing suit my grandmother knitted for me was uncomfortable. For more appropriate uses of the craft, turn to "The On-line Knitting Magazine." You'll discover resources that include knitting stores in the U.S., Canada, U.K., Ireland, Norway, and other countries; books and magazines for knitters; computer-knitting resources (including knitting newsgroups); and a calendar of upcoming knitting events. You also get digital patterns for sweaters, socks, hats, and scarves (thank God, no swimsuits). You'll also find information on knitting for dolls, a list of links addressing techniques that are a bit off the beaten path, and even spinning wheel FAQs (frequently asked questions)!

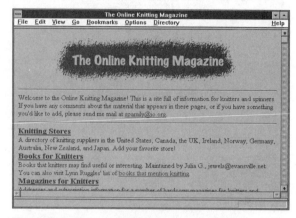

Figure 257 Knitters' Paradise.

Motorcycles Home Page

http://www.halcyon.com/moto/rec_moto.html

This Web spin-off of the Denizens of Doom Motorcycle Usenet Group has the coolest logo on the Internet, and the coolest slogan too: "Live to Flame, Flame to Live." Talk about attitude. If you've ever imagined yourself as a Peter Fonda or Dennis Hopper in *Easy Rider*, or dreamed about working security at a Stones concert, this is the cyberhangout for you. Ride out with your buddies and take over a few towns on the electronic frontier. Or, jump to bike and accessory reviews. Or, check out images of some of the hottest motorcycles ever invented.

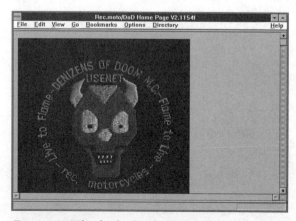

Figure 258 Who the devil is this?

Motorcycles: Harley-Davidson

http://www.hd-stamford.com/

Talk about brand loyalty. How many products do you know of that have customers so satisfied they tattoo the manufacturer's logo on to their chest? Well, you're right. More than a few computer users with Jamsa Press tattoos attend Comdex each year. But Harley-Davidson inspires even more body art, if you can believe it. Whether you are a Harley rider, a future Harley owner, or just want to fantasize about the Harley lifestyle and culture, stop off at this great site, where you can buy Harley clothing and collectibles, get great images of Harley bikes, and check schedules for Hog events near you.

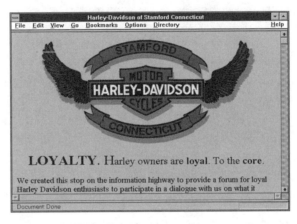

Figure 259 *Harley-Davidson page.*

Mountain Biking: *Dirt Rag*

http://cyclery.com/dirt_rag/index.html

Dirt Rag is a cool alternative to the mainstream mountain-bike magazines. As its publishers inform us, "The editors are not Gods, and *Dirt Rag* is not a bible. On the contrary, the content of *Dirt Rag* is driven by the very people who read it—serious mountain bikers. Real mountain bikers who live and breathe the sport." Turn to *Dirt Rag* for great stories about places to ride, mountain-bike (healthy) food-on-the-go, land access news, team and club news, event and race reports, and no-holds-barred product reviews. The style is witty, confrontational, and irreverent. The only loyalties at this site are to the bikes and the mountains.

Figure 260.1 *Dirt Rag.*

Figure 260.2 *A poem, of sorts.*

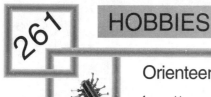
Orienteering & Rogaining Home Page

http://www2.aos.Princeton.EDU:80/rdslater/orienteering

I thought rogaining had something to do with desperate bald guys trying to get their hair back. But it is actually an extended form of orienteering. *Rogaining* is a sport of long distance, cross-country navigation by map and compass, in which teams of two to five members visit as many checkpoints as possible in the course of 24 hours. In other words, this rogaining makes you *lose* your hair. Visit this site for details on rogaining competitions and skills, as well as information on rogaining benign little brother orienteering. You'll find links to orienteering and rogaining organizations and resources worldwide. And you don't need a compass to find the site. All you need is the Web address.

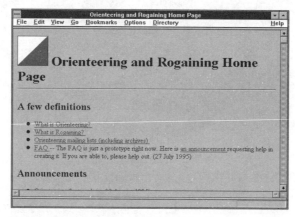

Figure 261 Orienteering and Rogaining home page.

The Photography Spot

http://www.cris.com/~Bubaluba/photo_spot.html

Stroll through the gallery of images submitted by your fellow photographers, or upload your own submissions to this digital museum. When you finish looking at pictures in the gallery, browse through a great list of links to other photography galleries and exhibits around the world, or look at the many products and services that are available to photographers on the Net. You can order film; shop for cameras, lenses, and tripods; and even test run a demo of some airbrush software. I'm getting inspired myself. Now hold it right there and say "cheese." :-)

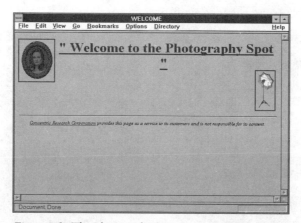

Figure 262 The Photography Spot.

The World Wide Quilting Page

http://ttsw.com/MainQuiltingPage.html

Be sure to check out the winner of the Worst Quilt in the World Contest. Yuck! Beyond that, you will find a rich array of options here. Look up diagrams and directions for many traditional quilt blocks. Read a brief history of quilting around the world. Check the schedules for quilting shows, exhibitions, and conventions worldwide (and get details on how to attend). Sample some of the best computer software specially geared for quilt designing. Or, visit a range of virtual stores in which you can buy fabric, patterns, tools, books, and magazines related to quilt creation. Design one for me with the Grateful Dead logo on it.

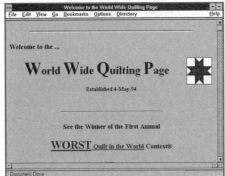

Figure 263.1 Quilters' heaven.

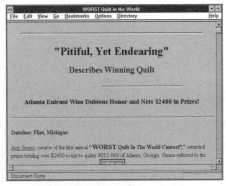

Figure 263.2 The worst quilt in the world.

The RC (Radio Control) Sailing Infocenter

http://honeybee.helsinki.fi/surcp/rcsail.htm

What is radio-control sailing? A sport in which you put a little sailboat in a pond and sail it, controlling the rudder and sail position using radio remote control. The boat actually sails, and you actually pilot it. You just don't have to go out on the water yourself, and you don't have to wear docksiders (unless you want to). This site gives you details on boat construction, racing rules, international and national RC-sailing events, RC-sailing authorities around the world, RC-sailing equipment providers, and more. One advantage to sailing these boats is that the mooring fees are *very* reasonable, even though the cabin space is tight.

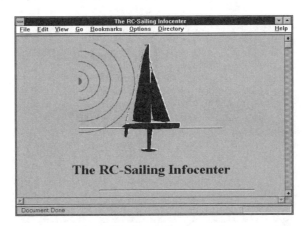

Figure 264 The RC Sailing Infocenter.

The Speleology Server

http://speleology.cs.yale.edu/

What? You don't know what speleology is? What rock have you been hiding under? Actually, if you've been hiding under a rock, you probably know that *speleology* is the study of caves. I'm not talking about Tom Sawyer and Becky Thatcher here. What I'm talking about is more like scientists with flashlights on their hard-hats, crawling down deep shafts while attached to safety harnesses to study cave geology and wildlife (a.k.a., bats). Here comes one now! Just kidding. Get up off the floor. You are *so* gullible. For more astute (albeit less whimsical) information on speleology, check out "The Speleology Information Server," you speleological devil you.

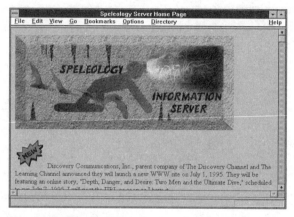

Figure 265 *The Speleology Server.*

Stamp Universe

http://www.stampworld.com/index.html

"Stamp Universe" is a veritable worldwide online mall of stamp dealers, shows, and Web resources for stamp collectors. Access information on stamp shows and conventions around the globe. Review reference databases of the latest prices paid for various rare collectibles. Survey upcoming issues from the U.S. and other postal services, and order first-day-of-issue sheets. You can also advertise stamps from your own collection for sale. Or, you can get a free, online appraisal of either just a few items or a whole lifetime's collection. Hey, I'll give you 32 cents for that one.

Figure 266 *Stamp universe.*

Unicycling Home Page

http://nimitz.mcs.kent.edu/~bkonarsk

That's right. Unicycling is not just for circus performers anymore. You can unicycle to work or school. You can even go on unicycling dates (although it is damned hard to make-out on those relatively uncomfortable seats). Some maniacs (or should I say masochists) even ride (what they call) unicycle trail bikes. To find out more, visit the "Unicycling Home Page." You get comparative unicycle product reviews, instructions on how to ride a unicycle (no mean feat), and suggestions of games you can play on a unicycle (such as unicycle hockey). I remember what my brother said when he tried unicycling: "Ouch!" Actually, that's not what he said. But it is close enough.

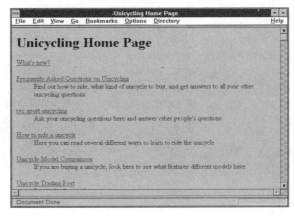

Figure 267 *Unicycling page.*

Woodworking

http://www.cs.rochester.edu/u/roche/wood.html

For the craftsman in you, this site includes such useful items as a wood toxicity table, information on woodworking for kids, a fine woodworking index, and designs for woodworking projects. You can also order wood from the Curtis Lumber Company, tools and patterns from the *Woodworking Catalog*, and more. Whenever my father needed something handy done around the house, he wrote a check. My brother and I have the same approach. If you are more interested in wood and tools than the Renehan men are, this is the site for you. Timber!

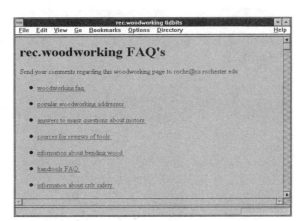

Figure 268 *Woodworking FAQs.*

More Hobbies

As you surf the Web, you may find that one or more of the site addresses listed in this book have changed. In such cases, connect to Jamsa Press at http://www.jamsa.com and click on the icon that corresponds to the *1001 Really Cool Web Sites* book. Jamsa Press will list replacement addresses (when possible) for sites that have moved. In addition, you can also use the following site list as you search for information on hobbies:

Golden Mailing List Info	http://www-acs.ucsd.edu/home-pages/wade/golden.html
Fish Information Service (FINS) Index	http://www.actwin.com/fish/index.html
The World-Wide Web Virtual Library: Fish	http://www.actwin.com/WWWVL-Fish.html
cAVe Rock 100 Amateur Radio Repeater	http://www.ccnet.com/~rwilkins/
UK Student SF Societies Directory	http://www.cl.cam.ac.uk/users/gdr11/uk-sf-societies.html
Statistics for the Kites pages	http://www.ensta.fr/~germond/data/kites_stat.html
Add a kite event to the list	http://www.ensta.fr/~germond/kites/event_add.html
The events page	http://www.ensta.fr/~germond/kites/events/
Pins for rec.kiters	http://www.ensta.fr/~germond/kites/pins.html

269

Live from Antarctica

http://quest.arc.nasa.gov/livefrom/livefrom.html

Experience one of the coldest and most scientifically interesting places on the planet: Antarctica. Access field journals written by scientists in the *Live from Antarctica* project, the great lab/TV partnership for bringing actual scientific fieldwork right into classrooms worldwide. You can also access files regarding astronomy and infrared light at the South Pole, get up-to-the-minute (and frightening) ozone layer information, and search a comprehensive bibliography of resources concerning the history, geology, and biology of the southernmost continent.

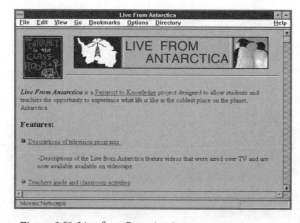

Figure 269 Live from Penguin city.

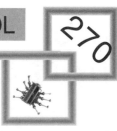

A Tourist Expedition to Antarctica

http://http2.sils.umich.edu/Antarctica/Story.html

This great hypermedia exhibit describes the author's experiences on the Grand Antarctic Circumnavigation cruise of the MV Marco Polo, which took place in early 1994. As documented by the author's splendid prose and beautiful photographs, the expedition visited sites on the Antarctic Peninsula and in the Ross Sea, traveling from Punta Arenas, Chile, to Christchurch, New Zealand. The exhibit includes the author's journal entries, photos, and audio records from the trip. This site also contains reproductions of pre-cruise materials that Orient Lines distributed, as well as a useful Internet resource guide to Antarctic-related information. Antarctica is more than just ice and penguins.

Figure 270 Just one of the beautiful photos.

Australia: ArtServe

http://rubens.anu.edu.au/

The Australian National University art server offers you 16,000 architectural images unavailable elsewhere. The collection consists of 2,800 images of prints from the 15th to 19th centuries, and over 13,000 images of Mediterranean architecture and architectural sculpture from all periods up to the 19th century. Additionally, "ArtServe" lets you access these images through a very friendly database interface. Although the images are of moderate quality (approximately 740x540 pixels on average), they're improving all the time.

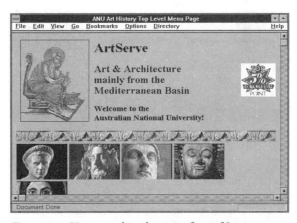

Figure 271 You guessed it: the many faces of Jesus.

Australia Home Page

http://info.anu.edu.au/aiwg/index.html

Just as Antarctica is more than penguins, Australia is far more than kangaroos. From this site, Australia's national homepage, you can link to a wide range of Australian Internet resources, including government and academic gophers that provide national news, statistics, and GIF files. Among the sites you can visit: the library of the Australian National University, various map and geology resources, zoological reference sites, and several detailed historical databases. Even a few Renehans found their way to Australia, willingly or not, from Ireland in the 18th and 19th centuries. The name *Renehan* is associated with some measure of accomplishment in that quarter. Greetings, cousins.

Figure 272 An Australian Bambi.

Australian Botanical Garden

http://155.187.10.12/index.html

At this site, the Australian Centre for Plant Biodiversity Research and the Australian National Botanic Garden team up to provide an astonishingly valuable collection of botanical information. Link to the Australian Nature Conservation Agency, the Tropical Forest Research Centre, the Australian Network for Plant Conservation, or the Australian Systematic Botany Society. Other options include the Biodiversity Information Network, the Australian Environmental Resources Information Network, and the Tasmanian Parks and Wildlife Service.

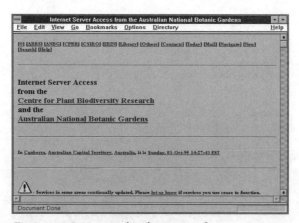

Figure 273 Boring graphics but great info.

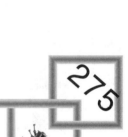

Austria: Hikes Around Vienna

http://tph.tuwien.ac.at/~svozil/wan/wan.html

That's right. Hike the trails that Freud hiked. Your host, a dedicated Viennese hiker by the name of Karl Svozil, shows you the way with maps, photographs, and detailed prose descriptions that take you to the top of the Bisamberg, to the northwestern edge of the Viennese woods, and to the South Styrian hill-range around Leutschach. Karl also provides an exhaustive illustrated account of the premier walk, "Der Antrittsmarsch." In the photos, vistas as beautiful as they are ancient open to your gaze and invite you to partake of the peaceful, cherished (and therefore largely protected) countryside that surrounds one of the great cities of the world.

Figure 274 A walk on the wild(life) side.

Austria Home Page

http://www.ifs.univie.ac.at/austria.html

Click on the Austrian map and access an extensive list of links to academic and government servers in the city you've selected. You can choose Linz (Hitler's hometown!), Vienna, Salzburg, Innsbruck, Graz, or three other locations. You can also get tourist information, releases from the Austrian Press and Information Service, an electronic edition of the Austrian phone book, and even electronic editions of the Austrian train schedules. Additionally, you'll find census and economic data; details about Austria's climate, geography, natural resources and, of course, ski reports.

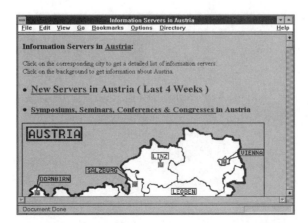

Figure 275 I never realized Austria was an island.

INTERNATIONAL COOL

Beautiful Cultural European Home Pages

http://s700.uminho.pt/cult-europ.html

This site will help you plan a tour through all the major western European countries. Access information about travel routes, hotels, museums, sports events, hostels, festivals, currency exchange rates, train and plane schedules, and more. Impressive links take you to Web sites that contain information about specific cities, such as Paris, London, Vatican City, Edinburgh, Dublin, Prague, Hamburg, and Madrid. If you love the countryside, see the walking-tour information, which includes hikes along the Thames, outside of Rome, and along that "civilizing river," the Seine.

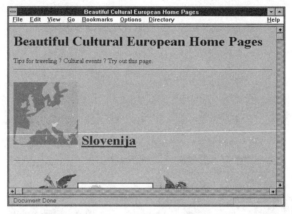

Figure 276 Two options: Slovenija and Paris.

A Journey Through Bulgaria and Romania

http://Alpha.Solutions.Net/rec-travel/europe/romania/trip.harris.html

"Journeys become stories to tell," writes Melissa Harris in the opening of her beautifully crafted hypertext account. "And my recent trip into Eastern Europe is one such story. I decided early in my tenure as an exchange professor in Vienna that I should take this trip during my time in the gateway city. Friends tried to intervene: 'Why Romania? It is very difficult there.' Guidebooks also advised skipping Romania: a rather ominous warning." Bucharest, Ms. Harris decided, was a town she must see. At this site, Ms. Harris' elegant prose transports us to Bucharest without exacting from us the physical and emotional discomfort that was her price of admission.

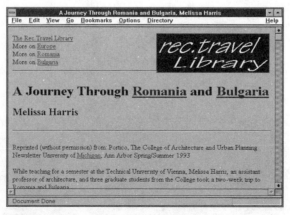

Figure 277 National Lampoon's Bulgarian Vacation.

Canadian Heritage Information Network

http://www.chin.gc.ca/

The "Canadian Heritage Information Network" (CHIN) is a computer-based network that serves museums, libraries, and other heritage institutions internationally. CHIN has an array of reference databases on topics ranging from Canadian folk-artists to international heritage law. This database collection includes the Canadian National Database of Museum Collections, which contains information on over 25 million objects and specimens found in Canadian museums from the Atlantic to the Pacific. CHIN also provides access to the Conservation Information Network.

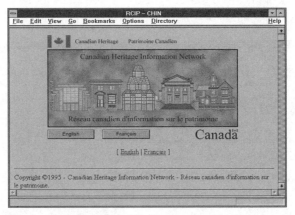

Figure 278 Where digital heritages are archived.

Canadian Football League

http://www.CFL.ca/

Who's up for some football? At this site, you have one-stop shopping for every possible morsel of information you could ever crave about the teams, schedules, players, rules, and coaches of the Canadian Football League. Revel in player and team statistics, league schedules, television broadcast schedules, game results, and league standings. You also get press releases, information on the featured "player of the week," and a glossary of CFL terms. Additionally, you'll find information on The Grey Cup, the history of the CFL, the CFL Hall of Fame, and more. If that is not enough, consider shopping for some CFL merchandise. A team shirt? A pennant? How about an autographed football?

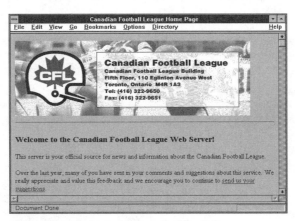

Figure 279 The home of Canadian football.

INTERNATIONAL COOL

CanadaNet

http://www.visions.com/netpages

Ranked in the top 5% of all World Wide Web sites by *Point Survey*, "CanadaNet" is the most comprehensive Internet resource for information on Canadian business, technology, and finance. Check the CanadaNet financial pages for detailed information on mutual funds and quotations for Canadian stocks. If you seek employment, check "CanadaNet" for career opportunities. Interested in a Canadian getaway (or an investment in a Canadian hotel)? Look up information on the CanadaNet tourism file. At the same time, you can search an extensive database of Canadian businesses that offer their goods and services online. At the end of the day, if you aren't in the mood for business, consider a visit to the CanadaNet art gallery, where some astonishingly beautiful, cleverly inspired images await you.

Figure 280.1 CanadaNet home page.

Figure 280.2 Information on CanadaNet.

Canadian Public Works & Government Services

http://www.Pwc-Tpc.ca/

Numerous government bureaus in Canada and elsewhere have, begrudgingly in some cases, put their organizations online. However, few have done so with either the skill or the spirit found at the homepage of the Canadian Public Works and Government Services Group. At this site, a clickable map provides thorough, useful information on Canadian Public Works and Government Services by region, including links to related government and academic Web servers. Choose an English or French language option on the initial page, and then get to know the builders, buyers, engineers, printers, architects, auditors, clerks, telecommunications specialists, environmental scientists, and many other professionals who comprise this remarkable 18,000-member organization.

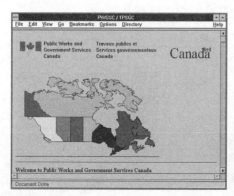

Figure 281.1 Canadian Public Works.

Figure 281.2 Details on Canadian Services.

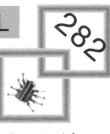

Champlain: Canadian Information Explorer

http://info.ic.gc.ca/champlain/champlain.html

Champlain is so hot off the griddle, it sizzles. This new service (which, as I write, is still in its Beta stage) lets you search for Canadian information across the Internet in an efficient and easy manner. Champlain contains information about all known Canadian-government sites (Federal, Provincial, and Municipal) and Canadian legal-information sites. The service is named after Samuel de Champlain, the French explorer of many of the lands that now make up Canada. This latter-day Champlain will prove a model for similar site engines around the globe. At least I hope so.

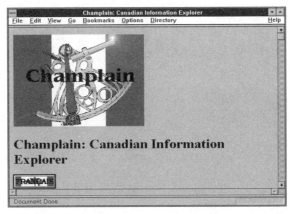

Figure 282 *Let Champlain help you navigate.*

Chile: A Clickable Map

http://www.dcc.uchile.cl/chile/chile.html

At this site, a clickable map lets you access a range of regional servers throughout Chile, as well as Chilean news, tourist information, GIFs, and more. The tourist information includes lots of great data about summer skiing on Chile's splendid mountain ranges. The season peaks in August. You also get links to many colleges and universities; details on Chilean law and government; and digital renderings of highway, town, and city maps. Additionally, you'll have access to census figures, health and demographic statistics, economic data, and reams of information on the environment, religions, language, culture, and folklore of this complex country.

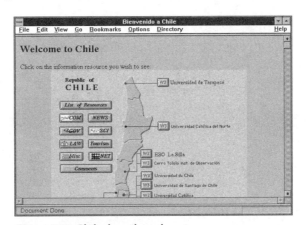

Figure 283 *Chile: long, lean, but not mean.*

284

China (Taiwan): Academia Sinica

http://www.sinica.edu.tw/

Located in Taiwan, the Academia Sinica houses one of the finest computing centers in the world. Available in both Chinese and English versions, this site includes details on not only the Academia Sinica's computing center, but also its High Energy Physics Institute and its biomedical science, ethnology, modern (Chinese) history, earth science, information science, economics, and molecular science institutes. Whether you want to apply to the school or just sample some of the great resources "Academia Sinica" has to offer, this site promises to be an engaging stopping-point.

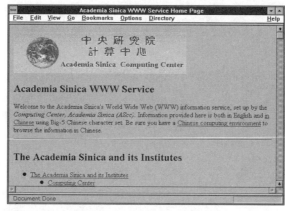

Figure 284 From Taiwan to you.

285

Support Democracy in China

http://www.christusrex.org/www1/sdc/sdchome.html

Support Democracy in China (SDC) is a volunteer community organization whose mission is to promote human rights in China through peaceful means. SDC promotes the use of digital information technology to advance the cause of freedom. Come here for a vivid pictorial history (273 images) of the events at Tiananmen Square in May, 1989. You may join the "Adopt a Dissident" program and begin writing letters demanding that the Chinese government release political prisoners. You may also want to read the 1995 Amnesty International report on China, accounts of extreme human rights violations in Tibet as well as within Chinese prisons. Yes, such places still exist.

Figure 285 Lady Liberty, and a clear message.

China News Digest

http://www.cnd.org/

Assembled by Chinese students and scholars exiled in Canada, this antidote to official Chinese news-groupthink includes detailed information on the Nanjing Massacre, a directory of Chinese student and scholar organizations around the world, digital versions of numerous masterpieces of classic Chinese literature (not a few of them banned in China), and scenic photographs and engravings of Chinese architecture and countryside. Reading through these hyperpages is an education in tyranny, in faith, in constancy, and in the simple but devastating power of the truth. Come to this site not just for information, but for inspiration.

Figure 286 Another view of the World Wide Web.

Commonwealth Games

http://freenet.victoria.bc.ca/XVCommonwealth.html

At this site, you'll find the complete results of the 1994 Commonwealth Games; the Goodwill Games held at St. Petersburg, Russia, and Atlanta, Georgia; the 1994 Winter Olympics; and more. A clickable map lets you zero in on the various Commonwealth Game venues for 1994. You'll also find convenient links to the "Global Network Navigator" sports page; results from all past Commonwealth Games; and the *Fifth British Empire and Commonwealth Games (1954) Research Guide*. This page is essential mind-candy for the Web surfer with a sports-trivia sweet tooth.

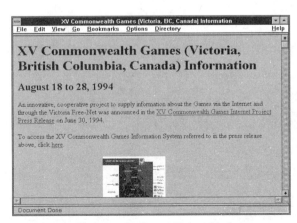

Figure 287 All the results from 1994 and before.

Denmark Home Page

http://info.denet.dk/denmark.html

Visit this site for answers to all your questions about Denmark, a kingdom in Northern Europe that lies between the North Sea and the Baltic on the Jutland peninsula and includes approximately 400 associated islands. Sorry, not fast enough. Bone-up on your Danish trivia at this site. You'll find all the facts on Danish geography (43,092 square kilometers, 75% arable land, 10% forests, 5% moors, 10% developed), geology, climate, and history. The capital? Copenhagen, of course. The chief of state? Queen Margrethe II. And the state religion? Evangelical Lutheran. If you want to know more, you will have to do the homework yourself, but this page makes it easy.

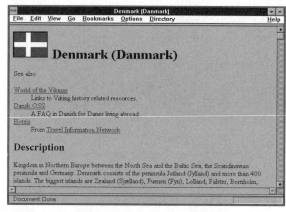

Figure 288 Denmark home page.

Steen Hansen's Denmark Page

http://www.us.ohio-state.edu/~steen/dk

Visit Steen Hansen's elegantly designed "Denmark Page" for Danish facts, trivia, and graphics. Did you know that the Danish flag, called *Dannebrog*, is the oldest national flag in the world? It is said to have fallen from heaven during a battle in 1219 in the small Baltic country of Estonia. Want to access an image of a collection of Danish stamps? Or, does a short picture tour of Copenhagen sound engaging? How about "a few pictures of what Danes do when they let loose?" Want to try some delectable recipes for Danish dishes? You'll find all these things and more at the "Denmark Page." You'll also find links to the Technical University of Denmark, the Royal Library, and several Danish language servers (including the online edition of a Danish-language daily newspaper).

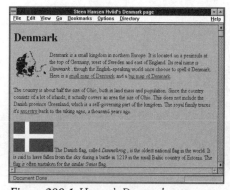

Figure 289.1 Hansen's Denmark page.

Figure 289.2 Information on the royal family.

The Denmark Page

http://info.denet.dk/dkmap.html

While site 288 fills you in on Danish governance, geography, history, and statistics, the "Denmark Page" provides all the information you need on Danish pop culture. We're talking music, clubs, contemporary literature, visual arts, and colleges and universities. This site is your access point for the best Danish galleries featuring some of the hottest contemporary Danish artists, the hippest bands in Copenhagen and its environs, the best in new Dane fiction and poetry, and more. Pick up details on numerous Danish-based business firms, non-Danish firms with significant Danish business connections, and Danish Internet and Web providers. "The Denmark Page" has everything that is new, young, fresh, and vigorous in Denmark, both socially and culturally. Treat yourself to a taste.

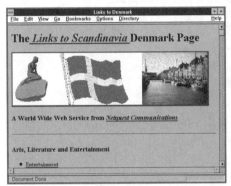

Figure 290.1 Denmark's "pop" page.

Figure 290.2 Danish music resources.

Egyptian Art & Archaeology

http://www.memphis.edu/egypt/main.html

Go to New York's Central Park to see Cleopatra's Needle, but visit this Web site to see the rest of Egypt's architectural and sculptural wonders. Download pictures of the Sphinx, the Nile, the Temple of Osiris, and the tomb of King Tut. Take a short illustrated tour of Egypt, enjoying color photographs of all the great pyramids, the busy city of Cairo, the beautiful Nile, and other wonders. Or survey an exhaustive digital exhibit of Egyptian artifacts. Then, point your mouse at the file that will tell you more about your host: the Institute of Egyptian Art and Archeology at the University of Memphis. (Now you know where Elvis went whenever he felt he needed a little taste of ancient Mediterranean culture. But how often could that have been?)

Figure 291.1 Ancient Egypt goes digital.

Figure 291.2 A color tour.

Figure 291.3 And some artifacts.

Egypt Interactive

http://www.channel1.com/users/mansoorm/index.html

"Egypt Interactive" gives equal attention to the Egypt of today and the Egypt of yesterday. This site provides you with links to information on all aspects of both ancient and modern Egypt including travel, history, religion, culture, and Egyptology. You'll find details about the contemporary social and political situation in Egypt; accounts of modern history that embrace such personalities as the great Anwar Sadat; and information on contemporary Egyptian demographics, economics, population trends, religion, and more. You also get tourism information: where to stay, how to get there, exchange rates, local customs, local cuisine, how to dress, and so on.

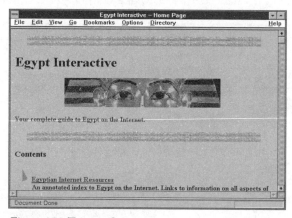

Figure 292 Tut, tut. Stop staring.

Europe Online

http://www.eo.net/

Think of this site as a digital mini-mall with a European flavor. However, this mall features not only retailers, but also business-service providers ranging from investment bankers to car leasing outlets. At this site, citizens from EEC (European Economic Community) member countries can meet, greet, buy, and sell. A piece of "Europe Online" was just recently sold to the German conglomerate, Axel Springer. For a diversion from business, visit the link to "Luxembourg: European City of Culture 1995" and partake of that town's museums, music halls, and yes, shops.

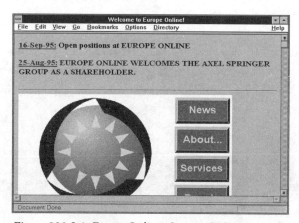

Figure 293 Is it Europe Online? Or is it CBS?

Hostels of Europe

http://www.tardis.ed.ac.uk/~og/hostels.html

One discriminating Web surfer describes this site as a "fun, plain-speaking message board where you can find the skinny on some of Europe's best and worst hostels (supervised, inexpensive lodgings for young travelers)." Read "reports from the trenches," which describes and reviews hostels in the U.K., Ireland, the Benelux countries, France, Spain, Switzerland, Italy, Greece, Scandinavia, and Eastern Europe. To save yourself some time, just go right to the file that features "The Worst Hostels in Europe" to read about hovels in Istanbul, Venice, Rome, Crete, and Munich.

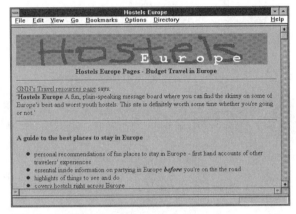

Figure 294 The inexpensive travel alternative.

I'm Europe

http://www.echo.lu/home.html

The "I'm Europe" server supports the European Commission in stimulating the European electronic-information services market and European multimedia-related industries. At this site, you'll find comprehensive information about the European Union, the European Parliament, the Economic and Social Committee of the European Union, and specific electronic programs related to the European information market. You'll also find details on all current programs that aim to maximize European investment in digital information technologies and leverage unique technological strengths within various member nations.

Figure 295 A site with an emphatic "in-your-face" kind of name.

Finland: FuNET

http://www.funet.fi/

This site is your launch pad into a large number of Finnish government, academic, and commercial servers. "FuNET" pages are in English, but most server sites to which these pages link are in Finnish. The array of information, however, is staggering. You will find information on the geology, demographics, climate, population, culture, history, economy, traditions, and religions of the country and links to resources on Finnish folklore, folkmusic, and folkdance. A few nice photo galleries offer gorgeous images of landscape and architecture, and reveal a profoundly beautiful place.

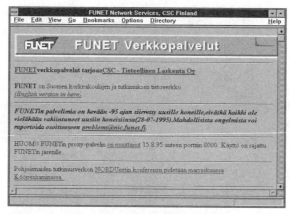

Figure 296 We're talking Finland!

Flags

http://www.adfa.oz.au/CS/flg/col/Index.html

Want to use Brazil's flag for wallpaper? From this site, you can download in full color almost any national flag. Sure, the index page from which you make your selections is a bit dull to look at, but the images that feed down on to your hard drive are vivid and realistic. An unreformed-hippie friend of mine has the Vietnamese flag (what was the North Vietnamese flag during the 60s and early 70s) flashing up on his monitor whenever he leaves the keyboard alone for more than three minutes. Which is fairly often, because he is easily distracted from his work. Yes Tex, I'm talking about you. And why do they call you Tex anyway? You're from New York.

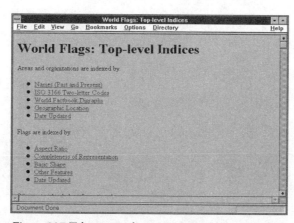

Figure 297 Take your pick.

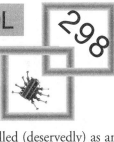

French Multimedia Tours

http://web.culture.fr/index-en.html

Tour French cities, museums, and countryside. Recent additions to this site include a tour billed (deservedly) as an "exceptional archeological discovery." This multimedia tour takes you to see Paleolithic cave paintings recently discovered in the French countryside. Other recently added digital exhibits include rare documents from the history of French archeology and an exploration of the Age of Enlightenment as revealed in the paintings of France's national museums. If you can't get to Paris any time soon, these splendid tours are a reasonable substitute, if not an equivalent.

Figure 298 *From the French Ministry of Culture.*

France: Louvre Home Page

http://mistral.enst.fr/louvre/

This remarkable Web site offers you a multimedia guide to the revolving shows and permanent collections of the Louvre. For example, you can view the paintings of Paul Cezanne, and read a detailed biography of the painter, in-depth scholarly articles, critical reviews, and references. The site includes all the French impressionists, of course, as well as Van Gogh and the Dutch masters who preceded him. Ranging from ancient canvases to the last great abstractions of the dying Picasso, the Louvre's massive collection of inspiration and excellence is appropriately mirrored in the "Louvre Home Page," the museum's digital counterpart. And to think art is only a few keystrokes away.

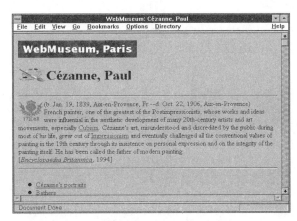

Figure 299 *A Paul Cezanne biography.*

INTERNATIONAL COOL

300

The French Page

http://www.acs.appstate.edu/~griffinw/french.html

Created and maintained by the French department at Appalachian State University (Boone, North Carolina), the "French Page" is the place for anything French—language, history, society, culture, politics, and so on. Select a link to get road guides to various regions of France. Choose another link and get a biography of Charlemagne. Choose yet another link and take a virtual walking tour of the Cathedral of Aachen. You get the picture. Whatever you do, check out the RealAudio links to French-Canadian broadcasts (download the player here as well!).

Figure 300 *From North Carolina, the ultimate French page.*

301

HAPAX: French Resources on the Web

http://hapax.be.sbc.edu/

HAPAX is an experimental server that features links to French-related Web resources of interest to university instructors and students. Among your options are a Cezanne exhibition, a multimedia exploration of French film, a link to the French Studies Web at NYU, and access to the French embassy servers in Washington and Ottawa. You also get French cooking guides, reviews of French restaurants, an exhaustive digital file on the siege of Paris and the Commune, French cartoons, and a super-fast hypersurfing English-French dictionary. Want more? How about the Voltaire Foundation Web server, the French Collection at the University of Virginia, and a digital edition of Fontaine's fables?

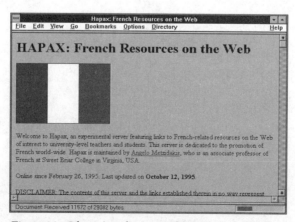

Figure 301 *I haven't a clue as to what Hapax stands for.*

Germany Home Page

http://www.chemie.fu-berlin.de/adressen/brd.html

Access the German News Service, as well as links to related sites and files on the country's geography, people, economy, government, and history. This site includes information on all of Germany's many and varied industries, details on the mechanics and fallout of reunification, exhaustive population demographics, and numerous resources that reveal the complexities of Germany's sometimes troubling past. Click cultural links that bring the Germany of Beethoven, Brahms, and Wagner to your keyboard. As if that were not enough, this site also has currency exchange rates, information on the German stock market, and even an English-German dictionary.

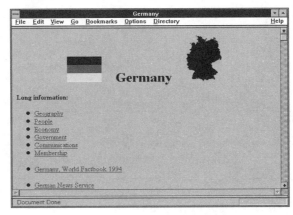

Figure 302 *The Germany home page.*

German Information Center

http://langlab.uta.edu/langpages/GIC.html

The "German Information Center" provides, in German and English, a weekly digital newsletter that summarizes current events in Germany. Each issue focuses on a different topic. One week, the newsletter focuses on unemployment. Another week, the German system of criminal law. Still another week . . . you get the idea. Recent issues have covered high-court rulings on the deployment of German armed forces, the process of German citizenship and naturalization, German/Israel relations, and the issue of German restitution for National Socialist crimes.

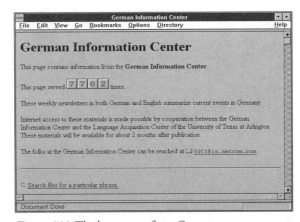

Figure 303 *The latest news from Germany.*

U.K. Guide

http://www.cs.ucl.ac.uk/misc/uk/intro.html

Dickens! Pubs! Big Ben! Stonehenge and the Abbey Road Studios! All things bright and beautiful and all things British are spotlighted at this site, which is a combination atlas and yearbook information source not only on England, but also Ireland, Wales, and Scotland. You'll find an exhaustive photo-file. To see this file, you click on the map that gives you access to regional Web servers. Then, you click on the section of country you would like to see, and special green sections on the map yield photographs of that location. Beautiful countryside opens up for you, as do the gates of classic old cathedrals and castles. Who could ask for more?

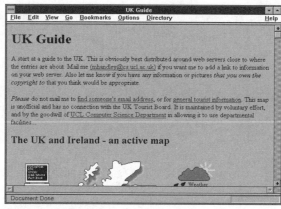

Figure 304 A clickable map for Ireland and the United Kingdom.

Great Britain: Natural History Museum

http://www.nhm.ac.uk/

The British National Natural History Museum of London is one of the premier institutions of its type in the world. At this site, you'll find a digital guide to the museum's exhibits, special events, seminars, and adult education courses. You also get images that show you the Natural History Museum's behind-the-scenes activities—four major research programs in earth and life sciences. Additionally, you get a virtual tour of the Walter Rothschild Zoology Museum at Tring and Down House, the home of Charles Darwin.

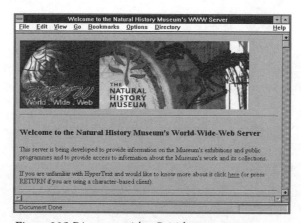

Figure 305 Dinosaurs with a British accent.

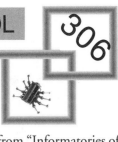

Hungary: The Prime Minister's Web Site

http://www.meh.hu

This site is the official, digital "mouthpiece" of the Hungarian Prime Minister's office. Choose from "Informatories of the Government sittings," "Statements by the Spokesman of the Foreign Ministry," and other intriguing topics. You get the picture. Wait! You can also take a virtual tour of the Hungarian Parliament that is fairly cool, read a summary of the Hungarian government's current (limited) leverage of information technology, and review the plans and procedures of the State Privatization and Holding Company. In other words, if you are one of those western (or eastern) capitalists looking to move in on a recently-liberated eastern-block country, this site is a good choice.

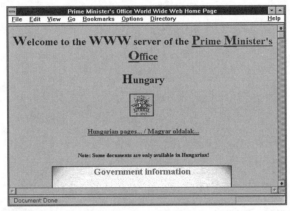

Figure 306 *Stick to Hungarian, guys.*

Icelandic WWW Servers

http://www.rfisk.is/english/sites.html

The good news: a clickable map gives you access to virtually every Icelandic Web server. The bad news: three servers. One in Reykjavik. One in Keflavik. And one in Akureyi. Let's say that once together: *Akureyi.* Very good. Now for more good news: the three servers have lots of cool stuff on them, and not just because they are in Iceland. You want it; the Icelandic servers have it—ski information, airline schedules, road maps, census data, demographics, and more. Best skiing on the planet, my friends. The very best. Tell them Ed sent you; but first check out these servers.

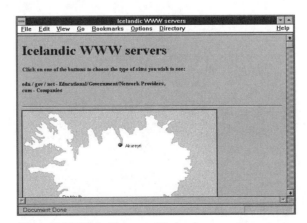

Figure 307 *Clickable map of Iceland.*

Ireland: The Internet Collection

http://itdsrv1.ul.ie/Information/Ireland.html

Ireland is more than shamrocks and leprechauns. The emerald isle is Oscar Wilde, James Joyce, William Butler Yeats, and my forbear, Laurence F. Renehan, scholar and ecclesiastic who served as President of the ancient and beautiful St. Patrick's College, Maynooth, County Kildare, in the 1850s. At this site, you'll find a dynamic collection of Irish heritage resources, as well as FTP sites where you can access back issues of *The Irish Emigrant*. You also get links to many Irish cultural institutions (*including* St. Patrick's at Maynooth) and more strikingly contemporary sites, such as the homepages for the Pogues and U-2, two bands that keep Ireland on the map.

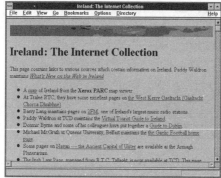

Figure 308.1 A cornucopia of resources.

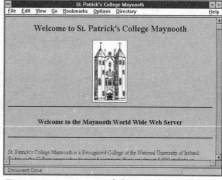

Figure 308.2 A seat of the Renehan tribe.

Ulysses: Internet Guide to Everything Irish

http://www.misty.com/ulysses

While site 308 gives you history and culture, "Ulysses" gives you commercial Ireland: tourism, pubs, stout, fishermen, knit sweaters, and Clancy Brothers records. This site shows Ireland for sale. To view blatant promotions for a range of Irish microbreweries, visit the Virtual Pub. To get the scoop on travel and hotel options across Ireland, visit the virtual tourist center. The interface is great, the navigation smooth, and the graphics impressive. You can buy (or at least see promotions for) everything from James Joyce posters to clay pipes that were probably made on an assembly line in a Chinese prison. But they sure *look* Irish. The Guinness? No, I *know* where they make that. I've been to the factory in Dublin, sacred ground. My Mecca.

Figure 309 Your guide to everything Irish.

Irish National Archives

http://147.252.133.152/nat-arch/

You might find a few interesting little knickknacks at this site. Not the *Book of Kells*. That's across town at Trinity College. (It's also at the other end of this book, under the Visual Arts category.) But you'll find a few items here that might prove interesting, such as Swift's original manuscript for *Gulliver's Travels*. Also noteworthy are census records and tax rolls that go back for centuries. I've found a few Renehans on such tax rolls. Such neat handwriting, Owen Renehan! Did everyone write like you in 1784, or did you have remarkably fine penmanship? Or, did some gentlemanly landlord record your name on the rolls for you right before he took your money? I think I know the answer.

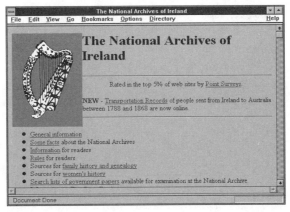

Figure 310 Look up your roots at the Irish National Archive.

Israel Information Service

http://www.israel.org/

The "Israel Information Service" is a clearinghouse for official and government information regarding the State of Israel and the Middle East. At this site, you'll find extensive resources on Israeli history, government, geography, health, education, science, and technology, as well as details on the Israeli economy, culture, and society. Be sure to look at the "Jerusalem 3000" illustrated exhibition, which includes a multimedia tour of the Biblical city, as well as a discussion of Jerusalem in early Christian times.

Figure 311 The Israel Information Service.

Sabra Home Page of Israel

http://www.csun.edu/~hfffl001/israel/sabra.html

"Sabra" is a splendid guide to contemporary Israeli business and culture. Visit this site and access hundreds of links related to the arts, agencies and institutions, celebrities, computer companies, cities and places, finance, and hobbies. Find information on languages, museums and exhibits, nature and wildlife, sports, religion, and universities. Get tourist information regarding hotels, cross-country travel options, and more. And, as icing on the cake, view (or download) a wonderful full-color map of Israel that vividly portrays the picturesque terrain. Additionally, check out the great photograph of David Ben Gurion reading the Declaration of Independence of Israel on May 14, 1948.

Figure 312 What is this supposed to be a picture of?

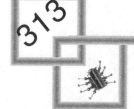

Web Servers of Israel

http://www.ac.il/

The title says it all. This site has links to many, if not all, of Israel's Web servers. Choose English or Hebrew as the language you want to work in. You can go to a clickable map and choose your sites by region, or browse with a word-search engine by topic. I have found these topics to be remarkably fruitful: kibbutz, anti-Semitism, Holocaust, Sadat, Golda Meir, and hydroponics. You also find terrific medical and mathematics resources and many links to universities in and around Jerusalem. Government servers offer, among other things, complete speech files for current and past prime ministers.

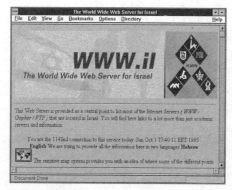

Figure 313.1 Web Servers of Israel.

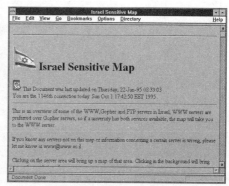

Figure 313.2 Clickable map of Israel.

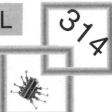

Tel Aviv Museum of Art

http://www.macom.co.il/ta-museum/index.html

This site offers the best of Israel's art and sculpture from the 1920s to the present day, as represented by the Museum's rich graphics collection of more than 20,000 prints and drawings. Check out the online Museum (and don't forget to see what's going on at the Helena Rubinstein Pavilion). When you finish looking at the online exhibits, stop by the Museum shop and pick up a memento. Perhaps some of the Museum's beautiful (and by now world-famous) notecards, or maybe a poster reproduction of one of the many beautiful works of art housed here at the "Tel Aviv Museum of Art," where beauty and refinement are one commodity.

Figure 314 One of the great art museums of the world.

Italian WWW Servers Map

http://www.mi.cnr.it/NIR-IT/NIR-map.html

Nearly 100 Italian cities await you, each with numerous server options to offer. You'll find links to a wealth of Italian resources: census data, population statistics, multimedia exhibitions, geography data, institutions of higher learning, and more. The Vatican server is one fantastically rich resource. Access the complete catalog of the Vatican's voluminous collections of rare books, artifacts, and paintings. Then, view one of the Vatican's digital, multimedia exhibitions. This site offers extensive medical resources—Italy is home to several of the very best medical schools in Europe.

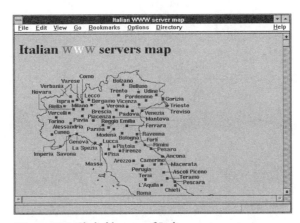

Figure 315 Clickable map of Italian servers.

INTERNATIONAL COOL

316

Japan Window

http://jw.stanford.edu/

This site is your launch pad to virtually everything Japanese on the Web. You'll find dozens of links to Japanese Internet sites and online resources at museums, universities, and private companies across Japan. And you'll get multimedia tours, complete text files of the Japanese Constitution, geographical facts, and more. The "Japan Window" is a collaborative research project of Stanford University and Nippon Telegraph and Telephone Corporation. Before you leave this site, make sure you visit "Kid's Window," a page that teaches children in America about Japanese culture and language.

Figure 316 Japan Window: Stunningly beautiful.

317

Kuwait Home Page

http://www.cs.cmu.edu/~anwar/kuwait.html

Visit this site to access hundreds of resources, including the *CIA World Factbook* data on Kuwait, the latest *American Heritage Encyclopedia* entry, the digital text of Kuwait's Constitution, and extensive maps of the country. For the traveler, this site provides guides to the hotels of Kuwait, U.S. Consular information, U.S. State Department advisories, and more. You'll discover a number of beautiful images of Kuwaiti landscape and architecture that you can download. You'll also see (a somewhat less beautiful) Gulf-War picture gallery.

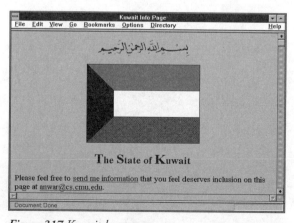

Figure 317 Kuwait home page.

Mexico Home Page

http://www.mty.itesm.mx/MexWeb/Info2/

Is there anything about Mexico that is not addressed at this site? I think not. You'll find information from the *CIA World Factbook*, as well as a beautifully organized site containing information from the newsgroup soc.culture.mexican. Choose your information about Mexican cities broken down by state, including Chihuaha, Colima, Guanajuato, Jalisco, Michoacan, Nuevo Leon, Yucatan, and Zacatecas. You want the inside scoop? Don't miss the multimedia exhibit entitled "Mexico Out of Balance," and another that spotlights the Zapatista movement. If you speak Spanish, you may also want to look at the online editions of four newspapers: *La Jornada, Reforma, El Norte,* and *El Nacional.*

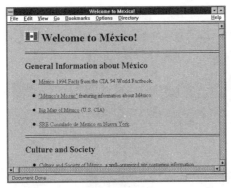

Figure 318.1 Mexico home page.

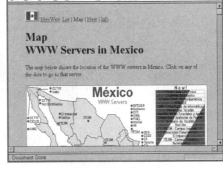

Figure 318.2 Clickable map.

The Netherlands Home Page

http://www.eeb.ele.tue.nl/map/netherlands.html

This page bills itself as "*The* meeting-point for The Netherlands." As its proprietors state, the page "connects the Dutch Web services with each other and to the outside world. Through a number of clickable maps, you are guided along the large number of Web-servers present in our little country." At this site, you'll find links to leisure and art, research and education, government and politics, media, and Internet resources. Use the "National Notebook" to locate people's phone numbers and addresses within the Netherlands. Or, access the "Internet Dutch Yellow Pages" to get addresses and phone numbers for business concerns within the Netherlands.

Figure 319 Netherlands home page.

INTERNATIONAL COOL

Norway Home Page

http://www.service.uit.no/homepage-no

At this site, a clickable map connects you with more than 100 servers in Norway and, at the same time, comprises an extensive cultural and social atlas of the country. Several different layers of the map give you quick information on conferences, festivals, universities, research centers, hospitals, and national parks. Useful links connect you to the range of academic, private, and governmental servers, the sum of which yields a wealth of data on all aspects of Norwegian life and culture. Whether you want information on ski resorts, annual profitability of the Norwegian fishing industry, maps of hiking trails in northern Norway, or guides to the restaurants of Oslo, you can find it at the "Norway Home Page"—a fabulous one-stop resource.

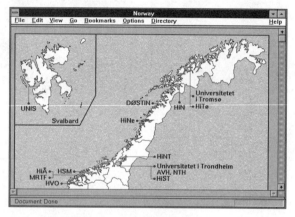

Figure 320 Clickable map of Norway.

Netherlands Museums

http://www.nbt.nl/holland/museums

This site contains virtually (no pun intended) every Netherlands museum link imaginable. Not only do you have access to the very largest and finest state-supported art and science museums, but also several local history establishments and small art collections. Additionally, you'll find links to scholarly resources that include history and art FTP sites, as well as extensive art, history, and science library reference files. A few pages are in Dutch only, but many have an English-language option, and some even a French option. Furthermore, you'll find links to major art schools worldwide.

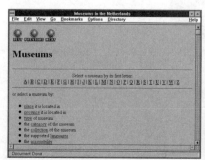

Figure 321.1 Netherlands Museums.

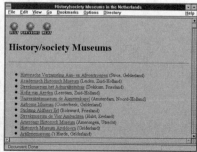

Figure 321.2 History Museums.

Figure 321.3 Nature Museums.

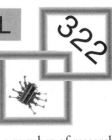

Norway Search

http://www.bibsys.no/english.html

BibSys is a reference database for all Norwegian University Libraries, the National Library, and a number of research libraries. The BibSys database includes 1.8 million bibliographic records (mostly monographs), and is free for all to use as a search space. As with any other extensive electronic library catalog, you can search by topic, title, author, or keyword. Citations show the location(s) of the work you request in any and all libraries across Norway. Given the intricacies of Norwegian spelling, those of you not familiar with the language should search using point-and-click topic menus, which seem well-designed and speed you to your answer fairly rapidly.

Figure 322 Hosted by the Norwegian University Libraries.

Norwegian Travel Information Network

http://www.oslonett.no/NTIN/NTIN.html

"Norwegian Travel Information Network" (NTIN) provides a virtual network of information for travelers and tourists visiting Norway. Thus, NTIN provides information on accommodations (hotels, motels, hostels), museums and exhibitions, restaurants, travel bureaus and tour operations, regional tourist attractions, transport options (bus, train, plane, ferries), and more. Many of these tourism-based businesses compensate NTIN for spreading the word about them; nevertheless, NTIN's advice seems completely unbiased. Start your trip to Norway with a trip to NTIN.

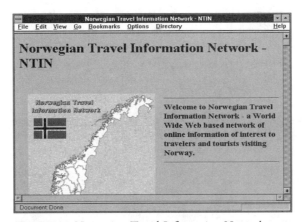

Figure 323 Norwegian Travel Information Network.

Portugal Home Page

http://s700.uminho.pt/Portugal/portugal.html

I was surprised to see that Portugal has a significant population. I'd assumed most of Portugal was living in my home state of Rhode Island, where many Portugese-Americans have for generations worked as fishermen on the Georges Bank. This excellent site includes a clickable map for accessing regional server resources in Portugal, a hypertext Portuguese news journal (in Portuguese), great mountain-biking news from the north of Portugal, satellite weather images, listings of Portuguese cultural events, and more. You'll also find facts on the Portuguese economy, census demographics, political news, U.S. State Department travel information for Portugal, and exchange rates.

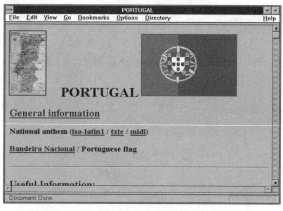

Figure 324 *Portugal information.*

Russia: Friends and Partners

http://solar.rtd.utk.edu/friends/home.html

Russians and Americans developed the "Friends and Partners" site to forge friendship and understanding between the two countries. At this site, the two countries share server resources on art, economics, education, student and cultural exchange, geography and geology, health and medicine, and history. You'll also find shared resources on literature, music, news, national and international law, and U.S. and Russian demographics. Read an in-depth newspaper article discussing the "Friends and Partners" project. This site is a fun, positive place that I encourage you to visit.

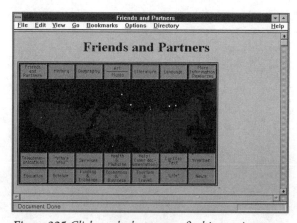

Figure 325 *Click on the button you find interesting.*

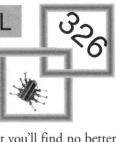

Little Russia: San Antonio

http://mars.uthscsa.edu/Russia/

San Antonio? That's right, the "Little Russia" page comes to you from San Antonio, Texas. But you'll find no better gathering of Russian information and resources anywhere in cyberspace: classic architecture, beautiful music, and fabulous literature. You also get a Russia travel page, clickable Russian network maps, Russian computer games and fonts, reprints from current Russian periodicals, and even Russian comics. Some of the site's most recent postings debate over exactly where to bury the newly identified bones of the Russian Imperial Family. Back in the anonymous pit where they've lain for nearly 80 years, or with the other tsars in one of the great cathedrals of Russia?

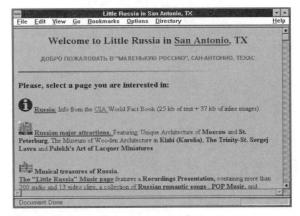

Figure 326 From San Antonio: Little Russia.

Slovakia Document Store

http://www.eunet.sk/slovakia/slovakia.html

Historically overshadowed by the Czech lands in general, and the Golden City of Prague in particular, Slovakia nonetheless maintains a distinct and fascinating culture that is worth investigating. What's waiting for you at this site? Travel information; radio sound clips from Slovakian news; a photo-documentary from the Slovak International Air Display; and facts on Slovakian government, cities, economy, nationalities/languages, religions, and much more. As for history, you can access either a short summary of milestones, or a longer, in-depth narration and analysis.

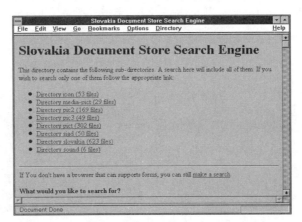

Figure 327 Slovakia Document Store. The price is right.

Slovenija Home Page

http://www.ijs.si/slo.html

Where is Slovenija, you ask? Immediately northeast of the northeastern border of Italy, that's where! Slovenija is the home of some of the finest hiking and alpine skiing in the world. This tiny nation of just two million souls has a culture and tradition that spans 1,500 years. Slovenija carries on a rich artistic heritage and, even today, contains 9 repertory theaters, 70 publishing houses, and 250 fine arts galleries. This small country also has 3,000 churches (for only two million people!) and over a million acres of woodland. Both these facts make the place sound ideally civilized to me. You'll find guides to all the towns, places, and people of Slovenija (sometimes spelled Slovenia). Oooh, a description of the Lasko brewery. Now we are getting somewhere . . .

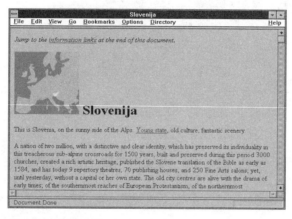

Figure 328 Slovenija home page.

South Africa-Related Resources

http://pantheon.cis.yale.edu/~jadwat/me/sa-resources.html

What a fantastic assortment of links. From this site, you can access the ANC Newswire, *The Independent* online edition, and several directories of South African web sites. You also get access to South African Human Rights Commission reports, the South African Freedom of Expression Institute, and a collection of excerpts from Nelson Mandela's biography, *Long Walk to Freedom*. Additionally, check out an enormous collection of U.S. print articles on the topic of South Africa and look at Intech's "Top Ten" South African Web sites.

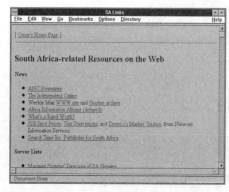

Figure 329.1 South African resources.

Figure 329.2 Mandela's autobiography.

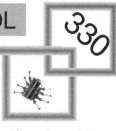

Cycle South Africa

http://www.gnn.com/gnn/meta/travel/features/willie/index.html

On a less official level, treat yourself to this site which chronicles the exploits of Willie Weir, self-proclaimed "long-distance cyclist extraordinaire." Willie recently completed a five-month bicycle journey along the coasts, over the mountains, and across the plains of South Africa. As he proceeded, he posted weekly dispatches describing his trip, along with photos, to this homepage. Read Willie's eloquently stated and beautifully photographed vignettes, which have titles such as "Beauties and the Beast," "Flamingo Silhouettes," "Swaziland Cowboy," "Video Night in Venda," and "Seatless." Guess what happens in that last episode. Ouch!

Figure 330 Go, Willie, go.

South Korea Servers

http://firefox.postech.ac.kr/map/Korea_map.html

At this site, a clickable map gives you access to numerous South Korean academic, private, and governmental servers in more than 25 different cities, from Mokpo in the south to Chunchon in the north. You'll also find detailed databases of information on Korean geography, history, politics, economics, and culture, as well as census data and demographic reports. As a bonus, you get *CIA World Factbook* information on the country, links to foreign sites where the study of Korean history and politics is a specialty, and an interactive Korean-English/English-Korean dictionary.

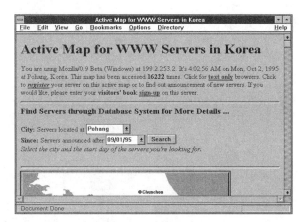

Figure 331 Clickable map of Korea.

Southeast Asian Archive

http://www.lib.uci.edu/sea/seahome.html

The "Southeast Asian Archive" collects materials related to the resettlement of Southeast Asian refugees and immigrants in the United States and around the world. Come here for vivid accounts and graphic illustrations of the plight of boat people and land refugees. Come here also for insightful analysis of the culture and history of Cambodia, Laos, and Vietnam. The "Southeast Asian Archive" is worth a visit if only to look at the very beautiful images, presented here in color GIFs, of Hmong *pa ndau* textiles from the mountain regions of, Vietnam and Laos. Also be sure to check out the Archive's quarterly newsletter, available in digital form.

Figure 332.1 The Southeast Asian Archive.

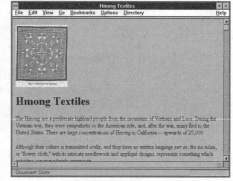

Figure 332.2 Images of Hmong pa ndau textiles.

Southeast Asia: The Virtual Tourist

http://www.ntt.jp/AP/asia-SE.html

At this site, a clickable map of all Southeast Asian countries gives you access to Web servers in Laos, Cambodia, Thailand, Vietnam, and other spots across Indochina. This map also provides "Virtual Tourist" guides for each country. You will find everything from information on walking tours to nightlife, from museums to restaurants. For the business person, you'll find special links to vital information on building business alliances in this up-and-coming region, as well as information on government regulations, taxation, tariffs, and other thorny issues. You also, of course, get resources relating to the history, culture, language, and religions of each country; census and demographic data; and guides to geography and natural resources.

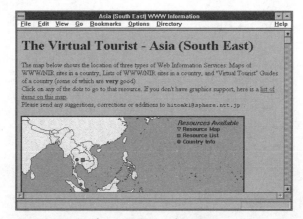

Figure 333 Southeast Asia virtual tourist.

Si, Spain

http://www.civeng.carleton.ca/SiSpain

Provided by the Embassy of Spain in Canada, "Si, Spain" is an interactive service promoting the free exchange of data on Spanish current affairs, history, and cultural development. You'll find the latest news and political analysis, details on Spanish foreign affairs, Spanish fisheries statistics, and more. How about a digital course in the Spanish language for beginners? How about a digital biography of King Juan Carlos, with photographs and sound files? How about a photographic tour of the city of Barcelona? Devour them all here. As my Mom used to say, "Come and get it."

Figure 334 Si, Spain home page.

WebFoot's Guide to Spain

http://www.webfoot.com/travel/guides/spain/spain.html

You've got lots and lots and lots of very cool Spanish stuff here. Let's start with the current, constantly updated, European satellite weather image for Madrid and the region around it. This image takes about eight years to load at 14.4 Kbps, and about four years to load at 28.8 Kbps, but is worth the wait. You also get a couple of great, illustrated travelogs that include Martin Heffels' *Foremtera, Pearl of the Mediterranean*. Let's see. What else? This site is packed: subway maps for Madrid and Barcelona, a complete Spanish Eurail map, a digital Spanish-English/English-Spanish Dictionary, references on Catalonian language and culture, and video clips of the Pamplona running of the bulls.

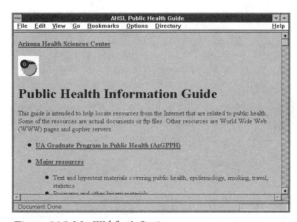

Figure 335 Mr. Webfoot's Spain.

Sweden on the Net

http://www.geopages.com/Hollywood/1200

"Sweden on the Net" offers virtually (no pun intended) any piece or parcel of information on (you guessed it) Sweden that you could possibly ever need. City information? Yup. Maps of various Swedish towns, cities, regions? Uh-huh. A guide to the best restaurants of Stockholm? Of course! The latest updates on Swedish political developments, both domestic and foreign? I'm surprised you even have to ask. And, of course, you also find extensive databases on Swedish culture, history, and language, as well as links to sites providing information on Swedish education and schools, newspapers and media, music and entertainment, and sports.

Figure 336 Sweden on the Net.

Aerial Views of Switzerland

http://www.eunet.ch/Customers/multimedia/index.html

Are there any sights in the world more impressive than those one sees when flying over the Swiss Alps? I don't think so. In an effort to promote what looks like a great CD-ROM that features 1,000 aerial photographs from the Photoswissair Archives, this Web site provides tantalizing mind-candy in the form of a small but splendid collection of sample images from the disk. You absolutely must check out these images. Some are in color, and some classic older photographs are, of course, in black-and-white. Several of the black-and-white images are available for a free download.

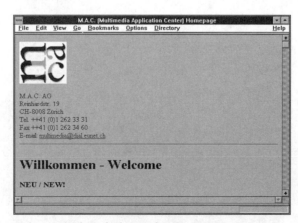

Figure 337 Flying high over the Alps.

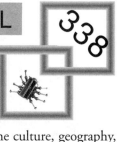

Switzerland Home Page

http://www.swisshome.ch/swisshome

This homepage is a great resource packed with GIFs, FAQs, timelines, maps, and essays on the culture, geography, history, and people of Switzerland. You'll also find a long list of resources on the Swiss language, the geography and geology of the Swiss Alps, tourism, and colleges and universities. If you are planning a ski holiday, this site is just the place to begin your quest for information. Link from here to sites that have complete slope and hotel listings, to maps of many of this alpine landscape's thousands of ski runs, and to beautiful GIFs of enticing resorts that cater to the wants of serious (and not so serious) skiers from around the globe. Check it out. The skiing is great!

Figure 338 *Digital Switzerland.*

Thailand Virtual Library

http://www.nectec.or.th/WWW-VL-Thailand.html

Yup, you're in Thailand. At this site, you'll find a clickable map to get you to Thai servers in various regions of the country, government documents and online information, and tourist information. You'll also find links dedicated to the documentation of Thai society, culture, geography, and history. An impressive list of links focuses on Thailand's extraordinary 20th century history, providing resources with which you can learn about the birth-pains of Thailand's modern nationhood and the contemporary attempts to cope with the messy afterbirth of the colonial tradition.

Figure 339 *Thailand Virtual Library.*

340

Turkey Home Page

http://www.metu.edu.tr:80/Turkey/

No, this page is not dedicated to guys like the turkey who lives next door who painted his house fluorescent green or the turkey who borrowed your bike in high school and then left it at the mall. This is about the *country* of Turkey. A clickable map gives you access to all Turkey's Web and Gopher sites, including colleges and universities, government servers, private Internet resource providers, and even a prison! Great, now you can hyperlink to a Turkish prison (just the place you've always wanted to go.). Other servers provide Turkish laws, census data, geographical and climate information, contact information for government officials, and more.

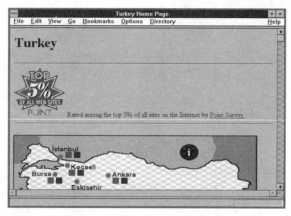

Figure 340 Your guide to everything Turkish.

341

WebFoot's Guide to the Vatican City

http://www.webfoot.com/travel/guides/vatican/vatican.html

Access beautiful color images of one of the great architectural and art treasures of the world: the Vatican. Explore the Vatican tombs where rest the Popes, many martyrs, and, rumors claim, St. Peter himself. Visit the awe-inspiring Sistine Chapel, where Michaelangelo's masterpiece will enthrall you. Delve deep into the rich archive of treasures that is the Vatican library. Explore illuminated manuscripts and ancient writings that date from the very beginning of the Church (and before). Of more contemporary interest, read digital editions of some of Pope John Paul II's writings, view the latest Vatican news-releases and announcements, and check the schedule of upcoming Vatican events.

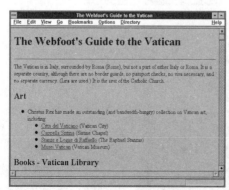

Figure 341.1 Mr. Webfoot's Vatican info.

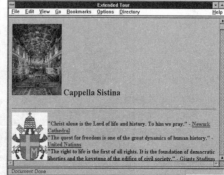

Figure 341.2 The Sistine Chapel, and wise words from John Paul II.

A Virtual Visit to Vietnam

http://grunt.space.swri.edu/visit.htm

"A Virtual Visit to Vietnam" focuses on supplying information about Vietnam (and travel in Vietnam) that is of interest to American veterans of the Vietnam War. Squad Leader John Rossie maintains this site, which includes photographs of Vietnam "taken by veterans and friends of veterans," diaries and trip reports from recent visits to Vietnam, and a *great* multimedia geography lesson on Vietnam. The site also includes an extensive (and I mean *extensive*) bibliography of items related to Vietnam and the war, a filmography structured along the same lines, and recommended reading/viewing lists for scholars, teachers, and students.

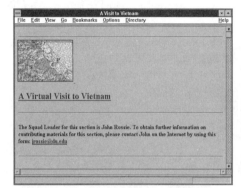

Figure 342.1 Vietnam information for vets.

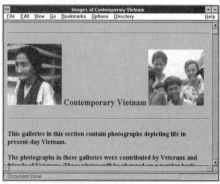

Figure 342.2 A gallery of images of Vietnam (the country, not the war).

Venezuela Web Server

http://venezuela.mit.edu/

Aloha, from Venezuela! Peruse information on everything from the hula to Maui-wowi marijuana and the Pearl Harbor naval base. Wait a minute. That doesn't sound like Venezuela. Let's try again. Let's just start over. MIT's Venezuela server page provides links to dozens of great sites both in and about Venezuela. A clickable map gives you access to various government, academic, and private servers in cities all over Venezuela; and a great list of links gives you access to Venezuelan resources throughout North and South America. Additionally, this site gives you access to information on Venezuelan climate, geography, economy, culture, politics, and history.

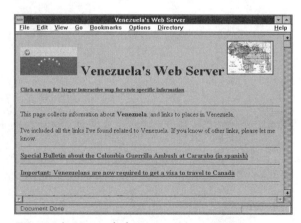

Figure 343 Venezuela home page.

Current Events in the Former Yugoslavia

http://futon.sfsu.edu/~vojin/Geopolitics.html

The world is watching Bosnia. Thus, this site is averaging 25,000 daily visits. Like everyone and everything in this bloody struggle, this site has its point of view: a Serbian point-of-view. However, regardless of *your* point-of-view, this site is definitely worth a visit. You'll find devastating photographs from Bosnia and Herzegovina, a detailed (albeit biased) account of the war for Krajina, and more. Visit the exhibit "Faces of Sorrow, Agony in the Former Yugoslavia." Also, access the Simon Wiesenthal Center's report on Jasenovac, covering Yugoslavian genocide from the region's last war, the Second World War. All told, this disturbing page deals with one of the great cataclysmic events of our century, a tragedy that is occurring right now. This site is not entertaining; it is hard to digest. And like so many things that are hard to digest, it is an education.

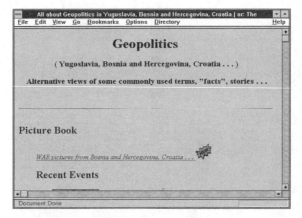

Figure 344 A Serbian perspective.

More International Cool

As you surf the Web, you may find that one or more of the site addresses listed in this book have changed. In such cases, connect to Jamsa Press at http://www.jamsa.com and click on the icon that corresponds to the *1001 Really Cool Web Sites* book. Jamsa Press will list replacement addresses (when possible) for sites that have moved. In addition, you can also use the following site list as you search for information on international sites:

University of Canberra	http://services.canberra.edu.au/
Infodienste an der UdS	http://sparlast.phil15.uni-sb.de/uebersicht.html
SunSITE at Hong Kong	http://sunsite.ust.hk/
Sakamura Laboratory Entrance Hall	http://tron.is.s.u-tokyo.ac.jp/
Yonezawa Lab WWW Server	http://web.yl.is.s.u-tokyo.ac.jp/
IAI Home Page External	http://wmwap1.math.uni-wuppertal.de/
WiLAN - Top Home Page	http://wvwd85.wifak.uni-wuerzburg.de/
Analysys	http://www.analysys.co.uk/
Aalborg University: General information	http://www.auc.dk/
University of Auckland	http://www.auckland.ac.nz/
KOMABA University of Tokyo	http://www.c.u-tokyo.ac.jp/

Download Netscape (and Other Tools)

http://metro.turnpike.net/Rene/tools.htm

The site entitled "Internet Tools, Browsers & Viewers" is the ideal starting point for downloading Netscape 1.2 (for Windows, Windows 95, Macintosh, and UNIX) and numerous other valuable tools. Here you can get Pretty Good Privacy (PGP), an encryption/privacy tool that you simply must have. You can also get the Netscape GhostScript graphics program, RealAudio utilities, MPEG players for Windows, WinZip, QuickTime for Windows/Mac/UNIX, and more! Although some of the downloads may take a while, all are easy and painless—a system of prompts tells you where to go and what to do. So have no fear; just go and gather the (sort-of) free software crop.

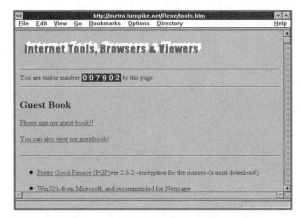

Figure 345 More than 16 great download options.

Easy Internet

http://www.futurenet.co.uk/netmag/Issue1/Easy/index.html

From *.net Magazine* in the U.K. comes this excellent primer that explains all the buzzwords: e-mail, infobahn, cyberspace, and more. At "Easy Internet," you will find out exactly what the Internet and the World Wide Web are all about and how and why they operate. The tutorial information provided here assumes absolutely no background knowledge of the Internet, modems, computers, or anything else more technically sophisticated than an electrical outlet. So feel welcome and at ease, Newbie. No one will make fun of you here.

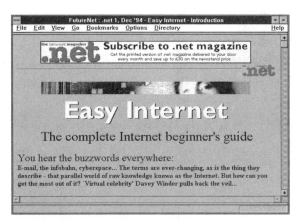

Figure 346 A tutorial for Newbies.

347

EFF's (Extended) Guide to the Internet

http://www.eff.org/papers/bdgtti/eegtti.html

A spot on the Web custom-designed for the edification and education of Newbies, this site explains how to hook up your hardware and configure your communications software for Web exploration. You'll also find tips on how to browse the Web, how to find the links you need in the most efficient manner possible, and even how to set up your own Web homepage. The prose is unassuming. The illustrations are easy to understand. And the hypertext Table-of-Contents navigation is easy to follow, as are the clear and concise instructions for downloading chapters.

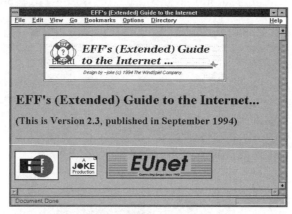

Figure 347 EFF's super-primer.

348

Global Village Internet Tour

http://www.globalcenter.net/gcweb/tour.html

If you really want an armchair introduction to the Internet and the World Wide Web, click into this interactive tour of cyberspace. But don't worry. You can't get lost on this tour because all the sites you visit are stored on Global Village's server. The tour starts with fundamentals, then shows you how to use the Internet to check the stock market, read news reports, research vendors, preview accounting software, hire a new employee, find a government, and even send birthday flowers (gee, you shouldn't have). Fear not. You won't really send anyone flowers. This tour is all a simulation. All in all, this is a great way to learn to swim without getting your feet wet, if you know what I mean.

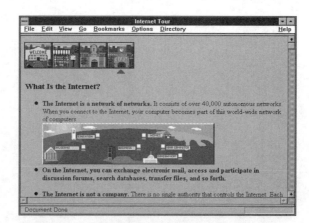

Figure 348 Global Village's "safe" tour.

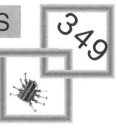

Glossary of Internet Terms

http://www.matisse.net/files/glossary.html

Newbie: A new Internet user who would be wise to use glossaries such as this, explore online tutorials, and access FAQs (see below) on Internet use before posting any queries to Web sites or newsgroups that might result in him or her being flamed (see below). *FAQ:* A "Frequently Asked Questions" list on any of a number of topics. *Flame:* an ungracious or insulting message most often sent from an experienced user to a Newbie when the Newbie asks a dumb question. This handy glossary may help you avoid many misunderstandings and perhaps some nastiness as well.

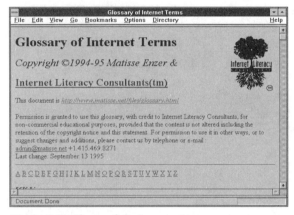

Figure 349 *Glossary from Internet Literacy.*

How to Publish on the Web

http://www.thegiim.org/

Many Web users are no longer content just visiting sites and downloading files. They want to publish and share their own information on the Web. Thus, the Global Institute launched these pages to help everyone publish. This site includes specific guidelines for various Web audiences: teachers, small business owners, community leaders, professionals, non-profit executives, and students. Additionally, because you'll need some technical guidance, the Global Institute maintains a registry of computer-science students who provide low-cost technical assistance to individuals and non-profit organizations who want to publish on the Web. Sounds like a great idea to me.

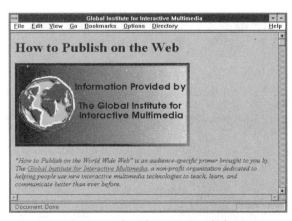

Figure 350 *Become a digital Rupert Murdoch.*

351

Imajika's Guide for New Users

http://www.sjr.com/sjr/www/bs/

Who is Imajika? I have no idea. Whoever he is, the guy has put together an impressive list of links for the new user. His emphasis is on basic knowledge. Here you'll find a new user's guide to the Internet, an FTP (File Transfer Protocol) primer, Usenet and e-mail FAQs, and an incredible hypertext tutorial entitled "Guide to Cyberspace 6.1." Also, check out the great online guide to the Eudora mail system, Stroud's consummate Winsock applications list, and CSUSM Windows World (an extensive software library for Windows users featuring tons of great stuff).

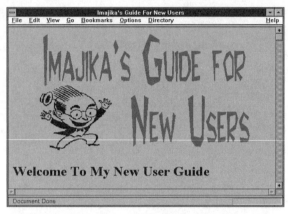

Figure 351 *What a happy little fellow.*

352

Internet E-Mail Syntax Guide

http://starbase.nse.com/~shoppe/mailgd4.htm

Although the Web's popularity has exploded, the most commonly used application on the Internet is electronic-mail (e-mail). This guide helps users send e-mail between the various network protocols that exist on the Internet. What is the proper syntax for sending mail from America Online to CompuServe? How about from CompuServe to NetCom? Or from AppleLink to Prodigy? Every one of these services has its own unique e-mail addressing and receiving system, and each requires a different sequence of characters to send and receive. This handy online guide gives you the key to such differences, and will doubtless save you a great deal of stress (not to mention lost e-mail).

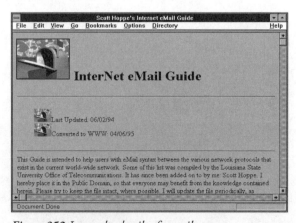

Figure 352 *Learn the details of e-mail.*

Internet Exploration Using Mosaic

http://www.math.udel.edu/MathResources.html

This site provides you with another guided tour of the Internet. The tour's developers characterize the excursion they created as a "voyage." They remind us that "the Internet is like an ocean. It is a great resource; it is huge; no one owns it. It is loaded with resources and wonderful islands." One can, of course, carry the analogy further. It also harbors pirates and is susceptible to pollution. And not a little territoriality goes on, as the island nations of this digital ocean extend their fishing limits further and further out into the sea. Lurking cyber submarines occasionally shoot torpedoes loaded with explosive viruses, while Netscape and other bold sailors provide depth charges in the form of security and encryption tools.

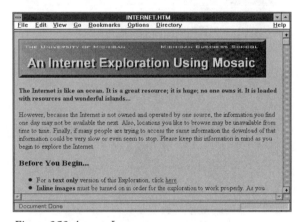

Figure 353 A great Internet tour.

Internet Foreplay

http://www.easynet.co.uk/pages/forepl/forepl.html

The good people at the EasyNet company in the U.K. bring you "Internet Foreplay," part of their cool "cyberia" site. "Internet Foreplay" is a collection of titillating facts and information about the Internet designed to better enable you to plunge into cyberspace. What are your digital erogenous zones? Your modem, your computer, and your service provider, of course. What are your accessories? Your alluring communications software, your shapely dialer, your see-through, transparent interface. The action, of course, is the main thing: the ultimate explosion of information as you finally reach that splendid place called "cyberia."

Figure 354.1 Click on errogenous zones.   *Figure 354.2 Then click on modem.*   *Figure 354.3 And come to this screen.*

Introduction to HTML

http://www.cwru.edu/help/introHTML/toc.html

HyperText Markup Language (HTML) is the tool that you use to create hypertext documents for the World Wide Web. Should you want to create your own homepage, you will want to learn how to use HTML. This site provides you with a splendid hypertext introduction to HTML created with HTML. You'll learn how to use document tags and work with basic text structures. You'll discover how to incorporate images into your HTML documents. The big surprise? HTML is not hard at all once "Introduction to HTML" explains this useful tool to you in a clear, straight-forward manner.

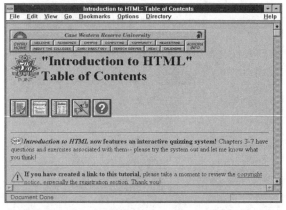

Figure 355 Your intro to HTML.

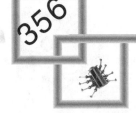

MecklerMedia Web Guide

http://www.mecklerweb.com/webguide/entry.htm

As the folks at Meckler point out, there's a big gap between simply having a Web connection and making good use of that connection. Their admirable ambition is to help you make that leap. A Usenet style guide is one of the best resources this site offers. You'll also find a wonderful, lucid, easy-to-understand explanation of PGP data encryption, tips on how to move graphics and movies across the Net, and a very amusing account of "The Art of the Flame." I heartily recommend this site to all new surfers on the Web sea. It will help you avoid the undertow.

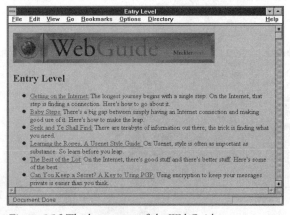

Figure 356 The base menu of the WebGuide.

Netscape Tutorial

http://w3.ag.uiuc.edu/AIM/Discovery/Net/www/netscape/index.html

If you are not using Netscape right now, you should go to Site 345, download Netscape, and then come here to Site 357 and learn to use it. Quicker than any other browser, Netscape lets you load files faster and thus gives you more time to explore the Web. Netscape also supports inline JPEG pictures and animation. Netscape lets you participate in newsgroups and send e-mail within the Netscape window. Netscape can also launch software applications. Bottom line: it is impossible to be cool without Netscape. And you *do* want to be cool, don't you?

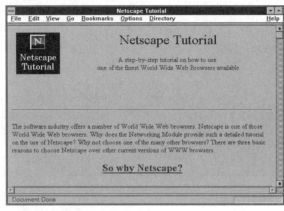

Figure 357 Netscape or die!

Winsock: A Beginner's Guide

http://sage.cc.purdue.edu/~xniu/winsock.htm

Winsock is a collection of Windows-based routines that Internet programs use. Winsock is popular because it is robust and reliable *once you get it configured*. But, simplicity is not one of its strong points. In fact, most of the best-selling Internet books dodge the question of how to set up Winsock. Their chapters on Internet dial-in connections begin with sentences like: "After you have Winsock configured, it is time to . . ." Xiaomu Niu's great hypertext tutorial and reference does not dodge the question (actually *questions*). It confronts them head-on, in clear prose that will ultimately let you, in turn, master the mysterious Zen (or is it Voodoo?) of Winsock.

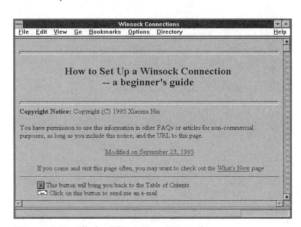

Figure 358 All the "skinny" on Winsock.

INTERNET EXPERTS RESOURCES

More Internet Beginners Resources

As you surf the Web, you may find that one or more of the site addresses listed in this book have changed. In such cases, connect to Jamsa Press at http://www.jamsa.com and click on the icon that corresponds to the *1001 Really Cool Web Sites* book. Jamsa Press will list replacement addresses (when possible) for sites that have moved. In addition, you can also use the following site list as you search for information on Internet resources:

Point of Presence Company	http://www.popco.com/
PSI HOME PAGE	http://www.psi.net/
Individual Services Page	http://www.psi.net/interramp/
QNSnet Home Page	http://www.qns.com/
NetPress (Micromedium)	http://www.rahul.net/netpress/
Primenet Services for the Internet WWW	http://www.ramp.com/
onLine Home Page	http://www.red.net/
LvNet-Teleport Information Services	http://www.riga.lv/

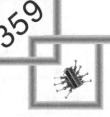

BizCafe: *Free* HTML Graphics!

http://www.bizcafe.com/freegrfx.html

What nice guys! "In the spirit of giving something back to the WWW community," the folks at the BizCafe Management Group make some great graphics available for you (yes, *you*) to download and use for free. Use them. Give them away. Have a ball. The only thing you can't do is sell them, capice? You will find an extraordinary library of great Web design tips, links to cool Web resources, and more. My suggestion: pick up the cool graphics here, plug them into your site, and tell your boss you did it all yourself. Then, demand a raise, a very big raise, the kind of raise an innovator and facilitator deserves. (Psst: By the way, for more free graphics, check out http://www.mccannas.com. But it's a secret, so don't tell anyone I told you, and don't tell anybody else. Okay?)

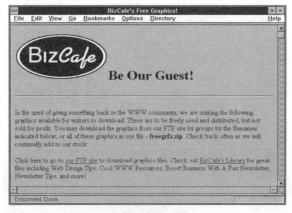

Figure 359 Help yourself to free graphics!

Booksite: Create Your Own Home Page

http://www.booksite.com/package.html

Of course you want your own homepage. Everyone does. And why not? I mean, the world deserves a page with your picture and biography on it. Especially your picture. I mean, you are just so darn good-looking! And clever, too. What you need is not just your picture up there, but a hypertext document packed with your wit and wisdom. And then you need links, lots of links, to those sites on your personal hot list, which are, by definition, the hippest places on the Internet. And, may I suggest a list of your favorite computer books as well (hint, hint)? Find everything you need to pull it off right here in Booksite's "Home Page Package."

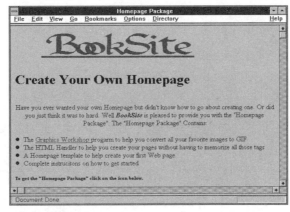

Figure 360 A great turn-key home page package.

Bolt, Beranek & Newman

http://www.bbn.com/

Bolt, Beranek & Newman provides contract research and development services related to the Internet. They design, build, and support a range of computer systems, including full Web server installations. In addition, they do network requirement assessment, architecture design and development, security audits, network optimization, and more. If your firm wants to get online, but has limited technical know-how in-house, you may want to touch base with Bolt, Beranek & Newman.

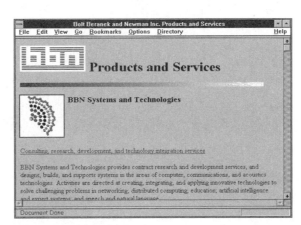

Figure 361 Beautiful graphics are one BBN specialty.

Center for Networked Information Discovery & Retrieval

http://kudzu.cnidr.org/welcome.html

The Center for Networked Information Discovery & Retrieval (CNIDR) is a non-profit group formed to promote and support the implementation and use of networked information discovery and retrieval software applications, such as the Wide Area Information Server (WAIS), the World Wide Web, the Internet Gopher, freeWAIS, and Archie. CNIDR collects and creates documentation and manuals, classifies protocol standards and compliance, and distributes educational and research materials. If you are a developer, this site is a vital connection.

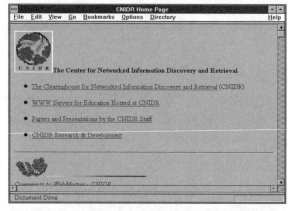

Figure 362 *One of the nicer logos I've seen lately.*

Computer-Mediated Communication Magazine

http://sunsite.unc.edu/cmc/mag/current/toc.html

A very, very cool zine (electronic magazine) for every Web professional, *The Computer-Mediated Communication Magazine* features well-written, hip articles on both practical and philosophical matters regarding Web content publishing. Okay, so you want some examples. In the current issue, Mich Doherty explores the linguistic and cultural roots of the term *cyberspace* in an article entitled "Marshall McLuhan Meets William Gibson in *Cyberspace*." Additionally, Louis Rosenfeld provides a perceptive analysis (and obituary) for Yahoo. These thinking-person's articles are not mind-candy, but they do entertain. This is great stuff. And it's published monthly, just for you.

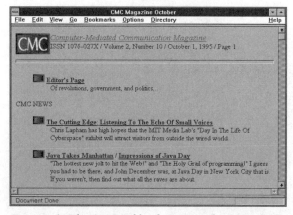

Figure 363 *The CMC Table of Contents for September.*

Creative Internet Solutions

http://creativeis.com

Specializing in Internet publishing and Web development, Creative Internet Solutions provides the tools and knowledge necessary to capitalize on the Internet's marketing potential. These days, when the simple text and images on the Web are becoming a snore, the future clearly belongs to those firms that have the vision to realize what is called for in the next phase of Web development: advanced database queries merged with real-time sound and video: real-time multimedia databases. You will find the expertise to make all this happen at Creative Internet Solutions.

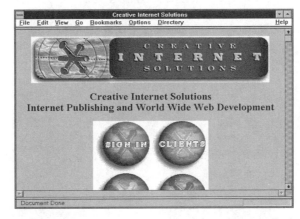

Figure 364 How's this for graphics?

Cyberleaf Internet Publishing

http://www.ileaf.com/ip.html

Cyberleaf is Interleaf's popular, practical, Web publishing alternative. With Cyberleaf, you use your favorite word processor (Word, WordPerfect, AmiPro, *even Xyrite*!) to create a document. Then, you use Cyberleaf, an easy and intuitive tool, to turn that same document into a Web hypertext document. Using Cyberleaf, you can create Web documents without ever going near anything like an HTML tag or flag or command. If you'd like to see some results of Cyberleaf Web projects, there is a set of links here you can check out, along with more information on the software.

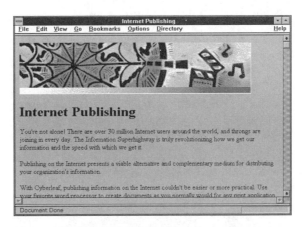

Figure 365 A musical Cyberleaf?

High-Five: Excellence in Design

http://www.highfive.com

In selecting his weekly features of well-done Web site designs, Dave Siegel does not always go for the most sophisticated site. He likes to honor businesspeople when they do something appropriate for their constituents; and he likes sites that bite off the right amount and chew it well. He dislikes mediocre solutions to hard problems. He does not care for pretentious or gratuitous use of Web capabilities. He says if you've got bells and whistles, fine. But make sure they ring and whistle for a reason, and that they serve as key parts of an elegant, ergonomically-correct design solution. In fact, reading his rationales for why he has selected a site as a model of excellence is a design lesson in itself.

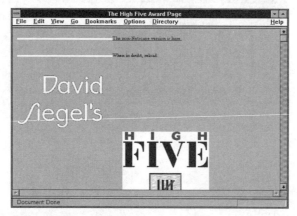

Figure 366 Dave Siegel's page is as well designed as those of some of his winners.

NetCom On-Line Communications Services

http://www.netcom.com

NetCom On-Line Communications Services is one of the leading providers of full-service, direct-Internet-access solutions in the United States. Come to this site for information about NetCom's products and services and their award-winning graphical interface NetCruiser. You also get a complete database of NetCom's local dial-up access points nationwide. NetCom may be the access provider for you, especially now that they no longer force-feed you NetCruiser, and have enabled Netscape usage on their network. Yeah!

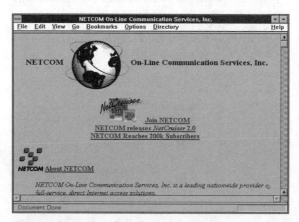

Figure 367 NetCom home page.

PC Week/Netweek Magazine

http://www.ziff.com/~pcweek/netweek/netweek.html

PC Week/Netweek magazine is a supplement to Ziff-Davis' *PC Week* newspaper. The sheet provides in-depth coverage of networking solutions for corporate America and targets as its audience IS managers, support staffmembers, LAN integrators and developers, and corporate executives. You not only get information on *Netweek*, but also links to Ziff-Davis' special reports of interest to computer professionals, *PC Week* lab reviews of hardware and software, and information on how to advertise in any of Ziff-Davis' many excellent computer-related publications. You'll also find great article reprints. When I visited, the pieces included product reviews for five virus-detection programs for LANs, and an article on what makes an anti-virus sleuth's engines "hum." I didn't even know they could carry a tune.

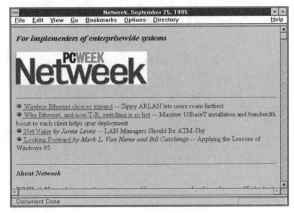

Figure 368 For the networker in you.

Presentation Imaging

http://www.jlc.net/~lrobert/ASF.html

Advertising themselves as the originators of creative Web design for all types and styles of sites, the folks at Presentation Imaging say they provide not just Web pages, "but integrated Web resources that can be used as the basis for presentations to your customers, [as] stand-alone presentations or integrated with Web pages." They seem to do it pretty well, as documented in the various samples of their clean, straightforward, intuitive work, posted for you to review. The homepage for the American Stage Festival of Nashua, New Hampshire, stands out among the samples. Presentation Imaging is, by the way, located in New Hampshire. But you can find them on the Web.

Figure 369.1 The Presentation Imaging page.   *Figure 369.2 And a sample of their work.*

INTERNET EXPERTS RESOURCES

370

Telecom Update

http://www.angustel.ca/up.html

This great weekly zine (electronic magazine) focuses on news of the telecommunications industry in Canada. The editorial range includes technical papers, but also extends to business news. Big news the week I visited: Worldlinx, a Bell Canada subsidiary, was backing away from an outrageous application to trademark the term *The Net*, which it uses for e-mail and related services. Another article revealed the acquisition of the DMR Group, one of Canada's largest systems integrators, by Amdahl Corporation for $120 million. You get the picture.

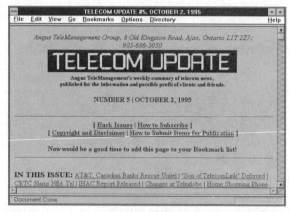

Figure 370 *Canadian telecommunications news.*

371

Top Ten Ways to Tell if You Have a *Sucky* Home Page

http://www.winternet.com/~jmg/topten.html

This guy is hilarious, as you can see in a quote from a letter he wrote to himself: "I'm always in a bad mood and I flame everyone everywhere! Someone has to put these people in their place. You holier-than-thou people really get my goat. What kind of cynical bastard are you to put up a list like this anyway? I don't even know how I ended up here. Oh, and another thing: If I see 'This page looks best when viewed with Netscape,' I'm gonna go nuts. What is it with you fascists? There's nothing wrong with me using AcmeWeb. It may be two years old, and it may not support inline JPEGs, Bookmarks or HTML 3.0, but it works just fine for me, and I refuse to 'jump on the bandwagon,' . . ."

Figure 371 *A very funny place on the Net.*

The Web Developer's Journal

http://www.awa.com/nct/software/eleclead.html

This great monthly journal (which looks best when viewed with Netscape!) contains news and reviews of the latest hypertext-authoring tools, modems, communications software, browsers, and more. *The Web Developer's Journal* covers subjects of interest to all businesses and individuals using electronic formats to communicate on the Internet. One very cool feature is their experimental pages, where they play with new design ideas and "wacky, Advanced Duct Tape HTML: the HTML your mother never told you about!" You will find links to super-cool Web games.

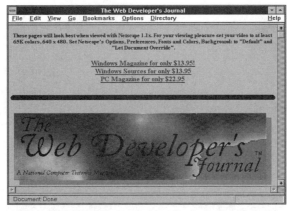

Figure 372 A great Web developer's resource.

Web Style Manual

http://info.med.yale.edu/caim/StyleManual_Top.HTML

Cole Porter had *style*. F. Scott Fitzgerald had *style*. A manual can't give you the kind of style these fellows had. But Web style is quite another thing. Pat Lynch's excellent interactive *Web Style Manual*, itself is a living example of a well-done HTML document. Succinct and navigationally simple, Lynch's style manual is precisely that, a style manual, and not a guide to HTML authoring. What Lynch tries to do (successfully, I think) is create a sort of *Strunk & White* for the Web: a succinct body of rules that, if followed, will inevitably lead to clear thinking and clear communication. Mr. Lynch's contribution is admirable and its guidelines are a must-read for Web designers.

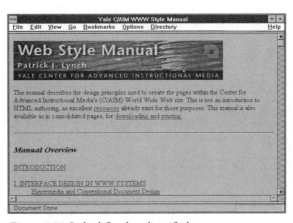

Figure 373 Style defined and rarified.

The Web Weaver's Warren

http://fox.nstn.ca/~tmonk/weaver/weaver.html

What do those little dwarfs, the Web weavers, talk about late at night in their secret tunnel beneath the stump of the dead tree? Mostly, they talk about how Tolkien never wrote a book about them. Lately, they've been talking a lot about the strange new wizardry of VRML, which a magician by the name of Marc Pesce has brought forth out of the forest. What to do with this strange new power? "It comes from the devil," one of them screamed a few months ago, when the thing was new. He ran off into the trees and has not been heard from since. But the others know it is not evil, but good. And the more they consider the power of VRML, the more interesting their ideas for using it become.

Figure 374 The little fellows come out at night.

Web Wonk

http://www.best.com/~dsiegel/tips/tips_home.html

Download a pleasant, minty-green Netscape background that is easy on your eyes and makes for far fewer trips to the Advil home page. Or, access information on the single-pixel GIF trick and learn how to gain control as browser programmers freak. Other goodies here include the full poop on horizontal white-space control, perspicuity (or, "The English Language in Cyberspace"), and, of course, a treatise on spelling in cyberspace. This site has a tone I like. The fellow, an elitist in the best sense of the word, insists on quality in design, in language, in *everything*.

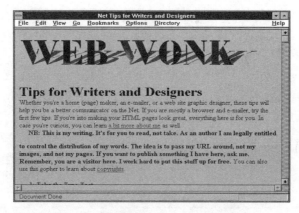

Figure 375 A healthy instinct to insist on quality.

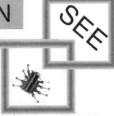

More Internet Experts Resources

As you surf the Web, you may find that one or more of the site addresses listed in this book have changed. In such cases, connect to Jamsa Press at http://www.jamsa.com and click on the icon that corresponds to the *1001 Really Cool Web Sites* book. Jamsa Press will list replacement addresses (when possible) for sites that have moved. In addition, you can also use the following site list as you search for information on Internet and Web resources:

Elm - Electronic Mail for UNIX	http://www.myxa.com/elm.html
Welcome to The North Bay Network	http://www.nbn.com/
A Beginner's Guide to URLs	http://www.ncsa.uiuc.edu/demoweb/url-primer.html
A Beginner's Guide to HTML	http://www.ncsa.uiuc.edu/General/Internet/WWW/HTMLPrimer.html
What's New With NCSA Mosaic	http://www.ncsa.uiuc.edu/SDG/Software/Mosaic/Docs/whats-new.html
The Internet Service Company	http://www.net-serve.com/isc.html
Net+Effects Home Page	http://www.net.effects.com/

An Ant Thology Home Page

http://www.ionet.net/~rdavis/antics.shtml

At this site, *ant*eractive cartoons of smiling, strange ants amuse you by performing tricks related to "ant" words. Of course, an ant word is any word containing the syllable *ant*. This site is a veritable *ant*hology of fun exercises. Look at an ant cartoon and guess which ant word goes with it. You've got twenty cartoons to choose from. Some answers are obvious, some are not. Your task is to guess their *ant*ymology. One cartoon shows an ant who has sp*ant* all his money; another, an ant who is flu*ant* in French. In one sketch, an ant *ant*ers a building; in another an ant meets The Who bassist John *Ant*whistle. Do you see the *ant*rigue? Do you get the system? Then take a mom*ant* to visit this site and play in Richard Davis' strange little world, a very *ant*ertaining place.

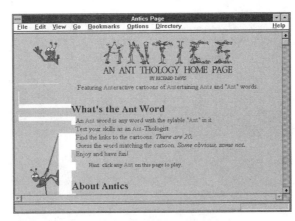

Figure 376 An Ant Thology home page.

Ask The Author

http://ipl.sils.umich.edu/youth/AskAuthor/

Wouldn't it be nice to sit down and talk with the authors and illustrators of your favorite children's books? Now you can. Some of the best of them (including Avi, Natalie Babbitt, Matt Christopher, Robert Cormier, Lois Lowry, Phyllis Reynolds Naylor, Jill Paton Walsh, Jane Yolen, and Charlotte Zolotow) have agreed to answer questions received through the Internet Public Library's "Ask the Author" program. The authors' answers to your questions become a permanent part of the Internet Public Library Youth Collection. In addition to the question-and-answer archive, the site also holds detailed biographies and bibliographies for each writer and illustrator, helping you get to know them even better. I was especially pleased to see Robert Cormier here, as my children and I have enjoyed his books.

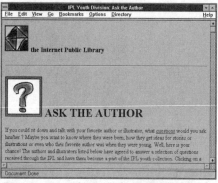

Figure 377.1 The "Ask the Author" page.

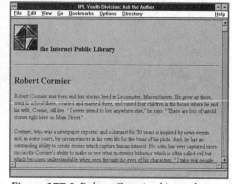

Figure 377.2 Robert Cormier biography.

Children's Literature

http://www.parentsplace.com/readroom/childnew/index.html

In an effort to improve children's literacy, the "Children's Literature" page helps parents select the cream of recently published children's literature. The editors of "Children's Literature" examine more than 5,000 new children's books each year and review the best of them in their newsletter. Additionally, they review electronic books and multimedia CD-ROMs. They also publish vivid, informative profiles of prominent (and soon to be prominent) authors and illustrators. To find out who's on file, just search through the site's online database of reviews and articles. This site is a very necessary stop for parents on the Information Super Highway.

Figure 378 The best of the best children's literature.

Children's Literature Web Guide

http://www.ucalgary.ca/~dkbrown/index.html

Created and maintained by the Doucette Library of Teaching Resources, University of Calgary, this great site provides critical links to Internet resources related to books for children and young adults. You'll find links to key information on conferences and book events, children's book awards, and online children's stories, as well as movies and television programs based on children's books. You'll also find resources for parents, teachers, storytellers, writers, and reviewers. As if that weren't enough, you also get bibliographies, research guides, and indexes to the best in children's literature.

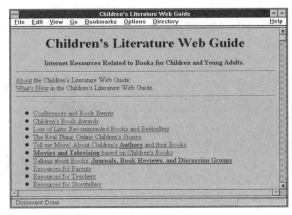

Figure 379 A wonderful set of literary links.

Children Now

http://www.dnai.com/~children

We must protect our children on so many fronts, and Children Now appears to have them all covered. Whether fighting to prevent Medicaid cuts that will hurt kids or stop television violence that already hurts kids, Children Now is active. In California, this organization has stirred up much controversy with its "Children are Watching Now" campaign to keep sexuality and violence off the airwaves during prime time. For this cause, Children Now has allied with many conservative organizations. Conversely, in efforts to stop federal spending cuts that would impact programs that help kids, the organization allies itself with liberals. Everyone should support Children Now!

Figure 380 Defending children on all fronts.

Children's Page

http://www.comlab.ox.ac.uk/oucl/users/jonathan.bowen/children

This delightful piece of cyberspace is put together by the Bowen family of Great Britain: Mummy, Daddy, Alice (9), and Emma (7). Each of the girls has her own homepage, as do Mummy and Daddy ("boring!" say the girls). Read a Daddy's story, "The Adventures of Tottles the Bear," and a sweet essay from Alice about her "Day Out." You'll also find sound recordings by Alice and Emma, an Advent Calendar by Alice, a "Children's Joke Page," and links to games on the Web that Alice and Emma enjoy and hope your children will too! The Bowens also share links to other cool family homepages, museums for children, movie clips, and more. Your children will love visiting the Bowens.

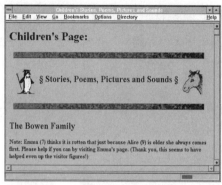

Figure 381.1 Cool stuff for kids.

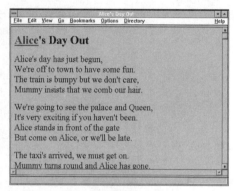

Figure 381.2 "Alice's Day Out."

Cinderella and the Glass Slipper

http://www.usm.edu/usmhburg/lib_arts/english/cinderella/cinderella.html

Treat your kids to a beautiful, illustrated, hypertext edition of this classic tale. The story takes on an added dimension as your children click on linked names of characters in the text to reveal sometimes-startling, sometimes-humorous, yet always-elegant illustrations. But explain this glass slipper routine to me. I mean, was this shoe really glass? I, for one, associate a certain measure of comfort with the term *slipper* that I'd certainly *not* associate with footwear made of glass. We're talking glass here! How do you walk on pavement without having the slippers shatter under your soon-to-be sliced and diced feet? Glass? You've got to be kidding me.

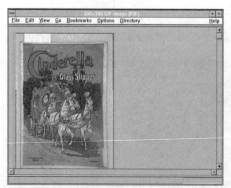

Figure 382.1 Cinderella and the Glass Slipper.

Figure 382.2 Text and illustrations.

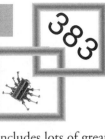

Cynthia & Winston's Family Home Page

http://www.webcom.com/~cynspot/kids.html

This great set of links for kids has two categories: serious fun and after-school fun. Serious fun includes lots of great sites where kids can learn about the environment, literature, mathematics, and the sciences. After-school fun includes the homepage of the Fox Kids' Network, the *Lion King* homepage, and great comics. Make sure you visit the reading corner, where you'll find digital texts for *Alice's Adventures in Wonderland, Anne of Green Gables, Tom Sawyer, The Scarlet Pimpernel* (sink me! it's a ripping tale!), and *The Wonderful Wizard of Oz*. Don't forget to stop at the "White Rabbit Toystore" homepage. While there, do not miss the absolutely fabulous digital display of Gund teddy-bears.

Figure 383 Link to excellent play and study sites.

The Walt Disney Company

http://www.disney.com

Kids will absolutely love this site right from the very first screen, when they are greeted by none other than Tinkerbell. At this site, you'll see video and sound clips from all the most recent Disney company movies. (When I visited, I viewed a scene from *A Kid in King Arthur's Court*.) Better yet, you'll find information about (and clips from) soon-to-be-released Disney films. As a bonus, you also get information on Disney television programs, including a comprehensive, digital, viewer's guide for the Disney Channel, as well as information about upcoming movies and soundtracks.

Figure 384 The latest on films from Disney.

Dr. Internet's Science Resources

http://ipl.sils.umich.edu/youth/DrInternet/

The "Dr. Internet" branch of the Internet Public Library helps children explore science and math through fun exercises. As the initial page explains, "Dr. Internet will help you to find stuff that can help with your homework or your science project or (that) is just cool!" One fun option is "Dr. Internet's Science Trivia." Who invented the radio? Does his name rhyme with *Macaroni*? Who invented the telephone? Does his name rhyme with *smell*? Then, discover several science projects with varying degrees of difficulty (and messiness!). After you clean up, go back to the computer and explore "Dr. Internet's" carefully selected set of science links for elementary-age children.

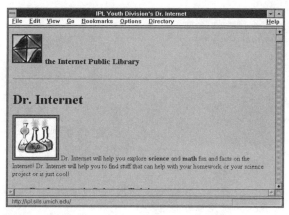

Figure 385 Dr. Internet's cool science options.

Lord Dunsany

http://rrnet.com/~nakamura/story/dunsany/index.html

To read Dunsany is to go through a secret door in a hidden garden and leave all the ugliness, cynicism, and calculation behind in favor of romantic myth. In "The Kith of the Elf-Folk," a Wild Thing proves he will do anything to get a soul, even become human. In "Where the Tides Ebb and Flow," a criminal's soul is left with nowhere to go when Heaven and Hell deny it entrance. And in "The Exiles Club," a startling secret is discovered in the world's most exclusive club. By now, this site will feature more tales from *A Dreamer's Tales* and *The Last Book of Wonder*.

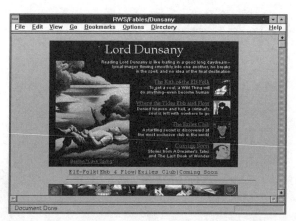

Figure 386 Illustrations by Benton, among others.

Family Planet

http://family.starwave.com

"Family Planet" is an absolutely fabulous resource, offering your family daily updates on education, legislation, toy recalls, and health and nutrition in a convenient summary format. Additionally, every Monday, you get practical medical advice from a world-renowned Harvard pediatrician, T. Berry Brazelton (who, by the way, was my wife's childhood doctor back in Belmont, Massachusetts—the Web makes a small world smaller). Each Tuesday, child-development expert Jan Faull considers the varied problems of school-age children. On Thursdays, family-issues expert Marguerite Kelly answers readers' questions. Finally, Joanna Conners and Jacquelyn Mitchard review family-oriented films and television programs. The cost? "Family Planet" is absolutely free, but nevertheless invaluable.

Figure 387.1 Family Planet home page.

Figure 387.2 Family Planet Table of Contents.

Family Surfboard

http://www.sjbennett.com/users/sjb/surf.html

Steve and Ruth Bennett created "Family Surfboard" to help parents help their children enjoy fun and educational computing at home. The Bennetts' make informed picks of the best Web sites for children, covering everything from museums and publishing projects to pages created at schools around the world. "Family Surfboard" also has a rich collection of online treasure hunts, puzzles, and games. For parents, the site includes the "Electronic Resource Center," where you can find answers to a variety of questions: how can I keep my children safe while they're online? What do people who produce educational or home software recommend to parents? What do educators and researchers have to say about making computers work for children in home and schools? Find out at Steve and Ruth Bennett's "Family Surfboard."

Figure 388.1 The Family Surfboard.

Figure 388.2 Best kidstuff on the Web.

Figure 388.3 Activities for kids.

389

FamilyWeb Home Page

http://www.familyweb.com

An ongoing project of Net Revolution, "FamilyWeb" provides a stem-to-stern reference that covers every aspect of pregnancy, childbirth, and baby care. Learn all about the Bradley Method, prenatal testing, preterm births, miscarriages, and natural family planning. After your baby's birth, come here for information on breast-feeding, circumcision, colic, crib and cradle safety, crib-to-bed transition, diaper rash, Sudden Infant Death Syndrome (SIDS), and toilet training. Additional information includes how to babyproof and childproof your house, the ins and outs of car seats, and medical recommendations. Thinking about having another baby? Read the tips on "Sibling Spacing." Actually, I've already read it, so perhaps I can save you some time: "Family Web" says three years is optimal.

Figure 389 FamilyWeb home page.

390

Family World

http://family.com

"Family World" is a collaboration between more than 40 monthly parenting publications, all members of a national trade association called *Parenting Publications of America*. At this site, you get the best of the best from each magazine. When I logged on, I saw an impressive menu of options that included a back-to-school safety quiz for kids, an informative article on healthy snacks and the importance of healthy breakfasts, and a great piece on how to interest your kids in the performing arts. Book reviews included considerations of *Sandbox Scientist* and *Don't Forget the Rubber Duckie: The Ultimate Book of Lists for Parents.*

Figure 390.1 Family World.

Figure 390.2 Your index of options.

Global Show-n-Tell

http://emma.manymedia.com/show-n-tell

This virtual exhibition lets children show off their favorite projects, possessions, accomplishments, and collections to kids (and adults) around the world. The exhibition consists of links to children's artwork in the form of multimedia pages that reside in Web or FTP servers. In addition to viewing what others have to show-n-tell, you can enter your child's or student's work in the exhibition. To learn more about this exhibition, visit the site.

Figure 391.1 Global Show-n-Tell.

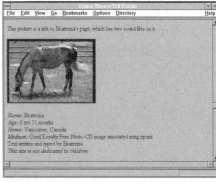

Figure 391.2 A future veterinarian.

Happy Puppy Games Onramp

http://happypuppy.com/games/kids.htm

What a great list of links to things any child is bound to love. One link takes you to the *Where's Waldo* game-preview slide-show at the "WarnerActive" archive. Another link transports you to "TeleRobot," a site where your child can operate a robotic arm in Australia and see the results on his or her home computer screen. Still other links connect you to sites where you can both play and download fantastic Macintosh and PC computer games, including the amazing "Lord Soth's Game Page." Want more? How about access to the enormous educational file area at Walnut Creek's CDROM.com. The "Happy Puppy" people, who hail from Australia and publish several excellent computer games themselves, should be proud of this site, which makes so many high-quality resources easily available to young people.

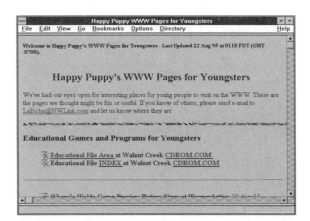

Figure 392 The games onramp.

Headbone Interactive

http://headbone.com

Headbone Interactive is a CD-ROM-software publisher that is creating a growing library of titles "for young thinkers everywhere." At this site, you will find powerful and entertaining interactive demos and games you can download. For ages 4 and up, the site includes *Alphabonk Farm*: "a barnyard romp from A-Z with over a hundred activities to get your noggin shakin'." Also, check out *Panysylvania*, which covers over a hundred children's activities that amuse and amaze and teach social studies, all at the same time (astonishing!). Other options include *Elroy Goes Bugzerk*, which lets you follow Elroy and his loyal bloodhound, Blue, on the trail of the mysterious Technoloptera. Stick close by them, because they need your help!

Figure 393.1 Headbone Interactive home page. *Figure 393.2 A great list of possibilities.*

The Homespun Web of Home Educational Resources

http://www.ictheweb.com/hs-web/

This service spins the thousands of Web and Internet educational resources into a golden opportunity for homeschoolers and anyone else who wants to incorporate the Net into the learning process. The site includes links to science, math, and reading resources, as well as curriculum guides, curriculum suppliers, newsgroups, and useful FTP locations. You also get access to digital and hypertext textbooks, databanks of examination materials, and links to digital editions of Department of Education pamphlets and manuals. Finally, "The Homespun Web of Home Educational Resources" provides chat areas where you can share your experiences with other homeschoolers. A virtual PTA, if you will.

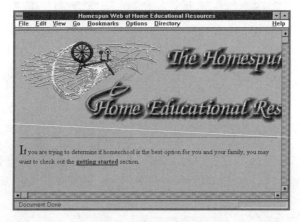

Figure 394 A home schooling cornucopia.

395

I Live on a Raft

http://www.digimark.net/iatech/books/rafttoc.htm

Jerzy Harasymowicz's "I Live on a Raft" is a great, beautifully illustrated collection of short, haiku-like verse for children. One of Poland's leading poets, Harasymowicz is noted for his unique personal mythology and the spontaneous fantasy inherent in all his works. Fantasy? Well, yes. You see, the raft is in fact an airplane that is out of gas, resting on a cloud indefinitely since no gas stations reside nearby. Navigating this site is simple and intuitive—just right for young children. Be sure to treat your child to the delightful experience of "I Live on a Raft."

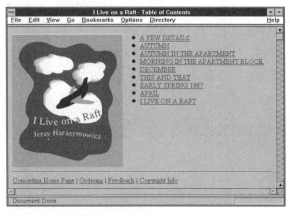

Figure 395 A fantasy on-high.

396

International Kids' Space

http://plaza.interport.net/~sachi

At this site, most pictures are clickable, and half the fun is finding their secrets! The main menu itself is one big picture. Click on the newspaper to get International Kids' news. Click on the radio to get sound files of cool kids' songs uploaded by children from around the world. Click on the picture that hangs on the wall to view artwork uploaded by kids from Singapore to Chicago, as well as to learn how to submit your own paintings and drawings. Click on the letter that lies on the table to send mail to the site proprietors. The storybook corner of the site, where you will always find something new to read, is available in both English and Japanese versions.

Figure 396 An international kids' space.

397

The Internet in the Classroom

http://quest.arc.nasa.gov/

The mission of NASA's K-12 initiative is to provide support and services for schools, teachers, and students that wish to fully utilize the Internet, and its underlying information technologies, as basic tools for learning. Supported by NASA centers around the country, K-12 Internet Initiative projects utilize online technology to let students interact with NASA scientists, researchers, and engineers. Trying to figure out how to bring the Internet to your school? Need ideas for classes? Want a helpful video guide to get you started? Find it all at "The Internet in the Classroom."

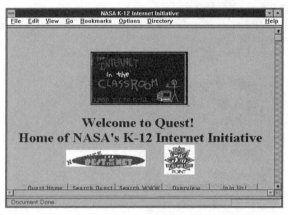

Figure 397 Internet in the Classroom, just where it belongs.

398

Ion Science

http://www.injersey.com/media/IonSci

That's *Ion* (eye-on) *Science*. Get it? Ho, ho, ho. Despite the name, this resource is fabulous. This new, graphic-based weekly magazine devotes itself to making sense of the latest news and trends in science. *Ion Science* demystifies complex topics, making them understandable for children. "Don't be surprised if we sometimes veer to the offbeat," their editor says. "We think science is fun." When I checked in, I found an article that discussed the history and dynamics of earthquakes. Another article explained this summer's rash of hurricanes. If you'd care to look something up, all past issues of this weekly reside in a searchable archive, which the site puts at your disposal. Now if they'd just lose that clunky name . . .

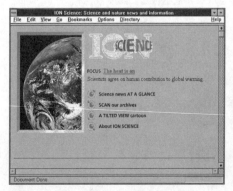

Figure 398.1 Tales of earthquakes and hurricanes.

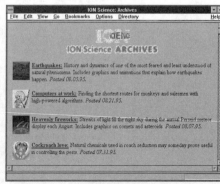

Figure 398.2 A new cartoon every week.

Kids' Corner

http://www.ot.com/kids/

"Kids' Corner" includes a great clickable puzzle page (see below), a sometimes-daunting digital version of Hangman, and more. The site also includes an ever-changing, interactive story—an engaging adventure that has kids pointing and clicking frantically while trying to solve problems and help a noble hero triumph over evil. Additionally, kids can leave their names in the guestbook and scan the names of others (from around the world) who visited the site before them. However, perhaps the most appealing aspect of "Kids' Corner" is its invitation to all children to upload their art for inclusion in the "Kids' Corner" gallery. Once a week, one lucky child gets his or her artwork chosen for the "Kids' Corner" cover page, which hundreds of users view each day. Quite a coup for a six-year-old!

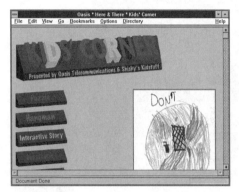

Figure 399.1 Put your picture on the cover.

Figure 399.2 A super-cool puzzle.

KidLit

http://mgfx.com/kidlit/

"KidLit" is designed for kids who want great stories to read, great illustrations to view, and great adventures to remember for a lifetime. What kind of adventures? Oh, the kind that Rudyard Kipling, Stephen Crane, or Robert Louis Stevenson excelled at creating. "KidLit" displays only the very best in juvenile fiction. Other names that float to the surface are C.S. Lewis (*The Chronicles of Narnia*) and Jack London, whose long-forgotten but nevertheless great juvenile fiction gains the attention it deserves here. Of course, you also have discussion of the best *contemporary* writers and illustrators of children's literature, together with related bibliographies, reviews, and filmographies.

Figure 400 A place for quality children's literature.

KIDSTUFF & K-12 EDUCATION

The Kids' Page

http://www.onramp.ca/~lowens/107kids.htm

"The Kids' Page" is a starting place on the Net for both the young and the young-at-heart, a jumping-in point for parents and children exploring the Web *together*. You'll find links to games, puzzles, brain-teasers, and competitions. Additionally, this site has links that will help a student develop a killer science fair project and achieve more trivial successes, such as obtaining immortality in a game of *Doom*. Virtually all the key resources are Canadian in origin, and many of the linked pages are available in English and French. But even non-Canadian kids will find it fun.

Figure 401 *Kidstuff from Canada.*

KidPub

http://www.en-garde.com/kidpub/

Would your child like to write a story and have it published on the Web for all the world to see? No problem. Just type the story and send it to "KidPub." Within two or three days, the work will be in HTML format and available for viewing. It's as simple as that. "KidPub is strictly a hobby," writes the site's Webmaster. "I don't earn any money from it, but I do get a lot of pleasure from it." "KidPub" subsists on a shoestring budget and resides on a I486 DX33 PC running Linux. "The machine has 8 Meg of RAM," writes the Webmaster, "and about a gigabyte of disk storage. It doesn't have a monitor or a keyboard. It sits quietly in a corner of my family room mumbling to itself."

Figure 402 *A place for kids to publish.*

KidsCom

http://www.kidscom.com

At "KidsCom," your child can find a "key pal," a boy or girl with similar interests to which your child can send messages across the Internet. Or, your child can write a one-line phrase on the site's "graffiti" wall (which, of course, is monitored to make sure its content is always suitable for children). Other fun options? The "Write Me A Story" program collects submissions for a weekly contest in which the kids themselves vote to decide which story is best (with the clear understanding that *all* who make the effort to write and submit are inherently winners). And, at the "Pet Arena," kids can post pictures and stories about their pet friends.

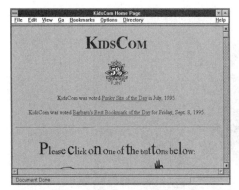

Figure 403.1 KidsCom home page.

Figure 403.2 The Parents' Place.

404

Stanislaw Lem

http://rrnet.com/~nakamura/story/lem/index.html

Every child is a fantasist. Thus, every child is well-positioned to enjoy the simple, sublime, and often naive fiction of Stanislaw Lem. Come here for three of Lem's greatest tales. Start with "The Seventh Voyage" and partake of hilarious time-travel adventures with the "Candide of the cosmos." Then, turn to "The Offer of King Krool," in which two inventors create the perfect beast in order to satisfy the ravings of a hunt-mad king. And finally, treat your child to "Automatthew's Friend," the story of a lonely little robot who, in desperation, purchases himself an "eternal" friend. Coming soon (perhaps by the time you read *1001 Really Cool Web Sites*): other Lem classics, including excerpts from *Tales of Prix* and *The Pilot*. These tales will delight young and old alike.

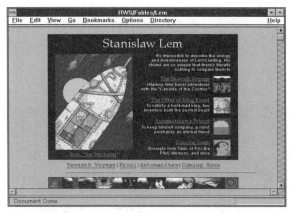

Figure 404 Lem's cosmic fantasies.

George MacDonald

http://rrnet.com/~nakamura/story/macdonald/index.html

Speaking of flights of fanciful exuberance, we cannot forget George MacDonald. C.S. Lewis (Remember him? *The Lion, The Witch,* and *The Wardrobe*) summed up MacDonald with the best brief, uncompromising estimate: "Nobody does fantasy better than MacDonald." And the three tales archived at this site exemplify MacDonald's virtuosity. "The Day Boy and the Night Girl" tells the story of a witch who raises a boy to see only day and a girl to know only night. In "The Light Princess," a princess experiences a surprising curse: the loss of all her gravity. And "The Golden Key" follows two children as they search for the country from which shadows fall.

Figure 405 *MacDonald's wild imaginings.*

The Magic Jungle

http://www.cais.com/djackson/jungle.html

"Zachary was a boy who was six years old. He was sitting on his back porch one lazy summer afternoon passing the time by counting clouds and comparing their relative shapes and sizes. How lovely these puffy clouds are, he thought, and from time to time a yard animal would distract his attention. Two young squirrels scrambled spirals down the old oak tree, one after the other, in an innocent game of young squirrel tag. He looked down at the two squirrels, who were temporarily frozen in place while they sized each other up." So begins "The Magic Jungle," a splendid illustrated story about a boy whose world suddenly gets turned upside down when he makes friends with a talking squirrel.

Figure 406 *Dinosaurs in the Magic Jungle.*

MidLink Magazine

http://longwood.cs.ucf.edu:80/~MidLink

MidLink Magazine is an electronic magazine for kids in the middle grades. You'll find writing by and for middle-school kids from around the globe. Links include cool school homepages; electronic portfolios from digital, middle-school artists; and an incredibly cool, ongoing competition entitled "Design an Alien." Additionally, the site regularly features celebrity visitors. When I visited the site, the theme for the issue, and the "assigned" topic for "The Write Spot," was "people of character." Students wrote about people who deserve admiration because of their high moral character—their honesty, trustworthiness, compassion, and loyalty. I cannot think of a better theme.

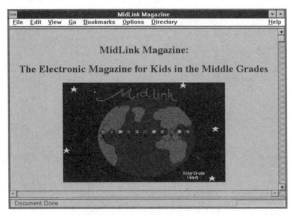

Figure 407 Middle-School e-publishing.

The Mole and the Owl

http://rrnet.com/~nakamura/mole/index.html

The Mole and the Owl is a splendid story. And the Web is the only place where you will find it, since one foolish publisher after another has rejected it. *The Mole and the Owl* is a romantic fable wherein an owl's love transforms a mole. When the owl mysteriously disappears, the mole overcomes his timid nature and journeys the world to find his friend. Your children will love the story. If *The Mole and the Owl* moves you or your child, feel free to leave a note to that effect in the "Mole's Scrapbook." The Mole is a sentimental little fellow and treasures such remembrances.

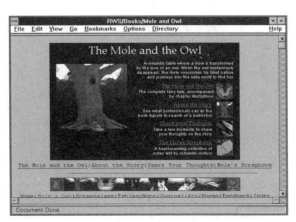

Figure 408 The tree where they live.

Muppets Home Page

http://www.ncsa.uiuc.edu/VR/BS/Muppets/muppets.html

The "Muppets Home Page" is an unofficial collection of information about Jim Henson's Muppets. This site includes a complete "Muppography" (the mother of all Muppet lists) and episode guides for several programs with which Jim Henson Productions has been associated, including *The Muppet Show*, *Fraggle Rock*, *Dinosaurs*, and *Sesame Street*. You'll also find images of various Muppet characters and a Muppet Wish List ("what we want next from Jim Henson Productions.") Any lover of the very lovable Muppets will enjoy this site, regardless of age.

Figure 409 *The late Henson with his friends.*

My Blue Suitcase

http://www.digimark.net/iatech/books/mbstoc.htm

"My Blue Suitcase" is a delightful story about a well-loved suitcase that travels on its own. The brief text has a poetic rhythm, and monotype prints beautifully depict the vehicles (planes, trains, and automobiles) that transport the suitcase. This thought-provoking story explores the themes of departure, separation, and return—themes that Sharon Katz's simple prose and potent images make comprehensible to the very young. When I showed the story to Katherine, my four-year-old daughter, she was enthralled, delighted, enamored. She would not give up the mouse. Back and forth we went, backing in and out of the story again and again, following the little blue suitcase.

Figure 410 *The indefatigable suitcase.*

KIDSTUFF & K-12 EDUCATION

Bill Nye, the Science Guy

http://www.seanet.com/vendors/billnye/nyelabs.html

Bill Nye, the Science Guy is the favorite television program of my son, Billy. So Billy was delighted to find Bill Nye's "on-line laboratory" on the Web. He has even sent Bill Nye a couple of e-mail messages and, much to his delight, received courteous responses. At this site, you'll find QuickTime video clips and prose summaries of experiments Nye performed in his public-television program. You'll also find some stuff that hasn't made it on to TV: Bill Nye's somewhat wacky "home videos." Add to that Bill Nye's offbeat take on current science news and nationwide listings for exactly when his program airs, and you have a cool site for a kid like my son who likes science and likes Bill Nye.

Figure 411.1 Bill Nye home page.

Figure 411.2 A few cool options.

On-line Children's Stories

http://www.ucalgary.ca/~dkbrown/storics.html

I'm not sure if these stories are very good. They're all rather obscure, and I've never heard of any of these authors. There's something called *The Hunting of the Snark* by a guy with a girl's last name: Lewis Carroll. Then, there's something called "The Cinderella Project," which provides a text and image archive for a dozen English-language versions, published between 1729 and 1912, of some story entitled "Cinderella." The site also includes poems for children by a few fellows of what must have been small reputation: Walter de la Mare, William Wordsworth, Charles Swinburne, and James Whitcomb Riley. And there's a weird-sounding book by somebody named Robert Louis Stevenson: *A Child's Garden of Verses*. I can't imagine it's worth pursuing. Oh, I have to go. It's time for *The Simpsons*.

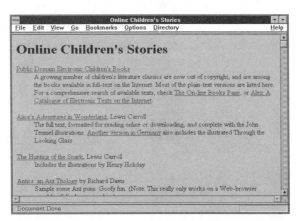

Figure 412 A rich collection of kids' literature.

The Parents' Resource Almanac

http://family.starwave.com/resource/pra/Table_of_Contents.htm

Wow! What a resource! This exhaustive, digital reference covers *all* aspects of parenthood, from healthy pregnancies to choosing (and paying for) a college. What isn't covered here? Language development? *Covered.* Birth order and only children? *Covered.* Emotional differences between genders? *Covered.* Crying? Diapering? Toilet training? *Covered. Covered. Covered.* You get the drift. Spoiling, self-esteem, anger, aggression, tantrums, fears—it's all here. I mean, this thing is extensive. If this site were a Jamsa Press book, they'd call it *1001 Parenting Tips*. I mean, this thing is so big that if it weren't a digital book, you'd need a strongman to pick it up. I mean, this thing is so huge that . . .

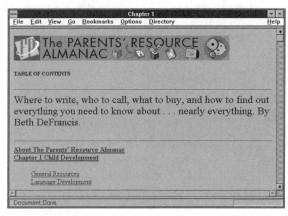

Figure 413 The Parents Resource Almanac.

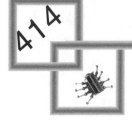

The *Peace in Pictures* Project

http://www.macom.co.il/peace/index.html

What does *peace* look like? Coming to you from Jerusalem, the "*Peace in Pictures* Project" is a game, contest, and collaboration that involves children from all over the world. "The *Peace in Pictures* Project" invites children of all ages to draw their impressions of peace. The project places these pictures on the Internet for people around the world to view and enjoy. Pictures uploaded thus far have titles like "The Hebrew soldiers and the American soldiers made friends," "The Soldiers are shaking hands and the people are hugging each other," "Everybody should hold hands and have peace," and "The soldiers should make friends and tell their other friends to make friends . . ." What does *peace* look like? Well, for one, it looks like this civilized and civilizing slice of cyberspace. Bravo.

Figure 414.1 Peace in Pictures.

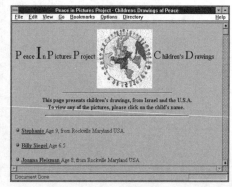

Figure 414.2 A few of the artists.

Pez Exhibit

http://www.best.com/~spectrum/pez/pezexhibit.html

Alright, I'm not really sure whether this site is cool or just weird. But in any event, I just couldn't pass it up. The opening screen includes a large group shot that contains virtually every Pez dispenser ever made. Below the group shot, extensive test keys give you the name of every dispenser, reading left to right by row. If you click on a dispenser's name or its image in the group shot, you get a closeup of that dispenser, further details about the character after which Pez modeled it, and distribution data. When I visited this site, I found some long out-of-date dispensers that I remember from my youth and haven't seen in more than thirty years.

Figure 415 Pez dispensers on parade.

Publications for Parents

http://www.ed.gov/pubs/parents.html

This site provides digital editions of several Department of Education publications, including the popular *Helping Your Child* series of pamphlets: *Helping Your Child Learn Math, Helping Your Child Learn to Read, Helping Your Child Learn History, Helping Your Child Get Ready for School, Helping Your Child Improve in Test Taking, Helping Your Child Learn to Write Well, Helping Your Child Use the Library, Helping Your Child Learn Geography,* and *Helping Your Child Learn Science*. You will also find *Preparing Your Child for College* which provides steps you can take throughout your son's or daughter's childhood and adolescence to prepare them for college (academically and financially).

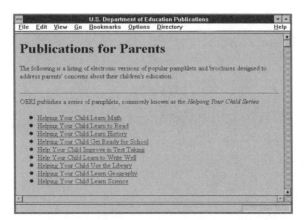

Figure 416 Literature to help you help your child.

417

Rain Forest Action Network

http://www.ran.org/ran/kids_action/index.html

This site lists several steps kids can take to protect endangered species and the rain forests. To name a few: 1) Don't let anyone in your family buy anything made of ivory, coral, reptile skins, tortoise shells, or cat pelts. 2) Ask your family not to buy tropical hardwoods unless they are certified as being from sustainable sources. 3) Choose cereals, cookies, and nuts made from rainforest products packaged by vendors who advertise their support for rainforest preservation. 4) Avoid fast-food hamburgers: the meat is likely from cattle raised on land that used to be rainforest. 5) Get everyone in your family to avoid buying products made by companies that destroy rainforests. I think that about says it.

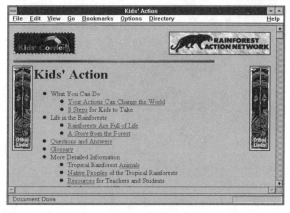

Figure 417 Kids saving the rainforest.

418

"60 Things to Do When Things Get a Little, um, Boring . . ."

http://www.tumyeto.com/tydu/foxy/60things.htm

Put lipstick on your cat. Eat a bug. Make kissy faces from the car window. Imagine the world without rubber cement. Change your name. Read a book about Sweden. Rent a movie with subtitles. Memorize the words to every Vanilla Ice song. Eat croutons. Talk with a British accent. Write a letter to someone you don't know. Laugh at everything. Tell the people next door you wish they would move. Visit the Pez exhibit on the Web. Write to Brian Wilson and tell him the Beach Boys were just a flash-in-the-pan. (After all, what have they done *lately*?) Teach a bear to ride a bike . . .

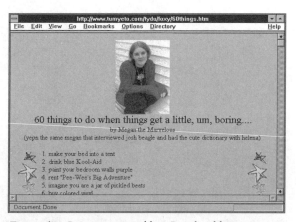

Figure 418 Paint your nose blue. Drink cold gravy.

The Song of Moses

http://www.digimark.net/iatech/books/guptoc.htm

Illustrated by Sharon Katz, Seymour Mayne's *The Song of Moses* offers novel readings and interpretations of such Biblical subjects as the stories of the golden calf, the blinding of Isaac, Noah and the great flood, and Adam and Eve in the Garden of Eden. Each chapter is a brief poem, albeit a prose poem. All the tales are from the Old Testament, and all are poignantly and beautifully expressed in language that shines new light into the previously dark corners of these ancient tales. This is not religious revisionism, but rather poetic expansion: rhapsodic variations on old and beautiful themes.

Figure 419 A new spin on Bible traditions.

Stage Hand Puppets

http://fox.nstn.ca/~puppets

"Stage Hand Puppets" is actually a commercial site (but a nice one) that sells child-oriented puppetry merchandise: puppets, puppet-making kits, puppet stages, books about puppetry, and so on. But there is some great free stuff here as well. For example, you can download (for free) paper patterns from which you can make puppets. Additionally, the site includes a great forum where kids can chat with other kids about their various puppet-related projects. You'll also find archives of information on making puppets from scrap materials, on the art of ventriloquism, and on Punch & Judy and other puppet traditions. While you are here, you may well want to check the commercial catalog because the wares are first rate.

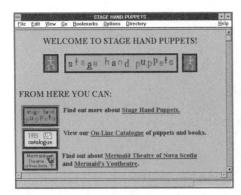

Figure 420.1 Puppets home page.

Figure 420.2 Great puppet projects.

Story Hour

http://ipl.sils.umich.edu/youth/StoryHour

At this site, you'll find three illustrated stories. The first, "Molly Whuppie," utilizes text, images, and a sound-file that contains a reading. Thus, the story takes about twenty-seven years to load, but is worth the wait. The remaining two stories are just straight text and illustrations, and load considerably faster. They are both very cute. "Do Spiders Live on the World Wide Web?" is an attempt to explain the Web to the very young. And "The Fishermen and His Wife" is a wonderful tale of separation and reunion. The books are brief and colorful—ideal for viewing by a toddler on your lap.

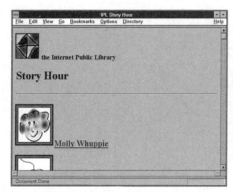

Figure 421.1 IPL's Story Hour.

Figure 421.2 A page from Do Spiders Live on the World Wide Web?

Summer Home Learning Recipes

http://www.ed.gov/pubs/Recipes

Want your kids to learn something during their summer vacation? Need some ways to inject learning into fun-starved, school-weary children? Then check out the great ideas at this site. I am talking about using excursions to the seashore to learn a little bit about oceanography and the environment or using hikes in the woods as an excuse to pick up some forestry knowledge. And how about a summer book-reading contest between competitive siblings? Whoever reads the most books by Labor Day gets . . . gets what? I don't know. Something cool. What other projects are good? How about putting together a family newspaper or a family journal of a vacation trip? Great concept. Great ideas.

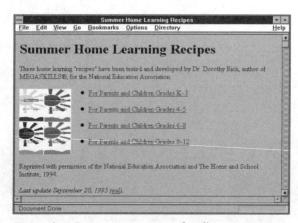

Figure 422 Great summer projects for all ages.

Theodore Tugboat

http://www.cochran.com/tt.html

The popular vessel of Canadian television, *Theodore Tugboat*, now has its own online activity center and homepage. Have your kids help Theodore decide what to do next in the wonderful interactive story (fully illustrated) that was custom-created for this Web site. Your child can also download pages from Theodore's online coloring book or register to receive a postcard signed by Theodore. You'll also find resources for parents and teachers, such as episode synopses and descriptions of the more than 30 characters that comprise Theodore's friends.

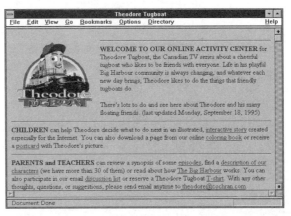

Figure 423 Great interactive fun with Theodore Tugboat.

Uncle Bob's Kids' Page

http://gagme.wwa.com/~boba/kids.html

Okay, so the first word in the site address is *gagme*. That doesn't mean anything. "Uncle Bob's Kids' Page" is still an excellent place on the Web. (In fact, *Point Survey* ranked it in the top 5% of all Web sites.) The links here could not be more extensive: unicycling, Sega Genesis, Sea World, ice sculpture, wooden toys, and even the "Michael Jordan Page," to name just a few. You also have links to the "Whale Watching Web," "Cool Word of the Day," "the Frisbee page," "Newton's Apple," "Mr. Potatohead," "Universal Cartoons," and many interactive Web games. So give Uncle Bob (that's Bob Allison, by the way) a break. He can't help it if he has an odd domain name.

Figure 424 You won't gag on this site.

Virtual Theater

http://www-ksl.stanford.edu/projects/cait/index.html

The Virtual Theater project provides a multimedia environment in which kids can play all roles associated with producing and performing plays and stories in an improvisational theater company. These roles include producer, playwright, casting director, set designer, music director, real-time director, and actor. In particular, in a typical production, animated actors perform the play in a multimedia set, all under the supervision of an automated "playmaster." Actors not only follow scripts and take interactive direction from the children, but also bring "life-like" qualities to their performances. For example, take note of the variability and idiosyncrasies in the actors' behavior. This is very wild. You *must* take a look.

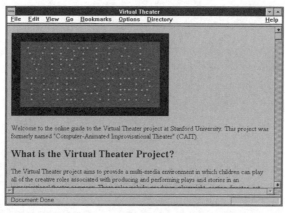

Figure 425 *The Virtual Theater.*

Wacky Web Tales

http://www.hmco.com/hmco/school/tales

This engaging spot in cyberspace is brought to you courtesy of Houghton Mifflin Publishing Company. At this site, you can experience seven different weird tales, each of them interactive. Here's how it works. First, you pick a story. Then, on an electronic form, you fill in the requested information, such as a boy's name, an adjective, a singular noun, a girl's name, a past tense verb, and so on. (If you like Mad-Libs, you'll love this site.) Finally, you run the story and it shapes and changes within the contours of the terms you prescribed. To see how vastly the same story can change, you can run it again with completely different terms.

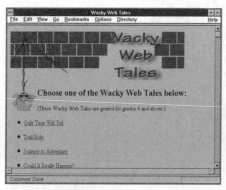 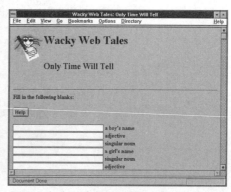

Figure 426.1 *Choose from seven stories.*   **Figure 426.2** *Then just fill in the blanks.*

Waking In Jerusalem

http://www.digimark.net/iatech/books/waketoc.htm

Recommended for children ages three to seven, Sharon Katz's *Waking In Jerusalem* is the story of a young boy who gets up before his parents and goes out to watch the city of Jerusalem wake for the day. Beautifully illustrated and written in brief lyrical prose, this digital book will delight both the young and the young-at-heart. The complete online version is a series of images, 10Kb-15Kb each, which combine the text and illustrations. Should you and your child enjoy the online edition of the book, you can order a bound copy for a nominal cost. Katherine, my four-year-old daughter, thoroughly enjoyed this book while Billy, my eight-year-old son, thought it was a snore. Thus, the publishers prescribed age group audience seems to be right on target.

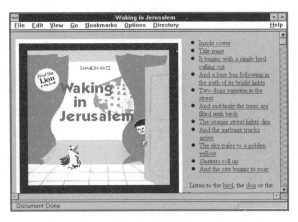

Figure 427 A beautiful tale of a town awakening.

The "Whole Frog" Dissection Project

http://george.lbl.gov/ITG.hm.pg.docs/Whole.Frog/Whole.Frog.html

Remember the ritual torture we suffered when our high school biology teachers made us dissect frogs? Well, this virtual dissection is a bit easier to endure. Thanks to 3-D surface and volume rendering, high-resolution MRI graphics, and mechanical sectioning, visitors to this site can explore a frog's anatomy without ever lifting a scalpel. Eventually, students will be able to enter the frog's virtual heart, fly down virtual blood vessels, and poke their heads out at any point to see the structure of surrounding anatomy. Cool. Is it lunchtime yet?

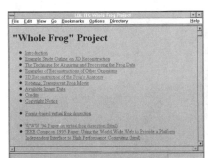 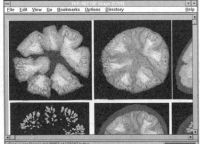 

Figure 428.1 The Whole Frog Project.   *Figure 428.2 MRI graphics.*   *Figure 428.3 A 3-D reconstruction.*

Wierenga Software Home Page

http://www.xmission.com/~wwwads/berts.html

From Australia comes a great collection of computer illustration and animation programs. Your kids will love *Bert's African Animals, Bert's Christmas, Bert's Dinosaurs, Bert's Prehistoric Animals,* and *Bert's Whales and Dolphins,* all of which your kids can color on your home PC screen. Little girls will enjoy *Rachel's Fashion Dolls.* And boys will go for *Peter's Warbirds,* which lets them color an array of fighter aircraft on the PC. All these programs come to you free, but they are shareware. So if your children try them, enjoy them, and continue to use them, you should pay whatever modest fee the shareware author requests. Of course, it's on the honor system, so let your conscience be your guide.

Figure 429 *Color the dinosaur on your computer.*

More Kidstuff & K-12 Education

As you surf the Web, you may find that one or more of the site addresses listed in this book have changed. In such cases, connect to Jamsa Press at http://www.jamsa.com and click on the icon that corresponds to the *1001 Really Cool Web Sites* book. Jamsa Press will list replacement addresses (when possible) for sites that have moved. In addition, you can also use the following site list as you search for stuff for kids or for educational resources:

Education	http://akebono.stanford.edu/yahoo/Education/
Educational Online Sources Front Door	http://archive.phish.net/eos1/
Kids' Stuff	http://crusher.bev.net:70/1/Schoolhouse/kids
The English Server	http://english-server.hss.cmu.edu/
APA Web Server	http://enterzone.berkeley.edu/
AskERIC Home Page	http://eryx.syr.edu/
Children (The Family)	http://galaxy.einet.net/galaxy/Community/The-Family/Children.html
Infants (The Family)	http://galaxy.einet.net/galaxy/Community/The-Family/Infants.html

Abbey's Web

http://www.abalon.se/beach/aw/abbey.html

Edward Abbey is the author of *Desert Solitaire* and more than ten other great books about nature, man, and the spiritual relationship between the two. He was born in 1927, and dropped out of Yale after two weeks of a graduate program, saying he hated the strictures of the Ivy League. In 1987, when offered the gold medal of the American Academy of Arts and Letters, he declined because he had plans to run a river in Idaho the week of the award ceremony. When he died in 1989, his friends transported his unembalmed body in the bed of a pickup truck to a spot in the desert near Saguaro National Monument in Arizona, where they had a beer-and-chili party and laid him in the ground according to his wishes. The tombstone he specified: "Edward Paul Abbey, 1927-1989, No comment."

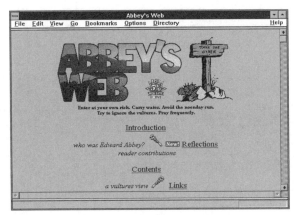

Figure 430 A site devoted to Edward Abbey.

The Academy of American Poets

http://www.he.net/~susannah/academy.htm

"To have great poets, there must be great audiences," Walt Whitman said to the more-or-less-unheeding ears of American educators in the 1880s. In 1934, The Academy of American Poets began to develop the audience that is necessary for great poets to thrive. Robert Penn Warren called the organization "ambitiously hopeful." And Stanley Kunitz has said, "I can think of no organization that has done more to foster, promote, and honor the poetry and poets of this country than The Academy of American Poets." To find out more, visit this informative Web site.

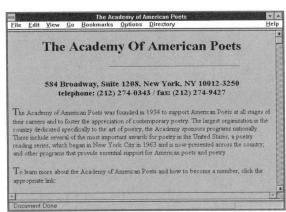

Figure 431 The on-line home of American poetry.

Jane Austen Information Page

http://uts.cc.utexas.edu/~churchh/janeinfo.html

The English novelist Jane Austen lived from 1775 to 1817. Her novels (which include *Pride and Prejudice, The Three Sisters*, and *Northanger Abbey*) are highly prized not only for their light irony, humor, and depiction of rural English life, but also for their underlying serious qualities of tension and moral confusion. This site has annotated hypertext editions of *Pride and Prejudice* and *Love and Friendship*, as well as straight (unannotated) HTML renderings of *Lady Susan, The Watsons, The Three Sisters, Frederic & Elfrida*, and *Northanger Abbey*. Additionally, you'll find a full biography of Jane Austen, several excellent drawings and paintings of Jane, the Austen family coat of arms, and a comprehensive bibliography of all writings by and about Austen. All this adds up to an excellent scholarly resource.

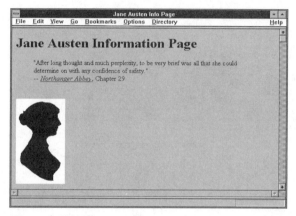

Figure 432 A silhouette of Jane greets you.

Author, Author

http://www.li.net/~scharf/author.html

Visit this site to access links to Web pages dedicated to the study and appreciation of well-known authors, such as Jane Austen (item 432), Tolkien, C.S. Lewis, Ernest Hemingway, F. Scott Fitzgerald, and Willa Cather. Additional links take you to resources concerning Nathaniel Hawthorne, Edith Wharton, Henry James, Owen Wister, Edna Ferber, Jack London, and Dubose Heyward. For most of these writers, you will find biographical information, comprehensive bibliographies, excerpts from their writings, guides to research materials, and portrait graphics.

Figure 433 The greatest collection of authors on the Web.

Bantam Doubleday Dell

http://www.bdd.com/

This homepage for one of the world's leading publishers, Bantam Doubleday Dell, offers you numerous options. View the publisher's catalog, examine books for young readers, access author interviews with the likes of John Grisham and Elmore Leonard, or complete the daily crossword puzzle. You can also check the schedules for tours and appearances of Bantam Doubleday Dell authors, participate in forums where you exchange views on various Bantam Doubleday Dell books with other readers, or browse new and forthcoming Bantam Doubleday Dell publications.

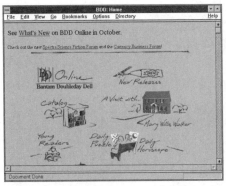

Figure 434.1 *The Web home of Bantam Doubleday Dell.*

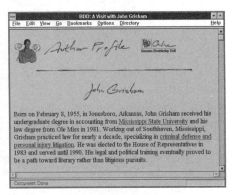

Figure 434.2 *An author profile.*

Banned Books On-Line

http://www.cs.cmu.edu/Web/People/spok/banned-books.html

Often, the books that end up on banned-book lists are great works of literary imagination. Just look at the masterpieces that have been ripped from bookstore and library shelves at various times: James Joyce's *Ulysses*, Voltaire's *Candide*, Mark Twain's *Huckleberry Finn*, Aristophanes' *Lysistrata*, Chaucer's *Canterbury Tales*, Whitman's *Leaves of Grass*, Pascal's *Provincial Letters*, and Rousseau's *Confessions*. Full digital texts of all these works and more are (thankfully) available here. In a town near my home, a teacher was recently fired from a high school for using a novel in her classroom that was "indecent" and, worse, dealt with homosexuality. The book was Gore Vidal's *The City and the Pillar*, a recognized classic. The fight against book banning and for freedom of speech is one that will never be over.

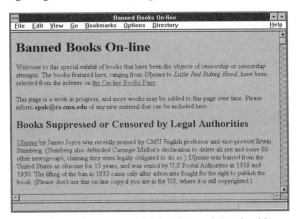

Figure 435 *Whenever any book is banned you should, on general principle, read it.*

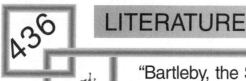

LITERATURE

"Bartleby, the Scrivener"

http://www.columbia.edu/acis/bartleby/bartleby.html

I call this luxury. A classic of American short fiction that I can call up on my computer screen with just a few keystrokes. I forget when I first read Melville's classic tale of a strange man in a dark back-office of lower Wall Street in the 1840s, but I suppose I may have been thirteen or fourteen. And I have loved it ever since. Bartleby is undoubtedly one of the most mysterious, tragic, and compelling characters Melville ever created.

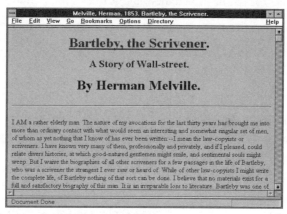

Figure 436 Melville's classic tale.

Madison Smartt Bell

http://www.goucher.edu/~mbell/

Imagine how pleased I was to discover that one of my favorite novelists has his own personal homepage. (Well, sort of personal. Goucher College, where Madison Smartt Bell is a writer-in-residence, maintains this page.) In addition to Bell's complete bibliography, you'll find selections from Bell's best books, including *All Soul's Rising* (1995), *Doctor Sleep* (1991), *Barking Man* (1990), and *Save Me, Joe Louis* (1993). As if that were not enough, you'll also find a copy of an unpublished short story entitled "Zigzag Wanderer." Other treats at this page: detailed information on the Goucher College Creative Writing Program (which is pretty good if Madison is involved) and links to Internet bookstores where you can purchase Madison's books.

Figure 437 If he's so smart, why doesn't he know how to spell it?

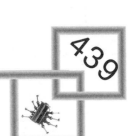

The Book Commons

http://www.bookport.com/welcome/piet

"The Book Commons" offers links to dozens of book-related sites, including the American Booksellers Association, *Publishers Weekly*, PIMA's resources for publishers, the Book Industry Study Group, and more. You also get connections to online e-text editions of classic and contemporary literature, links to publisher's homepages, and connections to literary journals and magazines available in digital form. If you love books, you can literally spend hours browsing through all these wonderful options, exploring reviews, excerpts, and interviews. You'll also find the links to author support resources, such as software tools for writers and online "Internet" book publicists you can hire.

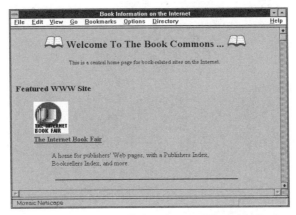

Figure 438 Check out all the options at The Book Commons.

BookWire

http://www.bookwire.com

"BookWire" bills itself as "the first place to look for book information on the World Wide Web." And friends, the billing is accurate—"BookWire" is an astonishingly fine resource. That "BookWire" made NetGuide's "Ultimate Hotlist" of the 50 best places to go online is no accident. "BookWire," wrote the NetGuide commentator, "demonstrates the natural affinity between book publishing and the Web. Be sure to show it to anyone who 1. scoffs at the future of the digital word, or 2. scoffs at the future of the printed word." At this site, you'll find many options, including a complete digital edition of *The Boston Book Review*, the BookWire Bestseller List Database, and the BookWire "Insider" (which offers the very latest news from the book publishing industry). Check it out.

Figure 439.1 A glorious place on the Web.

Figure 439.2 A new cartoon every day.

BookZone

http://ttx.com/bookzone/leaps.html

"BookZone" is a great set of links that embraces some arcane aspects of literature that the other sites tend to ignore. At this site, you'll find links for such esoteric areas as books about animals, antiquarian and rare books, audio books, literary awards, book clubs, comic books, history books, medical publishing, and pop-science. You'll also find links related to sports books, Sci-Fi, religious publishing, publishing industry employment, cookbooks, military resources, map and chart books, and that weird new age stuff (that's right, just call me Mr. Cynical).

Figure 440 *Take some literary leaps at the BookZone.*

British Poetry 1780-1910

http://www.lib.virginia.edu/etext/britpo/britpo.html

The University of Virginia's hypertext archive of scholarly editions incorporates works by Samuel Taylor Coleridge, Ann Batten Crystal, Richard Polwhele (including something called "The Unsex'd Females," 1798), Mary Robinson, and Dante Gabriel Rossetti. At this site, you'll also find Alfred Lord Tennyson's original manuscript for "The Charge of the Light Brigade" illuminated as a hypertext document, as well as hypertext editions of Oliver Goldsmith's "The Deserted Village," Andrew Marvell's *Miscellaneous Poems*, John Milton's *Paradise Lost* (1667), Sir Philip Sidney's "Defense of Poesie" (1595), Edmund Spenser's "Amoretti" and "Epithalamion," and Surrey's *Songs and Sonettes*. I congratulate the staff of the University of Virginia's Alderman Library on having created a wonderful tool for scholarship.

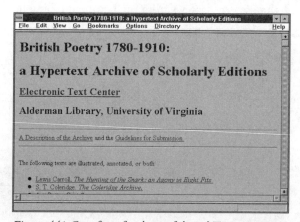

Figure 441 *Care for a few bytes of digital Tennyson?*

The William S. Burroughs InterNetWebZone

http://www.hyperreal.com/wsb/

A member of the Burroughs Business Machines family, William Seward Burroughs (born 1914) had, until recently, been best known for his novelizations of his experiences as a drug addict. These novels include *Junkie* (1953) and *The Naked Lunch* (Paris, 1959; New York, 1962). But Burrough's public image changed a year ago, when he appeared in television ads for Nike sneakers. (From the start, he seemed to me a strange choice for promoting anything associated with robust, healthy, outdoor physical achievement, but then I am too critical.) Long associated with the Beat movement, his bitter, existential tales include *The Exterminator* (1960), the *Soft Machine* (Paris, 1962), *Nova Express* (1964), and *The Wild Boys* (1971), a fantasy about revolutionary homosexuals. You'll find the entire scoop here.

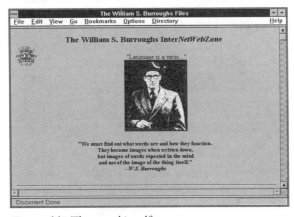

Figure 442 *The man himself.*

The Beat Generation

http://www.charm.net/~brooklyn/LitKicks.html

Speaking of the Beat writers, check out this huge collection of information. Levi Asher has created an invaluable archive of photographs, criticism, and text related to Jack Kerouac, Allen Ginsberg, Neal Cassady, William S. Burroughs, Gary Snyder, Lawrence Ferlinghetti, Gregory Corso, and Michael McClure. Also, you'll find pages of information on such topics as films about the Beats, the Beat connections in rock music, Buddhism (the Beat religion), and the origin of the term *Beat*. To top it all off, Mr. Asher has amassed a Beat bibliography with up-to-the-minute news briefs.

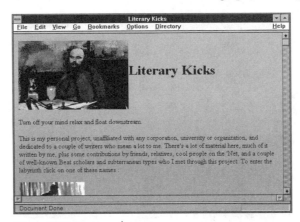

Figure 443 *Kerouac & company.*

The Blake Multimedia Project

http://luigi.calpoly.edu/Marx/Blake/Blakeproject.html

"The Blake Multimedia Project" operates on the (correct) assumption that William Blake, who lived two hundred years ago, was a multimedia artist. A gifted prose and poetry stylist and talented visual artist, Blake combined text with images to create works with powerful impact. At this site, you'll witness how multimedia liberates Blake's works and lets them enter their own proper medium. As David Erdman writes in "The Blake Multimedia Project," "we are learning at last to read Blake's pictorial language: to read its hieroglyphics, to see, hear, to follow its choreography, its music, its mental drama . . . to put fully into practice the dawning realization that all Blake's languages are one."

Figure 444 Blake's stunning illustrations and prose.

Lewis Carroll Home Page

http://www.students.uiuc.edu/~jbirenba/carroll.html

This site contains the Web's best list of resources on Lewis Carroll. Whether you are looking for Lewis Carroll organizations, worldwide events, bibliographies, research articles, graphics, or texts, this site is your launch pad to the other side of the looking-glass in cyberspace. Additionally, you can join in the compelling, ongoing forum discussion of an important question: are Carroll's children's books relevant to the youth of today? Feel free to come here with any opinions, or with empirical evidence (i.e., a 7 year old I know read *Alice in Wonderland* and said . . .). Additional tidbits include a biography of Carroll as mathematician and a vignette about Carroll and Queen Victoria.

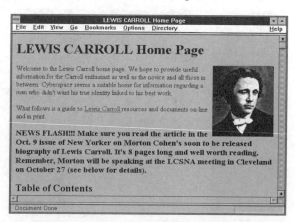

Figure 445 Point and click through the looking glass.

City Lights Publishers & Booksellers

http://town.hall.org/places/city_lights/

For several decades now, City Lights has clung steadfastly to the editorial fringe, always willing to publish the editorially dispossessed: the new, radical, experimental writers of each generation who, in pushing the edges of the creative envelope further than they've been pushed before, are generally not attractive to most mainstream publishers. Thus, the tradition of City Lights is one of advocacy, as well as publication. City Lights is committed to Ezra Pound's uncompromising dictum, "Make it new." The result: an eclectic list of publications well worth sampling.

Figure 446 The little logo guy perpetually waving for help.

The Devil's Dictionary

http://www.vestnett.no/cgi-bin/devil

"Edible, adj. Good to eat, and wholesome to digest, as a worm to a toad, a toad to a snake, a snake to a pig, a pig to a man, and a man to a worm." Thus runs the tone of the many witty, concise definitions in Ambrose Bierce's *The Devil's Dictionary*, first published as *The Cynic's Word Book* (1906) and retitled in 1911. What makes the definitions entertaining is that they reflect Bierce's profound sense of skepticism, pessimism, and irony. Bitter Bierce, as he was called, authored many other works, including the classic collection of stories entitled *Tales of Soldiers and Civilians* (1891). In 1913, Bierce announced that he was tired of American civilization. He bought a horse and wagon and drove into the heart of war-torn Mexico to seek "the good, kind darkness." No one knows what became of him.

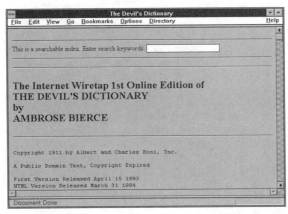

Figure 447 Bierce's bitter masterwork.

LITERATURE

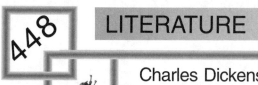

Charles Dickens

http://www.wonderland.org/Works/Charles-Dickens/

At this site, you'll find hypertext editions of three Dickens novels: *Great Expectations*, *A Christmas Carol*, and *The Chimes*. Through the years, who hasn't loved *A Christmas Carol* with its noble and direct message of compassion and generosity? On the novel's first page, Dickens made his didactic mission clear: "I have endeavored," he wrote, "in this Ghostly little book, to raise the Ghost of an Idea, which shall not put my readers out of humor with themselves, with each other, with the season, or with me. May it haunt their houses pleasantly, and no one wish to lay it." And, since 1843, when the "ghostly" little story took England by storm, the book has been a fundamental part of the tradition, spirit, and meaning of every Christmas.

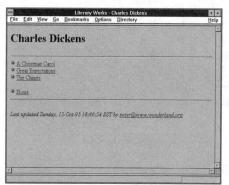

Figure 448.1 Your three splendid options.   *Figure 448.2 The holiday classic.*

Poems by Emily Dickinson

http://ww.columbia.edu/acis/bartleby/dickinson

She squints out at us from her photograph across the long decades. She is a strange, enigmatic woman. Wonderfully gifted and pathetically alone in a cosmic and spiritual, yet personal, sense, she dares us to match her gaze. And her poems dare us to contemplate, to encounter, and to joust with the riddles of man, spirit, and mind. At this site, you'll find Dickinson's "Belle of Amherst," which you may search by title or by opening line. And don't those opening lines say much about the nature of the poems they launch? A few of these openers: "Forbidden fruit a flavor has." "A word is dead." "My life closed twice before its close." "Hope is a subtle glutton." "Heaven is what I cannot reach."

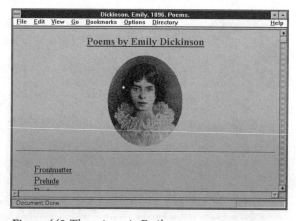

Figure 449 The enigmatic Emily.

Elements of Style

http://www.columbia.edu/acis/bartleby/strunk/

For decades, William Strunk Jr. and E.B. White's *Elements of Style* has been the touchstone reference and guide for writing well in English. Strunk and White's principles of composition are as true today as they ever were: use the active voice. Put statements in positive form. Omit needless words. Avoid a succession of loose sentences. Express coordinate ideas in similar form. Keep related words together. In summaries, keep to one tense. These simple guidelines alone will increase the quality of anyone's prose tenfold. Additionally, this hypertext edition of *Elements of Style* is a brilliant example of navigable HTML 3.0, which makes this site something of a style guide for HTML.

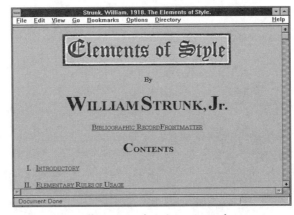

Figure 450 William Strunk, Jr.'s masterguide.

English Literary History

http://muse.jhu.edu/journals/elh/index.html

The Johns Hopkins University Press publishes *ELH,* the *Journal of English Literary History* online annually. Recent articles include Deirdre Coleman's "Conspicuous Consumption: White Abolitionism and English Women's Protest Writing in the 1790s," Talia Schaffer's "A Wilde Desire Took Me: the Homoerotic History of *Dracula*," and Mara H. Fein's "The Politics of Family in *The Pickwick Papers*." For a little bit of weirdness, look into "Eaten Alive: Slavery and Celebrity in Antebellum America." Also, check out Theodore B. Leinwand's "Redeeming beggary/buggery" (it is about time!) and Maureen Harkin Mackenzie's "Man of Feeling: Embalming Sensibility."

Figure 451 A great journal from Johns Hopkins.

Fiction

http://english-www.hss.cmu.edu/fiction.html

At this site, you'll find a long list of fiction resources embracing *hundreds* of options: author pages, e-texts, criticism, and scholarly journals. Just a few of the novels you can access from "Fiction" via Gopher: *Frankenstein, A Connecticut Yankee in King Arthur's Court, The Call of the Wild,* and *Uncle Tom's Cabin.* Authors represented include Louisa May Alcott, Nathaniel Hawthorne, Ambrose Bierce, Willa Cather, the Bronte sisters, Thackeray, Dickens, Oscar Wilde, Wilkie Collins, Owen Wister, Henry James, Edith Wharton, William Dean Howells, and Washington Irving. You'll also find links to author's organizations, fiction magazines, and novelist's and short story writer's homepages.

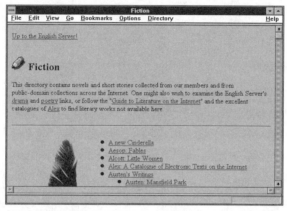

Figure 452 Find a long list of resources below the plume.

William Faulkner on the Web

http://www.mcsr.olemiss.edu/~egjbp/faulkner/library.html

From Faulkner's hometown of Oxford, Mississippi, this site includes criticism, interviews, and e-texts of Faulkner's novels and short stories. You can also hear the greatest speech ever made: Faulkner's Nobel Prize Address of December 10, 1950, penned just a few years after the creation of the atomic bomb. "I decline to accept the end of man," he wrote. " . . . [Man] is immortal, not because he alone among creatures has an inexhaustible voice, but because he has a soul, a spirit capable of compassion and sacrifice and endurance. The poet's, the writer's duty is to write about these things. It is his privilege to help man endure by lifting his heart, by reminding him of the courage and honor and hope and pride and compassion and pity and sacrifice which have been the glory of his past. The poet's voice need not merely be the record of man, it can be one of the props, the pillars to help him endure and prevail."

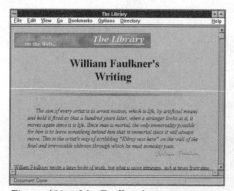

Figure 453.1 Mr. Faulkner's page.

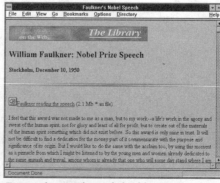

Figure 453.2 The Nobel address.

HarperCollins Publishers

http://www.harpercollins.com

J & J Harper was founded in New York in 1817. In 1832, the firm published the first American edition of *The Swiss Family Robinson*. In 1848, with a name change to Harper & Brothers, the firm introduced Thackeray to American readers. The firm launched *Harper's New Monthly Magazine* in 1850, *Harper's Weekly* in 1857, and *Harper's Bazaar* in 1867. The firm signed Mark Twain in 1895. In 1917, Harper began publishing Edna St. Vincent Millay. In 1932, Harper discovered Laura Ingalls Wilder and her *Little House* books. In 1937, Harper simultaneously published Thomas Wolfe's *The Web and the Rock* and *You Can't Go Home Again*. Next stop, 1952: E.B. White's *Charlotte's Web*. 1956: Kennedy's *Profiles in Courage*. 1963: Maurice Sendak's *Where the Wild Things Are*. 1976: Solzhenitsyn's *The Gulag Archipelago*. 1994: A name change to HarperCollins. And coming in 1997: another milestone—my book *Hitting the Line Hard: Theodore Roosevelt, His Family and Their Circle During the First World War*. Yes!

Figure 454.1 The HarperCollins home page.

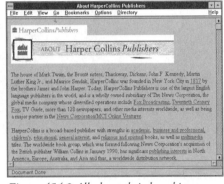

Figure 454.2 All about their long history.

The Odysseys of Homer

http://www.columbia.edu/acis/bartleby/chapman

At this site, you'll find a digital copy of the 1865 edition of George Chapman's classic 1614-16 translation of *The Odysseys of Homer*. "The Editor of the present volumes has the great gratification of being the first to restore to light a noble work which has been lying dormant for nearly two centuries," reads the 1865 edition's introduction. Coleridge, in a letter to Wordsworth, said he thought Chapman's version of *The Odyssey* finer than his *Iliad*, but Coleridge also preferred *The Odyssey* as literature. "He told us," remembered Mr. Payne Collier, "that he liked *The Odyssey*, as a mere story, better than *The Iliad*; *The Odyssey* was the oldest and finest romance that has ever been written." And it still is.

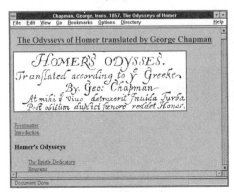

Figure 455.1 Not Homer Simpson.

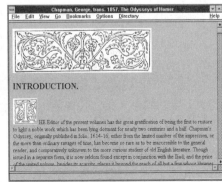

Figure 455.2 The introduction.

LITERATURE

Hungry Mind Review

http://www.iw.net/~mind/Review/index.html

Hungry Mind Review (HMR) is a quarterly book review founded in 1986 and distributed in more than 600 independent bookstores around the country. "HMR On-Line" offers a range of literary features, including biweekly reviews of books just published; selected reviews, essays, and interviews from back issues of the magazine; discussion areas on reading, writing, politics, and culture; and engaging articles on literary themes by such writers as E. Annie Proux, Quentin Crisp, and Kathleen Norris. Every edition of both *Hungry Mind Review* and "HMR On-Line" is profusely and beautifully illustrated with custom woodcuts, making for a very appealing look and feel.

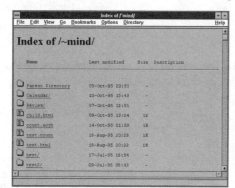

Figure 456.1 Scroll through Hungry Mind's home.

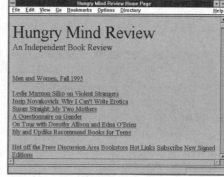

Figure 456.2 A book review.

The Search for Hyperfiction

http://is.rice.edu/~riddle/hyperfiction.html

Interested in postmodern narrative forms, Professor Edith Wyschogrod of the Department of Religious Studies, Rice University, started this project to study examples of interactive hypertext fiction on the Net. "It took quite a bit of looking before I found very much (interactive hypertext)," she writes. "There is plenty of postmodern fiction on the Net but it's mostly linear text . . . There is plenty of hypertext around but it's mostly nonfiction." What you'll find at "The Search for Hyperfiction" is the valuable result of Dr. Wyschogrod's sleuthing—a rich selection of links to genuine, honest-to-gosh hypertext fiction. This fiction includes *Adventures in the Great OutThere*, *The Book of Endings*, *The Doomsday Brunette*, *Girl Birth Water Death*, and, of course, Stuart Moulthrop's *Victory Garden*.

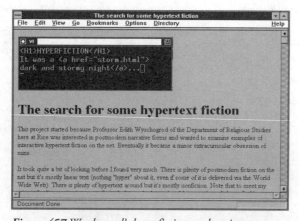

Figure 457 Wyschogrod's hyperfiction explorations.

James Joyce in Cyberspace: Work in Progress

http://astro.ocis.temple.edu/~callahan/joyce.html

Wouldn't James Joyce have loved hypertext? Imagine what he would have done with it. Conceived and maintained by R.L. Callahan of Temple University, "Work in Progress" is a constellation of resources available to enthusiasts and scholars of the work of James Joyce (Irish novelist and short story writer). At this site, you can browse through a hypertext journal of Joyce criticism, *Hypermedia Joyce Studies*, whose editorial board includes some of the most distinguished figures in Joycean scholarship. Another nice option: if you were unable to get to Dublin for Bloomsday, you can take a virtual tour of Joycean locations.

Figure 458 Yet another great Irish genius.

The Poetical Works of John Keats

http://www.columbia.edu/acis/bartleby/keats/

John Keats (1795-1821), a central figure of the Romantic Period in English literature, is one of the great British poets. I doubt that any undergraduate has gone through the basic English survey course work without reading Keats' "Hyperion," "Ode on a Grecian Urn," and "Ode to a Nightingale." Matthew Arnold commended Keats' "intellectual and spiritual passion" for beauty. This site contains virtually every poem Keats ever penned. In addition, you'll enjoy nice graphics and engravings from various editions of Keats' work. Among the fun stuff by Keats is the parody "Imitation of Spenser," the suggestive "To Some Ladies," and the strangely contemporary "Ode to Psyche."

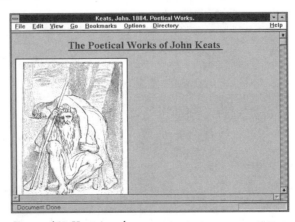

Figure 459 Keats in cyberspace.

Jack Kerouac

http://www.charm.net/~brooklyn/People/JackKerouac.html

Greenwich Village, 1948: Woody Guthrie and Jack Kerouac sit in a bar, drinking excessively with a number of people. Guthrie, the vagabond folksinger, has just published his autobiography *Bound for Glory*. The topic of Guthrie's book comes up. "Guthrie's not a writer. He's just a folksinger," Kerouac scoffs loud enough for Guthrie to hear. "He's not like me. I'm a poet, like Rimbaud." Guthrie breaks his guitar over Kerouac's head. And the fight that you'd expect to ensue, does. A friend of Guthrie's, who witnessed the event, told me this story. You won't find it at the Web site.

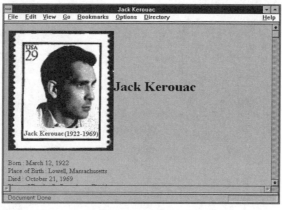

Figure 460 On the cyber-road with Kerouac.

Stephen King: *Umney's Last Case*

http://www.eunet.sk/king/king-intro.html

"It was one of those spring mornings so L.A.-perfect you keep expecting to see that little trademark symbol—®—stamped on it somewhere. The exhaust of the vehicles passing on Sunset smelled faintly of oleander, the oleander was lightly perfumed with exhaust, and the sky overhead was as clear as a hardshell Baptist's conscience. Peoria Smith, the blind paperboy, was standing in his accustomed place on the corner of Sunset and Laurel, and if that didn't mean God was in His heaven and all was jake with the world, I didn't know what did." So begins King's *Umney's Last Case*, a complete novella that appeared first on the Web before publication in print edition. The book is not one of King's supernatural adventures, but rather a straight L.A. down-and-out detective story. Give it a try. The price is right: free.

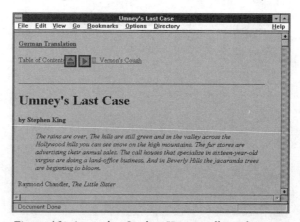

Figure 461 A complete Stephen King novella on-line.

Kipling: "The White Man's Burden" and Its Critics

http://web.syr.edu/~fjzwick/kipling/whiteman.html

Published in February of 1899, the Kipling poem "The White Man's Burden" appeared at a critical moment in the debate about imperialism in the United States. The Philippine-American War was raging, and the U.S. had just taken title to Cuba, Puerto Rico, and Guam as spoils from the Spanish-American War. Imperialists within the U.S. seized on the phrase "white man's burden" as a euphemism that justified imperialism as a noble enterprise. Anti-imperialists responded with parodies of the poem. In 1901, two years after the war in the Philippines, the anti-imperialist Mark Twain remarked: "The White Man's Burden has been sung. Who will sing the Brown Man's?" This page includes Kipling's poem, the parodies and editorials it inspired, and a well-reasoned analysis of all these things.

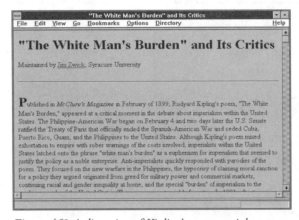

Figure 462 A discussion of Kipling's controversial poem.

The Knopf Publishing Group

http://www/randomhouse.com/knopf/index.html

This wonderful page introduces you to all the activities and imprints of the Knopf Publishing Group, including Knopf (founded by Alfred Knopf in 1915), Schocken Books (founded by Salman Schocken in Germany in 1933), Vintage Books (the paperback line created by Knopf in 1954), and Everyman's Library (initiated in 1905 by British publisher Joseph Malaby Dent, who aimed to provide the common man with well-produced, inexpensive editions of classics and other worthy books). One book this site features is Nicholas Negroponte's excellent *Being Digital*, which is particularly interesting to Web surfers, who are themselves very busy being digital.

Figure 463.1 The Knopf Publishing Group.

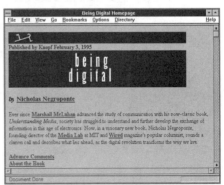

Figure 463.2 Being Digital.

Leaves of Grass

http://www.columbia.edu/acis/bartleby/whitman/

Hearing Walt Whitman sing "the body electric" in a digital edition of *Leaves of Grass* seems somehow appropriate. This site includes the complete text of the final deathbed edition of *Leaves*, an engine you can use to search the poems by titles and first lines, a biographical note on Walt Whitman, and a great gallery of images that includes Walt Whitman photographs and covers of various editions of his book. I like Whitman because the subject of my first book, the naturalist John Burroughs, was Whitman's friend for thirty years. Burroughs was one of Whitman's great defenders and the author of the first book-length study of Whitman ever published.

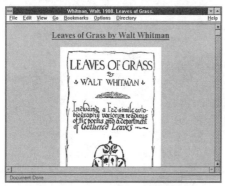

Figure 464.1 Whitman's masterpiece.

Figure 464.2 The many faces of Walt Whitman.

C.S. Lewis: Servant of Maleldil

http://www.scar.utoronto.ca/~94mcneim/100.html

If your knowledge of C.S. Lewis is limited to Anthony Hopkins' portrayal of him in Richard Attenborough's 1993 film *Shadowlands*, you may want to visit this Web page to learn something about Lewis the "Inkling" novelist, intellectual, and passionate spiritual journeyer. Like his fellow Inklings (J.R.R. Tolkien and Charles Williams among them), Lewis firmly endorsed the Augustinian view that evil cannot create, only corrupt. This thought lies at the heart of Lewis' classic *Chronicles of Narnia*. For the games-inclined, this site includes a link to something Lewis could never have imagined, the Narnia MUSH. You'll also, of course, find links to a complete Lewis bibliography, to some great online Lewis criticism, and to GIF-file photographs of Lewis, his friends, and family.

Figure 465.1 Illustration from Narnia.

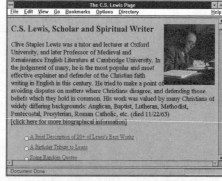

Figure 465.2 Discussing Lewis as a Christian voice.

Life and Works of Herman Melville

http://www.melville.org/melville.htm

An anecdote from Lewis Mumford: while working on a biography of Melville in the 1920s, Mumford interviewed Melville's elderly daughter, Eleanor Metcalf. Symbolic of the tension that existed between Melville, his work, and his family, his daughter had but one requirement before she would consent to an interview: under no circumstances was Mumford to mention Melville's name! This site contains links to complete electronic texts for most of Melville's more popular books (including *Moby Dick* and *Billy Budd*), estimates of Melville's writing from his contemporaries and from latter-day critics, a complete bibliography, observations of Melville by friends and family members, and even Melville's brief obituary notices (remember, Melville died in obscurity).

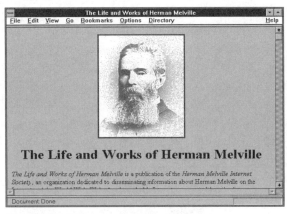

Figure 466 The creator of Moby Dick.

W.W. Norton & Company

http://www.wwnorton.com

W.W. Norton is the publisher of my friend Bill McFeely, author of the great *Frederick Douglass* and the Pulitzer Prize-winning *Grant: A Biography*. Additionally, Norton serves as publisher for Stephen Jay Gould, Peter Gay, Jonathan Spence, Christopher Lasch, and George F. Kennan, among others. Norton is also one of the few major houses to maintain a strong poetry list. Their poets include National Book Award winners Adrienne Rich and A.R. Ammons, as well as America's poet laureate, Rita Dove. Founded in 1923, Norton has published the likes of Bertrand Russell, Paul Henry Lang, and Sigmund Freud. To find out more about W.W. Norton & Company, visit this Web site.

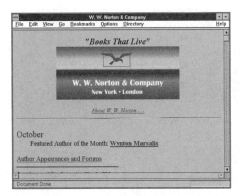 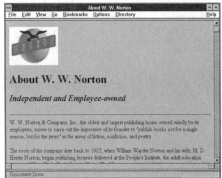

Figure 467.1 The Norton home page.   *Figure 467.2 A look at Norton's history.*

Walker Percy WWWsite

http://sunsite.unc.edu/wpercy

Alabama-born existentialist Walker Percy gave up a career in medicine in order to pursue a life in literature. Percy's first novel, *The Moviegoer*, won the National Book Award in 1961. His other books include *The Last Gentleman* (1966), *Love in the Ruins* (1971), *Lancelot* (1977), *The Second Coming* (1980), and *The Message in the Bottle* (1975). At this site, you'll find interviews, criticism, trivia, memoirs, GIFs, and symposiums designed to spotlight Percy's "critical perspective on the human crisis in the late 20th-century." This Web site comes to you courtesy of the University of North Carolina, Chapel Hill, which is the repository for the Walker Percy Papers.

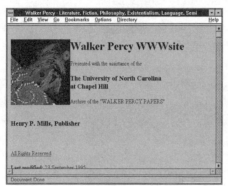

Figure 468.1 The Walker Percy page.

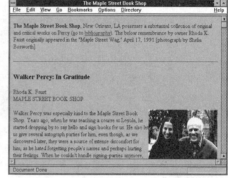

Figure 468.2 A personal memoir of Percy.

The Poe Page

http://138.232.92.2/sg/poe/poe.html

Who was stranger: Poe or the characters he created in his macabre poems and stories? Tough call. Dark and mysterious, Poe was 27 when he married his thirteen-year-old cousin in 1836. Soon after, he began composing his *Tales of the Grotesque and Arabesque*, which included "Ligeia" and "The Conqueror Worm." But Poe's descent into the macabre was only beginning. Soon he wrote "The Murders in the Rue Morgue," "Ascent into the Maelstrom," and "The Masque of the Red Death." We know that Poe attempted suicide at least once, experimented with drugs, and nursed a drinking problem through most of his adult life. We also know that Poe died penniless in Baltimore in 1849. Come to the "Poe Page" for more details on Poe's work, life, and times. Of course, you'll also find his complete works (prose, poems, and essays) in digital editions, searchable by title.

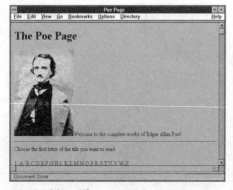

Figure 469.1 The strange Mr. Poe.

Figure 469.2 The Sleeper.

Poetry: 19th Century American Poetry

http://www.voyagerco.com/CD/ph/p.ampoetry.html

Want a chill to go down your spine? Listen to Allan Gurganus read Paul Laurence Dunbar's "When Malindy Sings." Or try Stanley Crouch reading "Casey at the Bat," or Cynthia Ozick matched with Poe's "The Conqueror Worm," or Garrison Keillor reciting some of Whitman's *Leaves of Grass*. Get all these sound files, plus screen-shots, hypertext pages, and biographical background on each poet and reader in this great online demo of Voyager's CD-ROM *American Poetry: The Nineteenth Century*. What else is here? Let's see. Melville's *Clarel*. Dickinson's "Vast Prairies of Air." Emma Lazarus' "In Exile." And works by Emerson, Bryant, Longfellow, Whittier, and Edith Wharton.

Figure 470 Hear great writers read great poets.

The Bertrand Russell Archives

http://www.mcmaster.ca/russdocs/russell.htm

Earl Bertrand Russell (1873-1970) was a leading British philosopher, mathematician, reformer, and pacifist. Widely known to the general public through his highly publicized campaigns for women's suffrage and world peace, Russell wrote many books and received the Nobel Prize for literature. Maintained by McMaster University in Canada, where the Bertrand Russell papers reside, this site includes Russell's correspondence, manuscripts, photographs, and a comprehensive directory to the entire Russell collection.

Figure 471 The Bertrand Russell Archives.

The Shakespeare Web

http://www.shakespeare.com

"The Shakespeare Web" is an interactive, hypermedia environment dedicated to increasing the popular understanding of Shakespeare's plays and poetry. At this site, you'll find extensive links to bibliographies and Shakespeare trivia contests; an extremely amusing feature entitled "Today in Shakespeare History;" and a fascinating work-in-progress: an in-depth, fully documented, and comprehensively annotated hypertext edition of all of Shakespeare's work. The first play to go online is *Twelfth Night*. Watch the document take shape and suggest improvements. Cool!

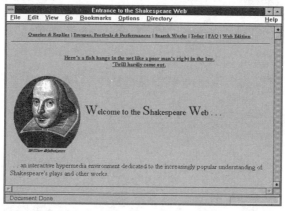

Figure 472 The indomitable Will.

George Bernard Shaw

http://wwwvms.utexas.edu/~edward/shaw.html

This page contains an essay summarizing the life and work of one of our greatest dramatists, wits, and social critics, George Bernard Shaw (1856-1950). Like most geniuses, Shaw was of Irish descent :-). Best known for the plays *Man and Superman* (1903), *Major Barbara* (1907), *Pygmalion* (1913), and *Heartbreak House* (1919), Shaw was also a social radical of some distinction. He attacked conventional morality routinely and gleefully, calling for free sex, open marriages, women's suffrage, birth control, and pacifism. The fact that he didn't drink and was an avowed vegetarian probably contributed to his longevity. Ninety-four when he died, Shaw was spry and active right up to the end.

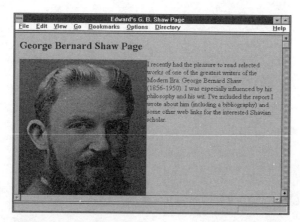

Figure 473 The Shaw page.

Complete Poetical Works of Percy Bysshe Shelley

http://www.columbia.edu/acis/bartleby/shelley

Percy Bysshe Shelley (1792-1822) got off to a rough start. His pamphlet, *The Necessity of Atheism,* resulted in his expulsion from Oxford. After his first marriage to Harriet Westbrook fell apart, Shelley ran away to Italy with two step-sisters, Mary Godwin and Claire Clairmont. Both women loved him, but he wound up marrying Mary, who would later write the novel *Frankenstein, or the Modern Prometheus* (1818). Settling in Italy, Shelley remained a radical, as the title of one of his books of poems (*The Mask of Anarchy*) suggests. He died in a boating accident, well before his time at age thirty. Visit this site to find the massive poetic output of Shelley's brief, passionate life.

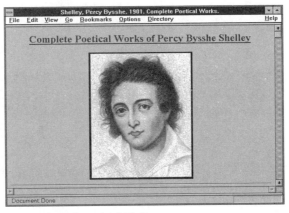

Figure 474 The radical Shelley.

CyberSaunter with Henry David Thoreau

http://umsa.umd.edu/thoreau/

Still under construction, this site holds great promise. As soon as you access it, you are greeted by one of the best Thoreau photographs I have ever seen. He looks straight-on, his earnest eyes connecting with yours. At this site, you'll find details on Thoreau's life and works, the facts surrounding his retreat to Walden Pond, a survey of his relatives and their involvement in his life, a description of his friends and love interests, a consideration of his formal education, and the history of his employment. You'll also find an image library containing GIFs of Thoreau, Concord, Walden Pond, and people who knew Thoreau, such as Franklin Sanborn, Ralph Waldo Emerson, and others.

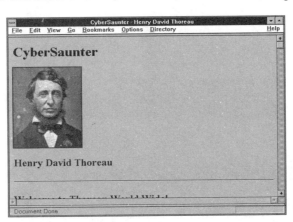

Figure 475 A cybersaunter with Thoreau.

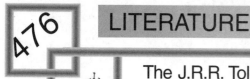

The J.R.R. Tolkien Information Page

http://www.math.uni-hamburg.de/.relippert/tolkien/rootpage.html

John Ronald Reuel Tolkien (1892-1973) is the author of *The Hobbit* (1937) and *The Lord of the Rings* (1954-57), both of them fantasies set in an imaginary Middle Earth peopled by hobbits and other strange races. Visit this site to learn more about Tolkien and the world he created. In addition to links to other Tolkien sites around the world, you'll find bibliographies, links to Tolkien societies on four continents, discussions of movies made from Tolkien's works, links to Tolkien newsgroups and Middle Earth language resources, and even links to Middle Earth MUSHes and MUDs!

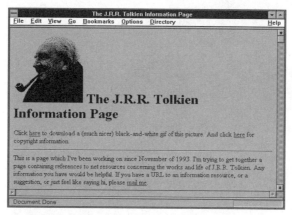

Figure 476 Tolkien with his trademark pipe.

Ever the Twain Shall Meet

http://www.lm.com/~joseph/mtwain.html

"Ever the Twain Shall Meet" provides you with online versions of several classic Mark Twain stories, including *The Adventures of Huckleberry Finn, The Tragedy of Pudd'nhead Wilson, What is Man and Other Essays, A Connecticut Yankee in King Arthur's Court*, and *The Adventures of Tom Sawyer*. Additional links bring you to downloadable zip files of *Tom Sawyer Abroad; Tom Sawyer, Detective; The Prince and The Pauper*; and *A Tramp Abroad*. You'll even find links to an exhaustive bibliography and GIF portraits of Twain. Rumor has it that more Twain texts are coming to the Web soon, including *Life on the Mississippi*, "The Man Who Corrupted Hadleyburg," and Twain's autobiography.

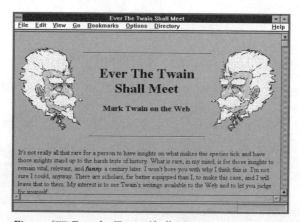

Figure 477 Ever the Twain Shall Meet.

Poems by Oscar Wilde

http://www.columbia.edu/acis/bartleby/wilde/

Is there any more tragic figure among American authors than Oscar Wilde? Ironically, his tragedy inspired much of his great later poetry—he turned his downfall, as he did all things, into high art. This site houses a complete collection of Wilde's poems, including those he composed in prison, his erotic verse, and his religious mediations. You'll also find poems from Helas, including "Sonnet to Liberty" and "Louis Napoleon." Search by poem title or via the index of first lines. I have recently finished reading Richard Ellman's master biography of Wilde and unreservedly recommend it to anyone who wants to learn more about this troubled genius.

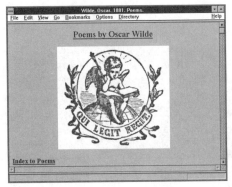

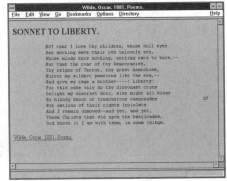

Figure 478.1 Search by titles or first lines.   *Figure 478.2 Sonnet to Liberty.*

William Wordsworth

http://www.columbia.edu/acis/bartleby/wordsworth

One of the great excursions in life is to visit the Lake District in central England, reading William Wordsworth's poems as you hike through the still beautiful (thank God) countryside. Wordsworth lived a life of "plain living and high thinking," composing romantic appreciations of his time and his place. At this site, you can read Wordsworth's poems in electronic editions, searchable by first lines and by poem titles. As an added bonus, for those who would like to travel step-by-step with Wordsworth in his development as a poet, the poems appear chronologically in the database.

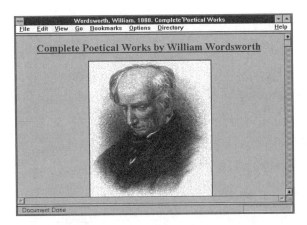

Figure 479 Romantic poet of the Lake District.

MUSIC

More Literature

As you surf the Web, you may find that one or more of the site addresses listed in this book have changed. In such cases, connect to Jamsa Press at http://www.jamsa.com and click on the icon that corresponds to the *1001 Really Cool Web Sites* book. Jamsa Press will list replacement addresses (when possible) for sites that have moved. In addition, you can also use the following site list as you search for information on literature:

The Ohio Literacy Resource Center	http://archon.educ.kent.edu/index.html
Thesaurus Linguarum Hiberniae	http://curia.ucc.ie/curia/menu.html
The Good Reading Guide - Index	http://julmara.ce.chalmers.se/SF_archive/SFguide/
Search SF & Fantasy reviews	http://julmara.ce.chalmers.se/stefan/WWW/saifai_search.html
Cambridge University Sci-Fi Society	http://myrddin.chu.cam.ac.uk/cusfs/
Charlie's Virtual Anthology	http://sf.www.lysator.liu.se/sf_archive/sub/Charles_Stross/index.html
The Commonplace Book	http://sunsite.unc.edu/ibic/Commonplace-Book.html
WorldWideWeb Virtual Library: Literature	http://sunsite.unc.edu/ibic/IBIC-homepage.html
Arthur C. Clarke Award Winners	http://thule.mt.cs.cmu.edu:8001/sf-clearing-house/awards/acc.html

480

The American Music Center

http://www.amc.net/amc/index.html

"The American Music Center"—a non-profit enterprise underwritten by the Lila-Wallace Reader's Digest Fund—has it all for professional musicians and composers. Want to know about grants, competitions, contracts, and rights agreements? Or maybe you need a list of composer organizations? Perhaps you're a jazz buff and need information on management and booking agencies. You'll find the answers at this site. The Center maintains a circulating collection of more than 55,000 scores and recordings, renders repertoire selection assistance, and maintains a database of works sorted by instrumentation, composers, and musical categories. The resources of information available at this site are mind-boggling!

Figure 480 AMC Jazz information.

The Band

http://www.-ia.hiof.no/~janh/TheBand.html

I've lived in the Catskill Mountains, in a place not far from the town of Woodstock, New York. When you drive between Woodstock and nearby Saugerties, you pass a nondescript house, commonly known as Big Pink, in which the Band made music history in the sixties. At this site, you'll find history on the house where the Band recorded *Music from Pink Pink* and *The Basement Tapes.* You'll also find bios and photographs of Robbie Robertson, Garth Hudson, Rick Danko, and Jim Weider; a discography and filmography for the group (remember Martin Scorsese's *The Last Waltz?*); and digital reprints of newspaper and magazine articles about the creation of an extraordinary musical legacy.

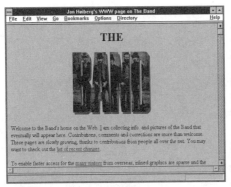

Figure 481.1 The Band home page.

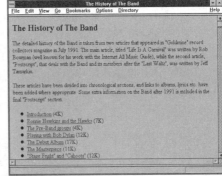

Figure 481.2 A Band biography.

Beethoven: Symphony No. 9

http://www.voyagerco.com/CD/ph/p.beethoven.html

Visit Voyager's online demo of their fantastic CD-ROM tour of Beethoven's last great work. *MacUser* called this CD-ROM "A brilliant multimedia experience that blurs the boundary between education and entertainment." The Vienna Philharmonic performs, accompanied by Joan Sutherland and Marilyn Horne. The CD-ROM offers scholarly commentary (which examines, measure by measure, the entire 68 minutes of the work) and includes the full text of *Ode to Joy* in your choice of either English or German. Visit Voyager's home on the Web for a taste of their fantastic multimedia accomplishment.

Figure 482 Beethoven by Voyager.

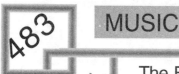
The Beatles

http://www.primenet.com/~dhaber/beatles.html

You'll run across a number of Beatles sites on the Web, all of them quite good. However, I think this one is the best. Click on capsule bios of John, Paul, George, and Ringo that include sound files and photographs. Click on similar bios for their late agent, Brian Epstein; their producer, George Martin; and Pete Best, the unlucky drummer who Ringo Starr replaced just as the band began its rise to the top of pop. A section of the page entitled "Do You Want to Know a Secret" provides a great reference library to Beatles-related articles. You'll also find a complete Beatles LP/CD discography, a singles and EP discography, and a song title cross-reference for both files. What else? How about sound files of behind-the-scenes outtakes from *The White Album*, and sound clips of never-released tracks?

Figure 483.1 The Fab Four.

Figure 483.2 Pete Best, unlucky drummer.

The Blue Highway

http://www.vivanet.com/~blues/

"The Blue Highway" is an excellent online resource to American blues information, both electric and acoustic. Detailed "tributes" provide comprehensive information on twenty great American bluesmen, including Sonny Rollins, Blind Lemon Jefferson, Willie McTell, Mississippi John Hurt, Lightnin' Hopkins, and Albert King. You'll also find extensive biographies and discographies for the likes of Otis Spann, Leroy Carr, Scrapper Blackwell, Bo Carter, Big Mama Thornton, Blind Boy Fuller, Jack Dupree, Mance Lipscomb, and the immortal Elmore James. Additionally, you'll find links to several blues-oriented record companies, a number of other blues-related sites, and the "Muddy's Cabin" chat-room, where you can exchange information and views with other blues enthusiasts.

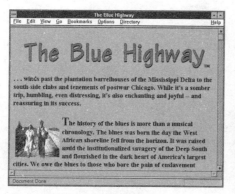

Figure 484.1 The Blue Highway.

Figure 484.2 Merging onto the Highway.

The Blue Note

http://users.aimnet.com/JAZZ/LABELS/BN/

Is there any other jazz record label as highly respected as Blue Note? I doubt it. Today, Blue Note brings forth the work of some of the best and brightest on the contemporary jazz scene: artists such as Chet Baker, Walter Davis, Jr., Lou Donaldson, Kurt Elling, and the incredible Rachelle Ferrell. At this site, you'll find information about all these artists, as well as new recordings from Grant Green, Fareed Haque, Andrew Hill, Freddie Hubbard, Charlie Hunter, Earl Klugh, and others. In addition to being noted for music, Blue Note is admired for its stunningly-designed album covers. If you see an album cover you like from among the many online at this site, feel free to download it.

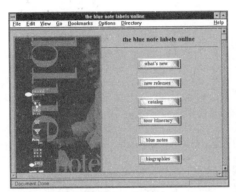

Figure 485.1 Blue Note Records.

Figure 485.2 New releases.

BluesNet

http://dragon.acadiau.ca/~rob/blues/blues.html

"BluesNet" is another exceptional blues site, focusing more on electric blues than acoustic. Among this site's gems is a copy of the last photograph taken of the legendary Albert King (B.B.'s cousin) at a club performance six days before his death. I remember seeing Albert King perform at the old Fillmore East in Manhattan, in 1973 or 1974. He was on a bill with John Mayall and John Hammond, Jr.; for me, seeing the three of them play together was a great, personal introduction to the blues. Mayall and Hammond still play clubs, and both are still phenomenal. Hammond is, of course, the son and namesake of the famous producer for Columbia Records. Like his father before him, Hammond is a Vanderbilt descendant, which makes you wonder why he's able to sing and play the blues so well.

Figure 486 BluesNet home page.

MUSIC

Harry Chapin Fan Page

http://www.fn.net/~jmayans/chapin/index.html

Harry Chapin was an acquaintance of mine from Long Island. We were both involved with various left-of-center, save-the-world organizations on Long Island and in the lower Hudson River Valley. Several of his hits, the most famous being *Taxi,* have become standards. This site contains lots of facts and trivia about Chapin's tragically short life, his songs, his social consciousness, and his legacy. You'll find a great assortment of photographs, a wonderful collection of Harry's poetry, and a comprehensive discography. You'll also find the script for Harry's Broadway show, *The Night That Made America Famous,* and information on the people in Harry's life, including his grandfather, the famous literary critic Kenneth Burke.

Figure 487.1 The immortal Harry Chapin.

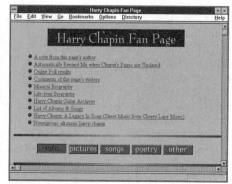

Figure 487.2 Some info on Harry.

John Coltrane Discography

http://www.siba.fi/~eonttone/trane.html

John Coltrane (1926-1967) made one of the most profound impacts on the development of American jazz. This exhaustive discography covers Coltrane's entire professional recording career, from 1949 until his death. The discography provides the date and place of each recording, the names of the tracks, a complete rundown on each track's performers, and more. The discography also covers other jazz greats who performed and recorded with Coltrane, among them Dizzy Gillespie, Joe Mitchell, Pinky Williams, Percy Heath, Stash O'Laughlin, Jimmy Hodges, Lawrence Brown, and Miles Davis.

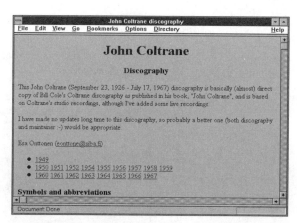

Figure 488 The early recordings.

Cybergrass

http://www.info.net/BG/

Cybergrass bills itself as "the Internet bluegrass magazine." And it is very cool! How cool? Well, Cybergrass "airs" bluegrass concerts and award shows via the Internet. Cybergrass also offers excellent articles by Bob Cherry and others on bluegrass personalities and record labels, as well as various "how-to" articles about bluegrass musicianship. Where else on the Web can you access a two-part tutorial entitled "More Than You Really Ever Wanted to Know About the Dobro?" And where else can you engage in an interactive chat session with Bill Munroe, or access an FAQs (frequently asked questions) file for The Greenbriar Boys? At this site, you'll also find a national bluegrass concert events calendar and a contact list for various bluegrass organizations across the country and around the world.

Figure 489.1 Cybergrass home page.

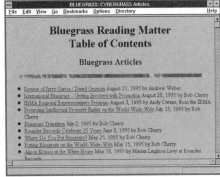

Figure 489.2 A few of your options.

Miles Davis CD Discography

http://www.wam.umd.edu/~losinp/music/md-list.html

This hypertext discography covers hundreds of discs for recordings from 1945 to 1991. On a primary screen system, the entries are arranged chronologically by recording date. Highlighted titles take you to files with information about those recordings—sidemen, location, original issues, and so on. For convenience, you can jump through the list by decade, or search by song title or label. As a bonus, you get a color gallery of Prestige LP covers. What was the date of Miles' first recording? April 24, 1945, of course. Everyone knows that. And the date of his last live recording? July 8, 1991, at Monteux, released by Warner Brothers. As Miles would say, Peace.

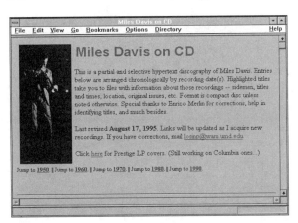

Figure 490 Miles Davis discography.

Dylan Information Page

http://www.ncl.ac.uk/~n328416/mate/

This site is your key to online information about everyone's favorite troubadour/mystic, Robert Zimmerman (aka, Bob Dylan). You'll find photographs of Dylan, as well as album covers and images of some of his associates. You'll also find a complete discography, as well as a bibliography of writings by and about Dylan, the man Jack Nicholson calls "Dr. Bob." Are you ready for Dylan trivia? Who discovered young Bob Dylan and signed him to Columbia Records? I'll give you a hint: he also signed every other major artist at Columbia from Bessie Smith through Bruce Springsteen.

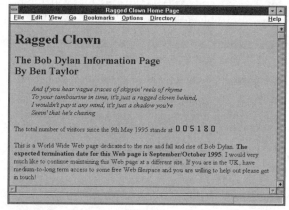

Figure 491.1 The man himself.

The Eagles Home Page

http://www.coc.powell-river.bc.ca/eagles/eagles.html

In 1980, when asked if the Eagles would get back together, one of its members said, "When Hell freezes over." In 1994, the temperature dropped and the music started. The Eagles reunited for a 37-tour concert sweep billed as the "Hell Freezes Over" tour. The site includes a discography, articles and interviews, GIF files, and sound files of "One of These Nights," "Hotel California," "The Long Run," "Heartache Tonight," and more. At this site, you'll also find links to an Eagles chat site and Geffen Records, as well as guitar tablature sheets for your favorite Eagles songs.

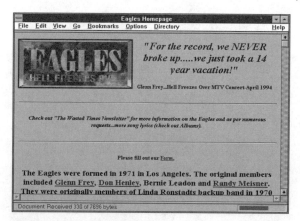

Figure 492 Hell freezes over.

FolkBook: Acoustic Music On-Line

http://www.cgrg.ohio-state.edu/folkbook

Looking for information on your favorite singer/songwriter? "FolkBook" is a one-stop information source on *almost* every contemporary folk artist. At this site, you'll find contact info, artist homepages, folk venue listings, folk record label information, and more. I say *almost*, because the site doesn't include my dear friend (of more than twenty years) Pete Seeger, the composer of "Where Have All the Flowers Gone?," "If I Had a Hammer," and "Turn, Turn, Turn." Not long ago, Pete appeared on an hour-long, nationally televised interview with Bill Moyers, yet he can't make the roster on this database. Interesting. But that's a nitpicky detail. The site is great otherwise. Go for it.

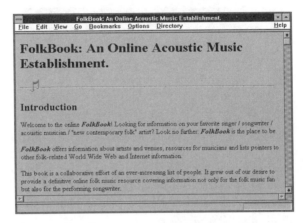

Figure 493 Folk sans Seeger.

The Grateful Dead Home Page

http://www.cs.cmu.edu/~mleone/dead.html

Visit this site for everything and anything related to the Grateful Dead. You'll find downloadable Dead graphics (including Dead icons for the Macintosh!), a complete database of song lyrics, image files, sound files, a Deadhead glossary, guitar tablatures for Dead songs, memorial tributes to Jerry Garcia, and more. You'll also find links to other Deadhead pages around the world (including a great one in Holland), as well as a depressingly empty file entitled "Tour Dates." Of course, nothing is happening. Is there a Grateful Dead after Jerry Garcia? Many wonder, and more than a few are pessimistic. But what a legacy!

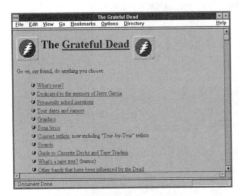

Figure 494.1 The Dead home page.

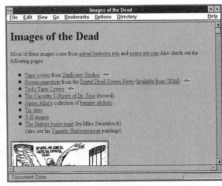

Figure 494.2 A great Dead gallery.

Nanci Griffith

http://www.perspective.com/frankf/nanci.html

My wife, Christa, and I have loved Nanci Griffith's music for about nine years now. We stumbled across her one night when she opened for Phil and Don Everly. Thereafter, we eagerly sought out her recordings. Originally from Texas, Nanci now divides her time between a farm in Franklin, Tennessee and a loft in Dublin, Ireland. She performs sporadically, records regularly, and generates an interesting mix of folk, country, and pop. She calls herself not a country singer, but a folksinger. She has recorded a dozen or so albums, all excellent. At this site, you'll find extensive information on Nanci and her music.

Figure 495 All about Nanci.

Guitar Resources: Harmony Central

http://harmony-central.mit.edu/Guitar

Consider this site the cyberspace guitar zone. The site includes a "Guitar Forum" with a hypernews page that hosts discussions on general guitar topics; a collection of lessons on guitar techniques and music theory; some chord charts; and a link to the "Guitar Chord of the Week" site. What else? How about links to sites where you can learn all about your favorite guitarists (from Segovia to Clapton), access guitar software (believe it or not) for Mac and DOS machines, and survey guitar and amplifier online "For-sale" advertisements. As a bonus, you'll also find links to the Gibson company, new and used guitar dealers, guitar magazines, and other commercial guitar sites.

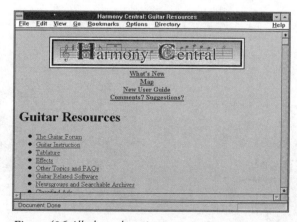

Figure 496 All about the guitar.

Jimi Hendrix: Digital Voodoo

http://www.lionsgate.com/music/hendrix

When we speak of guitarists, we can't ignore Hendrix. Dylan called him "the man who *really* wrote 'All Along the Watchtower.'" Clapton called him "a psychedelic genius." This site examines the soul and power of Hendrix's music, revealing both Hendrix's genius and the personal demons with which he wrestled all his life. Partitions on this page include "Jimi's Life and Death," "The Concert Experience," "Jimi's Life of Music," "Jimi in the Early Years," "Everlasting Visuals," and "The Control of Jimi's Soul." Also, you'll find a discography, interviews and reviews, photographs of Jimi on- and off-stage, and lyrics for such songs as "Wild Thing"and "Purple Haze." Jimi lives in cyberspace.

Figure 497 Hendrix lives.

Hootie and the Blowfish

http://www.tiac.net/users/longleyr/hootie.html

Visit this site to find out all you need to know about Darius Ricker (lead vocals and acoustic guitar), Mark Bryan (lead electric guitar), Jim "Soni" Sonefeld (drums), and Dean Felder (bass). You'll find photographs of the boys on and off stage, details on the records they've made for Atlantic, lyrics and guitar tablatures for Hootie songs, concert tour schedules, and links to three other Hootie and the Blowfish sites, not to mention the official Atlantic Records homepage. When did the members of *Hootie and the Blowfish* first meet? How long has the band been in existence? Where did the name *Hootie and the Blowfish* come from? Why didn't they just call themselves *Darius and the Flunkies*? Find out! Enter the Hootie and the Blowfish zone.

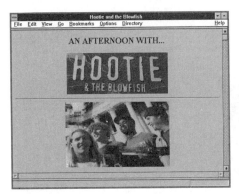 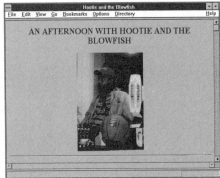

Figure 498.1 The Hootie home page.   *Figure 498.2 Davis gets a basketball.*

MUSIC

Hot Spots in World Music

http://www.webcom.com/~paf/wm/commint.html

From this site, you can access pages focusing on reggae, Afro-Caribbean sounds, Cuban music, and more. Tango? We've got it. Flamenco? Of course. Samba? For sure. But the real test is to have links that focus on truly esoteric specialties, such as Israeli music, sounds from the Brazilian underground, and Cape Verdian folk music, not to mention traditional music from Africa. Does "Hot Spots in World Music" pass this test? Yes, it most certainly does. You'll even find a page dedicated to Celtic music as found in Spain (yes, Spain. Not Ireland or England.) Another page addresses Jewish music from Uganda, called Abayudaya Music. Visit this site for something new and unique.

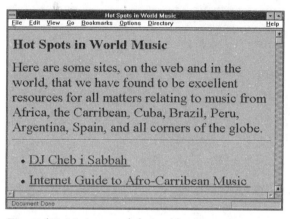

Figure 499 Music around the world.

House of Blues

http://underground.net/HOB/essential/

This site is a promotion for the House of Blue's first CD release, a compilation of 30 classic blues songs that features Elmore James, B.B. King, Howlin Wolf, Koko Taylor, Junior Wells, Albert King, Sonny Boy Williamson, Jimmy Reed, and others. The "House of Blues" site contains fantastic multimedia bios of all the performers on disk, plus James Brown, Slip Harpo, Albert Collins, Junior Parker, Katie Webster, Hound Dog Taylor, and many more. These bios include photographs, film footage, and sound files. The "House of Blues" is a great resource for the blues buff.

Figure 500 The House of Blues.

Hyperreal Rave Archives

http://hyperreal.com/

"Hyperreal" is the collaborative publishing effort of several dozen volunteers whose mission is to give a home to alternative culture, expression, and (most importantly) music, with particular attention to the worldwide rave scene. So what will you find here? You'll find the Rave Culture Archives, Rave regional mailing list archives, the "Spirit of Raving" archives, the Global Rave Calendar, and an electronic media clipping-service called "Raves in the News." You'll also find links to sites related to all types of techno and ambient music (including a link to *XLR8R*, the West Coast's best free rave/techno rag!) Check out this site.

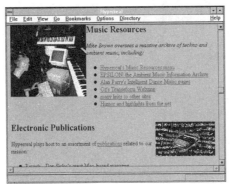

Figure 501.1 Hyperreal music sources.

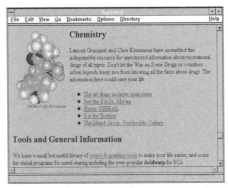

Figure 501.2 Beyond high-school chemistry.

JazzNet

http://www.dnai.com/~lmcohen/

"JazzNet" bills itself as "a compendium of jazz, blues, news, views, and information." And that it is. Packed with graphics and sound files, "JazzNet" includes the digital edition of *Jazz Now* magazine, which reports on jazz activities in Europe, Australia, and parts of North America. You'll also find a link to the official Monterey Jazz Festival page, information on U.S. Postal Service jazz stamps, and the DeCapo Press jazz/blues catalog. In addition, you'll find links to the Kuumbwa Jazz Center (Santa Cruz), the Tucson Jazz Society, the San Francisco *Jazz In Flight* newsletter, and many other jazz-related sites on the Web. So get hip, tune into "JazzNet," and immerse in one of the world's great art forms.

Figure 502.1 JazzNet home page.

Figure 502.2 Monterey fest info . . .

Figure 502.3 . . . and stamps.

The JazzWeb: Record Company Links

http://www.nwu.edu/WNUR/jazz/labels.html

Brought to you by the folks at Northwestern University Radio, WNUR, this fine site gives you links to the commercial pages of more than twenty great jazz record labels, including the AMM Group, Asian Improv Records, Beverly Records, DMP Records, ECM Records, and GRP Records. You'll also find connections to Impulse Records, Jazz Haus Musik, Jazz Focus Records, and MoJazz Records, as well as New Albion, Noteworthy Record Co., and PDCD Sonic Entertainment. At these commercial sites, you'll find artist bios, online catalogs, and pricing, of course.

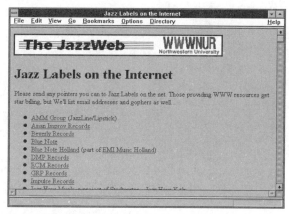

Figure 503 *The JazzWeb from Northwestern.*

Elton John

http://itchy.faa.uiuc.edu/elton.html

Put on your diamond-studded, gold-and-silver jumpsuit and click on over to this site. In addition to sound files, lyrics, discographies, and tour schedules, you'll find photographs of Elton in his numerous colored outfits. Want some photos of Elton's famous friends? They're here too: George Harrison, Eric Clapton, and Bernie Taupin. Additionally, you'll find a bibliography of books and articles about Elton, a directory of Elton fan publications and organizations, and "the 22nd row," which is a daily Internet digest of Elton's comings, goings, and preoccupations. Most importantly, this site includes a link to the homepage of the Elton John AIDS Foundation, endowed by Elton to promote AIDS research, help provide services for those afflicted with the disease, and educate the public.

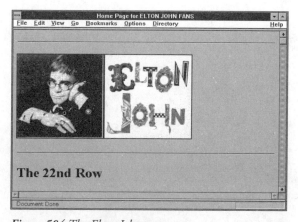

Figure 504 *The Elton John page.*

The Kinks

http://hobbes.it.rit.edu/kinks/kinks.html

This awesome site is dedicated to The Kinks, the band that brought us such classics as "Lola" and "I'm an Ape Man." A "News and Rumors" file keeps you up-to-date on all the latest Kinks news and gossip and gives you information about upcoming tours and recordings. A huge image collection gives you shots of the boys dating back to the band's earliest days. And, of course, you'll find the requisite sound clips, video clips, lyrics, bibliography, and discography. The site also includes FAQs (frequently asked questions) packed with trivia, a link to a Kinks newsgroup (alt.fan.kinks), guitar chords for Kinks songs, Kinks fan club information, and a link to a site where you can buy Kinks merchandise.

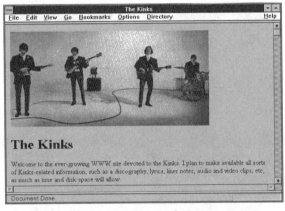

Figure 505 All about Ray Davies & company.

The Knitting Factory

http://www.knittingfactory.com

The Knitting Factory in New York is one of the world's premier performance spaces for music that hovers near or over the edge. And when I say over-the-edge music, I'm talking about Steve Turre and the Sanctified Shells, Matt Darriau's Paradox Trio, Abstract Truth, Verbana, and other such music-making organizations. If this site offered only performance schedules and ticket prices for The Knitting Factory, it would not rate as cool. What makes this site cool is an absolutely fantastic QuickTime virtual-reality tour of The Knitting Factory. Throughout the site, both in and out of the virtual-reality tour, the graphics are first-rate (and require Netscape).

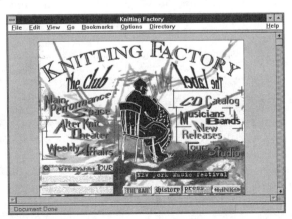

Figure 506 Knitting up something cool.

Motown Records

http://www.musicbase.co.uk/music/motown

This excellent page gives you complete information on Motown, yesterday and today. Along with information on new and upcoming releases, you'll find complete information on every musical legend that has been associated with this equally legendary record company. I'm talking about the likes of Marvin Gaye, Junior Walker, The Four Tops, Diana Ross and the Supremes, Stevie Wonder, Gladys Knight, Smokey Robinson, the Temptations, and Grover Washington, Jr., just to name a few. You'll see discographies, biographies, GIFs, bibliographies, and sound files for each performer. All combined, this site is something more than just a digital record catalog. It is a historical resource.

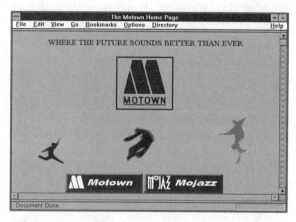

Figure 507 The Motown sound.

John Lennon Home Page

http://www.missouri.edu/~c588349/john-page.html

John Lennon has always been one of my great heros. Sam Choukri's great "John Lennon" "Homepage" includes biographical information, a complete bibliography, interview transcripts, and more. You'll find photographs (including a series of great candid photos of Lennon taken during the *Imagine* sessions), sound files, movies, original artwork by Lennon, and a comprehensive discography. You'll also find the text of Linda Keen's engaging book *John Lennon In Heaven*, as well as links to Steve Clifford's Beatle Page, Hri Satou's Beatles Page, and "The Toppermost of the Poppermost" site. All together, these features constitute a remarkable site profiling a totally cool personality whose impact on me, for one, was profound.

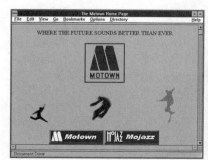

Figure 508.1 John Lennon Home Page.

Figure 508.2 John Lennon as a boy.

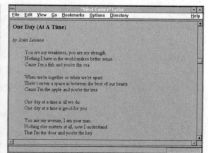

Figure 508.3 Lyrics for One Day (At a Time)

"Music That Doesn't Suck"

http://www.cs.utexas.edu/users/jwetzler/music.htm

"This is our collection of music that *does not* suck," reports the curator of this eclectic page. "If you've got a problem with these, then go listen to Stone Temple Pilots or even the David Matthews Band" whom, the inference is, *do suck*. (Perhaps so, although I can certainly think of worse bands.) This site lets you link to pages associated with the Dead Milkmen, They Might Be Giants, the Violent Femmes, Simon & Garfunkle, the Beatles, and the Doors. You'll also find connections to the "Punk Page," the "Pollstar Tour Database" (excellent), Sub-Pop Records, and several great image collections, including that of Beatles' photographer Ethan Russell, who shot the cover photos for *Abbey Road.*

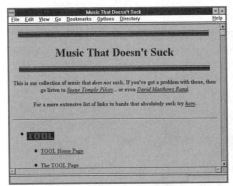

Figure 509.1 An uncompromising heading.

Figure 509.2 They Might Be Giants page.

Musicians On the Internet

http://www.escape.com/~rpiscn/MOIhomc.html

"Musicians on the Internet" is a wonderful concept: a virtual listening booth created and run by musicians on the World Wide Web. At this site, you will find music clips, films, photos, artwork, and other assorted items introducing the work of excellent, up-and-coming musicians. When I visisted, the line-up included Steve Packenham (a "complex, hypnotic, meditative" singer/songwriter), Red Miller ("a Boston musician and singer/songwriter with a bluesy edge"), the acoustic guitar duo Kick At Heaven, Chris Johnson ("somewhere between Melissa Etheridge, Sheryl Crow, Joni Mitchell, and Grace Slick"), and Flatus ("Loud Guitars! Crunchy Rhythms!"). My favorite was Psychedelic Steppenwolves, which seems the ideal band for a mid-life Dharma bum like me.

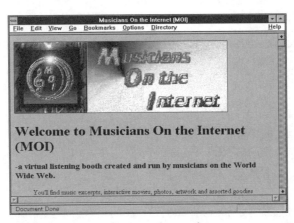

Figure 510 A great directory of new talent.

Phil Ochs

http://www.cs.pdx.edu/~trent/ochs/

What is this weird thing that success does to us? It's like, "Wow, I'm so happy I don't know what to do first—hang myself or drink myself to death." That was Phil Ochs' dilemma. I met Ochs only once, not long before he took his own life. We were in the office of concert promoter Harold Leventhal a few hours before a Pete Seeger performance at Carnegie Hall. I was at the office with Pete and Toshi Seeger when in came a shabby Phil. Marjorie Guthrie (the widow of Woody), who shared the office with Leventhal, thought Phil looked terrible, attempted to find out where he was living, and tried to talk him into staying with her at her apartment for a while. And then he was gone. But what songs he left! What a rich tradition of music! Find out more about Phil, his life, and his death at this page.

Figure 511 *Phil in the first flush of youthful success.*

OperaGlass

http://rick.stanford.edu/opera/main.html

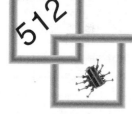

"OperaGlass" is the ideal spot on the Web for opera lovers. You'll find performance histories, synopses, and libretti for hundreds of great operas. Search for information by composer, librettist, opera name, opera companies, or conductors and performers. Links take you to a server with schedules for all the world's major companies, Lyle Neff's index to opera libretti and other vocal texts, *The Dictionary of Recorded Opera and Opera Arias*, and even the Verdi research papers. Additionally, you also find homepages and bios for many of operas greatest contemporary stars, as well as historic greats such as Enrico Caruso. In sum, the opera devotee will find this combination of resources invaluable.

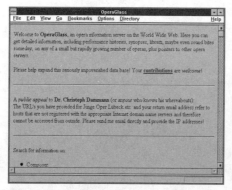

Figure 512.1 *The OperaGlass.*

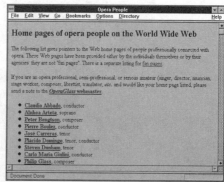

Figure 512.2 *Home pages of opera personalities.*

Pearl Jam

http://pages. prodigy.com/NY/music_man2/pj.html

Hey, Pearl Jam's not just Neil Young's back-up band, you know. They have their own life. Want the latest poop on Eddie Vedder (guitar/vocals), Mike McReady (guitar), Stone Gossard (guitar), Jeff Ament (bass), and Jack Irons (drums)? This site offers a complete discography, a bibliography of interviews and articles, concert tour information, and, of course, the very latest information on Pearl Jam's war with TicketMaster. You'll find lyrics and guitar chords for songs from the albums *Ten, Vs,* and *Vitalogy,* and links to several other sites dedicated to the band. Want more? Okay, an FTP link grabs sound files containing four songs: "Alive," "Evenflow," "Jeremy," and "Daughter." But be warned: each sound file is about 3 Mb in size, so prepare for a long transfer time if you're using a slow connection.

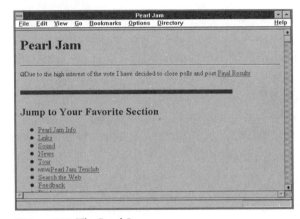

Figure 513 The Pearl Jam page.

The Recording Industry Environmental Task Force

http://www.musicpro.com/RIETF

The Recording Industry Environmental Task Force (RIETF) is a group of individuals and corporations concerned about the recording industry's impact on the environment. Comprised of professionals from all facets of the recording industry and environmental specialists, RIETF encourages recording companies to incorporate environmentally responsible practices in manufacturing, packaging, consumption, and reclamation. Similarly, RIETF works to improve the quality of the environment in regard to noise pollution (particularly music playback) levels in public places.

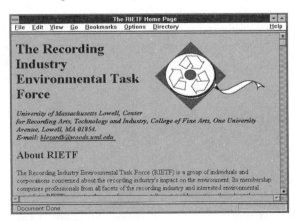

Figure 514 Eco-cops for the recording industry.

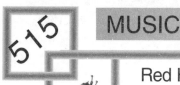

MUSIC

Red Hot & Cool: Jazz Resources

http://www.j51.com/~jayl/jazz

"Jazz Resources" contains more than 100 links to zines, lists, catalogs, newsletters, sounds, record labels, catalog stores, clubs, artists, radio stations, history, and more. Link to a digital biography of Albert Ayler, the "Atlantic Jazz Gallery" from Rhino Records, the "Billboard Jazz Top Ten List," and "The People of Jazz Index." Additional links connect you to such unique places on the Web as "The Trombone Home Page," "NetCetera" (jazz facts from the Netherlands), the "Montreux Jazz Festival," "Hot Clube de Portugal," "Jazz in France," and "Jazz On-line" (news, information, and other services). Additionally, you'll find discographies, performer profiles, tour and performance schedules, reviews of current and classic jazz releases, and even a filmography of movies related to jazz.

Figure 515 Red hot & cool jazz.

Rock n' Roll Hall of Fame

http://www.rockhall.com/

What a list of options! Click on "Inductees Live!" and listen to songs by rock legends, some of whom were around even before Dick Clark. Then, click on "The 500 Songs," which gives you *the* 500 songs that "shaped rock n' roll." Let's see, the list includes "My Girl," "In-A-Gadda-Da-Vida," and "Cryin' in the Rain." Okay, those make sense. Hey, wait a minute. What's "Cracklin' Rosy" doing here? (kidding) By the way, Pete Seeger did make this list, as a songwriter. Click on "Multimedia" and get an index to the video clips you can find in the "Rock n' Roll Hall of Fame" virtual inductees gallery. Or click on the "Bloodhound" icon to sniff out Rock 'n Roll people, places, and things.

Figure 516.1 The Rock Hall of Fame.

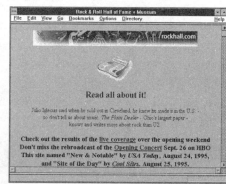

Figure 516.2 The latest rock news.

Rocktropolis

http://underground.net/Rocktropolis

The future of Rock n' Roll lies in the freedom of cyberspace. Welcome to "Rocktropolis," a Rock n' Roll fantasy theme park, a surreal city landscape inhabited by some of pop culture's greatest musicians and cult heroes, plus its new pretenders. "Rocktropolis," like the culture and tradition it depicts, is ferociously seductive at its best, absurd and tragic at its worst. At this site, you'll find glory, of course. But you'll also encounter evil, as represented by (among other icons) Rock's own Lee Harvey Oswald, Mark David Chapman. And no matter where you venture, you'll experience drama, emotion, and rhythm—the pulse, the backbeat, of life. Meet Buddy Holly in an alley, Janis Joplin up a corridor, Jimi Hendrix in a park. The past is present at Rocktropolis.

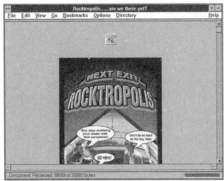

Figure 517.1 Welcome to Rocktropolis.

Figure 517.2 Rock Angels in Cyberspace.

The Rolling Stones: Voodoo Lounge

http://www.stones.com/

Welcome to the official Rolling Stones Web site which is cool not only for its association with Mick and the boys, but also because it uses some of the latest Web programming techniques and tools (including HotJava) to create a remarkable online multimedia experience. (Guess it is nice to have a big budget.) Visit "The Lounge," cool VideoStreamer boxes that let you download and print a chunk of Stones video, and view a *great* online collection of candid Polaroids shot by Ron Wood during the Voodoo Lounge tour. Additionally, you can access interviews with the Stones and download Stones artwork that include album covers and the famous tongue.

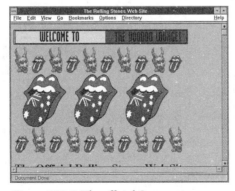

Figure 518.1 The official Stones pages.

Figure 518.2 Ron Wood's tour photos.

Frank Sinatra: Ring-a-Ding Dong!

http://www.io.org/~buff/sinatra.html

Word has it that Sinatra is not just famous for soliciting starlets for John Kennedy. He also, my friends tell me, has some small reputation as a singer. All kidding aside, this Web site has *everything* about Frank, including such esoteric goodies as Gay Talese's "Frank Sinatra Has a Cold" from the April 1966 *Esquire* (read it, it's great), and Bono's speech at the 1995 Grammies (where Sinatra received an award). "Ring-a-Ding Dong!" also includes a complete filmography and discography for Frank, details on Sinatra tracks recorded but unreleased, and an interesting essay on Sinatra the songwriter. Also check out the digital reprint of "Frank Sinatra Confidential: Gangsters in the Night Clubs" from the August 1951 *New American Mercury*, as well as Frank's *Playboy* interview for February 1963.

Figure 519 *The Sinatra site.*

Sony Music On-Line

http://www.music.sony.music.com/Music/MusicIndex.html

Sony Music's Web Server provides you with all the latest information on Sony artists, tours, videos, and more. At this site, "Featured Artists" highlights artists that have new albums, "or have slipped us enough promotional money that we decided to feature them." "Wire Taps" fills you in on the latest happenings at Sony Music. "Video Stuff" contains free downloadable screensavers and electronic press kits. You'll also find a page for each major Sony Music artist, graphics, videos, sound files, biography/discography, North America tour schedule, "current news" on works-in-progress, forthcoming albums, and more. In short, this site is an invaluable source for pop music fans.

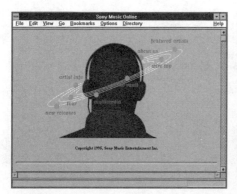

Figure 520.1 *Sony's home page.*

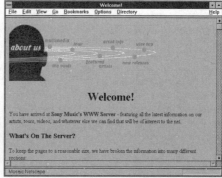

Figure 520.2 *A little information.*

Livingston Taylor: Singer/Songwriter

http://www.midcoast.com/~liv

James Taylor may play larger arenas, but brother Liv is the first of the two to show up on the Web. If you don't know Liv Taylor's music, you're missing something special. From his first album in 1970 through his latest (1995's *Unsolicited Material*), Liv has always been thoughtful, melodic, and eloquent. He tours coffeehouses and colleges nationwide, teaches occasionally at Boston's Berklee College of Music, and recently received an Honorary Doctorate of Music from St. Anselm College in Manchester, New Hampshire. Liv's Web page includes recent family photos and links to resources related to Martha's Vineyard, where Liv and many other Taylors (including James) live.

Figure 521 All about Liv.

10,000 Maniacs

http://spinning.com/maniacs/

This site contains graphics, sound files, discographies, and more about one of the best bands of this decade—10,000 Maniacs. You'll find a full biography for each band member; a comprehensive file of reviews, articles, and interviews; audio clips from every one of their albums plus some unreleased stuff; and a fantastic collection of images. From a gallery of thumbnails, choose the photographs and album covers you would like to download. Links connect to chat rooms where members of the band have been known to show up and mingle with their fans. The site also includes information on scholarships and grant programs the band has endowed in their home region (Jamestown, NY).

Figure 522 That's a lot of maniacs.

Texas A&M University Web Music Resources

http://orpheus.tamu.edu/music.favorite.html

The good folks at Texas A&M have put together a splendid array of links and resources. For a collection of traditional tunes from Europe and the United States, check out *Richard Robinson's Tunebook* from the University of Leeds in the United Kingdom. Or go to a demo of *Sheet Music On-Line* at the Lester S. Levy Collection, Johns Hopkins University. The complete Levy Collection consists of over 30,000 sheets of American music dating from 1780 to 1960. Access the University of North Carolina's "American Music Resource," which contains bibliographies and other research files about all styles of American music and related issues.

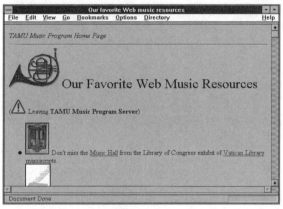

Figure 523 *A great set of links.*

524

Tom Waits

http://www.acns.nwu.edu/waits/

This site gives you extensive information on Tom Waits and what he's been up to over the past few years. What's he been doing? Besides acting in eight movies and producing his highly regarded concert film (and album) *Big Time*, he wrote the songs and music for the Robert Wilson production of the opera *The Black Rider*. (William Burroughs did the libretto.) Waits' songs have been recorded by Bruce Springsteen ("Jersey Girl"), Rod Stewart ("Downtown Train"), Marianne Faithful ("Stranger Weather"), the Bullet Boys ("Hang On St. Christopher"), Bob Seger ("Blind Love" and "New Coat of Paint"), Dion ("Heart of Saturday Night" and "San Diego Serenade"), and others.

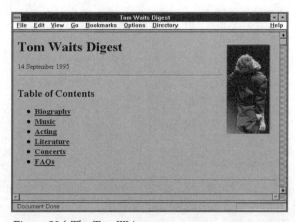

Figure 524 *The Tom Waits page.*

Warner Brothers Records

http://www.iuma.com/warner

Warner Brothers distributes the records of a few artists you may know: Eric Clapton, Little Texas, Madonna, American Music Club, Laurie Anderson, and, oh yes, Van Halen. At this site, you'll find complete information on these artists and more. You'll find detailed artist biographies and profiles, discographies, tour schedules, and online videos. Feel free to download some of the cool cover art, as well as portrait photographs of your favorite Warner musicians. Or, listen to portions of soon-to-be released songs that you won't hear anywhere else. Be the first on your block to hear the riffs on Eric Clapton's next single!

Figure 525.1 Warner Brothers Records page.

Figure 525.2 Click on the cover art.

Doc Watson: American Music Legend

http://sunsite.unc.edu/doug/DocWat/DocWat.html

Discovered in the heat of the sixties folk revival, Doc Watson is a legendary performer who blends traditional Appalachian folk music roots with blues, country, gospel, and bluegrass to create his unique style and expansive repertoire. Blind from infancy, Doc has spent his lifetime making music, and fans everywhere consider him one of the world's most accomplished flat-pickers. You'll find a comprehensive biography and discography for Doc, as well as his current concert schedule and two great sound files. The first contains sample recordings of Doc and Tom Ashley performing in 1961. The second sound file is Doc and his son, Merle, performing "Blue Railroad Train." (Merle served as Doc's backup guitarist and manager for many years and died tragically in 1985.)

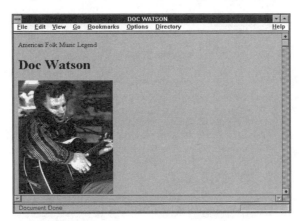

Figure 526 Doc in the 1960s.

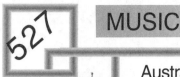

MUSIC

Australian Music Milieu

http://adam.com/au/~imerge/AMMIndex.html

What is Australian Music Milieu? The purpose of the Milieu is to let the world experience the vast pool of local Australian musical talent. The Milieu is always in a state of flux with new bands joining, existing bands changing their information, and regularly updated music industry news and reviews. Check out the featured artist of the month or view continuously updated performance schedules for clubs across Australia. Access cool links to other sites on the Web involved with the music industry as well as sites specifically dedicated to Australian music. Are you an Australian musical artist? Then find out about posting your own information on the Milieu.

Figure 527 Australian Music Milieu.

Neil Young Information Site

http://www.uta.fi/~trkisa/hyperrust.html

Neil is neither burning out nor rusting; he is just getting better with age. And this site documents every aspect of his career with a complete biography, long and short discography options, great graphics and sound files (including bootleg material), and tour schedules. Interested in playing Neil's songs yourself? Check out the songbooks, charts, tablatures, lyrics, and even tips for harmonica players. Find out all about *Mirror Ball*, Neil's album with Pearl Jam. You'll also find interviews with Neil, information on forthcoming releases, a list of Neil's appearances on other artists' records, and lists of Neil's songs that other artists and bands have recorded.

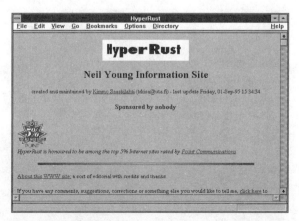

Figure 528 The Neil Young resource.

INTERNET EXPERTS RESOURCES

The Web Developer's Journal

http://www.awa.com/nct/software/eleclead.html

This great monthly journal (which looks best when viewed with Netscape!) contains news and reviews of the latest hypertext-authoring tools, modems, communications software, browsers, and more. *The Web Developer's Journal* covers subjects of interest to all businesses and individuals using electronic formats to communicate on the Internet. One very cool feature is their experimental pages, where they play with new design ideas and "wacky, Advanced Duct Tape HTML: the HTML your mother never told you about!" You will find links to super-cool Web games.

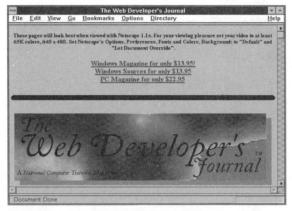

Figure 372 A great Web developer's resource.

Web Style Manual

http://info.med.yale.edu/caim/StyleManual_Top.HTML

Cole Porter had *style*. F. Scott Fitzgerald had *style*. A manual can't give you the kind of style these fellows had. But Web style is quite another thing. Pat Lynch's excellent interactive *Web Style Manual*, itself is a living example of a well-done HTML document. Succinct and navigationally simple, Lynch's style manual is precisely that, a style manual, and not a guide to HTML authoring. What Lynch tries to do (successfully, I think) is create a sort of *Strunk & White* for the Web: a succinct body of rules that, if followed, will inevitably lead to clear thinking and clear communication. Mr. Lynch's contribution is admirable and its guidelines are a must-read for Web designers.

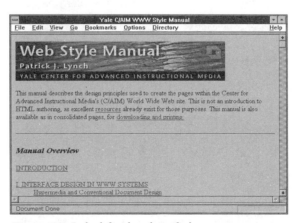

Figure 373 Style defined and rarified.

POLITICS

Lord Acton Book Shoppe

http://www.acton.org/books.html

Lord Acton, the great theorizer of freedom, said "Power corrupts; absolute power corrupts absolutely." In the small-government spirit of Acton, the Lord Acton Book Shop offers a variety of books and videos of interest to conservatives. For example, you'll find video interviews with William F. Buckley, Jr. on "Morality and American Society," Jeanne Kirkpatrick on "Humane Governance," Margaret Thatcher on "Faith and the Limitations of the State,"and Milton Friedman on the free-market resurrection of Eastern Europe. You'll also find videos of William Simon and Clarence Thomas. All interesting stuff for the Conservatively inclined.

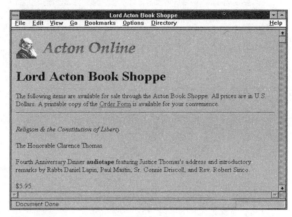

Figure 530.1 Books and videos for conservatives.

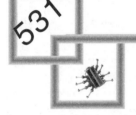

Americans for Democratic Action

http://www.fas.org/pub/gen/ada

The Americans for Democratic Action (ADA) cater to those at the liberal end of the political spectrum. Since 1947, the ADA has been successfully fighting for "the politically improbable," as its charter admits. The ADA was aligned against McCarthyism in the 1950s and against the Vietnam War in the 1960s. The ADA was also the first national political organization to call for the impeachment of Richard Nixon. Now the ADA fights against those it characterizes as the Nixons and McCarthys of the 1990s: Newt Gingrich, Jesse Helms, and the religious right. This page is a useful stop on the Information Super Highway for anyone with a similar point of view.

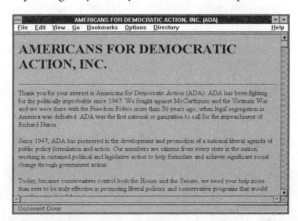

Figure 531.1 A resource for the left.

Amnesty International

http://www.io.org/amnesty/overview.html

At this very moment, thousands upon thousands of people languish in prisons and work-camps simply because they espouse political views their national leaders dislike. I am speaking of political prisoners in China, Iraq, North Korea, Afghanistan, and other places around the globe. Their only crime is free thought. And their only hope is the spotlight of outraged world attention. Amnesty International is a nonprofit organization that works to generate such attention. Politically, Amnesty International is non-partisan and works to free anyone (conservatives, liberals, and otherwise) incarcerated merely for expressing political views. Both Joan Baez and William F. Buckley, Jr. have, at various times, served on Amnesty International's Board-of-Directors. (And I suspect that supporting Amnesty International is the only thing about which Baez and Buckley will ever agree.) Stop by and join them in the good fight.

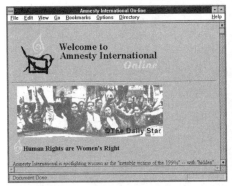

Figure 532.1 Amnesty International.

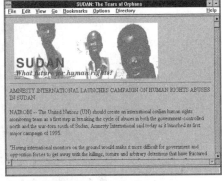

Figure 532.2 Fighting for freedom.

The Brookings Institution

http://www.brook.edu/

A private, independent, non-profit organization, the Brookings Institution is the nation's oldest think tank. To provide knowledge on emerging public policy issues facing the American people, the Institution conducts nonpartisan research in economics, government, foreign policy, defense strategy, and the social sciences. This site contains more information on the Institution, including biographies of Brookings scholars, survey reports of ongoing research programs, a catalog of executive education programs, digital reprints of Brookings publications, a large file of recent press releases, and an online catalog of the Brookings library. Presidents and senators have come to Brookings for the facts they need to make vital decisions; now you can, too.

Figure 533.1 The Brookings Institution page.

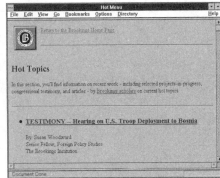

Figure 533.2 The latest from Brookings.

POLITICS

The Campaign for New Priorities

http://www.fas.org/pub/gen/cnp/index.html

If God sent you $2 billion and told you to use it in the best way possible to benefit your fellow citizens, would you rebuild 1,500 run-down schools? Or would you buy a nuclear submarine the Pentagon admits it doesn't need? Say you had $1 billion more. Would you increase funding for cancer, heart disease and AIDS research? Or would you use it for military spare parts the government's accountants say will never be used? Do you think the Pentagon, which plans to spend $1.5 trillion over the next six years, needs $25 billion more? If you'd fund school construction and medical research rather than advocate addtional military spending, you may want to stop off at "The Campaign for New Priorities," where you'll find like-minded people who have made a commitment to make a difference.

Figure 534 Fighting defense spending.

The Cato Institute

http://w3.ag.uiuc.edu/liberty/cato/index.html

Founded in 1977, the Cato Institute is a nonpartisan public-policy research foundation. The Institute takes its name from *Cato's Letters*, libertarian pamphlets that helped lay the philosophical foundation for the American Revolution. The Institute seeks to inject into the public policy debate more discussion of such traditional American principles as limited government, individual liberty, and peace. Toward that, the Institute promotes greater public involvement in questions of policy and the proper role of government. Libertarian political scientist and humorist P.J. O'Rourke sums up the program thus, "Government should be against the law. Term limits aren't enough. We need jail."

Figure 535.1 The Cato Institute page.

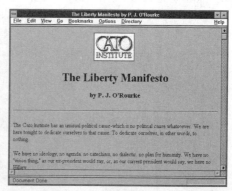

Figure 535.2 P.J. O'Rourke's Cato manifesto.

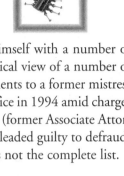

Clinton Administration Losers

http://www.crl.com/~jamesb/pres.html

No matter what you think about Bill Clinton, you must admit that he has surrounded himself with a number of people who, to put it mildly, have not served him well. This site takes a rather gleeful, critical view of a number of Clinton's appointees, including Henry Cisneros (who reportedly lied to the FBI about payments to a former mistress during his 1992 confirmation process), Mike Espy (former Agriculture Secretary who left office in 1994 amid charges that he accepted expensive gifts from firms his department regulated), and Webster Hubbell (former Associate Attorney General and long-time Clinton friend who resigned in March 1994 and subsequently pleaded guilty to defrauding his former law partners and clients out of nearly $400,000). And that, unfortunately, is not the complete list.

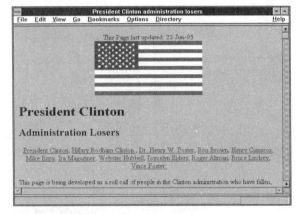

Figure 536 Clinton Administration losers.

Bill Clinton in '96

http://www.clinton96.org

Okay, you guessed it—this page is a joke. It claims to be the quasi-official page of the Clinton re-election effort, but it isn't. Instead, "Bill Clinton in '96" is a subtle comic masterpiece featuring such phrases as "One of the most essential jobs of a President is to make decisions." The page goes on to define what it says is Bill Clinton's personal philosophy: *In Epturum Omnistasis*. Oh yes, *Stasis* is the thing, "In 1992 . . . Clinton preached and believed in change . . . Still, over the past few years, Bill Clinton has matured personally and realized that things really aren't so bad." Whether you like Clinton or not, you'll like this spoof, which is all in good fun. Check it out.

Figure 537.1 Clinton in '96?

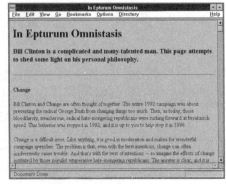

Figure 537.2 A philosophy, of sorts.

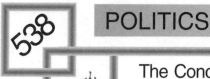

The Concord Coalition

http://sunsite.unc.edu/concord/

The Concord Coalition is a nonpartisan, grassroots movement to eliminate the deficit and bring entitlements down to a fair level for all generations. Founded by former Senators Warren B. Rudman and Paul E. Tsongas, the Concord Coalition has chapters in all 50 states and on many college campuses. You will find information on how to join the Concord Coalition, as well as news releases and the complete text of the Concord Coalition's Zero Deficit Plan for balancing the federal budget. If you are in the mood for some (serious) fun, stop and play one of the site's deficit-reduction games, which challenge you to balance the federal books yourself.

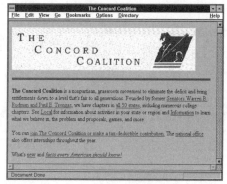

Figure 538.1 The Concord Coalition home page.

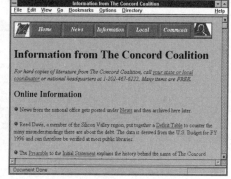

Figure 538.2 Details on the Coalition.

The Constitution of the United States

http://www.hax.com/USConstitution.html

The most perfect political document ever penned begins with one of the most beautiful sentences ever composed: "We, the people of the United States, in order to form a more perfect Union, establish justice, insure domestic tranquillity, provide for the common defense, promote the general welfare, and secure the blessing of liberty to ourselves and our posterity, do ordain and establish this Constitution for the United States of America." In this invaluable, hypertext edition of the U.S. Constitution, key phrases in each article and amendment link to subsequent articles and amendments that refine their scope, meaning, and validity. This clever, practical use of hypertext illuminates a document that is the foundation of the United States' political and legal system.

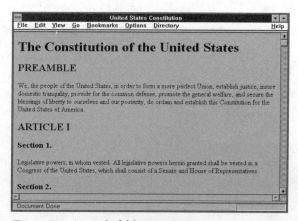

Figure 539 A wonderful hypertext resource.

Conservative Generation X

http://www.teleport.com/~pcllgn/cgx.html

No longer willing to accept a media and society that labels their generation a bunch of whiny, immature, Clinton-supporting slackers, three former college-radio disk jockeys decided to start *CGX*, the zine for, about, and by conservative Generation X. Published every two weeks, *CGX* discusses such topics as the past strengths and weaknesses of the Republican party, why liberals are "on the run," raising a family in the 1990s, and the ethics behind student loans. The zine's tone is thoughtful, reserved, and well-reasoned. You may not agree with the opinions expressed in *CGX*, but the writers' seriousness and sincerity deserve respect.

Figure 540.1 The CGX home page.

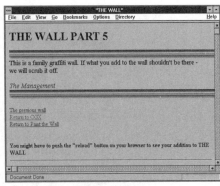

Figure 540.2 The graffiti board.

Digital Democrats

http://www.webcom.com/~digitals

If you are part of liberal Generation X, you may want to stop and visit "Digital Democrats." You'll find a wealth of useful links to Democratic Web pages across the country, Democratic-oriented Internet newsletters, and a national Democratic Party events calendar. You'll also find links to the Democratic forum on CompuServe, the Democratic Leadership Council, the Democratic National Committee, Democratic Party clubs around the United States, the Democratic Party Platform, and an entertaining site named "Republican Watch." In addition, cool links take you to the homepages of President Clinton, the White House, the Cabinet, Democratic senators and congressional representatives, governors, state and county party organizations, and more.

Figure 541 The Democratic Party page.

Department of State

http://dosfan.lib.uic.edu

Something new on the Net! The U.S. "Department of State" experimental World Wide Web server recently came online. This project is part of a cooperative effort between the University of Illinois at Chicago University Library and the Department of State. At this site, you'll find links to the "Electronic Embassy," which comprises a photographic tour of the U.S. Department of State. Addtionally, you can access DOSFAN (the Department of State Foreign Affairs Network Gopher) and other resources. DOSFAN contains mountains of reports and data that will prove invaluable to any journalist or student scrutinizing United States foreign policy.

Figure 542 U.S. Department of State page.

543

FAIR: Fairness & Accuracy in Reporting

http://www.igc.apc.org/fair/

FAIR (Fairness & Accuracy in Reporting) is a national media watch group that offers well-documented criticism in an effort to correct media bias and imbalance. FAIR focuses public awareness on the narrow, corporate ownership of the press, the media's allegiance to official agendas, and the media's "insensitivity to women, labor, minorities, and other public interest constituencies." FAIR, says the organization's charter, "seeks to reinvigorate the First Amendment by advocating greater media pluralism and the inclusion of public interest voices in national debates." At this site, you'll find details on the book *The Way Things Aren't: Rush Limbaugh's Reign of Error*, as well as regular reports FAIR publishes on media practices nationwide.

Figure 543.1 FAIR home page.

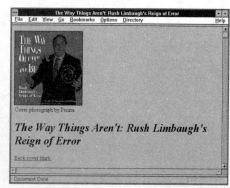

Figure 543.2 Shooting down Rush Limbaugh.

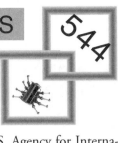

Foreign Affairs Agencies in the Executive Branch

http://www.embassy.org/feds.html

In addition to the State Department, the United States Information Agency (USIA), the U.S. Agency for International Development (AID), and the Arms Control and Disarmament Agency (ACDA) develop and execute U.S. foreign policy. This server provides information on each of the four agencies that make up the Executive Branch's foreign policy cadre. Visit this site to learn what these agencies do, how they interrelate, and how their roles overlap. You'll also find links to each agency, as well as to the USIA Web server, which provides complete details on Voice of America, Radio and TV Marti (broadcasting to Cuba), and other USIA ventures.

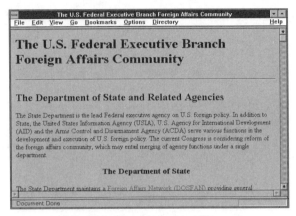

Figure 544 Executive Branch foreign affairs options.

Friends Committee on National Legislation

http://www.fas.org/pub/gen/fcnl/index.html

The Friends Committee on National Legislation (FCNL) is a nation-wide network of thousands of Quakers and like-minded people who work together to bring Friends' values (pacifism, equity, and social justice) to bear on the policies of the Federal government. Since 1943, FCNL has worked toward a non-military world order so firmly based on justice and voluntary cooperation that there would be no place for war. At the moment, FCNL seeks reconciliation among peoples, opposes militarism, advocates civil rights for all people, and supports self-determination for Native Americans.

Figure 545 Friends Committee home page.

Gingrich: Shining Knight of the Post-Reagan Right

http://www.cco.caltech.edu/~gpw/osborne.html

David Osborne's portrait of Newt from *Mother Jones* is less than complimentary, painting the Speaker as a back-stabbing opportunist and a cynical manipulator of conservative ideology who is more concerned with his own career than with advancing government reform. Osborne also mounts a damning attack on Gingrich's vision of a "conservative opportunity state" with the three pillars of free enterprise, high technology, and traditional values. At the same time, Osborne admits that Gingrich is a brilliant speaker and debater, an "effective guerrilla" on the House floor, and "a genuine political strategist and theorist, who by the force of his ideas has begun to reshape Republican politics."

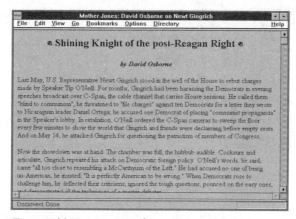

Figure 546 Newt uncovered.

NewtWatch

http://www.belguim-emb.org/newtwatch

"NewtWatch" is a profoundly anti-Newt news service. "Whether you're curious about Newt's Congressional voting record, interested in those ethics complaints you've heard so much about, or trying to learn who in *your* Zip Code contributed to Newt, you'll find it all here, and more, with more to come," says the site's Webmaster. Read the Newt's letter to the NRA, in which he promises to oppose all gun control legislation as long as he remains Speaker of the House. Review information on Newt's office expenditures and staff salaries, as well as an editorial note that points out that the fiscal conservative Gingrich needs 30% more cash to run his office than did the previous Speaker.

Figure 547 The Newtwit and his pals.

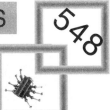

The Harvard Salient

http://www.fierce.net/salient

The Harvard Salient is a bi-weekly journal of political thought that categorizes itself as "naturally conservative but free from political allegiances." A group of Harvard students, who sought to provide a journalistic alternative to a predominantly liberal campus press, founded *The Harvard Salient* in 1981. *The Salient's* goal, they say, "is to return to the Harvard campus the principles of liberal education: tolerance, freedom of speech and thought, and above all, a respect for democracy." Articles address such topics as the continuing legacy of Vietnam, modern racism, politically correct pedagogy, and "liberal revisionism in college-level history curricula."

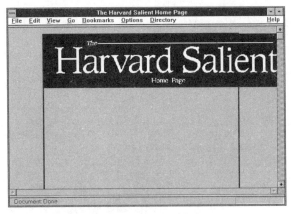

Figure 548 *Conservatism, Harvard style.*

The Hunger Project

http://www.igc.org/thp/

The tragedy of chronic, persistent hunger is staggering—35,000 of us succumb to this silent killer every day. Three-quarters of those who die from hunger are children under the age of five. Each day, slow starvation ravages the health, intelligence, and productivity of nearly one billion of our fellow human beings. The Hunger Project is chartered to mobilize leadership at all levels of society to confront the root causes of this problem. From remote villages in Africa and Asia to the corridors of power in Washington and Tokyo, The Hunger Project empowers women and men to discover their vision, express their leadership, and work together to create a future free from the holocaust.

Figure 549 *A simple plea: feed the hungry.*

550

International Federation of Liberal & Radical Youth

http://www.ftech.net/~worldlib/IFLRY_index.html

The International Federation of Liberal and Radical Youth (IFLRY) is a federation of 61 liberal and radical youth organizations from around the world. IFLRY organizes conferences, seminars, and delegation swaps for its member groups, as well as an annual "General Assembly." Most of the member organizations are far more than liberal. The emphasis is on radical. Members include Socialist and Marxist youth groups such as the Young Pioneers, the Youth Socialist Workers International, the Young Atheists League, and the Teens for Social Justice. Whether you are sympathetic to radical causes or not, I encourage you to read ILFRY's "Programme of Action" for the period 1993-1995.

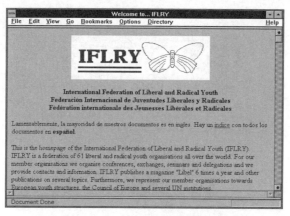

Figure 550 Supporting liberal youth worldwide.

551

The Interfaith Alliance

http://www.intr.net/tialliance

The Interfaith Alliance is a worldwide organization of ministers, priests, rabbis, and other clerics that confronts the extreme right-wing religious conservatism. This Web site provides the general public with the information and tools it needs to fight such extremism. For example, one link transports you to a digital hypertext document entitled "The Radical Religious Right in Their Own Words." This document archives "disturbing" quotations from Christian Coalition founder Pat Robertson, Executive Director Ralph Reed, "and several of their fellow extremists." Another file documents the Interfaith Alliance's fight against what they call "the Religious Coercion Amendment," which would allow prayer and religious symbols in public schools and other public buildings and institutions.

Figure 551.1 Interfaith Alliance home page.

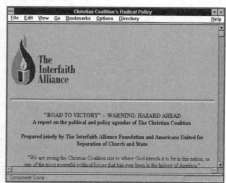

Figure 551.2 Details on their program.

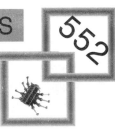

Sen. Edward Kennedy Home Page

http://www.ai.mit.edu/projects/iiip/Kennedy/homepage.html

This site is a great place to get information on the senior Senator from Massachusetts, Edward Moore Kennedy. At this site, you can find out what Kennedy is saying about the latest issues, access Kennedy's biographical information and committee assignments, or send him e-mail. Useful links connect you to other Federal offices (the President, senators, and congressional representatives). You'll also find links to a handy Washington, D.C. guide, a links list entitled "Massachusetts on the Web," and more. Coming soon: a link to the John F. Kennedy School of Government, as well as links to the John F. Kennedy Center for the Performing Arts and several other Kennedy-family sites.

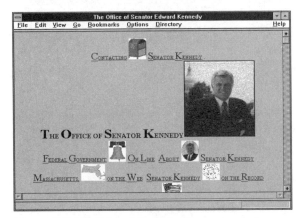

Figure 552 The Edward Kennedy home page.

Robert F. Kennedy Democratic Organization

http://www.webcom.com/~albany/rfk.html

The Robert F. Kennedy Democrats constitute the Democratic organization for Albany, New York's state capital. What makes this site interesting to those of us who don't live in upstate New York? Well, the site contains an impressive multimedia exhibit that documents the life and times of one of my great heroes, Robert F. Kennedy. You'll find a comprehensive collection of images and sound files (along with a copy of the RealAudio sound player you can download) that depict RFK at various high and low points in his life, including his famous remarks on JFK and on "this generation" at the 1964 Democratic National Convention.

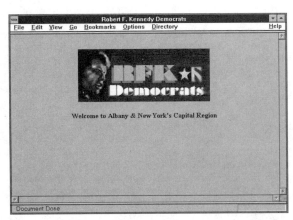

Figure 553 Home page of the RFK Democrats.

Legislative Schedules: Senate & House

http://sen.ca.gov/htbin/ca-legiss

Interested in U.S. political affairs? Then the "Legislative Schedules" is a great resource for you. At this site, two primary files—The Senate Daily File and The Assembly (House) Daily File—contain a date-by-date and committee-by-committee report of all scheduled hearings, as well as all bills or topics that appear on each hearing's agenda. View information chronologically or alphabetically by committee. The site also provides homepages and e-mail addresses for all senators and representatives and legislative calendars for the current and recently past legislative sessions.

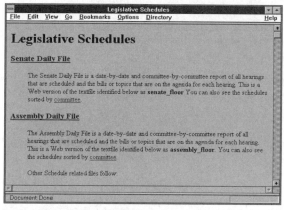

Figure 554 Capitol Hill schedules.

555

The Official Liberal Democrats Home Page

http://www.libdems.org.uk/

The Liberal Democratic Party is one of the leading political parties in the United Kingdom. And, according to a proud announcement on its home page, the organization is also Britain's "most wired" political party. "Our homepage is not just a shop window for the Liberal Democrats," the party's homepage says. "You will find mail links and telephone numbers throughout these pages. We want this service to make our party more accessible and responsive to the needs of ordinary people, so please make use of these links." Very well. At this site, you are privy to policy statements, party history, digital reprints of newspaper articles and interviews concerning the party, and more. You also get a quick and effective way to communicate with MPs (Members of Parliament), Councilors, and even the Leader of the Liberal Democrats, the Rt. Honorable Paddy Ashdown. Here, here!

Figure 555.1 Liberal Democrats home page.

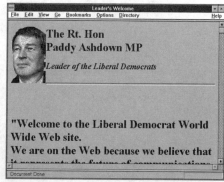

Figure 555.2 Paddy Ashdown, Party Leader.

World Wide Web Libertarian Pages

http://www.libertarian.com/wwlp/indexB.html

Libertarians do not believe in any single philosophy or creed. Within the Libertarian movement, you can find atheists and Christians, objectivists and subjectivists, Unitarians and advocates of natural rights, and many others. Libertarians are united in one thing: they see the state as the primary obstacle to individual freedom. The modern libertarian movement owes much to pre-twentieth century liberals, now known as classical liberals, such as Adam Smith and John Locke. Find out more at this site, which provides a comprehensive list of links to Libertarian literature, organizations, mailing lists, and more. The Libertarians seem right at home amid the informational anarchy of the Web.

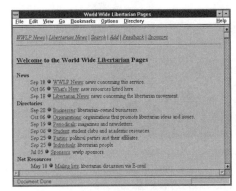

Figure 556.1 The world's Web home of libertarianism.

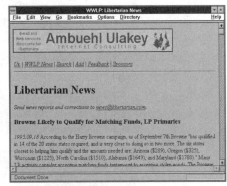

Figure 556.2 Libertarian News.

The George C. Marshall European Center for Security Studies

http://www.marshall.adsn.int/marshall.html

Founded in June of 1993, the Marshall Center seeks to become the leading institution within the Department of Defense for education and research on the rapidly changing European security environment. To ensure stability in Europe, the Marshall Center wants to create an enduring and ever-expanding network of national security officials who understand defense planning in democratic societies with market economies. In addition, the Marshall Center wants to provide those officials with greater opportunity to share their perspectives on current and future security issues. To advance its objectives, the Marshall Center created the valuable database of studies and raw data available to you via this server.

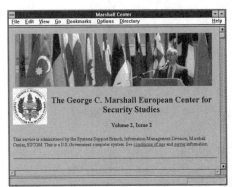

Figure 557.1 The George Marshall Center.

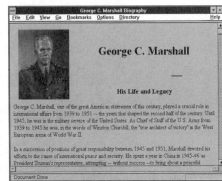

Figure 557.2 A bio of General Marshall.

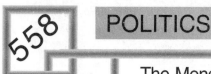

POLITICS

The Monday Lobby Group

http://www.clark.net/pub/gen/mlg

The Monday Lobby Group, a group of mostly left-wing peace and security organizations, meets weekly in Washington, D.C. The group discusses upcoming Congressional committee meetings, hearings, and votes on issues relating to arms and international security. The Monday Lobby Group also discusses various lobbying plans and divides related tasks among its participant organizations. The last time I visited this site, hot topics included lobbying efforts to defeat the Seawolf submarine, halt the Strategic Defense Initiative, and kill the B-2 "Stealth" Bomber.

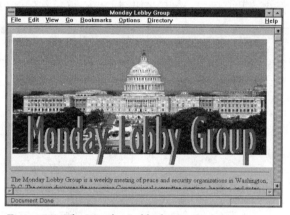

Figure 558 *The Monday Lobby home page.*

National Commission for Economic Conversion and Disarmament

http://www.fas.org/pub/gen/ncecd/index.html

The National Commission for Economic Conversion and Disarmament is a non-profit, nonpartisan organization dedicated to educating the public on the need and the means for an orderly transfer of military resources to civilian use. The Commision believes that the end of the Cold War gives America an unprecedented opportunity to reverse the arms race, build a new foundation for international security, and redirect billions of dollars in the defense budget to neglected domestic needs. The Commission advocates a massive program of economic conversion that emphasizes (1) planning for alternative production before defense industry cuts and layoffs occur, and (2) stimulating alternative markets for the products of post-conversion defense contractors. To find out more about this novel scheme, visit this site.

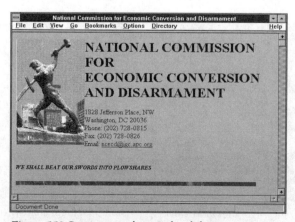

Figure 559 *Beating swords into ploughshares.*

National Security News Service

http://www.fas.org/pub/gen/nsns/index.html

The "National Security News Service" works to increase and improve the major news media's coverage of military, arms control, and international security stories. With funding from foundations and individual donors, the "News Service" develops stories from sources around the United States and abroad, including congressional, intelligence, and military sources; inside whistle-blowers; and expert scholars and researchers. The "News Service" investigates and documents stories, consults with scientific and arms control experts, provides information to individual journalists, and arranges briefings by recognized experts and government officials for reporters and editors.

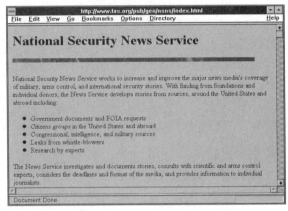

Figure 560 National Security News Service.

Richard Nixon Library & Birthplace

http://www.geninc.com/geni/USA/CA/Anaheim/travel/nixon.html

Located "15 minutes from Disneyland," the Richard Nixon Library promotes itself more as a tourist attraction than a library. In a presumed effort to compete with Disneyland's Space Mountain, the Library bills itself as "a high-tech roller coaster ride through half a century of California, U.S., and World History! Galleries, First Lady's Garden, Theaters, Memorial Garden, and the Restored Birthplace . . . A window on America's system of government, on the Presidency, and on the historic achievements of a senior statesman who was integrally involved with the most important issues, events, controversies, and personalities of our time." However, there are no mice signing autographs.

Figure 561 The Nixon Amusement Park.

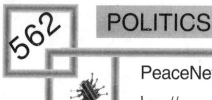

PeaceNet

http://www.peacenet.apc.org/peacenet

"PeaceNet" is a worldwide computer network serving organizations and individuals that work for positive change in the areas of peace, social and economic justice, human rights, and the struggle against racism. "PeaceNet" is a repository for current information on such issues as disarmament, economic justice, immigrant rights, the prison system, indigenous peoples, poverty, and children's rights. In addition to news and information, you'll find links to "PeaceNet's" many partner organizations in the Middle East, the Balkans, the Far East, the Pacific Basin, the former Soviet Union, and Latin America.

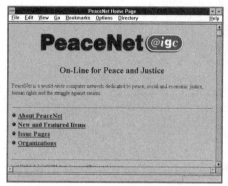 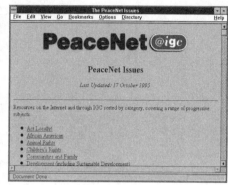

Figure 562.1 Options on the PeaceNet.   *Figure 562.2 PeaceNet issues pages.*

Physicians for Social Responsibility

http://www.psr.org:8000/

Winner of the Nobel Peace Prize for 1985, Physicians for Social Responsibility (PSR) is committed to eliminating weapons of mass destruction, preserving a sustainable environment, and reducing violence and its causes. The active conscience of American medicine, PSR uses its members' expertise and professional leadership, influence within the medical community, and strong links to policy makers to address what it perceives as the greatest threats to human welfare and survival. PSR is the U.S. affiliate of International Physicians for the Prevention of Nuclear War, a network of 200,000 physicians in 80 countries. With more than 90 local chapters and 20,000 U.S. members, PSR works to protect people from environmental health hazards and to shift government spending priorities away from what PSR considers wasteful military expenditures. To find out more about PSR, access the organization's Web site.

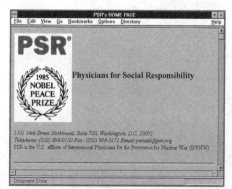 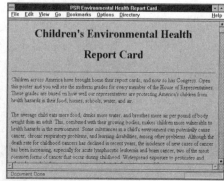

Figure 563.1 1985 Nobel Peace Prize winners. *Figure 563.2 What's the grade?*

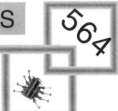

Political Parties Around the World

http://www.luna.nl/~benne/politics/parties.html

Talk about convenience! If you need information on a political party (I mean *any* political party *anywhere* around the globe), turn to this Web page. An easy tree-structure helps you isolate the information you need quickly and without hassle. To begin, you define a continent. Then, a country. At the country level, you click on your party of choice to access that organization's homepage. Of course, many of these pages are not in English. However, this set of links is still a wonderful resource. Benjamin den Butter, (benne@luna.nl), maintains this site. He deserves many thanks for a powerful political and governmental research tool.

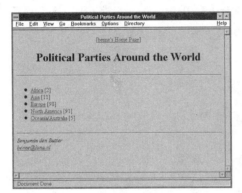

Figure 564.1 *Political Parties around the World.*

Figure 564.2 *British political parties.*

Political Science Links

http://spirit.lib/uconn.edu/PoliSci/polisci.htm

This site provides you with links to political science libraries; journals and collections of papers; research institutions, non-profit organizations, and government agencies; and a number of FTP servers, newsgroups, and listservs. Additionally, you'll find links to political science departments at colleges and universities across the country and around the world—Arizona State, the Australian Defense Force Academy, Brown, Caltech, Cornell, Duke, Flinders University of South Australia, Yale, Harvard, Princeton (including the Institute for Advanced Study), Northwestern, West Point, Annapolis, and more. In sum, this site lets you access a fantastic combination of powerful resources. Use it.

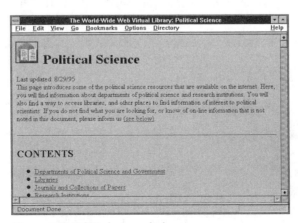

Figure 565 *Political science links.*

POLITICS

Johnston & Murphy's Presidential Footnotes

http://www.infi.net/jmshoe/

Johnston & Murphy designed this tongue in shoe (rather than cheek) consideration of Campaign '96 to help you stay in step with the candidates' stances and missteps. This information comes to you courtesy of Johnston & Murphy, maker of fine footwear for every U.S. President since Millard Fillmore. "Like you," the site says, "we want to know who'll fill the president's shoes." As Campaign '96 "kicks off," visit this site for witty commentary: "A horde of presidential hopefuls is attempting to follow in Clinton's footsteps and duplicate his amazing campaign feet of '92. Who could have predicted a barefoot boy from Hope, Arkansas, would successfully go to-to-toe with the then-popular Gulf War Commander-in-Chief? But a lackluster economy proved to be Bush's Achilles heel."

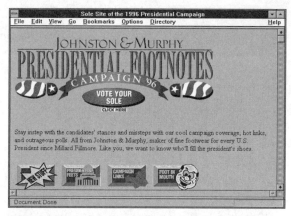

Figure 566 *Hoof on over to Presidential Footnotes.*

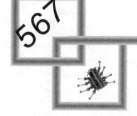

Project on Demilitarization and Democracy

http://www.fas.org/pub/gen/pdd/index.html

Call me crazy, but I suspect that a good way to guarantee you won't have democracy in the long term is to have total demilitarization in the short term. But if you disagree with me, you may like this Web page. The Project on Demilitarization and Democracy believes that the goals of demilitarization and democracy are linked. The organization believes that a dramatic reduction in the size and political power of armed forces in developing countries will spur progress toward full democratic rights, including freedom of speech, protection from human rights abuses, and fair elections. Perhaps they are correct. I am skeptical, but I would not mind if they proved me wrong.

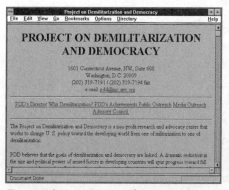

Figure 567.1 *An intro to the project.*

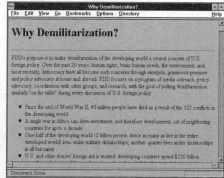

Figure 567.2 *An explanation of their rationale.*

The Right Side of the Web

http://www.clark.net/pub/jeffd/index.html

This site offers a long list of resources for the conservative. You'll find clear thinking, excellent writing, and valuable information along links such as "'96 Conservative Election Central" and "DeMOCKracy," which is an excellent new conservative comic strip. Also, to hear some well-reasoned arguments and debates, check out the "Conservative Reading Room." And be sure to treat yourself to some of the fun stuff. Stop by and help cast *Whitewater: The Miniseries*. Or, leave a message on the site's "Monument to the Clinton Presidency."

Figure 568 A conservative point of view.

Town Hall

http://www.townhall.com/

"Town Hall" is a new cooperative venture between Bill Buckley's *National Review* and The Heritage Foundation. Recently honored with *Point Survey's* "Top 5% of the Web" ranking, "Town Hall" is an excellently designed, graphically beautiful, information-rich resource. You'll find links to a broad range of conservative organizations and publications (but no Rush!). You'll also find many organizations here, including the American Conservative Union, Americans for Tax Reform, Empower America, The Family Research Council, The Leadership Institute, The National Commission on Economic Growth and Tax Reform, The Progress & Freedom Foundation, The Small Business Survival Committee, The Washington Times, and Young Americans for Freedom. The site is so well-done even a liberal will enjoy it.

Figure 569.1 The new conservative world.

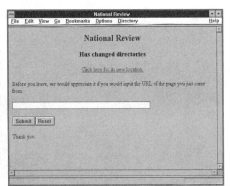

Figure 569.2 And an old conservative magazine.

Turn Left: The Home of Liberalism on the Web

http://falcon.cc.ukans.edu/~cubsfan/liberal.html

As the masthead for this site suggests, "when you know heading right is a dead end . . . Turn Left." Mike Silverman's excellent collection of links brings you organizations and publications concerned with social issues, government and policy issues, foreign policy, the economy, the presidency, and more. You also get links to homepages of some fairly well-known liberal types, including Tom Hayden and Jesse Jackson. At this site, you will find anti-nuclear, anti-gun, and women's rights organizations; civil rights lobbying groups (including the NAACP); consumer and public interest research organizations; environmental groups such as the Sierra Club and Friends of the Earth; and more.

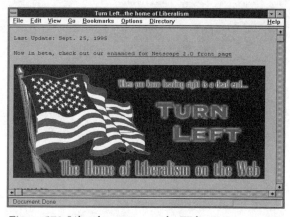

Figure 570 *Liberal resources on the Web.*

20/20 Vision

http://www.2020vision.org/brochure.html

One more for the lefties. If you are a lefty armed with more good intentions than you have time for, consider participating in the 20/20 program. Every month, "20/20 Vision" identifies the best way for you to spend 20 minutes to protect the environment and promote peace. "20/20" sends you a monthly action postcard with the information you need to write a brief letter or make a key phone call to policymakers facing crucial decisions. Your actions will help these leaders arrive at what "20/20" believes are the right choices for the earth and humankind. Every six months you will receive an update on the results of your actions. How many people are "20/20" participants? About 30,000. So you won't be alone. Joining with them gives you clout.

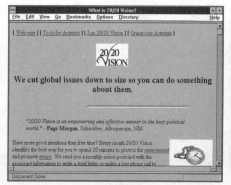

Figure 571.1 *20 minutes to a better world.*

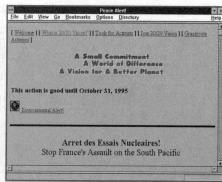

Figure 571.2 *A peace initiative.*

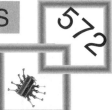

U.S. Government Hypertexts

http://sunsite.unc.edu/govdocs.html

This site provides an excellent collection of vital government documents in convenient hypertext editions. Your options are many: White House documents, the Report of the Bipartisan Commission on Entitlement and Tax Reform, Al Gore's National Performance Review (packed with recommendations on re-inventing government), the Clinton Administration's National Information Infrastructure Proposal, a valuable summary of the Clinton Administration's technology-related achievements, transcriptions of President Clinton's Saturday radio addresses, access to the National Trade Data Bank, and more. You might as well read this stuff; you paid for it.

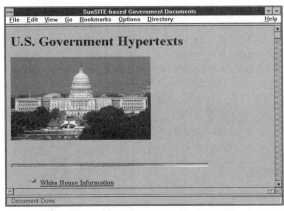

Figure 572 Important government documents on-line.

The United States Senate

http://policy.net/capweb/Senate/Senate.html

Want to write or telephone your Senator to whine about something? Not sure how to get in touch? You've come to the right place. This site includes homepage and e-mail links to every senator on Capitol Hill. Search by name of senator, state, committee, or party. Get the immediate gratification of knowing that ten seconds after you've finished writing your complaint, it will arrive at its destination and be read by some disinterested intern who will promptly send you a machine-signed (snail-mail) form letter in return. That is, unless you live in Rhode Island, the greatest and tiniest state in the country, where our two wonderful senators (Pell and Chafee) are on a first-name basis with just about everyone in the state. Oh, here comes Claiborne now . . .

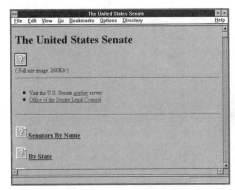

Figure 573.1 The Senate home page.

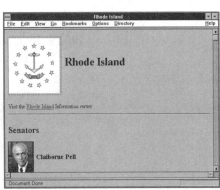

Figure 573.2 The best senators are always from Rhode Island.

Republican Web Central

http://republicans.vt.com/

"Republican Web Central" provides one-stop shopping for local, state, and national information by and about Republicans and their party. You'll find links to the homepages of hundreds of local Republican organizations and clubs across the country. Read detailed information on the (many) would-be Republican presidential candidates, with links to the homepages of Lamar Alexander, Phil Gramm, Arlen Specter, Richard Lugar, Pat Buchanan, Richard Dornan, and Malcolm Forbes, Jr., who I didn't even realize was running until I visited "Republican Web Central." You also get links to the official 1996 GOP Convention homepage, C-Span's homepage for coverage of the '96 campaign, and more. One interesting point: Bob Dole does not seem to have a campaign Web page.

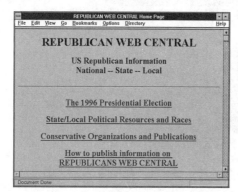

Figure 574.1 Republican Web Central.

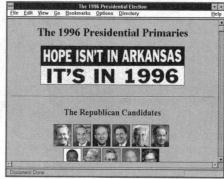

Figure 574.2 The Republican presidential field.

Women's Action for New Directions

http://www.fas.org/pub/gen/wand/index.html

Originally founded as Women's Action for Nuclear Disarmament by Dr. Helen Calidicott in the early 1980s, Women's Action for New Directions (WAND) seeks to empower women politically, reduce militarism and violence, and redirect military resources toward unmet human and environmental needs. WAND organizes female state legislators through WiLL, the Women Legislators' Lobby; works to elect women through the work of WAND-PAC; educates through the WAND Education Fund; and encourages and supports women in office through its media training workshops. Get more information at the WAND Web site.

Figure 575 The WAND home page.

Washington Weekly

http://dolphin.gulf.net

The *Washington Weekly,* a conservative, political-news magazine, is now available on the Web. To get an idea of the magazine's contents, try this sampling of titles from a few recent articles: "The Omnipresent Federal Thought Police," "Foster's Ties to Israelis Questions," and "Sam 'The Monkey' Loses Composure over Medicare." The periodical makes something of a hobby of tracking Bill Clinton on a daily basis, gleefully chronicling any gaff or embarrassment and, perhaps, making more of many of these incidents than is warranted. In any event, many readers will find the editorials here sensible and engaging, and the reporting to-the-point. One nice feature for me was the *Washington Weekly's* reprints of portions of *The Federalist Papers* in every issue.

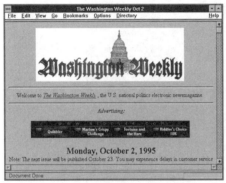

Figure 576.1 The Washington Weekly.   *Figure 576.2 All things political.*

The White House

http://www.whitehouse.gov/

You own the White House, so feel free to drop in any time. Come via the Web and you won't have to suffer the indignity of going through a metal detector. At "The White House" site, you get press releases, appointment schedules, speeches, and briefing sheets on international and domestic affairs, as well as executive orders and proclamations. Yes, you can also access the official repository of "Remarks during photo-ops." If you are not interested in Bill and Hill, you can drop by the vice-president's office to check in with Al and Tipper. Send e-mail to any or all of them (or to Socks the Cat, if you'd care to). You will invariably get a (form) response, even if you write to Socks.

Figure 577 Welcome to the White House.

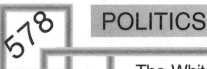

The Whitewater Scandal

http://dolphin.gulf.net/whitew.html

Whitewater started as a land development of river-front property in Arkansas in the 1980s. The Clintons received a large percentage of shares in the development without putting up any money. When the development went sour, additional capital infusions were needed. Some evidence and testimony suggests that these cash infusions were obtained illegally from the Federal Government and never paid back. That, in a nutshell, is the crux of the Whitewater issue. At this site, you will find complete details on the scandal, from its inception to the present day. This is, perhaps, the very best chronology of the events that comprise that strange, quirky thing labeled "the Whitewater scandal."

Figure 578 A conservative take on Whitewater.

World Liberalism

http://www.ftech.net/~worldlib/

Come here a set of links addressing national and international liberalism. "The idea of this server is not only to inform you about liberalism," writes the Webmaster. "We also provide lots of general political information. For example, check out our pages with links to media, governments and organizations worldwide." Of particular value are weekly news updates, including "World Liberalism's" portrait of a "political hotspot of the week." You also get a link to Liberal International, which is the world union of Liberal parties in over 48 countries, twenty of which are now in control of governments. Liberal International bases its work on basic documents, such as the Liberal Manifesto of 1947, and promotes democracy, pluralism, tolerance, human rights, and economy-based market principles.

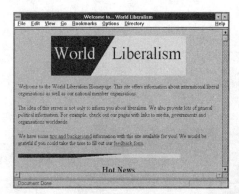 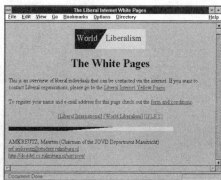

Figure 579.1 World Liberalism home page.   *Figure 579.2 E-mail prominent liberals.*

More Politics

As you surf the Web, you may find that one or more of the site addresses listed in this book have changed. In such cases, connect to Jamsa Press at http://www.jamsa.com and click on the icon that corresponds to the *1001 Really Cool Web Sites* book. Jamsa Press will list replacement addresses (when possible) for sites that have moved. In addition, you can also use the following site list as you search for information on politics:

California Electronic Government Info.	http://cpsr.org/dox/cegi.html
Ca. State Lands Commission Home Page	http://diablo.slc.ca.gov/
DOD's R&D CYCLE	http://dtic01.wpafb.af.mil/rdc.html
Minnesota E-Democracy Project	http://free-net.mpls-stpaul.mn.us:8000/govt/e-democracy/
Government Agencies (Government)	http://galaxy.einet.net/galaxy/Government/Government-Agencies.html
U.S. and Michigan Politics	http://garnet.msen.com:70/1/vendor/freep/lookhere
DOD WWW Servers	http://navysgml.dt.navy.mil/dodsites.html
MIT Political Science	http://polisci-mac-2.mit.edu/

APT Data Group

http://power.globalnews.com

APT Data Group publishes a range of market-leading magazines covering all aspects of computing. APT's titles include *PowerPC News* (a fortnightly which addresses IBM, Apple, and Motorola technology). APT also publishes *Unix News International*, the monthly online magazine for Unix and open-systems users and developers. A third online APT publication is *IBM System User International*, which provides up-to-date news and analysis on all major events in the PC world. At this site, you can register a free e-mail subscription for any of these electronic magazines, or access information on paper publications that include *Computergram International, Unigram X, Software Futures*, and *Computer Business Review*.

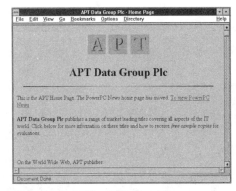

Figure 580.1 The APT Data Group.

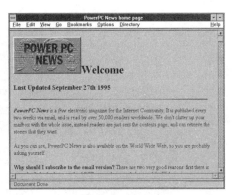

Figure 580.2 Power PC News.

The Arizona Daily Star

http://www.azstarnet.com/

Here at the cyberhome of *The Arizona Daily Star,* you can sample an online edition of one of the best newspapers in the country, view wire service reports updated every ten minutes, and see tomorrow morning's top stories tonight! This site gives a healthy taste of the resources that *The Arizona Daily Star* makes available through its online edition, which is not just an e-text edition of the standard daily, but rather an expanded interactive news database with real-time data (wire reports, stock market information, and more). For the value of the services you receive, this online edition's subscription fee is quite modest.

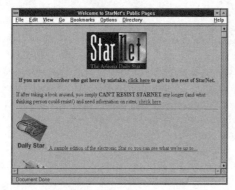

Figure 581.1 StarNet: The Arizona Daily.

Figure 581.2 Daily news updates.

The Box

http://lamar.colostate.edu/~kweed

The Box is a literary zine newly launched in the autumn of 1995 by a professor at the University of Colorado. At the time of this writing, one (astonishingly good) issue is off press, as it were. Check out the short stories "Penance" and "The Mission." And read the commentary on joyfully greeting the Lord's new day: "Every morning the clock radio blasts some Billy Ray Cyrus tune or farm reports that force me out of rapid eye movement and into the reality of another achy breaky, pork-bellied day. As the paper boy hurls my a.m. edition into the front yard, the subtleties of morning hit me in the face like a 16-point headline. Crawling to the front door, I wipe the schmutz from my eyes and retrieve the *Daily Chronicle,* not bothering to notice the ink blotches on my fingers while I rub away the sleep . . ." And so on.

Figure 582.1 The Box.

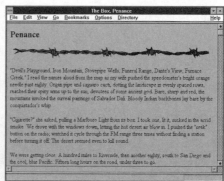

Figure 582.2 A great short story.

Buzz On-Line

http://204.119.182.202/FictionHome.html

Fiction has always been an integral part of *Buzz* magazine. In a section entitled "L.A. Tales," *Buzz* has published (and continues to publish) some of the most celebrated names in contemporary American fiction—Charles Bukowski, Kate Braverman, Bebe Moore Campbell, Thom Jones, and so on. As a result, *Buzz* is recognized as one of the top outlets in the United States for new short stories. *Buzz On-Line* continues that tradition with an electronic anthology of cutting-edge stories: some funny and some dramatic, but all with a distinctive L.A. twist. When I visited the site, the featured story was Donald Rawley's "Nirvana Drive," an acid-tinged portrait of an abandoned Beverly Hills wife who decides to celebrate her fiftieth birthday by killing her ex-husband.

Figure 583.1 Buzz home page.

Figure 583.2 A story titled "Nirvana Drive."

The Chicago Tribune

http://www.tribune.com/

The online edition of the *Chicago Tribune* is updated daily, giving you a complete run-down of page-one headlines and the entire texts of related articles. You'll find financial news and updates, the complete daily *Chicago Tribune* "Help Wanted" section in digital form, and more. More? Yup. I am talking about movie and book reviews, Chicago movie listings, restaurant reviews, and information about museums, concerts, and sports events around town. In sum, this fabulous Web site does justice to the outstanding newspaper it represents in cyberspace.

Figure 584.1 The Chicago Tribune home page.

Figure 584.2 Up-to-date financial information.

585

Computer Shopper

http://www.zdnet.com/~cshopper/

What could be more convenient than having an online edition of *Computer Shopper*? Perhaps a cold, fresh keg of Guinness propped next to my PC, but beyond that I couldn't say. Instead of turning the pages of huge bulky tabloids, leaf through the ads here in cyberspace. A word of caution, though: this site is the best place to get good prices on machines *only if you know exactly what you're shopping for*. You see, in return for cutting costs, most of these advertisers won't do much free consulting. As such, you should know exactly what you want to buy before you pick up the telephone. However, for anyone who is technically hip, this site is a fine resource.

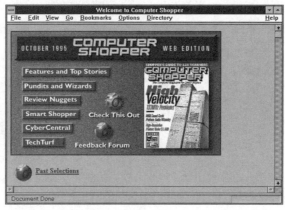

Figure 585 *Computer Shopper home page.*

586

Entertainment Week

http://www.timeinc.com/ew/

Well, you're too late. You've already missed the special *Melrose Place* issue of *Entertainment Week's* digital edition. That ran in mid-September. But if you scramble, you might be able to catch the issue dedicated to those attractive, though troubled, kids who live at Hollywood zip code 90210. In addition to coverage of television, the digital edition includes movie reviews, record reviews, concert and tour news for leading club and cabaret acts, and, of course, celebrity gossip. Was John Tesch seen with Barbara Streisand? Is Jack Nicholson having plastic surgery? What is Sly Stallone being paid to shoot up yet another hidden POW camp?

Figure 586 *Entertainment Week.*

The Houston Chronicle Interactive

http://www.chron.com/

The Houston Chronicle's interactive edition provides a good 80% of the print edition, including all the top stories, sports, reviews, and editorials. Additionally, it also provides special interactive features that are, as the editors say, "uniquely an online experience." These features include contests, instantly correcting crossword puzzles (when you finish, or before you finish the puzzle, click a button to see how your responses compare to the puzzle's correct answers), and video clips that accompany especially important front-page news stories (such as lawyers making summation speeches to the jury in the Simpson trial). As an extra perk, you'll find links to all of Houston's best community-oriented Internet sites.

Figure 587.1 Houston Chronicle.

Figure 587.2 All the day's top stories.

ImageSoup

http://www.emedia.net/imagesoup

This quarterly electronic publication of the New Media Arts Professionals Group contains tips, tricks, and techniques for creating fantastic visuals using Photoshop, MacroMedia Director, Fractal Design Painter, and countless filter packages. This zine is actually a vast palette of tools and strategies from concept to image. Even those who are not graphic artists will enjoy this zine because of the stunning graphics that decorate every page and serve as illustrations for the articles. So, if you want to view gorgeous pictures and add depth and dimension to your own work, visit *ImageSoup*.

Figure 588.1 ImageSoup.

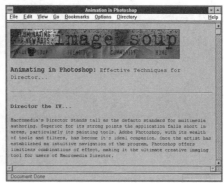

Figure 588.2 Creating animations in Photoshop.

Investor's Business Daily

http://ibd.ensemble.com/

Founded in 1984, *Investor's Business Daily* is a national daily newspaper headquartered in Los Angeles. The paper, now available in digital format, has a great reputation for delivering outstanding stock-market analysis and advice. The online edition includes summaries of all the day's important business stories, features articles on important concerns facing business people and investors, profiles some of the world's most successful business leaders, provides stock-market analysis and advice, and more. You'll even find "user-friendly" executive summaries on a range of computer and technology issues. Take advantage of the two-week free trial offer for the Windows edition of *Investor's Business Daily*. To find details, visit the *Investor's Business Daily* Web site.

Figure 589.1 Investor's Business Daily.

Figure 589.2 About IBD Electronic.

590

MacUser Web

http://www.macuser.ziff.com/~macuser/

Celebrating its one-year anniversary this autumn (1995), the online edition of *MacUser* offers its happy readers great articles, reviews, and forecasts. Ziff-Davis, *MacUser's* publisher, is best-known for the vigorous hardware and software testing its "PC Labs" unit conducts. In *MacUser*, as in other Ziff-Davis magazines, you'll find the results of these exhaustive product tests. In addition, you'll have the opportunity to read and critique the writings of John Dvorak, whose comments appear regularly in *MacUser* and other Ziff-Davis publications.

Figure 590.1 MacUser Web.

Figure 590.2 MacUser product reviews.

MacWeek Magazine On-Line

http://www.ziff.com/~macweek

Unlike its paper counterpart, *MacWeek's* online edition is updated throughout the week. Thus, you get frequent online exclusives. For example, when I visited this site recently, I read about a reorganization of the online services division that occurred only hours before. This site also includes reviews of Macintosh hardware and software, op-ed pieces on issues related to Macintosh computing, updates on the new series of PowerPC processors (some with speeds as fast as 600 Mhz) in development at Motorola and IBM, and more. No serious Mac user or developer should be without *MacWeek* in one form or another, either paper or digital. And if you are on the Web anyway, why not go digital?

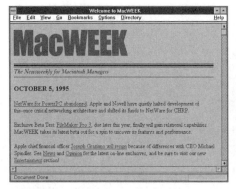 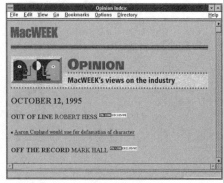

Figure 591.1 MacWeek Magazine.   *Figure 591.2 MacWeek editorials.*

Metropolis

http://virtumall.com/newstand/metropolis/main.html

Metropolis explores the ways design (architecture, industrial design, urban planning, and graphic design) shapes the world and the ways the world, in turn, shapes design. Neither a trade journal, a "how-to" magazine, nor a glossy "wish book," *Metropolis* focuses on the social, political, human, and aesthetic issues that inform every kind of design, from the schematics of a chair to the structure of network interfaces. For design professionals, *Metropolis* is a source of new ideas and a way to keep abreast of the changes shaping their professions. For design-conscious consumers, *Metropolis* provides an inside look at the man-made world around them. Visit this site to learn more about *Metropolis*, an exceptional magazine.

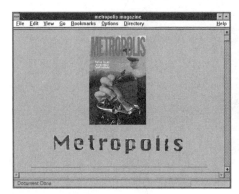 

Figure 592.1 Metropolis Magazine.   *Figure 592.2 The September 1995 issue.*

The Miami Herald

http://herald.kri.com/

When I first visited this site, it was something new—still under construction, but already looking cool. Perhaps the coolest of all the cool elements at this site is the archive of columns by *Miami Herald* humorist Dave Barry, who is running for president yet again. His motto for this electoral season: "Dave Barry for President. It's time we settled for less." When I e-mailed Barry and asked him for a brief campaign statement, he responded, "My platform is simple. What I say is that people who read Ed Renehan's *1001 Really Cool Web Sites* should be exempt from paying all federal, state, and local taxes. In fact, the government should give each and every one of Ed's readers a million dollars each just for buying the book. They don't even have to read it." Gosh, I hope he's not just telling you what you want to hear.

Figure 593.1 The Miami Herald On-line.

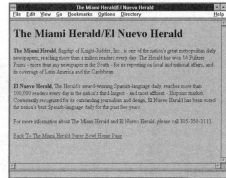

Figure 593.2 Your hosts, Knight-Ridder.

The Mississippi Review

http://sushi.st.usm.edu/~barthelm

One of the most prestigious literary magazines in the U.S. is now online with a digital edition. The staff of *The Mississippi Review* says they've entered cyberspace to "participate in the gonzo national dialog" taking place on the Information Super Highway. "We're starting with old-fashioned stories and poems (well, maybe they aren't old-fashioned, except in the sense that they are stories and poems, not buckets of peanut butter), but we're hoping to expand from this ground to more interactive components: parts where the readers contribute directly, or with editorial help; where collaborative efforts can take place; where whatever this Web grows into, we can grow as well."

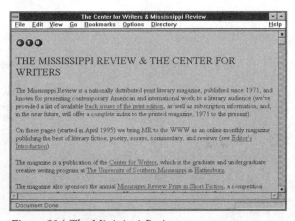

Figure 594 The Mississippi Review.

Mother Jones: The Mojo Wire

http://www.mojones.com/index.html

Stop here to check out the digital edition of the classic, radical-news magazine *Mother Jones*. This site includes digital reprints of many, though not all, of the articles that appear in the print edition, including scathingly splendid profiles of Phil Gramm, Rush Limbaugh, and other conservatives. The site also provides Mojo's special ongoing report on "The Race to the White House;" special reports on such topics as Phil Gramm's role in the Packwood scandal; Bob Dole's activities during the Watergate crisis; and a look at Newt Gingrich's attempts to increase the amount of federal entitlement money going to his home district while advocating cuts in nearly every other part of the federal budget. Visit this site and learn to love your mother. Your *Mother Jones,* that is.

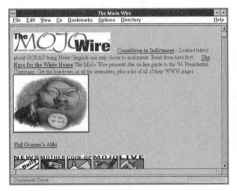
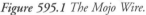

Figure 595.1 The Mojo Wire.

Figure 595.2 Your favorite radical rag.

The Mystery Zone

http://www.mindspring.com/~walter/mystzone.html

The Mystery Zone bills itself as "the Internet's first magazine of mystery, suspense, and crime fiction." This weekly digital magazine features reviews, short stories, interviews with writers of popular crime-fiction, excerpts from novels by new voices in mystery-fiction, and more. Be sure to stop at the "Deadly Image Vault," where you can revel in cover art from the tacky heyday of pulp-fiction. Copy some of the covers and use them as cool wallpaper on your computer. If you are sleuthing around looking for some good detective/crime fiction, burn *The Mystery Zone* into your hot list. Check it out!

Figure 596.1 The Mystery Zone.

Figure 596.2 Complete short stories.

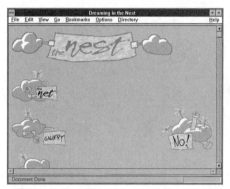

PUBLICATIONS/PERIODICALS

The *Net* On-Line

http://www.thenet-usa.com/

The editors of *The Net,* a great Generation X Internet magazine, have assembled a fantastic gallery of art for you to enjoy. When I visited this site, the Net featured the art of Richard Downs. (Primarily an editorial illustrator who works for national consumer and trade magazines, Downs is also exploring multimedia, and he recently finished working on a CD-ROM for Inscape entitled *The Dark Eye*.) In addition to art by contributors, you'll also find works that the Net's Web Rat stole from other sites. Before you leave this site, be sure to check out "Living with Matt & Jeff." It's not your average super-stale, rarely updated, here's-a-picture-of-my-cat Web page. No, "Living with Matt & Jeff" is the kind of Web page only *The Net* could deliver.

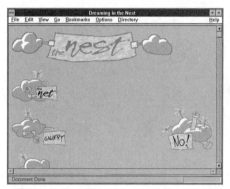
Figure 597.1 *The Net On-line.*

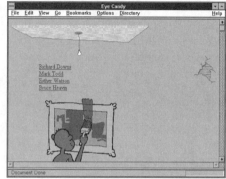
Figure 597.2 *The Net's gallery.*

The *Net Literary Journal*

http://www.webcom.com/~netjourn/

The treat for me in writing this book is discovering fantastic things on the Web, like *The Net Literary Journal*. When I visited this site, I found some of the finest short fiction that I've read in a very long time. The magazine features some of the best of America's largely unrecognized short fiction talents, including Michael Martin and Peter Simmons. On the poetry side, the work is refreshing and upbeat and, fortunately, doesn't exhibit the trivial content that so often characterizes contemporary verse. I recommend *The Net Literary Journal* for all who shine their lamp in various corners in search of something worth reading.

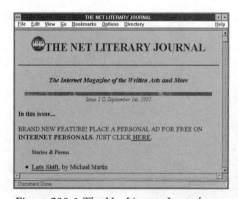
Figure 598.1 *The Net Literary Journal.*

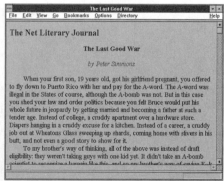
Figure 598.2 *Simmons' "The Last Good War."*

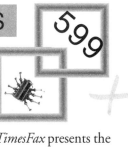
The New York Times

http://nytimesfax.com

TimesFax is an eight-page digest of *The New York Times* available now on the World Wide Web. *TimesFax* presents the highlights of front-page *Times* articles; foreign, national, and business news; sports; editorials and commentaries; and even the *Times* crossword puzzle! Designed to provide the reader with the look and feel of a newspaper, *TimesFax* is presented in Adobe Acrobat format. I have added this site to my hot list and come here every morning for my daily news. (By the way, *TimesFax* is more timely than the New York Times print edition. The site's content changes promptly at midnight, Eastern Standard Time. The print edition doesn't hit the stands until several hours later.)

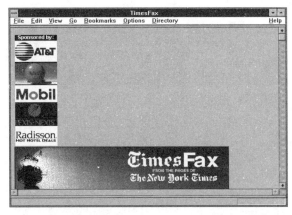

Figure 599 The Times on-line.

PC Computing On-Line

http://www.pc-computing.ziff.com/~pccomp

Read the online version of the magazine that has become known as the *Esquire* of computing. What a variety of useful items! Bugs gotcha down? Check Doug Vargas' "Bug Bytes" column regularly for the latest software fixes! Or, check out hot features on such topics as Windows 95, the Internet, and Newt Gingrich's Web hot-list. Then, take a few moments (actually, about sixty seconds) to survey the "One-Minute Guide" for a brief tutorial on a computer-related topic. The day I visited this site, the Guide's topic was "RealAudio for Your Browser." Do yourself a favor and visit.

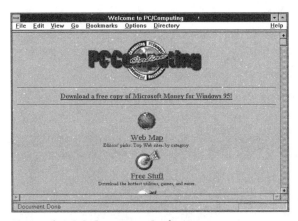

Figure 600 PC Computing On-line.

PUBLICATIONS/PERIODICALS

PC Week On-Line

http://www.pc-computing.ziff.com/~pcweek

PC Week is the touchstone industry-news magazine for all PC users, programmers, and administrators. Whether you need the latest news on who is developing what or who is buying whom, updates on forthcoming software releases, or analysis and reviews of new computer-related products, *PC Week* is the place to come. The online edition of *PC Week* includes news and special reports on such topics as "Novell, where change is the only constant" and "Windows 95: Proceed with Caution." You can also search current and back issues of *PC Week* by title, category, date, or author. Thus, the online edition is both a great source of current news and a splendid database of information on past industry events and issues.

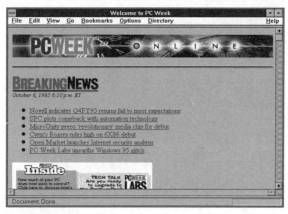

Figure 601 PC Week.

PC Magazine On-Line

http://www.pcmag.ziff.com/~pcmag/

PC Magazine is an excellent publication with some first-class writers who routinely have something intelligent and useful to convey. I am speaking most particularly of Jim Seymour, Don Willmott, and Michael Miller. Visit this site for their perceptive considerations of everything on the PC scene, including Windows 95 bugs, the new Intel P6, Web-based Groupware, and OS/2. In addition, you'll find great software downloads, including utilities such as Launch Control, which you can use to control DOS and Windows applications under Windows 3.1.

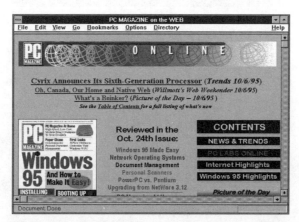

Figure 602 PC Magazine.

People Magazine

http://pathfinder.com/people

In this online edition of *People*, you'll find all the latest, most vital news on such important figures as Martha Stewart, Robert *Shapiro,* Connie Sellica, and Merv Griffin. You'll also find the "Passages" column, where you can read brief, illustrated notices about who among the famous has died, divorced, married, or given birth in the past week. And, of course, you get "Insider" gossip on who is sleeping with whom in Tinseltown or elsewhere in the pop firmament. Visit this site for great mind-candy.

Figure 603 People Magazine.

Playbill Magazine

http://www.webcom.com/~broadway

Playbill's international and national theater listings are by far the most up-to-date and comprehensive available anywhere on the Internet. *Playbill* recently added U.S. regional, London, and Paris listings to its roster, which already included Broadway, off-Broadway, and touring companies. *Playbill's* data bank now totals nearly 1,000 theaters worldwide, with more to come. In the very near future, this site will offer thirty-second video clips of Broadway and off-Broadway shows. Other options? You can search a *Playbill* database for bios of your favorite Broadway or off-Broadway actors; purchase original cast albums; and purchase theater memorabilia, books, posters, and even tickets. This site is a theater-lover's paradise.

Figure 604.1 Playbill Magazine.

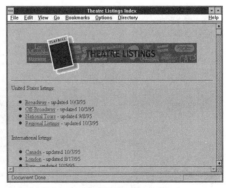

Figure 604.2 Theater listings.

605

Popular Mechanics: PM Zone

http://popularmechanics.com/

Come to the Web site of *Popular Mechanics*, the magazine that for 93 years has documented the dreams and deeds of those who believe technology will transform the world for the better. At this milepost on the Information Super Highway, past and future, medium and message, converge. *Popular Mechanics* has gone all out to make "PM Zone" a Web site unmatched in quality and depth of content. (You'll find more than 1,000 pages added every weekday.) And, in keeping with the *Popular Mechanics*' tradition of explaining the technically complex in easy-to-understand ways, this site tells you step-by-step how to make the most out of everything it contains. The result is very elegant, integrated hypertext and online multimedia.

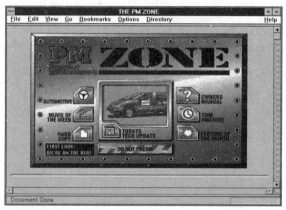

Figure 605 Do-it-yourself at the PM Zone.

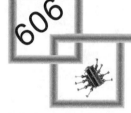

606

Pyramid Magazine

http://www.io.com/sjgames/pyramid

Published six times yearly, Pyramid Magazine gives you the best in gaming: the best articles, the best adventures, and the best entertainment. Past issues have featured material for such games as *GURPS, Champions, INWO, In Monine, Cyberpunk 2020, Car Wars, Toon,* and many other game systems. The print edition of the magazine comes bundled with game cards for *INWO, Galactic Empires, Everway, On the Edge: Arcana, Highlander, Towers in Time,* and other games not available anywhere else. Of course, the magazine also has games reviews, games-industry news and gossip, and more. Visit this site to get more details on this exciting magazine for the games enthusiast.

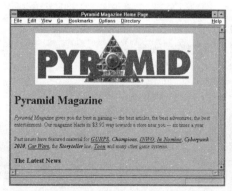

Figure 606.1 Pyramid Magazine.

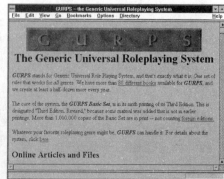

Figure 606.2 The game GURPS.

San Jose Mercury News

http://www.sjmercury.com/

One of California's most highly-regarded newspapers, The *San Jose Mercury News* delivers its digital edition at this Web site. You'll find the complete text of each daily edition and a comprehensive News Library of past editions that you can search by name, topic, or date. This site features international, national, and regional news; film, record, and book reviews; world and local sports; and classified advertising. The online edition of the real-estate classifieds is a remarkable resource for people from out-of-state who want (or need) to relocate to the San Jose area. All in all, the online edition of *The San Jose Mercury News* is, like the paper edition, a very useful daily.

Figure 607 Mercury Center Web.

608

San Francisco Chronicle/San Francisco Examiner: The Gate

http://www.sfgate.com

"The Gate" is the digital gateway to news developed cooperatively by *The San Francisco Chronicle* and *The San Francisco Examiner*. These two great dailies combine their talents to create what must be the most readable sports section on the Internet (Glenn Dickey on Tony La Russa's cloudy future with the A's, Ray Ratto on the cloudy future of the 49ers' kickers, and, of course, full 49ers and Raiders coverage.) You also get a great daily, "Silicon Valley Report," that includes the "Tomorrow" column by none other than Howard Rheingold. Columnists? Sure. How about Rob Morse, Jon Carroll, and Adair Lara? Not too shabby, eh? You'll also find reviews of art, music, culture, and civilization. (Note: both newspapers are very pro-culture and pro-civilization, which is a healthy sign though not necessarily the norm these days.)

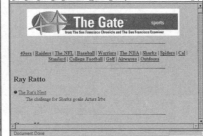
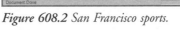
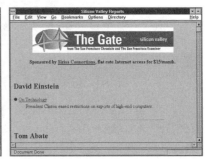

Figure 608.1 San Francisco news gate.   *Figure 608.2* San Francisco sports.   *Figure 608.3* Silicon Valley Report.

San Mateo Times

http://www.baynet.com/smtimes.html

The San Mateo Times, a 105-year-old daily, is the primary source of print information about and for the residents of San Mateo County, which is just south of San Francisco. This newspaper, which has a circulation of 45,000, is the only daily published in San Mateo County. And now portions of it are available in cyberspace. You'll find the business section (including daily stock quotes), weather, the weekly horoscope, real-estate sales and financing information, and the help-wanted ads. No sports, however. You'll have to rely on The Gate (site 607) for that. Such is life.

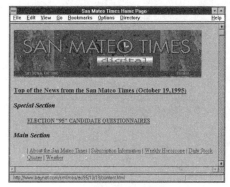

Figure 609.1 The San Mateo Times.

Figure 609.2 Back issues.

The Sewanee Review

http://www.sewanee.edu/sreview/Home.html

T.S. Eliot, this century's most influential man of letters, wrote in 1952, *"The Sewanee Review* has now reached the status of an institution, by which I mean that if it came to an end, its loss would be something more than merely the loss of one good periodical: it would be a symptom of an alarming decline in the periodical world at its highest level." What makes Eliot's statement remarkable is that it came just ten years after Andrew Lytle and Allen Tate transformed the *Review* from a modest humanities periodical to a major magazine presenting fiction and criticism by Robert Penn Warren, Cleanth Brooks, Randall Jarrell, Donald Davidson, and Robert Lowell. Today, *The Sewanee Review* continues its tradition of literary excellence. Visit this site to access the digital edition of this fine magazine.

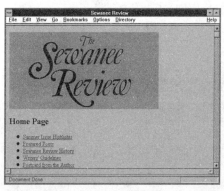

Figure 610.1 Sewanee Review.

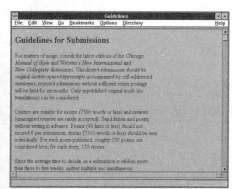

Figure 610.2 Writers' Guidelines.

Smithsonian Magazine

http://www.si.edu/img/resource/simag/start.htm

Some of the most innovative articles on the arts, environment, culture, history, and science are those which appear in *Smithsonian*, the magazine of that venerable institution in Washington where so many of the country's treasures are kept. The print edition of the magazine is, of course, absolutely splendid in every way. And the same is true for this digital reprint of various features from each monthly issue. The range is fantastic. In one issue, you'll find articles on Motown Records, hurricane chasers, Fenway Park, presidential photographs and photographers, the wildlife paintings of Walter Anderson, and Native American culture. The emphasis is on American culture and history broadly defined to embrace all these things and more. And now you can find it all online. Fabulous.

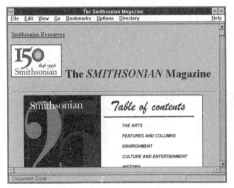

Figure 611.1 Smithsonian Magazine.

Figure 611.2 History in Smithsonian.

Sports Illustrated: Sports Access

http://www.timeinc.com/si/

No swimsuit issue at this site, so just forget it. But what "Sports Access" does have is excellent team and league coverage for a range of sports, including soccer, football, baseball, basketball, skating, skiing, and hockey. At this site, you'll find many, though not all, of the articles from each weekly print edition of *Sports Illustrated,* along with great graphics and even the occasional video and sound file. As in the print edition, you get coverage of both college professional leagues. Be sure to check out the special section of "Sports Access" entitled "Sports Illustrated for Kids," which contains interesting articles your children can read to learn more about the games they love.

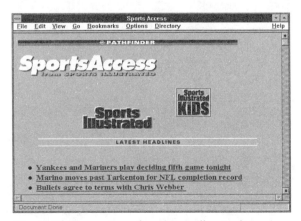

Figure 612 Sports Access from Sports Illustrated.

Stereo World: The Magazine of 3-D Imaging

http://www.tisco.com/3d-web/nsa/sw.htm

Stereo World, published bimonthly, is the official publication of the National Stereoscopic Association. *Stereo World* publishes original research on stereo photographers, their publishing histories, the historic events and subjects they depict, and their equipment and techniques. The magazine also features articles of interest to today's stereo photographers and students of 3-D imaging techniques and publishes reviews of cameras, projectors, viewers, and other 3-D equipment. To illustrate articles, the magazine prints stereo images from a variety of eras and formats as high-quality, side-by-side pairs. Visit this site to access *Stereo World's* online edition.

Figure 613.1 Stereo World.

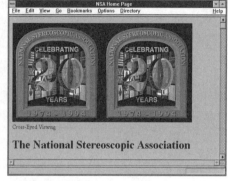

Figure 613.2 Your hosts.

Time: The Weekly News Magazine

http://www.timeinc.com/time/magazine/magazine.html

Is there another news weekly so highly regarded as *Time*? I doubt it. And now significant portions of *Time* are available online. At this site, you'll find digital reprints from both the United States and international editions of *Time* (they *are* different) and a searchable database of excerpts from past editions. What did *Time* have to say when John Kennedy was shot, or when Nixon resigned, or when the American hostages in Iran were released? With a few points and clicks, you can find out. Use an easy form to send letters to *Time's* editors, or use *Time's* convenient "Voter's Guide" search tool to find out who represents you in Congress and how to contact them.

Figure 614 Its about Time.

USA Today

http://www.usatoday.com/

"The nation's newspaper" is now available online, packed with articles, graphics, cartoons, and even video and sound files. Don't just read about Bill Clinton's latest remarks; listen to him make them. Don't just look at a static image of Bob Dole on the campaign trail; watch him meet and greet the voters. You also, of course, get extensive coverage of the sports, financial, and weather scenes, as well as television, record, book, and film reviews. In the autumn, *USA Today* specializes in covering college football; likewise, *USA Today* dedicates no small amount of server space to this pursuit. The articles in *USA Today* exhibit a lighter tone and less depth than those in *The New York Times*.

Figure 615 The nation's newspaper.

Windows Sources Magazine

http://www.winsources.ziff.com/~wsources

Enhanced with VRML, the Web site for *Windows Sources* magazine includes the very best, hippest, coolest-looking image map on the Web. The image map is so awesomely beautiful that, the first time you see it, you'll spend twenty minutes admiring it as a work of art. Of course, editorially, *Windows Sources* has a lot to say right now about Windows 95 (and its bugs!). But the magazine still covers Windows 3.1 extensively. So access this site for the news and views of the entire award-winning *Windows Sources* line-up of writers: Mark L. Van Name, Jim Louderback, Orson Scott Card, and Paul Bonner. The service is free. Jump in.

Figure 616 A gorgeous image map.

Ziff-Davis Magazine Subscriptions

http://www.pc-computing.ziff.com/~zdsubs/

Come here to subscribe to any or all of Ziff-Davis' many computer-related magazines. At this site, you'll find the site gives you information on great deals for subscribing to the print editions of *Computer Life*, *Computer Gaming World*, *Computer Shopper*, *FamilyPC*, *MacUser*, *PC Magazine*, *PC Magazine/CD*, *PC/Computing*, *PC/Computing CD*, and *Windows Sources*. Ziff-Davis offers these subscription deals at a discount of 50% or more off the newsstand price. And many of these deals include free CD-ROMs and other premium gifts when you enroll. You can subscribe via convenient forms the site provides; no credit card information is necessary.

Figure 617 Ziff-Davis subscription center.

Wired Magazine: Hot Wired!

http://www.hotwired.com

The online edition of *Wired* doesn't contain the same amount of prose and images as the paper edition, but it is still notoriously cool. You'll find all the standard columns, including "Rants and Raves" (reader feedback), "Electric Word" (bulletins from the front line of the digital revolution), "Scans" (people, companies, and ideas that matter), "Fetish" (technolust), "Reality Check" (the future of nanotechnology), "Raw Data" (lots and lots of stats), and more. You'll also find the "Geek Page," considerations of Cyber Rights, and profiles of the personalities involved in creating, defining, and refining the new frontier of cyberspace.

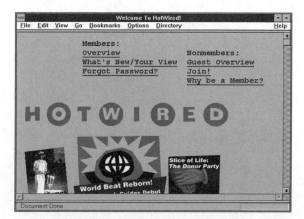

Figure 618 HotWired!!!

Zines

http://www.etext.org/Zines

John Labovitz has called this site "the definitive e-zine resource," and he is right. "Zines" contains links to virtually every zine (electronic magazine) on the Web that is worth reading. Constantly updated and expanded, the site includes links to *eScene* (offering some of the world's best online fiction), *InterText* (a bi-monthly electronic fiction magazine read by thousands of people on six continents), *Quanta* (a highly-regarded Sci-Fi zine), *Kudzu* (a quarterly digital magazine specializing in fiction, poetry, and essays), *The Lady in the Radiator* (hypertext version of a popular print journal that contains art, photographs, poetry, and interviews) and many, many other electronic publications.

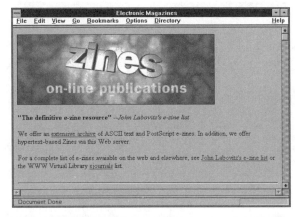

Figure 619 *The Zines connection.*

More Publications/Periodicals

As you surf the Web, you may find that one or more of the site addresses listed in this book have changed. In such cases, connect to Jamsa Press at http://www.jamsa.com and click on the icon that corresponds to the *1001 Really Cool Web Sites* book. Jamsa Press will list replacement addresses (when possible) for sites that have moved. In addition, you can also use the following site list as you search for information on zines:

Journalism Resources	http://garnet.msen.com:70/1/vendor/freep/jresource
University of Idaho's Electronic Publications	http://gopher.uidaho.edu/11/e-pubs
Electronic Documents (E-Journals & E-Books)	http://gopher.uidaho.edu/11/libraries/e-texts
EJS Home Page	http://gpu.srv.ualberta.ca:8010/home1.htm
Harvest User's Manual	http://harvest.cs.colorado.edu/harvest/doc.html
Harvest Papers	http://harvest.cs.colorado.edu/harvest/papers.html
CityLive! Contents Page [Editor: Kirk Bowe]	http://info.city.ac.uk/citylive/
Connectivityin landscapes and ecosystems	http://life.anu.edu.au/people/dgg/esa93.html
Complexity International	http://life.anu.edu.au:80/ci/ci.html
The Art Book - Price List	http://mmm.wwa.com/tab/tabsales.htm

REFERENCES

Worldwide Acronym and Abbreviation Finder

http://curia.ucc.ie/info/net/acronyms/acro.html

An *acronym* is a word formed from the initial letters of other words. This efficient, easy-to-use search engine links to the list of acronyms and abbreviations in the Network Acronym and Abbreviation Server. At this site, you can search for an acronym and see its expansion, search for a word in the expansions and see the related acronyms, and submit an acronym for inclusion in the database. You can also see a list of failures (acronyms not found) if you like. Peter Flynn (plflynn@curia.ucc.ie) established, and now maintains, this site. Peter, many thanks for a fun reference tool on the Web.

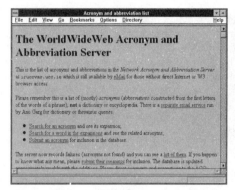

Figure 620.1 Acronym heaven.

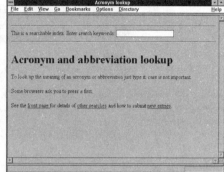

Figure 620.2 The search screen.

American National Standards Institute

http://www.ansi.org/

Founded in 1918, the American National Standards Institute (ANSI) is a private, non-profit membership organization that coordinates the U.S. voluntary consensus standards system and approves American National Standards. ANSI consists of approximately 1,300 national and international companies, 30 government agencies, 20 institutional members, and 250 professional, technical, trade, labor, and consumer organizations. ANSI establishes consistent sets of consensus-based standards for a variety of disciplines, including computers. At the ANSI Web site, you will find a comprehensive, searchable database containing all ANSI standards and standards-related information.

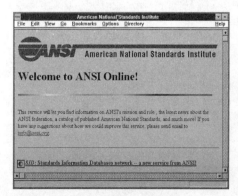

Figure 621.1 The ANSI home page.

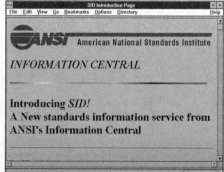

Figure 621.2 The SID network.

Bartlett's Familiar Quotations

http://www.cc.columbia.edu/acis/bartleby/bartlett

To use this fully searchable hypertext edition of *Bartlett's Familiar Quotations,* you type a word (or words) into the search engine and see what famous quotes use the terms you've entered. Or, put in phrases and see what rises to the surface. These quotes have wit, and no small amount of wisdom. Sir Humphrey Gilbert: "We are as near to heaven by sea as by land!" Kepler: "So long as the mother, Ignorance, lives, it is not safe for Science, the offspring, to divulge the hidden causes of things." And James Howell: "All work and no play makes Jack a dull boy."

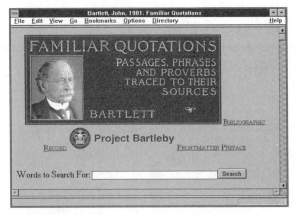

Figure 622 Bartlett certainly looks cheerful.

Britannica On-Line

http://www.eb.com

Britannica On-Line, is a service of *Encyclopedia Britannica* and Britannica Advanced Publishing, Inc. that recently won *Database Magazine's* Product of the Year award. *Britannica On-Line* is a searchable multimedia encyclopedia that gives you the full weight and depth of information you have always expected from *Encyclopedia Britannica* and much more. For example, in the discussion of John F. Kennedy, you'll find films and sound-files of JFK delivering his Inaugural Address. In the discussion of Walt Whitman, you'll see an entire gallery of photographs and hear theatrical recitations from *Leaves of Grass.*

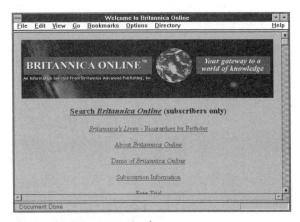

Figure 623 Britannica On-line.

REFERENCES

The British Library On-Line

http://portico.bl.uk/

This site is the hypertext front-end for the many varied online resources of The British Library. The British Library's collections are among the world's finest, and this site provides many excellent services that help you access and utilize these collections. Via the World Wide Web, the Library sends out more than five million documents each year to remote users. In the same amount of time, they typically add more than half a million items to their collections and online catalog records. As a result, this site is a marvelous resource for printed and manuscript musical scores and maps, philatelic material, sound recordings and videograms, Western and Oriental manuscripts, materials from the archives of the former British India Office, and more.

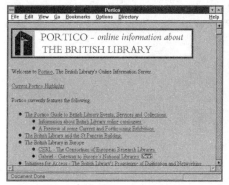

Figure 624.1 *The British Library on-line.*

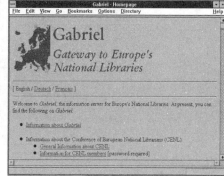

Figure 624.2 *Gateway to Europe's libraries.*

1995 CIA World Factbook

http://www.odci.gov/cia/publications/95fact/index.html

The fully searchable "CIA World Factbook" is updated annually and includes comprehensive information on virtually every country in the world. This site contains maps and location details, but that is just the beginning. You can look up total-square-kilometer area reports; total-square-mile land-area reports; comparative area reports (i.e., Angola is slightly less than twice the size of Texas); specific latitude and longitude land-boundary information; coastline mileage; and maritime claims. You can find information on current international disputes, climate, terrain, natural resources, and land use. You can also find population counts, age and gender demographics, population growth rates, birth rates, death rates, net migration rates, and infant mortality rates.

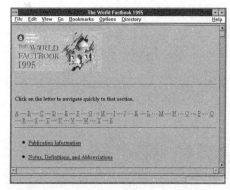

Figure 625.1 *The CIA World Factbook.*

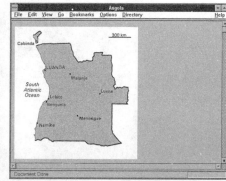

Figure 625.2 *All about Angola!*

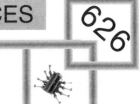

Eisenhower Center

http://history.cc.ukans.edu/heritage/abilene/ikectr.html

This site is the ideal place for reference information on one of the United States' great postwar presidents, Dwight David Eisenhower. You'll find links to Ike's presidential library at the University of Kansas; an Eisenhower family history; an audio file of Ike's "Farewell Address," in which he warned of the dangers inherent in the "military-industrial complex;" and a biography of Mamie Doud Eisenhower. The Eisenhower Library link gives you digital access to the complete set of Ike's presidential papers, as well as his family and military papers. A special group of files gives you direct access to key information about D-Day and Ike's (significant) role in its planning and execution.

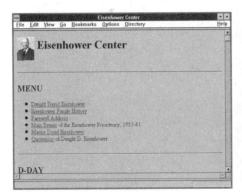

Figure 626.1 Eisenhower Center.

Figure 626.2 Ike's biography.

English-French Dictionary

http://mlab-power3.uiah.fi/EnglishFrench/avenues.html

Parlez vous Franciais? No? Me neither. I mean, I know how to order drinks, which probably gives you a clue as to what my priorities are. But beyond that, I am lost. However, this site houses a fantastic English-French (and French-English, for that matter) dictionary. Type in the English word (or, better yet, the English phrase) and get the French equivalent, and vice versa. Then, your only challenge is to pronounce the word or phrase that the dictionary dishes up! Sorry, you won't find any audio files at this site. That's something to recommend for the next revision, I guess. In addition to keyword searches, you can also browse a bit via a topics tree search pattern. I'm trying to figure out how to say "You know, Jerry Lewis really isn't all that funny."

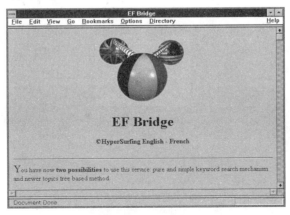

Figure 627 A great English-French Dictionary.

The Free On-Line Dictionary of Computing

http://wombat.doc.ic.ac.uk/

Isn't it frustrating when all your Turbogeek friends sit around the bar and speak in computer jargon without thinking twice about the fact that you and most of the other people on the planet just can't understand a word they're saying? Isn't it awful, that gnawing feel of inadequacy that eats at you: maybe I am too *stupid* to learn the language of megahertz, throughput, and object-orientation. Well, the solution to your problem awaits you on the Net. Spend a few hours with the automated *Free On-Line Dictionary of Computing* and then go back to that bar and amaze and delight your friends with the depth of your technical vocabulary! Let's see who, in the end, stumps whom!

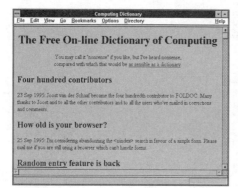

Figure 628.1 *Dictionary of Computing.*

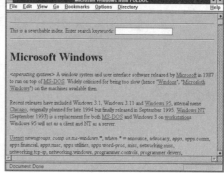

Figure 628.2 *The definition of Windows.*

Gerald R. Ford Presidential Library

http://www2.sils.umich.edu/FordLibrary/

This site is a complete reference source for information on the Ford Presidency and other aspects of Gerald Ford's long public career, including his participation in the Warren Commission investigation of John F. Kennedy's assassination. When you visit here, enjoy a great multimedia presentation entitled "A Day In the Life of a President," which combines photographs, films, and sound files to recreate a typical day in the Ford presidency. The presentation contains but one inaccuracy: nowhere do I see the accident-prone Jerry falling down a flight of stairs or hitting a secret service agent in the back of the head with a golf ball.

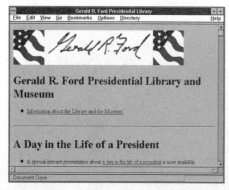

Figure 629.1 *The Gerald Ford Library.*

Figure 629.2 *A Day in the Life.*

Georgetown University Libraries

http://gulib.lausun.georgetown.edu/

This site gives you access not only to Georgetown's Lauinger Library, but also the Blommer Science Library. You can browse the comprehensive card catalogs of these institutions using "George," Georgetown University's automated text-search engine. You can search the catalog by topic, title, author, or ISBN. Whatever you can't find amid Georgetown's impressive holdings, you can look for elsewhere via Georgetown's impressive "Virtual Library," which gives you links to dozens of other excellent academic library servers across the United States and around the world. (P.S.: I've checked and Georgetown already has all my books.)

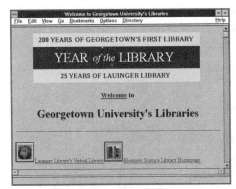
Figure 630.1 The Georgetown Libraries.

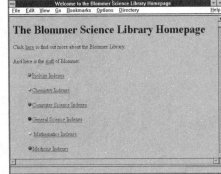
Figure 630.2 The Science Library.

631

The National Archives

http://www.nara.gov

The National Archives and Records Administration (NARA) preserves the permanently valuable records of the United States government and educates the public about the history of the nation. At this site, NARA displays online exhibits, some of its rich and varied holdings, beautiful reproductions of the 1945 document of Japanese surrender, the Declaration of Independence, poster art from World War II, and more. You'll also find a digital edition of the complete *Federal Register*, which is the U.S. Government's central publication tool for all laws, presidential documents, proposed and final executive branch regulations, and other legal notices. It is an extremely useful reference.

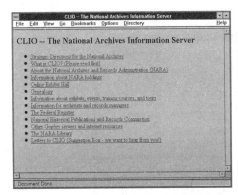
Figure 631.1 The National Archives.

Figure 631.2 National Archives Exhibits.

REFERENCES

National Mapping Information

http://www-nmd.usgs.gov/

Through its National Mapping Program, the U.S. Geological Survey (USGS) provides accurate and up-to-date cartographic data and information for the United States. This mapping information provides the "framework of spatial information" that federal, state, and local government agencies, as well as the private sector, need to deal with such problems as conserving our natural resources, identifying and mitigating environmental hazards, defining and studying ecosystems, and supporting economic development. In particular, educators and students can benefit from special resources dedicated to the teaching of cartography, geography, and related subjects.

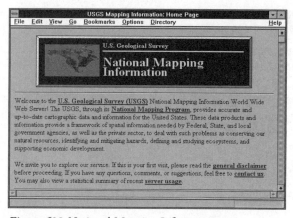

Figure 632 National Mapping Information.

Who's On-line

http://www.ict.trieste.it/Canessa/whoiswho.html

"Who's On-line" bills itself as a "collective experiment toward a non-commercial, decentralized HYPERbiographical database of people on the Internet." Want to have some fun? Browse for the great and near-great, the famous and infamous. Then, if you wish, add your own homepage listing to the databank—simply follow the directions on the site's initial screen. When I visited this site, I stumbled on to Marvin Minsky, William F. Buckley, Jr., Jerry Garcia (RIP), Roman Polanski, Fran Lebovitz, and even several members of the European nobility (although Prince Charles is yet to be online).

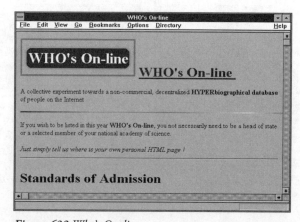

Figure 633 Who's On-line.

The Yale University Libraries

http://www.library.yale.edu/

Enjoy the Yale University libraries without having to put up with the lousy (and I mean *lousy*) parking situation that afflicts most of them! At this site, you can access a record of the libraries' complete holdings, which encompass more than 10,000,000 bound volumes, as well as vast collections of maps, manuscripts, sound recordings, musical scores, art works, coins, microforms, ancient clay tablets, and other unique research material. The link includes connections to every one of Yale's many libraries, including Sterling Memorial, the Art and Architecture Library, the Beinecke Rare Book and Manuscript Library, the Chemistry Library, the Classics Library, the Cross Campus Library, the Divinity School Library, the Drama Library, the Engineering Library, the Epidemiology and Public Health Library, the Lewis Walpole Library, and libraries addressing law, mathematics, medicine, geology, and forestry.

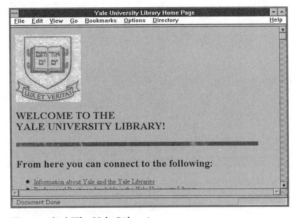

Figure 634 *The Yale Libraries.*

SEE

More References

As you surf the Web, you may find that one or more of the site addresses listed in this book have changed. In such cases, connect to Jamsa Press at http://www.jamsa.com and click on the icon that corresponds to the *1001 Really Cool Web Sites* book. Jamsa Press will list replacement addresses (when possible) for sites that have moved. In addition, you can also use the following site list as you search for information on reference materials:

IEEE INSTITUTE Homepage	http://www.ieee.org/ti.html
Campaign and Elections	http://www.infi.net/camelect/
eye — Toronto's Arts Newspaper	http://WWW.Interlog.COM/eye/
InfoWorld Home Page	http://www.internet.net/stores/infoworld/index.html
Axcess Magazine Home Page	http://www.internex.net/axcess/
Pixel Express Home	http://www.internex.net/pixel/Home.HTML
Realization Reports by Issue	http://www.itd.nrl.navy.mil/ONR/realization_report/rosenblum.toc.html
Journalism and Communications	http://www.jou.ufl.edu/commres/jouwww.htm
Architronic	http://www.kent.edu/Architronic/homepage.html

Anglicans On-Line

http://infomatch.com/~haibeck/anglican.html

Well organized and updated weekly, this site provides links and news for members of the Anglican community worldwide. Check out the "Newsroom" (updated Anglican news from around the world), "Canada News" (the Anglican Church of Canada and Gen. Synod '95), "USA Resources" (the Episcopal Church of the United States of America), "World Resources" (The Church of England and other provinces), and "General Resources," which includes reference links, Bible study, and ecumenical partners. Get the latest details on the British Church's current restructuring. Read about recent activities at the Canterbury International Liturgy Conference in Dublin. Stay up-to-date on the movement of Lutherans toward full communion with Canadian Anglicans.

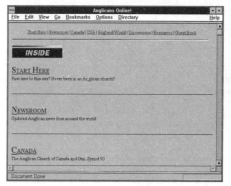

Figure 635.1 Digital Anglicans.

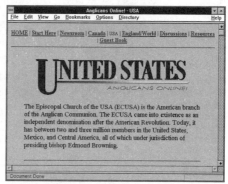

Figure 635.2 U.S. Anglicans.

636

The Hypertext *King James Bible*

http://saturn.colorado.edu:8080/Christian/KJV/kjv.html

This wonderful digital edition of the *King James Bible* lets you search the *Old Testament*, the *New Testament*, and the *Apocrypha* by name, psalm number, or any other keyword. You can search for quotations on a given theme (for example, greed, pestilence, famine, or redemption). You can also specify limitations to searches (for example, you can search only the *Old Testament* or only the book of *Lamentations)*. All in all, this site is a splendid application of HTML that illuminates one of our greatest pieces of literature.

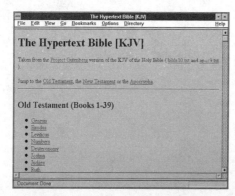

Figure 636.1 The King James Bible.

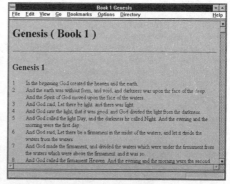

Figure 636.2 The Old Testament.

The Journal of Buddhist Ethics

http://www.psu.edu/jbe/jbe.html

Have you ever met an unethical Buddhist? Me neither. *The Journal of Buddhist Ethics* is the first academic journal dedicated entirely to Buddhist ethics. This journal is innovative in that it's entirely electronic; there is no print edition. However, in most other respects, it functions as a traditional scholarly journal. All submissions (research articles, discussions, and critical notes) are subject to blind peer review. *The Journal* addresses the application of Buddhist ethics to medicine, philosophy, human rights, psychology, ecology, politics, anthropology, and other aspects of modern life. *The Journal* also explores all aspects of Buddhist monastic discipline, providing comparative studies of the Vinayas (monastic disciplines) of different schools.

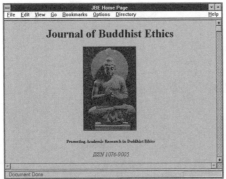

Figure 637.1 Not just for ethical Buddhists.

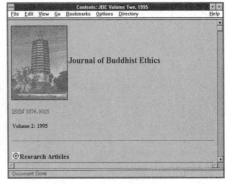

Figure 637.2 The current issue.

Catholic Answers

http://www.catholic.com/~answers/

Maintained by members of the Catholic Church, this useful and informative Web site provides basic information for people who wish to learn more about the Church. You can read recent articles from *The Rock*, which at the moment is the only magazine of practical apologetics and evangelization for Catholics. You'll also find the full text of two useful booklets: *Pillar of Fire, Pillar of Truth,* and *12 Painless Ways to Evangelize.* For those considering conversion, a lucid hypertext document entitled "Why Be a Catholic?" is particularly useful. "Catholic Answers" also includes links to other Catholic web sites because, as the Webmaster says, "Catholic Answers isn't the only good Catholic group around, you know."

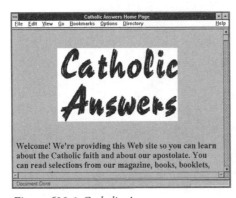

Figure 638.1 Catholic Answers.

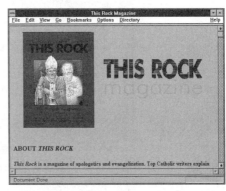

Figure 638.2 This Rock Magazine.

Celtic Christianity

http://www2.gol.com/users/stuart/celtihs.html

Visit this site for information and discussion on St. Patrick, St. Columba, the Isle of Iona, the Holy Island, and other topics related to Celtic Christianity. One especially good item at this site is the digital text for *The Lorrha Missal*. This *Missal* is a translation from the Latin and Gaelic *Missal* transcribed at Lorrha Monastery in the Ninth Century. The liturgy, baptism services, and unction ceremonies in *The Lorrha Missal* reflect Celtic practice and tradition prior to 650 A.D. This site also includes excellent research related to the twelve saints who brought Christianity to Glastonbury (St. Joseph of Arimathea and his group of twelve), the origin and art of Celtic crosses, and more.

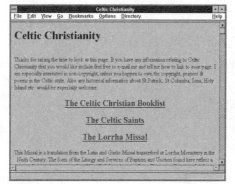 

Figure 639.1 Celtic Christianity home page.   *Figure 639.2 Celtic saints.*

The Christian Reformed Church

http://www.grfn.org/religion/crc/crc.html

Want to find out about the Christian Reformed Church? Visit this site for valuable information files that explain what members of the Christian Reformed Church believe (Ecumenical Creeds), what they see as their mission and vision, how they put their ideas into action, which institutions of higher education they support, and more. You'll find indexes to Christian Reform Church publications, mission news, synodical and other news releases, links to local congregation homepages, and the *Heidelberg Catechism* reading schedule for 1996. Special links bring you to the homepages of the Christian Reform Church in Canada and the Gospel Communications Network.

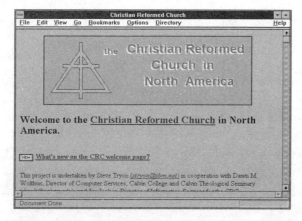

Figure 640 The Christian Reformed Church.

The Episcopal Church

http://www.ai.mit.edu/people/mib/anglican/anglican.html

This excellent but unofficial homepage serves as a repository for information relevant to the Episcopal Church in the USA and other provinces of the Anglican Communion. At this site, you'll find answers to common questions such as: what is the Episcopal Church? How do Episcopalians worship? What do Episcopalians believe? You'll also find liturgical and religious texts, including *The Book of Common Prayer*. In addition, links take you to the Anglican Communion News Service, the Brotherhood of St. Gregory, the unofficial homepage for the Anglican Church of Canada, and Roman Catholic resources on the Web.

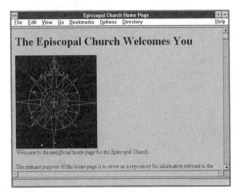

Figure 641.1 More Anglicans on-line!

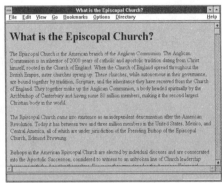

Figure 641.2 What is the Episcopal Church?

Global Hindu Electronic Network

http://rbhatnagar.csm.uc.edu:8080/buddhist_info.html

Sponsored by the Hindu Students Council, this site gives you great links to Buddha Dharma sites, Zen Buddhist texts, the Asynchronous School of Buddhist Dialectics, the "Buddhist Studies World Wide Web Virtual Library," the "Tiger Team Buddhist Information Network," and the "Asian Classic Input Project." You'll find the latest news of interest to the Hindu community, as well as Hindu scriptures and complete hypertext guides to Hindu organizations and temples. You'll also find a stunningly comprehensive list of classic Zen Buddhist texts available in hypertext editions on the Web.

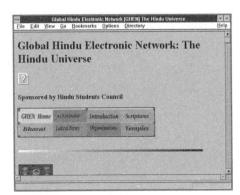

Figure 642.1 Hindu Universe.

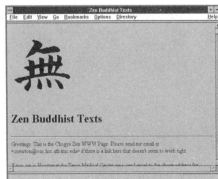

Figure 642.2 Zen Buddhist texts.

RELIGION

Documents of Jewish Belief

http://www.netaxs.com/~expweb/jewish_belief.html

This page and its underlying documents are the first steps in an ambitious effort to provide an archive of Judaica texts on the World Wide Web. You'll find Solomon Schechter's seminal 1896 essay on "The Dogmas of Judaism," a biography of Rabbi Abraham Isaac Ha-Kohen Kook, and documents from the reform movement, including 1885's "Pittsburgh Platform," 1937's "Columbus Platform," and 1976's "Reform Judaism: A Centenary Perspective." You'll also find a link to a great exhibit at Vanderbilt University's Divinity Library entitled "Franz Rosenzweig, His Life and Work." This exhibit includes pix, essays, and biographical material. This page is under continuous development, so stop in and see what's new.

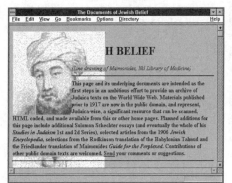

Figure 643.1 Documents of Jewish belief.

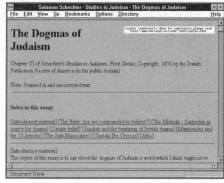

Figure 643.2 The Dogmas of Judaism.

Jews for Jesus

http://www.jews-for-jesus.org

Jews for Jesus. The name says it all, shortly and sweetly. The name tells you, without any doubt, exactly who the members of this group are and what their agenda is. You'll find the group's publications (online books, pamphlets, and magazines), testaments, resources, and links all gathered toward the end of converting even more Jews to Jesus. In addition to individual testimonies by former Jews, you'll also find a Jews for Jesus music and concert schedule, addresses and phone numbers of Jews for Jesus offices around the world, and links to other Christian resources.

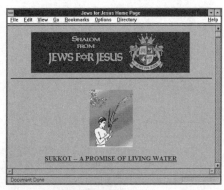

Figure 644.1 Shalom!

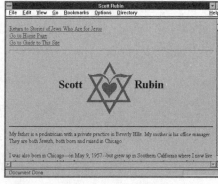

Figure 644.2 A testament from Scott Rubin.

Jewish News Links

http://www.netaxs.com/~expweb/test3.html

This site includes links to *The Jerusalem Post* (full text of selected articles), *The Haaretz Daily* (a Hebrew-language paper), RealAudio files of *Voice of Israel* broadcasts, Israeli lottery results, daily news summaries in Hebrew, and more. Additional goodies include digital reprints of Israel-related editorials and op-eds from major newspapers in New York and Chicago; the bi-weekly *Jerusalem Report*; the *Weekly Jewish Bulletin of Northern California*; the bi-weekly *Jewish Review of Portland, Oregon*; *Jewish Week*; *Tikkun Magazine*; *The Israeli Intelligence Digest*; *The Middle East Newswire*; and the Zionist Organization of America's *Israel News*.

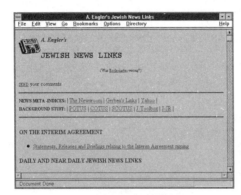

Figure 645.1 Jewish News Links.

Figure 645.2 The Jerusalem Post.

The Judaica Web World

http://www.nauticom.net/users/rafie/judaica-world.html

Enter the Jewish global village and check out the options. For some great Lubavitch links, check out "Chabad Web." For general information on Jewish thought, history, and culture, look into the "A-Z of Jewish & Israeli Related Resources." You'll find an absolutely splendid downloadable monthly Judaic Calendar for your Macintosh computer, as well as downloadable photos of past and present Rabeyim. Also be sure to treat yourself to the site's most delicious option, "The Reasoning and Seasoning of Jewish Cooking," which has many kosher recipes and other Jewish cooking information. And treat your children to the fun stuff in "Judaica Web World Kids."

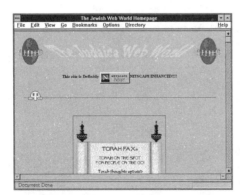

Figure 646.1 The Judaica Web World.

Figure 646.2 Judaism.com.

RELIGION

The Lesbian and Gay Christian Movement

http://www.dur.ac.uk/~dth2mnv/lgcm.html

This useful and informative list of links, which originates in the United Kingdom, includes a detailed study entitled "Homosexuality and the Bible." At this site, find the "Lesbian and Gay Christian Movement News Service;" a sermon preached by Archbishop Desmond Tutu in which he affirms all Christians (regardless of sexual orientation) in front of the primates of the Anglican Communion; and the announcement of the launch of AGLO (Action for Gay and Lesbian Ordination). Or, take links to an extensive bibliography on homosexuality and theology, the homepage of The Centre for Religious Tolerance, "The Lesbian and Gay Guide to Great Britain," and the "Queer Resources Directory."

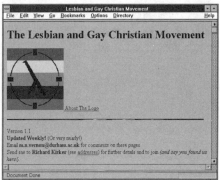

Figure 647.1 The Lesbian and Gay Christian Movement.

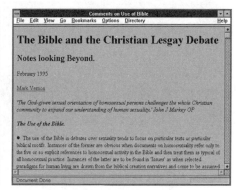

Figure 647.2 Gays in the Bible.

Evangelical Lutheran Church in America

http://www.elca.org/

The Evangelical Lutheran Church in America (ELCA) resulted from a union of three North American Lutheran church bodies: the American Lutheran Church, the Association of Evangelical Lutheran Churches, and the Lutheran Church of America. The three churches agreed to unite in 1982. They formed a 70-member Commission for a New Lutheran Church, which planned the merger. Church conventions held in 1986 approved the plan. The ELCA constituting convention was held in 1987, and the church actually began operations on January 1, 1988. Find out more about ELCA's beliefs, programs, and publications at this homepage.

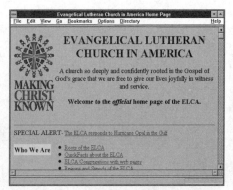

Figure 648.1 Evangelical Lutheran Church.

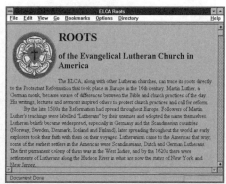

Figure 648.2 Roots of Evangelical Lutheranism.

Mennonite Resources On-Line

http://www.prairienet.org/community/reglion/mennonite/menno.html

A *Mennonite* is a member of one of the Christian groups derived from the Anabaptist movement, which stressed discipleship, community, and an ethic of love and nonresistance. Mennonites are historically distinctive in North America for their simplicity of life and rejection of military service, public office, and oaths. For some, being Mennonite is a chosen spiritual identity; for others, the term Mennonite merely describes a personal ethnic or historical connection. "Mennonite Resources On-Line" is a clearinghouse for information for, by, and about Mennonites. It contains a collection of links to Web and Gopher sites for Mennonite congregations, organizations, and schools.

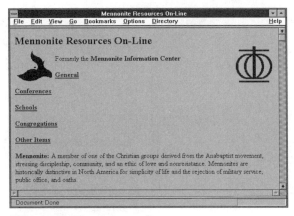

Figure 649 Mennonites on-line.

Monks, Monks, and More Monks

http://www.efn.org/~russelln

Monks? Yeah, you know, *monks*. Like Thomas Merton, the eloquent Trappist of Tennessee. This site contains exhaustive information on monks, monasticism, and monasteries, as well as abbots, cloisters, scriptoriums, and more. I spent part of my youth living next door to an Episcopal monastery, the Order of the Holy Cross. This particular monastery was a rather liberal establishment as those things go. The monks took no vows of silence and they led fairly active social lives as teachers. Although the men had taken vows of poverty and chastity, those obligations didn't seem to weigh heavily on them. For information on the monks of the Holy Cross and elsewhere, visit this informative Web site.

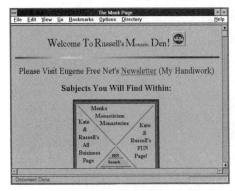

Figure 650.1 Digital monks.

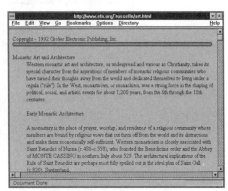

Figure 650.2 Monastery art and architecture.

RELIGION

The Book of Mormon

http://www.sci.dixie.edu/mormon/contents.html

Followers of Joseph Smith believe that *The Book of Mormon* is a volume of holy scripture comparable to the Bible. Their teachings hold that *The Book of Mormon* is a record of God's dealings with the ancient inhabitants of the Americas and contains, as does the Bible, the fullness of the everlasting gospel. The crowning event recorded in *The Book of Mormon* is the personal ministry of Jesus Christ among the peoples of the Americas soon after his resurrection. This record puts forth the doctrines of the Mormon gospel, outlines a plan of salvation, and tells men and women what they must do to gain peace in this life and eternal salvation in the life to come. At this site, you can read a hypertext edition of *The Book of Mormon*.

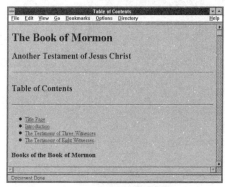

Figure 651.1 The Book of Mormon.

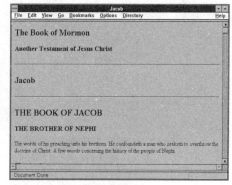

Figure 651.2 The Book of Jacob.

Foundation for Ancient Research and Mormon Studies

http://kolmogorov.che.psu.edu:2222/farms/farms.html

To learn about the Mormons, I suggest you first read portions of *The Book of Mormon*. Then, if you have questions about Joseph Smith and the church he founded, turn to the Foundation for Ancient Research and Mormon Studies (FARMS). At this site, you'll find publications that include *The Journal of BOOK OF MORMON Studies* and *Reviews of Books on THE BOOK OF MORMON*. You'll also find criticism, papers, and transcripts from the *THE BOOK OF MORMON Lecture Series*. Finally, this site give you access to the complete FARMS catalog of publications, a hypertext edition of the works of Mormon theologian Hugh Nibley, and a comprehensive set of links to related Web sites.

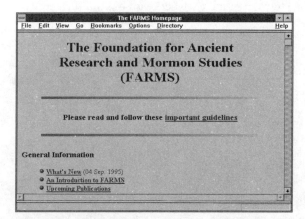

Figure 652 All about Mormonism.

New Advent Catholic Web Page

http://www.knight.org/advent/

"The New Advent Catholic Web Page" is a wonderful source for all kinds of information about the teachings, organization, and mission of the Roman Catholic Church. This site gives you details on all aspects of Catholic dogma, including God (his existence, nature, and the Blessed Trinity), Creatures (creation, angels, and humans), the three offices of the Church (the Teaching, Governing, and Sanctifying offices), the role and meaning of Mary and the Saints, and more. In addition, you'll find explanations of the Holy Mass, the notion of predestination, public and private Divine revelation, and grace and salvation. This page is less a link site for Catholic resources than it is a one-stop information source on the Catholic Catechism. And as such, it is well done.

Figure 653.1 New Advent.

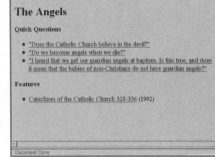

Figure 653.2 All about angels.

The Peregrine Foundation

http://www.matisse.net/~peregrin/

Founded in 1992, the Peregrine Foundation assists families and individuals living in or exiting from experimental social groups, such as high-demand religious groups and totalitarian sects. The Peregrine Foundation's extensive collection of literature on cults and their practices is an essential resource for anyone with a loved one involved in a cult, as well as anyone wishing to escape cult strictures and influence. This site includes discussions of "cult warning signs," the legalities involved in the "kidnapping" of cult members, religious brainwashing, and many other related topics. Very interesting.

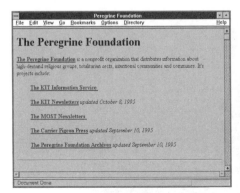

Figure 654.1 The Peregrine Foundation.

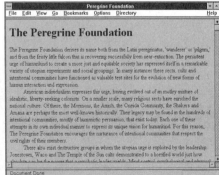

Figure 654.2 Details on the Foundation.

RELIGION

Pope John Paul II

http://www.zpub.com/un/pope/

Pope John Paul II is the most recognized person in the world. He is the most traveled pope in the 2,000 year history of the Church and speaks eight languages. When he became pope in 1978, he was the first non-Italian chosen in 456 years and the youngest pope selected this century. In 1994, he was *Time's* "Man of the Year." At this site, you can read many of Pope John Paul II's most famous writings and encyclicals, including "Letter to Women" (June 29, 1995), "That All May Be One" (the Pope's encyclical on the reunification of the Christian churches), and "As the Third Millennium Draws Near" (in which the Pope proposes a jubilee for the year 2,000).

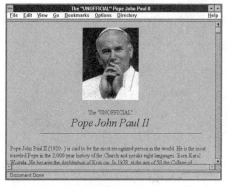

Figure 655.1 John Paul II online.

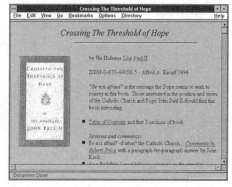

Figure 655.2 Crossing the Threshold of Hope.

The Religious Archive

http://www.lysator.liu.se/religion/index.html

"The Religious Archive" offers links and resources related to the entire range of religious practices, including Christianity, Discordianism, Islam, Neopaganism, Satanism, Tariqas, and Zen Buddhism. "What is Discordianism?" I hear you asking. I didn't know either. Quickly: Discordianism is a fairly new religion (late 1950s), mainly concerned with the balance between order and chaos. Its main deity is Eris, the Greek Goddess of Discord. The system also includes numerous saints. For a quick introduction to Discordianism, read a file at this site entitled "The Turkey Case." And Neopaganism? This is a group of 20th century religions based on the works of Gerald Gardener, Doreen Valiente, and Alex Sanders in Britain. Read the file for more details.

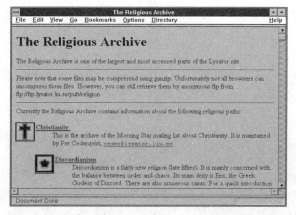

Figure 656 The Religious Archive.

Religious Freedom

http://northshore.shore.net/rf

One of my favorite things: religious freedom. To each his own. One person's ceiling is another's floor. This non-denominational, informational Web site offers historical background on the concept of religious freedom, as well as access to the exact text of established laws that protect this right. In addition, "Religious Freedom" explores legislative and court activities that (sometimes subtly) challenge the practice of religious freedom both in the United States and elsewhere. Of special value at this site is the detailed, in-depth analysis of the U.S. Constitution and Supreme Court decisions that impact the right to worship freely. By the way, The Christian Science Committee on Publication sponsors this page.

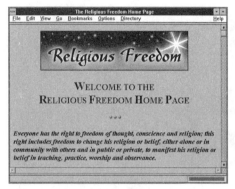

Figure 657.1 Religious freedom, my cup of tea.

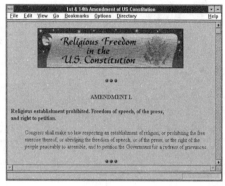

Figure 657.2 The Constitution, also my cup of tea.

Shamash: Jewish Resources

http://shamash.nysernet.org

"Shamash" offers a rich variety of links related to Jewish religion, history, and culture. From this conveniently located beach, you can surf to any number of wonderful places including "Hillel: The Foundation for Jewish Campus Life," the Orthodox Jewish Union (including Pirchei Shoshanim and the Jewish Burial Society), and "Project Genesis: Torah on the Information Super Highway." Other links take you to the "American Jewish Congress On-Line," the United Synagogues of Conservative Judaism, and the National Jewish Committee on Scouting. Additionally, you'll find links to the 1-800-Judaism bookstore and dozens of Jewish pages based in Europe and the United Kingdom.

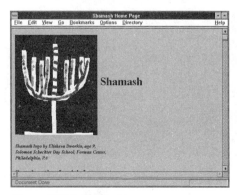

Figure 658.1 Shamash.

Figure 658.2 Torah Judaism.

RELIGION

Taoism

http://www.cnu.edu/~patrick/taoism.html

What is Taoism? Founded by Lao-tzu, Taoism is a religion that has as its central concept and goal the Tao, an elusive term denoting the force inherent in nature and, by extension, the code of behavior that is in harmony with the natural order. This graphically elegant page provides an invaluable list of resources on Taoism. Among the options you'll find at this site are two electronically available English versions of the *Tao Teh Ching* (Taoism's most sacred scripture), an English translation of Sun-tzu's *The Art of War*, and an English translation of the *I Ching* by Richard Le Mon. You'll also find links to many other sources of information on Taoism and Taoist practice.

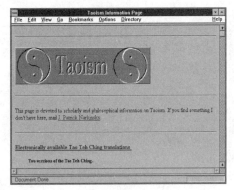

Figure 659.1 Digital Taoism.

Figure 659.2 Tao Teh Ching translations.

Eyebeams: Unitarian Universalism

http://www.wolfe.net/~uujim/eyebeams/magazine.htm

"Read the language of these wandering eyebeams," wrote Emerson. "The heart knoweth." *Eyebeams* is an experimental zine of Unitarian Universalist opinion. Thoughtful, polite discourse is the order of the day. Checkout *Eyebeams* to learn more about the Unitarian Universalist church which, after two centuries of fermentation in Poland and elsewhere, emerged in England when T. Lindsey seceded from the Church of England in 1773. Learn how the church influenced the rhetoric of such 19th century figures as Theodore Parker, James Freeman Clarke, and Ralph Waldo Emerson. Fascinating stuff.

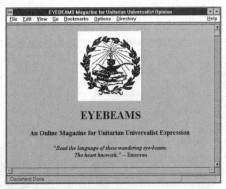

Figure 660.1 Eyebeams.

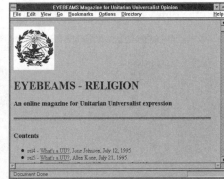

Figure 660.2 Religious issues.

Unitarian Universalist Hotlist

http://www.wolfe.net/~uujim/uusrc.html

Unitarians believe in the authority of reason and conscience. They believe that the ultimate arbiter in religion should not be a church, or a document, or an official, but rather the personal choice and decision of the individual. They also believe in the unity of experience—that there is no fundamental conflict between faith and knowledge, religion and the world, the sacred and the secular, since they all have their source in the same reality. A few famous Unitarians? Emerson, Thoreau, Clara Barton, Frank Lloyd Wright, Adlai Stevenson, and the current Secretary of Defense, William J. Perry. Visit this site, as well as site 660, for more information on this enlightened approach to faith.

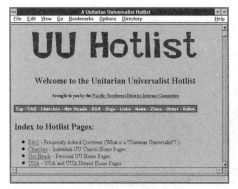

Figure 661.1 Unitarian Hotlist.

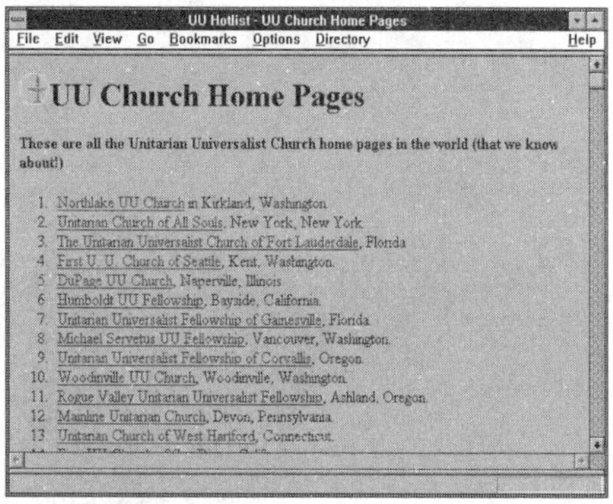

Figure 661.2 Unitarian FAQ.

Walk Away: A Resource for Ex-Fundamentalists

http://www.crocker.com/~ifas/wa/

Launched by The Institute for First Amendment Studies, "Walk Away" is a resource that offers support to those wrestling with the fear and guilt often associated with Christian fundamentalism. "Admittedly," the editors of *Walk Away* write, "some people are quite satisfied in Christian fundamentalism or other forms of ultra-conservative Christian doctrine. We strongly support religious freedom and have no quarrel with these people. *Walk Away* is not for fundamentalists. It is not our intention to convince anyone that their faith is invalid. *Walk Away* is for those who have already left fundamentalism or some extreme form of Bible-based belief, and are seeking support in their new decision to walk away."

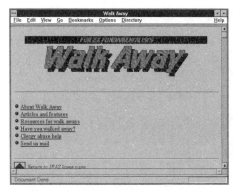

Figure 662.1 Walk Away.

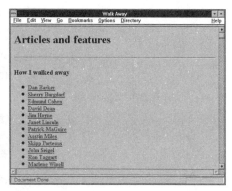

Figure 662.2 Articles and features.

RELIGION

The World Council of Churches

http://193.73.243.3/oikumene.HTML

The World Council of Churches embraces more than 324 flavors of religion from more than 120 countries. You'll find an ecumenical prayer calendar, a member church list, the official World Council of Churches' Rwanda crisis situation reports, the World Council of Churches calendar of meetings, and World Council of Churches press releases. You'll also find e-mail directories for World Council of Churches members, a link to Ecumenical News International, and information of World Council of Churches aid and relief projects around the globe.

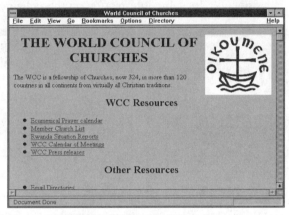

Figure 663 *The World Council of Churches.*

Zen in the American Grain

http://www.teleport.com/~ldotm/zhd.shtml

This page holds the opening chapter of a wonderful hypertext book that begins: "The necessity of faith in religious life and practice is something the 'faithful' take for granted. The 'Awakening of Faith' is considered an essential step in Buddhism, and while Zen may be thought of as nonconformist by some, on this point there really can be no disagreement. After all, taking up a practice that leads toward 'enlightenment,' a state that cannot be known until experienced, implies a faith that such an experience really does exist. Yet faith, as understood in Buddhism, is a very simple thing. It is gentle, flexible, and does not depend upon belief systems." Come here for a gentle, reasoned introduction to Zen Buddhism from one who lives it every day.

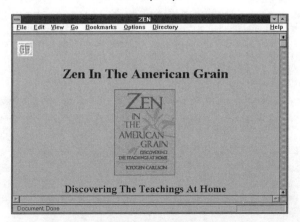

Figure 664 *Zen in the American Grain.*

More Religion

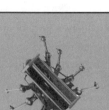

As you surf the Web, you may find that one or more of the site addresses listed in this book have changed. In such cases, connect to Jamsa Press at http://www.jamsa.com and click on the icon that corresponds to the *1001 Really Cool Web Sites* book. Jamsa Press will list replacement addresses (when possible) for sites that have moved. In addition, you can also use the following site list as you search for information on religion:

Religion and Philosophy	http://dewey.lib.ncsu.edu/disciplines/religion.html
University of Virginia KJV Bible Search	http://etext.virginia.edu/kjv.query.html
Religion Page	http://hakatai.mcli.dist.maricopa.edu/smc/ml/religion.html
Christian Resource List	http://saturn.colorado.edu:8080/Christian/list.html
Dead Sea — Introduction	http://sunsite.unc.edu/expo/deadsea.scrolls.exhibit/world.scrolls.html
Judaism and Jewish Resources	http://www.acm.uiuc.edu/signet/JHSI/judaism.html
The WWW Bible Gateway	http://www.calvin.edu/cgi-bin/bible
Christian Resources on the Internet	http://www.calvin.edu/christian-resources.html

Earthlife Africa

http://www.gem.co.za/ELA

Earthlife Africa is an activist organization dedicated to preserving the natural envrionment in Africa and around the world. In other words, the organization's members don't just talk about problems, they go out and accomplish something. For example, Earthlife Africa helped expose the toxic presence of Thor Chemicals at Cato Ridge and brought public attention to the proposed Iscor Steel Mill in the ecologically sensitive Saldahna region. Additionally, the organization tackles a wide range of environmental issues: from the environmental consequences of the toxic waste trade to the future of Africa's Table Mountain. Earthlife has ten branches in South Africa, with additional branches in Namibia and Uganda. Visit this site to find out more about this vibrant organization.

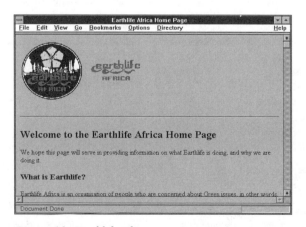

Figure 665 Earthlife Africa.

SAVE THE PLANET

666

EcoNews Africa

http://www.web.apc.org/~econews/

EcoNews Africa analyses global environment and development issues from an African perspective and reports on local, national, and regional activities that contribute to global solutions to environmental problems. EcoNews Africa is a joint project of the Africa Water Network (AWN), Climate Network Africa (CNA), the Environment Liaison Center International (ELCI), and the International Outreach Program. It is supported by the Netherlands' Humanistic Institute for Cooperation with Developing Countries (HIVOS) and NGONET based in Montevideo, Uruguay. To learn more about EcoNews Africa, visit this site.

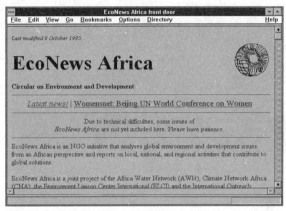

Figure 666 EcoNews Africa.

667

National Audubon Society

http://www.audubon.org/audubon/contents.html

The National Audubon Society is one of the United States' most popular and respected conservation organizations. In 1886, George Bird Grinnell, outraged by the senseless slaughter of birds associated with the plume trade, founded the organization and named it after his boyhood idol, John James Audubon. (Lucy Audubon, John James' wife, had been Grinnell's elementary school teacher.) The mission of the Audubon Society, then and now, is to prevent the extinction of species. Today, more than 570,000 Audubon members work on behalf of the environment in 518 communities across the United States. The organization spreads its message through a beautiful monthly magazine and educational programs that include splendid Audubon prints.

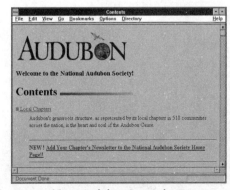

Figure 667.1 Audubon Society home page.

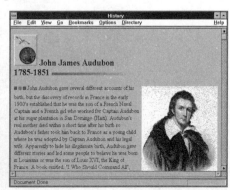

Figure 667.2 Information on the original Audubon.

Biodiversity Action Network

http://www.access.digex.net/~bionet

Biological diversity, or *biodiversity*, relates to the variety and variability of life on Earth and the natural complex of relationships between different life forms. Biodiversity has three main elements: 1) *genes* of individual organisms and the genomes of species; 2) *species* of animals, plants, and microorganisms; and 3) *ecosystems* and other larger biomes (the critical interrelationships that species form). No one is certain how many living species exist on Earth. Scientifically informed estimates range between 10 and 50 million. To date, scientists have named and classified only about 1.5 million separate forms of life. Visit this site to discover more about the complexities and politics of biodiversity.

Figure 668.1 Biodiversity Action Network.

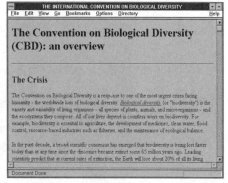

Figure 668.2 The Convention on Biological Diversity.

Byrd Polar Research Center

http://www-bprc.mps.ohio-state.edu/

Named in honor of one of America's most famous explorers, the Byrd Polar Research Center at Ohio State University is internationally recognized as a leader in polar and alpine research. Major research themes include climatic reconstruction of glacial and post-glacial times; the dynamics, history, and ice-atmosphere interactions of polar ice-sheets; high-latitude landform evolution, soils, and hydrology; the geologic evolution of Antarctica; and the history of polar exploration. Also, the Center conducts environmental studies in Alaska and Russia to examine hydrologic and geochemical cycles in permafrost terrains. To find out more about these fascinating and important activities, visit this site.

Figure 669 Byrd Polar Research Center.

Canadian Wildlife Federation

http://www.toucan.net/cwf-fcf

Founded in 1962, the Canadian Wildlife Federation (CWF) seeks to foster awareness and enjoyment of Canada's natural environment. To accomplish this objective, CWF provides public education about the impact of destructive human activities on the environment, encourages the sustainable use of natural resources, conducts and sponsors wildlife environmental research, recommends legislative measures to protect wildlife and its habitat, and cooperates with organizations and government agencies having similar environmental goals. Through its extensive education and conservation programs, CWF encourages a future in which Canadians may live in harmony with the natural world. To learn more about CWF, visit this site.

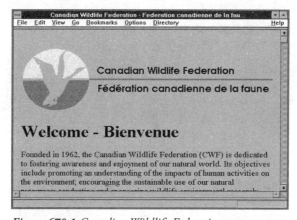

Figure 670.1 Canadian Wildlife Federation.

Chesapeake Bay Trust

http://www2.ari.net/home/cbt

The Chesapeake Bay Trust is a nonprofit organization created in 1985 by the Maryland General Assembly to promote public awareness and participation in the restoration and protection of Chesapeake Bay. To accomplish this mission, the Trust seeks contributions from the business community and private citizens. The Trust, in turn, distributes those contributions in the form of financial support grants to groups undertaking projects to help the Bay. A special file offers information and resources for educators wishing to teach about the history and importance of the Chesapeake Bay watershed and ecosystem.

Figure 671.1 Chesapeake Bay Trust.

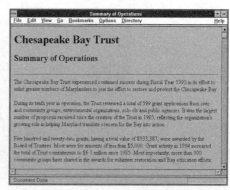

Figure 671.2 Summary of Trust activities.

Citizen's Clearinghouse for Hazardous Waste

http://www.essential.org/orgs/CCHW/CCHW.html

The Citizen's Clearinghouse for Hazardous Waste (CCHW) was founded in 1981 by Love Canal residents who successfully fought for relocation of their families. Through organization, leadership development, research, and technical assistance, CCHW gives individuals the skills and information they need to start local environmental groups, strengthen existing groups, and develop networks that protect public health and the environment. Over the past fourteen years, CCHW has developed a network of more than 24,000 individuals and 8,000 community organizations that work at the local, regional, and national level to protect health and stop environmental degradation.

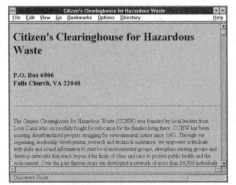

Figure 672.1 *Clearinghouse home page.*

Figure 672.2 *The campaign to stop dioxin exposure.*

Earth Pledge Foundation

http://www.earthpledge.org/epfhome.html

The Earth Pledge Foundation was established to promote the vision of sustainable development that emerged from the Earth Summit held in Rio de Janeiro in 1992. At Earth Pledges' cyberspace home (this site), you'll find lots of cool stuff. For example, you'll find information on "sustainable tourism," or, in other words, "how to structure foreign travel so you don't support nature's plunders (i.e., avoid tennis courts where once there were rain forests)." Also, be sure to check out the beautiful art gallery which, at the time I visited, featured work that acclaimed artist Robert Rauschenberg created specifically for the Foundation.

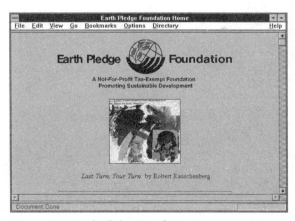

Figure 673 *Earth Pledge Foundation.*

SAVE THE PLANET

Earthwatch

http://gaia.earthwatch.org

Earthwatch sponsors cultural and environmental research by inviting concerned citizens to invest in the future of our planet. A nonprofit, membership organization founded in 1972, Earthwatch has enlisted over 40,000 people to assist noted scientists and scholars with projects that range from coral reef surveys to public health studies. Interested in signing up? At the moment, you can choose from more than 150 scientific field expeditions. For example, you can help preserve public art in Venice, track timber wolves in Minnesota, or build solar ovens in Kenya. At this site, you can search projects by scientific discipline, time of year, geographic location, or your skills and interests. You can also find out about Earthwatch grants you can obtain to fund your own expeditions.

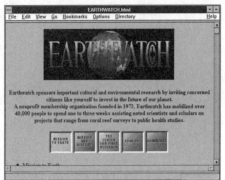

Figure 674.1 Earthwatch.

Figure 674.2 Over 150 expeditions.

EcoMall

http://www.ecomall.com/ecomall

EcoMall offers you a chance to help save the earth while you shop. At this site, you'll find guides to ecologically correct restaurants, products, stocks, businesses, and more. You'll also discover ecologically correct approaches to heating (or cooling) your home or office and purchasing office supplies. This site also includes information on how to locate goods suppliers and service providers who are committed to conducting business in a manner that minimizes environmental impact. Want more? You can find stock tips about up-and-coming businesses that make a nice profit without destroying nature. In short, visit the EcoMall for the ultimate "positive" shopping experience.

Figure 675.1 EcoMall.

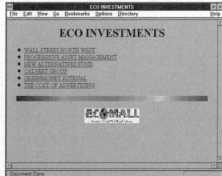

Figure 675.2 Eco Investments.

EcoNet

http://www.econet.apc.org/econet/

EcoNet serves organizations and individuals working for environmental preservation and sustainability. More specifically, EcoNet builds coalitions and partnerships with individuals, activist organizations, and non-profit organizations to help them utilize electronic communications. For example, EcoNet Gopher lets EcoNet members disseminate news and information about their projects and campaigns. The EcoNet Gopher is also an Internet browser on environmental issues. Another example: the EcoNet Issue Resource Center lists and sorts by category all the environmental resources available on the Internet. All told, this site is one-stop-shopping for the ecologically-sensitive surfer.

Figure 676 EcoNet main screen.

Ecotrust

http://www.well.com/user/ecotrust/

Ecotrust is a private, nonprofit organization established in 1991 to promote conservation-based development, beginning in the temperate rain forests *of North America*. The mission of Ecotrust is to conserve and restore the ecosystems that support life on Earth by helping local communities develop their ability to balance human needs and ecological integrity. The organization's hope is to contribute in small, but significant, ways to building functional examples of conservation-based development in those coastal temperate rain forests that stretch from the Alaskan Peninsula to central Oregon and include the dryer coast redwoods of southern Oregon and northern California's fog belt.

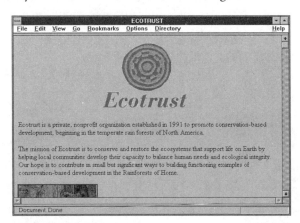

Figure 677 Ecotrust home page.

SAVE THE PLANET

Environmentally Sound Products

http://virtumall.com/ESP/ESPmain.html

By spending their individual dollars carefully, consumers can have a major and positive impact on the production and distribution of environmentally safe products. However, because advertising and marketing claims are often deceptive and unclear, it is sometimes hard to choose products that are 100% environmentally sound. Through intensive research, Environmentally Sound Products offers a wide variety of products that it guarantees are good environmental choices. Thus, as you read this catalog and make selections that suit your needs, you *know* you are a part of "the solution" to our planet's environmental woes. You'll find everything from toothpaste to vacuums, and rugs to toasters. Shop with a clear conscience.

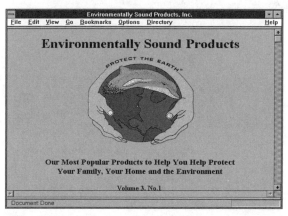

Figure 678 *Environmentally sound shopping.*

Friends of the Earth

http://www.essential.org/FOE.html

Founded in 1969 and headquartered in Washington, D.C., Friends of the Earth is a tax-exempt, environmental advocacy organization. One of its high profile programs is the Green Scissors Campaign. This campaign, a part of the organization's "Economics for the Earth" program, promotes economic reform to protect the earth and its people. Visit this site for free access to the Green Scissors report. Want to know the shocking details about what some of your favorite corporations (national and multinational) are doing to the planet and how they are (or aren't) getting away with it? Read the report entitled "Dirty Little Secrets." To learn more about Friends of the Earth, visit this site.

Figure 679.1 *What the earth needs, friends.*

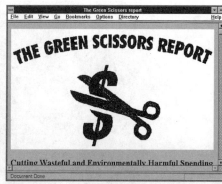

Figure 679.2 *Green Scissors report.*

Global Rivers Environmental Education Network

http://www.igc.apc.org/green/green.html

The Global River Environmental Education Network (GREEN) seeks to better people's lives by improving the quality of watersheds and rivers. GREEN seeks to build an international network of people and institutions that practice and promote global cooperation and resource sharing. GREEN develops programs that foster respect for, and sensitivity to, cultural differences and thus contribute to a more peaceful and ecologically sound environment. Visit the GREEN site for a great catalog of educational materials about the environment, online conferences, and links to watershed resources on the Internet.

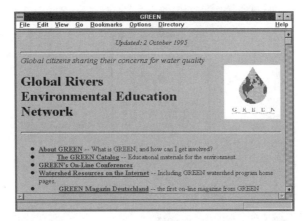

Figure 680 Global Rivers Environmental Education Network.

Greenpeace

http://www.greenpeace.org

Greenpeace is an international, independent campaign organization that uses non-violent, creative confrontation to expose global environmental problems and force solutions that are essential to a green and peaceful future. Greenpeace's overall goal is to ensure the earth's ability to nurture life in all its diversity. The organization's specific goals include preventing further pollution of oceans, land, air, and fresh water; ending all nuclear threats; and promoting world peace, global disarmament, and non-violence. This site offers information on current Greenpeace action campaigns, photo and video galleries, data on the Greenpeace ships afloat worldwide, and more.

Figure 681.1 Greenpeace home page.   *Figure 681.2* Current action campaigns.   *Figure 681.3* Photo & video gallery.

International Arid Lands Consortium

http://ag.arizona.edu/OALS/IALC/Home.html

The International Arid Lands Consortium (IALC) explores the problems (and solutions) unique to arid and semiarid regions. An independent, nonprofit organization, the Consortium offers hands-on expertise in arid and semiarid lands research. Its founders are the University of Arizona, the University of Illinois, New Mexico State University, South Dakota State University, Texas A&M University, the Jewish National Fund, and the USDA Forest Service. At this site, you'll find information on water conservation and harvesting, development of stress-tolerant plants, agroforestry, range management, fire control, drought mitigation, and other remedies to desertification and famine.

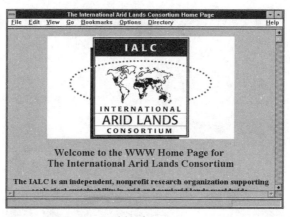

Figure 682 Saving arid lands.

League of Conservation Voters

http://www.econet.apc.org/lcv/lcv_info.html

The League of Conservation Voters is the bipartisan political arm of the environmental movement. Unlike any other national environmental organization, the League has but one mission: to use politics to protect the environment. League members believe legislative action by the United States Congress is responsible for many environmental improvements that have occured since the publication of Rachel Carson's *Silent Spring*. Visit this site to learn how senators and congressional representatives vote on environmental issues and how, in 1994, the League donated over $1 million to public-office candidates who pledge to protect the earth.

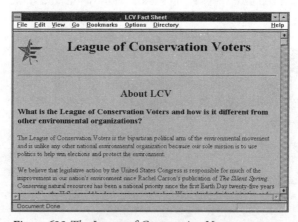

Figure 683 The League of Conservation Voters.

National Environmental Information Resources Center

http://www.gwu.edu/~greenu/

This provides one-stop, user-friendly access to a broad range of information about environmental matters. In fact, the types of information this site provides are as richly diverse as the hundreds of organizations that participate in National Environment Information Resources Center (NEIRC) activities. You can access information about conservation, ecology, education energy, economics, "green" buildings, health, laws and regulations, research, sustainability, environmentally conscious manufacturing, environmentally preferable products, pollution prevention, national and international policies, wildlife, and more. Y

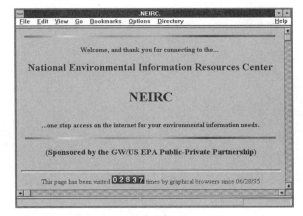

Figure 684 Environmental info cornucopia.

National Parks and Conservation Association

http://www.npca.com/pub/npca/

The National Parks and Conservation Association (NPCA) is the United States' only private, nonprofit citizens' organization dedicated solely to protecting, preserving, and enhancing the U.S. National Park System. An association of "Citizens Protecting America's Parks," NPCA was founded in 1919 and today has more than 450,000 members. Lately, NPCA has been defending the park system from the war declared on it by the 104th Congress. This site chronicles all the heated politics of Congress' war, providing coverage of the ongoing debate over park closing. Additionally, you'll find a digital reprint of the latest edition of *National Parks* magazine.

Figure 685 National Parks & Conservation Association page.

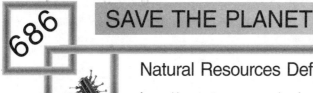

SAVE THE PLANET

Natural Resources Defense Council

http://www.igc.apc.org/nrdc

The Natural Resources Defense Council (NRDC) is a national, nonprofit organization dedicated to protecting the world's natural resources and ensuring a safe and healthy environment. In courtrooms, legislative chambers, regulatory agencies, and the public arena, NRDC defends the environment from pollution, exploitation, and destruction. From acid rain to global warming, ozone depletion to deforestation, energy overconsumption to habitat destruction, NRDC's scientists and attorneys have been working since 1970 to solve critical environmental problems. Visit this site for complete information on NRDC's varied and useful activities.

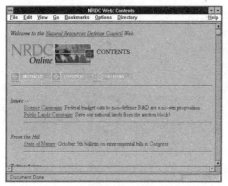

Figure 686.1 Defending the planet.

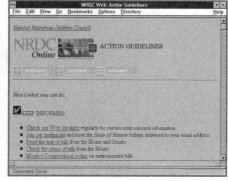

Figure 686.2 NRDC action guidelines.

National Wildlife Federation

http://www.nwf.org/nwf/prog

The National Wildlife Federation is the United States' largest member-supported conservation group. The Federation unites individuals, organizations, businesses, and governments interested in protecting nature, wildlife, and the planet. Through grassroots member organizations, the Federation educates and inspires people to establish and uphold a strong tradition of conservation. The Federation's common-sense approach to environmental protection balances the demands of a healthy economy with the need for a healthy environment, ensuring a brighter future for people and wildlife. Visit the Federation's site for more information on the organization's programs.

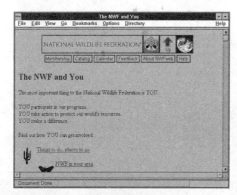

Figure 687.1 National Wildlife page.

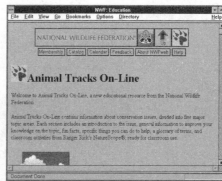

Figure 687.2 Viewing animal tracks.

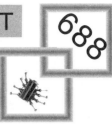

Natural History Book Store

http://www.nhbs.co.uk/

The Natural History Bookstore (NHBS) offers the world's largest inventory of environmental books. This site features "NHBS BookNet," a descriptive catalog of over 40,000 in-print or forthcoming environment-related books, CD-ROMs, and other materials. Browse "NHBS BookNet" (by subject or geographical area), or use the online catalog's powerful search facilities to find titles on global ecosystems, oceanography, forestry, pollution control, biosphere studies, endangered species, the history of the conservation movement, and more. NHBS, a UK-based organization, offers books and CD-ROMs from around the globe for a market that most assuredly embraces the world.

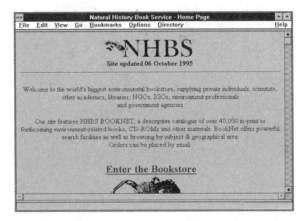

Figure 688 Natural history books on-line.

Ozone Action

http://www.essential.org/orgs/Ozone_Action/Ozone_Action.html

Depletion of the stratospheric ozone layer, the earth's protective shield, is one of the worst environmental disasters we face. Despite the 1987 enactment of the Montreal Protocol, an international agreement designed to protect the deteriorating ozone layer from man-made chemicals, the ozone layer is depleting, and ultraviolet radiation levels are increasing at astounding rates. In fact, ozone depletion has outstripped the predicted rate of ozone loss for the past three years, and scientists expect the problem to worsen over the next two decades. Find out more of the bad news, and what you can do about it, at the "Ozone Action" site.

Figure 689.1 Ozone Action.

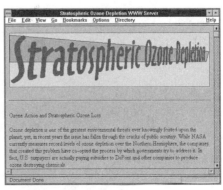

Figure 689.2 Stratospheric ozone depletion.

690

Ozone Depletion over Antarctica

http://icair.iac.org.nz/ozone/index.html

Ozone levels in the Antarctic vary throughout the year. During the Southern hemisphere winter, levels remain relatively static. However, each spring, as the sun returns to the Antarctic, up to 50% of the ozone disappears and returns only gradually over the coming months. Why does this ozone disappear? Why does it matter? Why is it a tragedy? To answer these questions, this site includes a document that explains the significance of the ozone problem. You'll also find a graph of the seasonal variation of ozone in the Antarctic for the year 1993; at that time, the graph already looked ominous. It is worse today.

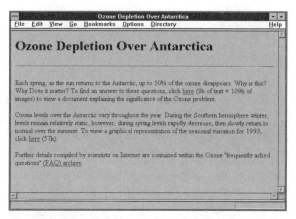

Figure 690 Ozone depletion above the penguins.

691

Sierra Club

http://www.sierraclub.org/

Founded by John Muir in 1892, the Sierra Club is one of the oldest and most highly respected environmental organizations in the United States. This extensive, well-designed site provides complete information on the organization and its activities, including action alerts, new member information/applications, contact information for local Sierra Club chapters, information on national Sierra Club outings, and more. You'll also find details on Sierra Club Books, the Sierra Club's ecoregions program, Sierra Club conservation policies, the Sierra Student Coalition, and affiliated Sierra Club organizations. As an added bonus, the site includes a great multimedia presentation that traces the proud history of the Sierra Club from 1892 up to present day.

Figure 691.1 Sierra Club home page.

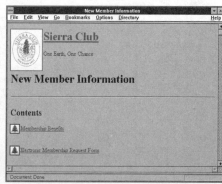

Figure 691.2 Membership information.

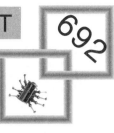

U.S. Fish and Wildlife Service

http://bluegoose.arw.r9.fws.gov

This site provides information about the National Wildlife Refuge System, wildlife and natural resources management, and current and pending conservation legislation, as well as links to other U.S. Fish and Wildlife Service resources. What wildlife refuges are near you? What educational programs and recreational resources do they offer? What is the current U.S. budget for new refuge acquisition? What are the procedures for deciding whether a site is appropriate for refuge status? Visit this site to get the answers to all these questions and more.

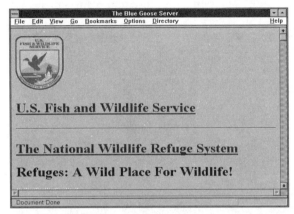

Figure 692 Wildlife refuge information.

Adopt a Whale Program

http://www.webcom.com/~iwcwww/whale_adoption/waphome.html

My two kids are the proud adoptive parents of a humpback whale named "Granny." We have a photograph of her distinctive tail, which my son Billy has posted on the bulletin board in his bedroom. From the excellent background information that accompanied Granny's adoption papers, we have details on Granny's annual migration pattern. Thus, at any time of year, we know approximately where Granny is and what she's doing. We are somewhat in awe of Granny when we realize the many miles she logs in the course of a year and contemplate the complex social structure in which she participates. As a result of their experience with Granny, my kids have learned (and continue to learn) a great deal about whales and marine ecosystems. It's an exercise I highly recommend.

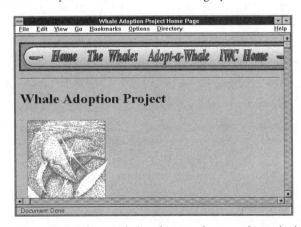

Figure 693 Adopt a whale today! But first get a bigger bathtub.

694

The Wilderness Society

http://town.hall.org/environment/wild_soc/wilderness.html

Now celebrating its 60th anniversary, the Wilderness Society is a non-profit conservation group dedicated to the protection of America's wild lands and wildlife. As part of that mission, the Society works to foster a land ethic based on broad ecosystem management and biodiversty. To advance its objectives, the Wilderness Society relies on a combination of public education, advocacy, and economic and ecological analysis. Lately, the Society has been striving to build new constituencies using, among other outreach programs, this Web site. For more information on the Wilderness Society, its "National Forest" program, and ecosystem management, visit this site.

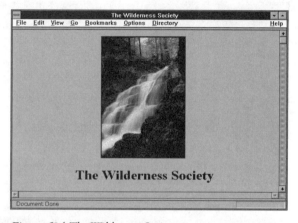

Figure 694 The Wilderness Society.

695

WhaleNet

http://whale.simmons.edu

"WhaleNet" is an interdisciplinary, hands-on, collaborative telecomputing project designed to foster excitement and learning about the natural world in schools around the world. "WhaleNet" is a combined project of the biology departments at Simmons and Wheelock Colleges, with support from the National Science Foundation and technical assistance from MuseNet (the Multi-User Science Education Network). Although splendid, "WhaleNet" is currently under construction by *biologists* who are learning HTML as they go. Thus, while "WhaleNet" remains a work-in-progress, you may occasionally experience a link that doesn't link or an image that doesn't resolve. But for all of that, the site is still impressive.

  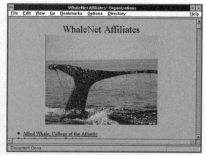

Figure 695.1 WhaleNet home page.   *Figure 695.2 An overview of the project.*   *Figure 695.3 WhaleNet affiliates.*

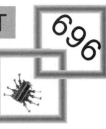

World Conservation Monitoring Center

http://www.wcmc.org.uk/

The World Conservation Monitoring Center (WCMC) specializes in information on biodiversity conservation. With more than 12 years' experience in this field, the Center has provided advice and information services to development-aid agencies, UN agencies, international convention secretariats, governmental and non-governmental organizations, commercial entities, scientists, and the media. WCMC is a non-profit organization, independent of governmental funding and public membership. At this site, you'll find information on protected areas, species and habitats, international agreements and programs, geographical information systems, and more.

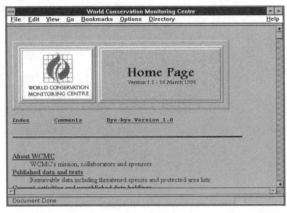

Figure 696 World Conservation Monitoring Center.

697

World Wildlife Fund

http://www.envirolink.org/orgs/wqed/wwf/wwf_home.html

For more than three decades, the World Wildlife Fund (WWF) has led international efforts to conserve the diversity of life on earth. WWF's passion for nature, the driving force behind all their work, is grounded in science and shaped by an understanding that addressing human needs is critical to successful long-term conservation. The WWF mission is simple and direct: the conservation of nature. It uses five broad strategies to fulfill this mission: creating and preserving protected areas, linking conservation and human needs, building capacity through education and training, protecting species, and reducing resource consumption and pollution.

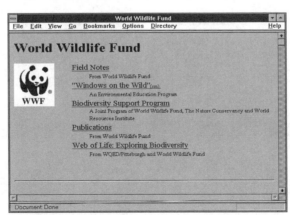

Figure 697 The famous Panda logo of the World Wildlife Fund.

More Save the Planet

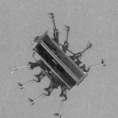

As you surf the Web, you may find that one or more of the site addresses listed in this book have changed. In such cases, connect to Jamsa Press at http://www.jamsa.com and click on the icon that corresponds to the *1001 Really Cool Web Sites* book. Jamsa Press will list replacement addresses (when possible) for sites that have moved. In addition, you can also use the following site list as you search for information on saving the planet:

The EPA WASTEWI$E PROGRAM	http://cygnus-group.com/ULS/Waste/epa.html
The EnviroArts Gallery	http://envirolink.org/arts/
The Virtual Environmental Library	http://envirolink.org/elib/
All Environmental Web Resources	http://envirolink.org/envirowebs.html
Other Projects on the EnviroWeb	http://envirolink.org/projects.html
nformation Center for the Environment	http://ice.ucdavis.edu/about_ICE.html
Earth and Environmental Science	http://info.er.usgs.gov/network/science/earth/index.html

698

Isaac Asimov

http://www.clark.net/pub/wmcbrine/html/Asimov.html

This site is an amazingly complete Web resource for fans and devotees of the late science-fiction writer Isaac Asimov, who was perhaps the most prolific practitioner in his field. This great page provides information on hundreds of Asimov's books and includes the short story "Eyes Do More Than See." You'll find a chronology of the *Foundation* series, reviews and critical essays concerning Asimov's work, and several obituaries. Additionally, this site contains two essays, Asimov's "Saving the Earth" and "The Impact of Science on Society," you won't find elsewhere. Finally, the page provides a searchable bibliography of all Asimov's novels and short stories, as well as a reference sheet on planets mentioned in the *Foundation* series.

Figure 698.1 Asimov himself.

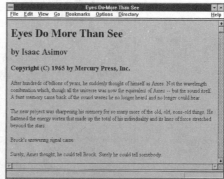

Figure 698.2 A complete short story.

Lurker's Guide to *Babylon 5*

http://www.hyperion.com/lurk/lurker.html

Who, by this time, is not acquainted with the television program *Babylon 5*? This Web page provides an extensive assortment of facts, trivia, and details concerning the show. You'll find information on *Babylon 5*'s setting and characters, an episode guide complete with schedules and synopses, a behind-the-scenes guide that provides information about *Babylon 5*'s creators, and pointers to other *Babylon 5* information (online and off). Additionally, you'll find digital reprints of U.S. and Canadian reviews of the program. Created and maintained by Webmaster Steven Grimm, "The Lurker's Guide to *Babylon 5*" is an excellent resource for all *B5* fans.

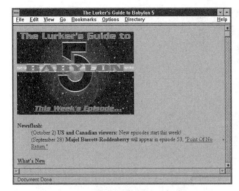

Figure 699.1 Everything about Babylon 5.

Figure 699.2 The show and its characters.

Century Magazine

http://www.supranet.com/century/

Century is a bimonthly magazine of stories that combine elements of science fiction, magic realism, fantasy, surrealism, and mainstream fiction. *Century* is not a zine, but a print magazine available by subscription and at bookstores around the country. However, *Century* posts sample stories and critical essays at its site to give you a free taste of what the magazine has to offer. When I visited this site, I found stories by Michael Shea, Maya Kathryn Bohnhoff, Carol Emshwiller, David Phalen, Avram Davidson, Kelly Link, and Gerald Pearce. Stop by and find out why Don D'Ammassa, writing in *Science Fiction Chronicle*, called *Century* "very impressive indeed, filled with high quality fiction . . . exceptional stories."

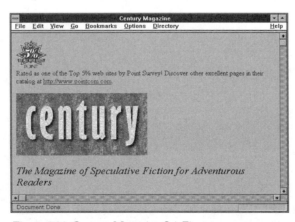

Figure 700 Century Magazine Sci-Fi.

Arthur C. Clarke Unauthorized Homepage

http://www.lsi.usp.br/~rbianchi/clarke

Arthur C. Clarke is one of the most celebrated science fiction authors of our time. He has written more than sixty books (with more than 50 million copies in print) and won all the field's highest honors. In 1962, he won the Kalinga Prize for science writing. In 1968, he shared an Oscar nomination with Stanley Kubrick for the film version of *2001: A Space Odyssey*. In 1969, he co-broadcasted the Apollo 11 mission with Walter Cronkite and Wally Schirra for CBS. And, in 1986, the Science Fiction Writers of America named him "Grand Master." At this site, you'll find a number of interviews with Clarke and critical essays about Clarke and his work.

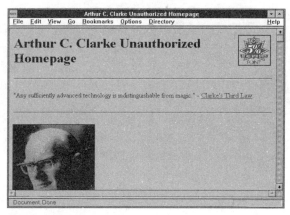

Figure 701 Arthur C. Clarke home page.

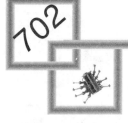

Del Rey Books

http://www.randomhouse.com/delrey/

Del Rey Books began as an imprint of Ballantine Books in 1977 with Terry Brooks' best-selling *The Sword of Shannara*. Founded by editor Judy-Lynn del Rey with the editorial assistance of her husband (author/editor Lester del Rey), Del Rey Books quickly grew into the most robust science fiction/fantasy imprint in the field. Over the years, Del Ray has published the work of Arthur C. Clarke, Isaac Asimov, Stephen Donaldson, Anne McCaffrey, David Eddings, Larry Niven, Katherine Kurtz, Barbara Hambly, and many others. Visit this site to find out about Del Rey's featured and forthcoming titles, their *Star Wars* publishing program, and their *Discovery Program,* which showcases new authors and first novels.

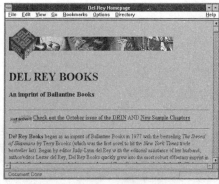

Figure 702.1 Del Rey Books page.

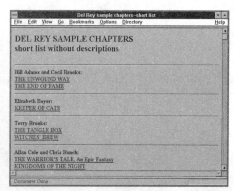

Figure 702.2 Sample chapters.

E-scape: Digital Journal of Speculative Fiction

http://www.flinthills.com/escape.html

September 1995 saw the premier issue of *E-scape*, a free magazine of speculative fiction. *E-scape* is published in Adobe Acrobat format, so you'll need Adobe's Acrobat Reader 2.0 or later (which you can download for free at this site) to read it. *E-scape* publishes science fiction, fantasy and horror fiction, articles, game reviews, and convention schedules/announcements. The premier issue features such stories as "The Choice" by Glenn Sixbury, "Finding Warren" by David Phalen, "Waypost" by Aaron Humphrey, and "Sirens in the Dark" by J.D. Bishop. Get in on the ground floor of something special. Check out *E-scape*.

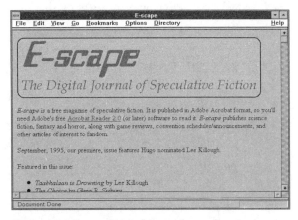

Figure 703 E-scape Digital Journal.

Future Fantasy Bookstore

http://futfan.com/home-text.html

Located in Palo Alto, California, the Future Fantasy Bookstore is one of the premier bookstores for connoisseurs of fantasy fiction. And now, for those of you who don't live near Palo Alto, the store has opened a branch office in cyberspace. At this site, you can browse or search an extensive list of thousands of available titles. Search by author, title, category, or genre. Then, order your books online and enjoy a 10% discount off the list price. Also, if the Palo Alto store hosts an author book-signing for a title you purchased online, you can (at no extra charge) have the store's staff set your copy aside for inscription and then ship it to you later.

Figure 704 Future Fantasy Bookstore.

House of Speculative Fiction

http://cyberus.ca/specific/

The near-legendary House of Speculative Fiction has just begun its seventeenth year of selling science fiction and fantasy in Canada's national capital, Ottawa. To celebrate, they've just opened up a sister store on the Web! At this site, you can order online from a wonderful, huge, searchable selection of the best science fiction and fantasy. Additionally, through the "What's Coming" report, you can get the inside scoop on forthcoming titles, order books before they're published, and become "the first kid on your block" to own great new works of science fiction. The store is founded on a beautiful principle: "There are some knightly souls who make their visits to bookshops not because they need a certain volume, but because they feel that there may be some book that needs them."

Figure 705 House of Speculative Fiction.

H.P. Lovecraft Page

http://www.primenet.com/~dloucks/hplpage.html

Howard Phillips Lovecraft (1890-1937) was a writer of weird fiction. He is best known for his "Cthulhu Mythos" stories, but many believe his voluminous correspondence is his greatest accomplishment. Maintained by dedicated Lovecraft-fan Donovan Loucks, this site includes a biography of Lovecraft, a chronological list of all of Lovecraft's tales, an illustrated guide to Lovecraft sites throughout New England, a bestiary of the creatures inhabiting the dark universe of Cthulha Mythos, an essay dispelling common misconceptions about Lovecraft, and more. You also get a file entitled "The Necronomicon and other Grimories," which provides quotes from Lovecraft's letters and tales.

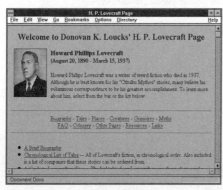

Figure 706.1 A Lovecraftian place in cyberspace.

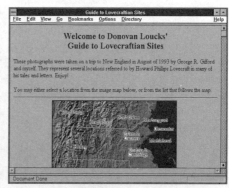

Figure 706.2 And a guide to Lovecraftian places in (nonvirtual) reality.

Nebula Awards, 1965-1994

http://www.lm.com/~lmann/awards/nebulas/nebulas.html

The Science Fiction Writers of America (SFWA) administers and presents the Nebula Awards to acknowledge excellence in science fiction. Laurie Mann, (lmann@telerama.lm.com) maintains this useful hypertext version of the awards list, which you can search (for novel, novella, novelette, and short story) by decade, genre, winner, or nominees. Among the winners you will find at this site are Mike Resnick, Connie Willis, Harlan Ellison, Ray Bradbury, Frank Herbert, Arthur C. Clarke, William Gibson, Orson Scott Card, and the indomitable Kate Wilhelm. Thanks, Laurie, for a wonderful resource.

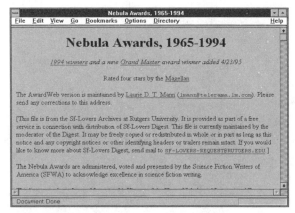

Figure 707 Nebula Awards: the best in Sci-Fi.

Quanta

http://www.etext.org/Zines/Quanta/

Quanta, the online magazine of science fiction and fantasy, has been publishing since 1989 and is highly regarded by sci-fi buffs. The magazine fosters a unique concept—shareword. If you read and enjoy *Quanta*, the editor asks that you send a five-dollar donation. "*Quanta* does cost money to produce, and that money comes solely from out of my pocket and from readers like yourself," writes editor Dan Appelquist. "Note that donations, while appreciated, are not in any way a requirement for subscription, or for reading *Quanta* stories." Recent stories include "Virtual Immortality" by R.E. Smeraglia, "In the City" by Jacqueline Carey, "Robotroubles" by Ken Kousen, and "The Plains of Meer" by Simon Joseph.

Figure 708.1 Quanta Sci-Fi.

Figure 708.2 A sample TOC.

University of Michigan Fantasy & Science Fiction Pages

http://www.umich.edu/~umfandsf/

Ranked in the top 5% of all Web sites by *Point Survey*, the "University of Michigan Fantasy & Science Fiction Pages" serves scholars and sci-fi buffs all over the world. At this site, you'll find bibliographies, filmographies, critical essays, author biographies, and references, as well as links to other sci-fi stops on the Web. From Asimov to Wilhelm, from H.G. Wells' *War of the Worlds* to the very latest novels and stories on the cutting-edge of the sci-fi literary tradition, this site has it all. Search for information by author, topic, genre, or specific title. Access sound files of interviews with Arthur Clarke and Isaac Asimov. And, download classic sci-fi cover art.

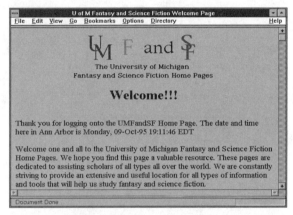

Figure 709 Fantasy & Sci-Fi page.

The New England Science Fiction Association

http://www.panix.com/NESFA/home.html

The New England Science Fiction Association (NESFA) is one of the oldest science fiction clubs in the northeast United States. At this site, you'll find details on upcoming NESFA events (such as the 1996 NESFA Short Story Contest for new writers), a catalog of great books from NESFA Press, recommended reading lists, and reviews by NESFA members. Additionally, links take you to science fiction resource guides, the "Lysator Science Fiction & Fantasy Archive," and information on science fiction campaigns across the United States and around the world. This site also provides links to NESFA's sister organizations in California, Oregon, Texas, Maryland, and elsewhere.

Figure 710.1 NESFA on the Web.

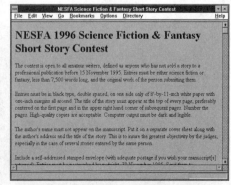

Figure 710.2 Enter the contest!

Science Fiction Links

http://boris.qub.ac.uk/edward/SciFi.html

Maintained by the U.K.'s Edward Smyth (E.SMYTH@qub.ac.uk), this great list of science fiction links gives you resources related to television shows, films, novels, and short stories. For example, no less than 19 links connect you to *Star Trek*. Eleven links take you to *The X Files* pages. Still other links transport you to resources related to *Babylon 5*, *Lost In Space*, *The Prisoner*, and *Dr. Who*. You'll also find materials related to Frank Herbert's *Dune*, the Hugo Awards, *Alien 3*, *Star Wars*, and every major sci-fi author and novel for the past one hundred years. Additional links take you to some of the Web's best science-fiction and speculative-fiction zines. "Science Fiction Links" is a splendid launch pad into sci-fi on the Net. Thank you, Ed Smyth!

Figure 711.1 *Smyth's Science Fiction page.*

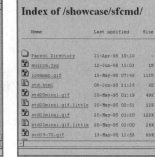

Figure 711.2 *One of your options.*

Science Fiction and Fantasy Links

http://www.ee.ucg.ie/science_fiction.html

At this site, you'll find pages dedicated to fifteen leading sci-fi authors, including Douglass Adams, Piers Anthony, Iain Banks, David Brin, Philip Dick, Edgar Rice Burroughs, Frederick Pohl, and Orson Scott Card. You'll find a comprehensive Heinlein bibliography, great studies of how science fiction has portrayed the Moon and Mars, a link to the MIT Science Fiction Library, a guide to Hugo Award Winners 1953-1995, and more. Additionally, the site includes detailed information on Larry Niven, E.E. "Doc" Smith, J.R.R. Tolkien, Roger Zelazny, and Vernon Vinge; filmographies; and some of the best downloadable graphics on the Web.

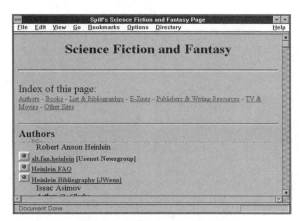

Figure 712 *Sci-Fi and fantasy pages.*

713

Science Fiction and Fantasy Writers of America

http://www.sfwa.org

Visit the cyberhome of the leading professional organization for science fiction and fantasy writers. This site is not a sci-fi trivia page, nor a bibliographical or critical reference, but rather a dynamic, professional resource for writers. Want fair compensation for your work of imagination? Visit this site to find recommended hardcover and paperback publisher contracts, model anthology rights contracts, and other such tools. Want to see what your fellow writers (even the famous ones) are up to? Click on links to their personal home pages. Need to gather some material for an upcoming novel or short story? Use this site's excellent research links to reach resources in science and mythology.

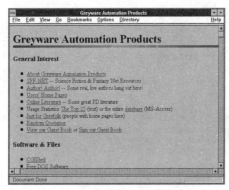

Figure 713.1 For professional writers.

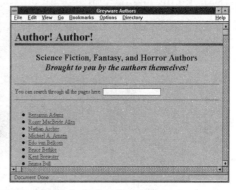

Figure 713.2 Author home pages.

714

The Science Fiction Gallery

http://www.onestep.com

This Web site, which focuses on television and film sci-fi, isn't a place of business and has no corporate sponsor (movie studio, television production group, or otherwise). Instead, fans and enthusiasts maintain the "Science Fiction Gallery." The site does not have a lot of flashy downloadable graphics, as do some pages that media companies subsidize. But it does have interesting viewpoints about recent sci-fi offerings, as well as interesting perspectives on classics. "Our goal is to incite discussions on serious science fiction topics, works, and new ideas," writes the Webmaster. So visit this site for interesting coverage of everything from the pioneering sci-fi flicks of the silent film era to the latest sci-fi television shows and movies.

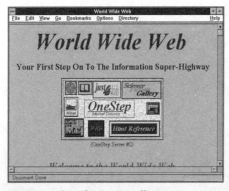

Figure 714.1 The Sci-Fi gallery.

Figure 714.2 The Writer's Gallery.

SCI-FI & FANTASY BOOKS/ZINES

The Science Fiction Shop

http://www.tagsys.com/Ads/SciFiShop

The "Science Fiction Shop" offers international ordering for virtually all science fiction, fantasy, and supernatural horror paperbacks, hardcovers, audio cassettes, and illustrated novels. The Shop carries most small press offerings, specialty publisher's titles, and magazines. The Shop also offers signed editions, first editions, and collectible comic books. To find the book you want, you can search the site's extensive database offerings by author name, title, genre, or publisher. (When I searched the database, I found such works *as Chaos Mode, Ring of Swords, Positronic Man, Bred for War*, and *Matter's End*.) Additionally, if you're someone who likes to devour a book as soon as it comes out, you can order forthcoming titles and have them shipped to you immediately upon publication.

Figure 715 The Sci-Fi Shop.

Science Fiction Weekly

http://www.mordor.com/sfw/

This outstanding digital weekly brings you the very latest news on sci-fi literature, authors, and publishing. One recent article considered (and provided samples of) Groiler Electronic Publishing's new *Science Fiction: The Multimedia Encyclopedia of Science Fiction* CD-ROM, which includes 1,700 images, 33 author sound bites, and more than 70 film clips. Another recent article announced that Michael Dorn will join the cast of *Star Trek: Deep Space Nine,* where he will revive the role of Lt. Commander Worf that he made famous in seven seasons on *Star Trek: The Next Generation*. You get the idea. Everything in "*Science Fiction Weekly*" is hot off the griddle. Take a bite.

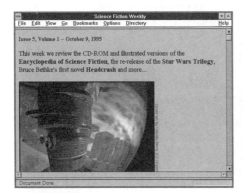 

Figure 716.1 Sci-Fi Weekly.   *Figure 716.2* Features complete short stories.

Tor Science Fiction & Fantasy

http://www.tor.com

Tor Books, an imprint of Tom Doherty Associates, Inc., is a New York-based publisher committed (although not limited) to science fiction and fantasy literature. Between their extensive hardcover and trade-softcover lines, Tor Books annually publishes what is arguably the largest and most diverse line of science fiction and fantasy literature in the world. Books from Tor have won every major award in the science fiction and fantasy fields. And, for the last eight years in a row, Tor has been named "Best Publisher" in the *Locus* Poll, the largest consumer poll in science fiction. Visit this site for information on all of Tor's great books, including sample chapters from works by Jonathan Lethem, Melissa Scott, John Barnes, and Nancy Kress.

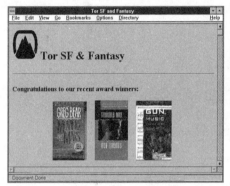

Figure 717.1 Tor Books home page.

Figure 717.2 Sample chapters!

718

The Vampire Chronicles

http://www.xroads.com/pages/gpalmer/vampire.html

Ranked in the top 5% of Web sites by Point Communications, *The Vampire Chronicles* site offers all the trivia, GIFs, and news you can swallow related to Anne Rice's famous *Vampire Chronicles*. You will find extensive information on the lonely existential narrator of *Interview With a Vampire*, as well as Lestat and all the other notable characters that have sprung from the mind of Anne Rice. And you'll get the scoop on the novels, as well as backlot chat and gossip from the making of the film *Interview With a Vampire*. All Anne Rice fans will find this Web site exciting and engaging, if not addicting.

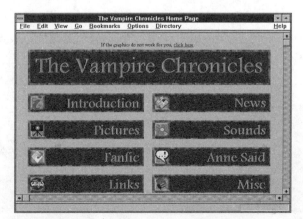

Figure 718.1 Bats and things.

The X Files

http://www.rutgers.edu/x-files.html

Is there anything more addicting than *The X Files*? I know my son is hooked. What supernatural or extraterrestrial lunacy will those two special agents encounter next week? To that question (and only that question), you'll find no answer at this site. Every other aspect of *The X Files* is painstakingly documented here. You'll find FAQs (frequently asked questions), character biographies (long and extensive life histories for the series' two adventurous FBI agents), cast and director biographies, and more. You'll also find GIFs, sound files, episode synopses, and even Acrobat files containing annotated scripts from the director's desk!

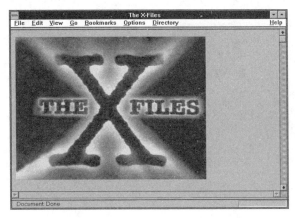

Figure 719 The big X.

More Sci -Fi & Fantasy Books/Zines

As you surf the Web, you may find that one or more of the site addresses listed in this book have changed. In such cases, connect to Jamsa Press at http://www.jamsa.com and click on the icon that corresponds to the *1001 Really Cool Web Sites* book. Jamsa Press will list replacement addresses (when possible) for sites that have moved. In addition, you can also use the following site list as you search for information on Sci-Fi:

UK Magazine	http://www.paragon.co.uk/
Scallywag	http://www.demon.co.uk/xyz/Scallywag/index.html
Newsbytes	http://www.islandtel.com/newsbytes/
NandO Time	http://www2.nando.net/nt/world/
Techno Online	http://www.techno.de
London Magazine	http://www.londonmall.co.uk
Blue Planet	http://www.demon.co.uk/blueplanet
Italian Football	http://wwwedu.cs.utwente.nl/~capoccia/soccer.html
West Ham	http://www.iafrica.com/~paulw/westham.html

American Astronomical Society

http://www.aas.org

The American Astronomical Society (AAS) is the major professional organization in North America for scientists and others interested in astronomy. At this site, you'll find information on every division of the society, including the High Energy Astrophysics Division, the Historical Astronomy Division, the Solar Physics Division, the Planetary Sciences Division, and the Dynamical Astronomy Division. You'll also find information on the Society's education programs, electronic publishing projects, and grants program. Of special value is the online edition of the *Astrophysical Journal*, which provides you with up-to-date results from the Society's ongoing research projects.

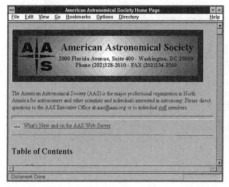

Figure 720.1 *The American Astronomical Society.*

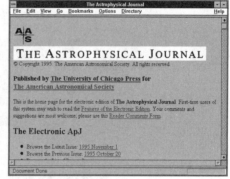

Figure 720.2 *The Society's Journal.*

Anthropology Virtual Library

http://www.usc.edu/dept/v-lib/anthropology.html

This site provides one-stop shopping for virtually every important anthropology resource on the Web. From the "Anthropology Virtual Library," you can connect to sites ranging from Rice University's "Anthropology and Culture Archives" to Peabody Museum at Yale. Additional connections take you to the Center for Advanced Studies, Research, and Development in Sardinia; The Institute for Egyptian Art and Archaeology; the Anabaptist Sociology and Anthropology Association; and the University of New Mexico's Maxwell Museum of Anthropology.

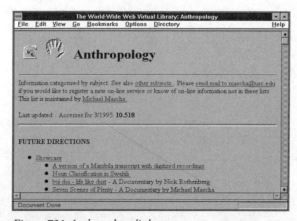

Figure 721 Anthropology links.

Armagh Observatory

http://star.arm.ac.uk/

Armagh Observatory is an astronomical research institution founded in 1790 and situated in the city of Armagh, North Ireland. The observatory is one of two sites that form the Northern Ireland Node of the international Starlink network of observatories. The other site is located at the Astrophysics and Planetary Science Division of the Queen's University, Belfast. Armagh Observatory has a long, distinguished tradition of excellence in groundbreaking astronomical research. (In other words, in astronomy as in so many other things, the Irish have outgunned the rest of mankind.) In addition to housing a splendid observatory, Armagh is also home to an outstanding planetarium.

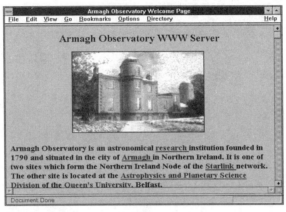

Figure 722 The Armagh Observatory.

Astronomy Magazine

http://www.kalmbach.com/astro/astronomy.html

Read by over 300,000 astronomy enthusiasts each month, *Astronomy Magazine* is the world's most popular English-language magazine for astronomy. Visit this site to sample some of the great articles and graphics from each monthly issue of *Astronomy Magazine*. What is NASA's new plan for analyzing the moon's surface? In what way do the ghostly remains of long dead stars highlight a new image of M31? How might neutrinos and gravitons help astronomers see beyond the microwave background barrier? And why does an otherwise normal binary star seem to contradict Einstein's theory of relativity? To find the answers to all these questions and more, stop by this site.

Figure 723.1 Astronomy Magazine.

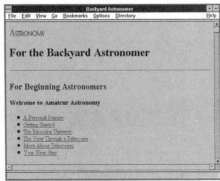

Figure 723.2 Info for the backyard astronomer.

The European Space Agency

http://www.esrin.esa.it/

The European Space Agency (ESA) seeks to promote cooperation among European nations in space research and technology. ESA's ultimate goal is to use the acquired knowledge for peaceful scientific purposes, such as developing communication and weather satellites. To achieve this objective, ESA defined and put into effect a long-term policy that will allow Europe to become and remain competent in the field of space technology. To boost the effectiveness of its programs, ESA also pools resources and shares work with various partners, such as NASA.

Figure 724 The European Space Agency.

The Evolution of Terrestrial Ecosystems Consortium

http://eteweb.lscf.ucsb.edu/

Formed by a group of paleontologists (scientists who study fossils and ancient life forms), The Evolution of Terrestrial Ecosystems Consortium (ETE Consortium) oversees all aspects of the ETE Database, a computerized database for research in evolutionary paleoecology. The Consortium members believe that we cannot fully comprehend long-term patterns of evolutionary change without knowing ecological changes that have occurred over geologic time periods, and understanding the interaction between ecological and evolutionary processes. Thus, the Consortium is interested in how the environment and ecosystems have changed and how these changes have affected species evolution over the past 400 million years.

Figure 725 The ETE Consortium.

Florida Museum of Natural History

http://www.flmnh.ufl.edu/

Come to the Web site of the Florida Museum of Natural History for a sample of its rich collections in archaeology and the natural sciences. On the archaeological front, access images and text files that reveal the Museum's holdings related to Caribbean archaeology, environmental archaeology, and ceramic technology. On the natural sciences front, consider the Museum's excellent holdings (beautifully presented here) related to mammals, birds, reptiles and amphibians, fishes, mollusks, butterflies, plants, and more. You'll also find wonderful material on invertebrate and vertebrate fossils.

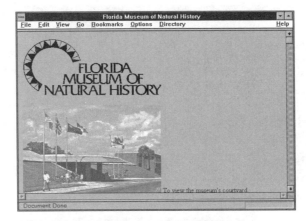

Figure 726 The Florida Museum of Natural History.

The Field Museum of Natural History

http://www.bvis.uic.edu/museum/

The Field Museum of Natural History in Chicago, Illinois, is an educational institution that provides collection-based research and learning for greater public understanding and appreciation of the natural world and cultures in which we live. The Museum's collections, public-learning programs, and research serve a diverse public of various ages, backgrounds, and education levels. At this site, you'll find many great features, including two multimedia tours: "Life Before Dinosaurs" and "Dinosaurs!" Both you and your kids will love these tours. And your kids will love "Teeth, Tusks and Tarpits!" with its movies, sound files, and games.

Figure 727.1 The Field Museum of Natural History.

Figure 727.2 Field Museum exhibits.

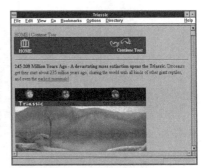

Figure 727.3 Dinosaur exhibits.

Gemini: An International Project

http://www.gemini.edu

What is Gemini? Two high-performance, 8-meter aperture optical/infrared telescopes in development as part of an international partnership between the United States, the United Kingdom, Canada, Chile, Argentina, and Brazil. The two telescopes will be positioned in the northern and southern hemispheres at Mauna Kea, Hawaii, and Cerro Pachon, Chile. The planned completion date for the project is 1998-2000. And the goal, of course, is to exploit the best natural observing conditions in the world so that scientists from the partner countries can initiate a broad range of astronomical research programs that were heretofore impossible. To find out more about the project, visit this site.

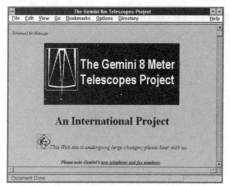

Figure 728.1 *Gemini Project information.*

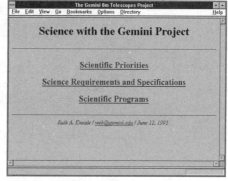

Figure 728.2 *Gemini science projects.*

Geological Society of America Bulletin

http://www.aescon.com/geosociety/pubs/bulletin.htm

You know how it is. You are trying to watch basketball but you just can't focus. You've got all those questions nagging at you. What is the status of quaternary soils and dust deposition in southern Nevada and California? What are the long-term results of water-rock interactions in modern coastal mixing zones? What are the major effects of synorogenic crystal fluids in the southern Omineca Belt of British Columbia, Canada? In what ways is the Bench Canyon shear zone of central Nevada typical of shear zone development during magnetic arc construction? And what are the constraints from low-altitude aeromagnetics vis-a-vis the tectonic of the Portland-Vancouver area? Find the answers at this Web site. Then, sit back and enjoy the game.

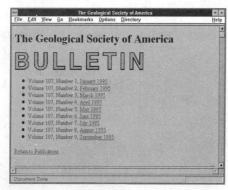

Figure 729.1 *The Geological Society of America.*

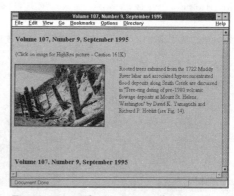

Figure 729.2 *The Society's Bulletin.*

Infrared Space Observatory Home Page

http://isowww.estec.esa.nl

As I write, the Infrared Space Observatory is about to launch. The projected date is November 8, 1995. The Infrared Space Observatory, a fully approved and funded project of the European Space Agency, will operate at wavelengths from 2.5 to 240 microns. A unique facility of unprecedented sensitivity, the Infrared Space Observatory will help astronomers study and explore the objects of our universe, from earth's neighboring planets to faraway galaxies. The instrument complement is an imaging photo-polarimeter, a camera, a short wavelength spectrometer, and a long wavelength spectrometer. To find out more about this cutting-edge project, and get to images and other results as the observatory transmits them, visit this site.

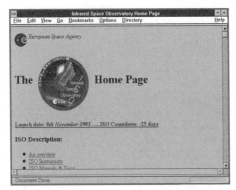 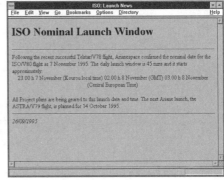

Figure 730.1 The Infrared Space Observatory.   *Figure 730.2 Launch information.*

The Natural History Museum of Los Angeles County

http://cwis.usc.edu/lacmnh/default.html

The Natural History Museum of Los Angeles County exists to advance knowledge and to enable people of all ages, backgrounds, and interests to appreciate their natural and cultural heritage. The Museum assembles, conserves, interprets, and holds in trust collections of irreplaceable objects from natural and human history. These collections reveal the history of the Earth and the evolution and diversity of life and culture. The Museum sustains our planet's geologic research and education programs, sponsors exhibits, and promotes scholarly publication. Visit this site for a number of resources, not the least of which is a splendid virtual tour of the Natural History Museum. Additional options give you access to the Museum's collections in paleontology and other important fields.

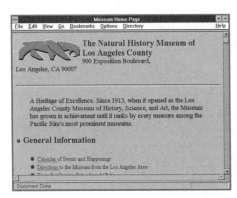 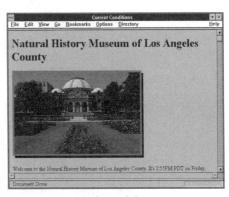

Figure 731.1 L.A. Natural History.   *Figure 731.2 A photo of the museum.*

National Museum of Natural History

http://nmnhwww.si.edu/nmnhweb.html

Compiled and maintained by the staff of the National Museum of Natural History, this site contains documents and data about the Museum's research and collections, which comprise more than 120 million scientific specimens and cultural artifacts from around the world. You'll also find information about the Museum's programs and projects, as well as news about collaborative efforts between the Museum and other organizations that support its missions (to understand the natural world and our place in it). You'll also find information on all departments of the Museum, including anthropology, botany, entomology, invertebrate zoology, palaebiology, and vertebrate zoology.

 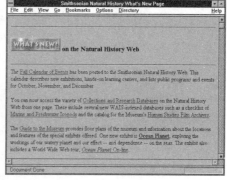

Figure 732.1 National Museum of Natural History.

Figure 732.2 What's New.

733

The Natural History Museum, Berne

http://www-nmbe.unibe.ch/

Daniel Sprungli (1721-1801) was vicar in Stettlen, Switzerland and a private scientist on his country estate "im Baumgarten" in Berne. Through his personal research, Sprungli became a naturalist of world reknown. After Sprungli's death, a gentlemen intent on forming a new institution, a Swiss Museum of Natural History, purchased Sprungli's extensive paleontological and zoological collections, among them his famous collection of Swiss birds. From that modest start, the Natural History Museum of Berne, Switzerland has expanded over the years to become one of the great museums of the West.

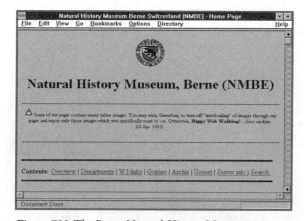

Figure 733 The Berne Natural History Museum.

The Oceanography Society

http://www.tos.org/

The Oceanography Society, founded in 1988, disseminates knowledge of oceanography and its application to promote communication among oceanographers and provide a constituency for consensus-building across all disciplines of the field. The Oceanography Society is a non-profit, tax-exempt organization incorporated in the District of Columbia. Visit this site for information on the Society and its many branches at the numerous Sea Grant colleges across the United States. In addition, you'll find a digital edition of the popular magazine *Oceanography*, as well as access to the Society's regularly updated news bulletin board and anonymous FTP server.

Figure 734 The Oceanography Society.

Palaeontological Association

http://www.nhm.ac.uk/paleonet/PalAss/PalAss.html

The Palaeontological Association is one of the most active and prominent of the numerous societies that cater to palaeontological interests. Founded in 1957 in the United Kingdom, the Association aims to further the study of palaeontology through publication of academic journals (*Palaeontology* and *Special Papers in Palaeontology*), newsletters, and field guides. In addition, the Society hosts regular meetings and field excursions. Visit this site to access the Association's valuable newsletter, as well as abstracts and papers from the Association's Annual Meeting in Galway. You can also find out how to become a member and submit papers to the Association's various publications.

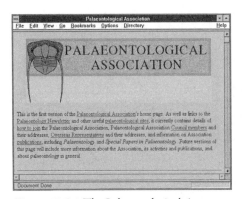

Figure 735.1 The Palaeontological Assoc.

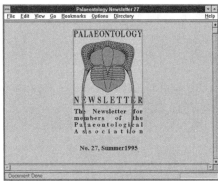

Figure 735.2 The Palaeontology Newsletter.

The PaleoNet Pages

http://www.nhm.ac.uk/paleonet/

What is "PaleoNet?" "PaleoNet" is a system of listservers, WWW pages, gopherholes, and FTP sites designed to enhance electronic communications among paleontologists. While primarily designed as a resource for paleontological professionals and graduate students, "PaleoNet" welcomes input and participation from all persons interested in the study of ancient life. You'll find the "PaleoNet" gopherhole the ideal place for all dinosaur-oriented cyber-rodents. You'll also find "CollectionsNet" (which covers the care and feeding of paleontological collections) and "TrainingNet" (which covers the training of paleontologists and those interested in paleontology at all educational levels).

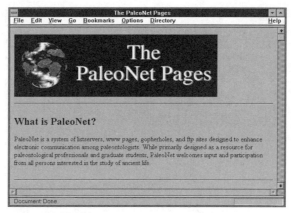

Figure 736 The PaleoNet Pages.

Santa Barbara Museum of Natural History

http://www.rain.org/~inverts/

Set in historic Mission Canyon, the Santa Barbara Museum of Natural History is one of the United States' most beautiful small museums by virtue of its natural setting and gracious Spanish-style buildings and grounds. At this site, staff experts in anthropology, entomology, invertebrate and vertebrate zoology, and other fields address your question or direct you to resources at the Santa Barbara Museum and elsewhere. You'll also find a multimedia tour of exhibits and information on the Museum's Sea Center, Cartwright Insectary, and the Astronomy Center. When you visit, also take the time to read the digital reprint of the Museum's informative bulletin.

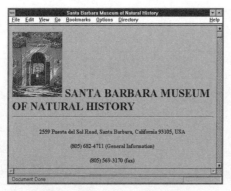

Figure 737.1 Museum of Natural History.

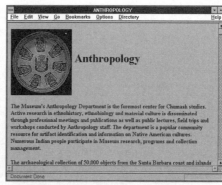

Figure 737.2 Anthropology at the museum.

Satellite Oceanography Laboratory

http://satftp.soest.hawaii.edu/spectacular.html

Are you prepared to view some of the most beautiful images you have ever seen in your life? The stunning gallery at the Satellite Oceanography Laboratory of Hawaii is where you will find them. See the moon setting over Siberia, as viewed by the satellite GMS-4. For oceanographic images, see an infrared shot of the California Current, AirSAR images of the California Current, and more. Meteorology? How about satellite images of hurricane Fernanda, or wake clouds in the lee of Kauai during a northerly wind event? Volcanology? How about pictures of lava flowing from Kilauea? Put on your cool shades and check it out.

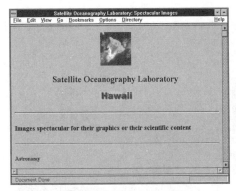

Figure 738.1 Satellite oceanography.

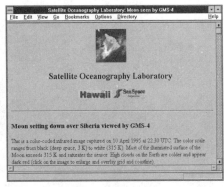

Figure 738.2 Moon-set over Siberia.

Scripps Institution of Oceanography Library

http://orpheus.ucsd.edu/sio/index.html

The library of the Scripps Institution of Oceanography provides an impressive set of links to electronic bibliographies, periodicals and texts; oceanographic and earth science institutes (research activities, personnel directories, data sets, satellite images, image/graph generation, tide predictions, and so on); and more. You'll also have access to the extensive Scripps Institution of Oceanography archives of images and datasets for the greater northeastern Pacific; real-time remote-sensor reports of "San Diego's ocean" (waves, ocean temperature, tide, weather); and direct links to the Woods Hole Oceanographic Institution, the Marine Biological Laboratory, and other important institutions and laboratories.

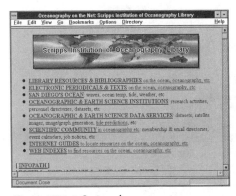

Figure 739.1 Scripps home page.

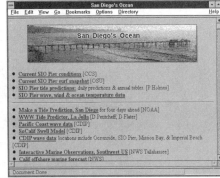

Figure 739.2 San Diego's Ocean.

Student Astronomers at Harvard-Radcliffe: STAHR

http://hcs.harvard.edu/~stahr

The Student Astronomers at Harvard-Radcliffe (STAHR) is a student organization at (yes, you guessed it) Harvard-Radcliffe. At this site, STAHR provides an excellent set of astronomy-related links to virtually every important observatory and astronomical society across the country and around the world. They also let you access Harvard's own extensive collection of sky-images, which documents more than 100 years of star-gazing at Harvard. So enter the astronomical tradition in which abided Percival Lowell. And while you visit this site, check out the absolutely fabulous, continually updated file entitled "What's up tonight?" This pithy guide to the night sky is bound to give your star-gazing more direction than it has ever had before.

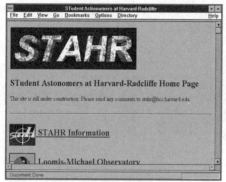

Figure 740.1 STAHR home page.

Figure 740.2 What's up tonight?

Swedish Museum of Natural History

http://www.nrm.se/

The Swedish Museum of Natural History is a state-run museum that operates as an independent government agency. The Museum's large collections of natural history material are reknowned throughout the world. Exhibitions and educational programs present the human environment from the wide definition of the universe as a whole down to the complex, compact, tiny subparticles of DNA. The Museum conducts ongoing research into the history and development of animals, plants, fossils, rocks, and minerals. At this site, in both Swedish- and English-language records, you'll find beautifully illustrated results of many of these research projects.

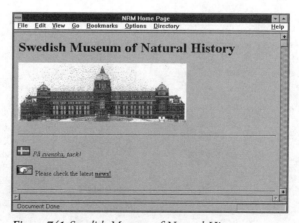

Figure 741 Swedish Museum of Natural History.

UMASS Astronomy Image Library

http://donald.phast.umass.edu/gs/wizimlib.html

After you view the first image this site offers, Van Gogh's *Starry Night*, you'll discover a sense of poetry in the arrangement of these otherwise methodical scientific images. Then, you'll move on to the equally beautiful, although more technically useful, images captured by a range of satellites and explorer spacecraft. At this site, you'll find a hyperlinked tour of the Lynds 1641 molecular cloud near Orion; a library of images of molecular line maps of star-formation regions; a three-color infrared image of the Ophiuchus region; a three-color infrared image of the central section of the Serpens Star Forming region; and an infrared cluster associated with the NGC2024 nebula (you know, where Flash Gordon used to get into trouble). If all that weren't enough, the gallery also includes an awe-inspiring image of Jupiter captured with the NICMASS Camera.

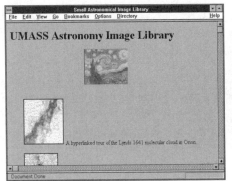

Figure 742.1 UMASS Astronomy Image Library.

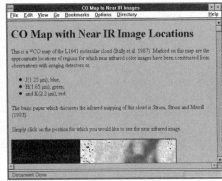

Figure 742.2 Molecular cloud on Orion.

Woods Hole Oceanographic Institution

http://www.whoi.edu/

The Woods Hole Oceanographic Institution is the largest independent marine science research facility in the United States. Founded in 1930, the Institution is dedicated to the study of all aspects of marine science and to the education of marine scientists. The Woods Hole Scientific Community consists of the Woods Hole Oceanographic Institution, the Marine Biological Laboratory, the USGS Branch of Atlantic Marine Geology, and the National Marine Fisheries Service Sea Education Association. To find out more about the Institution, stop by this site. And, while you're here, be sure to view the file that describes Woods Hole's new and beautiful research vessel, *Atlantis*, now under construction.

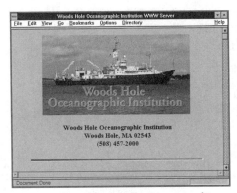

Figure 743.1 Woods Hole Oceanographic.

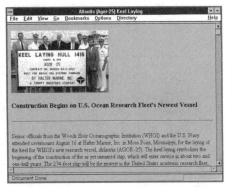

Figure 743.2 The new boat.

More Science, Natural & Otherwise

As you surf the Web, you may find that one or more of the site addresses listed in this book have changed. In such cases, connect to Jamsa Press at http://www.jamsa.com and click on the icon that corresponds to the *1001 Really Cool Web Sites* book. Jamsa Press will list replacement addresses (when possible) for sites that have moved. In addition, you can also use the following site list as you search for information on science:

MSTB Home Page	http://ndb1.larc.nasa.gov:80/
Science	http://nearnet.gnn.com/wic/sci.toc.html
NASA Ames Biocomputation Center	http://neuron.arc.nasa.gov:80/
MMRRCC Home Page	http://nmrsg.biophys.upenn.edu:8080/
Rapid Development Lab (RDL)	http://ollie.jsc.nasa.gov:80/
NASA Physical OceanographyGroup	http://oraac.gsfc.nasa.gov:80/
Univ. of Oregon Materials Science Institute	http://oregon.uoregon.edu/~lbiggs/msi.html
POC Lab MacHTTP Server	http://pekkel.uthscsa.edu/default.html
The Hopkins Ultraviolet Telescope	http://praxis.pha.jhu.edu/hut.html
MIT Computational Aerospace Sciences Lab	http://raphael.mit.edu/casl.html

744

Antique Marketplace

http://www.fred.net/dmaserv/

The "Antique Marketplace" provides what is, perhaps, the largest collective group of antique dealers on the Web. Dealers from around the corner and around the world, all with their own unique specialties, offer their wares at this site. Whether your interest is Edwardian cupboards or Victorian window boxes, early American doll houses or Louis XIV chairs, you'll find a dealer with a catalog of goods to suit your needs. A splendid "value-added" feature is *Antique Insights*, a regularly updated digital newsletter that features news and views from all over the world of antiques, provides price estimating guidelines, and more. You'll also find links to other antique-related resources on the World Wide Web and elsewhere on the Internet. This site is a splendid place in cyberspace for the antique-crazed to call home.

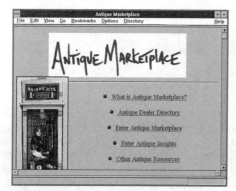

Figure 744.1 Antique Marketplace.

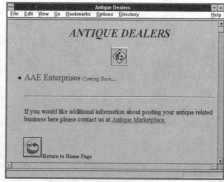

Figure 744.2 Antique dealer directory.

Antiques Online

http://www.rway.com/aoi/

"Antiques Online" offers a new and exciting way for antique dealers and collectors to advertise—through the World Wide Web. At this site, you'll find some of the very best in (mostly American) antiques. The site's offerings are especially strong in antique photographs and frames, Tiffany lamps and related period-items, Revolutionary-era firearms and sabers, and turn-of-the-century luggage. This site also includes some nice features. For example, the "Advertisement of the Week" showcases a particularly interesting antique, such as a piece associated with a famous personage or a rare representative item from a cherished school of workmanship.

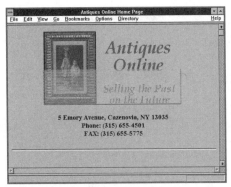

Figure 745.1 Antiques Online.

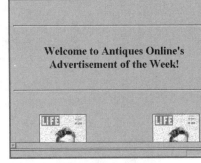

Figure 745.2 Ad of the week.

AutoExpress

http://www.mind.net/jfs/autox/index.html

It hardly matters what type of vehicle you want to buy. "AutoExpress" can get that vehicle for you at bottom-line prices with no hassle. You'll find details on all the latest models from Toyota, Honda, Lincoln, Saturn, Dodge, Chrysler, Mazda, Plymouth, Isuzu, Pontiac, Suzuki, Jeep, Mercury, and Eagle. The site amply represents the American and Japanese auto makers, but it doesn't give you access to (or information about) the products of great European car companies. Despite that deficiency, the site provides a lot of good information on performance ratings, optional accessories, gas/mileage efficiency, and other details. Even if you don't buy from "AutoExpress," this site is still a great place to learn more about a car without a salesperson breathing down your back.

Figure 746 AutoExpress.

Avant-Garde Virtual Marketplace

http://www.infoanalytic.com

What doesn't the "Avant-Garde Virtual Marketplace" have? Visit this site for business products and services, computers and software, gifts, clothing, specialty items, health and safety products, professional services, and even vacations! A few samples: "Databoat" lets you view clips of over 200 yacht charter adventures; the "Gallery of American Artisans" displays an elegant, hand-crafted gift collection featuring stained glass, jewelry, pewter, pottery, and more; and "Crazy Lou's Lingerie for All the Pretty Ladies" offers, well, you know. Search "Avant-Garde" by store, product category, or even price! How's that for a way to quickly come up with a great gift at moderate expense?

Figure 747 Avant-Garde virtual marketplace.

748

Baby Joy Toys

http://www.pacific.net/~joy/bjt/

"Baby Joy Toys'" creator, Joy Calonico, best describes the site: "When I gave birth to my only child, a daughter, I spent time, money, and energy seeking products that didn't exist. Though there were many things available for babies and young children, I wanted a more personal touch. I resorted to altering my daughter's clothes and toys to make them fit, or make them fun for her. Soon I was creating my own designs and sharing my ideas with others. In the process I found an untapped well of treasures. The designs in this catalog were created by parents and people who love children. These unique items are available by mail order, and through select stores that sell specialty products for children." At this site, you'll find one-stop shopping for a quality selection of the best toys for your kids.

Figure 748.1 Baby Joy Toys.

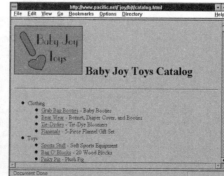

Figure 748.2 Toy catalog.

Small Computer Book Club and the Mac Professionals' Book Club

http://booksonline.com/

Newbridge Communications, the parent company of the highly-regarded Small Computer Book Club and Mac Professionals' Book Club, has collected an outstanding selection of computer-related books for their World Wide Web store. And they're available to you at attractive discounts. How attractive? You'll receive three new, up-to-date computer books of your choice for just $1 apiece when you agree to join either the Small Computer Book Club (for PC users) or the Mac Professionals' Book Club. Choose from more than three hundred titles online. Search by author, title, topic, or keyword to find just the right books. You won't find a better deal anywhere on the Web!

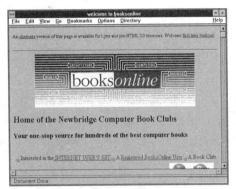

Figure 749.1 Newbridge Book Clubs home page.

Figure 749.2 News about great deals.

Branch Mall

http://www.branch.com

At "Branch Mall," you'll find hundreds of merchants offering such items as flowers and plants, gifts and decorations, toys and novelties, clothes, jewelry and accessories, eyewear, sports and fitness products, books and magazines, music and videos, cosmetics, medical and health products, computers and software, travel and vacations, big-screen televisions, and even professional services and real estate. Oh, and if you're looking for business opportunities, you can find them here too. In short, the "Branch Mall" is one-stop shopping for everything you could possibly want. Everything legal, anyway.

Figure 750 Branch Mall.

CDNOW

http://cdnow.com

Until I actually accessed this site, I presumed it was a place to purchase certificates of deposit that the National Organization for Women had endorsed. However, I now realize that this site is what we used to call, in the ancient daze of my youth, a record store. But this is better than a record store, isn't it? Yes, it is. Where else can you listen to portions of an album before you invest your hard-earned cash? Where else can you view JPEG videos of your favorite bands? Where else can you find what I'm sure some kid somewhere describes with the following quaint assembly of words: "Like, man, like it is like the biggest selection of discs like that I've ever, like, seen man." Like, do you dig it? Everything is always in stock, and they'll send whatever your order. Go for it.

Figure 751.1 CDNOW home page.

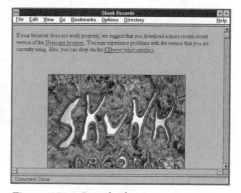

Figure 751.2 Details about store.

ClickShop Com

http://clickshop.com

"Clickshop Com" provides products and services for the home-office. At this site, you'll find everything from paper clips to fax machines, from stationary to scanners. Get excellent prices on computers, printers, writing utensils, laser-printer paper, rubber stamps, swivel chairs, desks . . . you name it. When you visit this site, check out the unique selection of "Talking Products" (talking clocks, talking cups), as well as the downloadable literature and software useful to home-office workers. Also, you can download a copy of EZ Com, which, the site announces, is "the absolutely easiest way to transmit files between PCs!" So point and click your way to "Clickshop Com" for some easy home-office solutions.

Figure 752.1 ClickShop Com home page.

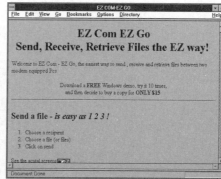

Figure 752.2 An easy file transmission utility.

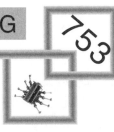

Cohasset Birdhouses Gift Shop

http://www.birdhouses.com/birdhouses/

Cohasset Birdhouses Gift Shop is located in Cohasset, Massachusetts, a small town on the Atlantic coast. The rugged Cohasset shoreline and frequent N'oreaster storms provide the driftwood and tope used in some of the unique birdhouses the Cohasset Birdhouses Gift Shop offers. The shop actually offers a number of products, but the most popular by far are their hand-crafted birdhouses (available in both Yankee and contemporary styles) and birdfeeders. The birdhouses, which you can view at this site, are beautiful to say the least, but also functional and durable; they'll stand up against many long winters and hot summers, providing an inviting retreat for your feathered friends.

Figure 753.1 Cohasset Birdhouses.

Figure 753.2 Contemporary birdhouses.

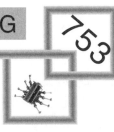

Cybercalifragilistic Shopping & Entertainment

http://www.webcom.com/~getagift/

The hype for "Cybercalifragilistic" says this site offers the most original collection of computer-themed goods and entertainment on the World Wide Web. And the hype seems accurate, in this case. A few examples? Okay. How about an "Email@ddict" tie-dye T-shirt? How about solid chocolate diskettes and CDs? What else? Well, you can get either a sculpted coffee mug that looks like a computer, a Geek Survival Kit (don't ask), or a Mr. CompuPotatohead. You'll find lots of other stuff along these lines for the lovable turbo-geek in your life. Come see it all at "Cybercalifragilistic."

Figure 754.1 Cybercalifragilistic!

Figure 754.2 Some cool stuff.

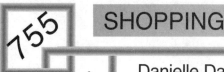

Danielle Dane Body Care Products

http://www.mdle.com/dana1.htm

Danielle Dane is a family-owned-and-operated business that specializes in the production of high quality vegetable-based soaps. Danielle Dane's precise (and secret) combination of olive oil, coconut oil, soy bean oil, spring water, sodium hydroxide, and herbs and fragrances yields a rich-lathering, sweet-smelling, mild soap. I know what you are wondering. I'll let the proprietors answer: "Yes, our soaps are cruelty free! Prior to introduction to the marketplace our soaps are tested exclusively on human beings and contain no ingredients derived from animals." Come to this site for great cruelty-free scents, soaps, moisturizers, and creams. And yes, gift baskets are available.

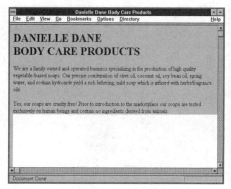

Figure 755.1 Danielle Dane Body Care.

Figure 755.2 Gift items.

Downtown Anywhere

http://awa.com

This cybermall has the same options as virtually (no pun intended) any other. Additionally, you'll find a great collection of museum shops from some of the finest art museums. Thus, you can come to "Downtown Anywhere" not only for canoes and roller-skates and pajamas, but also for wonderful collectibles and gifts (posters, stationary, sculpture reproductions, calendars, books, and more) from the shops of institutions such as the Museum of Modern Art, the Metropolitan Museum of Art, the Smithsonian's Freer Gallery, the Art Institute of Chicago, the Louvre, and many other notable institutions. That fact alone gives "Downtown Anywhere" an edge over its cybermall competitors.

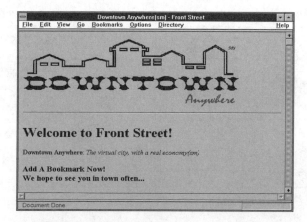

Figure 756 Downtown Anywhere.

Empire Mall: Your Global Storefront

http://empire.na.com

Ranked in the top 5% of Web sites by *Point Survey*, "Empire Mall" features a variety of stores that offer an assortment of products and services. Looking for imported compact discs? Look no further. Want to run your boss over (with your mouse)? Come here to order a custom imprinted mouse pad. Need some Russian transport helicopters (that's right, Russian transport helicopters!) for a weekend wilderness outing? Yup. They're here too. For those on more modest budgets than it takes to purchase a helicopter (even a Russian one), you have your choice of Omaha Steaks, Salsa Express, Diamonds by Van-Daaz, Hammacher Schlemmer, Bub's Bargain Basement, FTD Flowers, Insurance On-line, and even a lawyer-referral service. So pull on up to the "Empire Mall." There's plenty of parking.

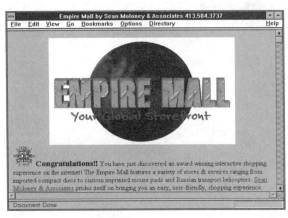

Figure 757 Empire Mall.

eduMall: The Shopping Mall for Educational Products

http://edumall.com

For quality educational materials and services, visit "eduMall," which bills itself as "your shopping mall for educational products." From distance learning to books, from educational software to travel and study programs, you will find the educational product you need at "eduMall." The site is the work of Magellan University, which offers its own educational services here, as well as those from other institutions. I should emphasize that "eduMall" addresses all levels of education, from the primary grades to the college level. In addition, you'll find college catalogs online, see offerings of educational games and toys for the very young, and more. So visit "eduMall" and take your knowledge-base to the next level.

Figure 758.1 EduMall.

Figure 758.2 Welcome to EduMall.

Figure 758.3 EduMall options.

Flower Stop

http://www.flowerstop.com/

Anniversary coming up? Mothers' Day? Aunt Agatha's birthday? Have you just heard your neighbor's cousin has just slipped into a coma? Think your horse might win the Kentucky Derby? For all your flower needs, turn to "Flower Stop," which bills itself as "your on-line fresh flower market." Send roses long-distance. Or, browse a rich catalog of beautiful floral arrangements presented in color and available for delivery anywhere in the United States or Canada. Whether the order is to celebrate, commemorate, or console, the "Flower Stop" offers convenient online shopping and fast, reliable delivery.

Figure 759 Flowerstop.

Ford Worldwide Connection

http://www.ford.com/home.html

Come to the "Ford Worldwide Connection" to find out about all Ford Motor Company products, including their automobiles (of course), and the products of the Ford Financial Services Group. See vivid color GIFs of all the latest models of Ford cars. Review performance statistics, pricing information, and credit terms for these automobiles. Take interactive tours of the "Ford Historical Library," the new "Jaguar Historical Library," and the "Ford Story," which includes details on the Ford family's involvement with the company through the decades. You also get the weekly digest *Ford News Briefs* and reports from Ford's international divisions in "Ford Around the World."

Figure 760.1 Ford Motor Company.

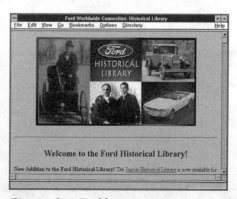

Figure 760.2 Ford history.

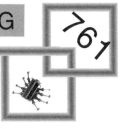

Ideal Internet Imaging and Shopping Mall

http://www.ideal.com

The "Ideal Internet Imaging and Shopping Mall" is the place to come for one-stop shopping for scanners, printers, and the full range of imaging software and hardware. You'll find catalogs and offerings from Hewlett-Packard, Autodesk, Cordant, CADalyst, Product Data Management, and others. You'll also find digital editions of *CADalyst Magazine*, *AutoCAD World*, and (coming soon) *Document Management and Business Systems Magazine*. The various publications and catalogs provide reviews of, and pricing for, literally hundreds of imaging, scanning, and printing products.

Figure 761 Ideal Internet Imaging Shopping Mall.

The Internet Antique Shop

http://rivendell.com/antiques/

In a sense, this interesting stop on the Information Super Highway is misnamed. Although the "Internet Antique Shop" does include many antiques dealers, it also contains products for other types of collectors. For example, you can purchase stamps, coins, comic books, and even those kitchy little figurines from the Franklin Mint. So, in addition to shops like "Gene Purdum Antiques and Funtiques," you'll also find "The Sterling Shop" (sterling and silverplate), "Incredible Collectibles," and a host of magazines, including *American Country Collectibles, Baby Boomer Collectibles, Coin Prices, Coins Magazine, Collector's Mart, Comic Buyer's Guide, DISCoveries, Military Trader, Old Cars, Sports Card Price Guide, Sports Collector's Digest*, and the *Toy Collector and Price Guide*.

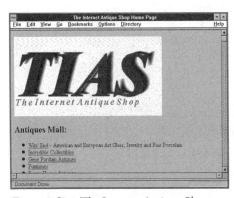

Figure 762.1 The Internet Antique Shop.

Figure 762.2 Wits" End Antiques.

SHOPPING

Kids Only

http://www.io.org/kidsonly/

Every parent knows the sound of those groans. "Come on, kids," you say. "We're going to the mall to buy you some clothes." And then come the groans, the moans, the pouts. "This is *boring!* I hate *this!*" they say as they retire from the much-loved mud-pile and climb into the car. So you resort to catalog shopping, but even this has its setbacks: all those busy signals, all that background music while you hold for the next available service representative, all that waiting while your service rep types product codes into a computer to see whether the item you want to buy is on back-order (and it always is). Now, at "Kids Only" online emporium, you can scan a great digital catalog of kids' clothes and then check for yourself to see if the item is available. Check it out.

Figure 763.1 Kids Only Clothing.

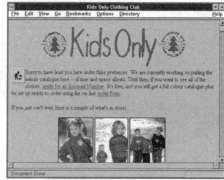

Figure 763.2 A wide selection.

Lands' End Direct Merchants

http://www.landsend.com

Who doesn't get the Lands' End catalog in their mailbox umpteen times a year? Perhaps if we all shop often enough using the company's online catalog and online ordering option, they'll stop sending out the print catalog, and save several thousands of acres of forest land. The clothing that Lands' End offers, of course, is quite attractive, well-made, and beautifully depicted in this elegant online catalog. You'll find men's, women's, and children's clothing for both formal and play situations, not to mention luggage, shoes, bedding, and more. Order (and even track the progress of your order) online. And, when and if you encounter any problems, chat with online customer-service reps.

Figure 764 Lands' End: the familiar logo.

Lexington Furniture

http://www.infi.net/lexington.com/lexington

Lexington Furniture Industries is the collective name for a group of manufacturing companies founded as early as 1901. In 1987, Masco Home Furnishing purchased the group and consolidated them into a single company. A producer of quality home furnishings, Lexington Furniture Industries operates 18 factories in North Carolina and employs more than 5,000 skilled artisans. Lexington offers nearly 50 different furniture collections, including wood furniture made from a range of fine hardwoods, upholstered products using fashionable fabrics and leather, and both indoor and outdoor wicker furniture made from rattan, woven wicker, metal, and teak.

Figure 765.1 Lexington Furniture.

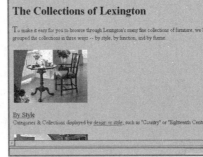

Figure 765.2 A view of Lexington's collections.

Magic Windows Shopping

http://biggulp.callamer.com/~mwinfo/

"Magic Window Shopping" started off on the Web offering fine wines, then gourmet foods. Now, the site brings even more products and services to your computer screen. Browse through the digital windowpanes and check out the attractive store displays of vendors such as "Milky Whey" (goat milk soaps), "Music Magic" (including Boona Music, Moonridge Records, and Vain Records), "Lonesome Posters," real-estate marketers, and software vendors. Of course, you will still see the fine shops with which "Magic Window Shopping" first experienced success—"Wine On-line," the "Paso Robles Wine Region," and "Naturally California Gourmet" still cater to visitors in search of good spirits and great food.

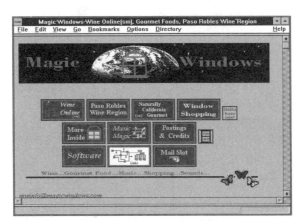

Figure 766 Magic Window.

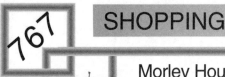

Morley House Home Shopping Catalogue

http://www.sofcom.com.au/Morley/

Visit this site for stuff you just won't find anywhere else. I am talking about anti-snore pillows, personalized port crocks, triple-edge wipers, personal breath alcohol analyzers, personalized micro breweries, knitting machines, sundials, gray-away combs, cat birdfeeders (I don't know what they are and I don't want to know), dog and cat repellent, dash-lite flashlites, electronic watch dogs, "foods that cause you to lose weight" (once again, I don't want to know), foot massagers, shock absorber heels, karaoke kits, workout gyms, inflatable doll houses, inflatable sleds, and more.

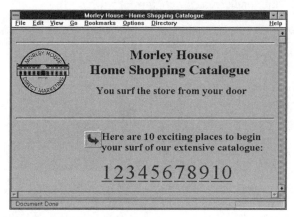

Figure 767 Morley House catalog.

On S'amuse Dollhouses

http://www.internet-eireann.ie/toyshop/house.html

Although this great Dublin toy store offers a range of items, its most notable products are wood dollhouses. These houses offer access from all sides and thus let several children enjoy play at one time. Furthermore, the houses' interior walls move, which lets children alter a house's floor plan whenever they wish. Finally, each section of roof lifts off easily to give attic access. The store also stocks various styles of doll furniture, traditional and modern, and "robust enough to be played with." Properly sized dolls, perfect for the occupation of these beautiful homes, are also available. So if any of your kids (or even you) wants to become a homeowner, check out this site.

Figure 768 Beautiful doll's houses.

Pecans: Plain & Fancy

http://www.icw.com/sunny/sunny.html

Access the homepage of Jane and Harry Willson from Sunnyland Farms. Who are they? They are a large by-mail shipper of pecans, other nuts, dried fruits, and related products. "We ship the brightest, freshest nuts and fruits you've ever tasted at direct-from-the-grove-to-you prices, just as we've done for the last 46 years," they write. Browse the Willson's online store and take your pick of choice pecan halves, pecan pieces, walnuts and holiday boxes, jumbo cashews and royal mixes, pistachios and "P'Nutty Mixes Deluxe," royal macadamias, gift assortments, Sunnyland's homemade candies, "Holly-Day" bags, extra-fancy dried fruits, and more. Lord, I'm starting to get hungry!

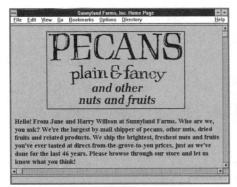

Figure 769.1 Pecans plains & fancy.

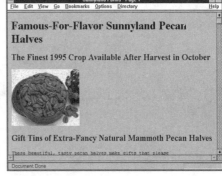

Figure 769.2 Pecan halves.

rSTMall: a Mall of Malls

http://polaris.net/~trexcom/shop.html

I can't figure out what "rST" stands for, but I can tell you what's at this site. "rSTMall" is both a mall of malls and a collection of great direct-marketers. This site contains links to "AcmeWeb Mall," "Condom Country" (a wide selection), the "Mammoth Records Internet Center," "MarketPlace.com," "NetMarket!," a great online bookstore, "Romance Elegant Lingerie and Keepsake Gifts," and more. Through "rSTMall," you can find just about any product that Web merchants sell. You'll also find links to clothes manufacturers and marketers (including several factory-direct discount organizations) and to banking and other financial services available over the Internet.

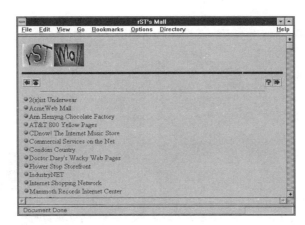

Figure 770 rSTMall.

Sam's Wine Warehouse

http://www.ravenna.com/sams/

After decades of catering to a worldwide market of wine connoisseurs, Chicago's number 1 wine merchant (Sam) has taken his act to the World Wide Web! Ranked in the top 5% of all Web sites by Point Communications, this site lets you browse and order fine wines online (by the bottle or the case) and read great reviews of various wines written by Sam's wine-worldly staff. In addition, you can sign up to receive Sam's informative electronic newsletter via e-mail. Or, you can even design your own wine labels online which Sam will print out and place on each bottle you order in the future! How's that for *style*?

Figure 771.1 Sam's Wine Warehouse.

Figure 771.2 Wine-notes from Sam's staff.

The Shopping Expressway

http://shopex.com

"The Shopping Expressway" is an extensive marketing and ordering service. It is *the place to go* for consumers and *the place to sell* for vendors and marketers in all businesses. Browse alphabetically by vendor name or by product category. Among the products you'll find at this site are Classic Cartoons, Mega Memory Brain Booster, the *New Webster's Deluxe Comprehensive Library*, the International Star Registry, the American Silver Coin Collector's Series, Playboy videos, DidiSeven Stain Remover, Duzzit Handy Hanger, Easy Stripper (as in for woodworking), and NoWet Wonder Foam (a carpet and upholstery cleaning system). Let your fingers do the walking, across your keyboard, to the stores at the "Shopping Expressway."

Figure 772.1 The Shopping Expressway.

Figure 772.2 The Mall.

The South African Wine Express

http://www.aztec.co.za/biz/africa/wine.htm

Now that South Africa has turned around politically, we can in good conscience enjoy some of the fine wines that come from that distant southern tip of Africa. The mission of "South African Wine Express" is to introduce the world to the pleasure and quality of South African wines. Visit this site for wine ratings and comments from South African author John Platter's renowned *1995 New South African Wine Guide*. Although all prices are quoted per bottle in South African rands, you don't need to check currency exchange rates before you order. The good people at "South African Wine Express" have provided a Global Currency Converter you can use to calculate the accurate price.

Figure 773.1 South African Wine Express.

Figure 773.2 A cornucopia of choices.

Specialty Gourmet Foods

http://www.iea.com/~cschin/catalogs/index.html

Come to this site for vegetarian foods, certified kosher products, and pickled garden-fresh vegetables (including tomatoes, mushrooms, baby corn, carrots, garlic cloves, snap peas, asparagus, and pearl onions). You'll also find specialty shaped pastas (bikes, stars, dolphins, hearts, sports balls, and trees), specialty breads (beer, corn, and sourdough), gift baskets, soups (chilies, organic, pasta, and bean), health foods, low-sodium foods, fat-free foods, organically-grown foods, and more. Along with the products you can purchase, you'll even find an absolutely wonderful (and free) directory of recipes for cooking (and rendering delectable) everything from pot roast to soyburgers, celery to marmalade.

Figure 774.1 Specialty Gourmet Foods.

Figure 774.2 Buckeye Beans & Herbs, Inc.

SHOPPING

Spencer Gifts

http://www.btg.com/spencer/

This site offers esoteric, sometimes-rare items you can't find elsewhere. For example, you can purchase a limited-edition photograph of the Beatles playing at the Cavern Club with their original drummer, Pete Best, who autographed the photo. You can also get lava lights, a limited-edition Star Trek telephone, a limited-edition Kurt Cobain portrait (poor Kurt), and a limited-edition framed facsimile of a letter autographed by Elvis Presley. Neon? Sure, they've got neon! Specifically, a Budweiser neon sign, a Coca-Cola neon sign, a neon shark, and so on.

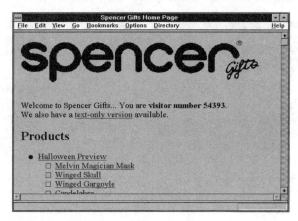

Figure 775 Spencer Gifts.

Sugarbush Gourmet Gift Baskets

http://www.on-library.com/friends/sgr_bush/sb_home.html

Need a memorable business gift? Send Sugarbush Gourmet Gift Baskets to your clients, suppliers, or associates. Sugarbush carefully designs their baskets to accommodate businesses that send client or employee gifts. Recipients will love the luscious selections that fill these baskets, and remember the sender (hopefully, you) fondly. Browse through Sugarbush's digital catalog and order right online. (Be sure to check out Sugarbush's great "Pick of the Crop" basket, which includes hearty apples, juicy citrus, and a special treat or two, such as mouthwatering pears and luscious kiwifruit.) Whether you need one gift basket or one-hundred, Sugarbush makes ordering fast and easy.

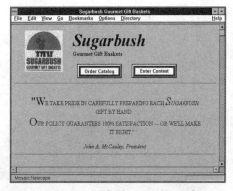 

Figure 776.1 Sugarbush Gourmet Gifts.   *Figure 776.2 The Sugarbush Catalog.*

Super Mall Directory

http://supermall.com

Come to the "Super Mall" for, quite simply, everything and anything. You'll find Internet services, CD-ROMs, cars and motorcycles, books and magazines, software, videos, gifts, televisions and radios, food and beverages, and more. You'll also find toys, gadgets, real estate, financial services, legal services, health services, antiques and collectibles, employment opportunities, flowers, and even furniture (both indoor and outdoor). The "Super Mall" features more than 475 product and store listings that you can search by store name, product or service name, and product or service category. You can also choose to see U.S.-only or Canada-only businesses, if you wish.

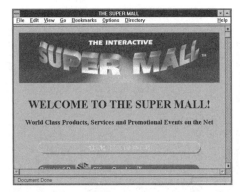

Figure 777.1 The Super Mall Directory.   *Figure 777.2* Enter the Mall.

Video Disc International

http://www.thesphere.com/VDI/

"Video Disc International" is the Web's first searchable laser-disc catalog. "Our company's goal is to make the excellent quality of laser video discs affordable," says the manager of this virtual store. "Our company specializes in the used laser disc market. We buy, sell, and trade used laser discs. Every disc we sell comes with our guarantee to play like new or we will refund your money. It is our goal to have the largest selection of used laser discs in perfect condition available to the general public." In addition to selling you discs, the company also wants to buy your old ones. And they'll even send you a free "Disc Plus Restorer" kit to help you remove scratches from your laser discs. Check it out.

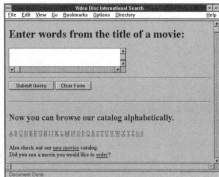

Figure 778.1 Video Disc International.   *Figure 778.2* Search the listings.

Virtual Furniture Mall

http://www.cato.com/ncnetworks/fur-mall.html

The State of North Carolina is known for furniture design and manufacturing. North Carolina produces over 60% of U.S. manufactured furniture. Each year, thousands of visitors tour the state's numerous discount stores, galleries, and home furnishings centers. Now, you can stay at home and still get furniture at the same low prices as North Carolinians. How? Visit the "Virtual Furniture Mall." From this site, you can connect to such noted North Carolina retailers as Alman's Home Furnishings, The Atrium Furniture Mall, Better Homes Discount Furniture, Cannon Village, Furniture Galleries, Inc., Hudson's Discount Furniture, Parkway Furniture Galleries, Stevens Furniture, and the Sutton-Council Furniture Company.

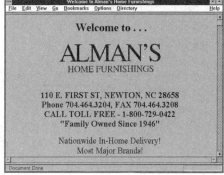

Figure 779.1 Virtual Furniture Mall.   *Figure 779.2 Alman's Home Furnishings.*

VirtuMall

http://virtumall.com/

Come to this site for great food, computers, software, entertainment, services, hobby merchandise, household items, magazines, books, and clothes. But also come for some amusement. The "VirtuMall" has assembled a fabulous assortment of downloadable software that includes some useful (free) utilities. Additionally, the site includes an impressive list of links to games on the Web. Thus, like most other highway malls, this one has an arcade! But you don't have to keep popping quarters into the slot. And you don't have to worry about your car being stolen out of the parking lot while you shop or play. Have a ball! Bring your credit card and bring Netscape for secure transactions.

Figure 780 VirtuMall.

White Rabbit Toys

http://www.toystore.com

Located in Ann Arbor, Michigan, White Rabbit Toys specializes in high quality toys that help children create, learn, imagine, and explore. White Rabbit's toys come from all over the world, and the store offers such international favorites as Brio (Sweden), Ravensburger (Germany), and Primetime Playthings and Creativity for Kids (USA). Want your order gift-wrapped? No problem. Want your order shipped within 48 hours of receipt on the Web? No problem. Want great links to other child-related sites? No problem. This site, ranked in the top 5% of Web sites by *Point Survey*, offers you all those features and more.

Figure 781.1 White Rabbit Toys.

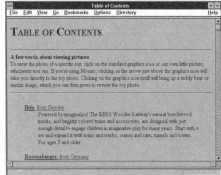

Figure 781.2 Select from the best.

The World Square

http://www.w2.com/

The "World Square" offers goods and services from all around the world to clients and customers all around the world. Let's see, what are a few of the hundreds of options at this site? You can browse the online catalog of Barnes & Noble Bookstores; buy concert and theater tickets for shows in New York, London, Paris, San Francisco, and Chicago; subscribe to your choice of more than fifty great magazines; access financial services ranging from MasterCard to stock brokerages; purchase musical instruments direct from manufacturers (such as Baldwin Pianos) at substantial discounts; get information on automobiles, medicine, and health products; (gasp!) and more.

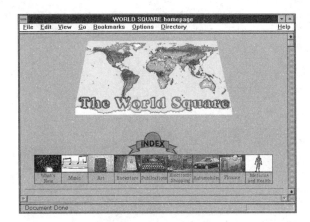

Figure 782 The World Square.

SHOPPING

Zadia Fine Jewelry

http://www.tribnet.com/shop/zadia.htm

This site is your online source for exclusive, beautiful jewelry. The good people at "Zadia Fine Jewelry" offer custom-designed rings, pendants, earrings, and bracelets, as well as loose diamonds and gemstones, pearls, 14kt and 18kt gold jewelry, expert jewelry repair, appraisals, and more. Sign up to receive *Facets Newsletter*, a periodic e-mail publication that addresses such questions as: what differentiates a generic ruby from a sapphire? Why does platinum cost so much more than gold? What is tourmaline? If you are like me, you've laid awake nights wondering the answer to that last one. Well, rest easy. Tourmaline is a rather common mineral that comes in virtually all colors and thus is popular with jewelry designers.

Figure 783.1 Zadia Fine Jewelry.

Figure 783.2 The Facets Newsletter.

More Shopping

As you surf the Web, you may find that one or more of the site addresses listed in this book have changed. In such cases, connect to Jamsa Press at http://www.jamsa.com and click on the icon that corresponds to the *1001 Really Cool Web Sites* book. Jamsa Press will list replacement addresses (when possible) for sites that have moved. In addition, you can also use the following site list as you search for information on shopping:

Bigfoot	http://ccnet.com/~crick/bigfoot.html
Display Tech Multimedia (computers to video)	http://ccnet.com/~dtmi/welcome.html
Dainamic Consulting	http://cnn.acsys.com:5050/~sims/kayak/kayak.html
Lerma Nagal Swartz Realtor	http://cruzio.com/bus/realestate/lermas/lermas.html
Mary Kay Cosmetics Cosmetics	http://cyberzine.org/html/Cosmetics/cosmetics2.html
Earth Spirit Designs Home Page	http://cyberzine.org/html/EarthSpirit/index.html
Earth Spirit Designs Home Page	http://envirolink.org/espirit/
Branch Mall	http://florist.com:1080/
Compact Disc Connection	http://galaxy.einet.net/hytelnet/OTH104.html
Compact Disc Europe	http://galaxy.einet.net/hytelnet/OTH131.html

SPECIAL, SUPERCOOL SITES

Adobe Acrobat On-line Publishing Kit

http://www.adobe.com

It's one thing to get your corporate information online. It's quite another to successfully transfer the richness of your visual identity to your Web site, as *The New York Times* (*TimesFax*), JP Morgan, the Internal Revenue Service, and several other "cool" sites in this book have. How did they do it? How does *TimesFax* manage to still look and feel like *The New York Times* that you read on the train? The *Times* does it, as do the others, with Adobe Acrobat. Visit this site to get your free Adobe Acrobat On-line Publishing Kit and learn how you can use Adobe products to maintain your company's image online. While you're here, be sure to download a free Adobe Acrobat Reader.

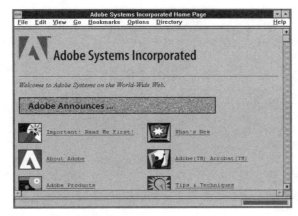

Figure 784 Adobe home page.

City University Distance Learning

http://www.cityu.edu/inroads/welcome1.html

Want to get an MBA? Or finish your bachelor's degree? Or study for your Microsoft Certified Professional designation? Now you can through the Web. City University offers college degrees online: electronically, interactively, seriously. They call their new Web-based program INROADS, for Information Resource and On-line Academic Degree System. Using a Web browser, you'll participate in discussions with faculty and guest lecturers. You'll also do online research, receive and send assignments, and correspond with your instructors and other students via e-mail. A diploma mill? No way. City University is accredited by the Northwest Association of Schools and Colleges (NASC).

Figure 785 City University on-line.

SPECIAL, SUPERCOOL SITES

Cool Word of the Day

http://www.dsu.edu/projects/word_of_day/word.html

At this site, the "cool" word changes every day, and it's always challenging. Click on a button to learn the definition. Click on another to view past cool words of the day. And if you have a suggestion for another "cool" word, feel free to submit it. However, make sure your suggestion is a challenging word. To get some an idea of what I am talking about, just look at some past "cool" words: soporific, unctuous, autochthonous, cynosure, spiegeliesen, schwa, zygotic, malversation, ritardando, declivitous, defenestration, achromatic, saturnalia, plinth, zymurgy, sciolism, nobble, and adiabatic. I can't define them all for you, but I do know what soporific means: *causing or tending to cause sleep*.

Figure 786.1 Cool Word of the Day.   *Figure 786.2 Past words.*

Cows Caught in the Web

http://www.brandonu.ca/~ennsnr/Cows/Welcome.html

Welcome to the strange but engaging page maintained by Neil Enns, who writes: "I have a pretty nifty cowlection of cow artifacts: posters, a porcelain cow, juggling cows, my pet cow Opt, a cow throw rug, and a plastic cow in my garden, among others." In short, this site is the spiritual home of the cowmania movement. Neil extols the pure Zen calm of these placid, grass-eating machines. Reportedly, Opt, Neil's pet cow, maintains the Web site. And Opt has assembled an impressive gallery of bovine portraits. The gallery not only includes shots of Opt himself, but also many of his pals in the cow-world. For more cow stuff, check out http://yay.tim.org and http://www.lysator.liu.se/pinball (which includes not only great information on pinball, but also on cows).

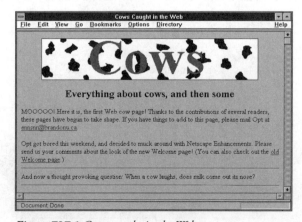

Figure 787.1 Cows caught in the Web.

SPECIAL, SUPERCOOL SITES

IDT Internet Online Services

http://www.iia.org/

IDT Internet Online Services (IOS) is a commercial provider of Internet access located in northern New Jersey. IOS is a division of International Discount Telecommunications, one of the largest privately-held telecommunications companies in the United States. IOS is dedicated to bringing low-cost full-featured Internet connectivity to users across the United States and around the world. At affordable prices, they offer Internet e-mail, Usenet news, complete World Wide Web access (including home page hosting), Internet Relay Chat, and FTP file transfer via both SLIP and PPP connections. IOS also offers dedicated connections including 56kbps, T1 and Frame Relay.

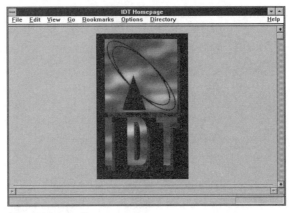

Figure 788 Welcome to IDT.

Electronic Arts

http://www.ea.com/eastudio.html

Put your pulse in overdrive. Come to the "Electronic Arts" homepage and see a preview of Delphine Software's *Fade to Black*, the adrenaline-pumping sequel to Delphine's *Flashback*. *Fade to Black* is a game that utilizes fluid, life-like animation and gives players complete control over seemingly unlimited character movements. Along the way, multiple camera angles mirror every heart-stopping turn. Even the sound and music score won't give you a moment's peace. That is, until you rest in eternal peace. You will find screens from *Fade to Black* and a 2.8 Mb demo version of the game. Check out *Fade to Black*; it is awe-inspiring.

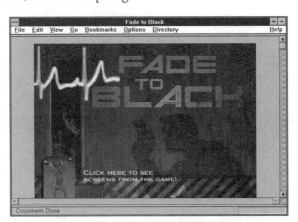

Figure 789 Electronic Arts home page.

eWorld

http://www.eworld.com/

Apple's little virtual community, eWorld, storms the online world with bigger and better services and an impressive calendar of special events for its members. Recent additions to eWorld include an herb store, a digital science forum, and Charlot Software, which designs programs to assist teachers in grading and keeping student records. eWorld also has been exploring cultural and ethnic diversity. This spring, it held Mexican folklore forums in Spanish and conducted an online forum for people wanting to brush up on their German language skills. Full Internet access is on its way shortly—an event that may well make eWorld the ideal Web launch pad for Macintosh platforms.

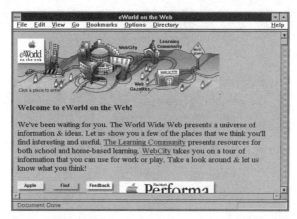

Figure 790 eWorld on the Web.

791

Enhanced for Netscape Hall of Shame

http://www.meat.com/netscape_hos.html

Chris Pearce (yyz@europa.com) maintains this collection of visually-awful Web sites, created by design-challenged businesses and individuals who've "fallen prey to Netscape 1.1 enhancements," as he puts it. Pearce's collection highlights sites that have tons of blinking text, all-centered copy, gruesome backgrounds, animated images surrounded by three-dimensional boxes, and more. To top it all off, the "Hall of Shame" sports an area called "Texture Land," which offers 60 eye-whacking backgrounds sure to devastate your visual senses. So, whether you want an odd type of negative inspiration, or simply wish to feel better about how your own page looks, check out the "Hall of Shame."

Figure 791 Hall of Shame.

InContext Spider

http://www.incontext.ca

It seems everybody wants to put something on the Web. And the InContext Spider makes it easy to do so. Both an HTML editor and Web browser, InContext Spider lets you combine dynamic page creation with the freedom of cruising the Web. InContext Spider talks directly to the browser, giving you the power to create and integrate Web pages simply and dynamically. Do everything your heart desires in no time—from editing text to creating amazing Web pages linked to sites all over the world. Learn how you can rule the Web with the bug that knows it best: InContext Spider, the next wave in electronic communications. It's lethal. And it's for Windows.

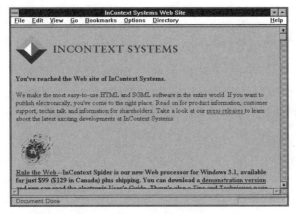

Figure 792 InContext Spider home page.

Lotus Tech Support

http://www.lotus.com

To show you its products in action, Lotus has used its Lotus Notes and the Lotus InterNotes Web Publisher software to place the company's technical support division on the World Wide Web. At this site, you'll find screens full of product information, a fully searchable database, and FTP access to help-specific files. Additionally, you'll find tech-support information for 1-2-3, Ami Pro, and the range of other Lotus products beyond Notes and InterNotes. Check it out. It's more than an infomercial.

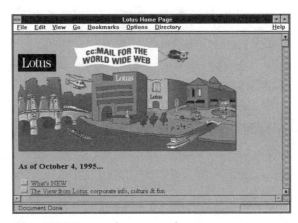

Figure 793 Lotus tech support online.

Mama's Cucina (from Ragu)

http://www.eat.com/

This site is the cyberhome of Ragu, the folks who bring you all those great sauces for pasta. You'll find a lot of great stuff there. Start with a fantastic Italian cookbook packed with wonderful recipes for raviolis, pastas, pizzas, and more. Then, check out the hints and tips for learning Italian phrases (including sound files). You can even enter to win a trip to Italy, courtesy of Mama. "Go! Mama will take care of everything. A trip for two. A nice, big, shiny airplane . . . You even get breakfast and dinner every day. (Would Mama let you go hungry?)" Additionally, you can enter your own experiences and favorite places from your own tours of Italy.

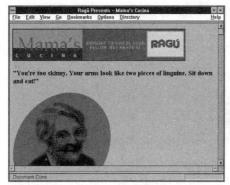

Figure 794.1 "Mama" from Ragu.

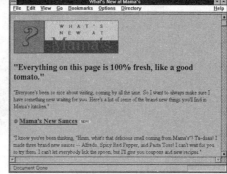

Figure 794.2 What's new with Ragu?

Microsoft Internet Assistant

http://www.microsoft.com

Come to Microsoft's Web site to learn about a product I've decided is just fantastic: Internet Assistant. This product turns Word for Windows into not only a WYSIWYG (What You See Is What You Get) HTML editor, but also a live World Wide Web browser, so long as you have a connection to the Internet. Basically, with Internet Assistant, Word for Windows 6.0 becomes a tool that lets code-fearful users create, view, and edit HTML in one application. Additionally, Internet Assistant takes advantage of Word's style-sheet analogy. As such, Internet Assistant lets you apply HTML codes as if they were styles. To learn more about Internet Assistant, visit this site.

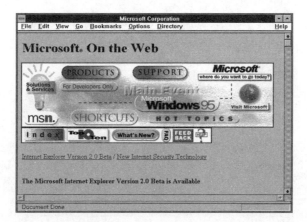

Figure 795 Microsoft home page.

Mortal Kombat Web Extravaganza

http://www.mortalkombat.com/kombatbegins

Mortal Kombat movie fans now have a Web site to help feed their tournament hunger. Provided by New Line Cinema, this site uses characters from the *Mortal Kombat* film to taunt and prod you to new levels of cyberspace adventure. The site includes behind-the-scenes footage, press kit materials, actor photos, animation, audio and video clips, special promotions, and more. However, this isn't your typical Web site; it's more like a game. In other words, the Outworld is out of this world and is a place in cyberspace you should visit. Arm yourself accordingly, and then submerge.

Figure 796.1 Mortal Kombat Web Extravaganza.

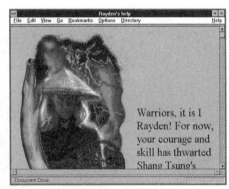

Figure 796.2 More cool stuff.

NewsPage

http://www.newspage.com

Now you have a better way to get your news. Just surf to this hot web site. Each night, "NewsPage" filters over 15,000 stories from over 500 leading news sources and categorizes these stories by industry and topic. To use "NewsPage," you simply bookmark the topics you like. Then, every day by 8:00 A.M., you'll receive news on only those topics you selected, without all the junk that causes information overload. Scan clear, concise briefs in seconds. Then, if you have the time and inclination, drill down to get the whole story. You can even link to the electronic publication from which the story originates. "NewsPage" is a fast, easy way to keep up with rapidly changing technologies and other important information.

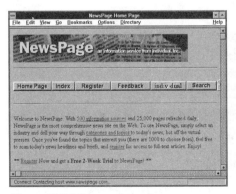

Figure 797.1 A great news digest.

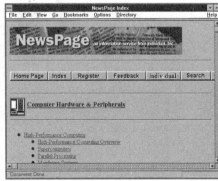

Figure 797.2 The index of stories.

NetNoir: Cybergateway to Afrocentric Culture

http://www.netnoir.com

"Imagine an hourglass, with all Afrocentric culture at the top. NetNoir is then the middle, the point at which all the sand falls through and is distributed. NetNoir will digitize, archive, and distribute Afrocentric culture," writes E. David Ellington, CEO and president of NetNoir, Inc. Last fall, NetNoir was one of the first groups chosen to receive funding from America Online's Green House project. Since then, the company has worked day and night to design and build a unique service that provides content (both inclusive and global) relating to Afro-American, Afro-European, Afro-Latino, and continental African culture. Check out the result of that effort.

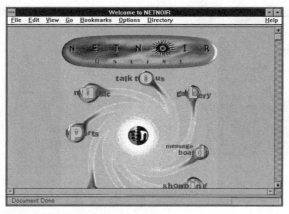

Figure 798 NetNoir home page.

RealAudio Player

http://www.realaudio.com

The RealAudio Player is both entertaining and downright revolutionary. The Player lets you use a conventional multimedia computer system and voice-grade telephone lines to browse, select, and play back audio-based, Web site content. And it's as easy to use as a standard cassette player! Currently, anyone with a 14.4 Kbps modem, Windows or a Macintosh, and a browser other than Netcom's Netcruiser can download a beta version of the RealAudio Player for free. The Player can stand alone or run through your existing Web browser. The Player is easy to install—just download it from the Web site and follow the friendly step-by-step instructions.

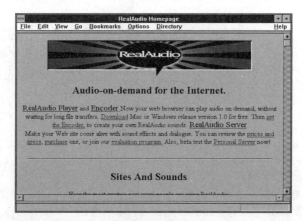

Figure 799 RealAudio download FREE!

Situationist International Archive

http://www.nothingness.org/SI/index.html

The Situationist Movement was born in France in the 1950s. Its proud parents were Deboard and Raoul Vaneigem, who combined art and politics into a movement that, as one critic points out, "scarred the face of capitalism with one of the largest and least talked-about civil rebellions in history," which occurred in Paris in 1968. The online "Situationist International Archive" is a great place to look for references and resources regarding philosophy, politics, art, and revolution. Additionally, you'll find (in both French and English) many of the original essays and manifestos the Vaneigems wrote. "Vive la Revolution!"

Figure 800.1 Situationist International Archive.

Figure 800.2 Links and resources.

SlipKnot: Graphical Web Browser for Windows

http://www.interport.net/slipknot/

In the past, if you weren't able to afford a SLIP or PPP account, you couldn't enjoy all the Web has to offer. Sure, you could browse with Lynx or WWW, but you couldn't view any graphics; or, you could use a SLIP emulator, but only if the sites you accessed supported it. Fortunately, a new day has come. Now, using SlipKnot, a graphical Web browser for Windows, you can Webwalk visually with a standard shell account. Find out more about Slipknot at this Web site. Then, download it. Version 1.0 (slnot100.zip) and the 1.08 beta upgrade (snup108.zip) are both available through FTP at ftp.netcom.com in/pub/pb/pbrooks/slipknot. Registering costs about $30, but trying is free.

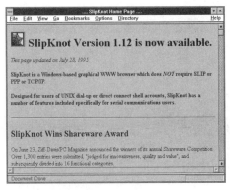

Figure 801.1 SlipKnot info.

Figure 801.2 SlipKnot product reviews.

Snake Oil: Kooky Kontemporary Kristian Kulture

http://fender.onramp.net/~analyst/snake/Snakeoil.html

"Paranoia is just a higher state of consciousness," believes Brother Randall, creator of *Snake Oil.: Kooky Kontemporary Kristian Kulture*. And what is the origin of *Snake Oil*? "It grew out of a fanzine I was doing about my favorite televangelist, Robert Tilton. I started out just being fanatical about Tilton, and then I got into the whole scene. Religious show business is much more fascinating to me than secular show biz, because you get that extra layer of hypocrisy and intrigue." Don't forget to check out the special files on David Koresh, including the photographs of the wet David-Koresh-tee-shirt contest. Also, check the many files on Bob Tilton's multi-million dollar ministry. *Hallelujah!*

Figure 802.1 *Guide to (enterprising) Fundamentalist nuts.*

Figure 802.2 *All Gospel gossip grapevine.*

The Utne Lens

http://www.utne.com

The Utne Lens is a bi-weekly World Wide Web periodical from *The Utne Reader*. *The Utne Lens* provides a gathering place to discuss challenging ideas, includes real-time panel discussions with leading thinkers, and incorporates engaging and entertaining essays, art reviews, and interviews. Recent articles include "A New Kind of History," in which writer Mary Carr discusses the power of memoir, and "This is the End, My Friend?" which addresses whether people are getting more upbeat about death. You will also hear from Barry Lopes on the real cost of developing the American West.

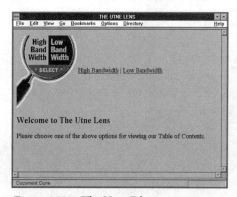

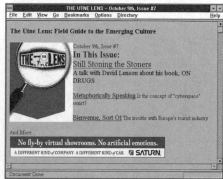

Figure 803.1 *The Utne Filter.*

Figure 803.2 *The Utne Lens.*

Who's Cool in America/Who's Cool International Project

http://www.getcool.com/~getcool/

Come check out the "Who's Cool in America" and the "Who's Cool International" projects. With 10,418 pages on the Web that mention the word "cool," this site's creators have been appointed by the Board of Cool (hereafter referred to simply as "CoolBoard") to distinguish the truly cool from the pretenders. "As our title implies," they write, "our mission is to arbitrate precisely who is cool through an esoteric, objective methodology too complicated to mention here." Are you cool? To be officially cool, someone ELSE must say you are. This is why the CoolBoard exists. Do you have the guts to find out whether or not you are truly cool? Apply within.

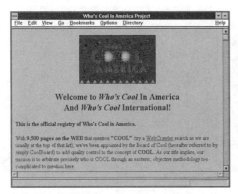

Figure 804.1 Who's cool?

Figure 804.2 The Board is cool.

SEE

More Special, Supercool Sites

As you surf the Web, you may find that one or more of the site addresses listed in this book have changed. In such cases, connect to Jamsa Press at http://www.jamsa.com and click on the icon that corresponds to the *1001 Really Cool Web Sites* book. Jamsa Press will list replacement addresses (when possible) for sites that have moved. In addition, you can also use the following site list as you search for information on special sites:

Positive Planet	http://cyberzine.org/html/HIV/mainpage.html
Friends of OSHO	http://earth.path.net/osho/
Michael Mauldin	http://fuzine.mt.cs.cmu.edu/mlm/home.html
Genealogy Online	http://genealogy.emcee.com/
Home Page for the Pegasus	http://pegasus.cc.ucf.edu/
Rice University personal	http://riceinfo.rice.edu/webshare_all.html
Food Family and Home	http://sfgate.com/~sfchron/homeplate/hoindex.html
Alpha Phi Alpha Fraternity Inc.	http://www-leland.stanford.edu/group/APhiA/
Russ Jones Business Card	http://www.digital.com/info/rjones.html
EFF Homepages	http://www.eff.org/homes/homes.html

SPORTS

U.S. Air Hockey Association

http://homepage.interaccess.com/~tweissm

Since Air Hockey's beginnings in 1972, the sport has grown steadily each year. Today, enthusiasts purchase thousands of tables every year, and millions of people have played this unique game. Find out more about "the world's fastest sport" at the homepage of the U.S. Air Hockey Association. The site includes official rules; listings of national, state, and local tournaments; and information about the 4-man team Carter Cup Competition. You'll find bios of some of the sport's top players, past and present. This site also contains precise definitions of Air Hockey terminology. For example, what is a *stuff* and why is it so humiliating? Find out at this site.

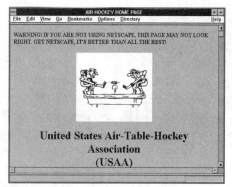

Figure 805.1 U.S. Air Hockey Association.

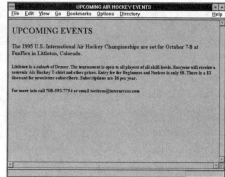

Figure 805.2 U.S. Air Hockey Events.

Howard A. Landman's Aikido Index

http://www.hal.com/~landman/Aikido/

Aikido is a non-violent martial art. Aikido's founder, Morihei Ueshiba, derived the art partly from the Daito-Ryu Jujitsu that he learned from Sokaku Takeda. Aikido, as an art, uses no punches or kicks. Instead, Aikido relies on various throws (projections) and joint locks. All Aikido's techniques, when properly performed, produce no lasting harm to the attacker. At this site, you'll find a complete list of Aikido-related links and resources. Topics range from the elementary (how to put on a gi) to the complex (the technique of kotegaeshi). You'll also find links to a great Aikido FAQ (frequently asked questions), the University of Pennsylvania Aikido Club, a valuable Aikido FTP site, and Aiki Jujitsu pages from Colorado, California, and elsewhere.

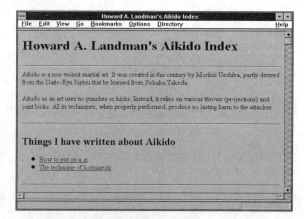

Figure 806 The Aikido Index.

America's Cup '95

http://www.ac95.org/

I live in Rhode Island, America's Cup country. One of the premier America's Cup yacht builders has a boatyard and workshop just a stone's throw from where I live. And in season, the talk is all about boats, races, and crews. In nearby Newport, they have even gone so far as to christen a street "America's Cup Boulevard." That is the mania with which the South County region of Rhode Island approaches the America's Cup competition. At this official America's Cup site, you will find race results, individual boat design and performance statistics, captain and crew biographies, a useful FAQ (frequently asked questions), and even a photo album of America's Cup yachts present and past. As a bonus, this site also includes real-time weather and tide information for San Diego.

Figure 807 A local Rhode Island preoccupation.

Archery Web Server

http://www.hsr.no/~morten-b/archery.html

Did you know that archery is actually an Olympic sport? I didn't. I thought archery was something semi-dangerous that kids did at summer camp (in my case, Camp Wauwepex on Long Island). Come to this Web page to learn about what, I now realize, is actually a fascinating sport with complex rules and a rich tradition. For starters, the file labeled "The Essentials of Archery" will clue you in to the rules and authorized equipment as specified by the international committee that oversees the sport. Also, you'll find a gallery of archery competition images, a link to an archery page in the Netherlands, and a link to a page dealing with the archery competition at the 1996 Olympics in Atlanta.

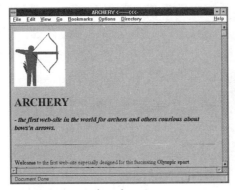

Figure 808.1 Archery home page.

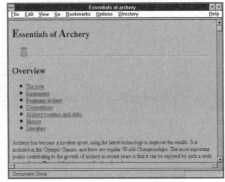

Figure 808.2 Another interesting archery page.

The Badminton Home Page

http://mid1.external.hp.com/stanb/badminton.html

Hey, cut out the attitude. If this sport were for wimps, it would not be called *Bad*minton. Before you jump to the conclusion that Badminton is a bore, check out the file headed "So you think you know about Badminton?" This site also contains information on the rules of Badminton, Round Robin tournament formats, and Swiss Ladder (an alternative tournament format). You'll find lessons on stretching and flexibility, sport psychology, and Badminton backhand. To top it all off, you get links to the United States Badminton Association, the Ontario Badminton Association, the Badminton Association of England, the Danish Badminton Federation, the Finnish Badminton Association, and the Hungarian Badminton Association.)

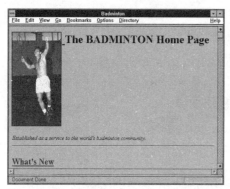

Figure 809.1 Not for wimps.

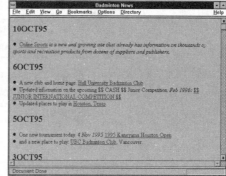

Figure 809.2 The latest events.

Ballooning Online!

http://sunsite.unc.edu/ballooning/

This site is your source for ballooning information on the Web. At this site, you can access schedules for various national and international events where you can see 50, 100, or even 600 balloons in flight at the same time. Links take you to dozens of ballooning clubs across North America and around the world. You'll find a regional breakdown of ballooning information that you can search by country, state, or province. You'll also find a valuable glossary (so when your ballooning buddies ask you to "Work the mouth," you'll know what they mean) and weather information, both national and international, to help you make your weekend ballooning plans. And most importantly, "Ballooning Online!" provides you with ballooning safety tips. (Tip number one in my book: stay on the ground.)

Figure 810.1 Up, up and away!

Figure 810.2 The latest ballooning news.

Baseball Server

http://www2.nando.net/SportServer/baseball/

"The Baseball Server" provides one-stop shopping for anyone who wants information on American baseball, past and present. You'll find stats, schedules, and personnel and coaching information for the National and American Leagues. You'll also find lists of World Series winners, baseball card collectors information, and up-to-the-minute news on major-league action. Want more? This site also has National and American League game previews, summaries of each day's games and starting pitchers, and even farm league stats. Make sure you check out the multimedia tribute entitled "The Mick, 1931-1995." And browse "The Baseball Server's" coverage of the 1994-95 strike.

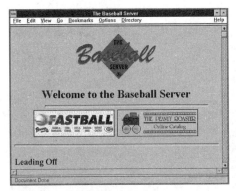

Figure 811.1 *The baseball page.*

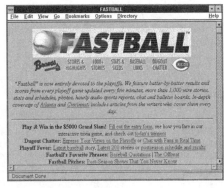

Figure 811.2 *Fastball news.*

Brown Curling Club Home Page

http://www.brown.edu/Students/Brown_Curling_Club/

Curling. What is it? Well, it's that weird sport you saw the Beatles playing in the famous snow-and-ice scene from *Help!* You know, I'm talking about guys in funny hats lobbing kettles of boiling water across the ice of a frozen lake to see who can throw them the farthest. I'm also talking about other guys dusting snow off the ice with brooms to make a clear path for the steaming pots. The whole enterprise gets all the more interesting the more schnapps you drink. You'll find no better place to get all the esoteric details on this most esoteric of sports than at the homepage of the Brown University Curling Club. This site provides a complete history of Curling, links to other Curling sites (yes, they do exist, believe it or not), and tips on the best curling hardware and the best curling sites in various regions.

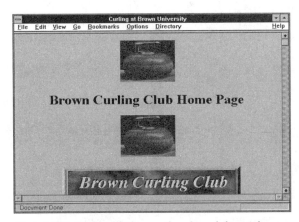

Figure 812 *Curl up with a good curling club tonight.*

Bass Fishing Home Page

http://wmi.cais.com/bassfish

This page covers bass fishing equipment, guides, tournaments, reports, locations, and stories (as in, "The One That Got Away"). "Bass Fishing" also includes a fantastic list of equipment manufacturers and dealers. Additionally, at this site, you can submit your own fishing report to the "Bass Fishing Home Page Report System." Are they biting at Saranac Lake? What is the best season on Tahoe? Upload or download the information as you see fit. You are also invited to share information about your favorite (or least favorite, for that matter) lures, reels, and rods. Make sure you check out the Lake Okeechobee Report, as well as regular reports from Plulpot (Kentucky), the Adirondack Mountains of New York, the Potomac River, Lake Winnipesaukee (New Hampshire), and other popular bass locations.

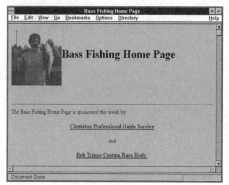

Figure 813.1 Bass Fishing Home Page.

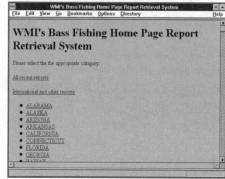

Figure 813.2 Fishing reports.

Boxing Page

http://lemur.cit.cornell.edu/boxing/boxing.html

Is there anything about boxing that this Web site does not cover? I don't think so. For starters, you'll find bios of all the current contenders, including Charles Murray, Reggie Green, Glenwood Brown, Julio Caesar Green, Hector Camacho, Jeff Passero, Michael Nunn, Charles Oliver, Henry Maske, Graciano Rocchigiani, Francis Ampofo, Robbie Regan, and even "Iron" Mike Tyson. You get gossip on the men behind the fighters, most notably the controversial Don King. And you'll also find boxing-match schedules for heavyweights, welterweights, middleweights, featherweights, and junior featherweights. Finally, "The Boxing Page" provides results from past fights, rankings of fighters by division, and even fight reviews.

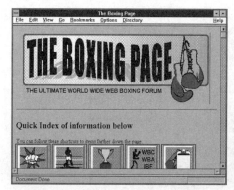

Figure 814.1 O.J.'s favorite sport.

Figure 814.2 The best of the best.

VeloNet: Global Cycling Network

http://cycling.org

This Web page covers every kind of cycling, including mountain biking, long-distance cycle racing, and even unicycling! You'll find a calendar of competition dates and times, notices from marketers of bikes and bike-hardware, mountain biking maps and tour offerings, and links to many excellent regional biking pages. You'll also find resources related to bicycle safety, tandem riding, and bike touring vacations. And "VeloNet" provides information on triathlons, duathlons, and other multisport events in the United States, Japan, France, England, Germany, Ireland, Canada, Spain, and Scotland. Whether you are a weekend biker or a die-hard cycle racer, "VeloNet" has something for you.

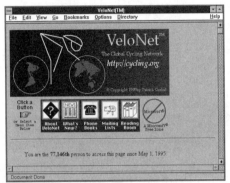

Figure 815.1 VeloNet home page.

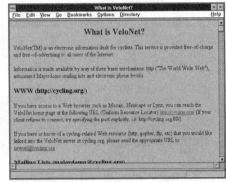

Figure 815.2 What is VeloNet?

ESPNet SportsZone

http://espnet.sportszone.com/

Courtesy of ESPN, this great Web site gives you all the information you need on professional baseball, football, soccer, hockey, and other sports. You'll find sports industry insider news, audio interviews with coaches and players, a great fantasy football league where you manage your own virtual team, and more. Check out reports from leading sports columnists, including David Robinson on why he is not going to miss Dennis Rodman, Tom Jackson on how the race issue allowed a guilty O.J. Simpson to escape justice, and Frank DeFord on why so many of us need to fib about our athletic prowess. Of course, "ESPNet SportsZone" provides all the scores, game schedules, and game analysis you can handle. What more could you ask for besides a big screen TV and a keg of Harp?

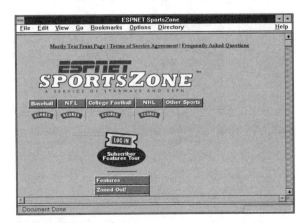

Figure 816 Enter the zoo.

Footbag WorldWide

http://www.footbag.org/

You've seen them: the kids in line for the rock concerts and on college campuses across the planet. They stand in groups of two to six kicking a beanbag between them, never touching it with their hands, trying to keep it up in the air for as long as possible. Did you know that this strange sport has its own Web server? Yup! Courtesy of the [San Francisco] Bay Area Footbag Foundation. At this site, you'll find links to footbag clubs and leagues across the United States, Canada, Europe, and Australia. You'll also find links to extensive information on Footbag equipment (footbags, special shoes, and so on). And don't forget to check out the details on Footbag rules (that's right, formalized rules), tournaments (that's right, tournaments), and international competitions (right again!).

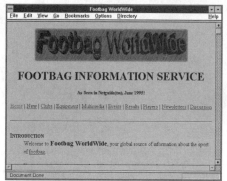

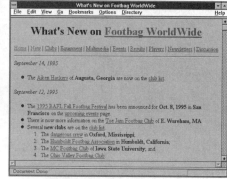

Figure 817.1 Footbag (not to be confused with Bodybag) home page.

Figure 817.2 What's New?

RSFC Home Page (College Football)

http://www.engr.wisc.edu/~dwilson/rsfc/

Maintained by David Wilson, "RSFC" provides weekly results for the top 25 college teams, game summaries, scores by date, player performance ratings, Darryl Marseed's useful ratings and predictions, and even a link to the National Football League Recruiting Center. You'll also find historical stats going back to the dawn of the contemporary college football divisions, stadium seating and parking information, and more. Now me, I'm more of a Division III man myself. As I write, we've got the Harvard-Brown game coming up in a few weeks; I just love to see those future doctors, lawyers, and investment bankers (not to mention the occasional would-be novelist) rough each other up.

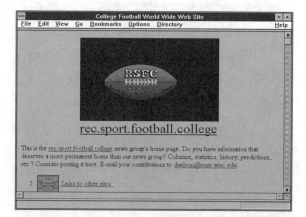

Figure 818 Are you ready for some football?

National Football League Links

http://www.tns.lcs.mit.edu/sports/nfl/home-pages.html

This site is your launch pad to the homepages of your favorite National Football League teams. Your options include the New England Patriots, Buffalo Bills, Dallas Cowboys, Miami Dolphins, Denver Broncos, Pittsburgh Steelers, Kansas City Chiefs, San Diego Chargers, Oakland Raiders, Arizona Cardinals, New York Giants, Green Bay Packers, Detroit Lions, Jacksonville Jaguars, and more. Additionally, you'll find player biographies, team stats, game schedules, and such esoterica as the official NFL/AFL rulebook, league equipment specifications (does your pigskin match up?), and great historical biographies of the NFL's greatest all-time players.

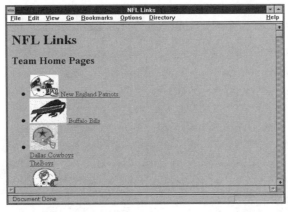

Figure 819 National Football League links.

Golf on the Web

http://www.gdol.com/

Whether you want maps of the great golf courses of the world or online biographies of Arnold Palmer and other great golfers, you have come to the right site. You'll find everything you want to know about golf at "Golf on the Web." Additionally, you'll find links to retailers that offer a broad selection of golf books, videos, equipment, and even software! One extremely valuable feature is the NBC Golf Tour information, which includes details on all upcoming tournaments, a handy course locator, and more. Care to order one of those supercool Ryder Cup hats? Do so here. Want to search the "Golf Resort Database" for your dream golf vacation? Do so here.

Figure 820 Links to the links.

The National Hockey League's Teams' Home Pages

http://maxwell.uhh.hawaii.edu/hockey/teams.html

This site provides links to homepages for teams in each of the four divisions of the National Hockey League. Check out all your favorite teams. You'll find links to teams in the Atlantic Division (New Jersey Devils, New York Islanders, New York Rangers, Philadelphia Flyers, Tampa Bay Lightning, and Washington Capitals), the Northeast Division (Boston Bruins, Buffalo Sabres, Hartford Whalers, Montreal Canadians, Ottawa Senators, and Pittsburgh Penguins), Central Division (Chicago Blackhawks, Dallas Stars, Detroit Red Wings, St. Louis Blues, Toronto Maple Leafs, and Winnipeg Jets) and the Pacific Division (Anaheim Mighty Ducks, Calgary Flames, Edmonton Oilers, Los Angeles Kings, San Jose Sharks, and Vancouver Canucks).

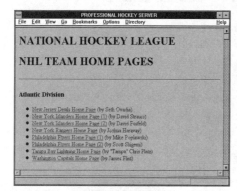

Figure 821.1 NHL team pages.

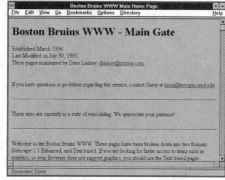

Figure 821.2 Your team stinks. Go Bruins!

National Hockey League Players' Association

http://www.nhlpa.com/

Find out who is playing for whom this season, courtesy of the National Hockey League Players' Association. Check out the biography, photograph, and stats of the player of the day. Take part in the Association's trivia challenge. Access RealAudio interviews with the players themselves. Read the players' side of the story concerning last year's notorious NHL strike. And, view a marvelous photo archive that includes a nostalgic gallery of the NHL greats from the past, such as Bobby Orr. You are invited to download all these items, as well as the National Hockey League Players' Association logo.

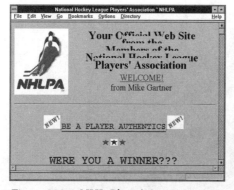

Figure 822.1 NHL Players' Association.

Figure 822.2 Welcome from Mike Gartner.

National Hockey League Schedule

http://www.cs.ubc.ca/nhl/

This useful Web site provides an easily-navigable interface to the complete National Hockey League schedule. You can see what games are playing today, or you can check the dates for particular team matches in the past and future. This site is particularly handy for the traveler. Going to be in Chicago on the 15th of the month and want to know if a good game is playing that night? Use this site's city-and-date search feature. The database, of course, covers all 26 teams for all four league divisions: Atlantic, Central, Northeast, and Pacific.

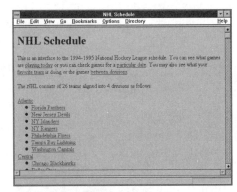

Figure 823.1 NHL Schedule.

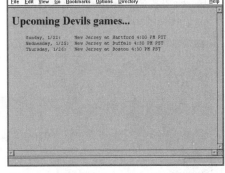

Figure 823.2 New Jersey Devils' schedule.

Horseracing: Churchill Downs

http://www.win.net/derby/

Who doesn't know Kentucky's beautiful Churchill Downs track (if not from personal experience, then from annual television exposure during the fabled Run for the Roses, the Kentucky Derby)? Is there any track in the country as steeped in tradition as Churchill? Is there any more dignified establishment in all of North America for the practice of the sport of gentlemen, horse racing? I don't think so. At this site, you'll find a complete history of the track, information on various upcoming meets, Kentucky Derby results information, a guide to locations for simulcast wagering, and more.

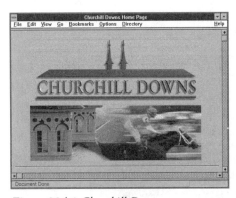

Figure 824.1 Churchill Downs.

Figure 824.2 Derby information.

SPORTS

825

Hugh Finn's Horse Racing

http://www.horseraces.com

I am, perhaps, revealing my horse racing illiteracy when I tell you that I haven't the slightest idea who Hugh Finn is, although I do know that his great-grandfather Huck was a colorful character. Nevertheless, Mr. Finn's page is marvelous and covers every aspect of North American horseracing. At this site, you'll find breaking industry news, including actual obituaries for great horses of the past who have gone to their reward, as well as listings for newly arrived sons and grandsons of such famous studs as Secretariat. You'll also find Cup competition information, weekly columns that include handicapping from John Asher and Bill Doolittle, industry reporting from John Harrell, and breeding information gathered by the voyeuristic Stacy Berkoff, who tells you which barnyard shenanigans are most likely to pay off with the birth of tomorrow's champions.

Figure 825.1 Hugh Finn's horse news.

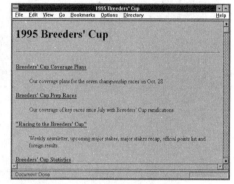

Figure 825.2 Breeders' Cup information.

826

The Olympics: Atlanta 1996

http://www.atlanta.olympic.org/

These are, of course, not just any Olympic Games. They are the centennial Olympics, celebrating one hundred years of formalized competition between the nations of the world. As such, the spectacle will be even greater than usual. The Olympics are more than just a sporting event. When approached in the right spirit (as they usually are), they are an antidote to a cynical age. The young people who work so diligently and loyally, striving always for the pinnacle of excellence, are (or should be) models for all. They should be held up for their perseverance, team spirit, and sense of single-minded duty to an honorable purpose. These are far more than just games.

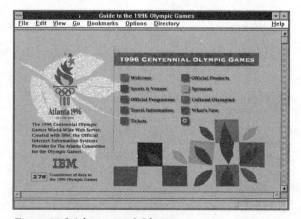

Figure 826 Atlanta 1996 Olympics.

The XVIII Olympic Winter Games

http://www.linc.or.jp/Nagano/index.html

The Winter Olympics began several decades after the summer games; thus, we have no centennial to celebrate at this site, at least not yet. I know that the Games in Nagano, Japan will be marvelous. But something about the idea of the Winter Olympics at this moment in history makes me profoundly sad. Whenever I think of the Winter Olympics, I think of not so many years ago, when the then-captivating and happy city of Sarajevo hosted the games. Today, of course, Sarajevo is the dominion of death and suffering and cynicism—a dark spot on the map where civilians suffer the blows of a war waged in the name of racial hatred.

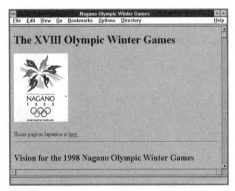

Figure 827.1 The 1998 Winter Games.

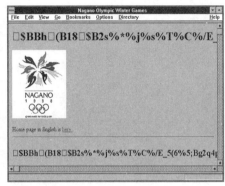

Figure 827.2 The same thing in Japanese.

American Racing Scene

http://www.racecar.com/index.html

Don't feel like going to Indy to watch the fabled 500? Like the races, but hate the exhaust fumes and the smell of burning rubber? Then stay home and visit this site, which provides daily racing results, statistics, details on world and national records, and more. NASCAR fans can check out all the track-side action on the "NASCAR Page." And the "IndyCar Page" provides weekend reports. You'll also find photography by Gary Toriello and Peter Burke. "'The American Racing Scene' is committed to providing timely information to IndyCar and NASCAR fans throughout the world," writes the Webmaster. "We will do our best to keep information accurate and up to date." And they seem to do an excellent job.

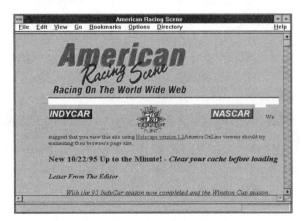

Figure 828 Your guide to crash dummies.

The U.S. Professional Racquetball Association

http://emporium.turnpike.net/~cyberguy/uspra.html

The United States Professional Racquetball Association was founded to help promote the sport of racquetball and the racquetball teaching profession. This site serves as a forum for the exchange of information, ideas, and experiences among Association members and others interested in racquetball as a sport. "Our goal," the Association says, "is to increase racquetball participation through increased awareness of the sport." At this site, you'll find a vast array of information, including details on official rules, major upcoming tournaments, current women's and men's pro rankings, the International Racquetball tour, Gregg Peck's backhand tips, and more.

 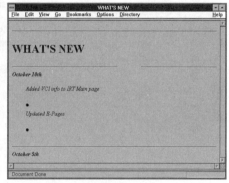

Figure 829.1 The US Racquetball Association. *Figure 829.2 The latest news.*

International Rugby League

http://www.brad.ac.uk/~cgrussel

Long ago, in my wild and woolly youth, I had a bumper sticker on my beat-up old car that said, "Give blood. Play Rugby." And Rugby really is like that. I don't know of a more violent sport; at the same time, I don't know of a sport I enjoyed more back in the days when I could run and kick (and punch and maul) with the best of them. At this site, you'll find a wonderful set of links to International Rugby League associates in Australia, Britain, the United States, Canada, and elsewhere. You'll also find links to the rules of the International Rugby League, a brief history of the league, league landmark events and records, and star-player biographies.

 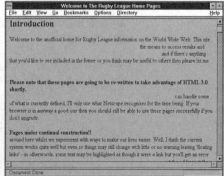

Figure 830.1 International Rugby. *Figure 830.2 More on the League.*

Saltwater Fishing Home Page

http://wmi.cais.com/saltfish/

In my part of Rhode Island, many people are very big on saltwater fishing, both as a sport and as a livelihood. This outstanding Web page covers saltwater fishing equipment, competitions, and more. "Saltwater Fishing" also provides information on fishing at various ports-of-call, including Ocean City (Maryland), Santa Cruz (California), Boca Raton (Florida), Cape Hatteras (North Carolina), Cancun (Mexico), Cape May (New Jersey), and dozens of other places. Useful links take you to fishing magazines and newspapers, fishing equipment suppliers, boat brokers, and even a number of fly-fishing-related sites.

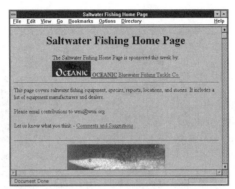
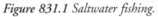

Figure 831.1 Saltwater fishing.

Figure 831.2 A word from the sponsor.

Aquanaut: Scuba

http://www.halcyon.com/jong/scuba/scuba.html

Aquanaut is the Internet's first and largest online magazine dedicated to the recreational and professional Scuba community. At this site, you'll find articles, files, and links related to dive destinations, underwater maps (and mapping), underwater photography, organized dive-tour-groups, scuba courses, certification tests, and more. You'll also find guides to diving the coasts of California, Massachusetts, North Carolina, Rhode Island, Mexico, Italy, the United Kingdom, and Florida. Coming soon: a newly designed "Wreck Database," which you can use to learn about wonderful old hulls, many fathoms below the surface, that are worth exploration.

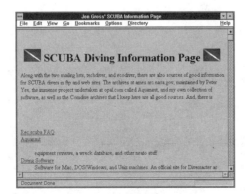

Figure 832.1 Aquanaut home page.

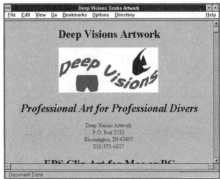

Figure 832.2 Scuba clip art.

The Skate.Net

http://www-unix.oit.umass.edu/~jona/skate/skate.html

Actually, we're talking skateboards, man, as in baggy pants, kids hangin' in the school parking lot or on a city street corner. Anywhere they can find a bit of inclined asphalt. You dig? I mean, we're talkin' bike skateboards, 60/40 skateboards, Alien Workshop skateboards, Capital skateboards, Element Skateboards, Foundation Super skateboards, Liquor skateboards, Maple Skateboards, Planet Earth skateboards, Stereo skateboards, Think skateboards, and Toy Machine skateboards. Before I checked out this site, I had no idea there were so many different makes and models of skateboards, man. You dig? I'm gonna buy me one of these babies and go hang with the dudes, rolling up walls and doing somersaults.

Figure 833.1 The Skate.Net.

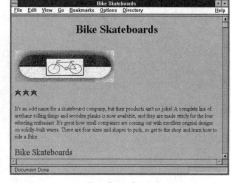

Figure 833.2 Skateboards a'plenty.

SkiWeb

http://www.sierra.net/SkiWeb/

Written for skiers and snow boarders by skiers and snow boarders, "SkiWeb" is your guide to the world of snow sports. You'll find plenty to check out at this site, which is really putting me in the mood as I sit, on a semi-crisp early-Autumn day, writing away. Hey, I mean the season is really already here. They're already making turns in Banff. And the northern slopes of Colorado received a foot of powder just a few days ago. At Tahoe, the nights are getting colder; soon the snow-making machines will begin to hum. Come to this site for great information on conditions around the world, details on excellent deals for transportation, lift-tickets, and more.

Figure 834.1 Ski Web.

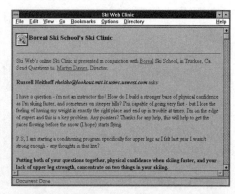

Figure 834.2 Just one information option.

Skydive!

http://www.afn.org/skydive/

Come on you chicken, do it! What's the matter? *Afraid?* If I were you, *I'd* do it. And I wouldn't even bother to check the parachute first. But I'm not you, so I'll just enjoy the sport vicariously. This site provides links to the Australian Parachute Federation, the Canadian Sport Parachute Association, the Parachute Industry Association, the Swiss Skydiving Federation, the United States Parachute Association, and many other groups. You'll also find links to a complete book about skydiving (*United We Fall* by Pat and Jan Works), details on competitive formation skydiving, parachute equipment manufacturers, parachute training programs, and more.

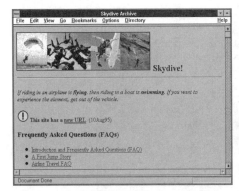

Figure 835.1 Skydiving is for you!

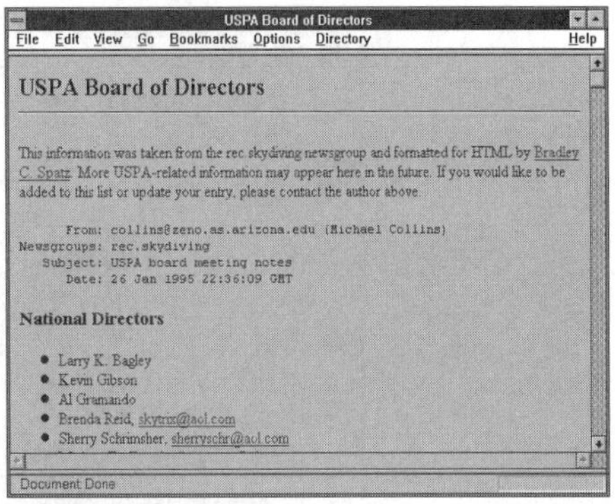

Figure 835.2 Be sure to take a parachute.

International Soccer Server

http://sigwww.cs.tut.fi/riku/soccer.html

At this site, you'll find frequently updated soccer scores and information from many European countries, including Italy, France, Germany, the United Kingdom, Denmark, Sweden, Austria, Belgium, Bulgaria, Finland, Greece, Hungary, Iceland, Netherlands, Ireland, Norway, Poland, Portugal, Romania, Scotland, Spain, Switzerland, and Turkey. You'll also find international rules and regulations, schedules, stats, links to additional soccer servers, and soccer-star biographies and updates. What's Pele doing these days? What is his favorite color? Where did he get that name? To find out, stop by.

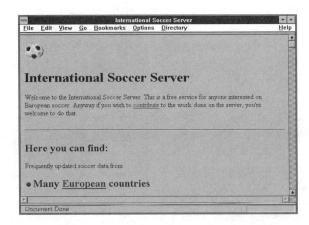

Figure 836 International soccer server.

SPORTS

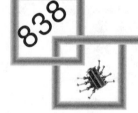

Open Entry to Sports around the World

http://open.entry.com/sports/index.html

This server provides you with information on professional and amateur hockey, football, basketball, baseball, soccer, tennis, fishing, cycling, rugby, lacrosse, boxing, cricket, volleyball, and even fencing at Harvard. At this site, you'll find complete rules for each league addressed, comprehensive tournament schedules and results, detailed statistics, and extensive schedules for amateur and professional leagues around the globe—the works, as the hot-dog vendors say. (By the way, what did Buddha say to the hot dog vendor at Yankee Stadium? Answer: "Make me one with everything.") Come here for one-stop-shopping sports information.

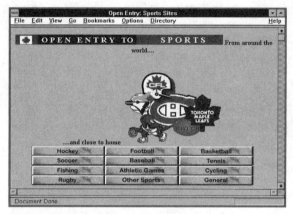

Figure 837 Open Entry to Sports.

The Internet Squash Federation

http://www.ncl.ac.uk/~npb/

Squash is one of the most satisfying and exhausting of all sports. It strengthens the legs, builds the upper body, and develops the heart and lungs. Furthermore, a game of squash is a taxing test of your mental agility as you battle to outwit your opponent. "To walk back to the dressing room as weak as a kitten with the sweat dripping off you but with your mind as clear as tomorrow's dawn is better than five reefers or a trip on LSD," says a once enthusiastic player. This applies whatever your age. Squash is just plain good for you! You'll find all the history and rules of the game, equipment reviews, contact information for regional squash federations, tournament information, and more.

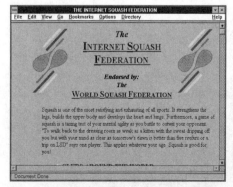 

Figure 838.1 The Internet Squash Federation.   *Figure 838.2 Info on the organization.*

Sumo Information Page

http://akebono.stanford.edu/users/jerry/sumo/

Pour yourself a beer, grab some popcorn, and sit back to enjoy watching overweight Japanese guys bouncing bellies and trying to knock each other down. Sure, you could be reading a classic novel, or listening to a great symphony, or hiking through a wooded landscape, but Sumo is definitely the way to go. Visit this site for a Sumo FAQ, a picture archive containing GIFs of Sumo wrestlers, and results (Natsu Basho, Haru Basho, Hatsu Basho, Kyushu Basho, Aki Basho, and Nagoya Basho). You'll also find a QuickTime movie of Takanohana vs. Akebono (November 28, 1994) and an MPEG movie of Chiyonofuji vs. Hokutoumi (July 20, 1994).

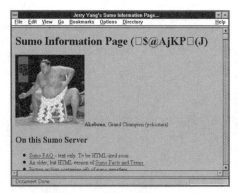

Figure 839.1 Fat guys in diapers.

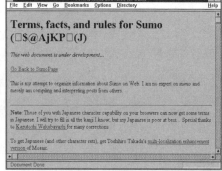

Figure 839.2 Sumo FAQ.

George Ferguson's Ultimate Page

http://www.cs.rochester.edu/u/ferguson/ultimate

Ultimate is a non-contact sport in which two seven-player teams, armed with only a frisbee, attempt to score goals. The player holding the frisbee at a given moment cannot take any steps; he or she must pass the disc to a teammate. Any time a pass is incomplete, intercepted, knocked-down, or contacts an out-of-bounds area, a turnover occurs, and the disc immediately changes possession. To score a goal, a player must pass the disc to a teammate in the opposing team's end zone. For official rules of the game, information about leagues around the world, and much more, visit this site.

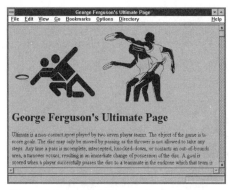

Figure 840.1 The Ultimate home page.

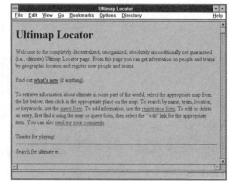

Figure 840.2 A great sport.

SPORTS

841

Volleyball Worldwide

http://www.volleyball.org/

"Volleyball Worldwide" is your source of information about the sport of volleyball. At this site, you'll find a complete history of the sport, rules of the game, tips for refereeing, tips on training for and coaching the game, and more. You also get guides to books, magazines, and volleyball television coverage, as well as reviews of balls, shoes, nets, and other volleyball equipment. In addition, you'll find a link to the USA Volleyball Association, as well as links to volleyball associations and clubs worldwide, including the Federation Internationale de Vulley-Ball and the Professional Volleyball League.

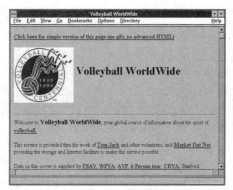

Figure 841.1 Volleyball Worldwide.

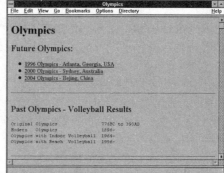

Figure 841.2 Volleyball as an Olympic sport.

842

World Wide Web of Sports

http://www.netgen.com/sis/sports.html

The NetGen Sports Information Server is an amazing resource, and I suppose this is why it won the Best Entertainment Site Award in the Best of the Web '94 Contest. This informative site offers extensive coverage of virtually every professional sport activity around the globe. You can access data about professional teams in a wide variety of sports, including baseball, hockey, basketball, football, soccer, lacrosse, volleyball, and others. Want information on schedules, scores, player bios, team and player stats? It's here. If you include only one sports site on your hot-list, make it the "World Wide Web of Sports."

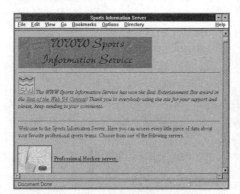

Figure 842.1 WWW of Sports.

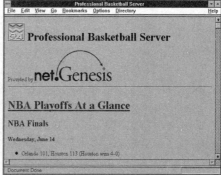

Figure 842.2 NBA information.

Amateur Wrestling

http://www.coe.uncc.edu/~jrlareau/

While professional wrestling is a kitchy drama of violence, amateur wrestling is a serious sport. I wrestled in high school, as did John Irving, who gave a vivid portrayal of the seriousness and drama of the sport in *The World According to Garp*. At this site, you'll find complete details on star college and high school wrestling teams across the United States; an e-mail directory of "Who's Who" in amateur wrestling; wrestling-related zines that include *The American Grappler, Amateur Wrestling News*, and *Wrestling USA*; and details on the development of the '96 U.S. Olympic freestyle team, including the selection of a head coach.

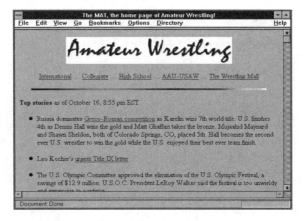

Figure 843 John Irving's favorite sport.

More Sports

As you surf the Web, you may find that one or more of the site addresses listed in this book have changed. In such cases, connect to Jamsa Press at http://www.jamsa.com and click on the icon that corresponds to the *1001 Really Cool Web Sites* book. Jamsa Press will list replacement addresses (when possible) for sites that have moved. In addition, you can also use the following site list as you search for information on sports:

Aladdin Sailing Index	http://www.aladdin.co.uk/sihe/
Cleveland Sports	http://www.apk.net/sports
Go Dodger Blue	http://www.armory.com/~lew/sports/baseball/dodgers.html
Rec.Sports.Soccer - The WEB Page	http://www.atm.ch.cam.ac.uk/sports/
World-Wide Web Virtual Library: Sport	http://www.atm.ch.cam.ac.uk/sports/sports.html
Saint-James Sportfishing Adventures	http://www.boatnet.com/boatnet/charter/Saint-James/STJames.html
NFL Playoff Races	http://www.cacs.usl.edu:80/~jkj/nfl/
Tennis Rankings	http://www.cdf.toronto.edu/DCS/FUN/ATP.html
ATP/WTA Doubles	http://www.cdf.toronto.edu/DCS/FUN/double.html
Tennis Rankings	http://www.cdf.toronto.edu/DCS/FUN/WTA.html
Boris Becker FAQ	http://www.cdf.toronto.edu/personal/chris/tennis/becker.html

Adventurous Traveler Bookstore

http://www.gorp.com/atb/hiking.htm

The "Adventurous Traveler Bookstore" gives you literally hundreds of wonderful books on outdoor sports and recreation activities around the world. At this site, you'll find illustrated guides to biking in Ohio, hiking in Yosemite, and rock climbing in the Adirondacks. You'll also find guides to hiking in Oregon's coast range, the Hudson Valley, the Magdalen Islands, the Swiss Alpine Pass, the Catskills, the Rocky Mountains, and on the Appalachian Trail. Do you prefer water adventures? This site has canoeing and rafting guides for waterways ranging from the Snake River to the upper Hudson. And for the mountain goats, "Adventurous Traveler Bookstore" includes climbing guides for mountains in the Bernia Alps, the Alaskan Brooks Range, Scotland, and elsewhere.

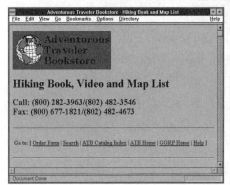 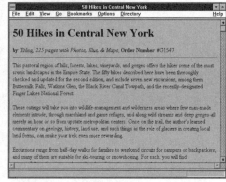

Figure 844.1 *Are you an adventurous traveler?* ***Figure 844.2*** *A sample book description.*

Airline Tickets WholeSale

http://www.tagsys.com/Ads/NetSale/

"Airline Tickets Wholesale" is brought to you by Travel Discounters, Inc., who say they will save you 17% to 30% on domestic United States airline fares above $300, guaranteed. Will you still qualify for mileage credit and reserved seating assignments? Absolutely! "Airline Tickets Wholesale" offers discounts on flights within the 48 contiguous states on such airlines as Delta, Continental, TWA, American, and Northwest. Additional discounts are available for children under twelve years of age traveling with at least one adult. Best of all, you can reserve your tickets right online at the Airline Tickets Wholesale Web site and have them delivered to your door. Reliable? Sure. Based in San Francisco, Travel Discounters, Inc., has been in business for more than 14 years.

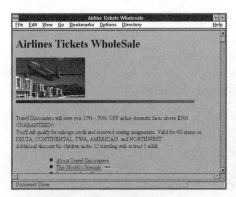 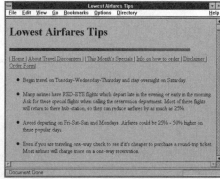

Figure 845.1 *Airline tickets cheap!* ***Figure 845.2*** *Lowest affair (oops, airfare) tips.*

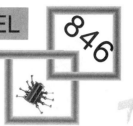

United States Airlines

http://w3.one.net/~flyba/AIRLINES/OAL/airlines.html

Links at this site take you to the homepages of Continental, Delta, Northwest, Southwest, TWA, United Airlines, Aloha, Carnival Airlines, Frontier Airlines, Presidential Air, Reno Air, ValuJet, Western Pacific, Aloha Island, American Eagle, Atlantic Southeast, Business Express, COMAIR, Gulfstream International, and Reeve Aleutian. You'll also find links to Skywest, First American, Haines Airways, New England Airlines, Air Cruise America, Air Kauai Helicopter Tours, Alaska Air Taxi, Bear Lake Air Service, Big Island Air, Classic Aviation Corporation, Eagle Canyon Airlines, Falcon Flight, and dozens more large and small carriers.

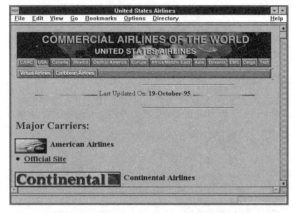

Figure 846 United States Airlines.

Airport Servers

http://acro.harvard.edu/GA/airports.html

Connect to the homepages of airports worldwide and get real-time information on arrivals, departures, and weather conditions. The list includes links to Amsterdam Airport, Atlanta International, Austin City Airport, Cleveland Hopkins International, Denver International, Entebbe International (yes, *that* airport), Heathrow (London), the Houston airports, Kansai International, McCarran International (Las Vegas), Moscow International, Narita Airport (Tokyo), Nashville International, Oakland International, Ontario International, Orly International (Paris), San Antonio International, San Jose International, Sugarbush Airport (Vermont), Tulsa International, and many more sites.

Figure 847 Airport servers at your service.

Amtrak's Great American Vacations

http://www.amtrak.com/agav.htm

Did you know that Amtrak offers many great customized vacations and tours? With dozens of destinations, hotels, travel options, and sightseeing packages to choose from, Amtrak's vacation package makes it easy to create your dream trip (and easy to book with one-call-does-it-all reservations and information). Another interesting option is Amtrak's Air-Rail Travel Plan, the economical choice for travelers with limited time. This plan offers the excitement of the train in one direction and the speed of air travel in the other. Also of interest is Amtrak's "Great Escapes" program, which offers quick, fun, and easy short trips. Make sure you check out Amtrak's escorted motorcoach tour vacations: eight comprehensive tours in motorcoach comfort—a great way to explore everything a region has to offer.

Figure 848 Amtrak's great vacation options.

Arizona Gold

http://204.31.168.10/travel/arizona

This page is your gateway to the one of the most beautiful places on earth: Arizona. At this site, you'll find links to pages with information on the Grand Canyon National Park, Nature Conservancy preserves in Arizona, Grand Canyon river running and rafting, the Arizona Mountaineering Club, the Arizona Four-Wheel Drive Association, fly fishing in Arizona, and the Sunrise Peak ski resort. This site also provides information on Grand Canyon area hotels. As soon as my son gets a few more years on him, he and I are running at least a part of the Grand Canyon, and I am expecting the rush of a lifetime.

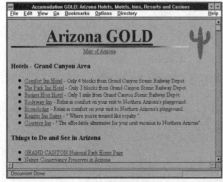

Figure 849.1 All about Arizona.

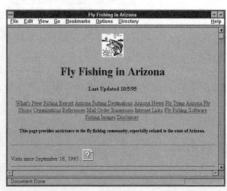

Figure 849.2 Fly fishing in Arizona.

Australia: Commonwealth Department of Tourism

http://tourism.gov.au/welcome.html

At this site, the Commonwealth Department of Tourism, an Australian government agency, provides a potpourri of information you can use to plan a trip to the land of wonder, the land down under. You'll find details on flight schedules and airfares from various points of departure around the world, hotel information, and facts about various tour and rental-car options (not to mention rail options) for getting around Australia. You'll also find complete information on the rich history and culture of Australia as represented in numerous historical museums, art galleries, and performance spaces throughout the country. As well, you get information on the great restaurants of Sydney (there are many) and other cities.

Figure 850.1 Australian tourism.

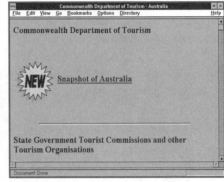

Figure 850.2 Want to know more?

Berkeley: Hotel Durant

http://cyber.cclims.com/comp/hdur/hdur.html

Step into the virtual lobby of the Hotel Durant and return to a bygone era of elegance and luxury. Located just one block from the campus of the University of California, Berkeley, and near the downtown business district, the hotel has been a Berkeley landmark for a hundred years. This richly restored hotel offers 140 spacious rooms and suites designed in a stately tradition. While the Hotel Durant provides the perfect setting for business meetings, conferences, or social events, it is also home to Berkeley's most popular and congenial gathering place, Henry's Publick House & Grille. To find out more about the Hotel Durant's many attractions, visit this informative site.

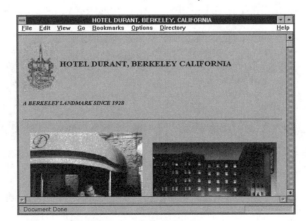

Figure 851 The elegant Hotel Durant.

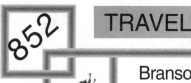

Branson-USA Online

http://www.usa.net/branson/default.html

Twenty years ago, no one had heard of Branson, Missouri. Now, it is the entertainment capital of the Northwest. At "Branson-USA Online," you'll find information on Lawrence Welk's Champagne Theatre, the Grand Palace (where you'll regularly find Yakov Smirnoff, Kenny Rogers, and Barbara Mandrell), Mickey Gilley's Theater, the Osmond Family Theater, the Andy Williams "Moon River" Theater, the Anita Bryant Theater, the Bobby Vinton Theater, the Charley Pride Theater (where you'll find not only Charley, but also Jimmy Travis and the Oak Ridge Boys), the Glen Campbell Goodtime Theater (where in addition to Glen you will also find Eddie Rabbitt), the Wayne Newton Theater, the Jim Stafford Theater, the Mel Tillis Theater, the Tony Orlando "Yellow Ribbon" Theater, and other similar institutions.

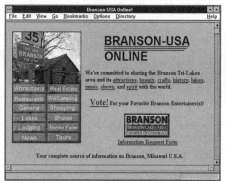

Figure 852.1 Branson-USA Online.

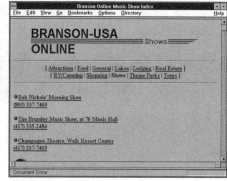

Figure 852.2 Branson music.

Boca Raton

http://bocaraton.com/index.html

Where should you go when the days get cold and you just don't like the cold? Why, Boca Raton, of course. This beautiful city in southeastern Florida sports wonderful beaches, great hotels, and friendly natives. Boca Raton also sports a splendid Web site that tells you about all these things and more. Can't you just feel the soft, warm ocean breeze? Can't you just see the palm trees sway? Can't you picture the gorgeous roller bladers down by the beach? Would you like to attend some of the regular concerts at the splendid Conservatory of Music (the Harid Conservatory) and dine at a few of the hundreds of fine eateries in the greater Boca Raton area? If the answer is yes, visit this site.

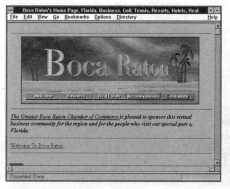

Figure 853.1 Life's a beach.

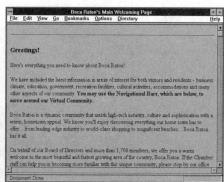

Figure 853.2 Welcome to Boca.

Canada Tourism & Travel Information Network

http://www.achilles.net/~tiac/homepage.html

The Tourism Industry Association of Canada is pleased to present the "Canada Tourism and Travel Information Network." This page links all Canadian tourism-related information on the Internet. You'll find links to resources that help you select transportation, hotels, and destinations within Canada. You'll also find city-by-city, province-by-province information on events and attractions, as well as a complete comparative run-down of Canadian hotel and motel options broken down by price-range and region. Additionally, the site links you to rail and air-travel schedules and prices, along with information on your rental car options across Canada.

Figure 854 Canadian tourism.

Connecticut Tourism

http://www.connecticut.com/tourism/

Here's to one of the most beautiful states in the Union—Connecticut. What a rich history! A history that includes some of the worst and most important fighting of the Revolutionary War. A history that includes no one less than Mark Twain, who in his later years made his home just outside of Hartford. Near me, right by the Rhode Island/Connecticut border, lies beautiful Stonington and the world-renowned Mystic Seaport Museum. And, in the northeast part of the state, you'll find the beautiful Connecticut River Valley, home of Dean Acheson and other twentieth-century movers and shakers. To find all about Connecticut tourism, visit this extensive and useful site.

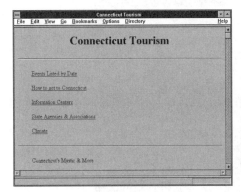

Figure 855.1 Connecticut tourism.

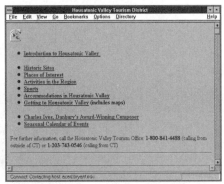

Figure 855.2 The Housatonic Valley.

Exploring Costa Rica

http://infoweb.magi.com/calypso/parks.html

When the Costa Rican government founded the Costa Rica Tourism Institute in 1955, it also established a two-kilometer zone around every volcano in the country and declared such zones national parks. This event marked the birth of the Costa Rican National Park System. In 1963, the government created the Cabo Blanco Absolute Natural Reserve (1,172 hectares of land and a 1,790 hectare area of the Pacific Ocean at the southern tip of the Puntarenas province). You will find maps, hiking and rafting guides, and information on how to arrange visits to the Costa Rican wilderness. To learn more about Costa Rica's natural resources and well-preserved ecosystems, visit this site.

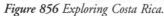

Figure 856 Exploring Costa Rica.

Fodor's WorldView

http://gnn.com/gnn/bus/wview/index.html

Fodor's WorldView is the publisher of custom, time-sensitive travel information. "Our writers," the publisher tells us, "gather travel news from hundreds of correspondents and thousands of sources worldwide and then organize that information into the Destinations and Interest Categories of our database. Each month you can view a representative Fodor's WorldView Travel Update for one of our destinations. You can also review a brief sampling of this month's events for all of our destinations." Pick from destinations in Canada, the United States, Europe, the Middle East, Latin America, the Caribbean, and the Pacific Rim.

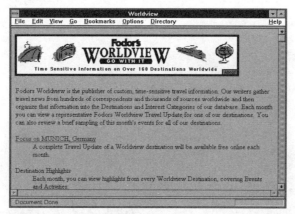

Figure 857 Fodor's Worldview.

GNN Traveler's Center

http://gnn.com/gnn/meta/travel/index.html

This site offers an interesting mix of travel-related items, including field reports from travelers in all sorts of exotic destinations. For example, you'll find Carla King's dispatches from her ongoing motorcycle journey across North America. Read about Carla's encounters with monuments and cities, as well as her more subtle adventures, such as a mechanical breakdown that leads to "a touching encounter with a blue-eyed mechanic named Ken." You'll also find Morris Dye's "Editor's Notes" column (in which he reviews Web sites designed to make travel-information accessible), a link to Mountain Travel Sobek (a firm specializing in providing active outdoor experiences), and more.

Figure 858.1 GNN Travel.

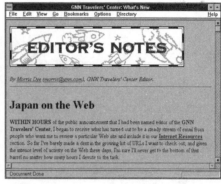

Figure 858.2 What's new.

Harpers Ferry National Historical Park

http://www.nps.gov/hafe/hf_visit.htm

My 1995 book *The Secret Six: The True Story of the Men Who Conspired with John Brown* documents the conspiracy that lay behind the famous anti-slavery raid by John Brown and his militia at Harpers Ferry, Virginia (now West Virginia) in October of 1859. The Harpers Ferry National Historical Park (located at the confluence (meeting point) of the Potomac and Shenandoah rivers in the states of West Virginia, Virginia, and Maryland) comprises 2,300 acres and is steeped in history. Thomas Jefferson, Stonewall Jackson, Frederick Douglass, and John Brown are but a few of the prominent people who left their mark on this place. To learn about Harpers Ferry and plan a trip to the area, check out this site.

Figure 859.1 You'll get a warmer welcome than John Brown did.

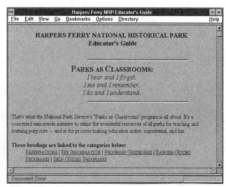

Figure 859.2 Educator's Guide to Harpers Ferry.

Harrah's - Las Vegas

http://harrahs.lv.com/

At Harrah's in Las Vegas, they guarantee that you will have "a great time every time." (That is, until you run out of money.) They do seem to have some first-class entertainment for those who are hip enough to stay away from the gaming tables and one-armed bandits. At this site, you'll find details about shows that include such great stars as Don Rickles, the Amazing Randi, Jay Leno, Dean Martin, Mort Sahl, Kenny Rogers, Tony Bennett, Florence Henderson, John Davidson, Barry Manilow, Liza Minnelli, and even Willie Nelson. You'll also find information on hotel pricing and reservations; the latter you can make right online. Harrah's will even help you make flight arrangements. They ask only one thing: when you come, bring your bankcards.

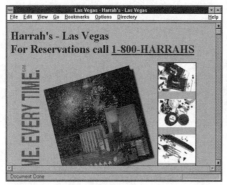

Figure 860.1 Come and lose your money.

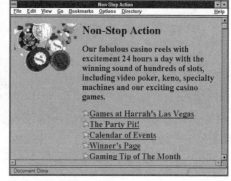

Figure 860.2 The "fun" never stops.

Hostelling International

http://gnn.com/gnn/bus/ayh/index.html

American Youth Hostels, Inc., offers "Hostelling International," which provides information on hostelling both in the United States and elsewhere around the world. The organization is nonprofit and dedicated to helping all, especially the young, gain a greater understanding of the world and its people through hostelling. You will be interested to know about the hostels in 77 countries around the world, as well as the 192 hostels in the United States. Whether in the U.S. or abroad, these hostels provide clean, safe, moderately-priced accommodations for those traveling on a shoe-string budget. Find out more at this useful and interesting site.

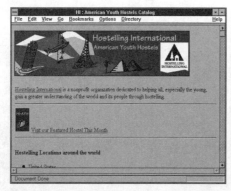

Figure 861.1 Hostelling International.

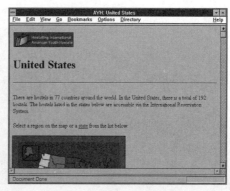

Figure 861.2 A guide to US hostels.

All the Hotels on the Web

http://www.digimark.net/dundas/hotels

What an astonishing resource! This site contains links to the homepages of 6,504 hotels worldwide. Search by price, hotel name, city, state, or province. Choose from U.S. hotels in such cities as Atlanta, Boston, Chicago, Dallas, Denver, Detroit, Los Angeles, Miami, New Orleans, New York City, Philadelphia, San Diego, San Francisco, Seattle, and Washington. Also, check out links to hotels in the Middle East, Asia, Africa, Australia/New Zealand, South America, Central America, the Caribbean, and Europe (including Andorra, Austria, Belgium, Croatia, Cyprus, Czech Republic, Denmark, Finland, France, Germany, Greece, Hungary, Iceland, Ireland, Italy, Latvia, Monaco, the Netherlands, Norway, Portugal, Russia, Serbia, Slovenia, Spain, Sweden, Switzerland, Turkey, and the United Kingdom).

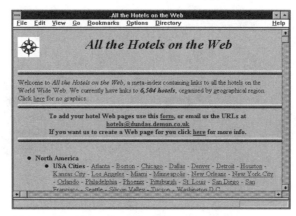

Figure 862 All hotels on the Web.

Hotel Net

http://www.u-net.com/hotelnet

If site 862 doesn't help you find the European hotel you need, check out "Hotel Net." Start with the clickable map of Europe. Click on the country you want to visit. Then, zero-in on the city and province. "Hotel Net" lets you choose the area you want to stay in and then quickly scan the available hotel options. Additionally, you can see pictures of the hotels or take a tour. This site includes hotels in Finland, France, Germany, Great Britain, Greece, Hungary, Ireland, Italy, Latvia, Liechtenstein, Luxembourg, Malta, the Netherlands, Poland, Portugal, Slovenia, Spain, Sweden, Switzerland, Turkey, Denmark, Estonia, Austria, and Belgium.

Figure 863.1 Hotel Net.

Figure 863.2 Austrian hotels.

Southern Illinois Tourism Council

http://www.intrnet.net/~sitc

This organization should be named the "Land of Lincoln" tourism council. The information this site provides is, of course, valuable to anyone who wishes to travel through Southern Illinois; but the fact of the matter is that the region's main tourism draw is "the Lincoln trail," which winds enticingly through the countryside. In Springfield, Lincoln matured, married, developed a successful legal career, and founded a prosperous household that is now a museum. In New Salem (now a historical park), he spent his early manhood and began to find his way in the world as an adult. And in a cabin out on the prairie (now a museum), he spent his late adolescence. Springfield also houses Lincoln's tomb, of course. Find out more at this site.

Figure 864.1 Land of Lincoln.

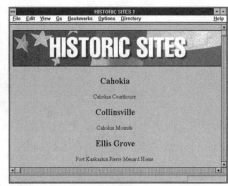

Figure 864.2 Historic sites.

Imagine Tours: Affordable Cycling Adventures

http://vvv.com/imagine/index.html

Imagine Tours has recently expanded their cycling program to offer tours in new and exotic places, as well as classic favorites. Come to this site for information on bicycle tours in Nova Scotia, New England, the Colorado Rockies, the Sonoma Valley wine country (including Jack London state park, located on the former Jack London ranch), Israel, Europe (including Holland and Belgium), and Baja, California. With over a dozen different rides throughout the year, through a variety of countries and terrain, Imagine Tours has something for everyone. Come to this Web site for more information.

Figure 865.1 Great cycling.

Figure 865.2 Affordable prices.

International Travel Group

http://www.airmail.net/~biztrvlr

If you or others in your firm travel internationally and you don't have direct airline contracts, take a moment to check out this site. It may save you some money. International Travel Group focuses on providing discount international airfares and discount domestic hotel rates for business travelers only. Because an airline seat and a hotel room are both perishable commodities, the airlines and hotels have discount contracts with select travel companies (not retail travel agencies), such as the International Travel Group. Today, the annual discount international airfare market in the United States exceeds $1.4 billion; similarly, the discount domestic hotel market exceeds $400 million. How much of this benefit are you getting? If your company doesn't have the volume for a direct airline contract, turn to the International Travel Group to get your slice of the discount pie.

Figure 866 International Travel Group.

Irish Tourism

http://www.ireland.net/marketplace/tourism.html

Ah! Ireland. You have gathered, from other portions of this book, my affinity for this ancient place. So by now, I'm sure, you've decided to actually make a visit and see for yourself what I'm talking about. This site contains all the information you need to do just that. You'll find details on hotels, motels, and bed-and-breakfasts all across Ireland; flight schedules and prices from major points of departure; hiking and climbing guides for Ireland's several beautiful wilderness areas; a special page dedicated to Kinsale visitor information; and even a Gaelic language reference center.

Figure 867.1 All roads lead to Ireland.

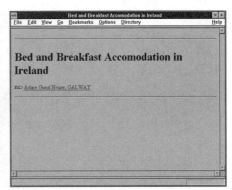

Figure 867.2 Irish bed and breakfasts.

Israel Tourism Online

http://www.pirsonet.co.il/TOURISM.html

Israel's tourism industry rests on three fundamental cornerstones. First, the country is the Land of the Bible and thus very important to the world's three great monotheistic religions. Second, the place has a rich historical and archaeological heritage which speaks volumes about the events that shaped civilizations and cultures. Last, Israel's geography and climatic conditions offer a splendid year-round tourism destination. Tel Aviv, in fact, contains some of the best beaches found anywhere. Come to "Israel Tourism Online" for information. You'll find hotel and flight information, lists of tours of everything from religious shrines to nightclubs, and other great resources for the would-be traveler.

Figure 868 Israel tourism.

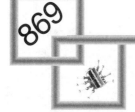

IVAN: International Vacation Network

http://www.sunbelt.net/ipi/ivan/ivan.htm

The "International Vacation Network (IVAN)" provides information about unique vacation opportunities worldwide. At IVAN, you'll find information on cruises, family vacations, scuba vacations, fishing vacations, mountain biking vacations, New York City vacations, Appalachian vacations, southeastern U.S. vacations, golf vacations, ecology vacations, water skiing vacations, snow skiing vacations, white-water rafting vacations, New England vacations, southwestern U.S. vacations, and more. This site also contains state and regional tourist information, official State Department travel advisories, a great guide to bed-and-breakfasts both in the United States and Europe, and even a step-by-step guide on how to get a United States passport.

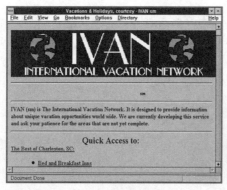

Figure 869.1 IVAN International.

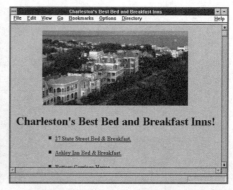

Figure 869.2 Charleston bed and breakfasts.

Accommodations in Central London

http://www.cs.ucl.ac.uk/misc/uk/london/hotels.html

This page provides you with information on all the best hotels in one of the world's greatest cities, London. At this site, you will find details on facilities, pricing, and reservations for the Tavistock Hotel (Tavistock Square), the Russell Hotel (Russell Square), the Hotel Ibis Euston (Cardington Street near Euston Station), the Grafton Hotel (129 Tottenham Court Road), the Academy Hotel (17-21 Gower Street), the Crescent Hotel (at Cartwright Gardens), the Celtic Hotel (Guilford Street), the Grenville House Hotel (Guilford Street), the Hotel President (Russell Square), the Avalon Hotel (Cartwright Gardens), the Bedford Hotel (Southampton Row), the Bonnington Hotel (Southampton Row), the Jenkins Hotel (Cartwright Gardens), and the Thanet Hotel (Bedford Place).

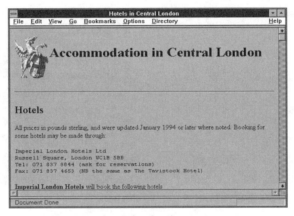

Figure 870 Central London hotels.

Maine Tourism Web Site

http://www.state.me.us/decd/tour/welcome.html

This site provides you with well-organized, helpful information about all the things that make Maine a wonderful place for recreation, exploration, and relaxation. You'll find information on all the regions of Maine, including the south coast, the western lakes and mountains, the mid-coast, the Kennebec and the Moose River valleys, Acadia, Katahdin, the "Sunrise Coast," and Aroostook County. You'll also find guides to special attractions (such as lighthouses, covered bridges, and Acadia National Park), and great activities that include hiking, sea kayaking, windjammer cruises, hunting, fishing, white-water rafting, museums, and historical sites.

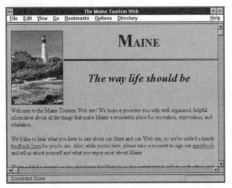

Figure 871.1 Maine: the way life should be.

Figure 871.2 What's new.

Travel Massachusetts

http://ftp.std.com/NE/masstravel.html

From the Berkshires to Boston, from Cape Ann to Cape Cod, Massachusetts has something for everyone. "Travel Massachusetts," your online guide to the Bay State, includes information on Boston/Cambridge, the Berkshires, Cape Ann, Cape Cod and the coastal islands (Nantucket and Martha's Vineyard), the Minuteman National Historic Park at Concord, old Plymouth, Salem (of witch-trial fame), and great state parks and forests. Of special interest is the information on the Freedom Trail in Boston, which includes the home of Paul Revere, the U.S.S Constitution, the Bunker Hill National Monument, and Boston Common. Check out a beautiful Web site that provides information on one of the most beautiful states of the Union: Massachusetts.

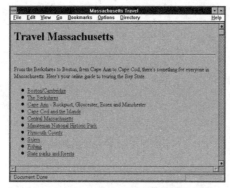

Figure 872.1 Massachusetts tourism.

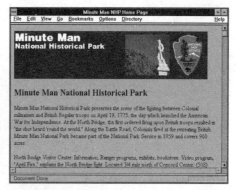

Figure 872.2 Minuteman National Park.

The Minnesota Office of Tourism

http://tccn.com/mn.tourism/mnhome.html

In my college years, I became acquainted with Mary Welsh Hemingway, who to my mind was distinguished less by the fact that she was the last wife of Ernest Hemingway than by the fact that she was a remarkably gifted writer and editor in her own right. She was one of the best correspondents of World War II and a particular favorite of the newspaper czar Lord Beaverbrook. Mary came from Minnesota and was always harkening back to her childhood in that land of a thousand lakes. Someday, I shall go to Minnesota to see what she was raving about. Should you decide to do the same, first visit this Web site, where you will find outstanding guides to the natural resources, hotels, highways, and byways of this splendid state.

Figure 873.1 Minnesota tourism.

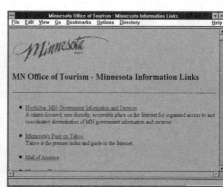

Figure 873.2 More Minnesota info.

Nebraska Tourism

http://www.ded.state.ne.us/tourism.html

Lots of great and sometimes strange stuff in Nebraska. Stuff I'd have never guessed was there. For example, Nebraska is home to Carhenge, a unique replica of the world-famous Stonehenge, constructed of old cars in 1987 by six local families on the occasion of their family reunion. On the more mundane (or is it *sane?*) side, Nebraska offers visitors the Knight Museum (which features cavalry equipment and Native American artifacts), the Harlan County Reservoir, the Anselmo Mineral Spring and Spa, the Arapahoe shrine to Our Lady of Fatima, the Arthur Township Courthouse Museum (listed in *Ripley's Believe It or Not* as the world's smallest courthouse), Aurora's Plainsman Museum (which features an exhibit on the strobe light, invented by Aurora's Harold Edgerton), the Nebraska State Historical Society museum in Bancroft, and the 1910 Living History Farm in Bayard.

Figure 874.1 Nebraska tourism.   *Figure 874.2 Travel details.*

Ski New England

http://obi.std.com/NE/neskiing.html

At this site, you'll find great guides to skiing throughout New England and especially in Maine, New Hampshire, and Vermont. This site contains guides to Maine's Sugar Loaf and Sunday River resorts; New Hampshire's Loon Mountain resort; and Vermont's Ascutney Mountain, Burke Mountain, Jay Peak, Killington, Mad River Glen, Smugglers Notch, Stowe, Stratton, and Sugarbush resorts. "Alpine Ski Report" details events and special pricing at various resorts throughout the region. These are all great places, of course. My wife and I have enjoyed Stowe and Stratton in particular, and my wife reports that New Hampshire's Loon Mountain is a "blast." (Christa went to college in New Hampshire and, I suspect, majored in skiing if only unofficially.)

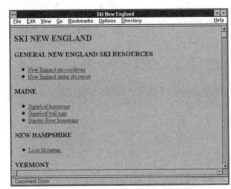

Figure 875.1 New England Skiing.   *Figure 875.2 Loon Mountain, New Hampshire.*

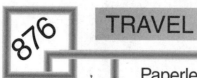
Paperless Guide to New York City

http://www.mediabridge.com/nyc/

I have only recently escaped the life of a high-powered, high-pressure publishing executive in New York City. Thus, I am jaded and should be ignored when I say that the place has little attraction for me at the moment. However, I will admit that New York City, though a lousy place to live, is an extraordinary place to visit. Think of the history: the Statue of Liberty, the Empire State Building, Lincoln Center, the Museum of Modern Art, Central Park, and more. Should you decide to visit New York City anytime in the near future, start first at "The Paperless Guide to New York City," a Web site packed with useful information for the tourist planning to take a bite out of the Big Apple.

Figure 876 New York City tourism.

Northwest Tourism

http://www.dmi.net/uspacnw

Come to this site for information on everything and anything involving tourism in the states of Washington, Oregon, Idaho, Montana, or Wyoming. Want to find a dude ranch where they won't beat you up or laugh at you too much? Find it here. Want to find great rock-climbing and hiking? Find it here. Want to discover some of the greatest trout fishing in the world? Find it here. In particular, find it in Idaho, where Ernest Hemingway, lured there by the trout, spent his last year. To discover all the stuff the Northwest has to offer (on and off the beaten track), visit this site.

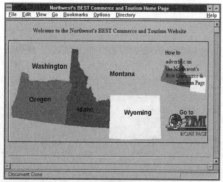

Figure 877.1 Northwest tourism.

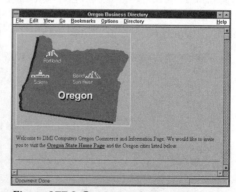

Figure 877.2 Oregon tourism.

Oklahoma Tourism

http://www.oklaosf.state.ok.us/~odt/

Oklahoma, where the wind comes roarin' down the plain, and where the corn is as high as an elephant's eye. Oklahoma, where Woody Guthrie was born and raised (in Okemah, to be precise). Of course, the corn wasn't as high as an elephant's eye when Guthrie came into his early manhood. The place was a dustbowl, the same dustbowl chronicled by Guthrie in his songs and by Steinbeck in *The Grapes of Wrath*. (If you want a great evocation of those days in Oklahoma, see either the Henry Fonda film, *The Grapes of Wrath,* or the David Carradine film of Guthrie's autobiography, *Bound for Glory*.) For contemporary information on this state, check out the "Oklahoma Tourism" web site.

Figure 878.1 Oklahoma: home of Woody Guthrie.

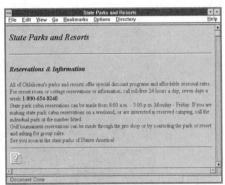

Figure 878.2 State parks and resorts.

Orlando: USA Tourist

http://magicnet.net/usatravel

What American parent hasn't been afflicted with Orlando? I've been there, at Disney World, on more than one occasion. My eight-year-old son knows his way around the Magic Kingdom as if he works there. In particular, he knows *the* shortest route around the triangle defined by Splash Mountain, Space Mountain, and the Haunted Mansion. These attractions, of course, are the three things in the Magic Kingdom that interest him the most. They are also the three rides that come the closest to seeming dangerous. Come to this site for discounts and reservations at Orlando-area hotels, as well as discount tickets for Disney World, Sea World, and a host of other attractions.

Figure 879 Orlando tourism.

Ottawa Information

http://www.tourottawa.org/index_e.html

The "Ottawa Information" page provides details on a number of excellent Ottawa attractions, including the Canadian National Aviation Museum, the Billings Estate Museum, the Bytown Museum, the Rideau Canal (a 19th century engineering marvel featuring 24 lock stations), the Currency Museum, the Laurier House National Historic Site (residence of Canadian Prime Ministers Laurier and King), and the Canadian Museum of Civilization (housing a vast collection of archaeological, and historical artifacts). You'll also find information on the Canadian Museum of Contemporary Photography, the Canadian Museum of Nature, the National Gallery of Canada, and the Royal Canadian Mounted Police Stables. (My attitude on the latter? Forget the horses. I want to meet Rin Tin Tin.)

Figure 880 Ottawa tourism.

Paris Hotels and Tourism

http://199.170.0.155/paris.html

Visit this site to receive excellent room rates at a number of fine hotels in Paris, including the Place de la Republique Holiday Inn, the Bel Air (Rue Rampon), the Hotel Plaza Etoile (Avenue de Wagram), and the Yllen Hotel (Rue de Vaugirard). You'll also find information on Embassy and Consular services, currency exchange rates, and more. Want to know what I think is the coolest thing to do in Paris? Go to Pere Lachaise Cemetery and check out Jacob Epstein's fascinating monument above the grave of Oscar Wilde. While you are there, stop by and visit Jim Morrison, who is planted not far away. His grave, decorated with years of psychedelic graffiti left by countless visitors, is hard to miss.

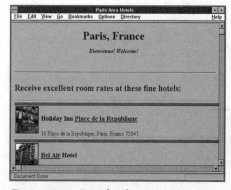

Figure 881.1 Paris hotels.

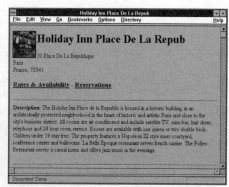

Figure 881.2 One of your options.

PC Travel

http://www.pctravel.com/

You can still find cheap airline tickets if you play your cards right. If you can purchase your tickets at least seven days before flying, and don't mind that they're non-refundable, PC Travel can save you some money. They are, in fact, one of the largest travel agencies in the country. At this site, you can conduct your own search of schedules, fares, and tickets for over 700 airlines worldwide via PC Travel's "Apollo" reservation system. Then, you can reserve and pay for your tickets right online. No hassle. The tickets are either sent to you or held for pickup at the airline ticket counter.

Figure 882 PC Travel.

Pikes Peak Country

http://electricstores.com/pikes-peak/default.htm

A friend of mine, 95-year-old Henry Villard, was a Red Cross ambulance driver in Italy during World War I and a good friend of Hemingway's. He was, in fact, the model for a minor character in *A Farewell to Arms*. Henry's grandfather, another Henry Villard, emigrated to the U.S. from Bavaria in the 1850s, settled at Springfield, Illinois, and became a close friend of the lawyer Abe Lincoln. He left Springfield to join in the Pikes Peak Gold Rush. He later became a founder of the Edison General Electric Company. Villard married Fanny Garrison, daughter of abolitionist William Lloyd Garrison (who is thus my friend Henry's great grandfather). To find out about the Pikes Peak country where that first Henry Villard came of age, access this interesting site.

Figure 883 Pikes Peak Country!

Pocono Mountains Tourism

http://www.pocono.com

This site is your source for complete Pocono Mountains tourist information, including details on resorts, lodging, golf, skiing, restaurants, side trips, and entertainment. In the winter, of course, the Poconos are noted for exceptional skiing at a host of fine resorts. In the spring and summer, they boast great canoeing, rafting, and tubing through the Delaware Water Gap. And in the autumn, they are known for exquisite displays of Fall color. Few places on the planet are more beautiful than the Poconos. Particularly lovely, to my mind, is Stroud Township in Monroe County, Pennsylvania, where you'll find some of the best hiking in the world. Go check it out before the developers show up.

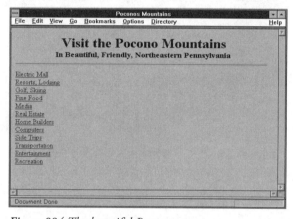

Figure 884 *The beautiful Poconos.*

Newport, Rhode Island

http://surf.aqua.net/newport.html

I live about ten miles from Newport, on the opposite shore and further up into Narragansett Bay. And I am here to tell you that Newport is one beautiful town. But don't take it from me. Instead, seize the evidence found at this Web site, which displays the architectural and cultural excellence that defines Newport. Start with a virtual tour of the seashore mansions, not the least of which is the famous Vanderbilt home, The Breakers. Then, check out the great guides to the many Newport museums, libraries, boatyards, and hotels. You'll also find details concerning the Naval War College (which features an excellent museum) and many other sites of interest.

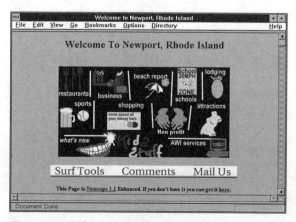

Figure 885 *Welcome to Newport!*

San Francisco Reservations

http://www.hotelres.com/

"San Francisco Reservations" provides you with a tool for finding the just-right accommodations in the San Francisco area, and then making reservations quickly and easily online (usually at the lowest rates available). Click on the map to choose from hotels in the Marina area, the Fisherman's Wharf area, Nob Hill, the Financial District, Union Square, the Moscone Center area, midtown, the Civic Center area, or near the airport. You can search by price range or by hotel type (suites vs. single rooms, hotels vs. motels, etc.) What I'm looking for is a cool, relaxing, nostalgic place down around Haight Ashbury, something with green floors and purple walls, the faint scent of cannabis wafting down the hallway, along with the sliding tin sound of a bottleneck blues guitar. I wonder, how I do a search for that?

Figure 886.1 San Francisco reservations.

Figure 886.2 Search hotels by price.

887

Seattle Information

http://www.pan.ci.seattle.wa.us/business/tda/tda.htm

At this site, you'll find trade and investment information, as well as tourist information. "Seattle Information's" purpose is to attract businesses and tourists to Seattle. The Web page itself was put together by the Trade Development Alliance of Greater Seattle, which is a partnership between the Port of Seattle Authority, the Metropolitan King County Government, the Snohomish County Government, the City of Seattle, and the Greater Seattle Chamber of Commerce. So, along with details on hotels, highways, and attractions, you'll find interesting information on population and work-force demographics, and other business-related information. By the way, this information is available in Chinese, Malaysian, Indonesian, Spanish, Tagalog, Japanese, Korean, Russian, Thai, and Vietnamese.

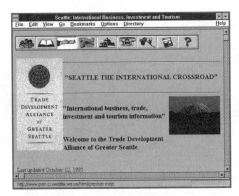

Figure 887.1 Everything about Seattle.

Figure 887.2 Seattle tourism.

Scotland Hotels

http://www.ibmpcug.co.uk/~ecs/hotel.html

Take your pick from any of the beautiful hotels presented on these lushly-illustrated pages. Check out the Ardanaiseig (Argyll), the Craigellachie (Speyside), the Balbirnie House (Fife), the Culloden House (Inverness), the Marcliffe at Pitfodels (Aberdeen), the Kinloch Hotel (Perthshire), and the Hebridean Princess (in the western Highlands). Note that the Marcliffe at Pitfodels is the hotel where Mikhail Gorbachev stayed in 1993 when the city of Aberdeen awarded him the Key to the Freedom of the City. Another featured hotel, Ardo House of Aberdeen, is a baronial mansion on 17 acres with magnificent views over the Dee Valley. You'll also find details on the "Tartan Collection," which comprises twenty-four more excellent hotels in the Grampian Highlands and Aberdeen.

Figure 888 Scottish hotels.

South African Tourism and Travel

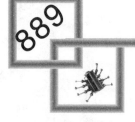

http://africa.com/docs/satravel.htm

Come to this Web site for everything you need to plan a trip to South Africa, that once-infamous place occupying the southernmost part of the African continent. You'll find complete details on South Africa's administrative capital, Pretoria; the seat of legislature, Cape Town; the nation's diamond region; its splendid wine country; and other areas of interest. You can review airline and hotel information, as well as details on the history of any place you'd like to visit. More to the point, you get information on South Africa's recent transformation from Apartheid to a free society with a black president and great hopes for the future. A great deal of work must still be done, but at least it has begun.

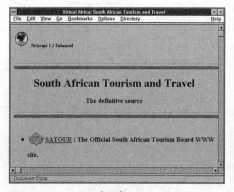

Figure 889.1 South African tourism.

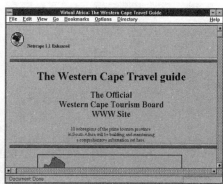

Figure 889.2 A wealth of information.

Small Luxury Hotels of the World

http://www.ibmpcug.co.uk/~ecs/hotel/slh/slh.htm

Now, you've come upon something interesting. Not just a guide to luxury hotels, but a guide to a specific type of luxury hotel with a particular feel and ambiance: the small luxury hotel. At this site, you will find an exceptional selection of the world's finest small hotels, each featuring superior hospitality, service, and cuisine. "When choosing from our rare collection of hotels," writes the Webmaster, "from the grandest to the most intimate, you are sure to enjoy the feeling of being a privileged guest in a luxurious personal residence. Wherever you travel, allow us to welcome you to Small Luxury Hotels." Choose from a wonderful assortment of options, from tiny pensions in Madrid to quiet, elegant getaways in London or Paris. They are all waiting, elegantly. Bring your checkbook.

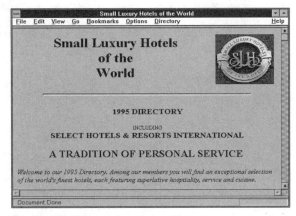

Figure 890 Your guide to petite elegance.

Texas Tourism

http://TravelTex.com/home/@56P374

When you think of Texas you probably think of cowboy country. But what you might not know is that Texas is also beach country. And canyon country. And mission country. And, of course, oil (Kuwait Koolaid) country. In Texas you will find everything from sparkling cities to quiet country lanes, from fresh Gulf seafood to authentic Tex-Mex. And you can easily preview Texas through this outstanding Web site, which would make J.R. Ewing proud. Start by choosing a city on the interactive map. Then, choose from a host of engaging information options. It's just that easy. So whether you want hotel information for Dallas or a calendar of musical events for Lubbock, check out this site.

Figure 891.1 Texas tourism.

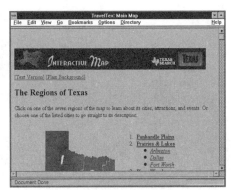

Figure 891.2 Clickable map of Texas.

TRAVEL

Travel Bank

http://www.travind.com/travelbank/

"Travel Bank" is a great guide to resources that help you plan all sorts of trips, whether across the state or around the world. You'll find a great tutorial entitled "Net Travel: Using the Internet to prepare for a trip." Another feature, "Destination Finder," provides excellent information on cities and provinces in Asia, Australia, the United States, British Columbia, India, Italy, Monaco, the Netherlands, France, the United Kingdom, and Southeast Asia. Other useful resources include links to airlines, travel agencies, Amtrak, and rental car companies, as well as references on languages, international currency exchange, visas, passports, and entry requirements. So get in the know before you go—visit the "Travel Bank" Web site.

Figure 892.1 Travel Bank home page.

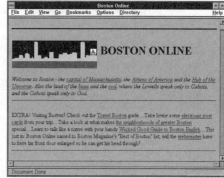

Figure 892.2 Boston details.

Traveller's World: UK Tourism

http://www.cpoint.co.uk/tw/

"Traveller's World" is the first concerted effort to concentrate tourism information from the whole United Kingdom in one place on the World Wide Web. The result of this effort is a valuable resource. Financed by a host of British hotels and tourism bureaus, "Traveller's World" includes information on all the major towns and cities in the United Kingdom, as well as road, rail, air, and sea travel routes for England, Wales, Scotland, and the Isle of Man. At this site, clickable country maps, divided into tourism regions, let you just point and click on an area for more information. Or, you can simply give the name of the county or town about which you want to know more. In addition to tourism information for the selected area, the site displays a selection of hotels at which you can stay and a summary of their prices and facilities.

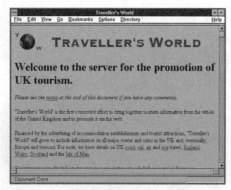

Figure 893.1 Traveller's World.

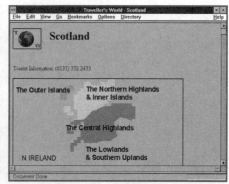

Figure 893.2 Scotland details.

Tropicana: Paradise Found

http://tropicana.lv.com/index.html

All of Las Vegas' decadence and greed is summed up excellently by the Tropicana. Two 35-foot tall Moai gods greet visitors to the new entrance of the Tropicana Resort and Casino, which includes a colorful "Caribbean Village" facade. The new front entrance also features a 25-foot waterfall, Kalanui (the god of money), a Polynesian long house, and spectacular nightly laser-light shows. Want to see a show? How about the *Follies Bergere*? Want to see a comedian? Stop off at The Comedy Stop (or just view the 1.9Mb Quicktime video of the joint that you'll find here online). Want to hand over every cent you have to the millionaires who own the Tropicana and have nothing at all to show for it? Go to the gaming tables. Have fun.

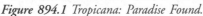

Figure 894.1 Tropicana: Paradise Found.

Figure 894.2 Gambling is for fools.

Utah's National Parks

http://sci.dixie.edu/NationalParks/nationalpark.html

Few people realize that Utah embraces no less than five national parks, six national monuments, two national recreation areas, and one national historic site. The national parks include the Arches National Park, the Bryce Canyon National Park, the Canyonlands National Park, the Capitol Reef National Park, and the Zion National Park. Among Utah's many national monuments: the Cedar Breaks National Monument, the Dinosaur National Monument, the Hovenweep National Monument, the Natural Bridges National Monument, the Rainbow Bridge National Monument, and the Timpanogos Cave National Monument. Recreation areas include the Flaming Gorge National Recreation Area and the Glen Canyon National Recreation Area. And the state's one historic site is the Golden Spike National Historic Site, where the continent was linked by rail for the first time.

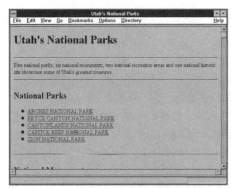

Figure 895.1 Utah's National Parks.

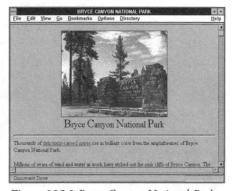

Figure 895.2 Bryce Canyon National Park.

Vacation Home Exchange

http://204.137.145.254/vacation/

Everyone seeks to get the most out of life. Why not get the most out of your second home? Is your second home vacant for part of the year? Would you like to vacation in other parts of the world and stay for free? "Vacation Home Exchange" (VHE) provides this service and does all the work for you. "VHE" coordinates the exchange of vacant time in your second home for an equal amount of vacant time in some other member's vacation home. And you can use your vacation "time credit" whenever it is convenient for you. "VHE" assumes the responsibility of coordinating the use of your property. Just request a time period and location, and they will do the rest.

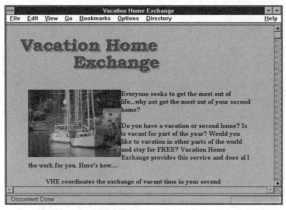

Figure 896 *Vacation home exchange.*

The Virtual Tourist: United States

http://wings.buffalo.edu/world/usa.html

The "Virtual Tourist" offers the ultimate in Web surfing for the tourist planning expeditions near or far. Start with the sequence of maps. Click on the state you want to visit, then the county or city, and then on one of the many lists of options that include information on everything from hotels to bus schedules, from attractions to flight schedules. This site is your access point for dude ranches in Wyoming, ski resorts in Vermont, beaches in southern California, gambling dens in Vegas, sailing off the coast of Texas, rafting on the upper Mississippi, historical sites in Ohio, and museums in New York and Chicago. You'll find it all here—everything. Surf to what you need.

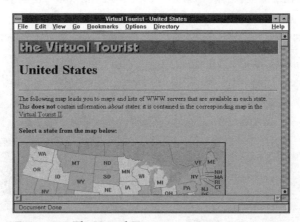

Figure 897 *The Virtual Tourist.*

Vacation Internationale

http://accessone.com/~vi/

Enter the awesome world of Vacation Internationale, the leaders in the timeshare vacation business since 1974. Their resorts in the mainland U.S. and Canada include the Clock Tower (Whistler, British Columbia), the Embarcadero (Newport, Oregon), the Elkhorn (Sun Valley, Idaho), the Kingsbury of Tahoe (Stateline, Nevada), the Marina Inn (Oceanside, California), the Oasis (Palm Springs, California), the Pines at Sunriver (Bend, Oregon), the Point Brown Resort (Ocean Shores, Washington), and a great place at Steamboat Springs, Colorado. The company also has no less than ten resorts in Hawaii and two in Mexico. Via Vacation Internationale, more than 31,000 satisfied owners enjoy these splendid resorts annually. To find out about joining them, access Vacation Internationale's beautiful Web site.

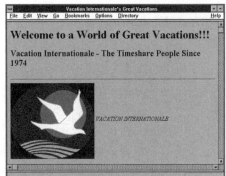

Figure 898.1 Vacation Internationale.

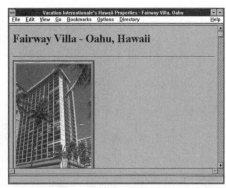

Figure 898.2 Just one of the many resorts.

Westin Hotel Listings and Reservations

http://www.westin.com/listings/listings.html

This Web travel guide gives you a comprehensive listing of all the services and amenities available at every Westin Hotel and Resort worldwide. At this site, you'll find information on everything from room accommodations to business services, tennis courts to children's activities. And soon, you'll have access to even more details, such as golf-course layouts and handicaps, conference-room floor plans, and even suggestions from Westin and other guests for dining and shopping. Be sure to check out the special offers for Westin hotels in the United States, Brazil, Canada, China, Germany, Guatemala, and Japan. You can even make reservations right online. And you can take virtual tours of several Westin hotels around the globe.

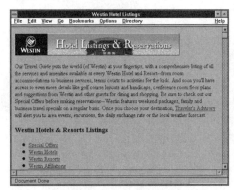

Figure 899.1 Westin Hotels listings and reservations.

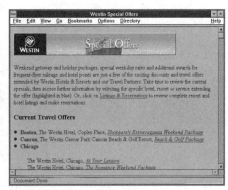

Figure 899.2 Special offers.

TRAVEL

Yosemite National Park

http://www.compugraph.com/yosemite/index.html

This is a site in development; but I include it because, when it releases on Christmas Day 1995, it will be one of the most beautiful Web sites ever developed. Believe me. I know what I'm talking about. I have seen betas for a number of the site's screens. This site will delight you with absolutely gorgeous depictions of Half Dome, El Capitan, Yosemite Falls, Bridalveil Falls, and Glacier Point. You'll find splendid park maps, graphical depictions of Yosemite Village services, campground reservations information, suggested travel routes, and an extensive calendar of events. You'll also find information on photographic safaris, Yosemite tours, river rafting, bicycle rentals, hiking, and climbing. Have yourself a merry little Christmas at the Yosemite National Park Web site.

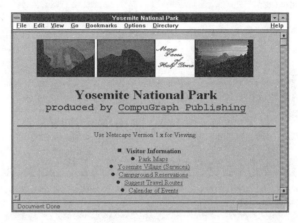

Figure 900 Yosemite National Park: a beauty.

More Travel

As you surf the Web, you may find that one or more of the site addresses listed in this book have changed. In such cases, connect to Jamsa Press at http://www.jamsa.com and click on the icon that corresponds to the *1001 Really Cool Web Sites* book. Jamsa Press will list replacement addresses (when possible) for sites that have moved. In addition, you can also use the following site list as you search for information on travel:

Chesapeake Virginia's home page.	http://hampton.roads.net/nhr/chesapeake/
Hampton Virginia	http://hampton.roads.net/nhr/hampton/
The Norfolk Virginia home page.	http://hampton.roads.net/nhr/norfolk/
City of Portsmouth	http://hampton.roads.net/nhr/portsmouth/
City of Virginia Beach Information Guide	http://hampton.roads.net/nhr/vabeach/
Montclair Home Page	http://haven.ios.com/~armstron/montclair.html
STATE OF HAWAII	http://hinc.hinc.hawaii.gov/soh_home.html
Kuwait Sensitive Map	http://hsccwww.kuniv.edu.kw/
Panama	http://lanic.utexas.edu/la/ca/panama/
PARIS GUEST BOOK	http://meteora.ucsd.edu:80/~norman/paris/Guestbook/page330.html

The Alvar Aalto Museum

http://jkl21.jkl.fi/aalto

The Alvar Aalto Museum of Finland specializes in architecture. The museum preserves, researches, and maintains a permanent display related to the work of Alvar Aalto as an architect and designer. The Museum also oversees conservation of many of Aalto's unique buildings, arranges traveling exhibitions, and distributes information principally on topics related to Aalto. The Museum's architectural collection features over 1,000 original models and artifacts designed by Alvar Aalto, an extensive picture archive, and a steadily growing selection of reproductions of Aalto's original drawings. The Alvar Aalto Museum also has an extensive collection of twentieth-century Finnish art. Visit this site for GIFs of many Aalto drawings, as well as images from the Museum's art gallery.

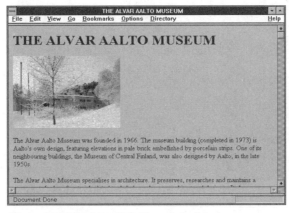

Figure 901 The beautiful Alvar Aalto Museum.

The American Institute of Architects

http://199.170.0.130/about.htm

The American Institute of Architects' purpose is to organize and unite in fellowship the members of the architectural profession of the United States of America. Along with this objective, the Institute seeks to promote the aesthetic, scientific, and practical efficiency of the profession; to further the science and art of planning and building by advancing the standards of architectural education, training, and practice; to facilitate communication between the building industry and the architecture profession to improve the indoor and outdoor environments in which people live; and to make the architecture profession of ever-increasing service to society.

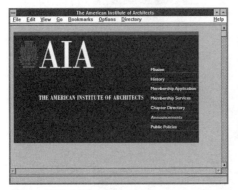

Figure 902.1 The American Institute of Architects.

Figure 902.2 The history of the Institute.

903

Architectural Photographs

http://rampages.onramp.net/~blitz/lreens/ap.html

Louis Reens is one of the leading architectural photographers in the world. Every month at Reens's homepage, you will find new photographs of different architectural subjects from around the world. When I visited, the city in focus was New Orleans. Among the gorgeous photographs on display was a view of Jackson Square in the French Quarter. In that photograph, St. Louis Cathedral was flanked by two almost identical buildings: the Cabildo in the foreground and the Presbitere on the far side. (The Cabildo was, by the way, the site of the signing of the Louisiana Purchase in 1803.) The site also included a beautiful photograph of the interior of St. Louis Cathedral, which was built in 1795.

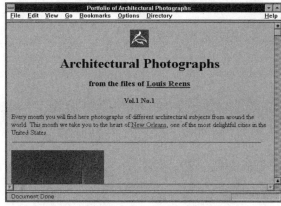

Figure 903 Architectural photos from Lou Reens.

904

@art

http://gertrude.art.uiuc.edu/@art/gallery.html

"@art" is a digital art gallery sponsored by the School of Art and Design of the University of Illinois at Urbana-Champaign. At this site, the exhibits change regularly. When I visited, the exhibit was entitled "Transitions" and featured the work of artists Tom Kovacs, Sarah Krepp, and Bea Nettles. In accepting the invitation to create new pieces of work explicitly for distribution on the Web, each artist created a different structure and made different decisions regarding images, text, and sound. Nevertheless, Kovac's *Journey* and Krepp's *White Noise* both addressed the general complexity of everyday life, as did Nettle's *The Moonsisters* through the mirror of family relationships.

Figure 904 The @art home page.

Ansel Adams: Fiat Lux

http://bookweb.cwis.uci.edu:8042/SlicedExhibit.html

Ansel Adams is world-renowned for his photographs of western forest and mountain landscapes. Nevertheless, in 1966, Adams took on the assignment of creating photograph portraits of all the campuses of the University of California in honor of its 1968 Centennial celebration. At this site, you'll find all the photographs from that project, as well as Melinda Wortz's provocative critique entitled "Ansel Adams and the University of California." You'll also see a great chronology of the life and work of Ansel Adams assembled by James Alinder. The digital exhibition is divided into five major areas: Northern UC Campuses, Southern UC Campuses, Agricultural Centers and Field Stations, Natural Reserve System, and Organized Research Units.

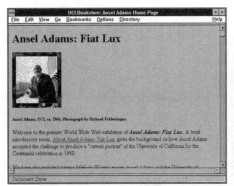

Figure 905.1 The man himself.

Figure 905.2 A tour of the exhibit.

Art Gallery Links

http://escher.cs.ucdavis.edu:1024/art.html

At this site, you'll find an array of links, including some that take you to Le WebLouvre, Access Art, the Uni High ArtSpace, Nathan Wagoner's Digital Studio, the FineArt Forum WWW Resource Directory, Drux Electronic Art, the La Trobe University Art Museum, the Krannert Art Museum, the Enrique Vega homepage, the Digital Image Center, and the Sunsite Mathematical Art Gallery. You'll also find the dynamic art search, a great feature that lets you search for images on the Web by specific artwork name, category, artist, or topic. From Leonardo to Picasso, from Rubens to Alexander Calder, from the Dutch Masters to Andy Warhol, you will find it all at the "Art Gallery Links."

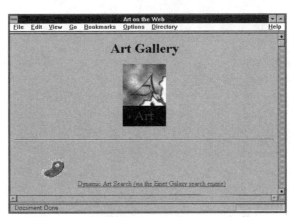

Figure 906 A great online art gallery.

907

Arthole

http://www.mcs.net/~wallach/arthole.html

"Arthole," a digital art gallery, has been curated by Harlan Wallach (wallach@mcs.com) since April of 1994. You will find a great deal of cool stuff at this site. Check out "Travel Documents: Guatemala 1993" (a pinhole/composite/35mm photography exhibit), "Colors" (a web color tone poem), and *Eightball* (a collection of collaborative Web images). Also check out the pinhole photograph exhibits that include "Paris Dream Journal," "New York Postcards," "Roadside Attractions," "Chicago Murder Sites," "Firenze: New Photographs of Florence," and "Destruction of the Temple." Want more? Then consider "The Internet Trans-Global Exquisite Corpse Project," "Emotions on the Streets of Paris," and "Balinese Shadow Puppets." Sound weird? It is.

Figure 907.1 Dig down into the Arthole.

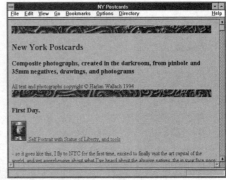

Figure 907.2 New York Postcards.

908

African Art: Aesthetics and Meaning

http://www.lib.virginia.edu/dic/exhib/93.ray.aa/African.html

Often, exhibits of African artifacts focus solely on the artifacts' cultural context or practical use. Only recently have exhibits started to emphasize the formal aesthetic aspects of the objects and the moral and religious ideas they express. The African aesthetic generally has a moral basis, as indicated by the fact that in many African languages the same word means "beautiful" and "good." As such, African art is intended not only to please the eye, but also to uphold moral values and standards. To see what I mean, visit this online exhibit presented by the Bayly Art Museum of the University of Virginia, Charlottesville.

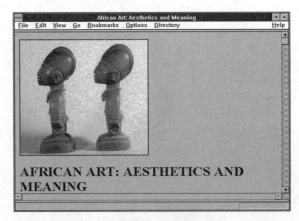

Figure 908 Who are these guys anyway?

Alamkara: 5000 Years of Indian Art

http://www.ncb.gov.sg/nhb/alam

Alamkara, a Sanskrit word meaning ornamentation or decoration, describes an enduring characteristic that has permeated Indian visual art, performance art, and literary art through the ages. The exhibit "Alamkara: 5000 Years of Indian Art" explores this notion of ornamentation in the context of objects that Indians made for use in domestic, religious, and courtly settings. The exhibit groups these objects into sections that focus on various aspects of Indian life, including the cooking, dress and jewelry, past-times, and devotional pursuits. Various sections of the exhibit are entitled "The Ideal of Ornament," "The Enduring Image," "Adorning the Self," "The Heroic Ideal," "Stream of Devotion," "From Pot to Palate," "The Pursuit of Pleasure," and "Mortal Women and Celestial Lovers."

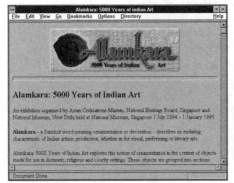 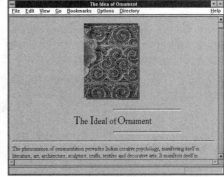

Figure 909.1 5000 years of Indian art. *Figure 909.2 The Ideal of Ornament.*

The Allen Memorial Art Museum

http://www.oberlin.edu/wwwmap/allen_art.html

I can't decide what is best at Oberlin College's Allen Memorial Art Museum: the beautiful collection, which is one of the best small collections in the country, or the marvelous Cass Gilbert building of 1917 that houses it. Gilbert worked very hard to achieve a warm, alluring building that encompassed beauty without monumentality. Gilbert designed the low horizontal scale, deep rhythmic shadows of the terraced loggia (roofed open gallery), and broad overhang of the roof toward this end. Touches of blue in the roof's rafter extensions, rich frieze, and the loggia's vaulting complement the warm buff and red sandstone patterns of the exterior walls, roof, and brickwork of the approach walks. Gilbert worried a bit about the bold color contrasts of the scheme. But he need not have. Check out both the building and the collection at this wonderful site.

Figure 910.1 Cass Gilbert's beautiful building. *Figure 910.2 Images from the museum.*

Alternative Virtual Biennial

http://plaza.interport.net/avb/

The purpose of this exhibit is to present visual art that is based on an alternative new aesthetic that rejects middle-brow pop culture and insists on forms that encompass wit, intelligence, and complexity. The idea here is to stay away from commercially popular visual approaches that cater to a low-culture aesthetic and appeal to a broad audience by tuning in on the lowest common denominator. The "Alternative Virtual Biennial" focuses, therefore, on art by and for the intelligentsia. Yup, there's a real snob-element to this site. Do you make the cut? I'm sure you do.

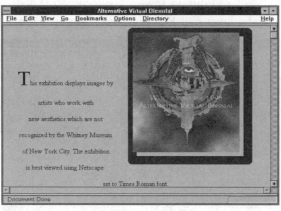

Figure 911 The Alternative Virtual Biennial.

Ancestry: Religion, Death, and Culture

http://gort.ucsd.edu/mw/bdl.html

Belinda Di Leo's paintings in the digital exhibition "Ancestry: Religion, Death, and Culture" document her native Appalachian culture, portraying Di Leo's sense of that place's "spiritual reality." Through the juxtaposition of a variety of images, Di Leo's paintings explore the interrelationship between religion and the inevitability of death as the mountain people of West Virginia perceive it. Titles of the various works include *The Place of Ancestors, Family Center, Room in the House of the Ancestors, The Room Upstairs, Virginian Funeral Fan, Interior Space/Grandparents,* and *Sister and I.* All the pictures are of Di Leo's family farm, where her people have lived and worked since the Revolutionary War. "To me, the land was a sacred place," said Di Leo. From this emotion, her pictures emerge.

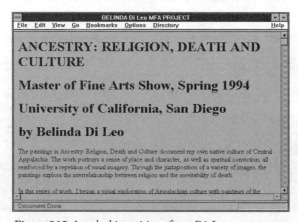

Figure 912 Appalachian visions from Di Leo.

Apparitions

http://www-apparitions.ucsd.edu/

"Apparitions" is both a physical installation at the UC San Diego Art Gallery and a computer-generated virtual environment. "Apparitions" is a collaboration between a group of artists and programmers working under the name *Vital Signs*. Visitors engage in activities that call into question notions of "real" and "virtual" by interacting with physical objects, exploring ideas on the Web, and moving through a virtual environment via large-scale video projections. As a new technology of representation, virtual reality raises a host of questions about how we perceive ourselves and our world, as well as how others perceive us. It is these questions that "Apparitions" is meant to explore.

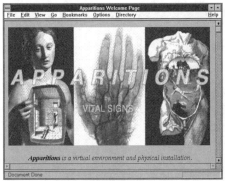
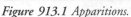

Figure 913.1 Apparitions.

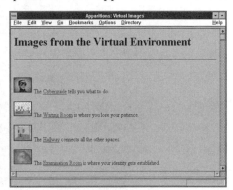

Figure 913.2 Images from the virtual environment.

ArtAIDS Link

http://artaids.dcs.qmw.ac.uk:8001/entrance/

"ArtAIDS Link" is a collaborative Internet art-event that invites all digital artists to commemorate and celebrate the fight against AIDS. The ArtAIDS Project facilitates the storage and transfer of computer-based art objects between remote users, encouraging them to collaborate in order to create and refine new art objects that increase awareness and raise funds for AIDS research and related activities. The "ArtAIDS Link" started December 1, 1994, on World AIDS Day, with specially commissioned images by twenty internationally known artists. Each piece of art served as a starting point intended to inspire other artists to respond, add, or incorporate elements into their own work in order to create an infinite chain of images that continues to this day.

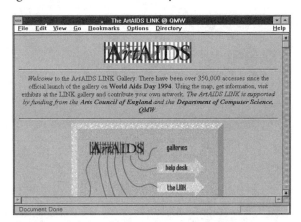

Figure 914 The ArtAIDS Project.

915

Art Crimes: The Writing on the Wall

http://www.gatech.edu/graf/index/Index.Art_Crimes.html

If you have ever read and enjoyed Norman Mailer's *The Faith of Graffiti*, you will want to roam through this large gallery of graffiti from around the world. Separate links let you access graffiti collections that originate in more than 30 different cities, from Prague to Fresno. The self-proclaimed goal of the site is to "help preserve and document the constantly disappearing works of the graffiti-art movement, and to help spread the word that graffiti writers are not gang members. The art they create can't hurt you, and they are not violent. So stop shooting them!" A reasonable request, it seems. One nice plus is that there seems to be no place at this site for "hate graffiti," such as swastikas.

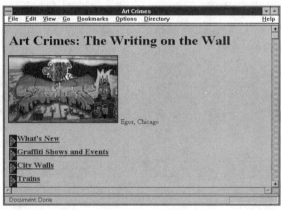

Figure 915 Graffiti heaven.

916

Art & Design at California Polytechnic

http://louise.libart.calpoly.edu/index.html

This site is the homepage for the Art and Design Department at the California Polytechnic State University at San Luis Obispo. What makes this site interesting is that in addition to details about the department and its programs (including details on both their graphic design and photography concentration programs), you'll also find a wonderful gallery of images from the University's impressive collection and a large array of homepages that feature the works of students and faculty. As a bonus, you can download almost all of the remarkably beautiful images. View thumbnails on the various homepages or in the gallery. Then, simply click on the images you'd like to download.

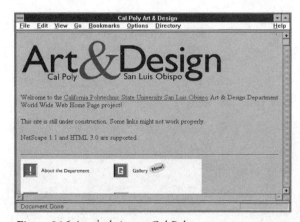

Figure 916 Art & design at Cal Poly.

Artix: The Web Site for Galleries

http://www.artix.com/biz/artix

"Artix: The Web Site for Galleries" provides links to the homepages for a host of New York City's absolutely finest art galleries. Be sure to have your American Express card handy when you check into the elegant homepages of such art impresarios as Paoli Baldacci, Sandra Gering, Nancy Hoffman, Luhring Augustine, Marlborogh Dealers, James McCoy, Schmidt Bingham, Allan Stone, and Thea Westreich. Along with today's greatest working artists, you'll also find works by Picasso, Dali, John Singer Sargent, James Whistler, Alexander Calder, Max Hoffman, Jasper Johns, Edward Hopper, and many other noted artists of the past. To browse is free; to buy is prohibitive; to sin is human.

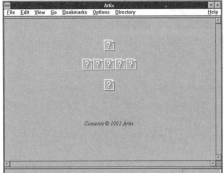

Figure 917.1 Artix.

Figure 917.2 Your list of options.

ArtsUSA

http://www.artsusa.org/

This site is the homepage for the American Council for the Arts. Founded in 1960, the American Council for the Arts conducts programs that promote public policies that advance and document the contributions of the arts and individual artists to American life. The Council is the only national organization that works to ensure that both public and private sectors support *all* the arts. The Council provides leadership in promoting quality arts education and plays an active role in the fight to maintain the National Endowment for the Arts and the Corporation for Public Broadcasting. To find out more, visit this site.

Figure 918 The ArtsUSA home page.

VISUAL ARTS & ARCHITECTURE

919

ArtsWire

http://www.tmn.com/Oh/Artswire/www/awfront.html

Although the New York Foundation for the Arts maintains this site, "ArtsWire" provides information of interest to artists and art organizations nationwide. The main emphasis of "ArtsWire" seems to be grants: what art grants are available, exactly who is qualified to receive the grants, and how to apply. For this function alone, "ArtsWire" is easily labeled indispensable. But there is more. Among the features of "ArtsWire" is an extremely useful weekly summary of news in the arts entitled *The Current*. This digital news digest often focuses on government threats to the budgets of profoundly important arts institutions, including the dire threat to the National Council on the Arts. Come to "ArtsWire" for particularly useful information on several fronts.

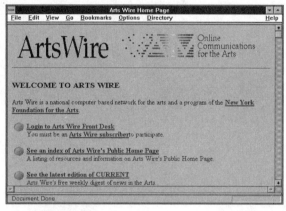

Figure 919 ArtsWire.

920

The ArtVark Gallery

http://www.fwi.uva.nl/~boncz/artvark/

"The ArtVark Gallery" is an interactive, digital gallery-space that features not only paintings, drawings, objects, photographs, and computer images, but also viewers' reactions to them. So when you stop in, don't just look at the works of art; read the comments on them as well. And then leave your own comments—either about the works of art themselves or about what others have said. That way, each piece becomes an ongoing work-of-art kept alive by, and evolving in meaning with, the various reactions of those who view it. The art is always interesting, as is the banter and occasional argument. All in all, "ArtVark" is a thoroughly engaging slice of cyberspace.

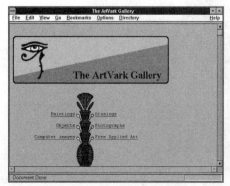 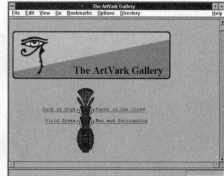

Figure 920.1 The ArtVark Gallery.   *Figure 920.2 ArtVark paintings.*

Asian Arts

http://www.webart.com/asianart/index.html

"Asian Arts" comprises a great online forum for the study and exhibition of the arts of Asia. At this site, you'll find links to digital exhibitions such as *Lao Textiles Revisited* (sponsored by the Fashion Institute of Technology), *Mongolia: The Legacy of Khan* (sponsored by the Asian Art Museum), *Heaven's Embroidered Cloths: One Thousand Years of Chinese Textiles* (sponsored by the Hong Kong Museum of Art), *Images of Faith* (sponsored by John Eskenazi, Ltd., London), and *Early Tibetan Mandalas* (sponsored by The Rossi Collection, London). You'll also find links to interesting articles and references on Asian arts, including Terese Tse Bartholomew's "Introduction to the Art of Mongolia" and a fascinating account of Tibetan miniature ritual paintings.

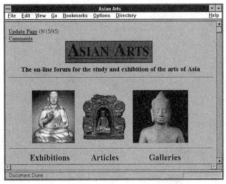

Figure 921.1 Asian Arts.

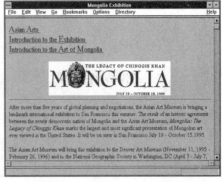

Figure 921.2 Mongolian treasures.

The Michael C. Carlos Museum of Art, Emory University

http://www.cc.emory.edu/CARLOS/carlos.html

The permanent collection of Emory University's Michael C. Carlos Museum includes more than 15,000 objects and spans nearly 9,000 years—from the prehistoric cultures of seventh millennium B.C. to the 20th century. Now, via this wonderful Web site, you can take a digital tour through the museum's 45,000-square-foot building designed by internationally renowned architect Michael Graves. You may explore each floor and click on rooms or galleries that interest you. You can also go behind the scenes to discover the people who work hard to catalog and care for these priceless art objects, design the exhibitions, and do the vast array of tasks to support the museum's operation.

Figure 922 Art at Emory University.

Christus Rex et Redemptor Mundi

http://www.Christusrex.org/

What's the matter? Can't translate it? Okay, I'll translate it for you: *Christ King and Redemptor of the World.* And that's the name of this site devoted to various aspects of Roman Catholic theology. I include "Christus Rex" in this book's "Visual Arts" section because the site contains gorgeous GIFs of some of the greatest works of art ever created, including the collections of the Vatican living quarters and study chambers, the many paintings that make up Michaelangelo's Sistine Chapel, Raphael's *Stanze* and *Loggia*, the art of the Vatican museums (596 images), art associated with the Marian Movement, and more. The site also contains a photo documentary entitled "The Splendors of Christendom" that documents the greatest pieces of art in various Catholic churches around the world.

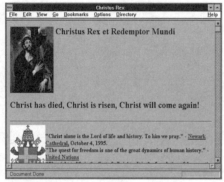

Figure 923.1 Christus Rex.

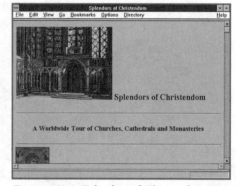

Figure 923.2 Splendors of Christendom.

Dia Center for the Arts

http://www.diacenter.org/

Dia Center for the Arts is a multi-disciplinary, contemporary-arts organization. The name *Dia*, taken from the Greek word meaning "through," was chosen as the name of the center to suggest its role as the conduit or means for realizing extraordinary projects. At this site, you'll find several Dia projects designed specifically for the Web. For the exhibit entitled "Most Wanted Paintings," several artists interpreted market-research surveys about aesthetic preferences and tastes in painting and then created works to match those preferences. You'll also find "Fantastic Players," a collaboration of artist Tony Oursler, writer/performer Constance DeJong, and musician/composer Stephen Vitiello.

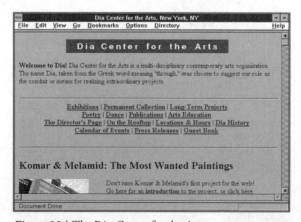

Figure 924 The Dia Center for the Arts.

VISUAL ARTS & ARCHITECTURE

Digital Image Center

http://www.lib.virginia.edu/dic/

The Digital Image Center currently makes available what it calls "a limited collection" of about 400 images of Renaissance and Baroque architecture, all of them free from copyright restrictions. But the Center is looking to do more, much more, in the very near future. The Digital Image Center is a fairly new program of the University of Virginia Library. Its charter is to create, collect, and provide access to digital images to support teaching and research in the humanities. The Center is undertaking a variety of projects, such as producing Internet-accessible, digital-image collections to support specific courses at the University of Virginia and elsewhere, making electronic exhibitions available on the University's Gopher and Web servers, and so on.

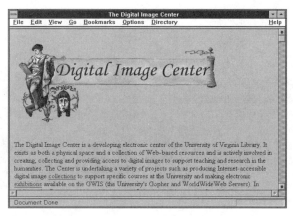

Figure 925 The Digital Image Center.

Digital Photography '94

http://www.bradley.edu/exhibit/index.html

The world of photography has expanded beyond the realm of the darkroom and into the arena of pixels and digital algorithms. Sponsored by the Peoria (Illinois) Art Guild and Bradley University, this competitive exhibit sought entries from photographers across the United States involved in digital (i.e., computer) photography. Digital photographers begin their work with the lens-imaging camera and complete each piece on a computer screen. The various results are fascinating, to say the least, combining traditional and modern technologies to create works that are new in more ways than one.

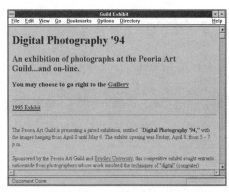

Figure 926.1 Photography from Peoria.

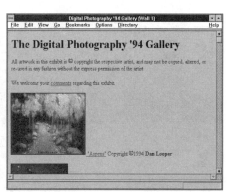

Figure 926.2 Step into the gallery.

The Age of Enlightenment in the Paintings of France's National Museums

http://dmf.culture.fr/files/imaginary_exhibition.html

The Age of Enlightenment can be situated roughly between the death of Louis XIV in 1715 and the coup of the 18th Brumaire (November 9, 1799), when the future emperor Napoleon Bonaparte took power. The Age may be divided into several stages: first, the Regency (1715-1723); then, the reigns of Louis XV (1723-1774) and Louis XVI (1774-1791); and, finally, the French Revolution (1789-1799). In this digital exhibition, these various stages are documented through the arts and artists of the era, including Eteine Allegrain, Christoph Gluck, Marie Leszczynska, Nicolas Bertin, Joseph Bidauld, Charles Antoine Coypel, Louis David, Gabriel Francois Doyen, and Francois Eisen.

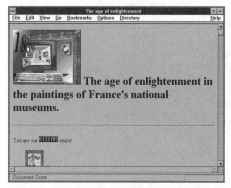

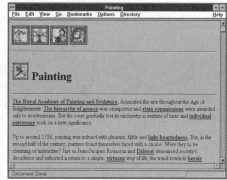

Figure 927.1 The Age of Enlightenment home page.

Figure 927.2 Paintings.

The FineArt Forum Gallery

http://www.msstate.edu/Fineart_Online/gallery.html

The "FineArt Forum Gallery" is a place both to view wonderful contemporary works of visual art and to exhibit your own work. (Actually, you can participate in the "FineArt Forum Gallery" in three ways: you can trade reciprocal links with "FineArt Gallery" to an existing online gallery you have developed. Or, you can propose an exhibition that the "FineArt Forum Gallery" will then create (if the curator likes your idea, of course). Or, you can submit your own individual works to the "Open Gallery," which comprises one of the pages in the "FineArt Forum Gallery" document. Current shows include the artists Wendy Mills, Stelarc, Joseph DeLappe, Helaman Ferguson, Celeste Bignac, and Paul Brown.

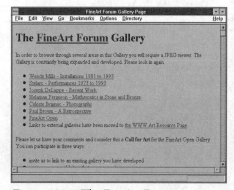

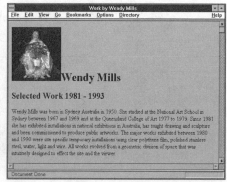

Figure 928.1 The FineArt Forum.

Figure 928.2 The art of Wendy Mills.

Mattison FitzGerald Art Exhibition

http://www.cc.swarthmore.edu/~sjohnson/mattison/

Can you feel it rumbling? From the heart of Silicon Valley comes a dynamic synergy (combination) of art and technology: a synergy that quakes and resonates as though it were a prelude to the next millennium. The disturbance in the atmosphere is painter Mattison FitzGerald opening his digital bicoastal exhibition, which comprises the first "real-time" (as he calls it) fine-art, Internet connection between San Jose and New York City. The connection links Mattison's San Jose gallery/studio with the Carib Art Gallery in New York's Soho. And you're in the middle, on the Internet. Choose one of two versions of the exhibition: a Netscape version and (yes, you guessed it) a non-Netscape version. And tell Mattison (mattart@netcom.com) what you think of the show.

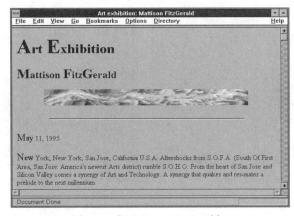

Figure 929 The art of Mattison FitzGerald.

Fuse

http://www.worldserver.pipe.com/fuse94/fuse94.html

Launched in 1991, *Fuse* is an interactive magazine that sets out to challenge our assumptions about typographic and visual language in an age of ever-changing communications technology and media. Each issue of *Fuse* provides four experimental typeface fonts (each the work of leading international designers) and several downloadable poster images that show the typefaces in witty, creative applications. (Be sure to download the cool sign that reads, "Due to budget cuts, the light at the end of the tunnel will be turned off immediately.") By the way, *Fuse's* editors are the good people at Fontworks, Ltd. in the United Kingdom.

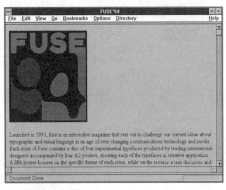

Figure 930.1 Fuse home page.

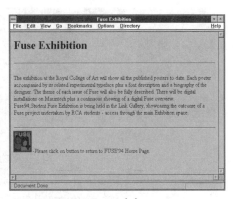

Figure 930.2 A Fuse exhibit.

The Getty Art History Information Program

http://www.ahip.getty.edu/ahip/home.html

The Getty Art History Information Program (AHIP) works to enrich the content of the computer networks of the future by encouraging those who wish to preserve cultural heritage to collaborate in building a cultural information infrastructure. While glad that technical barriers to global connectivity are disappearing, AHIP points out correctly that electronic links do not solve the problem of content. How can we gather, digitize, store, process, and distribute massive bodies of information from dissimilar sources? This is the key problem that AHIP strives to address through art history resources.

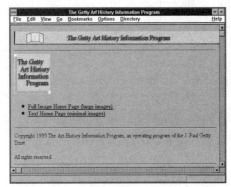

Figure 931.1 Getty Art History.

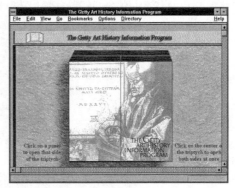

Figure 931.2 A few images.

The High Museum of Art

http://isotropic.com/highmuse/highhome.html

Located in Atlanta, Georgia, the High Museum of Art holds a permanent collection of more than 10,000 objects, including a significant collection of nineteenth-century American paintings and works by major contemporary artists. The American collection includes paintings, sculptures, and drawings from the West Foundation Collection, which is on extended loan. The Museum's critically acclaimed collection of decorative arts includes the Virginia Carroll Crawford Collection of American Decorative Arts, which comprehensively documents styles from 1825 through the early twentieth century, and the Francis and Emory Cocke Collection of English Ceramics. To top it off, you'll also find a significant collection of European paintings and sculpture from the fourteenth through the eighteenth centuries.

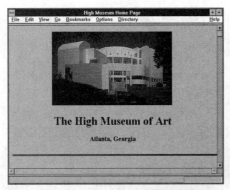

Figure 932.1 The High Museum of Art.

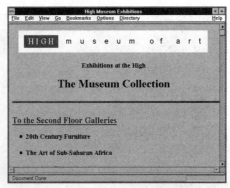

Figure 932.2 The permanent collection.

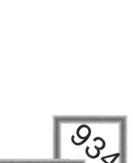

Huntsville Museum of Art

http://www.hsv.tis.net/hma/

The first time I ever heard of Huntsville, Alabama was when I was a kid in the mid 1960s. My Dad was part of a business group awarded a lucrative contract from NASA to build tracking stations at various points around the globe. The tracking stations were a part of Project Apollo. NASA strategically postioned each station to enable constant radio-and-tracking contact with Apollo flights as the earth turned. I remember they built one of the stations in the heart of the Australian outback, and several others at a number of exotic outposts. And they built one at Huntsville, which my father described at the time as a rather lonely spot. Now Huntsville thrives and sports one of the finest small art museums in the country: one that is about to move to a brand new, greatly enlarged building.

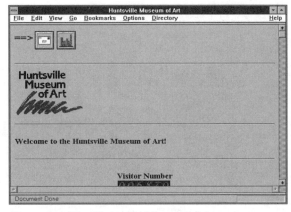

Figure 933 *The Huntsville Museum of Art.*

HypArt

http://rzsun01.rrz.uni-hamburg.de/cgi-bin/HypArt.sh

This site has an interesting concept. "HypArt" is intended to be the artistic equivalent of hypertext. Here's the concept: several people collaborate to create a single picture. The image is divided into squares and each artist does his or her thing on each individual square. But, since the aim is to get a single congruent picture as a result, the parts are not created simultaneously but rather chronologically. Each square-making artist views and reacts to the other parts of the picture created by those who have gone before him. It's easy to take part. Just select an image in progress and jump in.

Figure 934 *The HypArt Project.*

IAMfree

http://www.artnet.org/iamfree/IAMFREE/html/mappg.html

"IAMfree" is a gallery embarking on an ever-changing series of exhibits in modern art, "bereft of the pitfalls and commercialization that is currently stifling art." The Webmaster further informs us that "the key to 'IAMfree' is the exhibition of art that is complete. We offer only large picture files that are rich in content and size . . . No excerpts, no tasters, no thumbnails, no way baby . . . Bounce around; don't be daunted by download times; we think it is worth the wait. Whether you browse, surf, look or listen, we hope you keep an open mind and enjoy the future presented at this site. Though you have come this far, you still have a ways to go." Capice? We are talking *cool*. Let your instincts (not your conscience) be your guide.

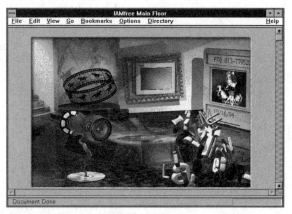

Figure 935 A wild image.

Architecture Image Library

http://mirror.syr.edu/soaimage.html

This site has what must be the most extensive collection of architectural images anywhere on the planet. You'll find images of Renaissance and Baroque architecture, contemporary and classical French architecture, contemporary architecture in Hong Kong, Greek architecture, contemporary architecture in Melbourne (Australia), and more. You'll also see collections of images from the works of Louis Sullivan, Frank Lloyd Wright, Stanford White, I.M. Pei, and many other architectural greats. Also, the site includes text files of architectural criticism by the likes of Lewis Mumford and Brendan Gill, each of whom has taken turns writing the "Skylines" column for *The New Yorker*.

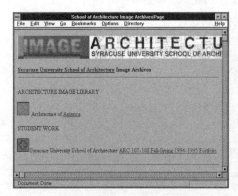

Figure 936.1 Architecture Image Library.

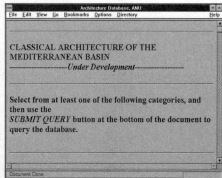

Figure 936.2 Classical Mediterranean.

interARTisrael

http://www.macom.co.il/interart/

"interARTisrael" is the first virtual gallery in Israel. In fact, it is the first in the entire Middle East. "Our main purpose," writes the Webmaster, "is to bridge the gap between our area and the West, and introduce the work of local artists to professionals such as curators, collectors, and galleries, as well as art lovers in general throughout the world. Through the Internet we wish to bring these artists closer to the international art community, and hopefully foster the recognition they deserve." "interARTisrael" is constantly changing, constantly innovating. New Israeli (and Palestinian) artists are added regularly, and the pages are adding up. But they are all so excellent.

Figure 937.1 interARTisrael home page.

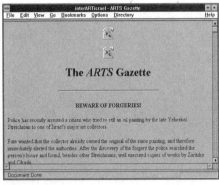

Figure 937.2 One of your options.

Los Angeles County Museum of Art

http://www.lacma.org/

The Los Angeles County Museum of Art is the largest art museum west of the Mississippi River. Within its more than 200,000 square feet of exhibition space, the Museum presents an international collection of art that dates from prehistory to the present day. This impressive display of human creativity offers the possibility of discovery to viewers of all ages, tastes, and backgrounds. The collection consists of more than a quarter of a million objects, including Greek and Roman art, European paintings, sculpture, and decorative arts from the Middle Ages through the twentieth century. Also, the collection includes American paintings, sculpture, and decorative arts from colonial times to the present. Use this impressive Web site to get more details.

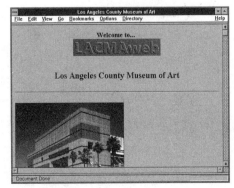

Figure 938.1 Los Angeles County Museum of Art.

Figure 938.2 Alexander Calder's "Hello Girls."

Leonardo

http://www.leonardo.net/main.html

Actually, Leonardo is only his first name. Yes, the world is on a first-name basis with this greatest of artists. At this site, you will find an enormous collection of images from his varied career, including *The Annunciation* (painted for the convent of San Bartolomeo di Moneoliveto between 1475 and 1478), the uncompleted *Visitation of the Magi*, the unfinished *St. Jerome* from around 1482, *The Virgin of the Rocks*, *The Virgin and Child with St. Anne*, the *Mona Lisa* (1503), *The Last Supper* (1497), *Baptism of Christ* (1470), *The Benois Madonna* (1480), and *Virgin and Child with Vase of Flowers* (1478). You'll also find more than 100 additional images, all of which you can download.

Figure 939.1 *All about Leonardo.*

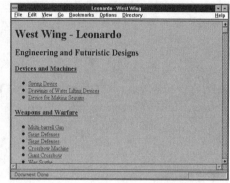

Figure 939.2 *Your entre to a superb collection.*

Montreal Museum of Fine Arts

http://www.interax.net/tcenter/tour/mba.html

Over the past 130 years, the Montreal Museum of Fine Arts has assembled one of North America's finest encyclopedic collections of art, which totals over 25,000 pieces. Founded in 1860 (nine years before the Metropolitan Museum of Art in New York City and ten years before the Boston Museum of Fine Arts), the Montreal Museum of Fine Arts is guided by a commitment to educate the citizens it serves. The Museum is especially strong in the areas of decorative arts, Canadian art, and nineteenth-century prints and drawings. Other areas of unique strength are the Museum's important collections of ancient textiles, English porcelain, and the world's largest collection of Japanese incense boxes.

Figure 940.1 *The Montreal Museum of Fine Arts.*

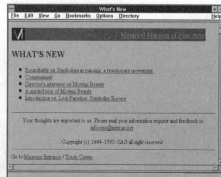

Figure 940.2 *What's new.*

Museum Moderner Kunst Stiftung Ludwig Wien

http://www.mmkslw.or.at/MMKSLW

Liechtenstein's Museum Moderner Kunst Stiftung Ludwig Wien includes two fine exhibition buildings and one outstanding cyberspace annex. At this site, you will find a large and wonderful collection of GIFs representing such great twentieth-century European artists as Giacomo Balla, Andre Derain, Franz Gertsch, Jorg Immendorff, Oskar Kokoschka, Rene Magritte, Joan Miro, Bruce Nauman, Hermann Nitsch, Pino Pascali, Pablo Picasso, and Arnulf Rainer. Choose either German- or English-language text files to see critical analyses of the artworks and capsule biographies of the artists. You may also download many of the site's full-color images.

Figure 941 Immendorff's portrait of the museum interior.

National Museum of American Art

http://www.nmaa.si.edu/

At this site, you can view the work of many wonderful artists: Frederick Remington, Thomas Cole, Asher Brown Durrand, John Singleton Copley, and old Gilbert Stuart, who was born right up the road from where I live. Thomas Cole was perhaps the greatest of the Hudson River School painters. Several of his works hang in the National Museum of American Art, the Metropolitan, and the White House. Currently, I am unsuccessfully trying to purchase and restore (and thus save from the wrecking ball) Thomas Cole's former home in the Catskill Mountains. Can I buy it and prop it up before the coming winter? Agh! That is the question. For you see, the house is on the verge of collapse already. It will probably be replaced by a mini-mart.

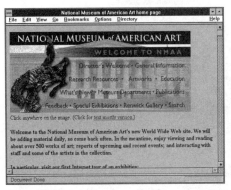 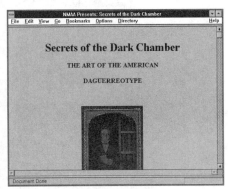

Figure 942.1 A Remington sculpture greeting.   *Figure 942.2 The American daguerreotype.*

Net in Arcadia

http://www.parnasse.com/net.in.arcadia.html

The virtual museum of the school of Contemporary Classicism, "Net in Arcadia" exhibits works by Alfred Russell, Andre Descharnes, their students, and their close circle (including their daughter, Elsie Russell). These like-minded artists share a humanistic and atemporal vision unique in the post-war world of Modernist Art. To express the human condition, they explore various aspects of the Western Figurative Tradition. Nicolas Poussin's *Et in Arcadia Ego*, which Alfred Russell copied in the Louvre in 1956, symbolizes this complex vision. Come to this site for images that both emerge from the classical tradition and uniquely reflect modern concerns and themes.

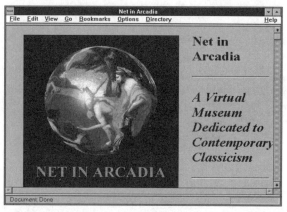

Figure 943 Contemporary classicism home page.

The Ohio State University Art Gallery

http://www.cgrg.ohio-state.edu/mkruse/osu.html

Established in 1968, the Ohio State University's Newark Art Gallery now makes its exhibitions available to the worldwide community via the Web. Their pages are impressive! You can even view an MPEG movie that shows you parts of the gallery's interior. Online exhibitions include "Roy Lichtenstein Pre-Pop 1948-1960" and works by Ralph Rosenfeld, Nathaniel Larrabee, and Halena Cline. And the gallery adds new exhibitions regularly. At this site, you'll find many images you can download, as well as links to over 600 additional arts-related resources, including museums, galleries, exhibitions, publishers, and more.

Figure 944 The Ohio State Art Gallery.

Ornitorrinco in Eden

http://www.uky.edu/Artsource/kac/kac.html

Ornitorrinco in Eden is the first telerobotics art work realized on the Internet. Devised by Eduardo Kac and Ed Bennett, this work of art "bridged the placeless space of the Internet" between physical locations in Seattle, Chicago, and Lexington, Kentucky. The piece consists of three nodes of active participation, as well as multiple nodes of observation worldwide. The active participants in Seattle and Lexington controlled and simultaneously shared the body of the mobile and wireless telerobot Ornitorrinco, which resided in Chicago. Via the Internet, they created the work with Ornitorrinco's limbs and watched it evolve through the robot's eyes. Now you can get a full account of this exercise in art on the Internet, including MPEG films of the event.

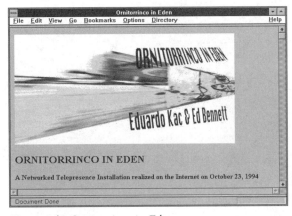

Figure 945 *Ornitorrinco in Eden.*

The OTIS Artchives

http://sunsite.unc.edu/otis/gallery.html

The "OTIS Artchives" sorts images in two ways: medium and content. For example, when you ask the site to sort by a medium (such as paintings), the site provides a list of artists who worked in that medium. When you select an artist, "OTIS Artchives" gives you a list of all the images that it contains by him or her. Medium selections include collages, drawings, paintings, automata, ray-traces, math-art, morphs, photo-manipulations, etchings (want to see mine?), carvings, video, jewelry, body art, animation, and collaborations. Content options include abstracts, nudes, animals, landscapes, political, portraits, techno (robots and cyborgs), flora and fauna, and comics.

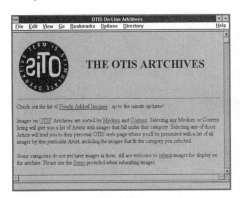

Figure 946.1 The Otis home page.

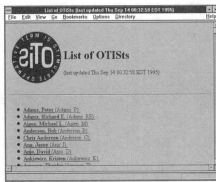

Figure 946.2 Your access point for images.

VISUAL ARTS & ARCHITECTURE

Complete Writings & Pictures of Dante Gabriel Rossetti

http://jefferson.village.virginia.edu/rossetti/rossetti.html

The "Rossetti Archive" is a hypermedia environment for studying the works of the Pre-Raphaelite poet and painter Dante Gabriel Rossetti (1828-1882). The archive is a structured database that holds digitized images of Rossetti's works (poetical manuscripts, early printed texts, drawings, and paintings). The site's materials are marked up for electronic search and include scholarly annotations and notes. The materials are made available with the help and permission of the British Library, the Duke University Library, the Fitzwilliam Museum and Library, the Fogg Museum, Princeton University Library, and the Tate Gallery.

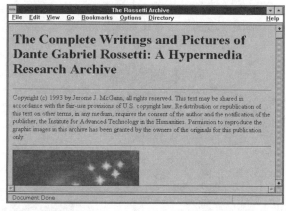

Figure 947 Detail from "The Blessed Damozel."

San Francisco Museum of Modern Art

http://gw2.pacbell.com:1995/

Digital gallery exhibitions include "William de Kooning: The Late Paintings/1980s," "From Matisse to Diebenkorn: Works from the Permanent Collection of Painting and Sculpture," "Enter a New Museum: Recent Gifts and Other Acquisitions of Contemporary Art," "Subjects and Objects: The Chrysler Award for Innovation in Design," "Selections from the Permanent Collection of Architecture and Design," "Paul Klee: Themes and Variations," "The Photographic Condition," and "Picturing Modernity: Photographs from the Permanent Collection." Upcoming exhibitions include "An Everyday Modernism: The Houses of William Wurster," "Andrea Zittel: New Work," "Wild Design: Designs for the Wild," and "Lebbus Woods: The San Francisco Project."

Figure 948.1 A modern logo for a modern museum.

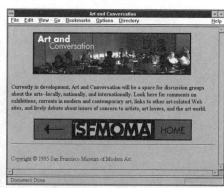

Figure 948.2 Art and Conversation.

Santa Barbara Museum of Art

http://artdirect.com/sbma/

Enter the Santa Barbara Museum of Art. A quick step through the Museum's digital archways of Ludington Court, and you're transported into the classical world, where you can stare into the eyes of a Roman general or admire the grace and form of Greek athletes. A few points and clicks take you to the other side of the world. Now you're in Asia, where you'll find ancient deities captured in stone or wood, and delicately painted silk scrolls that reveal the physical wonders of China and Japan. Turn the corner, and you're surrounded by American history depicted by colorful paintings that reflect development from Revolutionary times to contemporary life. A few more clicks, and you're in 19th century France with such artists as Monet, Rousseau, Dufy, Sisley, Boudin, Chagall, and Fantin LaTour.

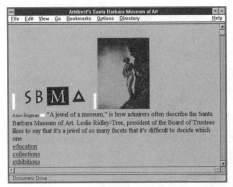 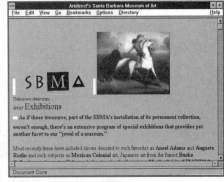

Figure 949.1 Santa Barbara Museum of Art.   *Figure 949.2 A peak into the gallery.*

Sculpture Tour

http://loki.ur.utk.edu/sculpture/sculpt.html

Enjoy a digital edition of the "Sculpture Tour" (a famous walking-tour at the University of Tennessee, Knoxville Gallery of Art), where works on display change annually. Organized by Dennis Peacock with the capable assistance of Monica Thomeczek, Karen Beall, April Franklin, and Kenneth Marshall, the current sculpture tour includes Benson Warren's *In Search of Noah*, Margery Amdur's *All She Ever Wanted*, Brian Rust's *Red Earth Ariel*, William Sapp's *Kingdom of Dog*, and Jonathan Kirk's *Neptune's Horn*. On average, each annual tour includes twenty-six sculptural works. This site also gives you numerous images from the permanent collection of the University of Tennessee, Knoxville, Gallery of Art, including paintings and photographs.

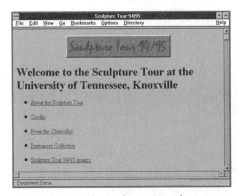 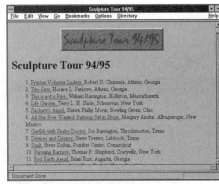

Figure 950.1 The Sculpture Tour home page.   *Figure 950.2 Current works of art.*

The David and Alfred Smart Museum of Art, University of Chicago

http://csmaclab-www.uchicago.edu/SmartMuseum/default.html

Named for the founders and publishers of *Esquire* magazine, The David and Alfred Smart Museum of Art opened in 1974 at the University of Chicago. This jewel of a museum houses a permanent collection that began in the 1890s, the first decade of the University's founding. Now numbering over 7,000 objects, the collection spans five centuries of both Western and Eastern civilizations. The Smart Museum features special exhibitions and educational programming year-round. Take a virtual tour of the Smart Museum's cyberspace galleries. With over 400 images available, it's the next best thing to being there.

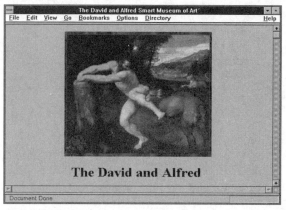

Figure 951 *David Smart being attacked by wild tigers.*

Stuart Collection

http://gort.ucsd.edu/sj/stHome.html

The Stuart Collection of Sculpture at the University of California, San Diego, seeks to enrich the cultural, intellectual, and scholarly life of cybervisitors to its digital space. You will see a 1.5Mb video of Mary Beebe, director of the Stuart Collection, that introduces you to the works on display. You will also find photographs of such notable sculptures as Terry Allen's *Trees*, Michael Asher's *Untitled*, Jackie Ferrara's *Terrace*, Ian Hamilton Finlay's *UNDA*, Richard Fleischner's *La Jolla Project*, Jenny Hozer's *Green Table*, Robert Irwin's *Two Running Violet V Forms*, and more.

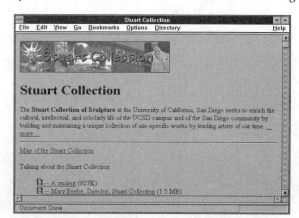

Figure 952 *The Stuart Collection of Sculpture home page.*

Surrealism!

http://pharmdec.wustl.edu/juju/surr/surrealism.html

Surrealism began primarily as a literary movement based on radical ideas that gained momentum in the 1920s. Naturally, where words flow, images soon follow; it is perhaps for the many paintings associated with the movement that Surrealism has received most of its notoriety. At this site, you will find an outstanding collection of links that take you to all sorts of information about Surrealist painters and their work, as well as writers and musicians who helped define the movement. You will take a digital tour of the Dali Museum and read an extensive online reference on Dada and Surrealism, compiled by Julie Cencebaugh and Carl Merchant.

Figure 953 Where things are not always what they seem.

University of California, Riverside, Museum of Photography

http://cmp1.ucr.edu/

This amazing Web space includes photographic art by Edward Beardsley *(Imaginary Places - One)*, Helen Sanematsu *(Greetings from Riverside)*, Stephen Axelrad *(Letter to Pati)*, Mark Alice Durant *(The River and the Bridge: An Inventory of Romantic Gestures)*, Lisa Bloomfield *(Random Readings)*, Nancy Buchanan *(Home: Developing the Whole Picture)*, and Kevin Boyle *(Rolling the Dice)*. This site is wonderful for admirers of art photography. I, myself, am more into photojournalism. I had the privilege of knowing the great *Life* magazine photographer W. Eugene Smith when he was in New York in the 1970s. One of the inventors of the photo-essay form, Smith created the famous *Life* photo-essay on the theme of a country doctor's work. He is also noted for providing a photographic record of the results of industrial poisoning at Minimata, Japan.

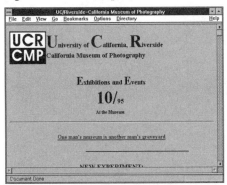 

Figure 954.1 Photography at UC Riverside.   *Figure 954.2 The work of Edward Beardsley.*

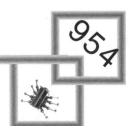

955

Paintings by Jan Vermeer

http://www.ccsf.caltech.edu/~roy/vermeer

The painter Jan Vermeer (1632-1675) created luscious canvases of limited scope: generally women and men in seventeenth-century rooms, but also occasional outdoor, allegory, and religious themes. His work intricately combines light, color, proportion, and scale in ways that enhance the moods and reality of the subjects. At this site, you will find many great Vermeer images in small, medium, and large JPEG formats. View a file of thumbnails. Then, click on those pictures you would like to view in larger formats, or download. You can also click on a database that lets you find the locations of non-virtual Vermeer paintings in museums around the world.

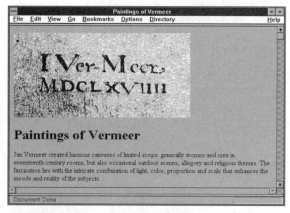

Figure 955 Vermeer, a real Dutch Master.

956

Virtual Ceramics Exhibit

http://www.uky.edu/Artsource/vce/VCEhome.html

Utilizing the Internet as gallery space, this site offers an exhibition of contemporary ceramics. You will find works by such noted ceramic artists as Michael Farnsworth, Sheilah Norris, Betty Crampton, Felix Michaels, Tricia Haris, Paul Cronin, Kelley Mylod, Peter Lentini, Frank Gates, Norman Henry, Michael Dulles, Elizabeth Cummings, Jake Atwater, Judy Farmer, Martin Rusk, James Benton, Violet Grant, Shelley Woodward, Peter Collier, Henry Larabee, Michael Miller, Daphne Halberstam, Martin Green, Paula Sheehan, and Kevin Starr. You'll also find statements by organizers, jurors, and artists, as well as brief resumes of the artists.

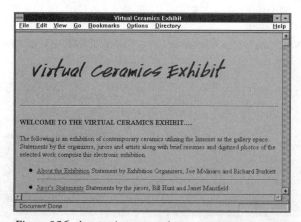

Figure 956 A ceramic cornucopia.

The World's Women Online!

http://www.asu.edu/wwol/

This site is an electronic art network project associated with the United Nations' Fourth World Conference on women, held at Beijing, China in 1995. Using the Internet as a global exhibition format, this site features art from women around the world: from Brazil to Mongolia, from San Diego to Prague, and from the Cape of Good Hope to Hudson's Bay. At this site, you'll see clickable thumbnails of hundreds of art works available for download, plus full biographies for all the artists the show represents. This site also has a video entitled "The World's Women Online!," which consists of images uploaded by women from around the world. The video intermingles these images to create one great cooperative piece of art on a "video wall."

Figure 957.1 The World's Women electronic art project.

Figure 957.2 Artist Muriel Magenta.

WebMuseum, Paris

http://sunsite.unc.edu/louvre/paint/

This "Famous Paintings Exhibition" from the "WebMuseum, Paris" includes paintings from the Gothic Period (1280-1515); the Italian Renaissance (1420-1600); the Northern Renaissance (1500-1615); the Baroque Period (1660-1790); the Age of Revolution and Restoration in France, Germany, and England (1740-1860); the advent of Impressionism (1860-1900); and the twentieth century (with attention to Fauvism, Matisse, Expressionism, artistic emigres, Picasso and the Cubists, the move towards abstraction, Paul Klee, the art of the fantastic, pre-war American painting, abstract expressionism, and pop art). From Van Dyke to Warhol, from Leonardo to Picasso, from Van Gogh to Klee—you will find it all at this site.

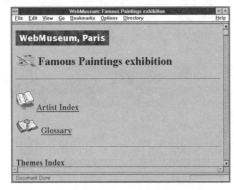

Figure 958.1 WebMuseum, Paris.

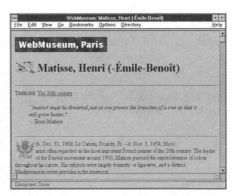

Figure 958.2 Matisse, master of color.

959

Frank Lloyd Wright in Wisconsin

http://flw.badgernet.com:2080/

Frank Lloyd Wright (1869-1959) was the leading exponent of "organic" architecture, advocating a close relationship between building, landscape, and the nature of the materials used. The "prairie" style houses he built in Wisconsin, with their long, low, horizontal lines and visual merging of an unbroken interior with the surrounding landscape, revolutionized American domestic architecture in the first decade of the twentieth century. His public spaces and office buildings were shaped by a similar philosophy. You will see not only family dwellings, but also the Johnson Wax Administration building, the Annunciation Greek Orthodox Church, and the A.D. German Warehouse.

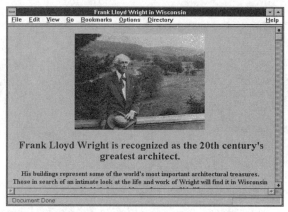

Figure 959 Wright photographed in Wisconsin.

960

Yale University Art Gallery

http://www.cis.yale.edu/yups/yuag/lobby.html

I am here to tell you that the Yale University Art Gallery is probably one of the most ugly physical structures on the East Coast, and is certainly the ugliest structure on the Yale campus. That being said, the place houses one of the finest small collections in the country and hosts a fascinating series of special exhibitions. For example, from October 20, 1995 through January 7, 1996, the gallery will present an exhibit devoted entirely to the Futurist art of the Italian painter Gino Severini (1883-1966). Embracing new technologies and their impact on everyday life, Severini found his subjects in cities, on trains, around war machinery, and as dancers with frenetic energy. At the Yale show, a selection of 35 oil paintings details his achievement. To find out more about this exhibition and other shows, visit this site.

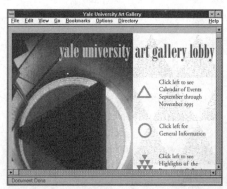

Figure 960.1 Yale University Art Gallery.

Figure 960.2 Calendar of events.

SEE

More Visual Arts & Architecture

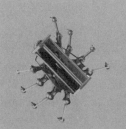

As you surf the Web, you may find that one or more of the site addresses listed in this book have changed. In such cases, connect to Jamsa Press at http://www.jamsa.com and click on the icon that corresponds to the *1001 Really Cool Web Sites* book. Jamsa Press will list replacement addresses (when possible) for sites that have moved. In addition, you can also use the following site list as you search for information on art and architecture:

Art:Exhibits	http://akebono.stanford.edu/yahoo/Art/Exhibits/
Art on the web	http://altair.stmarys-ca.edu:70/1s/art
Drama	http://english-server.hss.cmu.edu/Drama.html
just outside the place	http://gertrude.art.uiuc.edu/ludgate/the/place.html
BELINDA Di Leo	http://gort.ucsd.edu/mw/bdl.html
The Heard Museum	http://hanksville.phast.umass.edu/defs/independent/Heard/Heard.html
David Voth's Home Page	http://haven.uniserve.com/~dvoth
Artists and Works	http://lydia.bradley.edu/exhibit/artists.html
PARIS.ARCHIVE.LOUVRE	http://meteora.ucsd.edu:80/~norman/paris/Musees/Louvre/Treasures/gifs
ANU Art History	http://rubens.anu.edu.au/index.html

961

Your Absolutely First VRML Stop

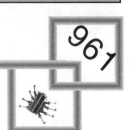

http://www.artificia.com/html/vrml.htm

VRML (Virtual Reality Modeling Language) is a new standard on the Web that lets you model and navigate within a 3-D environment that mimics the real world and, consequently, is as intuitive an exercise as walking down the street or up a flight of stairs. However, before you can experience VRML firsthand, you need a VRML-compatible extension for your browser. Fortunately, this site provides such browsers. Here, you can download WebSpace (for Windows 3.1 and Macintosh), Whirlwind (especially for the PowerMac), Pueblo (for Windows 95), and SDSC Web View (for SGI/Unix). Download one of these browsers before you visit any of the sites that this section of *1001 Really Cool Web Sites* describes.

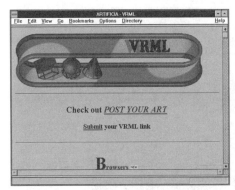

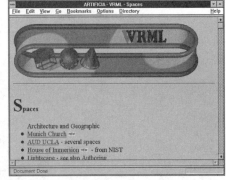

Figure 961.1 A great set of VRML resources.   *Figure 961.2 A fine collection of VRML spaces.*

962

Architecture & Urban Design at UCLA Using VRML

http://www.gsaup.ucla.edu/vrml/

One of the most valuable uses of VRML is in architectural modeling. VRML lets architects and planners create virtual models of buildings and view these models from every angle on a computer screen. At this impressive Web site, you will find astonishingly great VRML images that depict such buildings as the African American Unity Center in Los Angeles, Orchestra Hall in Los Angeles, the inside of the UCLA Tower, the basement of the UCLA School of Public Policy and Research, Scott Lelieur's cool imagined space named Zepher Point, the Equitable Building in downtown Los Angeles, the Gas Building in downtown Los Angeles, and many other engaging structures and spaces.

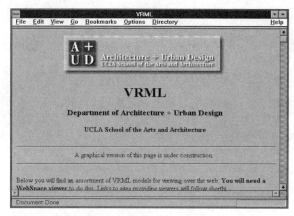

Figure 962 *Architecture and Urban Design home page.*

963

Calendar of VRML Events

http://www.sdsc.edu/SDSC/Partners/vrml/events.html

This calendar is a wonderful tool for the VRML professional. Regularly updated, the site highlights such events as the VRML '95 Symposium, as well as the annual IEEE Visualization Conference, the annual ACM Multimedia Conference, the twice-annual Comdex show, the annual Symposium on User Interface Software and Technology, the annual Cyberspace show, the Workshop on New Paradigms in Information Visualization and Manipulation, Edugraphics, the Compugraphics Convention, the annual International World Wide Web Conference, the Virtual Reality World trade-show and conference, the annual Eurographics Convention, and, of course, the always-cool SIGGRAPH.

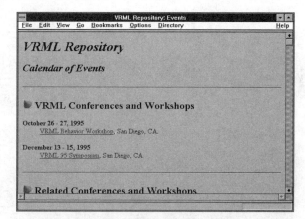

Figure 963 *Calendar of VRML events.*

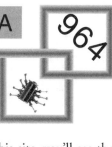

Chemical Examples of VRML

http://www.ch.ic.ac.uk/VRML/

This site offers a splendid collection of VRML images that model chemical compounds. At this site, you'll see the world's first ever VRML model of a molecule, the 3-CRO Protein; a ribbon representation of a protein; a Connoly surface of a protein; and a VRML model of an oxygen/chlorobenzene interaction. You'll also find great writings, including an essay entitled "VRML in Protein Structure Determination." When you visit this site, be sure to try creating your own membranes using the "Interactive VRML Membrane Scene Builder," developed by Alan Robinson and Barry Hardy at the University of Oxford.

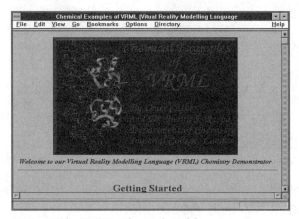

Figure 964.1 VRML Chemical modeling.

Clip Art for VRML

http://vrml.wired.com/vrml.tech/vrml.art

This is the deal. On 90% of the VRML-related Web sites, the same banner logo appears even though unrelated organizations develop and maintain the sites. Why? Because the logo looks reasonably cool, downloads free, and has no usage restrictions. All these various logos and symbols are in the public domain. You need no permission to use them, resell them, or distort them. Although no official VRML logo exists, Kevin Hughes (kevinh@eit.com) offers these pieces as benchmark icons. The various banners and buttons are available in files customized to fit both Mosaic for X and standard Netscape browsers. At the moment, the images are not 3-D, although this is coming soon.

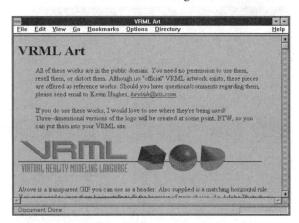

Figure 965 VRML logo clip-art.

VRML & HOT JAVA

966

The Cybernaut Station

http://www.mayavr.com/maya/maya.html

Visit "The Cybernaut Station," a virtual-reality space station that promises to be the ultimate launching point for the whole VR (virtual reality) universe. Maya, a firm that provides Internet services, runs this project. Via the "Cybernaut Station," Maya is moving to the forefront of the commercial use of VRML. Rest assured, the whole VRML community, not to mention the entire Web marketing community, is watching Maya's development with great interest.

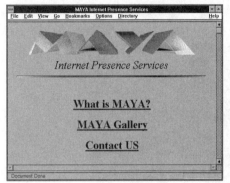

Figure 966.1 Cybernaut Station.

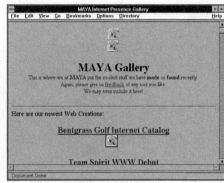

Figure 966.2 The Maya Gallery.

967

Example VRML Applications

http://www.sdsc.edu/SDSC/Partners/vrml/examples.html

At this site, you can experience more than a hundred great examples of VRML use in many different disciplines, including architecture, art, astronomy, computer science, computer engineering, entertainment (i.e., games programming), environmental science (natural systems modeling), history (modeling of historical sites), interactive scene building (such as a virtual maze generator), topography and maps, mathematics, music, physics, and more. Check out the interior of an Italian castle, a Lightscape model of the Jerusalem City Hall, a complete cybertown with numerous streets and shops, a VRML model of a black hole, a VRML-based biodiversity reserve for digital organisms, or the VRML-based Westworld Saloon. You can also wander through a 3-D model of Stonehenge or drive drunk on a digital road. Good luck.

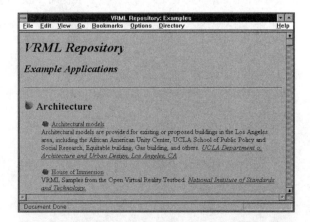

Figure 967 Example VRML applications.

Experimenting with VRML

http://amber.rc.arizona.edu/vrml.html

Marvin Landis created all the great VRML objects, scenes, and converters at this site. Three objects of his, in particular, are worth noting. The first is a Polynesian platform bird feeder containing 1,658 polygons. The second is a three-string mountain dulcimer containing 5,018 polygons. And the third is a Pirogue Cajun canoe containing 4,016 polygons. Landis has also created a great 3-D logo for the University of Arizona that contains 5,060 polygons. The letters in the logo are links to various HTML pages at the University of Arizona. Additionally, Landis has provided a great utility that lets you view a time series dataset with WebSpace, as well as another that translates Lightwave objects into images readable by the popular Open Inventor program. He provides both these programs at this site for you.

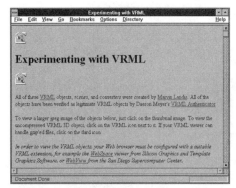 

Figure 968.1 Experimental VRML images.   *Figure 968.2 The artist.*

Fractals in VRML

http://kirk.usafa.af.mil/~baird/vrml

Use WebSpace (which you can download at this site) to view these fractals. The closer you zoom in on the fractal, the more details appear. The site also provides something for those using the WorldView browser. (WorldView cannot yet display fractals, but it can display a small pseudofractal. This pseudofractal is identical to a fractal at a distance; it just has less detail close-up.) You can also view a mountain with 4, 16, 64, or 256 surfaces, and a fractal terrain defined by a mesh of elevation data before and after being converted to a psuedofractal by a C-program, which has equations derived by Mathematica. This is really the cutting-edge of cool.

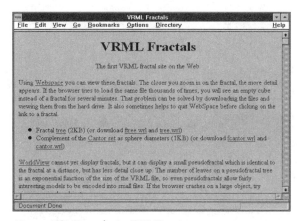

Figure 969 Fractals in VRML.

HotJava

http://java.sun.com

While VRML lets you create navigable 3-D images on the Web, Sun Microsystem's new HotJava programming language takes things a step further—HotJava animates those same static VRML images and enables them to move and act. At this site, you can download the HotJava Developer's Kit and the HotJava browser, which is a dynamic, extensible WWW browser that showcases the capabilities of the HotJava Programming Language. Additionally, Sun provides a comprehensive hyperlinked directory of HotJava resources, releases of the HotJava Developer's Kit for Spark Solaris and Windows 95, a complete source-code release, documentation, and details of HotJava technology licensing. This is the future of the Web, gang. Come taste the HotJava, if you dare.

Figure 970 *Sun's HotJava home page. Take a sip.*

IVL: A Language for Creating and Manipulating VRML Scenes

http://www.ocnus.com/ivl.html

At this site, you can experiment with IVL, a new language that is still in development. After you run through the hypertext tutorial on IVL, and perhaps download and read the valuable postscript paper (84 Kb) on IVL, you may want to goof around at this site and try to make things happen. Just type IVL commands into the box on the page. A linked IVL-language interpreter will translate your commands and the resulting VRML image will appear on your screen. Fun! If you'd care to, grab one of the pre-written IVL scripts, toss it to the interpreter, and see what happens.

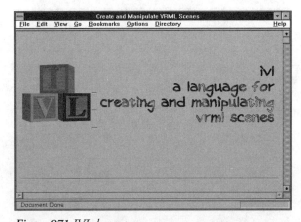

Figure 971 *IVL home page.*

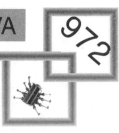

MathMol Library of 3-D Molecular Structures

http://www.nyu.edu/pages/mathmol/library/libray.html

This site contains 3-D structures of many molecules discussed in modern K-12 science textbooks. Of course, to view these images, you must have a VRML viewer, such as WebSpace (which you can download at this site), or a PDB viewer, such as RasMol (also available to download). Current 3-D structures include ice and water molecules, simple carbon compounds, solid-material molecules, DNA molecules, and (my personal favorite) drug molecules. Additionally, you'll find links to advanced molecular databases that employ VRML, including "The IMB Iena Image Library of Biological Molecules" and a cool document entitled "Hyperactive Molecules." Too much HotJava perhaps?

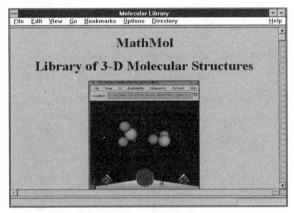

Figure 972 MathMol 3-D srtructures.

Sample VRML Objects

http://coney.gsfc.nasa.gov/Mathews/Objects

If you don't care much about the details of how cool VRML images are created . . . if you don't want to mess with the programming and the math . . . if all you want to do is view some great images, this is the site for you. You'll find images of a cube, a simple house, a park bench, a banana, a glass, a red Camaro, a Volkswagen, a teapot, a WWI biplane, a soccer ball, a Ford Taurus (yuck!), an X-29 Fighter, an F-117 Fighter, the Space Shuttle, the U.S.S. Enterprise, the Galileo Shuttlecraft, a Klingon Battle Cruiser, a Romulan Warbird, an X-Wing Fighter, a Millennium Falcon, and a Star Destroyer. The warplanes and the spacecraft are cool to begin with. They are cooler in 3-D.

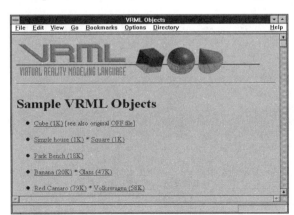

Figure 973 But what is the object of these objects?

VRML Object Supermarket

http://www.dcs.ed.ac.uk/generated/package-links/objects/vrml.html

This page lets you view and download all the WRL format objects stored at the U.K. VR-SIG 3-D Object Archive. (The WRL format is an open, platform-independent file format for 3-D graphics on the Internet.) Available objects include a pear, a small cannon, a colorful deck chair, a gray man made out of cubes, a window frame section, a colorful and decorated box with the lid open, a simple card folder, a pavilion building with a pool, a pencil, the Silicon Graphics logo in e-D (cool), a slot machine, a child's spinning top, two theater-type spot lights, an imaginary monument (to what?), a helicopter, a set of rooms, a circuit board, a toy gun, part of a room with an overhead light, a man made out of VRML spheres, and more. You can choose from more than sixty images.

Figure 974 Everything from cannons to pencils.

Interactive Origami in VRML

http://www.neuro.sfc.keio.ac.jp/~aly/polygon/vrml/ika

Of course, *origami* is the traditional and intricate Japanese art of folding paper into decorative shapes (i.e., not just airplanes). At this site, you can learn to use VRML to fold virtual pieces of 3-D paper into a number of attractive virtual items, including airplanes, houses, birds, ducks, octopi, trees, shrubs, and more. Now why you would possibly want to spend time doing this is an entirely different matter. Nevertheless, the application of VRML is cool and has implications for HotJava interactivity in the near future.

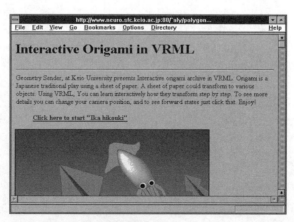

Figure 975 Origami for geeks.

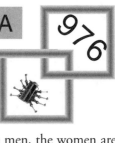

OZ

http://www.oz.is/OZ/Misc/VRML.html

I don't think we're in Kansas anymore, Toto. Nope, we're in Silicon Valley where the men are men, the women are women, and the smog is everywhere. Oz is a leading company (in fact, one of the few pioneering companies) in the area of Web space development using VRML. OZ is the originator of SOFTIMAGE 3-D Extreme and the SOFTIMAGE To VRML Translator, both of which are increasingly popular tools for e-D animators and Web programmers. Oz takes an active interest in VRML standards development. This interest is so active, in fact, that they sponsor a discussion mailing to which you may subscribe (and in which you may participate) for free.

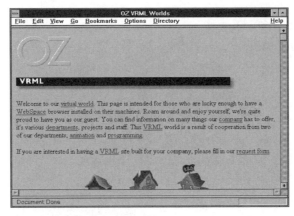

Figure 976 An escape from Kansas.

Paper Software Does VRML

http://www.paperinc.com/vrml.html

Paper Software, Inc., specializes in advanced, object-oriented, user-interface technologies with special attention to 3-D user interfaces and 3-D information spaces. "When VRML came along," the company writes, "we saw our first opportunity to make our research available in consumer form. Our first step was to provide world class VRML viewing, authoring, and multi-user capabilities on Windows, Macintosh and UNIX platforms. Our next step, though, is far more interesting . . ." To find out more about Paper's next step, which involves a host of exciting VRML extensions, visit this interesting Web site.

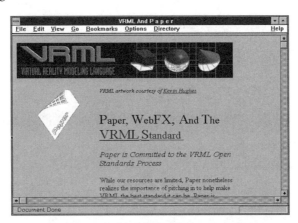

Figure 977 Paper Software's VRML home page.

978

ParaGraph's Home Spaces

http://www.us.paragraph.com/3Dsite/3Dsite.htm

"ParaGraph's Home Spaces" contains scenes created with ParaGraph's Home Space Builder 1.0, a tool for both VRML and MUS formats. This site includes a specially commissioned set of VRML images by Andrei Kryukov. Born in Moscow in 1959, Kryukov graduated from the First Moscow City Children's Art School (1976), the Moscow Art College (1980), and the Surikov Moscow State Art Institute (1987). His works are in private collections and galleries in the United States, Germany, the Netherlands, England, Cyprus, Bulgaria, Norway, Austria, Italy, and Spain. And now they're also on display in cyberspace, where the only price of admission is a VRML browser. Check them out.

Figure 978 ParaGraph's Home Spaces.

979

Programming Tools for VRML

http://vrml.wired.com/vrml.tech/qv.html

This VRML programming library, called QvLib, is a set of C++ routines that can parse VRML files. The output is a *parse tree* that a program can traverse to generate a *view* (or a translation) of a VRML environment. Versions of this library are currently available for IRIX, SunOS4.1x, LINUX, and Windows NT. Oh, stop whining. Macintosh, Windows 95, and Solaris versions are coming soon. I hear you asking: "Are there release notes?" Yes, you'll find release notes. "Where are the release notes?" *At this site*, of course. "Can I download the tool kit for free?" Yes, yes, yes. "What's the catch?" There is no catch!

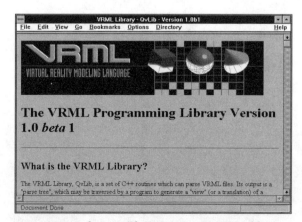

Figure 979 A fantastic [free] C++ programming library.

VRML testbed

http://nemo.ncsl.nist.gov/~sressler/OVRThome.html

I know what you're thinking. I can relate. I guess we've all tested a few beds in our day. But actually, this site has nothing to do with beds my friends, nor with testing anything so far as I can tell. What you'll find here is simply a cool VRML implementation that is worth a virtual stroll. The joint is called "The Temple of Slack," and you can view it in either Windows 3.1 (WorldView) or NT (WebSpace) versions. "The Temple of Slack," by the way, is part of a large cathedral dubbed "The Church of the Sub-Genius," which is the seat of what the church's programmers call "the religion of the 90s." So when you come to this temple, bring your browser.

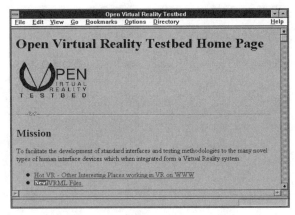

Figure 980 Visit the Temple of Slack at testbed.

Virtual COHO: Space Physics in 3-D

http://nssdc.gsfc.nasa.gov/cohoweb/vrml/coho.html

NASA created these 3-D scientific visualizations with VRML to depict various space phenomena and spacecraft, including Helios-1, Helios-2, Omni, Pioneer 10, Pioneer 11, Pioneer 12, Ulysses, Voyager 1, and Voyager 2. The visualizations of planetary bodies include Saturn with her rings, the moon, Mars, Pluto, Halley's Comet, Jupiter, Neptune, and Mercury. You'll see models of space phenomena that include black holes, supernovas, and more. In addition to a VRML browser, you also need Netscape for this document, which is based on HTML 3.0. No other browser will work.

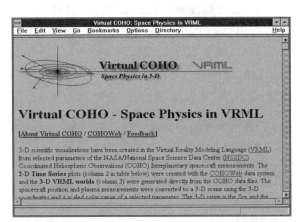

Figure 981 Space physics in VRML 3-D.

VRML Reference Information

http://wintermute.gmd.de:8000/vrml/

Come to "VRML Reference Information" for all the standard, benchmark VRML documentation. At this site, you'll find the final version of the VRML 1.0 specification, as well as the official FAQ (frequently asked questions) for VRML. You'll also find interesting information on a new, multi-user approach to HTTP/VRML. This new approach uses a smooth extension of the protocols that lets existing browsers participate in VRML graphics. The approach calls for the use of multi-casting to achieve an acceptable performance in large-scaled, multi-user virtual worlds. If you're a VRML programmer or developer, you'll find this material indispensible. You won't be able to work without it.

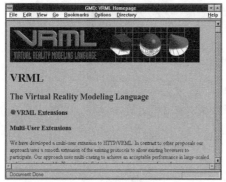

Figure 982.1 Modeling Langauge resources.

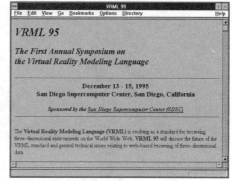

Figure 982.2 San Diego VRML Symposium.

VRML/WebOOGL Zoo of Mathematical 3-D Objects

http://www.geom.umn.edu:80/software/weboogl/zoo

From Tamara "Love Triangle" Munzner at The Geometry Center comes the great "VRML/WebOOGL Zoo of Mathematical 3-D Objects." Now, I am not sure why this site is called a zoo. After all, the site contains objects, not beasts. I couldn't find one animal at the "Zoo." That said, what I did find at this site is cool. Each object is available in both VRML and WebOOGL format, and in iterations that embrace various amounts of data. You'll find an everting sphere, archimedean and platonic solids, 59 stellations of an icosahedron, and (this is the cool thing) a full trefoil icosahedron. Download these babies. Use them as PC screen wall-paper. Print them out and pin them to walls for something to stare at when you're sitting back sipping way too much Jose Cuervo. You get the picture.

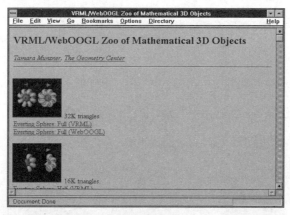

Figure 983 VRML/WebOOGL Zoo.

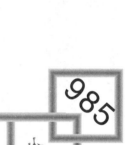

Virtual Soma

http://www.hyperion.com/planet9/vrsoma.htm

Planet 9 Studios, using a specially modified portion of their larger San Francisco model, has created Virtual Soma, the first 3-D city-model displayed in real time on the Internet. Soma (South of the Market Street Area) is the neighborhood in San Francisco where most of the Internet software and animation development happens. In Virtual Soma, you can walk (or fly, if you prefer) down actual San Francisco streets. Click on hyperlinked buildings to walk inside, play animations, or leap to the homepage of the structure's occupants. Virtual Soma is continually expanding, so keep visiting as they add more spaces to this compelling virtual world!

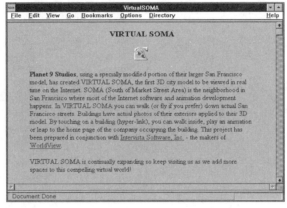

Figure 984 Stroll through VirtualSOMA.

Virtual World Factory

http://www.virtpark.com/theme/factinfo.html

Use "Virtual World Factory" to create your own worlds, without programming! All you need to do is fill-in-the-blanks and out pops your world, rendered in VRML. Okay. Let's design a world. I think I'll put one bar over here, and another over there, and another next to the ballpark. Then, on the other side of town, I think we should have a few taverns. Hmmm. What else do we need? Wait a minute. I know. Liquor stores! I'll put one liquor store up the road from the vineyard, and I'll put another next door to the brewery. I suppose I should add a bank with a cash-machine so I can get money to spend in the bars and the liquor stores. Oh, and we need a hospital for when my liver goes out.

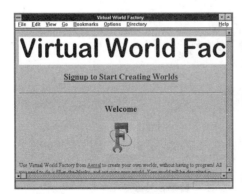

Figure 985.1 Virtual World Factory.

Figure 985.2 Example worlds.

WEIRD, VERY WEIRD

More VRML & Hot Java

As you surf the Web, you may find that one or more of the site addresses listed in this book have changed. In such cases, connect to Jamsa Press at http://www.jamsa.com and click on the icon that corresponds to the *1001 Really Cool Web Sites* book. Jamsa Press will list replacement addresses (when possible) for sites that have moved. In addition, you can also use the following site list as you search for information on technical compputing applications such as Hot Java and VRML:

VRML Forum	http://vrml.wired.com
Leap the Gap	http://www.arc.org/
Hot Virtual Sites	http://nemo.ncsl.nist.gov/~sressler/hotvr.html
Partnerships and Coll.	http://www.sdsc.edu/1/Parts_Collabs/parts_collabs.html
The Geometry Sender	http://synap.neuro.sfc.keio.ac.jp/~aly/polygon/polygon.html
Web Developer	http://www.charm.net/~web/About.html

986

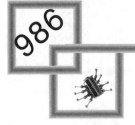

The Bigfoot Research Project

http://www.teleport.com/~tbrp/

This is the deal. The people who maintain this site actually believe in Bigfoot. "Although many years of research into the Bigfoot phenomenon now lie behind us," they write, "much of what we believe we know comes mainly from prudent speculation." In other words, it does not come from scientific evidence. Nevertheless, they have drawn many conclusions. Not only does Bigfoot exist, they say, but he is more man-like than ape-like, and he possesses "unusual intelligence, on a level possibly close to our own . . . This extraordinary hominid may well be the mysterious wild man that the great Swedish scientist, Carolus Linnaeus (1707-1778) called Homo Nocturnus, the Man of the Night." I know where to find plenty of examples of Homo Nocturnus, but it's not in the Alaskan wilderness.

Figure 986 Stalking Bigfoot.

Cereal Hall of Fame

http://198.3.117.222/index.html

Breakfast cereal is the stuff Americans love to hate. Everyone complains about the high cost and the low nutritional value of cereal. Yet, more people have cereal in their homes than have televisions. Like it or not, we Americans are what we eat, and we eat a lot of breakfast cereal. The "Cereal Hall of Fame" is your virtual cereal box, bringing you cereal facts, entertainment, and more. The Webmaster writes, "We are an independent group of cereal enthusiasts who delight in the celebration of America's breakfast cereal culture. From the origin of Tony the Tiger to the explosive properties of grain dust, we will be presenting timely, well-researched information on a regular basis." I think the site is lots of fun. Tony the Tiger would most certainly characterize it as GR-R-REAT!

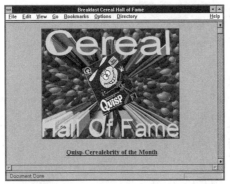

Figure 987.1 Cereal Hall of Fame.

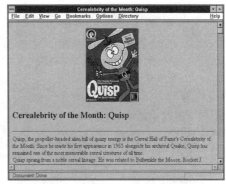

Figure 987.2 Quisp-Cerealebrity of the Month.

Conspiracies: the 50 All-Time Greatest

http://www.webcom.com/~conspire/

Visit this site to read about the Air Force cover-up of a reported UFO crash in Georgia; the Kennedy connection in the (some believe) murder of Marilyn Monroe; the CIA's backing of the Charles Manson death cult; the role of the Beatles as secret agents for Her Majesty, the Queen; the secret mechanisms by which Aristotle Onassis ruled as supreme world overlord; the "one-world-blueblood Rockefeller cabal;" FDR's involvement with the planning of the Japanese raid on Pearl Harbor; the secret whereabouts of an extremely old Adolf Hitler in Paraguay; the secluded Pacific Island where John F. Kennedy lives out his life after being hideously deformed (but not killed) by the shots fired in Dallas; George Bush's links to John Hinkley; and other absurdities.

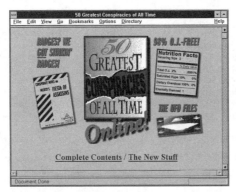

Figure 988.1 The 50 greatest conspiracies.

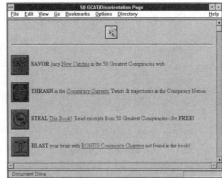

Figure 988.2 A few of your options.

WEIRD, VERY WEIRD

The Dark Side of the Web

http://www.cascade.net/dceme.html

What a den of morbidity! Shop at the "Bone Clones Skeleton Shop," walk through the virtual museum of dead rock stars, take a dip in the dead pool, view online casket catalogs, access crime archives that detail the deeds of serial killers, identify corpses in a virtual morgue, or join the "Hearse Car Club." You can also shop for tombs and gravesites, view obituary notices from newspapers around the world, learn precisely how and when various celebrities bought the farm, and even get a cultural history of grave robbing. On a lighter side, you'll find a funny file that fills you in on "30 ways to be offensive at a funeral," as well as a soppy collection of terrible verses from Victorian sympathy cards.

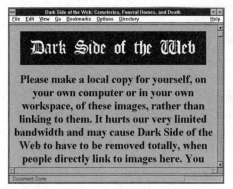

Figure 989.1 Dark Side of the Web.

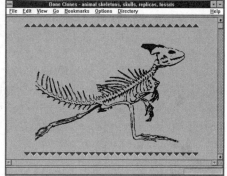

Figure 989.2 The Bones Clones Skeleton Shop.

Druid Science Reading Room

http://www.generality.wis.net//Druid.html

The "Druid Science Reading Room" has nothing to do with Druidism and very little to with science! It does, however, have lots to do with reading and provides many cool, off-the-wall stories of the abnormal and the supernatural, including something absolutely fabulous entitled "A Buffalo in Winter." Also worth a look is "Tomorrow Belongs to We." This site also contains a neat item, still under construction, called Cyberia. A description? You are standing in a virtual alley in a large city by the ocean. A street runs east-west. At the end of the alleyway is a midnight blue door. A neon sign above it reads: Cyberia. But be careful. Poets are inside. And some have been drinking. Enter at your own risk.

Figure 990.1 Druid Science Reading Room.

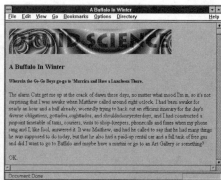

Figure 990.2 A Buffalo In Winter.

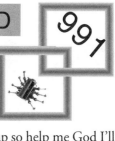

50 Fun Things for Non-Christians to Do in Church

http://nmt.edu/~tobias/church.html

If you hear a crying baby, go over and tell the mother, "If you don't shut that Goddamn thing up so help me God I'll kill it!" At a church dinner, scoop up a forkful of mashed potatoes, stare at it for a moment, and announce that you can see a miraculous image of Jesus. Make the sun reflect off your watch into the preacher's face. *Discreetly* position a number of bottle rockets on the floor in front of the altar and then *discreetly* light them. Fake a demonic possession. Distribute condoms. Speak in tongues. Ask where the nearest ashtray is. Ask someone what they think about the Book of Peleponnesians and, after they tell you, inform them that there is no Book of Peleponnesians.

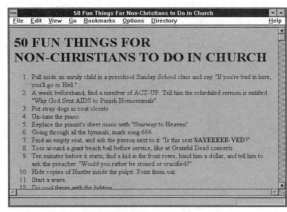

Figure 991 50 Fun Things.

FishCam Remote Sensor

http://www2.netscape.com/fishcam/fishcam.html

Somewhere in the world, a camera focuses on a small aquarium filled with perhaps a dozen fish: goldfish, angelfish, guppies, and miniature catfish. They swim back and forth, up and down, around and around. Occasionally, someone pinches fishfood into the tank, and they migrate near the surface to grab it. Then they settle down again. Back and forth. The image broadcasts live via the Internet, and you can grab it at this site. A point? There is no point. The technology is great, of course, for the remote study of weather, events at field locations, etc. But the fish? Well, they are just *there* and they are just weird. And they are almost as boring via the Web as they are in your own den.

Figure 992 Keep your eye on the fish.

Highgate Cemetery

http://www.worldserver.pipex.com/nc/Emlyn

The Bishop of London consecrated the Cemetery of St. James, Highgate, on May 20, 1839. The first inhumation (now, there's a word!) was that of Elizabeth Jackson, a 36 year-old spinster from Golden Square, Soho. In the years that followed, Highgate became the burial-place of choice for the most fashionable (dead) Victorian society. Perched on a hill above London, the cemetery's catacombs, labyrinth of sepulchers, and avenues of death have echoed with the entombment of poets, painters, and paupers. At this site, you see many members of the Dickens family (though not Charles, who is buried in Westminster Abbey), as well as George Eliot, Karl Marx, Dante Gabriel Rossetti, and many other notables. To visit them, take this site's virtual tour of Highgate. And don't worry about bringing flowers.

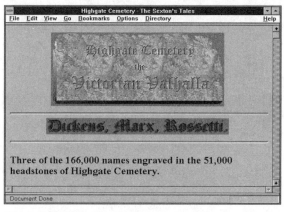

Figure 993 Highgate Cemetery.

Ghosts in the Machine

http://www.russellt.com/~paranorm

"Ghosts in the Machine" is a wonderful collection of supposedly-true urban legends about ghosts and other dark phenomena of the night. Check out such stories as "A Father's Final Love," "A Flurry of Voices," "A Haunted Light," "A Normal Looking House in Texas," "An Unearthly Visit," "California Indian Ghosts," "The Haunted Boarding House," "The Phantom Hitchhiker," "Mr. Edison's Necrophone," "Nevermore," "Night People," "The Creature in the Wall," "The Haunted Church," "The Lady in the Attic," and more. All the tales are weird, chilling, and extremely well-told. Don't read them in an old house, alone, late at night.

Figure 994.1 Ghosts in the Machine.

Figure 994.2 A Haunted Light.

The Captain James T. Kirk Sing-a-long Page

http://www.ama.caltech.edu/~mrm/kirk.html

Little known to the civilized world, the great William Shatner (Kirk on the original *Star Trek* TV series) recorded an album entitled *The Transformed Man* back in 1968. On this record, Shatner proves, with unwitting hilarity, that his skills as a Star Fleet captain do not extend to music. You haven't lived until you've heard Shatner belt out "Mr. Tambourine Man" and "Lucy in the Sky with Diamonds." But lucky you! At this site, you'll find audio files that give you a taste of what you missed. After hearing these cuts myself, I had but one thing to say: "Cap'n, stop yer singing! You've cracked the dilithium crystals! The engines can't take this very much longer!" (While you're at this site, be sure to check out the link to "The Music of Mr. Spock," which is equally wonderful.)

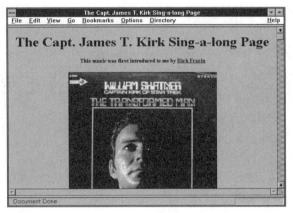

Figure 995 Sing-a-long with Shatner.

996

The Marshmallow Peanut Circus

http://www.circus.com

In a plush suburban home just north of Santa Cruz, a young woman named Dracon and her girlfriend, Goddess, are gathered around a computer in their living room. Picori, a friend who has stopped by to visit, plops down in front of another terminal on the floor beside her housemate, Banshee, who is already typing away on his laptop computer. The group is silent, save for an occasional fit of laughter. They are all partying, via modem, with some twenty other geeks from around the planet. The digital commune that links them is called a *Geekhouse*. The "Marshmallow Peanut Circus" is one of many such Geekhouses, where cyberpunks congregate and pursue their, ugh, work.

Figure 996.1 Marshmallow Peanut Circus.

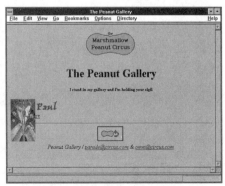

Figure 996.2 The Peanut Gallery.

Ollie's Home Page

http://maxwell.ucdavis.edu/~newquist/olliehome.html

In the beginning there was no Ollie. There were only the waters. But then from the waters came the One Egg. And thus the myth of Ollie (which some fundamentalists literally believe to be true) was born. Believers or not, we can all benefit from the wise, third-person sayings of this venerable ostrich. A few of them: Ollie realizes that Barbara Eden is NOT a real genie. Ollie really doesn't like our social pecking order. Ollie believes that Love is All You Need. Ollie thinks Cheryl Tiegs is a fox. Ollie's bark is worse than his beak. Ollie uses Certs—shouldn't you? Ollie's not afraid of Hillary Clinton. Ollie voted for Nixon and felt betrayed. Ollie thinks the Bee Gees deserve better. And he's right; they do!

Figure 997.1 Behold Ollie.

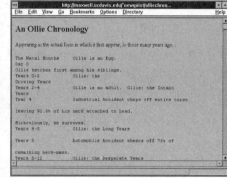

Figure 997.2 The Ollie chronology.

Pere Lachaise Cemetery Online

http://www.io.org/cemetery/e/lachaise.intro.html

Located in the eastern civil district of Paris, Pere Lachaise is without doubt the city's most beautiful burial ground. The cemetery, which covers 44 hectares, contains 100,000 burial plots and, since opening, has had over one million burials. At this site (cemetery), you will find Oscar Wilde, Frederick Chopin, Jim Morrison, Marcel Proust, Simone Signoret, and many others. Take the digital tour. Go through the main entrance on the boulevard. Pick up an electronic map showing famous grave sites. Then, travel through the cemetery, calling on the famous and non-famous, all of whom will be equally attentive to you. The monumental architecture is astonishing. Have a nice stroll.

Figure 998.1 A digital tour of Pere Lachaise.

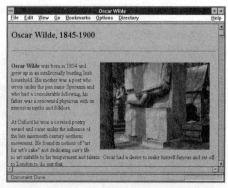

Figure 998.2 Wilde waits patiently for your visit.

The Principia Discordia

http://www.willamette.edu/webdev/principia/

This astonishingly great piece of literature, subtitled *How I Found the Goddess and What I Did To Her When I Found Her*, is nearly as wonderful as it is obscure. Some great books are recognized at once with all kinds of critical acclaim, like Joyce's *Ulysses*. Others don't receive recognition until decades after their first appearance, like *Moby Dick*. Such is the case with *The Principia Discordia*, which is only now coming into its own. The book is the work of a time-traveling anthropologist from the 23rd Century. He is currently passing among us as a computer specialist, bon vivant, and philosopher named Gregory Hill. I have it on good authority that he is one of the most accomplished time travelers in the galaxy and has visited earth many times in the past, using many different names.

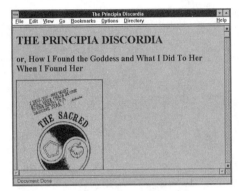

Figure 999.1 *The Principia Discordia.*

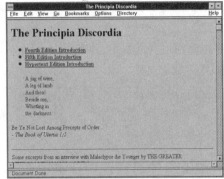

Figure 999.2 *The start of the prose.*

Strawberry Pop-Tart Blow-Torches

http://www.sci.tamucc.edu/~pmichaud/toast

Last year, well-known newspaper columnist Dave Barry noted that you can make Kellogg's Pop-Tarts emit flames "like a blow-torch" if you leave them in a toaster too long. Given previous work in the field of food-entertainment combustion, it was obvious that this was a new frontier requiring further exploration. Thus, the genesis of this Web site. (It is interesting to note that you need only two basic materials to cause Pop-Tart combustion: a toaster and some Pop-Tarts.) For the purposes of the research that the site's authors scrupulously document, they use Strawberry Pop-Tarts with Real Smucker's Fruit.

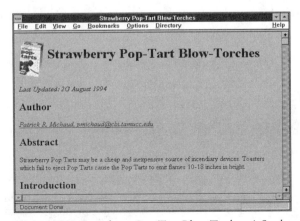

Figure 1000 *Strawberry Pop-Tart Blow-Torches: A Study.*

1001

WEIRD, VERY WEIRD

Vampyres: the Eternal Immortals

http://aloha.net/~alita/vampyre.html

Vampires. In many legends and tales, vampires are creatures of the night. They are demons and angels, darkness and light, despair and hope, all in one. As mortals, they viewed the world around them with indifference. As vampires, they see things mortals do not. No boundary of reality binds them. "Reality," the site's vampire Webmaster writes, "often proves the destroyer of worlds, as what you stop believing in ceases to exist within your mind. So reader. Open your mind to a world where the stakes are high, the blood runs thick, and where there is such a thing as vampires." At this site, you'll find stories, scholarly research, and even links to the homepages of individuals who claim to be actual living vampires. Open their coffins and take a peak.

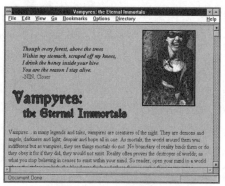

Figure 1001.1 Enter the world of vampires.

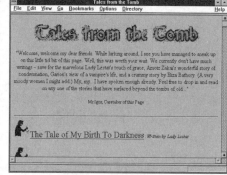

Figure 1001.2 Tales of the vampire.

SEE

More Weird, Very Weird

As you surf the Web, you may find that one or more of the site addresses listed in this book have changed. In such cases, connect to Jamsa Press at http://www.jamsa.com and click on the icon that corresponds to the *1001 Really Cool Web Sites* book. Jamsa Press will list replacement addresses (when possible) for sites that have moved. In addition, you can also use the following site list as you search for information on wierd things:

What Snooz	http://www.digimark.net/mfu/whasnooz.html
A Zen Web site	http://www.nomius.com/~zenyard/zenyard.htm
The Twinkie Project	http://www.rice.edu/~gouge/twinkies.html
FoodPlex	http://www.gigaplex.com/wow/food/index.htm
Tequila Home Page	http://www.io.com/~elvis/
Area 51	http://www.cris.com/~psyspy/area51/index.html
Mann's Point of View	http://wwwwhite.media.mit.edu/~steve/html9/myview.html
Spying on You	http://ciips.ee.uwa.edu.au/~hutch/Spy.html
The Green Iguana	http://iguana.images.com/dupecam.html
3D Riffle	http://cvs.anu.edu.au/andy/rid/riddle.html

INDEX

INDEX

INDEX

INDEX

INDEX

INDEX